Human Personality And Its Survival Of Bodily Death

ederic William Henry Myers, Leopold Hamilton Myers

HUMAN PERSONALITY

AND ITS SURVIVAL OF
BODILY DEATH

BY

FREDERIC W. H. MYERS

EDITED AND ABRIDGED
BY HIS SON
LEOPOLD HAMILTON MYERS

Cessas in vota precesque,
Tros, ait, Aenea, cessas ? Neque enim ante dehiscent
Adtonitæ magna ora domus. — VIRGIL.

"Nay !" quoth the Sybil, "Trojan ! will thou spare
The impassioned effort and the conquering prayer ?
Nay ! not save thus those doors shall open roll, —
That Power within them burst upon the soul."

LONGMANS, GREEN, AND CO.
91 AND 93 FIFTH AVENUE, NEW YORK
LONDON AND BOMBAY
1907

til 7069.07.25

First Edition, December, 1906
Reprinted, March, 1907

The Plimpton Press Norwood Mass. U.S.A.

DEDICATED

TO

HENRY SIDGWICK

AND

EDMUND GURNEY

CONTENTS

♥

EDITOR'S NOTE

NEARLY four years have elapsed since the first appearance of my Father's book "Human Personality and its Survival of Bodily Death." It cost two guineas and was published in two volumes, each of which was little under 700 pages in length.

The price and dimensions of such a work made the future issue of a more popular edition not improbable. Indeed, my Father himself indicated briefly the lines on which an abridgment could best be made. In accordance with his indications I have endeavoured to keep as closely as possible to the original scheme and construction of the book.

The task of abridging, however, must always be an ungrateful one. It is inevitable that somewhere or other I should disappoint the reader who, already acquainted with the unabridged edition, finds some admired passage curtailed in favour of others that are to him of secondary interest. This I cannot avoid. All I can hope to do is so to reconcile the principles of *omission* and *condensation* as least to do violence to the style while preserving as far as possible the completeness of the exposition.

One half of each volume in the unabridged edition consists of appendices containing examples of the various kinds of phenomena discussed and analyzed in the text. It has been possible to reduce considerably the number of these cases without, I think, detracting much from the value of the work for the purposes of the ordinary reader. Those cases, however, which are included in this edition are quoted in full, an abridged version having very little value.

It must be remembered that the author in his preface insists that "the book is an exposition rather than a proof," and the remark naturally applies with even greater force to this abridgment. Here the cases must be regarded simply as illustrative of the different types of the evidence upon which *in its entirety* the argument of the book ultimately rests.

The reader who may feel disposed to study this evidence will find numerous references given in the foot-notes. The cases, however, to which he is thus referred are scattered in many different publications, some of which will probably be less easy of access than the unabridged edition. In the many instances, therefore, where a case is quoted in the latter its place therein is indicated by means of a number or a number and letter in square brackets, thus [434 A]: these being in accordance with the plan of arrangement observed in the larger book.

I wish to express my sincere thanks to Miss Alice Johnson, who very kindly read over the whole of the proof of this abridgment. I have profited largely by her advice as well as from that given me by Miss Jane Barlow, to whom my thanks are also due.   L. H. M.

PREFACE

[This unfinished preface consists of several passages written at different times by the author, who died on January 17th, 1901. In 1896 he arranged that the completion of his book should be in the hands of Dr. Richard Hodgson in case of his death before its publication. In the meantime he had entrusted the general supervision of the press work and much of the detail in marshalling the Appendices to Miss Alice Johnson (now Secretary of the Society for Psychical Research), who was therefore associated with Dr. Hodgson also in the editorial work needed for the completion of the book, and much the greater part of the labour involved fell to her share.]

THE book which is now at last given to the world is but a partial presentation of an ever-growing subject which I have long hoped to become able to treat in more adequate fashion. But as knowledge increases life rolls by, and I have thought it well to bring out while I can even this most imperfect text-book to a branch of research whose novelty and strangeness call urgently for some provisional systematisation, which, by suggesting fresh inquiries and producing further accumulation of evidence, may tend as speedily as possible to its own supersession. Few critics of this book can, I think, be more fully conscious than its author of its defects and its lacunæ; but also few critics, I think, have yet realised the importance of the new facts which in some fashion the book does actually present.

Many of these facts have already appeared in *Phantasms of the Living ;* many more in the *Proceedings* of the Society for Psychical Research; but they are far indeed from having yet entered into the scientific consciousness of the age. In future years the wonder, I think, will be that their announcement was so largely left to a writer with leisure so scanty, and with scientific equipment so incomplete.

Whatever value this book may possess is in great measure due to other minds than its actual author's. Its very existence, in the first place, probably depends upon the existence of the two beloved friends and invaluable coadjutors to whose memory I dedicate it now.

The help derived from these departed colleagues, Henry Sidgwick

and Edmund Gurney, although of a kind and quantity absolutely essential
to the existence of this work, is not easy to define in all its fulness under
the changed circumstances of to-day.   There was indeed much which *is*
measurable; — much of revision of previous work of my own, of col-
laborative experiments, of original thought and discovery.   Large quota-
tions purposely introduced from Edmund Gurney indicate, although
imperfectly, how closely interwoven our work on all these subjects
continued to be until his death.   But the benefit which I drew from the
association went deeper still.   The conditions under which this inquiry was
undertaken were such as to emphasise the need of some intimate moral
support.   A recluse, perhaps, or an eccentric, — or a man living mainly
with his intellectual inferiors, may find it easy to work steadily and confidently at a task which he knows that the bulk of educated men will
ignore or despise.   But this is more difficult for a man who feels manifold
links with his kind, a man whose desire it is to live among minds equal
or superior to his own.   It is hard, I say, for such a man to disregard
altogether the expressed or implied disapproval of those groups of weighty
personages to whom in other matters he is accustomed to look up.

I need not say that the attitude of the scientific world — of all the
intellectual world — then was very much more marked than now.   Even
now I write in full consciousness of the low value commonly attached to
inquiries of the kind which I pursue.   Even now a book on such a subject
must still expect to evoke, not only legitimate criticism of many kinds,
but also much of that disgust and resentment which novelty and hetero-
doxy naturally excite.   But I have no wish to exalt into a deed of daring
an enterprise which to the next generation must seem the most obvious
thing in the world.   *Nihil ausi nisi vana contemnere* will certainly be the
highest compliment which what seemed to us our bold independence of
men will receive.   Yet gratitude bids me to say that however I might in
the privacy of my own bosom have 'dared to contemn things contempt-
ible,' I should never have ventured my amateurish acquirements on a
publication of this scale were it not for that slow growth of confidence
which my respect for the judgment of these two friends inspired.   Their
countenance and fellowship, which at once transformed my own share in

the work into a delight, has made its presentation to the world appear as a duty.

My thanks are due also to another colleague who has passed away, my brother, Dr. A. T. Myers, F.R.C.P., who helped me for many years in all medical points arising in the work.

To the original furnishers of the evidence my obligations are great and manifest, and to the Council of the S.P.R. I also owe thanks for permission to use that evidence freely. But I must leave it to the book itself to indicate in fuller detail how much is owing to how many men and women: — how widely diffused are the work and the interest which have found in this book their temporary outcome and exposition.

The book, indeed, is an exposition rather than a proof. I cannot summarise within my modest limits the mass of evidence already gathered together in the sixteen volumes of *Proceedings* and the nine volumes of the *Journal* of the S.P.R., in *Phantasms of the Living* and other books hereafter referred to, and in MS. collections. The attempt indeed would be quite out of place. This branch of knowledge, like others, must be studied carefully and in detail by those who care to understand or to advance it.

What I have tried to do here is to render that knowledge more assimilable by co-ordinating it in a form as clear and intelligible as my own limited skill and the nature of the facts themselves have permitted. I have tried to give, in text and in Appendices, enough of actual evidence to illustrate each step in my argument: — and I have constantly referred the reader to places where further evidence will be found.

In minor matters I have aimed above all things at clearness and readiness in reference. The division of the book into sections, with Appendices bearing the same numbers, will, it is hoped, facilitate the use both of syllabus and of references in general. I have even risked the appearance of pedantry in adding a glossary. Where many unfamiliar facts and ideas have to be dealt with, time is saved in the end if the writer explains precisely what his terms mean.

·   ·   ·   ·   ·   ·   ·   ·   ·

F. W. H. MYERS.

GLOSSARY

Aboulia. — Loss of power of willing.

After-image. — A retinal picture of an object seen after removing the gaze from the object.

Agent. — The person who seems to initiate a telepathic transmission.

Agraphia. — Lack of power to write words.

Alexia or *Word-blindness.* — Lack of power to understand words written.

Anaesthesia, or the loss of sensation generally, must be distinguished from *analgesia,* or the loss of the sense of pain alone.

Analgesia. — Insensibility to pain.

Aphasia. — Incapacity of coherent utterance, not caused by structural impairment of the vocal organs, but by lesion of the cerebral centres for speech.

Aphonia. — Incapacity of uttering sounds.

Automatic. — Used of mental images arising and movements made without the initiation, and generally without the concurrence, of conscious thought and will. *Sensory automatism* will thus include visual and auditory hallucinations. *Motor automatism* will include messages written and words uttered without intention (automatic script, trance-utterance, etc.).

Automnesia. — Spontaneous revival of memories of an earlier condition of life.

Autoscope. — Any instrument which reveals a subliminal motor impulse or sensory impression, *e.g.,* a divining rod, a tilting table, or a planchette.

Bilocation. — The sensation of being in two different places at once, namely where one's organism is, and in a place distant from it.

Catalepsy. — "An intermittent neurosis producing inability to change the position of a limb, while another person can place the muscles in a state of flexion or contraction as he will." (Tuke's *Dictionary of Psychological Medicine.*)

Centre of Consciousness. — The place where a percipient imagines himself to be. The point of view from which he seems to himself to be surveying some phantasmal scene.

Chromatism. — See *Secondary Sensations.*

Clair-audience. — The sensation of hearing an internal (but in some way veridical) voice.

Clairvoyance (Lucidité). — The faculty or act of perceiving, as though visually, with some coincidental truth, some distant scene.

Cœnesthesia. — That consensus or agreement of many organic sensations which is a fundamental element in our conception of personal identity.

Control. — This word is used of the intelligence which purports to communicate messages which are written or uttered by the *automatist, sensitive* or *medium.*

* *Cosmopathic.* — Open to the access of supernormal knowledge or emotion.

Cryptomnesia. — Submerged or subliminal memory of events forgotten by the supraliminal self.

* *Dextro-cerebral* (opposed to * *Sinistro-cerebral*) of left-handed persons as employing preferentially the *right* hemisphere of the brain.

Diathesis. — Habit, capacity, constitutional disposition or tendency.

Dimorphism. — In crystals the property of assuming two incompatible forms: in plants and animals, difference of form between members of the same species. · Used of a condition of alternating personalities, in which memory, character, etc., present themselves at different times in different forms in the same person.

Discarnate. — Disembodied, opposed to *incarnate.*

Disintegration of Personality. — Used of any condition where the sense of personality is not unitary and continuous: especially when secondary and transitory personalities intervene.

Dynamogeny. — The increase of nervous energy by appropriate stimuli, often opposed to *inhibition.*

Ecmnesia. — Loss of memory of a period of time.

. * *Entencephalic.* — On the analogy of *entoptic :* of sensations, etc., which have their origin within the brain, not in the external world.

Eugenics. — The science of improving the race.

Falsidical. — Of hallucinations *delusive, i.e.,* when there is nothing objective to which they correspond. The correlative term to *veridical.*

Glossolaly. — "Speaking with tongues," *i.e.,* automatic utterance of words not belonging to any real language.

Hallucination. — Any sensory perception which has no objective counterpart within the field of vision, hearing, etc., is termed a hallucination.

Heterœsthesia. — A form of sensibility decidedly different from any of those which can be referred to the action of the known senses.

Hyperboulia. — Increased power over the organism, — resembling the power which we call *will* when it is exercised over the voluntary muscles, — which is seen in the bodily changes effected by self-suggestion.

Hyperœsthesia. — Unusual acuteness of the senses.

Hypermnesia. — "Over-activity of the memory; a condition in which past acts, feelings, or ideas are brought vividly to the mind, which, in its normal condition, has wholly lost the remembrance of them." (Tuke's *Dict.*)

Hyperpromethia. — Supernormal power of foresight.

Hypnagogic. — *Illusions hypnagogiques* (Maury) are the vivid illusions of sight or sound — "faces in the dark," etc. — which sometimes accompany the oncoming of sleep. To similar illusions accompanying the *departure* of sleep, as when a dream-figure persists for a few moments into waking life, I have given the name *hypnopompic.*

Hypnogenous zones. — Regions by pressure on which hypnosis is induced in some hysterical persons.

Hypnopompic. — See *Hypnagogic.*

Hysteria. — "A disordered condition of the nervous system, the anatomical seat and nature of which are unknown to medical science, but of which the symptoms consist in well-marked and very varied disturbances of nerve-function" (*Ency. Brit.*). Hysterical affections are not dependent on any discoverable lesion.

Hysterogenous zones. — Points or tracts on the skin of a hysterical person, pressure on which will induce a hysterical attack.

Ideational. — Used of impressions which display some distinct notion, but not of sensory nature.

Induced. — Of hallucinations, etc., intentionally produced.

Levitation. — A raising of objects from the ground by supposed supernormal means; especially of living persons.

Medium. — A person through whom communication is deemed to be carried on between living men and spirits of the departed. It is often better replaced by *automatist* or *sensitive.*

Message. — Used for any communication, not necessarily verbal, from one to another stratum of the automatist's personality, or from an external intelligence to the automatist's mind.

Metallæsthesia. — A form of sensibility alleged to exist which enables some hypnotised or hysterical subjects to discriminate between the contacts of various metals by sensations not derived from their ordinary properties of weight, etc.

Metastasis. — Change of the seat of a bodily function from one place (*e.g.,* brain-centre) to another.

Metetherial. — That which appears to lie after or beyond the ether: the metetherial environment denotes the spiritual or transcendental world in which the soul may be supposed to exist.

Methectic. — Of communications between one stratum of a man's intelligence and another.

Mirror-writing (*écriture renversée, Spiegel-schrift*). — Writing so inverted, or, more exactly, *perverted*, as to resemble writing reflected in a mirror.

Mnemonic chain. — A continuous series of memories, especially when the continuity persists after an interruption.

Motor. — Used of an impulse to action not carrying with it any definite idea or sensory impression.

Negative hallucination or *systematised anæsthesia.* — Signifies the condition of an entranced subject who, as the result of a suggestion, is unable to perceive some object or to hear some sound, etc.

Number forms. — See *Secondary sensations.*

Objectify. — To externalize a phantom as if it were a material object; to see it as a part of the waking world.

* *Panmnesia.* — A potential recollection of all impressions.

Paræsthesia. — Erroneous or morbid sensation.

Paramnesia. — *All* forms of erroneous memory.

Paraphasia. — The erroneous and involuntary use of one word for another.

Percipient. — The correlative term to Agent; the person on whose mind the telepathic impact falls; or, more generally, the person who perceives any motor or sensory impression.

Phantasm and Phantom. — Phantasm and phantom are, of course, mere variants of the same word; but since phantom has become generally restricted to *visual* hallucinations, it is convenient to take phantasm to cover a wider range, and to signify any hallucinatory sensory impression, whatever sense — whether sight, hearing, touch, smell, taste, or diffused sensibility — may happen to be affected.

Phantasmogenetic centre. — A point in space apparently modified by a spirit in such a way that persons present near it perceive a phantasm.

Phobies. — Irrational restricting or disabling preoccupations or fears; e.g., *agoraphobia*, fear of open spaces.

Photism. — See *Secondary sensations.*

Point de repère. — Guiding mark. Used of some (generally inconspicuous) real object which a hallucinated subject sometimes sees as the nucleus of his hallucination, and the movements of which suggest corresponding movements of the hallucinatory object.

Polyzoism. — The property, in a complex organism, of being composed of minor and quasi-independent organisms. This is sometimes called "colonial constitution," from animal *colonies.*

Possession. — A developed form of motor automatism, in which the automatist's own personality disappears for a time, while there appears to be a more or less complete substitution of personality, writing or speech being given by another spirit through the entranced organism.

Post-hypnotic. — Used of a suggestion given during the hypnotic trance, but intended to operate after that trance has ceased.

Precognition. — Knowledge of impending events supernormally acquired.

Premonition. — A supernormal indication of any kind of event still in the future.

* *Preversion.* — A tendency to characteristics assumed to lie at a further point of the evolutionary progress of a species than has yet been reached; opposed to reversion.

* *Promnesia.* — The paradoxical sensation of recollecting a scene which is only now occurring for the first time; the sense of the *déjà vu.*

* *Psychorrhagy.* — A special idiosyncrasy which tends to make the phantasm of a person easily perceptible; the breaking loose of a psychical element, definable mainly by its power of producing a phantasm, perceptible by one or more persons, in some portion of space.

* *Psychorrhagic diathesis.* — A habit or capacity of detaching some psychical element, involuntarily and without purpose, in such a manner as to produce a phantasm.

Psycho-therapeutics. — "Treatment of disease by the influence of the mind on the body." (Tuke's *Dict.*)

Reciprocal. — Used of cases where there is both agency and percipience at each end of the telepathic chain, so that A perceives P, and P perceives A also.

* *Retrocognition.* — Knowledge of the past, supernormally acquired.

Secondary personality. — It sometimes happens, as the result of shock, disease, or unknown causes, that an individual experiences an alteration of memory and character, amounting to a change of personality, which generally seems to have come on during sleep. The new personality is in that case termed *secondary*, in distinction to the original, or *primary*, personality.

Secondary sensations (Secundärempfindungen, audition colorée, sound-seeing, synæsthesia, etc.). — With some persons every sensation of one type is accompanied by a sensation of another type; as for instance, a special sound may be accompanied by a special sensation of colour or light (*chromatisms* or *photisms*). This phenomenon is analogous to that of *number-forms*, — a kind of diagrammatic mental picture which accompanies the conception of a progression of numbers. See Galton's *Inquiries into Human Faculty.*

Shell-hearing. — The induction of hallucinatory voices, etc., by listening to a shell. Analogous to crystal-gazing.

Stigmatisation. — The production of blisters or other cutaneous changes on the hands, feet, or elsewhere, by suggestion or self-suggestion.

Subliminal. — Of thoughts, feelings, etc., lying beneath the ordinary *threshold* (*limen*) of consciousness, as opposed to *supraliminal*, lying *above* the threshold.

Suggestion. — The process of effectively impressing upon the subliminal intelligence the wishes of some other person. *Self-suggestion* means a suggestion conveyed by the subject himself from one stratum of his personality to another, without external intervention.

* *Supernormal.* — Of a faculty or phenomenon which transcends ordinary experience. Used in preference to the word *supernatural*, as not assuming that there is anything outside nature or any arbitrary interference with natural law.

Supraliminal. — See *Subliminal.*

Synæsthesia. — See *Secondary Sensations.*

Synergy. — A number of actions correlated together, or combined into a group.

Telekinesis. — Used of alleged supernormal movements of objects, not due to any known force.

**Telepathy.* — The communication of impressions of any kind from one mind to another, independently of the recognised channels of sense.

* *Telæsthesia.* — Any direct sensation or perception of objects or conditions independently of the recognised channels of sense, and also under such circumstances that no known mind external to the percipient's can be suggested as the source of the knowledge thus gained.

　* *Telergy.* — The force exercised by the mind of an agent in impressing a percipient, — involving a direct influence of the extraneous spirit on the brain or organism of the percipient.

　Veridical. — Of hallucinations, when they correspond to real events happening elsewhere and unknown to the percipient.

CHAPTER I

INTRODUCTION

Maior agit deus, atque opera in maiora remittit.
— Virgil.

In the long story of man's endeavours to understand his own environment and to govern his own fates, there is one gap or omission so singular that, however we may afterwards contrive to explain the fact, its simple statement has the air of a paradox. Yet it is strictly true to say that man has never yet applied to the problems which most profoundly concern him those methods of inquiry which in attacking all other problems he has found the most efficacious.

The question for man most momentous of all is whether or no he has an immortal soul; or — to avoid the word *immortal*, which belongs to the realm of infinities — whether or no his personality involves any element which can survive bodily death. In this direction have always lain the gravest fears, the farthest-reaching hopes, which could either oppress or stimulate mortal minds.

On the other hand, the method which our race has found most effective in acquiring knowledge is by this time familiar to all men. It is the method of modern Science — that process which consists in an interrogation of Nature entirely dispassionate, patient, systematic; such careful experiment and cumulative record as can often elicit from her slightest indications her deepest truths. That method is now dominant throughout the civilised world; and although in many directions experiments may be difficult and dubious, facts rare and elusive, Science works slowly on and bides her time, — refusing to fall back upon tradition or to launch into speculation, merely because strait is the gate which leads to valid discovery, indisputable truth.

I say, then, that this method has never yet been applied to the all-important problem of the existence, the powers, the destiny of the human soul.

Nor is this strange omission due to any general belief that the problem

1

is in its nature incapable of solution by any observation whatever which mankind could make. That resolutely agnostic view — I may almost say that scientific superstition — *"ignoramus et ignorabimus"* — is no doubt held at the present date by many learned minds. But it has never been the creed, nor is it now the creed, of the human race generally. In most civilised countries there has been for nearly two thousand years a distinct belief that survival has actually been proved by certain phenomena observed at a given date in Palestine. And beyond the Christian pale — whether through reason, instinct, or superstition — it has ever been commonly held that ghostly phenomena of one kind or another exist to testify to a life beyond the life we know.

But, nevertheless, neither those who believe on vague grounds nor those who believe on definite grounds that the question might possibly be solved, or has actually been solved, by human observation of objective facts, have hitherto made any serious attempt to connect and correlate that belief with the general scheme of belief for which Science already vouches. They have not sought for fresh corroborative instances, for analogies, for explanations; rather they have kept their convictions on these fundamental matters in a separate and sealed compartment of their minds, a compartment consecrated to religion or to superstition, but not to observation or to experiment.

It is my object in the present work — as it has from the first been the object of the Society for Psychical Research, on whose behalf most of the evidence here set forth has been collected, — to do what can be done to break down that artificial wall of demarcation which has thus far excluded from scientific treatment precisely the problems which stand in most need of all the aids to discovery which such treatment can afford.

Yet let me first explain that by the word "scientific" I signify an authority to which I submit myself — not a standard which I claim to attain. Any science of which I can here speak as possible must be a *nascent* science — not such as one of those vast systems of connected knowledge which thousands of experts now steadily push forward in laboratories in every land — but such as each one of those great sciences was in its dim and poor beginning, when a few monks groped among the properties of "the noble metals," or a few Chaldean shepherds outwatched the setting stars.

What I am able to insist upon is the mere Socratic rudiment of these organisms of exact thought — the first axiomatic prerequisite of any valid progress. My one contention is that in the discussion of the deeper problems of man's nature and destiny there ought to be exactly the same openness of mind, exactly the same diligence in the search for objective evidence of any kind, exactly the same critical analysis of results, as is habitually shown, for instance, in the discussion of the nature and destiny of the planet upon which man now moves.

Obvious truism although this statement may at first seem, it will presently be found, I think, that those who subscribe to it are in fact committing themselves to inquiries of a wider and stranger type than any to which they are accustomed; — are stepping outside certain narrow limits within which, by ancient convention, disputants on either side of these questions are commonly confined.

A brief recall to memory of certain familiar historical facts will serve to make my meaning clearer. Let us consider how it has come about that, whereas the problem of man's survival of death is by most persons regarded as a problem in its nature soluble by sufficient evidence, and whereas to many persons the traditional evidence commonly adduced appears insufficient, — nevertheless no serious effort has been made on either side to discover whether other and more recent evidence can or cannot be brought forward.

A certain broad answer to this inquiry, although it cannot be said to be at all points familiar, is not in reality far to seek. It is an answer which would seem strange indeed to some visitant from a planet peopled wholly by scientific minds. Yet among a race like our own, concerned first and primarily to live and work with thoughts undistracted from immediate needs, the answer is natural enough. For the fact simply is that the intimate importance of this central problem has barred the way to its methodical, its scientific solution.

There are some beliefs for which mankind cannot afford to wait. "What must I do to be saved?" is a question quite otherwise urgent than the cause of the tides or the meaning of the marks on the moon. Men must settle roughly somehow what it is that from the Unseen World they have reason to fear or to hope. Beliefs grow up in direct response to this need of belief; in order to support themselves they claim unique sanction; and thus along with these specific beliefs grows also the general habit of regarding matters that concern that Unseen World as somehow tabooed or segregated from ordinary observation or inquiry.

Let us pass from generalities to the actual history of Western civilisation. In an age when scattered ritual, local faiths — tribal solutions of cosmic problems — were destroying each other by mere contact and fusion, an event occurred which in the brief record of man's still incipient civilisation may be regarded as unique. A life was lived in which the loftiest response which man's need of moral guidance had ever received was corroborated by phenomena which have been widely regarded as convincingly miraculous, and which are said to have culminated in a Resurrection from the dead. To those phenomena or to that Resurrection it would at this point be illegitimate for me to refer in defence of my argument. I have appealed to Science, and to Science I must go; — in the sense that it would be unfair for me to claim support from that which Science in her strictness can set aside as the tradition of a pre-scientific age. Yet this one great tradition, as we know, has, as a fact, won the adhesion and reverence of the great majority of European minds. The complex results which followed from this triumph of Christianity have been discussed by many historians. But one result which here appears to us in a new light was this — that the Christian religion, the Christian Church, became for Europe the accredited representative and guardian of all phenomena bearing upon the World Unseen. So long as Christianity stood dominant, all phenomena which seemed to transcend experience were absorbed in her realm — were accounted as minor indications of the activity of her angels or of her fiends. And when Christianity was seriously attacked, these minor manifestations passed unconsidered. The priests thought it safest to defend their own traditions, their own intuitions, without going afield in search of independent evidence of a spiritual world. Their assailants kept their powder and shot for the orthodox ramparts, ignoring any isolated strongholds which formed no part of the main line of defence.

Meantime, indeed, the laws of Nature held their wonted way. As ever, that which the years had once brought they brought again; and every here and there some marvel, liker to the old stories than any one cared to assert, cropped up between superstition on the one hand and contemptuous indifference on the other. Witchcraft, Swedenborgianism, Mesmerism, Spiritism — these especially, amid many minor phenomena, stood out in turn as precursory of the inevitable wider inquiry. A very few words on each of these four movements may suffice here to show their connection with my present theme.

Witchcraft. — The lesson which witchcraft teaches with regard to the validity of human testimony is the more remarkable because it was so long and so completely misunderstood. The belief in witches long passed — as well it might — as the culminant example of human ignorance and folly; and in so comparatively recent a book as Mr. Lecky's "History of Rationalism," the sudden decline of this popular conviction, without argument or disapproval, is used to illustrate the irresistible melting away of error and falsity in the "intellectual climate" of a wiser age. Since about 1880, however, when French experiments especially had afforded conspicuous examples of what a hysterical woman could come to believe under suggestion from others or from herself, it has begun to be felt that the phenomena of witchcraft were very much what the phenomena of the Salpêtrière would seem to be to the patients themselves, if left alone in the hospital without a medical staff. And in *Phantasms of the Living*, Edmund Gurney, after subjecting the literature of witchcraft to a more careful analysis than any one till then had thought it worth while to apply, was able to show that practically all recorded first-hand depositions (made apart from torture) in the long story of witchcraft may quite possibly have been *true*, to the best belief of the deponents; true, that is to say, as representing the conviction of sane (though often hysterical) persons, who merely made the almost inevitable mistake of confusing self-suggested hallucinations with waking fact. Nay, even the insensible spots on the witches were no doubt really anæsthetic — involved a first discovery of a now familiar clinical symptom — the *zones analgésiques* of the patients of Pitres or Charcot. Witchcraft, in fact, was a gigantic, a cruel psychological and pathological experiment conducted by inquisitors upon hysteria; but it was conducted in the dark, and when the barbarous explanation dropped out of credence much of possible discovery was submerged as well.

Mesmer. — Again, the latent possibilities of "suggestion," — though not yet under that name, and mingled with who knows what else? — broke forth into a blaze in the movement headed by Mesmer; — at once discoverer and charlatan. Again the age was unripe, and scientific opposition, although not so formidable as the religious opposition which had sent witches to the stake, was yet strong enough to check for the second time the struggling science. Hardly till our own generation — hardly even now — has a third effort found better acceptance, and hypnotism and psycho-therapeutics, in which every well-attested fact of witchcraft or of mesmerism finds, if not its explanation, at least its parallel, are establishing themselves as a recognised and advancing method of relieving human ills.

This brief sketch of the development as it were by successive impulses, under strong disbelief and discouragement, of a group of mental tendencies, faculties, or sensibilities now recognised as truly existing and as often salutary, is closely paralleled by the development, under similar difficulties, of another group of faculties or sensibilities, whose existence is still disputed, but which if firmly established may prove to be of even greater moment for mankind.

At no time known to us, whether before or since the Christian era, has the series of *trance-manifestations*, — of supposed communications with a supernal world, — entirely ceased. Sometimes, as in the days of St.

Theresa, such trance or ecstasy has been, one may say, the central or culminant fact in the Christian world. Of these experiences I must not here treat. The evidence for them is largely of a subjective type, and they may belong more fitly to some future discussion as to the amount of confidence due to the interpretation given by entranced persons to their own phenomena.

But in the midst of this long series, and in full analogy to many minor cases, occurs the exceptional trance-history of Emmanuel Swedenborg. In this case, as is well known, there appears to have been excellent objective evidence both of clairvoyance or telæsthesia[1] and of communciation with departed persons; — and we can only regret that the philosopher Kant, who satisfied himself of some part of Swedenborg's supernormal[2] gift, did not press further an inquiry surpassed in importance by none of those upon which his master-mind was engaged. Apart, however, from these objective evidences, the mere subject-matter of Swedenborg's trance-revelations was enough to claim respectful attention. I cannot here discuss the strange mixture which they present of slavish literalism with exalted speculation, of pedantic orthodoxy with physical and moral insight far beyond the level of that age. It is enough to say here that even as Socrates called down philosophy from heaven to earth, so in a somewhat different sense it was Swedenborg who called up philosophy again from earth to heaven; — who originated the notion of science in the spiritual world, as earnestly, though not so persuasively, as Socrates originated the idea of science in this world which we seem to know. It was to Swedenborg first that that unseen world appeared before all things as a realm of law; a region not of mere emotional vagueness or stagnancy of adoration, but of definite progress according to definite relations of cause and effect, resulting from structural laws of spiritual existence and intercourse which we may in time learn partially to apprehend. For my own part I regard Swedenborg, — not, assuredly, as an inspired teacher, nor even as a trust-

---

[1] See glossary.

[2] I have ventured to coin the word "supernormal" to be applied to phenomena which are *beyond what usually happens* — *beyond*, that is, in the sense of suggesting unknown psychical laws. It is thus formed on the analogy of *abnormal*. When we speak of an abnormal phenomenon we do not mean one which *contravenes* natural laws, but one which exhibits them in an unusual or inexplicable form. Similarly by a supernormal phenomenon I mean, not one which *overrides* natural laws, for I believe no such phenomenon to exist, but one which exhibits the action of laws higher, in a psychical aspect, than are discerned in action in everyday life. By *higher* (either in a psychical or physiological sense) I mean "apparently belonging to a more advanced stage of evolution."

worthy interpreter of his own experiences, — but yet as a true and early precursor of that great inquiry which it is our present object to advance.

The next pioneer — fortunately still amongst us — whom I must mention even in this summary notice, is the celebrated physicist and chemist, Sir W. Crookes. Just as Swedenborg was the first leading man of science who distinctly conceived of the spiritual world as a world of law, so was Sir W. Crookes the first leading man of science who seriously endeavoured to test the alleged mutual influence and interpenetration of the spiritual world and our own by experiments of scientific precision.[1] Beyond the establishment of certain supernormal facts Crookes declined to go. But a large group of persons have founded upon these and similar facts a scheme of belief known as Modern Spiritualism, or Spiritism. Later chapters in this book will show how much I owe to certain observations made by members of this group — how often my own conclusions concur with conclusions at which they have previously arrived. And yet this work of mine is in large measure a critical attack upon the main Spiritist position, as held, say, by Mr. A. R. Wallace, its most eminent living supporter, — the belief, namely, that all or almost all supernormal phenomena are due to the action of spirits of the dead. By far the larger proportion, as I hold, are due to the action of the still embodied spirit of the agent or percipient himself. Apart from speculative differences, moreover, I altogether dissent from the conversion into a sectarian creed of what I hold should be a branch of scientific inquiry, growing naturally out of our existing knowledge. It is, I believe, largely to this temper of uncritical acceptance, degenerating often into blind credulity, that we must refer the lack of progress in Spiritualistic literature, and the encouragement which has often been bestowed upon manifest fraud, — so often, indeed, as to create among scientific men a strong indisposition to the study of phenomena recorded or advocated in a tone so alien from Science.

I know not how much of originality or importance may be attributed by subsequent students of the subject to the step next in order in this series of approximations. To those immediately concerned, the feeling of a new departure was inevitably given by the very smallness of the support

---

[1] Other servants of eminence — the great name of Alfred Russel Wallace will occur to all — had also satisfied themselves of the reality of these strange phenomena; but they had not tested or demonstrated that reality with equal care. I am not able in this brief sketch to allude to distinguished men of earlier date — Richard Glanvil, John Wesley, Samuel Johnson, etc., who discerned the importance of phenomena which they had no adequate means of investigating.

which they for a long time received, and by the difficulty which they
found in making their point of view intelligible to the scientific, to the
religious, or even to the spiritualistic world.   In about 1873 — at the
crest, as one may say, of perhaps the highest wave of materialism which
has ever swept over these shores — it became the conviction of a small
group of Cambridge friends that the deep questions thus at issue must be
fought out in a way more thorough than the champions either of religion
or of materialism had yet suggested.   Our attitudes of mind were in some
ways different; but to myself, at least, it seemed that no adequate attempt
had yet been made even to determine whether anything could be learnt as
to an unseen world or no; for that if anything were knowable about such a
world in such fashion that Science could adopt and maintain that knowledge, it must be discovered by no analysis of tradition, and by no manipulation of metaphysics, but simply by experiment and observation; — simply
by the application to phenomena within us and around us of precisely
the same methods of deliberate, dispassionate, exact inquiry which have
built up our actual knowledge of the world which we can touch and see.
I can hardly even now guess to how many of my readers this will seem
a truism, and to how many a paradox.   Truism or paradox, such a thought
suggested a kind of effort, which, so far as we could discover, had never
yet been made.   For what seemed needful was an inquiry of quite other
scope than the mere analysis of historical documents, or of the *origines*
of any alleged revelation in the past.   It must be an inquiry resting primarily, as all scientific inquiries in the stricter sense now must rest, upon
objective facts actually observable, upon experiments which we can repeat
to-day, and which we may hope to carry further to-morrow.   It must
be an inquiry based, to use an old term, on the uniformitarian hypothesis;
on the presumption, that is to say, that *if a spiritual world exists, and if
that world has at any epoch been manifest or even discoverable, then it ought
to be manifest or discoverable now.*

It was from this side, and from these general considerations, that the
group with which I have worked approached the subject.   Our methods,
our canons, were all to make.   In those early days we were more devoid
of precedents, of guidance, even of criticism that went beyond mere expressions of contempt, than is now readily conceived.   Seeking evidence
as best we could — collecting round us a small group of persons willing to
help in that quest for residual phenomena in the nature and experience of
man — we were at last fortunate enough to discover a convergence of experimental and of spontaneous evidence upon one definite and important
point.   We were led to believe that there was truth in a thesis which at

least since Swedenborg and the early mesmerists had been repeatedly, but cursorily and ineffectually, presented to mankind — the thesis that a communication can take place from mind to mind without the agency of the recognised organs of sense. We found that this agency, discernible even on trivial occasions by suitable experiment, seemed to connect itself with an agency more intense, or at any rate more recognisable, which operated at moments of crisis or at the hour of death. Edmund Gurney — the invaluable collaborator and friend whose loss in 1888 was our heaviest discouragement — set forth this evidence in a large work, *Phantasms of the Living*, in whose preparation Mr. Podmore and I took a minor part. The fifteen years which have elapsed since the publication of this book in 1886 have added to the evidence on which Gurney relied, and have shown (I venture to say) the general soundness of the canons of evidence and the lines of argument which it was his task to shape and to employ.[1]

Of fundamental importance, indeed, is this doctrine of telepathy — the first law, may one not say? — laid open to man's discovery, which, in my view at least, while operating in the material, is itself a law of the spiritual or *metetherial* world. In the course of this work it will be my task to show in many connections how far-reaching are the implications of this direct and supersensory communion of mind with mind. Among those implications none can be more momentous than the light thrown by this discovery upon man's intimate nature and possible survival of death.

We gradually discovered that the accounts of apparitions at the moment of death — testifying to a supersensory communication between the dying man and the friend who sees him — led on without perceptible break to apparitions occurring after the death of the person seen, but while that death was yet unknown to the percipient, and thus apparently due, not to mere brooding memory, but to a continued action of that departed spirit. The task next incumbent on us therefore seemed plainly to be the collection and analysis of evidence of this and other types, pointing directly to the survival of man's spirit. But after pursuing this task for some years I felt that in reality the step from the action of embodied to the action of disembodied spirits would still seem too sudden if taken in this direct way. So far, indeed, as the evidence from apparitions went, the series seemed continuous from phantasms of the living to phantasms of the dead. But the whole mass of evidence *primâ facie* pointing to man's survival was

---

[1] The Society for Psychical Research was founded in 1882, Professor W. F. Barrett taking a leading part in its promotion. Henry Sidgwick was its first President, and Edmund Gurney was its first Honorary Secretary — he and I being joint Honorary Secretaries of its Literary Committee, whose business was the collection of evidence.

of a much more complex kind. It consisted largely, for example, in written or spoken utterances, coming through the hand or voice of living men, but claiming to proceed from a disembodied source. To these utterances, as a whole, no satisfactory criterion had ever been applied.

In considering cases of this kind, then, it became gradually plain to me that before we could safely mark off any group of manifestations as definitely implying an influence from beyond the grave, there was need of a more searching review of the capacities of man's incarnate personality than psychologists unfamiliar with this new evidence had thought it worth their while to undertake.

It was only slowly, and as it were of necessity, that I embarked on a task which needed for its proper accomplishment a knowledge and training far beyond what I could claim. The very inadequate sketch which has resulted from my efforts is even in its author's view no more than preparatory and precursive to the fuller and sounder treatment of the same subject which I doubt not that the new century will receive from more competent hands. The truest success of this book will lie in its rapid supersession by a better. For this will show that at least I have not erred in supposing that a serious treatise on these topics is nothing else than the inevitable complement and conclusion of the slow process by which man has brought under the domain of science every group of attainable phenomena in turn — every group save this.

Let me then without further preamble embark upon that somewhat detailed survey of human faculty, as manifested during various phases of human personality, which is needful in order to throw fresh light on these unfamiliar themes. My discussion, I may say at once, will avoid metaphysics as carefully as it will avoid theology. I avoid theology, as already explained, because I consider that in arguments founded upon experiment and observation I have no right to appeal for support to traditional or subjective considerations, however important. For somewhat similar reasons I do not desire to introduce the idea of personality with any historical *résumé* of the philosophical opinions which have been held by various thinkers in the past, nor myself to speculate on matters lying beyond the possible field of objective proof. I shall merely for the sake of clearness begin by the briefest possible statement of two views of human personality which cannot be ignored, namely, the old-fashioned or common-sense view thereof, which is still held by the mass of mankind, and the newer view of experimental psychology, bringing out that composite or "colonial" character which on a close examination every personality of men or animals is seen to wear.

The following passage, taken from a work once of much note, Reid's "Essay on the Intellectual Powers of Man," expresses the simple *primâ facie* view with care and precision, yet with no marked impress of any one philosophical school:

The conviction which every man has of his identity, as far back as his memory reaches, needs no aid of philosophy to strengthen it; and no philosophy can weaken it without first producing some degree of insanity. . . . My personal identity, therefore, implies the continued existence of that indivisible thing which I call myself. Whatever this self may be, it is something which thinks, and deliberates, and resolves, and acts, and suffers. I am not thought, I am not action, I am not feeling; I am something that thinks, and acts, and suffers. My thoughts and actions and feelings change every moment; they have no continued, but a successive existence; but that *self* or *I*, to which they belong, is permanent, and has the same relation to all succeeding thoughts, actions, and feelings which I call mine. . . . The identity of a person is a perfect identity; wherever it is real it admits of no degrees; and it is impossible that a person should be in part the same and in part different, because a person is a *monad*, and is not divisible into parts. Identity, when applied to persons, has no ambiguity, and admits not of degrees, or of more and less. It is the foundation of all rights and obligations, and of all accountableness; and the notion of it is fixed and precise.

Contrast with this the passage with which M. Ribot concludes his essay on "Les Maladies de la Personnalité."

It is the organism, with the brain, its supreme representative, which constitutes the real personality; comprising in itself the remains of all that we have been and the possibilities of all that we shall be. The whole individual character is there inscribed, with its active and passive aptitudes, its sympathies and antipathies, its genius, its talent or its stupidity, its virtues and its vices, its torpor or its activity. The part thereof which emerges into consciousness is little compared with what remains buried, but operative nevertheless. The conscious personality is never more than a small fraction of the psychical personality. The unity of the Ego is not therefore the unity of a single entity diffusing itself among multiple phenomena; it is the co-ordination of a certain number of states perpetually renascent, and having for their sole common basis the vague feeling of our body. This unity does not diffuse itself downwards, but is aggregated by ascent from below; it is not an initial but a terminal point. Does then this perfect unity really exist? In the rigorous, the mathematical sense, assuredly it does *not*. In a relative sense it is met with, — rarely and for a moment. When a good marksman takes aim, or a skilful surgeon operates, his whole body and mind converge towards a single act. But note the result; under those conditions the sentiment of real personality disappears, for the conscious individual is simplified into a single idea, and the personal sentiment is excluded by the complete unification of consciousness. We thus return by another route to the same conclusion; *the Self is a co-ordination*. It oscillates between two extremes at each of which it ceases to exist; — absolute unity and absolute incoherence.

The last word of all this is that since the consensus of consciousness is subordinated to the consensus of the organism, the problem of the unity of the Ego is in its ultimate form a problem of Biology. Let Biology explain, if it can, the genesis of organisms and the solidarity of their constituent parts. The psychological explanation must needs follow on the same track.

Here, then, we have two clear and definite views, — supported, the one by our inmost consciousness, the other by unanswerable observation and inference, — yet apparently incompatible the one with the other. And in fact by most writers they have been felt and acknowledged to be even hopelessly incompatible. The supporters of the view that "The Self is a co-ordination," — and this, I need hardly say, is now the view prevalent among experimental psychologists, — have frankly given up any notion of an underlying unity, — of a life independent of the organism, — in a word, of a human soul. The supporters of the unity of the Ego, on the other hand, if they have not been able to be equally explicit in *denying* the opposite view, have made up for this by the thorough-going way in which they have *ignored* it. I know of no source from which valid help has been offered towards the reconcilement of the two opposing systems in a profounder synthesis. If I believe — as I do believe — that in the present work some help in this direction is actually given, this certainly does not mean that I suppose myself capable of stitching the threadbare metaphysical arguments into a more stable fabric. It simply means that certain fresh evidence can now be adduced, which has the effect of showing the case on each side in a novel light; — nay, even of closing the immediate controversy by a judgment more decisively in favour of *both* parties than either could have expected. On the one side, and in favour of the co-ordinators, — all their analysis of the Self into its constituent elements, all that they urge of positive observation, of objective experiment, must — as I shall maintain on the strength of the new facts which I shall adduce — be unreservedly conceded. Let them push their analysis as far as they like, — let them get down, if they can, to those ultimate infinitesimal psychical elements from which is upbuilt the complex, the composite, the "colonial" structure and constitution of man. All this may well be valid and important work. It is only on their *negative* side that the conclusions of this school need a complete overhauling. Deeper, bolder inquiry along their own line shows that they have erred when they asserted that analysis showed no trace of faculty beyond such as the life of earth — as they conceive it — could foster, or the environment of earth employ. For in reality analysis shows traces of faculty which this material or planetary life could not have called into being, and whose exercise even here and now involves and necessitates the existence of a spiritual world.

On the other side, and in favour of the partisans of the unity of the Ego, the effect of the new evidence is to raise their claim to a far higher ground, and to substantiate it for the first time with the strongest presumptive proof which can be imagined for it; — a proof, namely, that the Ego can and does survive — not only the minor disintegrations which affect it during earth-life — but the crowning disintegration of bodily death. In view of this unhoped-for ratification of their highest dream, they may be more than content to surrender as untenable the far narrower conception of the unitary Self which was all that "common-sense philosophies" had ventured to claim. The "conscious Self" of each of us, as we call it, — the empirical, the supraliminal Self, as I should prefer to say, — does not comprise the whole of the consciousness or of the faculty within us. There exists a more comprehensive consciousness, a profounder faculty, which for the most part remains potential only so far as regards the life of earth, but from which the consciousness and the faculty of earth-life are mere selections, and which reasserts itself in its plenitude after the liberating change of death.

Towards this conclusion, which assumed for me something like its present shape some fourteen years since,[1] a long series of tentative speculations, based on gradually accruing evidence, has slowly conducted me. The conception is one which has hitherto been regarded as purely mystical; and if I endeavour to plant it upon a scientific basis I certainly shall not succeed in stating it in its final terms or in supporting it with the best arguments which longer experience will suggest. Its validity, indeed, will be impressed — if at all — upon the reader only by the successive study of the various kinds of evidence to which this book will refer him.

Yet so far as the initial possibility or plausibility of such a widened conception of human consciousness is concerned; — and this is all which can be dealt with at this moment of its first introduction; — I have not seen in such criticism as has hitherto been bestowed upon my theory any very weighty demurrer.[2]

[1] See, for instance, *Proceedings* of the Society for Psychical Research (henceforth in this book referred to as the S.P.R.), vol. iv. p. 256, Jan. 1887.

[2] See, however, an article in *Proceedings* S.P.R., vol. xi. pp. 317 to 325, entitled

"Normally at least," says one critic, summarising in a few words the ordinary view, "all the consciousness we have at any moment corresponds to all the activity which is going on at that moment in the brain. There is one unitary conscious state accompanying all the simultaneous brain excitations together, and each single part of the brain-process contributes something to its nature. None of the brain-processes split themselves off from the rest and have a separate consciousness of their own." This is, no doubt, the apparent dictum of consciousness, but it is nothing more. And the dicta of consciousness have already been shown to need correction in so many ways which the ordinary observer could never have anticipated that we have surely no right to trust consciousness, so to say, a step further than we can feel it, — to hold that anything whatever — even a separate consciousness in our own organisms — can be proved *not* to exist by the mere fact that we — as we know ourselves — are not aware of it.

But indeed this claim to a unitary consciousness tends to become less forcible as it is more scientifically expressed. It rests on the plain man's conviction that there is only one of him; and this conviction the experimental psychologist is always tending to weaken or narrow by the admission of coexistent localised degrees of consciousness in the brain, which are at any rate not obviously reducible to a single state. Even those who would stop far short of my own position find it needful to resort to metaphors of their own to express the different streams of "awareness" which we all feel to be habitually coexistent within us. They speak of "fringes" of ordinary consciousness; of "marginal" associations; of the occasional perception of "currents of low intensity." These metaphors may all of them be of use, in a region where metaphor is our only mode of expression; but none of them covers all the facts now collected. And on the other side, I need not say, are plenty of phrases which beg the question of soul and body, or of the man's own spirit and external spirits, in no scientific fashion. There seems to be need of a term of wider application, which shall make as few assumptions as possible. Nor is such a term difficult to find.

The idea of a *threshold* (*limen*, *Schwelle*), of consciousness; — of a level above which sensation or thought must rise before it can enter into our conscious life; — is a simple and familiar one. The word *subliminal*, — meaning "beneath that threshold," — has already been used to define those sensations which are too feeble to be individually recognised. I propose to extend the meaning of the term, so as to make it cover *all* that takes place beneath the ordinary threshold, or say, if preferred, outside the

"Subliminal Self or Unconscious Cerebration," by Mr. A. H. Pierce, of Harvard University, with a reply by Mr. F. Podmore.

ordinary margin of consciousness; — not only those faint stimulations whose very faintness keeps them submerged, but much else which psychology as yet scarcely recognises; sensations, thoughts, emotions, which may be strong, definite, and independent, but which, by the original constitution of our being, seldom emerge into that *supraliminal* current of consciousness which we habitually identify with *ourselves*. Perceiving (as this book will try to show) that these submerged thoughts and emotions possess the characteristics which we associate with conscious life, I feel bound to speak of a *subliminal* or *ultra-marginal consciousness*, — a consciousness which we shall see, for instance, uttering or writing sentences quite as complex and coherent as the supraliminal consciousness could make them. Perceiving further that this conscious life beneath the threshhold or beyond the margin seems to be no discontinuous or intermittent thing; that not only are these isolated subliminal processes comparable with isolated supraliminal processes (as when a problem is solved by some unknown procedure in a dream), but that there also is a continuous subliminal chain of memory (or more chains than one) involving just that kind of individual and persistent revival of old impressions, and response to new ones, which we commonly call a Self, — I find it permissible and convenient to speak of subliminal Selves, or more briefly of a subliminal Self. I do not indeed by using this term assume that there are two correlative and parallel selves existing always within each of us. Rather I mean by the subliminal Self that part of the Self which is commonly subliminal; and I conceive that there may be, — not only *co-operations* between these quasi-independent trains of thought, — but also upheavals and alternations of personality of many kinds, so that what was once below the surface may for a time, or permanently, rise above it. And I conceive also that no Self of which we can here have cognisance is in reality more than a fragment of a larger Self, — revealed in a fashion at once shifting and limited through an organism not so framed as to afford it full manifestation.

Now this hypothesis is exposed manifestly to two main forms of attack, which to a certain extent neutralise each other. On the one hand it has been attacked, as has already been indicated, as being too elaborate for the facts, — as endowing transitory moments of subconscious intelligence with more continuity and independence than they really possess. These ripples over the threshold, it may be said, can be explained by the wind of circumstance, without assuming springs or currents in the personality deep below.

But soon we shall come upon a group of phenomena which this view

will by no means meet.   For we shall find that the subliminal uprushes, —
the impulses or communications which reach our emergent from our
submerged selves, — are (in spite of their miscellaneousness) often characteristically different in quality from any element known to our ordinary
supraliminal life.   They are different in a way which implies faculty of
which we have had no previous knowledge, operating in an environment
of which hitherto we have been wholly unaware.   This broad statement it is
of course the purpose of my whole work to justify.   Assuming its truth here
for argument's sake, we see at once that the problem of the hidden self
entirely changes its aspect.   Telepathy and telæsthesia — the perception of
distant thoughts and of distant scenes without the agency of the recognised
organs of sense; — those faculties suggest either incalculable extension of
our own mental powers, or else the influence upon us of minds freer and
less trammelled than our own.   And this second hypothesis, — which would
explain by the agency of discarnate minds, or spirits, all these supernormal
phenomena, — does at first sight simplify the problem, and has by Mr.
A. R. Wallace and others been pushed so far as to remove all need of what
he deems the gratuitous and cumbrous hypothesis of a subliminal self.

I believe, indeed, that it will become plain as we proceed that some
such hypothesis as this, — of almost continuous spirit-intervention and
spirit-guidance, — is at once rendered necessary if the subliminal faculties
for which I argue are denied to man.   And my conception of a subliminal
self will thus appear, not as an extravagant and needless, but as a limiting
and rationalising hypothesis, when it is applied to phenomena which at
first sight suggest Mr. Wallace's extremer view, but which I explain by the
action of man's own spirit, without invoking spirits external to himself.
I do not indeed say that the explanation here suggested is applicable in all
cases, or to the complete exclusion of the spirit-hypothesis.   On the contrary, the one view gives support to the other.   For these faculties of distant
communication exist none the less, even though we should refer them to
our own subliminal selves.   We can, in that case, affect each other at a
distance, telepathically; — and if our incarnate spirits can act thus in at
least apparent independence of the fleshly body, the presumption is strong
that other spirits may exist independently of the body, and may affect us
in similar manner.

The much-debated hypothesis of spirit-intervention, in short, still looms
behind the hypothesis of the subliminal Self; but that intermediate hypothesis should, I think, in this early stage of what must be a long inquiry,
prove useful to the partisans of either side.   For those who are altogether
unwilling to admit the action of agencies other than the spirits of living

men, it will be needful to form as high an estimate as possible of the faculties held in reserve by these spirits while still in the flesh. For those, on the other hand, who believe in the influence of discarnate spirits, this scheme affords a path of transition, and as it were a provisional intelligibility.

These far-reaching speculations make the element of keenest interest in the inquiry which follows. But even apart from its possible bearing on a future life, the further study of our submerged mentation, — of the processes within us of which we catch only indirect, and as it were, refracted glimpses, — seems at this time especially called for by the trend of modern research. For of late years we have realised more and more fully upon how shifting and complex a foundation of ancestral experience each individual life is based. In recapitulation, in summary, in symbol, we retraverse, from the embryo to the corpse, the history of life on earth for millions of years. During our self-adaptation to continually wider environments, there may probably have been a continual displacement of the threshold of consciousness; — involving the lapse and submergence of much that once floated in the main stream of our being. Our consciousness at any given stage of our evolution is but the phosphorescent ripple on an unsounded sea. And, like the ripple, it is not only superficial but manifold. Our psychical unity is federative and unstable; it has arisen from irregular accretions in the remote past; it consists even now only in the limited collaboration of multiple groups. These discontinuities and incoherences in the Ego the elder psychologists managed to ignore. Yet infancy, idiocy, sleep, insanity, decay; — these breaks and stagnancies in the conscious stream were always present to show us, even more forcibly than more delicate analyses show us now, that the first obvious conception of man's continuous and unitary personality was wholly insecure; and that if indeed a soul inspired the body, that soul must be sought for far beneath these bodily conditions by which its self-manifestation was clouded and obscured.

The difference between older and newer conceptions of the unifying principle or soul (if soul there be) in man, considered as manifesting through corporeal limitations, will thus resemble the difference between the older and newer conceptions of the way in which the sun reveals himself to our senses. Night and storm-cloud and eclipse men have known from the earliest ages; but now they know that even at noonday the sunbeam which reaches them, when fanned out into a spectrum, is barred with belts and lines of varying darkness; — while they have learnt also that where at either end the spectrum fades out into what for us is blackness, there stretches onwards in reality an undiscovered illimitable ray.

It will be convenient for future reference if I draw out this parallel somewhat more fully. I compare, then, man's gradual progress in self-knowledge to his gradual decipherment of the nature and meaning of the sunshine which reaches him as light and heat indiscernibly intermingled. So also Life and Consciousness — the sense of a world within him and a world without — come to the child indiscernibly intermingled in a pervading glow. Optical analysis splits up the white ray into the various coloured rays which compose it. Philosophical analysis in like manner splits up the vague consciousness of the child into many faculties; — into the various external senses, the various modes of thought within. This has been the task of descriptive and introspective psychology. Experimental psychology is adding a further refinement. In the sun's spectrum, and in stellar spectra, are many dark lines or bands, due to the absorption of certain rays by certain vapours in the atmosphere of sun or stars or earth. And similarly in the range of spectrum of our own sensation and faculty there are many inequalities — permanent and temporary — of brightness and definition. Our mental atmosphere is clouded by vapours and illumined by fires, and is clouded and illumined differently at different times. The psychologist who observes, say, how his reaction-times are modified by alcohol is like the physicist who observes what lines are darkened by the interposition of a special gas. Our knowledge of our conscious spectrum is thus becoming continually more accurate and detailed.

But turning back once more to the physical side of our simile, we observe that our knowledge of the visible solar spectrum, however minute, is but an introduction to the knowledge which we hope ultimately to attain of the sun's rays. The limits of our spectrum do not inhere in the sun that shines, but in the eye that marks his shining. Beyond each end of that prismatic ribbon are ether-waves of which our retina takes no cognisance. Beyond the red end come waves whose potency we still recognise, but as heat and not as light. Beyond the violet end are waves still more mysterious; whose very existence man for ages never suspected, and whose intimate potencies are still but obscurely known. Even thus, I venture to affirm, beyond each end of our conscious spectrum extends a range of faculty and perception, exceeding the known range, but as yet indistinctly guessed. The artifices of the modern physicist have extended far in each direction the visible spectrum known to Newton. It is for the modern psychologist to discover artifices which may extend in each direction the conscious spectrum as known to Plato or to Kant. The phenomena cited in this work carry us, one may say, as far onwards as fluorescence carries us beyond the violet end. The "X rays" of the psychical spectrum remain for a later age to discover.

Our simile, indeed — be it once for all noted — is a most imperfect one. The range of human faculty cannot be truly expressed in any linear form. Even a three-dimensional scheme, — a radiation of faculties from a centre of life, — would ill render its complexity. Yet something of clearness will be gained by even this rudimentary mental picture; — representing conscious human faculty as a linear spectrum whose red rays begin where voluntary muscular control and organic sensation begin, and whose violet rays fade away at the point at which man's highest strain of thought or imagination merges into reverie or ecstasy.

At both ends of this spectrum I believe that our evidence indicates a momentous prolongation. Beyond the *red* end, of course, we already know that vital faculty of some kind must needs extend. We know that organic processes are constantly taking place within us which are not subject to our control, but which make the very foundation of our physical being. We know that the habitual limits of our voluntary action can be far extended under the influence of strong excitement. It need not surprise us to find that appropriate artifices — hypnotism or self-suggestion — can carry the power of our will over our organism to a yet further point.

The faculties that lie beyond the *violet* end of our psychological spectrum will need more delicate exhibition and will command a less ready belief. The actinic energy which lies beyond the violet end of the solar spectrum is less obviously influential in our material world than is the dark heat which lies beyond the red end. Even so, one may say, the influence of the ultra-intellectual or supernormal faculties upon our welfare as terrene organisms is less marked in common life than the influence of the organic or subnormal faculties. Yet it is *that* prolongation of our spectrum upon which our gaze will need to be most strenuously fixed. It is *there* that we shall find our inquiry opening upon a cosmic prospect, and inciting us upon an endless way.

Even the first stages of this progress are long and labyrinthine; and it may be useful to conclude this introductory chapter by a brief summary of the main tracts across which our winding road must lie. It will be my object to lead by transitions as varied and as gradual as possible from phenomena held as normal to phenomena held as supernormal, but which like the rest are simply and solely the inevitable results and manifestations of universal Law.

Following then on this first or introductory chapter is one containing a discussion of the ways in which human personality disintegrates and decays. *Alternations of personality* and hysterical phenomena generally are in this connection the most instructive to us.

In the third chapter we utilize the insight thus gained and discuss the line of evolution which enables man to maintain and intensify his true normality. What type of man is he to whom the epithet of *normal*, — an epithet often obscure and misleading, — may be most fitly applied? I claim that that man shall be regarded as normal who has the fullest grasp of faculties which inhere in the whole race. Among these faculties I count subliminal as well as supraliminal powers; — the mental processes which take place below the conscious threshold as well as those which take place above it; and I attempt to show that those who reap most advantage from this submerged mentation are men of *genius*.

The fourth chapter deals with the alternating phase through which man's personality is constructed habitually to pass. I speak of *sleep;* which I regard as a phase of personality, adapted to maintain our existence in the spiritual environment, and to draw from thence the vitality of our physical organisms. In this chapter I also discuss certain supernormal phenomena which sometimes occur in the state of sleep.

The fifth chapter treats of *hypnotism*, considered as an *empirical development of sleep*. It will be seen that hypnotic suggestion intensifies the physical recuperation of sleep, and aids the emergence of those supernormal phenomena which ordinary sleep and spontaneous somnambulism sometimes exhibit.

From hypnotism we pass on in the sixth chapter to experiments, less familiar to the public than those classed as hypnotic, but which give a still further insight into our subliminal faculty. With these experiments are intermingled many spontaneous phenomena; and the chapter will take up and continue the spontaneous phenomena of Chapters III. and IV. as well as the experiments of Chapter V. Its theme will be the messages which the subliminal self sends up to the supraliminal in the form of sensory hallucinations: — the visions fashioned internally, but manifested not to the inward eye alone; the voices which repeat as though in audible tones the utterance of the self within.

These *sensory automatisms*, as I have termed them, are very often *telepathic* — involve, that is to say, the transmission of ideas and sensations from one mind to another without the agency of the recognised organs of sense. Nor would it seem that such transmission need necessarily cease with the bodily death of the transmitting agent. In the seventh chapter evidence is brought forward to show that those who communicated with us telepathically in this world may communicate with us telepathically from the other. Thus *phantasms of the dead* receive a new meaning from observations of the phenomena occurring between living men.

But besides the hallucinatory hearing or picture-seeing which we have classed as sensory automatisms, there is another method by which the subliminal may communicate with the supraliminal self.

In Chapter VIII., we consider in what ways *motor automatism* — the unwilled activity of hand or voice — may be used as a means of such communication. Unwilled writings and utterances furnish the opportunity for experiment more prolonged and continuous than the phantasms or pictures of sensory automatism can often give, and, like them, may sometimes originate in telepathic impressions received by the subliminal self from another mind. These motor automatisms, moreover, as the ninth chapter shows, are apt to become more complete, more controlling, than sensory automatisms. They may lead on, in some cases, to the apparent *possession* of the sensitive by some extraneous spirit, who seems to write and talk through the sensitive's organism, giving evidence of his own surviving identity.

The reader who may feel disposed to give his adhesion to this culminating group of the long series of evidences which have pointed with more and more clearness to the survival of human personality, and to the possibility for men on earth of actual commerce with a world beyond, may feel perhaps that the *desiderium orbis catholici*, the intimate and universal hope of every generation of men, has never till this day approached so near to fulfilment. There has never been so fair a prospect for Life and Love. But the goal to which we tend is not an ideal of personal happiness alone. The anticipation of our own future is but one element in the prospect which opens to us now. Our inquiry has broadened into a wider scope. The point from which we started was an analysis of the latent faculties of man. The point towards which our argument has carried us is the existence of a spiritual environment in which those faculties operate, and of unseen neighbours who speak to us thence with slowly gathering power. Deep in this spiritual environment the cosmic secret lies. It is our business to collect the smallest indications; to carry out from this treasury of Rhampsinitus so much as our bare hands can steal away. We have won our scraps of spiritual experience, our messages from behind the veil; we can try them in their connection with certain enigmas which philosophy hardly hoped to be able to put to proof. Can we, for instance, learn anything, — to begin with fundamental problems, — of the relation of spiritual phenomena to Space, to Time, to the material world?

As to the idea of Space, the evidence which will have been presented will enable us to speak with perhaps more clearness than could have been hoped for in such a matter. Spiritual life, we infer, is not bound and confined by space-considerations in the same way as the life of earth. But in what way is that greater freedom attained? It appears to be attained by the mere extension of certain licenses (so to call them) permitted to ourselves. We on earth submit to two familiar laws of the ordinary material universe. A body can only act where it is. Only one body can occupy the same part of space at the same moment. Applied to common affairs these rules are of plain construction. But once get beyond ponderable matter, — once bring life and ether into play, and definitions become difficult indeed. The orator, the poet, we say, can only act where he is; — but where is he? He has transformed the sheet of paper into a spiritual agency; — nay, the mere memory of him persists as a source of energy in other minds. Again, we may say that no other body can be in the same place as this writing-table; but what of the ether? What we have thus far learnt of spiritual operation seems merely to extend these two possibilities. Telepathy indefinitely extends the range of an unembodied spirit's potential presence. The interpenetration of the spiritual with the material environment leaves this ponderable planet unable to check or to hamper spiritual presence or operation. Strange and new though our evidence may be, it needs at present in its relation to space nothing more than an immense extension of conceptions which the disappearance of earthly limitations was certain immensely to extend.

How, then, does the matter stand with regard to our relation to Time? Do we find that our new phenomena point to any mode of understanding or of transcending Time fundamentally different from those modes which we have at our command?

In dealing with Time Past we have memory and written record; in dealing with Time Future we have forethought, drawing inferences from the past.

Can, then, the spiritual knowledge of Past and Future which our evidence shows be explained by assuming that these existing means of knowledge are raised to a higher power? Or are we driven to postulate something in the nature of Time which is to us inconceivable; — some co-existence of Past and Future in an eternal Now? It is plainly with Time Past that we must begin the inquiry.

The knowledge of the past which automatic communications manifest

is in most cases apparently referable to the actual memory of pe
existing beyond the tomb.   It reaches us telepathically, as from
which remote scenes are still imprinted.   But there are certain sce
are not easily assigned to the individual memory of any given sp
if it be possible for us to learn of present facts by telæsthesia as
telepathy; — by some direct supernormal percipience without the ____
tion of any other mind to which the facts are already known, — may there
not be also a retrocognitive telæsthesia by which we may attain a direct
knowledge of facts in the past?

Some conception of this kind may possibly come nearest to the truth.
It may even be that some World-Soul is perennially conscious of all its past;
and that individual souls, as they enter into deeper consciousness, enter
into something which is at once reminiscence and actuality.   But nevertheless a narrower hypothesis will cover the actual cases with which we have
to deal.   Past facts are known to men on earth not from memory only, but
by written record; and there may be records, of what kind we know not,
which persist in the spiritual world.   Our retrocognitions seem often a
recovery of isolated fragments of thought and feeling, pebbles still hard
and rounded amid the indecipherable sands over which the mighty waters
are "rolling evermore."

When we look from Time Past to Time Future we are confronted with
essentially the same problems, though in a still more perplexing form, and
with the world-old mystery of Free Will *versus* Necessity looming in the
background.   Again we find that, just as individual memory would serve
to explain a large proportion of Retrocognition, so individual forethought
— a subliminal forethought, based often on profound organic facts not
normally known to us — will explain a large proportion of Precognition.
But here again we find also precognitions which transcend what seems
explicable by the foresight of any mind such as we know; and we are tempted
to dream of a World-Soul whose Future is as present to it as its Past.   But
in this speculation also, so vast and vague an explanation seems for the
present beyond our needs; and it is safer — if aught be safe in this region
which only actual evidence could have emboldened us to approach — to
take refuge in the conception of intelligences not infinite, yet gifted with a
foresight which strangely transcends our own.

Closely allied to speculations such as these is another speculation,
more capable of subjection to experimental test, yet which remains still
inconclusively tested, and which has become for many reasons a stumbling-
block rather than a corroboration in the spiritual inquiry.   I refer to the
question whether any influence is exercised by spirits upon the gross

material world otherwise than through ordinary organic structures. We know that the spirit of a living man controls his own organism, and we shall see reason to conclude that discarnate spirits may also control, by some form of "possession," the organisms of living persons, — may affect directly, that is to say, some portions of matter which we call living, namely, the brain of the entranced sensitive. There seems to me, then, no paradox in the supposition that some effect should be produced by spiritual agency — possibly through the mediation of some kind of energy derived from living human beings — upon inanimate matter as well. And I believe that as a fact such effects have been observed and recorded in a trustworthy manner by Sir W. Crookes, the late Dr. Speer, and others, in the cases especially of D. D. Home and of W. Stainton Moses. If, indeed, I call these and certain other records still inconclusive, it is mainly on account of the mass of worthless narratives with which they have been in some sense smothered; the long history of so-called investigations which have consisted merely in an interchange of credulity and fraud. For the present the evidence of this kind which has real value is better presented, I think, in separate records than collected or discussed in any generalised form. All that I purpose in this work, therefore, is briefly to indicate the relation which these "physical phenomena" hold to the psychical phenomena with which my book is concerned. Alongside of the faculty or achievement of man's ordinary or supraliminal self I shall demarcate the faculty or achievement which I ascribe to his subliminal self; and alongside of this again I shall arrange such few well-attested phenomena as seem *primâ facie* to demand the physical intervention of discarnate intelligences.

I have traced the utmost limits to which any claim to a scientific basis for these inquiries can at present be pushed. Yet the subject-matter has not yet been exhausted of half its significance. The conclusions to which our evidence points are not such as can be discussed or dismissed as a mere matter of speculative curiosity. They affect every belief, every faculty, every hope and aim of man; and they affect him the more intimately as his interests grow more profound. Whatever meaning be applied to ethics, to philosophy, to religion, the concern of all these is here.

It would have been inconsistent with my main purpose had I interpolated considerations of this kind into the body of this work. For that purpose was above all to show that realms left thus far to philosophy or to religion, — too often to mere superstition and idle dream, — might in the end be brought under steady scientific rule. I contend that Religion and Science are no separable or independent provinces of thought or action;

but rather that each name implies a different aspect of the same ideal; — that ideal being the completely normal reaction of the individual spirit to the whole of cosmic law.

Assuredly this deepening response of man's spirit to the Cosmos deepening round him must be affected by all the signals which now are glimmering out of night to tell him of his inmost nature and his endless fate. Who can think that either Science or Revelation has spoken as yet more than a first half-comprehended word? But if in truth souls departed call to us, it is to them that we shall listen most of all. We shall weigh their undesigned concordances, we shall analyse the congruity of their message with the facts which such a message should explain. To some thoughts which may thus be generated I shall try to give expression in an Epilogue to the present work.

CHAPTER II

DISINTEGRATIONS OF PERSONALITY

θάνατός ἐστιν ὁκόσα ἐγερθέντες ὁρέομεν, ὁκόσα δὲ εὕδοντες, ὕπνος.
— HERACLITUS.

OF the race of man we know for certain that it has been evolved through many ages and through countless forms of change. We know for certain that its changes continue still; nay, that more causes of change act upon us in "fifty years of Europe" than in "a cycle of Cathay." We may reasonably conjecture that the race will continue to change with increasing rapidity, and through a period in comparison with which our range of recorded history shrinks into a moment.

The actual nature of these coming changes, indeed, lies beyond our imagination. Many of them are probably as inconceivable to us now as eyesight would have been to our eyeless ancestors. All that we can do is to note so far as possible the structural laws of our personality as deduced from its changes thus far; inferring that for some time to come, at any rate, its further changes will proceed upon similar lines.

I have already (Chapter I) indicated the general view as to the nature of human personality which is maintained in this work. I regard each man as at once profoundly unitary and almost infinitely composite, as inheriting from earthly ancestors a multiplex and "colonial" organism — polyzoic and perhaps polypsychic in an extreme degree; but also as ruling and unifying that organism by a soul or spirit absolutely beyond our present analysis — a soul which has originated in a spiritual or metetherial environment; which even while embodied subsists in that environment; and which will still subsist therein after the body's decay.

It is, of course, impossible for us to picture to ourselves the way in which the individual life of each cell of the body is reconciled with the unity of the central life which controls the body as a whole. But this difficulty is not created or intensified by the hypothesis of a separate and persistent soul. On no hypothesis can we really understand the collaboration and subordination of the cell-lives of any multicellular animal. It is as mysterious in the starfish as it is in Plato; and the "eight brains of Aurelia," with their individual and their common life, are as inconceivable as the life of the phagocytes in the philosopher's veins, in their relation to his central thought.[1]

I claim, in fact, that the ancient hypothesis of an indwelling soul, possessing and using the body as a whole, yet bearing a real, though obscure relation to the various more or less apparently disparate conscious groupings manifested in connection with the organism and in connection with more or less localised groups of nerve-matter, is a hypothesis not more perplexing, not more cumbrous, than any other hypothesis yet suggested. I claim also that it is conceivably provable, — I myself hold it as actually proved, — by direct observation. I hold that certain manifestations of central individualities, associated now or formerly with certain definite organisms, have been observed in operation apart from those organisms, both while the organisms were still living, and after they had decayed. Whether or no this thesis be as yet sufficiently proved, it is at least at variance with no scientific principle nor established fact whatever; and it is of a nature which continued observation may conceivably establish to the satisfaction of all. The negative thesis, on the other hand, is a thesis in unstable equilibrium. It cannot be absolutely proved by any number of negative instances; and it may be absolutely disproved by a single positive instance. It may have at present a greater scientific *currency*, but it can have no real scientific authority as against the view defended in these pages.

Leaving these questions, however, aside for the present, we may agree that in the organism as we can observe it in common life we have no complete or unchanging unity, but rather a complex hierarchy of groups of cells exercising vaguely limited functions, and working together with rough precision, tolerable harmony, fair success. That these powers ever work *perfectly* together we have no evidence. Our feeling of health is but a rough haphazard register of what is passing within us. Nor would it ever be possible to define a permanently ideal status in an organism in moving equilibrium, — an organism which lives by exploding unstable compounds, and which is constantly aiming at new ends at the expense of the old.

Many disturbances and disintegrations of the personality must presently fall to be discussed. But the reader who may follow me must remember the point of view from which I am writing. The aim of my

---

[1] The difficulty of conceiving any cellular focus, either fixed or shifting, has actually led some psychologists to demand a unifying principle which is not cellular, and yet is not a soul.

analysis is not to destroy but to fulfil; — or say, rather, my hope is that observation of the ways in which the personality tends to disintegrate may suggest methods which may tend on the other hand to its more complete integration.

Such improvements upon the natural conditions of the organism are not unknown. Just as the study of hysteria deals mainly with instabilities in the threshold of consciousness, so does the study of zymotic disease deal mainly with instabilities in the constitution of the blood. The ordinary object of the physician is to check these instabilities when they occur; to restore healthy blood in the place of vitiated. The experimental biologist has a further aim. He wishes to provide men with *better* blood than nature has bestowed; to elicit from virus and decay some element whose infusion into the veins may give immunity against microbic invasion. As the adult is safer against such attacks than the child by dint of his more advanced development, so is the immunised adult safer than the common man. The change of his blood which healthy maturity has induced has made him safe against whooping-cough. The change in his blood which we effect by injecting antitoxin makes him temporarily safe against diphtheria. We have improved upon nature; — and our artifice has been *prophylactic* by virtue of being in a certain sense *developmental*.

Even such, I trust, may be the achievement of experimental psychology in a later day. I shall be well content if in this chapter I can give hints for some future colligation of such evolutive phenomena as may lurk amid a mass of phenomena mainly dissolutive — phenomena whose records are scattered and imperfect, and have as yet only in some few directions, and by quite recent writers, been collated or systematised on any definite plan.

The discussion of these disintegrations of personality needs, I think, some little clearing of the ground beforehand, if it is to avoid confusion. It will be needful to speak of concurrent and alternating streams of consciousness, — of subliminal and supraliminal strata of personality and the like; — phrases which save much trouble when used with care, but which need some words of preliminary explanation. It is not easy to realise that anything which deserves the name of consciousness can be going on within us, apart from that central stream of thought and feeling with which we identify ourselves in common life. Something of definition is needed; — not indeed of any formal or dogmatic kind; — but enough to make clear the sense given to such words as consciousness, memory, personality, in the ensuing pages.

I begin, then, with the obvious remark that when we conceive any act other than our own as a conscious act, we do so either because we regard it as *complex*, and therefore *purposive*, or because we perceive that it has been *remembered*. Thus we call the fencer or the chess-player fully conscious; or, again, we say, "The man who seemed stunned after that blow on the head must really have been conscious all the time; for he afterwards recalled every incident." The *memorability* of an act is, in fact, a better proof of consciousness than its complexity. Thus consciousness has been denied both to hypnotised subjects and to dogs; but it is easier to prove that the hypnotised subject is conscious than that the dog is conscious. For the hypnotised subject, though he may forget the incidents of the trance when he awakes, will remember them in the next trance; or he may be trained to remember them in the waking state also; while with regard to the dog we cannot decide from the mere complexity of his actions how far he is conscious of their performance. With him, too, the best line of proof lies in his obvious memory of past acts. And yet, although all agree that our own memory, broadly speaking, proves our past consciousness, some persons would not admit that a dog's memory does so too. The dog's organism, they would say, responds, no doubt, in a new manner to a second repetition of a previous stimulus; but this is more or less true of all living organisms, or parts of organisms, even far below what we generally regard as a conscious level.

Reflections of this kind naturally lead to a wider conception of consciousness. It is gradually seen that the earlier inquiries which men have made about consciousness have been of a merely ethical or legal character; — have simply aimed at deciding whether at a given moment a man was *responsible* for his acts, either to a human or to a divine tribunal. Commonsense has seemed to encourage this method of definite demarcation; we judge practically either that a man is conscious or that he is not; in the experience of life intermediate states are of little importance.

As soon, however, as the problem is regarded as a psychological one, to be decided by observation and experiment, these hard and fast lines grow fainter and fainter. We come to regard consciousness as an attribute which may possibly be present in all kinds of varying degrees in connection with the animal and vegetable worlds; as the psychical counterpart of life; as conceivably the psychical counterpart of all phenomenal existence. Or, rather, we may say this of *mind*, to which, in its more elementary forms, consciousness bears somewhat the same relation as self-consciousness bears to consciousness, or some higher evolution may bear to self-consciousness.

This being so, I cannot see how we can phrase our definition more simply than by saying that any act or condition must be regarded as conscious if it is *potentially memorable*; — if it can be recollected, under any circumstances, by the subject concerned. It does not seem needful that the circumstances under which such recollection may occur should arise while the subject is still incarnated on this planet. We shall never on this planet remember the great majority of our dreams; but those dreams were presumably no less conscious than the dreams which a sudden awakening allowed us to keep in memory. Certain hypnotic subjects, indeed, who can be made to remember their dreams by suggestion, apparently remember dreams previously latent just as easily as dreams previously remembered. And we shall have various other examples of the unexpected recollection of experiences supposed to have been entirely devoid of consciousness.

We are bound, I think, to draw at least this negative conclusion: that we must not take for granted that our apparently central consciousness is something wholly different in kind from the minor consciousnesses out of which it is in some sense elaborated. I do indeed believe it to be in an important sense different; but this difference must not be assumed on the basis of our subjective sensations alone. We must approach the whole subject of split or duplicated personalities with no prepossession against the possibility of any given arrangement or division of the total mass of consciousness which exists within us.

Before we can picture to ourselves how that mass of consciousness may *disintegrate*, we ought, were it possible, to picture to ourselves how it is in the first instance *integrated*. That, however, is a difficulty which does not begin with the constitution of man. It begins when unicellular develop into multicellular organisms. It is, of course, a mystery how a single cell can hold together, and what kind of unity it can possess. But it is a fresh mystery when several cells cohere in a conjoint and independent life. `In the collective unity of certain "colonial animals" we have a kind of sketch or parody of our own complex being. Higher intelligences may possibly see us as we see the hydrozoon — a creature split up into different "persons," a "hydriform person" who feeds, a "medusiform person" who propagates, and so on — elements of the animal differentiated for different ends — interconnected from one point of view as closely as our stomach and brain, yet from another point of view separable existences, capable of detachment and of independent regeneration in all kinds of different ways. Still more composite, though less conspicuously composite, is every animal that we meet as we rise through the scale; and in man we reach the summit both of colonial complexity and of centralised control.

I need hardly say that as regards the inner nature of this close coordination, this central government, science can at present tell us little or nothing. The growth of the nervous mechanism may be to some extent deciphered; but how this mechanism is centrally governed; what is the tendency which makes for unity; where precisely this unity resides, and what is its exact relation to the various parts of the multicellular organism — all these are problems in the nature of *life*, to which as yet no solution is known.

The needed clue, as I believe, can be afforded only by the discovery of laws affecting primarily that unseen or spiritual plane of being where I imagine the origin of life to lie. If we can suppose telepathy to be a first indication of a law of this type, and to occupy in the spiritual world some such place as gravitation occupies in the material world, we might imagine something analogous to the force of cohesion as operating in the psychical contexture of a human personality. Such a personality, at any rate, as the development of higher from lower organisms shows, involves the aggregation of countless minor psychical entities, whose characteristics still persist, although in a manner consistent with the possibility that one larger psychical entity, whether pre-existent or otherwise, is the unifying continuum of which those smaller entities are fragments, and exercises over them a pervading, though an incomplete, control.

It is plainly impossible to say beforehand what will be the relation to the ordinary stream of consciousness of a personality thus composed. We have no right to assume that all our psychical operations will fall at the same time, or at any time, into the same central current of perception, or rise above what we have called the ordinary conscious threshold. We can be sure, in fact, that there will be much which will *not* so rise; can we predict what *will* rise?

We can only reply that the perception of stimuli by the supraliminal consciousness is a kind of exercise of function; and that here, as in other cases where a function is exercised, part of its range will consist of such operation as the primary structure of the organism obliges it to perform, and part will consist of such operation as natural selection (after the structure has come into being) has trained it to perform. There will be something which is structurally inevitable, and something which was not structurally inevitable, but which has proved itself practically advantageous.

Thus it may be inevitable — a necessary result of nervous structure — that consciousness should accompany unfamiliar cerebral combinations; — that the "fraying of fresh channels" should carry with it a perceptible tingle of novelty. Or it is possible, again, that this vivid consciousness of new cerebral combinations may be a later acquisition, and merely due to the obvious advantage of preventing new achievements from stereotyping themselves before they have been thoroughly practised; — as a musician will keep his attention fixed on a difficult novelty, lest his execution should become automatic before he has learnt to render the piece as he desires. It seems likely, at any rate, that the greater part of the contents of our supraliminal consciousness may be determined in some such fashion as this, by natural selection so operating as to keep ready to hand those perceptions which are most needed for the conduct of life.

The notion of the upbuilding of the personality here briefly given is of use, I think, in suggesting its practical tendencies to dissolution. Subjected continually to both internal and external stress and strain, its ways of yielding indicate the grain of its texture.

It is possible that if we could discern the minute psychology of this long series of changes, ranging from modifications too minute to be noted as abnormal to absolute revolutions of the whole character and intelligence, we might find no definite break in all the series; but rather a slow, continuous detachment of one psychical unit or element of consciousness after another from the primary synthesis. It is possible, on the other hand, that there may be a real break at a point where there appears to our external observation to be a break, namely, where the personality passes into its new phase through an interval of sleep or trance. And I believe that there is another break, at a point much further advanced, and not to be reached in this chapter, where some external intelligence begins in some way to possess the organism and to replace for a time the ordinary intellectual activity by an activity of its own. Setting, however, this last possibility for the present aside, we must adopt some arrangement on which to hang our cases. For this purpose the appearance of sleep or trance will make a useful, although not a definite, line of demarcation.

We may begin with localised psychical hypertrophies and isolations, — terms which I shall explain as we proceed; and then pass on through hysterical instabilities (where intermediate periods of trance may or may not be present) to those more advanced sleep-wakings and dimorphisms which a barrier of trance seems always to separate from the primary stream of conscious life. All such changes, of course, are generally noxious to the psychical organism; and it will be simpler to begin by dwelling on their noxious aspect, and regarding them as steps on the road — on one of the many roads — to mental overthrow.

The process begins, then, with something which is to the psychical organism no more than a boil or a corn is to the physical. In consequence of some suggestion from without, or of some inherited tendency, a small group of psychical units set up a process of exaggerated growth which shuts them off from free and healthy interchange with the rest of the personality.

The first symptom of disaggregation is thus the *idée fixe*, that is to say, the persistence of an uncontrolled and unmodifiable group of thoughts or emotions, which from their brooding isolation, — from the very fact of ·deficient interchange with the general current of thought, — become alien and intrusive, so that some special idea or image presses into consciousness with undue and painful frequency.

The fixed idea, thus originating, may develop in different ways. It may become a centre of explosion, or a nucleus of separation, or a beginning of death. It may induce an access of hysterical convulsions, thus acting like a material foreign body which presses on a sensitive part of the organism. Or it may draw to its new parasitic centre so many psychical elements that it forms a kind of secondary personality, co-existing secretly with the primary one, or even able at times (as in some well-known cases) to carry the whole organism by a *coup-de-main*. (Such changes, it may be noted in passing, are not always for the *worse*.) Or, again, the new quasi-independent centres may be merely *anarchical;* the revolt may spread to every cell; and the forces of the environment, ever making war upon the organism, may thus effect its total decay.

Let us dwell for a few moments on the nature of these fixed or insistent ideas. They are not generally or at the first outset extravagant fancies, — as that one is made of glass or the like. Rather will "fixed ideas" come to seem a mere expression for something in a minor degree common to most of us. Hardly any mind, I suppose, is wholly free from tendencies to certain types of thought or emotion for which we cannot summon any adequate check — useless recurrent broodings over the past or anxieties for the future, perhaps traces of old childish experience which have become too firmly fixed wholly to disappear. Nay, it may well be that we must look even further back than our own childhood for the origin of many haunting troubles. Inherited tendencies to terror, especially, seem to reach far back into a prehistoric past. In a recent "Study of Fears," which Professor Stanley Hall has based on a wide statistical collection,[1] it would seem that the fears of childhood often correspond to no existing cause for uneasiness, but rather to the vanished perils of primitive man. The fear of darkness, for instance, the fear of solitude, the fear of thunderstorms, the fear of the loss of orientation, speak of primitive helplessness,

---

[1] Stanley Hall's "Study of Fears," *American Journal of Psychology*, vol. viii., No. 2, January, 1897. See also "The Use of Hypnotism in the First Degree," by Dr. Russell Sturgis (Boston, 1894).

just as the fear of animals, the fear of strangers, suggest the fierce and hazardous life of early man. To all such instinctive feelings as these a morbid development is easily given.

Of what nature must we suppose this morbid development to be? Does it fall properly within our present discussion? or is it not simply a beginning of brain-disease, which concerns the physician rather than the psychologist? The psychologist's best answer to this question will be to show cases of fixed ideas *cured* by psychological means.[1] And indeed there are few cases to show which have been cured by any methods *except* the psychological; if hypnotic suggestion does not succeed with an *idée fixe*, it is seldom that any other treatment will cure it. We may, of course, say that the brain troubles thus cured were functional, and that those which went on inevitably into insanity were organic, although the distinction between functional and organic is not easily demonstrable in this ultra-microscopic realm.

At any rate, we have actually on record, — and that is what our argument needs, — a great series of *idées fixes*, of various degrees of intensity, cured by suggestion; — cured, that is to say, by a subliminal setting in action of minute nervous movements which our supraliminal consciousness cannot in even the blindest manner manage to set to work. Some such difference as exists on a gross scale between striped and unstriped muscle seems to exist on a minute scale among these smallest involved cells and fibres, or whatever they be. Some of them obey our conscious will, but most of them are capable of being governed only by subliminal strata of the self.

If, however, it be the subliminal self which can reduce these elements to order, it is often probably the subliminal self to which their disorder is originally due. If a fixed idea, say agoraphobia, grows up in me, this may probably be because the proper controlling co-ordinations of thought, which I ought to be able to summon up at will, have sunk below the level at which will can reach them. I am no longer able, that is to say, to convince myself by reasoning that there is no danger in crossing the open square. And this may be the fault of my subliminal self, whose business it is to keep the ideas which I need for common life easily within my reach, and which has failed to do this, owing to some enfeeblement of its grasp of my organism.

If we imagine these obscure operations under some such form as this, we get the advantage of being able to connect these insistent ideas in a coherent sequence with the more advanced phenomena of hysteria.

---

[1] For instances of such cures see Drs. Raymond and Janet's *Névroses et Idées fixes*.

We have seen that the presence of insistent ideas implies an instability of the conscious threshold; and this, in its turn, indicates a disorderly or diseased condition of the hypnotic stratum, — of that region of the personality which, as we shall see, is best known to us through the fact that it is reached by hypnotic suggestion.

Now we shall find, I think, that all the phenomena of hysteria are reducible to the same general conception. To understand their many puzzles we have to keep our eyes fixed upon just these psychological notions — upon a threshold of ordinary consciousness above which certain perceptions and faculties ought to be, but are not always, maintained, and upon a "hypnotic stratum" or region of the personality to which hypnotic suggestion appeals; and which includes faculty and perception which surpass the supraliminal, but whose operation is capricious and dreamlike, inasmuch as they lie, so to say, in a debateable region between two rules — the known rule of the supraliminal self, adapted to this life's experience and uses, and the conjectured rule of a fuller and profounder self, rarely reached by any artifice which our present skill suggests. Some of these conscious groupings have got separated from the ordinary stream of consciousness. These may still be unified in the subliminal, but they need to be unified in the supraliminal also. The normal relation between the supraliminal and the subliminal may be disturbed by the action of *either*.

Let us now see how far this view, which I suggested in the S.P.R. *Proceedings* as far back as 1892,[1] fits in with those modern observations of hysteria, in Paris and Vienna especially, which are transforming all that group of troubles from the mere opprobrium of medicine into one of the most fertile sources of new knowledge of body and mind.

First, then, let us briefly consider what is the general type of hysterical troubles. Speaking broadly, we may say that the symptoms of hysteria form, in the first place, a series of phantom copies of real maladies of the nervous system; and, in the second place, a series of fantasies played upon that system — of unreal, dreamlike ailments, often such as no physiological mechanism can be shown to have determined. These latter cases are often due, as we shall see, not to purely physiological, but rather to intellectual causes; they represent, not a particular pattern in which the nervous system tends of itself to disintegrate, but a particular pattern which has been imposed upon it by some intellectual process; — in short, by some form of self-suggestion.

Let us briefly review some common types of hysterical disability, —

[1] See vol. vii. p. 309.

taking as our first guide Dr. Pierre Janet's admirable work, *L'Etat Mental des Hystériques* (Paris, 1893).

What, then, to begin with, is Dr. Janet's general conception of the psychological states of the advanced hysteric? "In the expression *I feel*," he says (*L'Etat Mental*, p. 39), "we have two elements: a small new psychological fact, 'feel,' and an enormous mass of thoughts already formed into a system 'I.' These two things mix and combine, and to say *I feel* is to say that the personality, already enormous, has seized and absorbed this small new sensation; . . . as though the *I* were an amœba which sent out a prolongation to suck in this little sensation which has come into existence beside it." Now it is in the assimilation of these elementary sensations or affective states with the *perception personnelle*, as Janet terms it, that the advanced hysteric fails. His field of consciousness is so far narrowed that it can only take in the minimum of sensations necessary for the support of life. "One must needs have consciousness of what one sees and hears, and so the patient neglects to perceive the tactile and muscular sensations with which he thinks that he can manage to dispense. At first he could perhaps turn his attention to them, and recover them at least momentarily within the field of personal perception. But the occasion does not present itself, and the *psychological bad habit* is formed. . . . One day the patient — for he is now veritably a patient — is examined by the doctor. His left arm is pinched, and he is asked whether he feels the pinch. To his surprise the patient realises that he can no longer feel consciously, can no longer bring back into his personal perception sensations which he has neglected too long — he has become anæsthetic. . . . Hysterical anæsthesia is thus a fixed and perpetual distraction, which renders its subjects incapable of attaching certain sensations to their personality; it is a restriction of the conscious field."

The proof of these assertions depends on a number of observations, all of which point in the same direction, and show that hysterical anæsthesia does not descend so deep into the personality, so to say, as true anæsthesia caused by nervous decay, or by the section of a nerve.

Thus the hysteric is often *unconscious* of the anæsthesia, which is only discovered by the physician. There is none of the distress caused by true anæsthesia, as, for instance, by the "tabetic mask," or insensibility of part of the face, which sometimes occurs in *tabes dorsalis*.

An incident reported by Dr. Jules Janet illustrates this peculiarity. A young woman cut her right hand severely with broken glass, and complained of insensibility in the palm. The physician who examined her found that the sensibility of the right palm was, in fact, diminished by the section of certain nerves. But he discovered at the same time that the girl was hysterically anæsthetic over the whole left side of her body. She had never even found out this disability, and the doctor twitted her with complaining of the small patch of anæsthesia, while she said nothing of that which covered half her body. But, as Dr. Pierre Janet remarks, she might well have retorted that these were the facts, and that it was for the man of science to say why the small patch annoyed her while the large one gave her no trouble at all.

Of similar import is the ingenious observation that hysterical anæsthesia rarely leads to any accident to the limb; — differing in this respect, for instance, from the true and profound anæsthesia of syringomyelitis, in which burns and bruises frequently result from the patient's forgetfulness of the part affected. There is usually, in fact, a supervision — a *subliminal* supervision — exercised over the hysteric's limbs. Part of her personality is still alive to the danger, and modifies her movements, unknown to her supraliminal self.

This curious point, I may remark in passing, well illustrates the kind of action which I attribute to the subliminal self in many phases of life. Thus it is that the hypnotised subject is prevented (as I hold) from committing a real as opposed to a fictitious crime; thus it is that fresh ideas are suggested to the man of genius; thus it is — I will even say — that in some cases monitory hallucinations are generated, which save the supraliminal self from some sudden danger.

I pass on to another peculiarity of hysterical anæsthesiæ; — also in my eyes of deep significance. The anæsthetic belts or patches do not always, or even generally, correspond with true anatomical areas, such as would be affected by the actual lesion of any given nerve. They follow arbitrary arrangements; — sometimes corresponding to rough popular notions of divisions of the body, — sometimes seeming to reflect a merely childish caprice.

In these cases what is only a silly fancy seems to produce an effect which is not merely fanciful; — which is objective, measurable, and capable of causing long and serious disablement. This result, however, is quite accordant with my view of what I have termed the *hypnotic stratum* of the personality. I hold, as our coming discussion of hypnotism will more fully explain, that the region into which the hypnotic suggestion gives us access is one of strangely mingled strength and weakness; — of a faculty at once more potent and less coherent than that of waking hours. I think that in these cases we get at the subliminal self only somewhat in the same sense as we get at the supraliminal self when the "highest-level centres" are for the time inoperative (as in a dream) and only "middle-level centres" are left to follow their own devices without inhibition or co-ordination. I hold that this is the explanation of the strange contrasts which hypnosis makes familiar to us — the combination of profound power over the organism with childish readiness to obey the merest whims of the hypnotiser. The intelligence which thus responds is in my view only a fragmentary intelligence; it is a dreamlike scrap of the subliminal self, functioning apart from that self's central and profounder control.

What happens in hypnotism in obedience to the hypnotiser's caprice happens in hysteria in obedience to the caprice of the hypnotic stratum itself. Some middle-level centre of the subliminal self (to express a difficult idea by the nearest phrase I can find) gets the notion that there is an "anæsthetic bracelet," say, round the left wrist; — and lo, this straightway is so; and the hysteric loses supraliminal sensation in this fantastic belt. That the notion does not originate in the hysteric's supraliminal self is proved by the fact that the patient is generally unaware of the existence of the bracelet until the physician discovers it. Nor is it a chance combination; — even were there such a thing as chance. It is a dream of the hypnotic stratum; — an incoherent self-suggestion starting from and affecting a region below the reach of conscious will. Such cases are most instructive; for they begin to show us divisions of the human body based not upon local innervation but upon ideation (however incoherent); — upon intellectual conceptions like "a bracelet," "a cross," — applied though these conceptions may be with dreamlike futility.

In this view, then, we regard the fragments of perceptive power over which the hysteric has lost control as being by no means really extinguished, but rather as existing immediately beneath the threshold, in the custody, so to say, of a dreamlike or hypnotic stratum of the subliminal self, which has selected them for reasons sometimes explicable as the result of past suggestions, sometimes to us inexplicable. If this be so, we may expect that the same kind of suggestions which originally cut off these perceptions from the main body of perception may stimulate them again to action either below or above the conscious threshold.

We have already, indeed, seen reason to suppose that the submerged perceptions are still at work, when Dr. Janet pointed out how rare a thing it was that any accident or injury followed upon hysterical loss of feeling in the limbs. A still more curious illustration is afforded by the condition of the field of vision in a hysteric. It often happens that the field of vision is much reduced, so that the hysteric, when tested with the perimeter, can discern only objects almost directly in front of the eye. But if an object which happens to be particularly exciting to the hypnotic stratum — for instance the hypnotiser's finger, used often as a signal for trance — is advanced into that part of the hysteric's normal visual field of which she has apparently lost all consciousness, there will often be an instant subliminal perception, — shown by the fact that the subject promptly falls into trance.

In such cases the action of the submerged perceptions, while provoked by very shallow artifices, continues definitely *subliminal*. The patient *herself*, as we say, does not know why she does not burn her anæsthetic limbs, or why she suddenly falls into a trance while being subjected to optical tests.

But it is equally easy to devise experiments which shall call these submerged sensations up again into supraliminal consciousness. A hysteric has lost sensation in one arm: Dr. Janet tells her that there is a caterpillar on that arm, and the reinforcement of attention thus generated brings back the sensibility.

These hysterical anæsthesiæ, it may be added here, may be not only very definite but very profound. Just as the reality, — though also the impermanence, — of the hysterical retrenchment of field of vision of which I have been speaking can be shown by optical experiments beyond the patient's comprehension, so the reality of some profound organic hysterical insensibilities is sometimes shown by the progress of independent disease. A certain patient feels no hunger or thirst: this indifference might be simulated for a time, but her ignorance of severe inflammation of the bladder is easily recognisable as real. Throw her into hypnosis and her sensibilities return. The disease is for the first time felt, and the patient screams with pain. This result well illustrates one main effect of hypnosis, viz., to bring the organism into a more normal state. The deep organic anæsthesia of this patient was dangerously abnormal; the missing sensibility had first to be restored, although it might be desirable afterwards to remove the painful elements in that sensibility again, under, so to say, a wiser and deeper control.

What has been said of hysterical defects of sensation might be repeated for motor defects. There, too, the powers of which the supraliminal self has lost control continue to act in obedience to subliminal promptings. The hysteric who squeezes the dynamometer like a weak child can exert great muscular force under the influence of emotion.

Very numerous are the cases which might be cited to give a notion of dissolutive hysterical processes, as now observed with closer insight than formerly, in certain great hospitals. But, nevertheless, these hospital observations do not exhaust what has recently been learnt of hysteria. Dealing almost exclusively with a certain class of patients, they leave almost untouched another group, smaller, indeed, but equally instructive for our study.

Hysteria is no doubt a disease, but it is by no means on that account an indication of initial weakness of mind, any more than an Arctic explorer's frost-bite is an indication of bad circulation. Disease is a function of two variables: power of resistance and strength of injurious stimulus. In the case of hysteria, as in the case of frost-bite, the inborn power of resistance may be unusually great, and yet the stimulus may be so excessive that that power may be overcome. Arctic explorers have generally, of course, been among the most robust of men. And with some hysterics there is an even closer connection between initial strength and destructive malady. For it has often happened that the very feelings which we regard as characteristically civilised, characteristically honourable, have reached a pitch of vividness and delicacy which exposes their owners to shocks such as the selfish clown can never know. It would be a great mistake to suppose that all psychical upsets are due to vanity, to anger, to terror, to sexual passion. The instincts of personal cleanliness and of feminine modesty are responsible for many a breakdown of a sensitive, but not a relatively *feeble* organisation. The love of one's fellow-creatures and the love of God are responsible for many more. And why should it not be so? There exist for many men and women stimuli far stronger than self-esteem or bodily desires. Human life rests more and more upon ideas and emotions whose relation to the conservation of the race or of the individual is indirect and obscure. Feelings which may once have been utilitarian have developed wholly out of proportion to any advantage which they can gain for their possessor in the struggle for life. The dangers which are now most shudderingly felt are often no real risks to life or fortune. The aims most ardently pursued are often worse than useless for man regarded as a mere over-runner of the earth.

There is thus real psychological danger in fixing our conception of human character too low. Some essential lessons of a complex perturbation of personality are apt to be missed if we begin with the conviction that there is nothing before us but a study of decay. As I have more than once found need to maintain, it is his steady advance, and not his occasional regression, which makes the chief concern of man.

To this side of the study of hysteria Drs. Breuer and Freud have made valuable contribution. Drawing their patients not from hospital wards, but from private practice, they have had the good fortune to encounter, and the penetration to understand, some remarkable cases where unselfish but powerful passions have proved too much for the equilibrium of minds previously well-fortified both by principle and by education.[1]

"Wax to receive and marble to retain"; such, as we all have felt, is the human mind in moments of excitement which transcend its resistant powers.   This may be for good or for evil, may tend to that radical change in ethical standpoint which is called *conversion*, or to the mere setting-up of some hysterical disability.   Who shall say how far we desire to be susceptible to stimulus?   Most rash would it be to assign any fixed limit, or to class as inferior those whose main difference from ourselves may be that they feel sincerely and passionately what we feel torpidly, or perhaps only affect to feel.   "The term degenerate," says Dr. Milne Bramwell, "is applied so freely and widely by some modern authors that one cannot help concluding that they rank as such all who do not conform to some primitive, savage type, possessing an imperfectly developed nervous system."   Our "degenerates" may sometimes be in truth *progenerate;* and their perturbation may mask an evolution which we or our children needs must traverse when they have shown the way.

Let us pause for a moment and consider what is here implied.   We are getting here among the *hystériques qui mènent le monde.*   We have advanced, that is to say, from the region of *idées fixes* of a paltry or morbid type to the region of *idées fixes* which in themselves are reasonable and honourable, and which become morbid only on account of their relative intensity.   Here is the debateable ground between hysteria and genius. The kind of genius which we approach here is not, indeed, the purely intellectual form.   Rather it is the "moral genius," the "genius of sanctity," or that "possession" by some altruistic idea which lies at the root of so many heroic lives.

The hagiology of all religions offers endless examples of this type. That man would hardly be regarded as a great saint whose conduct seemed completely reasonable to the mass of mankind.   The saint in consequence is apt to be set unduly apart, whether for veneration or for ridicule.   He is regarded either as inspired or as morbid; when in reality all that his mode of life shows is that certain *idées fixes*, in themselves of no unworthy kind, have obtained such dominance that their impulsive action may take and retake, as accident wills, the step between the sublime and the ridiculous.

[1] See "Studien über Hysterie" (Leipsic, 1895), by Drs. Breuer and Freud. An account of two of these cases is given in the original edition.   Vol. i. pp. 51–6.

Martyrs, missionaries, crusaders, nihilists, — enthusiasts of any kind who are swayed by impulses largely below the threshold of ordinary consciousness, — these men bring to bear on human affairs a force more concentrated and at higher tension than deliberate reason can generate. They are virtually carrying out self-suggestions which have acquired the permanence of *idées fixes*. Their fixed ideas, however, are not so isolated, so encysted as those of true hysterics. Although more deeply and immutably rooted than their ideas on other matters, these subliminal convictions are worked in with the products of supraliminal reason, and of course can only thus be made effective over other minds. A deep subliminal horror, generated, say, by the sight of some loathsome cruelty, must not only prompt hallucinations, — as it might do in the hysteric and has often done in the reformer as well, — it must also, if it is to work out its mission of reform, be held clearly before the supraliminal reason, and must learn to express itself in writing or speech adapted to influence ordinary minds.

We may now pass from the first to the second of the categories of disintegration of personality suggested at the beginning of this chapter. The cases which I have thus far discussed have been mainly cases of *isolation* of elements of personality. We have not dealt as yet with *secondary personalities* as such. There is, however, a close connection between these two classes. There are cases, for example, where a kind of secondary state at times intervenes — a sort of bewilderment arising from confluent *idées fixes* and overrunning the whole personality. This new state is often preceded or accompanied by something of somnambulic change. It is this new feature of which we have here a first hint which seems to me of sufficient importance for the diagnosis of my second class of psychical disintegrations. This second class starts from sleep-wakings of all kinds, and includes all stages of alternation of personality, from brief somnambulisms up to those permanent and thorough changes which deserve the name of dimorphisms.

We are making here a transition somewhat resembling the transition from isolated bodily injuries to those subtler changes of diathesis which change of climate or of nutrition may induce. Something has happened which makes the organism react to all stimuli in a new way. Our best starting-point for the study of these secondary states lies among the phenomena of *dream*.

We shall in a later chapter discuss certain rare characteristics of dreams; occasional manifestations in sleep of waking faculty heightened, or of faculty altogether new. We have now to consider ordinary dreams in their aspect as indications of the structure of our personality, and as agencies which tend to its modification.

In the first place, it should be borne in mind that the dreaming state, though I will not call it the normal form of mentation, is nevertheless the form which our mentation most readily and habitually assumes. Dreams of a kind are probably going on within us both by night and by day, unchecked by any degree of tension of waking thought. This view — theoretically probable — seems to me to be supported by one's own actual experience in momentary dozes or even momentary lapses of attention. The condition of which one then becomes conscious is that of swarming fragments of thought or imagery, which have apparently been going on continuously, though one may become aware of them and then unaware at momentary intervals; — while one tries, for instance, to listen to a speech or to read a book aloud between sleep and waking.

This, then, is the kind of mentation from which our clearer and more coherent states may be supposed to develop. Waking life implies a fixation of attention on one thread of thought running through a tangled skein. In hysterical patients we see some cases where no such fixation is.possible, and other cases where the fixation is involuntary, or follows a thread which it is not desirable to pursue.

There is, moreover, another peculiarity of dreams which has hardly attracted sufficient notice from psychologists, but which it is essential to review when we are dealing with fractionations of personality.[1] I allude to their *dramatic* character. In dream, to begin with, we have an environment, a surrounding scene which we have not wittingly invented, but which we find, as it were, awaiting our entry. And in many cases our dream contains a *conversation* in which we await with eagerness and hear with surprise the remarks of our interlocutor, who must, of course, all the time represent only another segment or stratum of ourselves. This duplication may become either painful or pleasant. A feverish dream may simulate the confusions of insanity — cases where the patient believes himself to be two persons at once, and the like. [See R. L. Stevenson's dream, given in Appendix II. A.] These complications rarely cause the dreamer any surprise. One may even say that with the first touch of sleep the superficial unity of consciousness disappears, and that the dream world gives a truer representation than the waking world

[1] On this subject see Du Prel, *Philosophy of Mysticism*, Eng. trans., vol. i., *passim.*

of the real fractionation or multiplicity existing beneath that delusive simplicity which the glare of waking consciousness imposes upon the mental field of view.

Bearing these analogies in mind, we shall see that the development of somnambulism out of ordinary dream is no isolated oddity. It is parallel to the development of a secondary state from *idées fixes* when these have passed a certain pitch of intensity. The sleep-waking states which develop from sleep have the characteristics which we should expect from their largely subliminal origin. They are less coherent than waking secondary personalities, but richer in supernormal faculty. It is in connection with displays of such faculty — hyperæsthesia or telæsthesia — that they have been mainly observed, and that I shall, in a future chapter, have most need to deal with them. But there is also great interest simply in observing what fraction of the sleep-waker's personality is able to hold intercourse with other minds. A trivial instance of such intercourse reduced to its lowest point has often recurred to me. When I was a boy another boy sleeping in the same room began to talk in his sleep. To some slight extent he could answer me; and the names and other words uttered — *Harry, the boat*, etc. — were appropriate to the day's incidents, and would have been enough to prove to me, had I not otherwise known, who the boy was. But his few coherent remarks represented not facts but dreaming fancies — *the boat is waiting*, and so forth. This trivial jumble, I say, has since recurred to me as precisely parallel to many communications professing to come from disembodied spirits. There are other explanations, no doubt, but one explanation of such incoherent utterances would be that the spirit was speaking under conditions resembling those in which this sleeping boy spoke.

There are, of course, many stages above this. Spontaneous somnambulistic states become longer in duration, more coherent in content, and may gradually merge, as in the well-known case of Félida X. (see Appendix II. C) into a continuous or dimorphic new personality.

The transition which has now to be made is a very decided one. We have been dealing with a class of secondary personalities consisting of elements *emotionally selected* from the total or primary personality. We have seen some special group of feelings grow to morbid intensity, until at last it dominates the sufferer's mental being, either fitfully or continuously, but to such an extent that he is "a changed person," not precisely insane, but quite other than he was when in normal mental health. In such cases the new personality is of course dyed in the morbid emotion. It is a kind of dramatic impersonation, say, of jealousy, or of fear, like the case of "demoniacal possession," quoted from Dr. Janet in Appendix II. B. In other respects the severance between the new and the old self is not very profound. Dissociations of memory, for instance, are seldom beyond the reach of hypnotic suggestion. The cleavage has not gone down to the depths of the psychical being.

We must now go on to cases where the origin of the cleavage seems to us quite arbitrary, but where the cleavage itself seems even for that very reason to be more profound. It is no longer a question of some one morbidly exaggerated emotion, but rather of a scrap of the personality taken at random and developing apart from the rest.

The commonest mode of origin for such secondary personalities is from some access of sleep-waking, which, instead of merging into sleep again, repeats and consolidates itself, until it acquires a chain of memories of its own, alternating with the primary chain.[1]

And now, as an illustration of a secondary condition purely degenerative, I may first mention *post-epileptic* states, although they belong too definitely to pathology for full discussion here. Post-epileptic conditions may run parallel to almost all the secondary phases which we have described. They may to all outward semblance closely resemble normality, — differing mainly by a lack of rational *purpose*, and perhaps by a recurrence to the habits and ideas of some earlier moment in the patient's history. Such a condition resembles some hypnotic trances, and some factitious personalities as developed by automatic writing. Or, again, the post-epileptic state may resemble a suddenly developed *idée fixe* triumphing over all restraint, and may prompt to serious crime, abhorrent to the normal, but premeditated in the morbid state. There could not, in fact, be a better example of the unchecked rule of middle-level centres; — no longer secretly controlled, as in hypnotic trance, by the higher-level centres, — which centres in the epileptic are in a state not merely of psychological abeyance, but of physiological exhaustion.[2]

The case of Ansel Bourne is interesting in this connection.[3] Subject

---

[1] An old case of Dr. Dyce's (see *The Zoist*, vol. iv. p. 158) forms a simple example of this type. Dr. Mesnet's case (*De l'Automatisme de la Mémoire*, etc. Par le Dr. Ernest Mesnet, Paris, 1874. p. 18, seq.) should also be referred to here. In these instances the secondary state is manifestly a degeneration of the primary state, even when certain traces of supernormal faculty are discernible in the narrowed psychical field.

[2] See *The Zoist*, vol. iv. pp. 172–79, for a case showing the inevitable accomplishment of a post-epileptic crime in such a way as to bring out its analogy with the inevitable working out of a post-hypnotic suggestion.

[3] See *Proceedings* S.P.R., vol. vii. pp. 221–258 [225 A].

from childhood to fits of deep depression, and presenting in later life symptoms suggestive of epilepsy, Ansel Bourne was struck down in his thirty-first year by what was supposed to be a severe sunstroke. Connected with this event were circumstances which led to a profound religious conversion. At sixty-one years of age, being at that time an itinerant preacher, and living in the small town of Greene, in the State of Rhode Island, Ansel Bourne disappeared one morning, whilst apparently in his usual state of health, and remained undiscovered for a period of two months. At the end of this time he turned up at Norristown, Pennsylvania, where for the previous six weeks he had been keeping a small variety store under the name of A. J. Brown, appearing to his neighbours and customers as an ordinary normal person, but being, as it would seem, in a somnambulistic condition all the while. When he regained his ordinary waking consciousness, Ansel Bourne lost all memory of his actions while in his secondary state. In the year 1890, however, having been hypnotised by Professor James, he was able while in the trance state to give an account of his doings during the eight weeks that the Brown personality lasted.

In this case it is perhaps safest to regard the change of personality as *post-epileptic*, although I know of no recorded parallel to the length of time during which the influence of the attack must have continued. The effect on mind and character would suit well enough with this hypothesis. The "Brown" personality showed the narrowness of interests and the uninquiring indifference which is common in such states. But on this theory the case shows one striking novelty, namely, the recall by the aid of hypnotism of the memory of the post-epileptic state. It is doubtful, I think, whether any definite post-epileptic memory had ever previously been recovered. On the other hand, it is doubtful whether serious recourse had ever been had at such times to hypnotic methods, whose increasing employment certainly differentiates the latter from the earlier cases of split personality in a very favourable way. And this application of hypnotism to post-epileptic states affords us possibly our best chance — I do not say of directly checking epilepsy, but of getting down to the obscure conditions which predispose to each attack.

Next we may mention two cases reported by Dr. Proust and M. Boeteau. Dr. Proust's patient,[1] Emile X., aged thirty-three, was a barrister in Paris. Although of good ability and education in classical studies, both as a boy and at the university he was always nervous and over sensitive, showing signs, in fact, of *la grande hystérie*. During his attacks he ap-

[1] See *Revue de l'Hypnotisme*, March 1890, p. 267 [226 A].

parently underwent no loss of consciousness, but would lose the memory of all his past life during a few minutes or a few days, and in this condition of secondary consciousness would lead an active and apparently normal life. From such a state he woke suddenly, and was entirely without memory of what had happened to him in this secondary state. This memory was, however, restored by hypnotism.

M. Boeteau's patient, Marie M.,[1] had been subject to hysterical attacks since she was twelve years old. She became an out-patient at the Hôpital Andral for these attacks: and on April 24, 1891, being then twenty-two years old, the house physician there advised her to enter the surgical ward at the Hôtel-Dieu, as she would probably need an operation for an internal trouble. Greatly shocked by this news, she left the hospital at ten A.M., and lost consciousness. When she recovered consciousness she found herself in quite another hospital — that of Ste. Anne — at six A.M. on April 27. She had been found wandering in the streets of Paris, in the evening of the day on which she left the Hôpital Andral. On returning to herself, she could recollect absolutely nothing of what had passed in the interval. While she was thus perplexed at her unexplained fatigue and footsoreness, and at the gap in her memory, M. Boeteau hypnotised her. She passed with ease into the hypnotic state, and at once remembered the events which filled at least the earlier part of the gap in her primary consciousness.

These two cases belong to the same general type as Ansel Bourne's. There does not seem, however, to be any definite evidence that the secondary state was connected with epileptic attacks. It was referred rather by the physicians who witnessed it to a functional derangement analogous to hysteria, though it must be remembered that there are various forms of epilepsy which are not completely understood, and some of which may be overlooked by persons who are not familiar with the symptoms.

Another remarkable case is that of the Rev. Thomas C. Hanna,[2] in whom complete amnesia followed an accident. By means of a method which Dr. Sidis (who studied the case) calls "hypnoidisation," he was able to prove that the patient had all his lost memories stored in his subliminal consciousness, and could temporarily recall them to the supraliminal. By degrees the two personalities which had developed

[1] See the *Annales Médico-Psychologiques* for January 1892 [226 B].
[2] For full details of this, see Dr. Boris Sidis's work, *The Psychology of Suggestion: a Research into the Subconscious Nature of Man and Society* (New York, 1898), and *Multiple Personality* by Drs. Boris Sidis and S. P. Goodhart. London, 1905.

since the accident were thus fused into one and the patient was completely cured.

For another case of the ambulatory type, like Ansel Bourne's, but remarkable in that it was associated with a definite physical lesion — an abscess in the ear — the cure of which was followed by the rapid return of the patient to his normal condition, see Dr. Drewry's article in the *Medico-Legal Journal* for June 1896 [228 A].

Again, in a case reported by Dr. David Skae,[1] the secondary state seems to owe its origin to a kind of tidal exhaustion of vitality, as though the repose of sleep were not enough to sustain the weakened personality, which lapsed on alternate days into exhaustion and incoherence.

The secondary personalities thus far dealt with have been the spontaneous results of some form of *misère psychologique*, of defective integration of the psychical being. But there are also cases where, the cohesion being thus released, a slight touch from without can effect dissociations which, however shallow and almost playful in their first inception, may stiffen by repetition into phases as marked and definite as those secondary states which spring up of themselves, that is to say, from self-suggestions which we cannot trace. In Professor Janet's *L'Automatisme Psychologique* the reader will find some instructive examples of these fictitious secondary personalities [230 A and B].

Up to this point the secondary states which we have considered, however startling to old-fashioned ideas of personality, may, at any rate, be regarded as forms of mental derangement or decay — varieties on a theme already known. Now, however, we approach a group of cases to which it is difficult to make any such definition apply. They are cases where the secondary state is *not* obviously a degeneration; — where it may even appear to be in some ways an *improvement* on the primary; so that one is left wondering how it came about that the man either originally was what he was, or — being what he was — suddenly became something so very different. There has been a shake given to the kaleidoscope, and no one can say why either arrangement of the component pieces should have had the priority.

In the classical case of Félida X. the second state is, as regards health and happiness, markedly superior to the first. (See Appendix II. C.)

The old case of Mary Reynolds[2] is again remarkable in respect of the change of character involved. The deliverance from gloomy preoccupations — the childish insouciance of the secondary state — again illustrates

[1] Zoist vol. iv. p. 185 [229 A].
[2] See Professor W. James's *Principles of Psychology*, vol. i. pp. 381-84 [232 A].

the difference between these *allotropic* changes or reconstructions of personality and that mere predominance of a morbid factor which marked the cases of *idée fixe* and hysteria.   Observe, also, in Mary Reynolds's case the tendency of the two states gradually to *coalesce* apparently in a third phase likely to be preferable to either of the two already known.

We now come to spontaneous cases of multiple personality, of which Louis Vivé's is one of the best known.   Louis Vivé exhibited an extraordinary number and variety of phases of personality, affording an extreme example of dissociations dependent on *time-relations*, on the special epoch of life in which the subject was ordered to find himself.[1] Among various conditions of his organism — all but one of them implying, or at least simulating, some grave central lesion — any given condition could be revived in a moment, and the whole gamut of changes rung on his nervous system as easily as if one were setting back or forward a continuous cinematograph.   It is hard to frame a theory of memory which shall admit of these sudden reversions, — of playing fast and loose in this manner with the accumulated impressions of years.

Yet if Louis Vivé's case thus strangely intensifies the already puzzling notion of *ecmnesia* — as though the whole organism could be tricked into forgetting the events which had most deeply stamped it — what are we to say to Dr. Morton Prince's case of "Sally Beauchamp,"[2] with its grotesque exaggeration of a subliminal self — a kind of hostile bedfellow which knows everything and remembers everything — which mocks the emotions and thwarts the projects of the ordinary reasonable self which can be seen and known?   The case must be studied in full as it stands; its later developments may help to unravel the mysteries which its earlier stages have already woven.[3]

I quote in full in the text the next case, reported by Dr. R. Osgood

[1] For Dr. Camuset's account see *Annales Médico-Psychologiques*, 1882, p. 75; for Dr. Voisin's, *Archives de Neurologie*, September 1885.   The observations at Rochefort have been carefully recorded by Dr. Berjon, *La Grande Hystérie chez l'Homme*, Paris, 1886, and by Drs. Bourru and Burot in a treatise, *De la suggestion mentale*, &c. (*Bibl. scientifique contemporaine*), Paris, 1887 [233 A].

[2] See *Proceedings* S.P.R., vol. xv. pp. 466-483 [234 A] and the more complete account given in Dr. Morton Prince's *Dissociation of a Personality*.   New York and London, 1906.

[3] Besides the cases mentioned above see a remarkable recent case recorded by Dr. Bramwell in *Brain*, Summer Number, 1900, on the authority of Dr. Albert Wilson, of Leytonstone.   Dr. Wilson has given a detailed account of his patient, Mary Barnes, in *Proceedings* S.P.R., vol. xviii. pp. 352-416, where a full discussion of the case will also be found.   Mary Barnes developed sixteen different personalities with distinct memories and different characteristics.

Mason (in a paper entitled "Duplex Personality: its Relation to Hypnotism and to Lucidity," in the *Journal of the American Medical Association*, November 30th, 1895). Dr. Mason writes: —

Alma Z. was an unusually healthy and intellectual girl, a strong and attractive character, a leading spirit in whatever she undertook, whether in study, sport, or society. From overwork in school, and overtaxed strength in a case of sickness at home, her health was completely broken down, and after two years of great suffering suddenly a second personality appeared. In a peculiar child-like and Indian-like dialect she announced herself as "Twoey," and that she had come to help "Number One" in her suffering. The condition of "Number One" was at this time most deplorable; there was great pain, extreme debility, frequent attacks of syncope, insomnia, and a mercurial stomatitis which had been kept up for months by way of medical treatment and which rendered it nearly impossible to take nourishment in any form. "Twoey" was vivacious and cheerful, full of quaint and witty talk, never lost consciousness, and could take abundant nourishment, which she declared she *must* do for the sake of "Number One." Her talk was most quaint and fascinating, but without a trace of the acquired knowledge of the primary personality. She gave frequent evidence of supranormal intelligence regarding events transpiring in the neighbourhood. It was at this time that the case came under my observation, and has remained so for the past ten years. Four years later, under depressing circumstances, a third personality made its appearance and announced itself as "The Boy." This personality was entirely distinct and different from either of the others. It remained the chief alternating personality for four years, when "Twoey" again returned.

All these personalities, though absolutely different and characteristic, were delightful each in its own way, and "Twoey" especially was, and still is, the delight of the friends who are permitted to know her, whenever she makes her appearance; and this is always at times of unusual fatigue, mental excitement, or prostration; then she comes and remains days at a time. The original self retains her superiority when she is present, and the others are always perfectly devoted to her interest and comfort. "Number One" has no personal knowledge of either of the other personalities, but she knows them well, and especially "Twoey," from the report of others and from characteristic letters which are often received from her; and "Number One" greatly enjoys the spicy, witty, and often useful messages which come to her through these letters and the report of friends.

Dr. Mason goes on to say: —

Here are three cases [the one just given, that of another patient of his own, and that of Félida X] in which a second personality — perfectly sane, thoroughly practical, and perfectly in touch and harmony with its surroundings — came to the surface, so to speak, and assumed absolute control of the physical organisation for long periods of time together.

During the stay of the second personality the primary or original self was entirely blotted out, and the time so occupied was a blank.   In neither of the cases described had the primary self any knowledge of the second personality, except from the report of others or letters from the second self, left where they could be found on the return of the primary self to consciousness.   The second personality, on the other hand, in each case, knew of the primary self, but only as another person — never as forming a part of, or in any way belonging to their own personalities.   In the case of both Félida X. and Alma Z., there was always immediate and marked improvement in the physical condition when the second personality made its appearance.

The case of Mollie Fancher,[1] which, had it been observed and recorded with scientific accuracy, might have been one of the most instructive of all, seems to stand midway between the transformations of Louis Vivé — each of them frankly himself at a different epoch of life — and the "pseudo-possessions" of imaginary spirits with which we shall in a later chapter have to deal.

The case of Anna Winsor[2] goes so far further in its suggestion of interference from without that it presents to us, at any rate, a contrast and even conflict between positive insanity on the part of the organism generally with wise and watchful sanity on the part of a single limb, with which that organism professes to have no longer any concern.

The last case[3] that I shall mention is that of Miss Mary Lurancy Vennum, the "Watseka Wonder."

The case briefly is one of alleged "possession," or "spirit-control." The subject of the account, a girl nearly fourteen years old, living at Watseka, Illinois, became apparently controlled by the spirit of Mary Roff, a neighbour's daughter, who had died at the age of eighteen years and nine months, when Lurancy Vennum was a child of about fifteen months old.   The most extraordinary feature in the case was that the control by Mary Roff lasted almost continuously for a period of four months.

For the present we must consider this case as a duplication of personality — a pseudo-possession, if you will — determined in a hysterical child by the suggestion of friends, but at a later stage, and when some other wonders have become more familiar than now, we may find that this singular narrative has further lessons to teach us.

We have now briefly surveyed a series of disintegrations of personality

---

[1] *Proceedings* S.P.R., vol. xiv. 396–398 [236 A].
[2] *Proceedings of American* S.P.R., vol. i. p. 552 [237 A].
[3] For a detailed record of this case see the *Religio-Philosophical Journal* for 1879.   An abridgment is given in [238 A].   See also *Journal* S.P.R., vol. x. p. 99.

ranging from the most trifling *idée fixe* to actual alternations or permanent changes of the whole type of character. All these form a kind of continuous series, and illustrate the structure of the personality in concordant ways. There do exist, it must be added, other forms of modified personality with which I shall not at present deal. Those are cases where some telepathic influence from outside has been at work, so that there is not merely dissociation of existing elements, but apparent introduction of a novel element. Such cases also pass through a long series, from small phenomena of motor automatism up to trance and so-called possession. But all this group I mention here merely in order to defer their discussion to later chapters.

The brief review already made will suffice to indicate the complex and separable nature of the elements of human personality. Of course a far fuller list might have been given; many phenomena of actual insanity would need to be cited in any complete conspectus. But hysteria is in some ways a better dissecting agent than any other where delicate psychical dissociations are concerned. Just as the microscopist stains a particular tissue for observation, so does hysteria stain with definiteness, as it were, particular synergies — definite complexes of thought and action — more manifestly than any grosser lesion, any more profound or persistent injury could do. Hysterical mutism, for instance (the observation is Charcot's[1]), supplies almost the only cases where the faculty of vocal utterance is attacked in a quite isolated way. In aphasia dependent upon organic injury we generally find other word-memories attacked also, — elements of agraphy, of word-blindness, of word-deafness appear. In the hysteric the incapacity to speak may be the single symptom. So with anæsthesiæ; we find in hysteria a separation of sensibility to heat and to pain, possibly even a separate subsistence of electrical sensibility. It is worth remarking here that it was during the hypnotic trance, which in delicacy of discriminating power resembles hysteria, that (so far as I can make out) the distinctness of the temperature-sense from the pain-sense was first observed. Esdaile, when removing tumours under mesmerism in Calcutta, noticed that patients, who were actually undergoing capital operations without a murmur, complained if a draught blew in upon them from an open window.

Nor is it only as a dissecting agent that hysteria can aid our research. There are in hysteria frequent *acquisitions* as well as *losses* of faculty. It is not unusual to find great hyperæsthesia in certain special directions — of touch, hearing, perception of light, etc. — combined with hysterical loss of sensation of other kinds. This subject will be more conveniently

[1] *Revue de l'Hypnotisme*, July 1889.

treated along with the hyperæsthesia of the hypnotic trance. But I may note here that just such occasional quickenings of faculty were, in my view, almost certain to accompany that instability of psychical threshold which is the distinguishing characteristic of hysteria, since I hold that subliminal faculty habitually overpasses supraliminal. These also are a kind of capricious *idées fixes;* only the caprice in such cases raises what was previously submerged instead of exaggerating what was previously emergent.

And from this point it is that our inquiries must now take their fresh departure. We in this work are concerned with changes which are the *converse* of hysterical changes. We are looking for integrations in lieu of disintegrations; for intensifications of control, widenings of faculty, instead of relaxation, scattering, or decay.

Suppose, then, that in a case of instability of the psychical threshold, — ready *permeability*, if you will, of the psychical diaphragm separating the supraliminal from the subliminal self, — the elements of emergence tend to increase and the elements of submergence to diminish. Suppose that the permeability depends upon the force of the uprushes from below the diaphragm rather than on the tendency to sink downwards from above it. We shall then reach the point where the vague name of *hysteria* must give place to the vague name of *genius*. The uprushes from the subliminal self will now be the important feature; the down-draught from the supraliminal, if it still exists, will be trivial in comparison. The content of the uprush will be congruous with the train of voluntary thought; and the man of genius will be a man more capable than others of utilising for his waking purposes the subliminal region of his being.

Next in order to the uprushes of genius will come the uprushes of dream. All men pass normally and healthily into a second phase of personality, alternating with the first. That is *sleep*, and sleep is characterised by those incoherent forms of subliminal uprush which we know as dreams. It is here that our evidence for telepathy and telæsthesia will first present itself for discussion. Sleep will indicate the existence of submerged faculty of a rarer type than even that to which genius has already testified.

There are, moreover, other states, both spontaneous and induced, analogous to sleep, and these will form the subject of the fifth chapter, that on Hypnotism. Hypnotism, however, does not mean trance or somnambulism only. It is a name, if not for the whole *ensemble*, yet for a large group of those artifices which we have as yet discovered for the purpose of eliciting and utilising subliminal faculty. The results of hypnotic suggestion will be found to imitate sometimes the subliminal uprushes of genius, and sometimes the visions of spontaneous somnambulism; while they also open to us fresh and characteristic accesses into subliminal knowledge and power.

Further than this point our immediate forecast need not go. But when we have completed the survey here indicated, we shall see, I think, how significant are the phenomena of hysteria in any psychological scheme which aims at including the hidden powers of man. For much as the hysteric stands in comparison to us ordinary men, so perhaps do we ordinary men stand in comparison with a not impossible ideal of faculty and of self-control.

But apart from these broader speculations, it has become evident that disturbances of personality are not mere empty marvels, but psycho-pathological problems of the utmost interest: — no one of them exactly like another, and no one of them without some possible *aperçu* into the intimate structure of man.

The purpose of this book, of course, is not primarily practical. It aims rather at the satisfaction of scientific curiosity as to man's psychical structure; esteeming *that* as a form of experimental research which the more urgent needs of therapeutics have kept in the background too long. Yet it may not have been amiss to realise thus, on the threshold of our discussion, that already even the most delicate speculations in this line have found their justification in helpful act; that strange bewilderments, paralysing perturbations, which no treatment could alleviate, no drug control, have been soothed and stablished into sanity by some appropriate and sagacious mode of appeal to a *natura medicatrix* deep-hidden in the labouring breast.

CHAPTER III

GENIUS

Igneus est ollis vigor et cœlestis origo
Seminibus, quantum non noxia corpora tardant
Terrenique hebetant artus moribundaque membra.

— VIRGIL.

In my second chapter I made no formal attempt to define that human personality which is to form the main subject of this book. I was content to take the conception roughly for granted, and to enter at once on the study of the lapses of personality into abnormal conditions, — short of the lowest depths of idiocy or madness. From that survey it appeared that these degenerations could be traced to some defect in that central control which ought to clasp and integrate into steady manhood the hierarchies of living cells which compose the human organism. This insight into the Self's decay was the needed prerequisite to our present task — that of apprehending its true normality, and thereafter of analysing certain obscurer faculties which indicate the line of its evolution during and after the life of earth.

Strength and concentration of the inward unifying control — *that* must be the true normality which we seek; and in seeking it we must remember how much of psychical operation goes on below the conscious threshold, imperfectly obedient to any supraliminal appeal. What advance can we make in inward mastery? how far extend our grasp over the whole range of faculty with which we are obscurely endowed?

"Human perfectibility" has been the theme of many enthusiasts; and many utopian schemes of society have been and still are suggested, which postulate in the men and women of the future an increase in moral and physical health and vigour. And it is plain that in a broad and general way natural selection, sexual selection, and the advance of science are working together towards improvements of these kinds. But it is plain also that these onward tendencies, at least in comparison with our desires and ideals, are slow and uncertain; and it is possible to argue that the apparent advance in our race is due merely to the improvement which science has affected in its material environment, and not to any real development, during the historical period, in the character or faculties of man himself. Nay, since we have no means of knowing to what extent any genus has an inward potentiality of improvement, it is possible for the pessimist to argue that the *genus homo* has reached its fore-ordained evolutionary limit; so that it cannot be pushed further in any direction without risk of nervous instability, sterility, and ultimate extinction. Some dim apprehension of this kind lends plausibility to many popular diatribes. Dr. Max Nordau's works afford a well-known example of this line of protest against the present age as an age of overwork and of nervous exhaustion. And narrowing the vague discussion to a somewhat more definite test, Professor Lombroso and other anthropologists have discussed the characteristics of the "man of genius"; with the result of showing (as they believe) that this apparently highest product of the race is in reality not a culminant but an aberrant manifestation; and that men of genius must be classed with criminals and lunatics, as persons in whom a want of balance or completeness of organisation has led on to an over-development of one side of the nature; — helpful or injurious to other men as accident may decide.

On this point I shall join issue; and I shall suggest, on the other hand, that Genius — if that vaguely used word is to receive anything like a psychological definition — should rather be regarded as a power of utilising a wider range than other men can utilise of faculties in some degree innate in all; — a power of appropriating the results of subliminal mentation to subserve the supraliminal stream of thought; — so that an "inspiration of Genius" will be in truth a *subliminal uprush,* an emergence into the current of ideas which the man is consciously manipulating of other ideas which he has not consciously originated, but which have shaped themselves beyond his will, in profounder regions of his being. I shall urge that there is here no real departure from normality; no abnormality, at least in the sense of degeneration; but rather a fulfilment of the true norm of man, with suggestions, it may be, of something *supernormal;* — of something which transcends existing normality as an advanced stage of evolutionary progress transcends an earlier stage.

But before proceeding further I wish to guard against a possible misapprehension. I shall be obliged in this chapter to dwell on valuable aid rendered by subliminal mentation; but I do not mean to imply that such mentation is *ipso facto superior* to supraliminal, or even that it covers a large proportion of practically useful human achievement. When I say "The differentia of genius lies in an increased control over subliminal mentation," I express, I think, a well-evidenced thesis, and I suggest an important inference, — namely, that the man of genius is for us the best type of the normal man, in so far as he effects a successful co-operation of an unusually large number of elements of his personality — reaching a stage of integration slightly in advance of our own. Thus much I wish to say: but my thesis is not to be pushed further: — as though I claimed that all our best thought was subliminal, or that all that was subliminal was potentially "inspiration."

It is true, however, that the range of our subliminal mentation is more extended than the range of our supraliminal. At one end of the scale we find *dreams*, — a normal subliminal product, but of less practical value than any form of sane supraliminal thought. At the other end of the scale we find that the rarest, most precious knowledge comes to us from outside the ordinary field, — through the eminently subliminal processes of telepathy, telæsthesia, ecstasy. And between these two extremes lie many subliminal products, varying in value according to the dignity and trustworthiness of the subliminal mentation concerned.

This last phrase — inevitably obscure — may be illustrated by reference to that hierarchical arrangement of *supraliminal* action and perception which Dr. Hughlings Jackson has so used as to clear up much previous confusion of thought. Following him, we now speak of highest-level nerve-centres, governing our highest, most complex thought and will; of middle-level centres, governing movements of voluntary muscles, and the like; and of lowest-level centres (which from my point of view are purely subliminal), governing those automatic processes, as respiration and circulation, which are independent of conscious rule, but necessary to the maintenance of life. We can roughly judge from the nature of any observed action whether the highest-level centres are directing it, or whether they are for the time inhibited, so that middle-level centres operate uncontrolled.

Thus ordinary speech and writing are ruled by highest-level centres. But when an epileptic discharge of nervous energy has exhausted the highest-level centres, we see the middle-level centres operating unchecked, and producing the convulsive movements of arms and legs in the "fit." As these centres in their turn become exhausted, the patient is left to the guidance of lowest-level centres alone; — that is to say, he becomes comatose, though he continues to breathe as regularly as usual.

Now this series of phenomena, — *descending* in coherence and co-ordination from an active consensus of the whole organism to a mere automatic maintenance of its most stably organised processes, — may be pretty closely paralleled by the series of subliminal phenomena also.

Sometimes we seem to see our subliminal perceptions and faculties acting truly in unity, truly as a Self; — co-ordinated into some harmonious "inspiration of genius," or some profound and reasonable hypnotic self-reformation, or some far-reaching supernormal achievement of clairvoyant vision or of self-projection into a spiritual world. Whatever of subliminal personality is thus acting corresponds with the highest-level centres of supraliminal life. At such moments the *subliminal* represents (as I believe) most nearly what will become the *surviving* Self.

But it seems that this degree of clarity, of integration, cannot be long preserved. Much oftener we find the subliminal perceptions and faculties acting in less co-ordinated, less coherent ways. We have products which, while containing traces of some faculty beyond our common scope, involve, nevertheless, something as random and meaningless as the discharge of the uncontrolled middle-level centres of arms and legs in the epileptic fit. We get, in short, a series of phenomena which the term *dream-like* seems best to describe.

In the realm of genius, — of uprushes of thought and feeling fused beneath the conscious threshold into artistic shape, — we get no longer masterpieces but half-insanities, — not the Sistine Madonna, but Wiertz's Vision of the Guillotined Head; not *Kubla Khan*, but the disordered opium dream. Throughout all the work of William Blake (I should say) we see the subliminal self flashing for moments into unity, then smouldering again in a lurid and scattered glow.

In the realm of hypnotism, again, we sink from the reasonable self-suggestion to the "platform experiments," — the smelling of ammonia, the eating of tallow candles; — all the tricks which show a *profound* control, but not a *wise* control, over the arcana of organic life. I speak, of course, of the subject's *own* control over his organism; for in the last resort it is *he* and not his hypnotiser who really exercises that directive power. And I compare these tricks of middle-level subliminal centres to the powerful yet irrational control which the middle-level centres ruling the epileptic's arms and legs exercise over his muscles in the violence of the epileptic attack.

And so again with the *automatisms* which are, one may say, the subliminal self's peculiar province. Automatic script, for instance, may represent highest-level subliminal centres, even when no extraneous spirit, but the automatist's own mind alone, is concerned. It will then give us true telepathic messages, or perhaps messages of high moral import,

surpassing the automatist's conscious powers. But much oftener the automatic script is regulated by what I have called middle-level subliminal centres only; — and then, though we may have scraps of supernormal intelligence, we have confusion and incoherence as well. We have the falsity which the disgusted automatist is sometimes fain to ascribe to a devil; though it is in reality not a devil, but a dream.

And hence again, just as the epileptic sinks lower and lower in the fit, — from the incoordinated movements of the limbs down to the mere stertorous breathing of coma, — so do these incoherent automatisms sink down at last, through the utterances and drawings of the degenerate and the paranoiac, — through mere fragmentary dreams, or vague impersonal bewilderment, — into the minimum psychical concomitant, whatever that be, which must coexist with brain-circulation.

Such is the apparent parallelism; but of course no knowledge of a hierarchy of the familiar forms of nervous action can really explain to us the mysterious fluctuations of subliminal power.

When we speak of the highest-level and other centres which govern our supraliminal being, and which are fitted to direct this planetary life in a material world, we can to some extent point out actual brain-centres whose action enables us to meet those needs. What are the needs of our cosmic life we do not know; nor can we indicate any point in our organism (as in the "solar plexus," or the like), which is adapted to meet them. We cannot even either affirm or deny that such spiritual life as we maintain while incarnated in this material envelope involves any physical concomitants at all.

For my part, I feel forced to fall back upon the old-world conception of a *soul* which exercises an imperfect and fluctuating control over the organism; and exercises that control, I would add, along two main channels, only partly coincident — that of ordinary consciousness, adapted to the maintenance and guidance of earth-life; and that of subliminal consciousness, adapted to the maintenance of our larger spiritual life during our confinement in the flesh.

We men, therefore, *clausi tenebris et carcere cæco*, can sometimes widen, as we must sometimes narrow, our outlook on the reality of things. In mania or epilepsy we lose control even of those highest-level supraliminal centres on which our rational earth-life depends. But through automatism and in trance and allied states we draw into supraliminal life some rivulet from the undercurrent stream. If the subliminal centres which we thus impress into our waking service correspond to the *middle-level* only, they may bring to us merely error and confusion; if they correspond to the highest-level, they may introduce us to previously unimagined truth.

It is to work done by the aid of some such subliminal uprush, I say once more, that the word "genius" may be most fitly applied. "A work of genius," indeed, in common parlance, means a work which satisfies two quite distinct requirements. It must involve something original, spontaneous, unteachable, unexpected; and it must also in some way win for itself the admiration of mankind. Now, psychologically speaking, the first of these requirements corresponds to a real class, the second to a purely accidental one. What the poet feels while he writes his poem is the psychological fact in *his* history; what his friends feel while they read it may be a psychological fact in *their* history, but does not alter the poet's creative effort, which was what it was, whether any one but himself ever reads his poem or no.

And popular phraseology justifies our insistence upon this subjective side of genius. Thus it is common to say that "Hartley Coleridge" (for example) "was a genius, although he never produced anything worth speaking of." Men recognise, that is to say, from descriptions of Hartley Coleridge, and from the fragments which he has left, that ideas came to him with what I have termed a sense of subliminal uprush, — with an authentic, although not to us an instructive, inspiration.

As psychologists, I maintain, we are bound to base our definition of genius upon some criterion of this strictly psychological kind, rather than on the external tests which as artists or men of letters we should employ; — and which consider mainly the degree of delight which any given achievement can bestow upon other men. The artist will speak of the pictorial genius of Raphael, but not of Haydon; of the dramatic genius of Corneille, but not of Voltaire. Yet Haydon's Autobiography — a record of tragic intensity, and closing in suicide — shows that the tame yet contorted figures of his "Raising of Lazarus" flashed upon him with an overmastering sense of direct inspiration. Voltaire, again, writes to the president Hénault of his unreadable tragedy *Catilina:* "Five acts in a week! I know that this sounds ridiculous; but if men could guess what enthusiasm can do, — how a poet in spite of himself, idolising his subject, devoured by his genius, can accomplish in a few days a task for which without that genius a year would not suffice; — in a word, *si scirent donum Dei,* — *if they knew the gift of God,* — their astonishment might be less than it must be now." I do not shrink from these extreme instances. It would be absurd, of course, to place Haydon's "Raising of Lazarus" in the same *artistic* class as Raphael's "Madonna di San Sisto." But in the same *psychological* class I maintain that both works must be placed. For each painter, after his several kind, there was the same inward process, — the same sense of subliminal uprush; — that extension, in other words, of mental concentration which draws into immediate cognisance some workings or elements of the hidden self.

Let me illustrate this conception by a return to the metaphor of the " conscious spectrum " to which I introduced my reader in the first chapter. I there described our conscious spectrum as representing but a small fraction of the *aurai simplicis ignis*, or individual psychical ray; — just as our visible solar spectrum represents but a small fraction of the solar ray. And even as many waves of ether lie beyond the red end, and many beyond the violet end, of that visible spectrum, so have I urged that much of unrecognised or subliminal faculty lies beyond the red (or organic) end, and much beyond the violet (or intellectual) end of my imaginary spectrum. My main task in this book will be to prolong the psychical spectrum beyond either limit, by collecting traces of latent faculties, organic or transcendental: — just as by the bolometer, by fluorescence, by other artifices, physicists have prolonged the solar spectrum far beyond either limit of ordinary visibility.

But at present, and before entering on that task of rendering manifest supernormal faculty, I am considering what we ought to regard as the normal range of faculty from which we start; — what, in relation to man, the words *norm* and *normal* should most reasonably mean.

The word *normal* in common speech is used almost indifferently to imply either of two things, which may be very different from each other — conformity to a standard and position as an average between extremes. Often indeed the average constitutes the standard — as when a gas is of normal density; or is practically equivalent to the standard — as when a sovereign is of normal weight. But when we come to living organisms a new factor is introduced. Life is change; each living organism changes; each generation differs from its predecessor. To assign a fixed norm to a changing species is to shoot point-blank at a flying bird. The actual average at any given moment is no ideal standard; rather, the furthest evolutionary stage now reached is tending, given stability in the environment, to become the average of the future. Human evolution is not so simple or so conspicuous a thing as the evolution of the pouter pigeon. But it would be rash to affirm that it is not even swifter than any variation among domesticated animals. Not a hundred generations separate us from the dawn of history; — about as many generations as some microbes can traverse in a month; — about as many as separate the modern Derby-winner from the war-horse of Gustavus Adolphus. Man's change has been less than the horse's change in physical contour, — probably only because man has not been specially bred with that view; — but taking as a test the power of self-adaptation to environment, man has traversed in these thirty centuries a wider arc of evolution than separates the race-horse from the eohippus. Or if we go back further, and to the primal germ, we see that man's ancestors must have varied faster than any animal's, since they have travelled farthest in the same time. They have varied also in the greatest number of directions; they have evoked in greatest multiplicity the unnumbered faculties latent in the irritability of a speck of slime. Of all creatures man has gone furthest both in differentiation and in integration; he has called into activity the greatest number of those faculties which lay potential in the primal germ, — and he has established over those faculties the strongest central control. The process still continues. Civilisation adds to the complexity of his faculties; education helps him to their concentration. It is in the direction of a still wider range, a still firmer hold, that his evolution now must lie. I shall maintain that this ideal is best attained by the man of genius.

Let us consider the way in which the maximum of faculty is habitually manifested; the circumstances in which a man does what he has never supposed himself able to do before. We may take an instance where the faculty drawn upon lies only a little way beneath the surface. A man, we say, outdoes himself in a great emergency. If his house is on fire, let us suppose, he carries his children out over the roof with a strength and agility which seem beyond his own. That effective impulse seems more akin to instinct than to calculation. We hardly know whether to call the act reflex or voluntary. It is performed with almost no conscious intervention of thought or judgment, but it involves a new and complex adaptation of voluntary muscles such as would need habitually the man's most careful thought to plan and execute. From the point of view here taken the action will appear to have been neither reflex nor voluntary in the ordinary sense, but *subliminal;* — a subliminal uprush, an emergence of hidden faculty, — of nerve co-ordinations potential in his organism but till now unused, — which takes command of the man and guides his action at the moment when his being is deeply stirred.

This stock instance of a man's possible behaviour in moments of great physical risk does but illustrate in a gross and obvious manner, and in the motor region, a phenomenon which, as I hold, is constantly occurring on a smaller scale in the inner life of most of us. We identify ourselves for the most part with a stream of voluntary, fully conscious ideas, — cerebral movements connected and purposive as the movement of the hand which records them. Meantime we are aware also of a substratum of fragmentary automatic, *liminal* ideas, of which we take small account. These are bubbles that break on the surface; but every now and then there is a stir among them. There is a rush upwards as of a subaqueous spring; an inspiration flashes into the mind for which our conscious effort has not prepared us. This so-called inspiration may in itself be trivial or worthless; but it is the initial stage of a phenomenon to which, when certain rare attributes are also present, the name of genius will be naturally given.

I am urging, then, that where life is concerned, and where, therefore, change is normality, we ought to place our norm somewhat ahead of the average man, though on the evolutionary track which our race is pursuing. I have suggested that that evolutionary track is at present leading him in the direction of greater complexity in the perceptions which he forms of things without, and of greater concentration in his own will and thought, — in that response to perceptions which he makes from within. Lastly I have argued that men of genius, whose perceptions are presumably more vivid and complex than those of average men, are also the men who carry the power of concentration furthest; — reaching downwards, by some self-suggestion which they no more than we can explain, to treasures of latent faculty in the hidden Self.

I am not indeed here assuming that the faculty which is at the service of the man of genius is of a kind different from that of common men, in such a sense that it would need to be represented by a prolongation of either end of the conscious spectrum. Rather it will be represented by such a brightening of the familiar spectrum as may follow upon an intensification of the central light. For the spectrum of man's conscious faculty, like the solar spectrum, is not continuous but banded. There are groups of the dark lines of obstruction and incapacity, and even in the best of us a dim unequal glow.

It will, then, be the special characteristic of genius that its uprushes of subliminal faculty will make the bright parts of the habitual spectrum more brilliant, will kindle the dim absorption-bands to fuller brightness, and will even raise quite dark lines into an occasional glimmer.

But, if, as I believe, we can best give to the idea of genius some useful distinctness by regarding it in some such way as this, we shall find also that genius will fall into line with many other sensory and motor automatisms to which the word could not naturally be applied. Genius represents a narrow selection among a great many cognate phenomena; — among a great many uprushes or emergences of subliminal faculty both within and beyond the limits of the ordinary conscious spectrum.

It will be more convenient to study all these together, under the heading of sensory or of motor automatism. It will then be seen that there is no kind of perception which may not emerge from beneath the threshold in an indefinitely heightened form, with just that convincing suddenness of impression which is described by men of genius as characteristic of their highest flights. Even with so simple a range of sensation as that which records the lapse of time there are subliminal uprushes of this type, and we shall see that a man may have a sudden and accurate inspiration of what o'clock it is, in just the same way as Virgil might have an inspiration of the second half of a difficult hexameter.

For the purpose of present illustration of the workings of genius it seems well to choose a kind of ability which is quite indisputable, and which also admits of some degree of quantitative measurement. I would choose the higher mathematical processes, were data available; and I may say in passing how grateful I should be to receive from mathematicians any account of the mental processes of which they are conscious during the attainment of their highest results. Meantime there is a lower class of mathematical gift which by its very specialisation and isolation seems likely to throw light on our present inquiry.

During the course of the present century, — and alas! the scientific observation of unusual specimens of humanity hardly runs back further, or so far, — the public of great cities has been from time to time surprised and diverted by some so-called "calculating boy," or "arithmetical prodigy," generally of tender years, and capable of performing "in his head," and almost instantaneously, problems for which ordinary workers would require pencil and paper and a much longer time. In some few cases, indeed, the ordinary student would have no means whatever of solving the problem which the calculating boy unriddled with ease and exactness.

The especial advantage of the study of arithmetical prodigies is that in their case the subjective impression coincides closely with the objective result. The subliminal computator feels that the sum is right, and it *is* right. Forms of real or supposed genius which are more interesting are apt to be less undeniable.

An American and a French psychologist[1] have collected such hints

---

[1] Professor Scripture in the *American Journal of Psychology*, vol. iv., No. 1, April 1891; Professor Binet in the *Revue Philosophique*, 1895. Professor Binet's article deals largely with Jacques Inaudi, the most recent prodigy, who appears to differ from the rest in that his gift is auditile rather than visual. His gift was first observed in childhood. His general intelligence is below the average. Another recent prodigy, Diamanti, seems, on the other hand, to be in other ways quick-witted.

and explanations as these prodigies have given of their methods of working; methods which one might naturally hope to find useful in ordinary education. The result, however, has been very meagre, and the records left to us, imperfect as they are, are enough to show that the main and primary achievement has in fact been subliminal, while conscious or supra-liminal effort has sometimes been wholly absent, sometimes has super-vened only after the gift has been so long exercised that the accesses between different strata have become easy by frequent traversing. The prodigy grown to manhood, who now recognises the arithmetical artifices which he used unconsciously as a boy, resembles the hypnotic subject trained by suggestion to remember in waking hours the events of the trance.

In almost every point, indeed, where comparison is possible, we shall find this computative gift resembling other manifestations of subliminal faculty, — such as the power of seeing hallucinatory figures, — rather than the results of steady supraliminal effort, such as the power of logical analysis. In the first place, this faculty, in spite of its obvious connection with general mathematical grasp and insight, is found almost at random, — among non-mathematical and even quite stupid persons, as well as among mathematicians of mark. In the second place, it shows itself mostly in early childhood, and tends to disappear in later life; — in this resembling visualising power in general, and the power of seeing halluci-natory figures in particular; which powers, as both Mr. Galton's inquiries and our own tend to show, are habitually stronger in childhood and youth than in later years. Again, it is noticeable that when the power disap-pears early in life it is apt to leave behind it no memory whatever of the processes involved. And even when, by long persistence in a reflective mind, the power has become, so to say, adopted into the supraliminal consciousness, there nevertheless may still be flashes of pure "inspira-tion," when the answer "comes into the mind" with absolutely no per-ception of intermediate steps.

I subjoin a table, compiled by the help of Dr. Scripture's collection, which will broadly illustrate the main points above mentioned. Some more detailed remarks may then follow.

CHAPTER III

TABLE OF PRINCIPAL ARITHMETICAL PRODIGIES.

Name (alphabetically).	Age when gift was observed.	Duration of gift.	Intelligence.
Ampère	4	?	eminent
Bidder	10	through life	good
Buxton	?	?	low
Colburn	6	few years	average
Dase [or Dahse] . . .	boyhood	through life	very low
Fuller	boyhood	?	low
Gauss	3	?	eminent
Mangiamele . . .	10	few years	average ?
Mondeux	10	few years	low
Prolongeau	6	few years	low
Safford	6	few years	good
"Mr. Van R., of Utica" .	6	few years	average ?
Whately	3	few years	good

Now among these thirteen names we have two men of transcendent, and three of high ability. What accounts have they given us of their methods?

Of the gift of Gauss and Ampère we know nothing except a few striking anecdotes. After manifesting itself at an age when there is usually no continuous supraliminal mental effort worth speaking of, it appears to have been soon merged in the general blaze of their genius. With Bidder the gift persisted through life, but grew weaker as he grew older. His paper in Vol. XV. of the *Proceedings of the Institute of Civil Engineers*, while furnishing a number of practical hints to the calculator, indicates also a singular readiness of communication between different mental strata. "Whenever," he says (p. 255) "I feel called upon to make use of the stores of my mind, they seem to rise with the rapidity of lightning." And in Vol. CIII. of the same *Proceedings*, Mr. W. Pole, F.R.S., in describing how Mr. Bidder could determine mentally the logarithm of any number to 7 or 8 places, says (p. 252): "He had an almost miraculous power of seeing, as it were, intuitively what factors would divide any large number, not a prime. Thus, if he were given the number 17,861, he would instantly remark it was 337×53. . . . He could not, he said, explain how he did this; it seemed a natural instinct to him."

Passing on to the two other men of high ability known to have possessed this gift, Professor Safford and Archbishop Whately, we are struck with the evanescence of the power after early youth, — or even before the end of childhood.   I quote from Dr. Scripture Archbishop Whately's account of his powers.

There was certainly something peculiar in my calculating faculty. It began to show itself at between five and six, and lasted about three years. . . . I soon got to do the most difficult sums, always in my head, for I knew nothing of figures beyond numeration.   I did these sums much quicker than any one could upon paper, and I never remember committing the smallest error. *When I went to school, at which time the passion wore off, I was a perfect dunce at ciphering, and have continued so ever since.*

Still more remarkable, perhaps, was Professor Safford's loss of power. Professor Safford's whole bent was mathematical; his boyish gift of calculation raised him into notice; and he is now a Professor of Astronomy. He had therefore every motive and every opportunity to retain the gift, if thought and practice could have retained it.   But whereas at ten years old he worked correctly in his head, in one minute, a multiplication sum whose answer consisted of 36 figures, he is now, I believe, neither more nor less capable of such calculation than his neighbours.

Similar was the fate of a personage who never rises above initials, and of whose general capacity we know nothing.

"Mr. Van R., of Utica," says Dr. Scripture on the authority of Gall, "at the age of six years distinguished himself by a singular faculty for calculating in his head.   At eight he entirely lost this faculty, and after that time he could calculate neither better nor faster than any other person. *He did not retain the slightest idea of the manner in which he performed his calculations in childhood.*"

Turning now to the stupid or uneducated prodigies, Dase alone seems to have retained his power through life.   Colburn and Mondeux, and apparently Prolongeau and Mangiamele, lost their gift after childhood.

On the whole the ignorant prodigies seldom appear to have been conscious of any continuous logical process, while in some cases the separation of the supraliminal and subliminal trains of thought must have been very complete.   "Buxton would talk freely whilst doing his questions, that being no molestation or hindrance to him."[1]   Fixity and clearness of inward visualisation seems to have been the leading necessity in all these achievements; and it apparently mattered little whether the mental blackboard (so to say) on which the steps of the calculation were recorded were or were not visible to the mind's eye of the supraliminal self.

I have been speaking only of visualisation; but it would be interesting

[1] Scripture, *op. cit.*, p. 54.

if we could discover how much actual mathematical insight or inventiveness can be subliminally exercised. Here, however, our materials are very imperfect. From Gauss and Ampère we have, so far as I know, no record. At the other end of the scale, we know that Dase (perhaps the most successful of all these prodigies) was singularly devoid of mathematical grasp. "On one occasion Petersen tried in vain for six weeks to get the first elements of mathematics into his head." "He could not be made to have the least idea of a proposition in Euclid. Of any language but his own he could never master a word." Yet Dase received a grant from the Academy of Sciences at Hamburg, on the recommendation of Gauss, for mathematical work; and actually in twelve years made tables of factors and prime numbers for the seventh and nearly the whole of the eighth million, — a task which probably few men could have accomplished, without mechanical aid, in an ordinary lifetime. He may thus be ranked as the only man who has ever done valuable service to Mathematics without being able to cross the Ass's Bridge.

No support is given by what we know of this group to the theory which regards subliminal mentation as necessarily a sign of some morbid dissociation of physical elements. Is there, on the other hand, anything to confirm a suggestion which will occur in some similar cases, namely, that, — inasmuch as the addition of subliminal to supraliminal mentation may often be a completion and integration rather than a fractionation or disintegration of the total individuality, — we are likely sometimes to find traces of a more than common activity of the *right* or less used cerebral hemisphere? Finding no mention of ambidexterity in the meagre notices which have come down to us of the greater "prodigies," I begged the late Mr. Bidder, Q.C., and Mr. Blyth, of Edinburgh (the well-known civil engineer and perhaps the best living English representative of what we may call the calculating diathesis), to tell me whether their left hands possessed more than usual power. And I find that in these — the only two cases in which I have been able to make inquiry — there is somewhat more of dextro-cerebral capacity than in the mass of mankind.

We may now pass on to review some further instances of subliminal co-operation with conscious thought; — first looking about us for any cases comparable in *definiteness* with the preceding; and then extending our view over the wider and vaguer realm of creative and artistic work.

But before we proceed to the highly-specialised senses of hearing and sight, we must note the fact that there are cases of subliminal intensification of those perceptions of a less specialised kind which underlie our more elaborate modes of cognising the world around us. The sense of

...nd the sense of *weight*, or of muscular resistance, are ...ndest elements in our organic being. And the sense ...in several ways as a largely subliminal faculty. There ... show that it is often more exact in men sleeping than ...in men hypnotised than in men sleeping. The records ...nambulism are full of predictions made by the subject ...e, and accomplished, presumably by self-suggestion, ...from clocks, at the precise minute foretold. Or this ...may take shape in the imagery of dream, as in a case ...fessor Royce, of Harvard,[1] where his correspondent ...n in which I saw an enormous flaming clock-dial with ...g at 2.20. Awaking immediately, I struck a match, ...at my watch found it was a few seconds past 2.20." ...nd cases where the uprush of subliminal faculty is con- ...ep organic sensation of muscular resistance. We need ...direct or supernormal knowledge, — but merely a sub- ..., such as we see in the case of "arithmetical prodigies," expressing itself supraliminally, sometimes in a phantasmal picture, sometimes as a mere "conviction," without sensory clothing.[2]

Passing on here to subliminal products of *visual* type, I am glad to be able to quote the following passage which seems to me to give in germ the very theory for which I am now contending on the authority of one of the most lucid thinkers of the last generation.

The passage occurs in an article by Sir John Herschel on "Sensorial Vision," in his *Familiar Lectures on Scientific Subjects*, 1816. Sir John describes some experiences of his own, "which consist in the involuntary production of visual impressions, into which geometrical regularity of form enters as the leading character, and that, under circumstances which altogether preclude any explanation drawn from a possible regularity of structure in the retina or the optic nerve."[3] Twice these patterns appeared in waking daylight hours, — with no illness or discomfort at the time or afterwards. More frequently they appeared in darkness; but still while Sir John was fully awake. They appeared also twice when he was placed under chloroform; "and I should observe that I never lost

---

[1] *Proceedings* of American S.P.R., vol. i. No. 4, p. 360.

[2] See *Proceedings* S.P.R., vol. viii. p. 337 [§311].

[3] On this point see Professor James's *Principles of Psychology*, vol. ii. p. 84, note. Goethe's well-known phantasmal flower was clearly no mere representation of retinal structure. A near analogy to these patterns lies in the so-called "spirit-drawings," or automatic arabesques, discussed elsewhere in this chapter.

my consciousness of being awake and in full possession of my mind, though quite insensible to what was going on. . . . Now the question at once presents itself — What *are* these Geometrical Spectres? and how, and in what department of the bodily or mental economy do they originate? They are evidently not dreams. The mind is not dormant, but active and conscious of the direction of its thoughts; while these things obtrude themselves on notice, and by calling attention to them, *direct* the train of thought into a channel it would not have taken of itself. . . . If it be true that the conception of a regular geometrical pattern implies the exercise of thought and intelligence, it would almost seem that in such cases as those above adduced we have evidence of a *thought*, an intelligence, working within our own organisation distinct from that of our own personality." And Sir John further suggests that these complex figures, entering the mind in this apparently arbitrary fashion, throw light upon "the suggestive principle" to which "we must look for much that is determinant and decisive of our volition when carried into action." "It strikes me as not by any means devoid of interest to contemplate cases where, in a matter so entirely abstract, so completely devoid of any moral or emotional bearing, as the production of a geometrical figure, we, as it were, seize upon that principle in the very act, and in the performance of its office."

From my point of view, of course, I can but admire the acumen which enabled this great thinker to pierce to the root of the matter by the aid of so few observations. He does not seem to have perceived the connection between these "schematic phantasms," to borrow a phrase from Professor Ladd,[1] and the hallucinatory figures of men or animals seen in health or in disease. But even from his scanty data his inference seems to me irresistible; — "we have evidence of a *thought*, an intelligence, working within our own organisation, distinct from that of our own personality." I shall venture to claim him as the first originator of the theory to which the far fuller evidence now accessible had independently led myself.

Cases observed as definitely as those just quoted are few in number; and I must pass on into a much trodden — even a confusedly trampled — field; — the records, namely, left by eminent men as to the element of subconscious mentation, which was involved in their best work. Most of these stories have been again and again repeated; — and they have been collected on a large scale in a celebrated work, — to me especially distasteful, as containing what seems to me the loose and extravagant parody of important truth. It is not my business here to criticise Dr.

[1] See Professor Ladd's paper on this subject in *Mind*, April 1892.

Von Hartmann's *Philosophy of the Unconscious* in detail; but I prefer
to direct my readers' attention to a much more modest volume, in which
a young physician has put together the results of a direct inquiry addressed
to some Frenchmen of distinction as to their methods especially of imaginative work.[1] I quote a few of the replies addressed to him, beginning
with some words from M. Sully Prudhomme, — at once psychologist
and poet, — who is here speaking of the subconscious clarification of a
chain of abstract reasoning. "I have sometimes suddenly understood
a geometrical demonstration made to me a year previously without having
in any way directed thereto my attention or will. It seemed that the mere
spontaneous ripening of the conceptions which the lectures had implanted
in my brain had brought about within me this novel grasp of the proof."

With this we may compare a statement of Arago's — "Instead of
obstinately endeavouring to understand a proposition at once, I would
admit its truth provisionally; — and next day I would be astonished at
understanding thoroughly that which seemed all dark before."

Condillac similarly speaks of finding an incomplete piece of work
finished next day in his head.

Somewhat similarly, though in another field, M. Retté, a poet, tells
Dr. Chabaneix that he falls asleep in the middle of an unfinished stanza,
and when thinking of it again in the morning finds it completed. And
M. Vincent d'Indy, a musical composer, says that he often has on waking
a fugitive glimpse of a musical effect which (like the memory of a dream)
needs a strong immediate concentration of mind to keep it from vanishing.

De Musset writes, "On ne travaille pas, on écoute, c'est comme un
inconnu qui vous parle à l'oreille."

Lamartine says, "Ce n'est pas moi qui pense; ce sont mes idées qui
pensent pour moi."

Rémy de Gourmont: "My conceptions rise into the field of consciousness like a flash of lightning or like the flight of a bird."

M. S. writes: "In writing these dramas I seemed to be a spectator at
the play; I gazed at what was passing on the scene in an eager, wondering
expectation of what was to follow. And yet I felt that all this came from
the depth of my own being."

Saint-Saens had only to listen, as Socrates to his Dæmon; and M.
Ribot, summing up a number of similar cases, says: "It is the unconscious which produces what is vulgarly called inspiration. This condition
is a positive fact, accompanied with physical and psychical characteristics

[1] "Le Subconscient chez les Artistes, les Savantes, et les Ecrivains," par le Dr.
Paul Chabaneix, Paris, 1897.

peculiar to itself. Above all, it is impersonal and involuntary, it acts like an instinct, when and how it chooses; it may be wooed, but cannot be compelled. Neither reflection nor will can supply its place in original creation. . . . The bizarre habits of artists when composing tend to create a special physiological condition, — to augment the cerebral circulation in order to provoke or to maintain the unconscious activity."

In what precise way the cerebral circulation is altered we can hardly at present hope to know. Meantime a few psychological remarks fall more easily within our reach.

In the first place, we note that a very brief and shallow submergence beneath the conscious level is enough to infuse fresh vigour into supra-liminal trains of thought. Ideas left to mature unnoticed for a few days, or for a single night, seem to pass but a very little way beneath the threshold. They represent, one may say, the first stage of a process which, although often inconspicuous, is not likely to be discontinuous, — the sustenance, namely, of the supraliminal life by impulse or guidance from below.

In the second place, we see in some of these cases of deep and fruitful *abstraction* a slight approach to duplication of personality. John Stuart Mill, intent on his *Principles of Logic*, as he threaded the crowds of Leaden-hall Street, recalls certain morbid cases of hysterical *distraction;* — only that with Mill the process was an integrative one and not a dissolutive one — a gain and not a loss of power over the organism.

And thirdly, in some of these instances we see the man of genius achieving spontaneously, and unawares, much the same result as that which is achieved for the hypnotic subject by deliberate artifice. For he is in fact co-ordinating the waking and the sleeping phases of his existence. He is carrying into sleep the knowledge and the purpose of waking hours; — and he is carrying back into waking hours again the benefit of those profound assimilations which are the privilege of sleep. Hypnotic suggestion aims at co-operations of just this kind between the waking state in which the suggestion, say, of some functional change, is planned and the sleeping state in which that change is carried out, — with benefit persisting anew into waking life. The hypnotic trance, which is a *developed* sleep, thus accomplishes for the ordinary man what ordinary sleep accomplishes for the man of genius.

The coming chapters on Sleep and Hypnotism will illustrate this point more fully. But I may here anticipate my discussion of *dreams* by quoting one instance where dreams, self-suggested by waking will, formed, as one may say, an integral element in distinguished genius.

The late Robert Louis Stevenson, being in many ways a typical man of genius, was in no way more markedly gifted with that integrating faculty — that increased power over all strata of the personality — which I have ascribed to genius, than in his relation to his dreams (see "A Chapter on Dreams" in his volume *Across the Plains*). Seldom has the essential analogy between dreams and inspiration been exhibited in such a striking way. His dreams had always (he tells us) been of great vividness, and often of markedly *recurrent* type. But the point of interest is that, when he began to write stories for publication, the "little people who managed man's internal theatre" understood the change as well as he.

When he lay down to prepare himself for sleep, he no longer sought amusement, but printable and profitable tales; and after he had dozed off in his box-seat, his little people continued their evolutions with the same mercantile designs. . . . For the most part, whether awake or asleep, he is simply occupied — he or his little people — in consciously making stories for the market. . . .
The more I think of it, the more I am moved to press upon the world my question: "Who are the Little People?" They are near connections of the dreamer's, beyond doubt; they share in his financial worries and have an eye to the bank book; they share plainly in his training; . . . they have plainly learned like him to build the scheme of a considerate story and to arrange emotion in progressive order; only I think they have more talent; and one thing is beyond doubt, — they can tell him a story piece by piece, like a serial, and keep him all the while in ignorance of where they aim. . . .
That part [of my work] which is done while I am sleeping is the Brownies' part beyond contention; but that which is done when I am up and about is by no means necessarily mine, since all goes to show the Brownies have a hand in it even then.

Slight and imperfect as the above statistics and observations admittedly are, they seem to me to point in a more useful direction than do some of the facts collected by that modern group of anthropologists who hold that genius is in itself a kind of nervous malady, a disturbance of mental balance, akin to criminality or even to madness.

It is certainly not true, as I hold, either that the human race in general is nervously degenerating, or that nervous degeneration tends to a maximum in its most eminent members. But it can be plausibly maintained that the proportion of nervous to other disorders tends to increase. And it is certain that not nervous degeneration but nervous change or development is now proceeding among civilised peoples more rapidly than ever before, and that this self-adaptation to wider environments must inevitably be accompanied in the more marked cases by something of nervous instability. And it is true also that from one point of view these changes might form matter for regret; and that in order to discern what I take to be their true meaning we have to regard the problem of human evolution from a somewhat unfamiliar standpoint.

The nervous system is probably tending in each generation to become more complex and more delicately ramified. As is usual when any part of an organism is undergoing rapid evolutive changes, this nervous progress is accompanied with some instability. Those individuals in whom the hereditary or the acquired change is the most rapid are likely also to suffer most from a *perturbation which masks evolution* — an occasional appearance of what may be termed "nervous sports" of a useless or even injurious type. Such are the fancies and fanaticisms, the bizarre likes and dislikes, the excessive or aberrant sensibilities, which have been observed in some of the eminent men whom Lombroso discusses in his book on the Man of Genius. Their truest analogue, as we shall presently see more fully, lies in the oddities or morbidities of sentiment or sensation which so often accompany the development of the human organism into its full potencies, or precede the crowning effort by which a fresh organism is introduced into the world.

Such at least is my view; but the full acceptance of this view must depend upon some very remote and very speculative considerations bearing upon the nature and purport of the whole existence and evolution of man. Yet however remote and speculative the thesis which I defend may be, it is not one whit remoter or more speculative than the view which, *faute de mieux*, is often tacitly assumed by scientific writers.

In our absolute ignorance of the source from whence life came, we have no ground for assuming that it was a purely planetary product, or that its unknown potentialities are concerned with purely planetary ends. It would be as rash for the biologist to assume that life on earth can only point to generations of further life on earth as it would have been for some cosmic geologist to assume — before the appearance of life on earth — that geological forces must needs constitute all the activity which could take place on this planet.

Since the germ of life appeared on earth, its history has been a history not only of gradual *self-adaptation* to a known environment, but of gradual *discovery* of an environment, always there, but unknown. What we call its primitive simple irritability was in fact a dim panæsthesia; a potential faculty, as yet unconscious of all the stimuli to which it had not yet learnt to respond. As these powers of sensation and of response have developed, they have gradually revealed to the living germ environments of which at first it could have no conception.

of genius spring from a source one step nearer to primitive reality than
is that specialised consensus of faculties which natural selection has lifted
above the threshold for the purposes of working-day existence, then surely
we need not wonder if the mind and frame of man should not always
suffice for smooth and complete amalgamation; if some prefiguration of
faculties adapted to a later stage of being should mar the symmetry of
the life of earth.

And thus there may really be something at times *incommensurable*
between the inspirations of genius and the results of conscious logical
thought. Just as the calculating boy solves his problems by methods
which differ from the methods of the trained mathematician, so in artistic
matters also that "something of strangeness" which is in "all excellent
beauty," may be the expression of a real difference between subliminal
and supraliminal modes of perception. I cannot help thinking that such
a difference is perceptible in subliminal relations to speech; that the subliminal self will sometimes surpass conscious effort, if it is treating speech
as a branch of Art, in Poetry; — or else in some sense will fall short of
conscious effort, when it is merely using words as an unavoidable medium
to express ideas which common speech was hardly designed to convey.

Thus, on the one hand, when in presence of one of the great verbal
achievements of the race — say the *Agamemnon* of Æschylus — it is hard
to resist the obscure impression that some form of intelligence other than
supraliminal reason or conscious selection has been at work. The result
less resembles the perfection of rational choice among known data than
the imperfect presentation of some scheme based on perceptions which
we cannot entirely follow.

But, on the other hand, even though words may thus be used by genius
with something of the mysterious remoteness of music itself, it seems to
me that our subliminal mentation is less closely bound to the faculty of
speech than is our supraliminal. There is a phrase in common use which
involves perhaps more of psychological significance than has yet been
brought out. Of all which we can call genius, or which we can ally with
genius — of art, of love, of religious emotion — it is common to hear
men say that they *transcend the scope of speech*. Nor have we any reason
for regarding this as a mere vague sentimental expression.

There is no *a priori* ground for supposing that language will have
the power to express all the thoughts and emotions of man. It may indeed
be maintained that the inevitable course of its development tends to exhibit more and more clearly its inherent limitations. "Every language,"
it has been said, "begins as poetry and ends as algebra." To use the

possessor in the struggle for existence in a material world. The higher gifts of genius — poetry, the plastic arts, music, philosophy, pure mathematics — all of these are precisely as much in the central stream of evolution — are perceptions of new truth and powers of new action just as decisively predestined for the race of man — as the aboriginal Australian's faculty for throwing a boomerang or for swarming up a tree for grubs. There is, then, about those loftier interests nothing exotic, nothing accidental; they are an intrinsic part of that ever-evolving response to our surroundings which forms not only the planetary but the cosmic history of all our race.

What inconsistencies, what absurdities, underlie that assumption that evolution means nothing more than the survival of animals fittest to conquer enemies and to overrun the earth. On that bare hypothesis the genus *homo* is impossible to explain. No one really attempts to explain him except on the tacit supposition that Nature somehow tended to evolve intelligence — somehow needed to evolve joy; was not satisfied with such an earth-over-runner as the rabbit, or such an invincible conqueror as the influenza microbe. But *how much* intelligence, *what* kind of joy Nature aimed at — is this to be left to be settled by the instinct of *l'homme sensuel moyen?* or ought we not rather to ask of the best specimens of our race what it is that they live for? — whether they labour for the meat that perisheth, or for Love and Wisdom? To more and more among mankind the need of food is supplied with as little conscious effort as the need of air; yet these are often the very men through whom evolution is going on most unmistakably — who are becoming the typical figures of the swiftly-changing race.

Once more. If this point of view be steadily maintained, we shall gain further light on some of those strangenesses and irregularities of genius which have led to its paradoxical juxtaposition with insanity as a divergence from the accepted human type. The distinctive characteristic of genius is the large infusion of the subliminal in its mental output; and one characteristic of the subliminal in my view is that it is in closer relation than the supraliminal to the spiritual world, and is thus nearer to the primitive source and extra-terrene initiation of life. And earthly Life itself — embodied as it is in psycho-physically individualised forms — is, on the theory advanced in these pages, a product or characteristic of the etherial or metetherial and not of the gross material world. Thence in some unknown fashion it came; there in some unknown fashion it subsists even throughout its earthly manifestation; thither in some unknown fashion it must after earthly death return. If indeed the inspirations an external intelligence.[1] These complex and fanciful compositions — often absolutely automatic — appear to me like a stammering or rudimentary symbolism; as though the subliminal intelligence were striving to express itself through a vehicle perhaps more congenial to its habits than articulate language.

Returning, then, from these illustrations drawn from actual *automatism* to our proper subject of *genius*, — that happy mixture of subliminal with supraliminal faculty, — we may ask ourselves in what kind of subliminal uprush this hidden habit of wider symbolism, of self-communion beyond the limits of speech, will be likely to manifest itself above the conscious threshold.

The obvious answer to this question lies in the one word Art. The inspiration of Art of all kinds consists in the invention of precisely such a wider symbolism as has been above adumbrated. I am not speaking, of course, of symbolism of a forced and mechanical kind — symbolism designed and elaborated as such — but rather of that pre-existent but hidden concordance between visible and invisible things, between matter and thought, between thought and emotion, which the plastic arts, and music, and poetry, do each in their own special field discover and manifest for human wisdom and joy.

In using these words, I must repeat, I am far from adopting the formulæ of any special school. The symbolism of which I speak implies nothing of mysticism. Nor indeed, in my view, can there be any real gulf or deep division between so-called realistic and idealistic schools. All that exists is continuous; nor can Art symbolise any one aspect of the universe without also implicitly symbolising aspects which lie beyond.

And thus in the Arts we have symbolism at every stage of transparency and obscurity; from symbolisms which merely summarise speech to symbolisms which transcend it. Sometimes, as with Music, it is worse than useless to press for too close an interpretation. Music marches, and will march for ever, through an ideal and unimaginable world. Her melody may be a mighty symbolism, but it is a symbolism to which man has lost the key. Poetry's material, on the other hand, is the very language which she would fain transcend. But her utterance must be subliminal and symbolic, if it is to be poetry indeed; it must rise (as has been already hinted) from a realm profounder than deliberate speech; it must come charged, as Tennyson has it, with that "charm in words, a charm no words can give."

---

[1] Instances of this form of automatism are described in a book called *Spirit Drawings: a Personal Narrative*, by W. M. Wilkinson, some account of which is given in Appendix 8:1 A (Vol. II.) of the unabridged edition.

Here, too, we must dwell for a moment upon another and higher kind of internal visualisation. I have spoken of the arithmetical prodigy as possessing a kind of internal blackboard, on which he inscribes with ease and permanence his imaginary memoranda. But blackboards are not the only surfaces on which inscriptions can be made. There are other men — prodigies of a different order — whose internal *tabula* is not of blackened wood, but of canvas or of marble; whose inscriptions are not rows of Arabic numerals but living lines of colour, or curves of breathing stone. Even the most realistic art is something more than transcript and calculation; and for art's higher imaginative achievements there must needs be moments of inward idealisation when visible beauty seems but the token and symbol of beauty unrevealed; when Praxiteles must "draw from his own heart the archetype of the Eros that he made;" when Tintoret must feel with Heraclitus that "whatsoever we see waking is but deadness, and whatsoever sleeping, is but dream."

But when we reach this point we have begun (as I say) to transcend the special province to which, in Chapter I, I assigned the title of *genius*. I there pointed out that the influence of the subliminal on the supraliminal might conveniently be divided under three main heads. When the subliminal mentation co-operates with and supplements the supraliminal, without changing the apparent phase of personality, we have *genius*. When subliminal operations change the apparent phase of personality from the state of waking in the direction of trance, we have *hypnotism*. When the subliminal mentation forces itself up through the supraliminal, without amalgamation, as in crystal-vision, automatic writing, etc., we have *sensory or motor automatism*. In accordance with this definition, the *content* of the inspirations of genius is supposed to be of the same general type as the content of ordinary thought. We have regarded genius as crystallising fluid ideas; or, if you will, as concentrating and throwing upwards in its clear fountain a maze of subterranean streams. But we have not regarded it as modifying, in such operation, the ordinary alert wakefulness of the thinker, nor as providing him with any fresh knowledge, obtainable by supernormal methods alone.

It is plain, however, that such distinctions as those which I have drawn between genius, trance, automatism, cannot possibly be rigid or absolute. They are distinctions made for convenience between different phases of what must really be a continuous process — namely, the influence of the Self below the threshold upon the Self above it. Between each of these definite phases all kinds of connections and intermediate stages must surely exist.

Connections between *trance* and *automatism*, indeed, are obvious enough. The difficulty has rather lain in their clear separation. Trance, when habitual, is pretty sure to lead to automatic speech or writing. Automatism, when prolonged, is similarly apt to induce a state of trance.

The links between *Genius* and these cognate states are of a less conspicuous kind. They do, however, exist in such variety as to confirm in marked fashion the analogies suggested above.

And first, as to the connection between genius and automatism, one may say that just as anger is a brief madness, so the flash of Genius is essentially a brief automatism.

Wordsworth's moments of inspiration, when, as he says,

> "Some lovely image in the song rose up
> Full-formed, like Venus rising from the sea,"

were in effect moments of automatic utterance; albeit of utterance held fast in immediate co-operation with the simultaneous workings of the supraliminal self. Such a sudden poetic creation, like the calculating boy's announcement of the product of two numbers, resembles the sudden rush of planchette or pencil, in haste to scrawl some long-wished-for word.

Now extend this momentary automatism a little further. We come then to what is called the faculty of improvisation. How much is meant by this term? Is the extempore oration, "the unpremeditated lay," in truth a subliminal product? or have we to do merely with the rapid exercise of ordinary powers?

In the first place, it is clear that much of what is called improvisation is a matter of memory. The so-called secondary automatism which enables the pianist to play a known piece without conscious attention passes easily into improvisations which the player himself may genuinely accept as original; but which really consist of remembered fragments united by conventional links of connection. Thus also the orator, "thinking on his legs," trusts himself at first to the automatic repetition of a few stock phrases, but gradually finds that long periods flow unforeseen and unremembered from his tongue.

We thus get beyond the range of stereotyped synergies, of habituations of particular groups of nerve-centres to common action. There is some adaptability and invention; some new paths are traversed; adjustments are made for which no mere recurrence to old precedents will suffice.

The problem here resembles that well-known difficulty of explaining what goes on during the restoration or "substitution" of function after an injury to the brain. In that case, the brain-elements which remain uninjured slowly assume functions which they apparently never exercised before, — rearranging paths of cerebral communication in order to get the old efficiency out of the damaged and diminished brain-material. This recovery is not rapid like an extemporisation, but gradual, like a healing or re-growth, and it therefore does not suggest an intelligent control so much as a physiological process, like the re-budding on a certain pre-ordained pattern of the severed claw of a crab. Of course this restoration of brain-functions is inexplicable, as all growth is at present inexplicable. We may call it indeed with some reason the highest process of human growth. So viewed, it forms a kind of middle term between ordinary growth of bone or muscle, always on a predetermined plan, and that sudden creation of new cerebral connections or pathways which is implied in an inspiration of genius. Such a juxtaposition need not weaken my claim that the inspirations of genius represent a co-operant stream of submerged mentation, fully as developed in its own way as the mentation of which we are conscious above the threshold. The nature and degree of sub-liminal faculty must of course be judged by its highest manifestations. And this analogy between the hidden operations of *genius* and of *growth* would rather support me in regarding organic growth also as controlled by something of intelligence or memory, which under fitting conditions — as in the hypnotic trance — may be induced to co-operate with the waking will.

Moreover, the talent of improvisation, which suggested these analogies, will sometimes act much more persistently than in the case of the orator or the musician. There is reason to believe (both from internal style and from actual statements) that it plays a large part in imaginative literature. Various passages from George Sand's life-history, corroborated by the statements of other persons familiar with her methods of working, reveal in her an unusual vigour and fertility of literary outflow going on in an almost dream-like condition; a condition midway between the actual inventive dreams of R. L. Stevenson and the conscious labour of an ordinary man's composition.

What George Sand felt in the act of writing was a continuous and effortless flow of ideas, sometimes with and sometimes without an apparent *externalisation* of the characters who spoke in her romances. And turning to another author, as sane and almost as potent as George Sand her-self, we find a phenomenon which would have suggested to us actual in-sanity if observed in a mind less robust and efficient. If the allusions to the apparent independence of Dickens's characters which are scattered through his letters be read with our related facts in view, it will no longer be thought that they are intended as a mystification. Mrs. Gamp, his greatest creation, spoke to him, he tells us (generally in church) as with an inward monitory voice.

And note further that as scientific introspection develops we are likely to receive fuller accounts of these concurrent mental processes, these partial externalisations of the creatures of the romancer's brain. One such account, both definite and elaborate, has been published by M. Binet in *L'Année Psychologique* for 1894.[1]

This account, — contributed as serious evidence, as M. Binet's long article shows, — is thoroughly concordant with several other cases already known to us. It comes midway between Stevenson's dreams and the hysteric's *idées fixes*.

I have thus far endeavoured to show that Genius represents not only the crystallisation of ideas already existing in floating form in the supraliminal intelligence, but also an independent, although concurrent, stream of mentation, spreading often to wider range, although still concerned with matters in themselves cognisable by the normal intelligence.

Let us proceed to push the inquiry a step further. It has been claimed in this work for subliminal uprushes generally that they often contain knowledge which no ordinary method of research could acquire. Is this supernormal knowledge — we ought now to ask — ever represented in the uprushes to which we give the name of Genius?

What is the relation, in short, of the man of Genius to the sensitive?

If the man of Genius be, as I have urged, on the whole the completest type of humanity, and if the sensitive's special gift be in itself one of the most advanced forms of human faculty, ought not the inspirations of genius to bring with them flashes of supernormal knowledge as intimate as those which the sensitive — perhaps in other respects a commonplace person — from time to time is privileged to receive?

Some remarkable instances of this kind undoubtedly do exist. The most conspicuous and most important of all cannot, from motives of reverence, be here discussed. Nor will I dwell upon other founders of religions, or on certain traditional saints or sages. But among historical characters of the first mark the names of Socrates and of Joan of Arc are enough to cite. I believe that the monitions of the Dæmon of Socrates — the subliminal self of a man of transcendent genius — have in all probability been described to us with literal truth: and did in fact convey to that great philosopher precisely the kind of telæsthetic or precognitive information

[1] *L'Année Psychologique*, i. 1894, p. 124, F. de Curel, par A. Binet [§ 330].

which forms the sensitive's privilege to-day. We have thus in Socrates the ideal unification of human powers.

It must, however, be admitted that such complete unification is not the general rule for men of genius; that their inspirations generally stop short of telepathy or of telæsthesia. I think we may explain this limitation somewhat as follows. The man of genius is what he is by virtue of possessing a readier communication than most men possess between his supraliminal and his subliminal self. From his subliminal self, he can only draw what it already possesses; and we must not assume as a matter of course that the subliminal region of any one of us possesses that particular sensitivity — that specific transparency — which can receive and register *definite facts* from the unseen. *That* may be a gift which stands as much alone — in independence of other gifts or faculties — in the subliminal region as, say, a perfect musical ear in the supraliminal. The man of genius may draw much from those hidden wells of being without seeing reflected therein any actual physical scene in the universe beyond his ordinary ken.

And yet neither must we hastily assume that because the man of genius gets no *definite* impression of a world beyond our senses he does not therefore get any *true* impression, which is all his own.

I believe, on the contrary, that true, though vague, impressions of a world beyond the range of sense are actually received — I do not say by all men of genius, but by men of genius of certain types.[1]

A dim but genuine consciousness of the spiritual environment; that (it seems) is the degree of revelation which artistic or philosophic genius is capable of conferring. Subliminal uprushes, in other words, so far as they are intellectual, tend to become *telæsthetic*. They bring with them indefinite intimations of what I hold to be the great truth that the human spirit is essentially capable of a deeper than sensorial perception, of a direct knowledge of facts of the universe outside the range of any specialised organ or of any planetary view.

But this conclusion points the way to a speculation more important still. Telæsthesia is not the only spiritual law, nor are subliminal uprushes affairs of the intellect alone. Beyond and above man's innate power of world-wide perception, there exists also that universal link of spirit with spirit which in its minor earthly manifestations we call telepathy. Our submerged faculty — the subliminal uprushes of genius — can ex-

[1] In Wordsworth's *Prelude* we find introspective passages of extreme psychological interest as being deliberate attempts to tell the truth about exactly those emotions and intuitions which differentiate the poet from common men.

pand in that direction as well as in the direction of telæsthesia. The emotional content, indeed, of those uprushes is even profounder and more important than the intellectual; — in proportion as Love and Religion are profounder and more important than Science or Art.

That primary passion, I repeat, which binds life to life, which links us both to life near and visible and to life imagined but unseen; — *that* is no mere organic, no mere planetary impulse, but the inward aspect of the telepathic law. Love and religion are thus *continuous;* they represent different phases of one all-pervading mutual gravitation of souls. The flesh does not conjoin, but dissever; although through its very severance it suggests a shadow of the union which it cannot bestow. We have to do here neither with a corporeal nor with a purely human emotion. Love is the energy of integration which makes a Cosmos of the Sum of Things.

But here there is something of controversy to traverse before a revived Platonic conception of love can hope to be treated by the physiologist as more than a pedantic jest. And naturally so; since there is no emotion subliminal over so wide a range of origin, — fed so obscurely by "all thoughts, all passions, all delights," — and consequently so mysterious even to the percipient himself. At one end of its scale love is based upon an instinct as primitive as the need of nutrition; even if at the other end it becomes, as Plato has it, the ἑρμηνεῦον καὶ διαπορθμεῦον "the Interpreter and Mediator between God and Man." The controversy as to the planetary or cosmical scope of the passion of Love is in fact central to our whole subject.

It will give clearness to the question in dispute if I quote here a strong expression of each view in turn. For the physiological or materialist conception of the passion of love, — where love's subliminal element is held to be of the organic type, — set forth in no light or cynical spirit, but with the moral earnestness of a modern Lucretius, I can turn to no better authority than Professor Pierre Janet. The passage which follows is no mere *boutade* or paradox; it is a kind of culminating expression of the theory which regards the supraliminal man as the normal man, and distrusts all deep disturbance of his accustomed psychical routine.

It is commonly said that love is a passion to which man is always liable, and which may surprise him at any moment of his life from 15 to 75. This does not seem to me accurate; and a man is not throughout all his life and at every moment susceptible of falling in love (*de devenir amoureux*). When a man is in good physical and moral health, when he has easy and complete command of all his ideas, he may expose himself to circumstances the most capable of giving rise to a passion, but he will not feel it. His desires will be reasonable and obedient to his will, leading the man only so far as he wishes to go, and disappearing when he wishes to be rid of them. On the other hand, if a man is morally below the mark (*malade au moral*), — if in consequence of physical fatigue or excessive intellectual work, or of violent shocks and prolonged sorrow, he is exhausted, melancholy, distracted, timid, incapable of controlling his ideas, — in a word, *depressed*, — then he will fall in love, or receive the germ of some kind of passion, on the first and most trivial occasion. . . . The least thing is then enough; the sight of some face, a gesture, a word, which previously would have left us altogether indifferent, strikes us, and becomes the starting point of a long amorous malady. Or more than this, an object which had made no impression on us, at a moment when our mind was healthier and not capable of inoculation, may have left in us some insignificant memory which reappears in a moment of morbid receptivity. That is enough; the germ is sown in a favourable soil; it will develop itself and grow.

There is at first, as in every virulent malady, a period of incubation; the new idea passes and repasses in the vague reveries of the enfeebled consciousness; then seems for a few days to have disappeared and to leave the mind to recover from its passing trouble. But the idea has done its work below the surface; it has become strong enough to shake the body; and to provoke movements whose origin lies outside the primary consciousness. What is the surprise of a sensible man when he finds himself piteously returning beneath the windows of his charmer, whither his wandering feet have taken him without his knowledge; — or when in the midst of his daily work he hears his lips murmuring perpetually the well-known name! . . . Such is passion in its reality; not as idealised by fantastic description, but reduced to its essential psychological characteristics. (*L'Automatisme Psychologique*, p. 466.)

On the other side I will appeal to Plato himself, giving a brief sketch merely of one of the leading passages (*Symposium*, 192–212) where the Platonic conception of love is set forth.[1]

Plato begins by recognising, as fully as pessimist or cynic could do, the absolute inadequacy of what is called on earth the satisfaction of this profound desire. Lovers who love aright will feel that no physical nearness can content them, but what *will* content them they cannot say. "Their soul," says Plato, "is manifestly desiring something else; and what it is

---

[1] In the passage which follows some use has been made of Jowett's translation. It is noticeable that this utterance, unsurpassed among the utterances of antiquity, has been placed by Plato in the mouth of a woman — the prophetess Diotima — with the express intention, as I think, of generalising it, and of raising it above the region of sexual passion. There is nothing else in antiquity resembling the position thus ascribed to Diotima in reference to Socrates, — the woman being represented as capable of raising the highest and of illumining the wisest soul.

she cannot tell, only she darkly prophesies thereof and guesses it from afar. But if Hephæstus with his forging fire were to stand beside that pair and say: 'Is this what ye desire — to be wholly one? to be together by night and day? — for I am ready to melt you together and to make you grow in one, so that from two ye shall become one only, and in this life shall be undivided, and dying shall die together, and in the underworld shall be a single soul'; — there is no lover who would not eagerly accept the offer, and acknowledge it as the expression of the unknown yearning and the fulfilment of the ancient need." And through the mouth of Diotima, Plato insists that it is an unfailing sign of true love that its desires are *for ever;* nay, that love may be even defined as the desire of the *everlasting* possession of the good. And in all love's acts he finds the impress of man's craving for immortality, — for immortality whose only visible image for us on earth is the birth of children to us as we ourselves decay, — so that when the slow self-renewal of our own everchanging bodies has worn out and ceased, we may be renewed in brighter, younger bodies which we desire to be born to us from whomsoever we find most fair. "And then," says Plato, rising, as ever, from visible to invisible things, "if active *bodies* have so strong a yearning that an endless series of lovely images of themselves may constitute, as it were, an earthly immortality for them when they have worn away, how greatly must creative *souls* desire that partnership and close communion with other souls as fair as they may bring to birth a brood of lofty thoughts, poems, statues, institutions, laws, — the fitting progeny of the soul?

"And he who in his youth hath the need of these things in him, and grows to be a godlike man, wanders about in search of a noble and well-nurtured soul; and finding it, and in presence of that beauty which he forgets not night or day, brings forth the beautiful which he conceived long ago; and the twain together tend that which he hath brought forth, and are bound by a far closer bond than that of earthly children, since the children which are born to them are fairer and more immortal far. Who would not choose to have Homer's offspring rather than any sons or daughters of men? Who would not choose the offspring which Lycurgus left behind him, to be the very salvation of Lacedæmon and of Greece? or the children of Solon, whom we call Father of our Laws? or of other men like these, whether Greeks or barbarians, who by great deeds that they have done have become the begetters of every kind of virtue? — ay, and to these men's children have temples been set up, and never to any other progeny of man. . . ."

"He, then, who to this end would strive aright, must begin in youth to seek fair forms, and should learn first to love one fair form only, and therein to engender noble thoughts. And then he will perceive that the beauty of one fair form is to the beauty of another near akin; and that if it be Beauty's self he seek, it were madness not to account the beauty of all forms as one same thing; and considering this, he will be the lover of all lovely shapes, and will abate his passion for one shape alone, despising and deeming it but a little thing. And this will lead him on to see that the beauty of the soul is far more precious than any beauty of outward form, so that if he find a fair soul, though it be in a body which hath but little charm, he will be constant thereunto, and bring to birth such thoughts as teach and strengthen, till he lead that soul on to see the beauty of actions and of laws, and how all beauty is in truth akin, and the body's beauty is but a little matter; and from actions he will lead him on to sciences, that he may see how sciences are fair; and looking on the abundance of beauty may no longer be as the slave or bondman of one beauty or of one law; but setting sail into the ocean of beauty, and creating and beholding many fair and glorious thoughts and images in a philosophy without stint or stay, he may thus at last wax strong and grow, and may perceive that there is one science only, the science of infinite beauty.

"For he who hath thus far had intelligence of love, and hath beheld all fair things in order and aright, — he drawing near to the end of things lovable shall behold a BEING marvellously fair; for whose sake in truth it is that all the previous labours have been undergone: One who is from everlasting, and neither is born nor perisheth, nor can wax nor wane, nor hath change or turning or alteration of foul and fair; nor can that beauty be imagined after the fashion of face or hands or bodily parts and members, nor in any form of speech or knowledge, nor as dwelling in aught but in itself; neither in beast nor man nor earth nor heaven nor any other creature; but Beauty only and alone and separate and eternal, which, albeit all other fair things partake thereof and grow and perish, itself without change or increase or diminution endures for everlasting. And whoso being led on and upward by human loves begins to see that Beauty, he is not far, I say, from reaching the end of all. And surely then, O Socrates (said that guest from Mantinea), man's life is worth the living, when he beholds that Primal Fair; which when thou seest it shall not seem to thee to be made after the fashion of gold or raiment or those forms of earth, — whom now beholding thou art stricken dumb, and fain, if it were possible, without thought of meat or drink, wouldst look and love for ever. What would it be, then, were it granted to any man to see Very Beauty clear; — incorruptible and undefiled, not mingled with colour

't can consume away, but single and
' vision and beatitude, be poor or low?
then, that then alone it will be possible for this
away with those eyes by which it is spiritually
toward virtue, since that is no shadow to which
very truth, since he hath the very Truth in his
rearing Virtue as his child, he must needs
and if there be any man who is immortal,

here expressed in extreme terms, — the
term it, and the cosmical, — the choice is
I say that in our estimate of love is involved
for Religion should mean the sane response of
n of Cosmic Law. But Religion in the sense
— our emotional and ethical attitude towards
reality too closely parallel to Platonic Love to
who denies reality in the one to assume reality in
Platonic lover the image of the Beloved one — no
serious summons and imagination — has become
instinctive impulse to noble thought and deed. Even
r to a Theresa is the image of the Divinity whom they
claim that sometimes in moments of crisis they feel
e. a *communicatio idiomatum* with the Divine, we may
to the humbler, but more tangible, evidence which assures
seen souls still inhabiting and souls who have quitted the
exist a telepathic intercommunication and an impalpable
afar.

survey has been, it has served to indicate that the
to which we have applied the name of genius may be
every region of thought and emotion, as in each direction
day self may be more or less permeable to subliminal
Coming, then, to the question, "What is the origin of
cannot accept the ordinary explanation that it is a mere
mental by-product, occurring as physical "sports" do in the
evolution. The view which I hold, — the view which I am
ting, is in some sort a renewal of the old Platonic "reminis-
the light of that fuller knowledge which is common property
I hold that in the protoplasm or primary basis of all organic
must have been an inherent adaptability to the manifesta-
all faculties which organic life has in fact manifested. I hold,

of course, that "sports" or variations occur, which are at present unpredictable, and which reveal in occasional offspring faculties which their parents showed no signs of possessing. But I differ from those who hold that the faculty itself thus manifested is now for the first time initiated in that stock by some chance combination of hereditary elements. I hold that it is not initiated, but only revealed; that the "sport" has not called a new faculty into being, but has merely raised an existing faculty above the threshold of supraliminal consciousness.

This view, if pushed back far enough, is no doubt inconsistent with the way in which evolution is generally conceived. For it denies that all human faculties must have been evoked by terrene experience. It assumes a subliminal self, with unknown faculties, originated in some unknown way, and not merely by contact with the needs which the terrene organism has had to meet. It thus seems at first sight to be introducing a new mystery, and to be introducing it in a gratuitous way.

To this I reply in the first place that so far as the origin of man's known powers is concerned, no fresh mystery is in fact introduced. All human powers, to put the thing broadly, have somehow or other to be got into protoplasm and then got out again. You have to explain first how they became implicit in the earliest and lowest living thing, and then how they have become thus far explicit in the latest and highest. All the faculties of that highest being, I repeat, existed *virtually* in the lowest, and in so far as the admitted faculties are concerned, the difference between my view and the ordinary view may be said to be little more than a difference as to the sense which that word *virtually* is here to assume.

The real difference between the two views appears when the faculties which I have called unknown come to be considered. If they are held to be real, my view is certainly the better able to embrace them. I hold that telepathy and telæsthesia do in fact exist — telepathy, a communication between incarnate mind and incarnate mind, and perhaps between incarnate minds and minds unembodied; telæsthesia, a knowledge of things terrene which overpasses the limits of ordinary perception, and which perhaps also achieves an insight into some other than terrene world. And these faculties, I say, cannot have been acquired by natural selection, for the preservation of the race, during the process of terrene evolution; they were (as we may phrase it) the products of extra-terrene evolution. And if they were so, man's other powers may well have been so also. The specialised forms of terrene perception were not real novelties in the universe, but imperfect adaptations of protoplasm to the manifestation of the indwelling general perceptive power. The mathematical faculty, for instance (we may, perhaps, say with Plato), pre-existed. When Dase solved all those sums in his head, his power of solving them was not a fresh development in his ancestral stock, but depended on the accidental adaptation of his organism to the manifestation of the indwelling computative power. I do not indeed venture to follow Plato in his ontogenetic argument — his claim that the individual computator has had already an individual training in computation. I do not say that Dase himself learnt or divined the multiplication-table in some ideal world. I only say that Dase and all the rest of us are the spawn or output of some unseen world in which the multiplication-table is, so to speak, in the air. Dase trailed it after him, as the poet says of the clouds of glory, when he "descended into generation" in a humble position at Hamburg.

In him and in his ancestors were many faculties which were called out by the struggle for existence, and became supraliminal. But there were many faculties also which were not thus called out, and which consequently remained subliminal. To these faculties, as a rule, his supraliminal self could get no access. But by some chance of evolution — some sport — a vent-hole was opened at this one point between the different strata of his being, and a subliminal uprush carried his computative faculty into the open day.

Two things, of course, are assumed in this argument for which Science offers no guarantee. I assume in the man a soul which can draw strength and grace from a spiritual Universe, and conversely I assume in the Universe a Spirit accessible and responsive to the soul of man. These are familiar postulates. Every religion has claimed them in turn; although every religion in turn has so narrowed their application as grievously to narrow the evidence available for their support. But that which religions have claimed for their Founders or for their Saints — and what is sanctity but the genius of the ethical realm? — Psychology must claim for every form of spiritual indrawing, every form of spiritual response; for sleeping vision, for hypnotic rejuvenation, for sensory and motor automatisms, for trance, for ecstasy. The philosopher who has cried with Marcus Aurelius "Either Providence or atoms!" — who has declared that without this basis in the Unseen, "the moral Cosmos would be reduced to a Chaos"; — should he not welcome even the humblest line of research which fain would gather from every unsolved problem some hint as to the spiritual law unknown which in time may give the solution of all?

We know not in what directions — directions how definitely predetermined — even physical organisms can vary from the common type. We know not what amount of energy any given plant or animal can absorb and incorporate from earth and air and sun. Still less can we predict or limit the possible variations of the soul, the fulness which it may receive from the World-Soul, its possible heritage of grace and truth. But in genius we can watch at each stage the processes of this celestial nurture. We can imagine the outlook of joyous trustfulness; we can almost seem, with Wordsworth, to remember the child's soul entering into the Kingdom of Heaven. Childhood is genius without capacity; it makes for most of us our best memory of inspiration, and our truest outlook upon the real, which is the ideal, world.

From a greater distance we can watch the inward stir of mighty thought, the same for Æschylus, for Newton, for Virgil; — a stir independent of worldly agitation; like the swing and libration of the tide-wave across the ocean, which takes no note of billow or of storm.

Nay, we can see against the sun "the eagle soaring above the tomb of Plato," and in Paul, as in Plotinus, we can catch that sense of self-fulfilment in self-absorption, of rapture, of deliverance, which the highest minds have bequeathed to us as the heritage of their highest hours.

These our spiritual ancestors are no eccentrics nor degenerates; they have made for us the sanest and most fruitful experiment yet made by man; they have endeavoured to exalt the human race in a way in which it can in truth be exalted; they have drawn on forces which exist, and on a Soul which answers; they have dwelt on those things "by dwelling on which it is," as Plato has it, "that even God is divine."

CHAPTER IV

SLEEP

ὄλβιος δ' ἅπαντεν αἶσα λυσίπονον μεταωίσσονται τελευτάν.
καὶ σῶμα μὲν πάντων ἕπεται θανάτῳ περισθενεῖ,
ξωὸν δ' ἔτι λείπεται αἰῶνος εἴδωλον· τὸ γάρ ἐστι μόνον
ἐκ θεῶν· εὕδει δὲ πρασσόντων μελέων, ἀτὰρ εὑδόντεσσιν ἐν πολλοῖς ὀνείροις
δείκνυσι τερπνῶν ἐφέρποισαν χαλεπῶν τε κρίσιν.

                                                    — PINDAR.

THE preceding chapters have carried us two steps upon our way. In Chapter II. we gained some insight into the structure of human personality by analysing some of the accidents to which it is subject; in the third chapter we viewed this personality in its normal waking state, and considered how that norm should be defined, and in what manner certain fortunate persons had integrated the personality still further by utilising uprushes of subliminal faculty to supplement or to crystallise the products of supraliminal thought.

The review of these two chapters indicates clearly enough what my next step must be. It is obvious that in my review of phases or alternations of personality I have left out of sight the most constant, the most important alternation of all. I have thus far said nothing of *sleep*. Yet *that* change of personality, at least, has been borne in on every one's notice; — not, certainly, as a morbid curiosity, but as an essential part of life.

Let us then consider the specific characteristics of sleep. The definition of sleep is an acknowledged *crux* in physiology. And I would point out that the increased experience of hypnotic sleep which recent years have afforded has made this difficulty even more striking than before. A physiological explanation must needs assume that some special bodily condition, — such, for instance, as the clogging of the brain by waste-products, — is at least the usual antecedent of sound sleep. But it is certain, on the other hand, that with a large percentage of persons profound and prolonged sleep can be induced, in *any* bodily condition, by simple suggestion. Hypnosis, indeed (as Wetterstrand and others have shown) may be prolonged, with actual benefit to the sleeper, far beyond

93

the point which the spontaneous sleep of a healthy subject ever reaches. A good subject can be awakened and thrown into hypnosis again almost at pleasure, and independently of any state either of nutrition or of fatigue. Such sleep belongs to those phenomena which we may call nervous if we will, but which we can observe or influence from the psychological side alone.

We can hardly hope, from the ordinary data, to arrive at a definition of sleep more satisfactory than others have reached. We must defer that attempt until we have collected something more than the ordinary evidence as to what occurs or does not occur during the abeyance of waking life. One point, however, is plain at once. We cannot treat sleep, — as it has generally been treated, — in its purely *negative* aspect. We cannot be content merely to dwell, with the common text-books, on the mere *absence* of waking faculties; — on the diminution of external perception, the absence of controlling intelligence. We must treat sleep *positively*, so far as we can, as a definite phase of our personality, co-ordinate with the waking phase. Each phase, as I believe, has been differentiated alike from a primitive indifference; — from a condition of lowly organisms which merited the name neither of sleep nor of waking. Nay, if there were to be a contest as to which state should be deemed primary and which second-- ary, sleep might put forward its claim to be regarded as the more primitive phase. It is sleep rather than vigilance which prenatal and infantile life suggest; and even for us adults, however much we may associate ourselves in thought with the waking state alone, that state has at least thus much of secondary and adventitious that it is maintained for short periods only, which we cannot artificially lengthen, being plainly unable to sustain itself without frequent recourse to that fuller influx of vitality which slumber brings.

Out of slumber proceeds each fresh arousal and initiation of waking activities. What other activities may in slumber be aroused and initiated the evidence to be set forth in this chapter should help us to say. To some extent at least the abeyance of the supraliminal life must be the liberation of the subliminal. To some extent the obscuration of the noonday glare of man's waking consciousness must reveal the far-reaching faint corona of his unsuspected and impalpable powers.

Entering, then, upon a review of sleeping faculty, thus inevitably imperfect, we may best begin from the red end of our spectrum of consciousness; — the red end which represents the deepest power which waking effort can exert upon our physical organism.

Our survey of the efficacy of sleep, indeed, must make its beginning *beyond* that limit. For assuredly in sleep some agency is at work which far surpasses waking efficacy in this respect. It is a fully admitted, although an absolutely unexplained fact, that the regenerative quality of healthy sleep is something *sui generis*, which no completeness of waking quiescence can rival or approach. A few moments of sleep — a mere blur across the field of consciousness — will sometimes bring a renovation which hours of lying down in darkness and silence would not yield. A mere bowing of the head on the breast, if consciousness ceases for a second or two, may change a man's outlook on the world. At such moments, — and many persons, like myself, can fully vouch for their reality, — one feels that what has occurred in one's organism, — alteration of blood-pressure, or whatever it be, — has been in some sense discontinuous; that there has been a break in the inward *régime*, amounting to much more than a mere brief ignoring of stimuli from without. The break of consciousness is associated in some way with a potent physiological change. That is to say, even in the case of a moment of ordinary sleep we already note the appearance of that special recuperative energy which is familiar in longer periods of sleep, and which, as we shall presently see, reaches a still higher level in hypnotic trance.

This recuperative power, then, lies just beyond the red end of our spectrum of waking faculty. In that obscure region we note only added power; an increased control over organic functions at the foundation of bodily life. But when we pass on within the limits of our spectrum of waking consciousness; — when we come to control over voluntary muscles, or to sensory capacity, we find that our comparison between sleeping and waking faculty is no longer a simple one. On the one hand, there is of course a general blank and abeyance of control over the realm of waking energies; — or in partial sleep a mere fantastic parody of those energies in incoherent dream. On the other hand, we find that sleep is capable of strange developments, — and that night can sometimes suddenly outdo the most complex achievements of day.

Take first the degree of control over the voluntary muscles. In ordinary sleep this is neither possessed nor desired; in nightmare its loss is exaggerated, in quasi-hysterical fashion, into an appalling fear; while in somnambulism, — a kind of new personality developed *ad hoc*, — the sleeper (as we shall see later on) walks on perilous ridges with steady feet. I have already said that morbid somnambulism bears to sound sleep a relation something like that which hysteria bears to normal life. But between the healthy somnambulist and the subject of nightmare we find from another point of view a contrast resembling that between the man of genius and the hysteric. The somnambulist, like the man of genius, brings into play resources which are beyond ordinary reach. On the other hand, just as in many hysterics certain ordinary powers of movement have lapsed below voluntary control, so also the dreamer who dimly wishes to move a constrained limb is often unable to send thither a sufficient current of motor energy to effect the desired change of position. That nightmare inability to move, which we thus feel in dream, — "when neither he that fleeth can flee, nor he that pursueth pursue," — that sensation which both Homer and Virgil have selected as the type of paralysing bewilderment,[1] — this is just the *aboulia* of the hysteric; — the condition when it takes a man half an hour to put on his hat, or when a woman sits all the morning looking at her knitting, but unable to add a stitch.

"Somnambulism," however, is too vague and undefined a term for our present discussion. It will only be by a comparison with hypnotism, in the next chapter, that we can hope to get some clearer notion of "sleep-waking" states.

Let us pass on to consider *entencephalic sensory faculty,* — "mind's eye" faculty, — as shown in sleep or dream. Here too we shall find the same rule to prevail as with motor faculty. That is to say, on the whole the sensory faculty is of course dimmed and inhibited by sleep; but there are nevertheless indications of a power subsisting as vividly as ever, or with even added acuteness.

Baillarger in France and Griesinger in Germany (both about 1845) were among the first to call attention to the vivid images which rise before the internal vision of many persons, between sleep and waking. M. Alfred Maury, the well-known Greek scholar and antiquary, gave to these images a few years later the title of *illusions hypnagogiques*, and published a remarkable series of observations upon himself. Mr. Galton has further treated of them in his *Inquiry into Human Faculty;* and cases will be found in *Phantasms of the Living*, vol. i, pp. 390, 473, etc.

These visions may be *hypnopompic* as well as *hypnagogic;* — may appear, that is to say, at the moment when slumber is departing as well as at the moment when it is coming on; — and in either case they are closely related to dreams; the "hypnagogic illusions" or pictures being sometimes repeated in dream (as with Maury), and the hypnopompic pictures consisting generally in the persistence of some dream-image into the first moments of waking. In either case they testify to an intensified power of inward visualisation at a very significant moment; — a moment which is actually or virtually one of sleep, but which yet admits of definite

[1] *Iliad*, xxii. 199; *Æneid*, xii. 908.

comparison with adjacent moments of waking. We may call the condition one of cerebral or "mind's eye" hyperæsthesia, — an exalted sensibility of special brain-centres in response to those unknown internal stimuli which are always giving rise to similar but fainter inward visions even in broadly waking hours.

For those who are already good visualisers such phenomena as these, though striking enough, present no quite unique experience. For bad visualisers, on the other hand, the vividness of these hypnagogic pictures may be absolutely a revelation.

The degree of acuteness, not of the visualising faculty alone, but of all the senses in dream, is a subject for direct observation, and even — for persons who can at all control their dreams — for direct experiment. Some correspondents report a considerable apparent accession of sensory power in dream. Others again speak of the increased vividness of dramatic conception, or of what has been called in a hypnotic subject "objectivation of types." "In each of these dreams," writes one lady, "I was a man; — in one of them a low brute, in the other a dipsomaniac. I never had the slightest conception of how such persons felt or thought until these experiences." Another correspondent speaks of dreaming two disconnected dreams, — one emotional and one geometrical, — simultaneously, and of consequent sense of confusion and fatigue.

The "Chapter on Dreams," in R. L. Stevenson's volume, *Across the Plains* (already referred to in the last chapter), contains a description of the most successful dream-experiments thus far recorded. By self-suggestion before sleep Stevenson could secure a visual and dramatic intensity of dream-representation which furnished him with the motives for some of his most striking romances. His account, written with admirable psychological insight, is indispensable to students of this subject. I am mentioning these well-known phenomena, as the reader will understand, with a somewhat novel purpose — to show, namely, that the internal sensory perceptions or imaginative faculty of sleep may exceed that of vigilance in something the same way as the recuperative agency of sleep surpasses the *vis medicatrix* of waking hours.

I pass on to a less frequent phenomenon, which shows us at once intense imagination during sleep, and a lasting imprint left by these imaginations upon the waking organism; — an unintended self-suggestion which we may compare with Stevenson's voluntary self-suggestion mentioned just above.

The permanent result of a dream, I say, is sometimes such as to show that the dream has not been a mere superficial confusion of past waking experiences, but has had an unexplained potency of its own, — drawn, like the potency of hypnotic suggestion, from some depth in our being which the waking self cannot reach. Two main classes of this kind are conspicuous enough to be easily recognised — those, namely, where the dream has led to a "conversion" or marked religious change, and those where it has been the starting-point of an "insistent idea" or of a fit of actual insanity.[1] The dreams which convert, reform, change character and creed, have of course a *primâ facie* claim to be considered as something other than ordinary dreams; and their discussion may be deferred till a later stage of our inquiry. Those, on the other hand, which suddenly generate an insistent idea of an irrational type are closely and obviously analogous to post-hypnotic self-suggestions, which the self that inspired them cannot be induced to countermand. Such is the dream related by M. Taine,[2] where a gendarme, impressed by an execution at which he has assisted, dreams that he himself is to be guillotined, and is afterwards so influenced by the dream that he attempts suicide. Several cases of this kind have been collected by Dr. Faure;[3] and Dr. Tissié, in his interesting little work, *Les Rêves*, has added some curious instances from his own observation.

A striking illustration may be drawn from the following incident in the story of Krafft-Ebing's patient,[4] Ilma S., the genuineness of whose stigmata seems proved by that physician's care in observation, and by the painfulness of certain experiments performed upon her by students as practical jokes and against her will: —

May 6th, 1888. — The patient is disturbed to-day. She complains to the sister of severe pain under the left breast, thinks that the professor has burnt her in the night, and begs the sister to obtain a retreat for her in a convent, where she will be secure against such attacks. The sister's refusal causes a hystero-epileptic attack. [At length, in the hypnotic trance] the patient gives the following explanation of the origin of the pain: "Last night an old man came to me; he looked like a priest and came in company with a Sister of Charity, on whose collet there was a large golden B. I was afraid of her. The old man was amiable and friendly. He dipped a pen in the sister's pocket, and with it wrote a W and B on my skin under the left breast. Once he dipped his pen badly and made a blot in the middle of the figure. This spot and the B pain me severely, but the W does not. The man explained the W

---

[1] See Dr. Féré in *Brain* for January 1887.
[2] *De l'Intelligence*, vol. i. p. 119.
[3] *Archives de Médecine*, vol. i. 1876, p. 554.
[4] *An Experimental Study in Hypnotism*, by Dr. R. von Krafft-Ebing, translated by Dr. C. G. Chaddock, p. 91.

as meaning that I should go to the M church and confess at the W confessional."

After this account the patient cried out and said, "There stands the man again. Now he has chains on his hands."

When the patient woke into ordinary life she was suffering pain in the place indicated, where there were "superficial losses of substance, penetrating to the corium, which have a resemblance to a reversed W and B," with "a hyperæmic raised spot between the two." Nowhere in this peculiar neurotrophic alteration of the skin, which is identical with those previously produced experimentally, are there traces of inflammation. The pain and the memory of the dream were removed by the doctor's suggestion; but the dream self-suggestion to confess at the M church persisted; and the patient, without knowing why, did actually go and confess to the priest of her vision.

In this last case we have a dream playing the part of a powerful post-hypnotic suggestion. The meaning of this vague term "suggestion" we shall have to discuss in a later chapter. It is enough to notice here the great power of a subliminal suggestion which can make an impression so much stronger not only than the usual evanescent touch of dream, but than the actual experiences of waking day.

But this case may also serve to lead us on to further reflections as to the connection between dream-memory and hypnotic memory, a connection which points, as we shall presently see, towards the existence of some subliminal continuity of memory, lying deeper down than the evocable memory of common life — the stock of conscious reminiscences on which we can draw at will.

With regard to memory, as with regard to sensation, we seem in waking life to be dealing with a selection made for purposes of earthly use. From the pre-conscious unselective memory which depends on the mere organisation of living matter, it is the task of consciousness, as it dawns in each higher organism, to make its own appropriate selection and to develop into distinctness certain helpful lines of reminiscence. The question of self-preservation — What must I needs be aware of in order to escape my foes? — involves the question, What must I needs remember in order to act upon the facts of which I am aware? The selected currents of memory follow the selected avenues of sensation; what by disuse I lose the power of noticing at the time, I also lose the power of recalling afterwards.

For simpler organisms this rule may perhaps suffice. Man needs a more complex formula. For it may happen, as we have already seen, that two or more phases of personality in one man may each select from the mass of potential reminiscences a special group of memories of its own.

These special groups, moreover, may bear to one another all kinds of relations; one may include another, or they may alternate and may be apparently co-exclusive.

From these dissociations and alternations of memory there will be many lessons to learn. The lesson which here presents itself is not the least important. What is the relation of the sleeping state to these dissociated, these parallel or concentric memories? Is it the case that when one memory includes another it is the waking memory — as one might expect from that state's apparently superior vividness — which shows itself the deeper, the more comprehensive record?

The answer of actual experience to these questions is unexpectedly direct and clear. In every recorded instance — so far at least as my memory serves me, where there has been any *unification* between alternating states, so as to make comparison possible — it is the memory furthest from waking life whose span is the widest, whose grasp of the organism's upstored impressions is the most profound. Inexplicable as this phenomenon has been to observers who have encountered it without the needed key, the independent observations of hundreds of physicians and hypnotists have united in affirming its reality. The commonest instance, of course, is furnished by the ordinary hypnotic trance. The degree of intelligence, indeed, which finds its way to expression in that trance or slumber varies greatly in different subjects and at different times. But whensoever there is enough of alertness to admit of our forming a judgment, we find that in the hypnotic state there is a considerable memory — though not necessarily a complete or a reasoned memory — of the waking state; whereas with most subjects in the waking state — unless some special command be imposed upon the hypnotic self — there is no memory whatever of the hypnotic state. In many hysterical conditions also the same general rule subsists; namely, that the further we get from the surface the wider is the expanse of memory which we encounter.

If all this be true, there are several points on which we may form expectations definite enough to suggest inquiry. Ordinary sleep is roughly intermediate between waking life and deep hypnotic trance; and it seems *a priori* probable that its memory will have links of almost equal strength with the memory which belongs to waking life and the memory which belongs to the hypnotic trance. And this is in fact the case; the fragments of dream-memory are interlinked with both these other chains. Thus, for example, without any suggestion to that effect, acts accomplished in the hypnotic trance may be remembered in dream; and remembered under the illusion which was thrown round them by the hypnotiser. Thus Dr.

Auguste Voisin suggested to a hypnotised subject to stab a patient — really a stuffed figure — in the neighbouring bed.[1] The subject did so; and of course knew nothing of it on waking. But three days afterwards he returned to the hospital complaining that his dreams were haunted by the figure of a woman, who accused him of having stabbed and killed her. Appropriate suggestion laid this ghost of a doll.

Conversely, dreams forgotten in waking life may be remembered in the hypnotic trance. Thus Dr. Tissié's patient, Albert, dreamt that he was about to set out on one of his somnambulic "fugues," or aimless journeys, and when hypnotised mentioned to the physician this dream, which in his waking state he had forgotten.[2] The probable truth of this statement was shown by the fact that he did actually set out on the journey thus dreamt of, and that his journeys were usually preceded and incited by remembered dreams.

I need not dwell on the existence, but at the same time the incompleteness, of our dream-memory of waking life; nor on the occasional formation of a separate chain of memory, constructed from successive and cohering dreams. It should be added that we do not really know how far our memory in dream of waking life may have extended; since we can only *infer* this from our notoriously imperfect waking memory of past dreams.

A cognate anticipation to which our theory will point will be that dream-memory will occasionally be found to fill up gaps in waking memory, other than those due to hypnotic trance; such so-called "ecmnesic" periods, for instance, as sometimes succeed a violent shock to the system, and may even embrace some space of time *anterior* to the shock. These periods themselves resemble prolonged and unremembered dreams. Such accidents, however, are so rare, and such dream-memory so hard to detect, that I mention the point mainly for the sake of theoretical completeness; and must think myself fortunate in being able to refer the reader to a recent case of M. Charcot's which affords an interesting confirmation of the suggested view.[3]

I pass on to the still more novel and curious questions involved in the apparent existence of a dream-memory which, while accompanying the memory of ordinary life, seems also to have a wider purview, and to

[1] *Revue de l'Hypnotisme*, June 1891, p. 302.

[2] *Les Rêves*, p. 135. This remarkable patient afforded examples of many forms of communication of memory between different states of personality. See pp. 192-200 for a conspectus of these complex recollections.

[3] *Revue de Médecine*, February 1892. A full account and discussion of the same case is contained in Dr. P. Janet's *Névroses et Idées fixes*, vol. i. pp. 116 *et seq.* (§413).

indicate that the record of external events which is kept within us is far fuller than we know.

Let us consider what stages such a memory may show.

I. It may include events once known to the waking self, but now definitely forgotten.

II. It may include facts which have fallen within the sensory field, but which have never been supraliminally "apperceived" or cognised in any way. And thus also it may indicate that from this wider range of remembered facts dream-*inferences* have been drawn; — which inferences may be *retrospective, prospective*, or, — if I may use a word of Pope's with a new meaning, *circumspective*, — that is to say, relating not to the past or to the future, but to the present condition of matters beyond the range of ordinary perception. It is plain that inferences of this kind (if they exist) will be liable to be mistaken for direct retrocognition, direct premonition, direct clairvoyance; while yet they need not actually prove anything more than a perception on the part of the subliminal self more far-reaching, — a memory more stable, — than is the perception or the memory of the supraliminal self which we know.

These hypermnesic dreams, then, may afford a means of drawing our lines of evidence more exactly; of relegating some marvellous narratives to a realm of lesser marvel, and at the same time of realising more clearly what it is in the most advanced cases which ordinary theories are really powerless to explain.

As to the *first* of the above-mentioned categories no one will raise any doubt. It is a familiar fact — or a fact only sufficiently unfamiliar to be noted with slight surprise — that we occasionally recover in sleep a memory which has wholly dropped out of waking consciousness.

In such cases the original piece of knowledge has at the time made a definite impress on the mind, — has come well within the span of apprehension of the supraliminal consciousness. Its reappearance after however long an interval is a fact to which there are already plenty of parallels. But the conclusion to which some cases seem to me to point is one of a much stranger character. I think that there is evidence to show that many facts or pictures which have never even for a moment come within the apprehension of the supraliminal consciousness are nevertheless retained by the subliminal memory, and are occasionally presented in dreams with what seems a definite purpose. I quote an interesting case in Appendix IV. A.[1]

[1] See also *Journal* S.P.R., vol. iv. p. 142 (October 1889), and *Proceedings* of the American S.P.R., vol. i. No. 4, p. 363 [415 A and B].

The same point, as we shall hereafter see, is illustrated by the phenomena of crystal-vision. Miss Goodrich-Freer,[1] for example, saw in the crystal the announcement of the death of a friend; — a piece of news which certainly had never been apprehended by her ordinary conscious self. On referring to the *Times*, it was found that an announcement of the death of some one of the same unusual name was contained in a sheet with which she had screened her face from the fire; — so that the words may have fallen within her range of vision, although they had not reached what we broadly call her waking mind.

This instance was of value from the strong probability that the news could never have been supraliminally known at all; — since it was too important to have been merely glanced at and forgotten.

In these cases the dream-self has presented a significant scene, — has chosen, so to say, from its gallery of photographs the special picture which the waking mind desired, — but has not needed to draw any more complex inference from the facts presumably at its disposal. I have now to deal with a small group of dreams which reason as well as remember; — if indeed in some of them there be not something more than mere reasoning on facts already in some way acquired, — something which overpasses the scheme prescribed for the present chapter.

In the first place we cannot doubt that definite data already known may sometimes be treated in somnambulism or ordinary dream with more than waking intelligence. Such are the cases of mathematical problems solved in somnambulism, or of the skeletal arrangement discovered by Agassiz in common sleep for scattered bones which had baffled his waking skill. I give in Appendix IV. B. the striking case of Professor Hilprecht where dream-intelligence is carried to its highest point. Professor Romaine Newbold (who records the case) is well versed in the analysis of evidence making for supernormal powers, and his explanation of the vision as the result of "processes of associative reasoning analogous to those of the upper consciousness" must, I think, be taken as correct. But had the incident occurred in a less critical age of the world, — in any generation, one may say, but *this*, — how majestic a proof would the phantasmal Babylonian's message be held to have afforded of his veritable co-operation with the modern *savant* in the reconstruction of his remote past!

I repeat that with this case of Professor Hilprecht's we seem to have reached the utmost intensity of sleep faculty within the limits of our ordinary spectrum. In almost every region of that spectrum we have found

[1] *Proceedings* S.P.R., vol. v. p. 507.

that the sleeper's faculty, under its narrow conditions, shows scattered signs of at least a potential equality with the faculty of waking hours.

We have already seen this as regards muscular movements, as regards inward vision and audition, and as regards memory; and these last records complete the series by showing us the achievement in sleep of intellectual work of the severest order. Coleridge's *Kubla Khan* had long ago shown the world that a great poet might owe his masterpiece to the obscuration of waking sense.[1] And the very imperfection of *Kubla Khan* — the memory truncated by an interruption — may again remind us how partial must ever be our waking knowledge of the achievements of sleep.

May I not, then, claim a real analogy between certain of the achievements of *sleep* and the achievements of *genius?* In both there is the same triumphant spontaneity, the same sense of drawing no longer upon the narrow and brief endurance of nerves and brain, but upon some unknown source exempt from those limitations.

Thus far, indeed, the sleep-faculties which we have been considering, however strangely intensified, have belonged to the same class as the normal faculties of waking life. We have now to consider whether we can detect in sleep any manifestation of *supernormal* faculty — any experience which seems to suggest that man is a cosmical spirit as well as a terrestrial organism, and is in some way in relation with a spiritual as well as with a material world. It will seem, in this view, to be natural that this commerce with a spiritual environment should be more perceptible in sleep than in waking. The dogma which my point of view thus renders probable is perhaps, as a mere matter of history, the dogma of all dogmas which has been most universally believed by mankind.

"*Quod semper, quod ubique, quod ab omnibus*" — for how many narrow theological propositions have we not heard this proud claim — that they have been believed everywhere, and by everybody, and in every age? Yet what can approach the antiquity, the ubiquity, the unanimity of man's belief in the wanderings of the spirit in dream? In the Stone Age, the sceptic would have been rash indeed who ventured to contradict it. And though I grant that this "palæolithic psychology" has gone out of fashion for the last few centuries, I do not think that (in view of the telæsthetic evidence now collected) we can any longer dismiss as a mere *bizarrerie* of dream-imagery the constant recurrence of the idea of visiting in sleep some distant scene, — with the acquisition thereby of new facts not otherwise accessible.

Starting, then, not from savage authority, but from the evidential

[1] Cædmon's poem was traditionally said to have come to him in like fashion.

scrutiny of modern facts, we shall find, I think, that there are coincidences of dream with truth which neither pure chance nor any subconscious mentation of an ordinary kind will adequately explain. We shall find that there is a perception of concealed material objects or of distant scenes and also a perception of a communion with the thoughts and emotions of other minds. Both these phenomena have been noted sporadically in many ages and countries, and were observed with serious attention especially by the early French mesmerists. The first group of phenomena was called *clairvoyance* or *lucidité*, and the second *communication de pensées*, or in English, *thought-transference*. These terms are scarcely comprehensive enough to satisfy a more systematic study. The distant perception is not *optical*, nor is it confined even to the apparent sense of sight alone. It extends to all the senses, and includes also impressions hardly referable to any special sense. Similarly the communication between distant persons is not a transference of thought alone, but of emotion, of motor impulses, and of many impressions not easy to define. I ventured in 1882 to suggest the wider terms *telæsthesia*, sensation at a distance, and *telepathy*, fellow-feeling at a distance, and shall use these words in the present work. But I am far from assuming that these terms correspond with definite and clearly separated groups of phenomena, or comprise the whole field of supernormal faculty. On the contrary, I think it probable that the facts of the metetherial world are far more complex than the facts of the material world; and the ways in which spirits perceive and communicate, apart from fleshly organisms, are subtler and more varied than any perception or communication which we know.

I have hinted above at another line of demarcation which the dreamer's own sensations suggest, — the distinction between active psychical excursion or invasion and the passive reception of psychical invasion from without. But even here, as was also hinted, a clear line of division is hard to draw. For whether we are dealing with dream-perceptions of distant material scenes, or of distant living persons, or of discarnate spirits, it is often impossible for the dreamer himself to say either from what point he is himself observing, or where the scene of the vision is laid.

For the present I must confine myself to a brief sketch of some of the main types of supernormal dreams, arranged in a kind of ascending order. I shall begin with such dreams as primarily suggest a kind of heightening or extension of the dreamer's own innate perceptive powers, as exercised on the world around him. And I shall end with dreams which suggest his entrance into a spiritual world, where commerce with incarnate or discarnate spirits is subject no longer to the conditions of earthly thought.

I begin, then, with some dreams which seem to carry perceptive faculty beyond the point at which some unusual form of common vision can be plausibly suggested in explanation. Mr. Lewis's dream of the landing-order (Appendix IV. A) may be taken as an instance of such a dream.[1]

I will next refer to certain cases where the sleeper by clairvoyant vision discerns a scene of direct interest to a mind other than his own; — as the danger or death of some near friend. Sometimes there is a flash of vision, which seems to represent correctly the critical scene. Sometimes there is what seems like a longer gaze, accompanied, perhaps by some sense of *communion* with the invaded person. And in some few cases — the most interesting of all — the circumstances of a death seem to be symbolically *shown* to a dreamer, as though by the deceased person, or by some intelligence connected with him. (See Mrs. Storie's narrative p. 109.)

One of the best instances of the flash of vision is Canon Warburton's, which I quote from *Phantasms of the Living*, vol. i. p. 338 — a case whose remoteness is rendered less of a drawback than usual by the character of the narrator and the simplicity and definiteness of the fact attested.

The following is his account: —

THE CLOSE, WINCHESTER, *July 16th*, 1883.

Somewhere about the year 1848 I went up from Oxford to stay a day or two with my brother, Acton Warburton, then a barrister, living at 10 Fish Street, Lincoln's Inn. When I got to his chambers I found a note on the table apologising for his absence, and saying that he had gone to a dance somewhere in the West End, and intended to be home soon after one o'clock. Instead of going to bed, I dozed in an armchair, but started up wide awake exactly at one, ejaculating "By Jove! he's down!" and seeing him coming out of a drawing-room into a brightly illuminated landing, catching his foot in the edge of the top stair, and falling headlong, just saving himself by his elbows and hands. (The house was one which I had never seen, nor did I know where it was.) Thinking very little of the matter, I fell a-doze again for half an hour, and was awakened by my brother suddenly coming in and saying, "Oh, there you are! I have just had as narrow an escape of breaking my neck as I ever had in my life. Coming out of the ballroom, I caught my foot, and tumbled full length down the stairs."

That is all. It may have been "only a dream," but I always thought it must have been something more. W. WARBURTON.

In a second letter Canon Warburton adds: —

July 20th, 1883.

My brother was hurrying home from his dance, with some little self-reproach in his mind for not having been at his chambers to receive his

[1] The reader will find many similar cases in the *Journal* and *Proceedings* of the S.P.R. Several are quoted in Appendices to Section 421 in the unabridged edition.

guest, so the chances are that he was thinking of me. The whole scene was vividly present to me at the moment, but I did not note particulars any more than one would in real life. The general impression was of a narrow landing brilliantly illuminated, and I remember verifying the correctness of this by questions at the time.

This is my sole experience of the kind.

[The last words are in answer to the question whether he had had similar vivid visions which had *not* corresponded with any real event.]

The impression here produced is as though a jerk were given to some delicate link connecting the two brothers. The brother suffering the crisis thinks vividly of the other; and one can of course explain the incident, as we did on its first publication, as the endangered man's projection of the scene upon his brother's mind. The passive dozing brother, on the other hand, feels as though he were suddenly *present* in the scene, — say in response to some sudden call from the brother in danger, — and I am here bringing into relief *that* aspect of the incident, on account of its analogy with cases soon to be quoted. But the main lesson no doubt may be that no hard and fast line can be drawn between the two explanations.[1]

And here I feel bound to introduce a sample of a certain class of dreams, — more interesting, perhaps, and certainly more perplexing than any; — but belonging to a category of phenomena which at present I can make no attempt to explain. I mean precognitive dreams; — pictures or visions in which future events are foretold or depicted, generally with more or less of symbolism, — and generally also in a mode so remote from the previsions of our earthly sagacity that we shall find ourselves driven, in a later discussion, to speak in vague terms of glimpses into a cosmic picture-gallery; — or of scenic representations composed and offered to us by intelligences higher and more distant than any spirit whom we have known. I give in Appendix IV. C a thoroughly characteristic example; — characteristic alike in its definiteness, its purposelessness, its isolated unintelligibility.

Dr. Bruce's narrative, which I next give in Appendix IV. D, written by an intelligent man, while the facts were yet fresh, seems to me of high

---

[1] The case of Mr. Boyle, investigated by Edmund Gurney and printed in S.P.R. *Journal*, vol. iii. pp. 265, 266 [§423], is interesting in this connection. In this case the vision, which recurred twice, was of a simple kind, and might be interpreted as an impression transferred from the mind of one waking to the mind of one asleep.

Again, the single dream which a man has noted down in all his life stands evidentially in almost as good a position as a single waking hallucination. For cases of this kind see *Journal* S.P.R., vol. iii. p. 267 [§424]; *ibid.* vol. v. p. ⁷⁰ [424 A]; *ibid.* vol. v. p. 252 [424 C]; and *Phantasms of the Living*, vol. i. p. 443 [424 B].

importance. If we accept the rest of his story, we must, I think, suppose that the sense of spiritual presence with which the incident began was more than a mere subjective fancy. Shall we refer it to the murdered man's wife; — with whom the dreamer seemed afterwards to be in tele- . pathic relation? Or shall we interpret it as a kind of summons from the dying man, drawing on, as it were, his friend's spirit to witness the actual murder and the subsequent scene? The fact that another friend, in another locality apparently, had a vision of similar nature, tells somewhat in favour of the supposition that the decedent's spirit was operative in both cases; since we very seldom — if ever — find an agent producing an impression in two separate places at once — or nearly so — except at or just after the moment of death.

In this view, the incident resembles a scene passing in a spiritual world. The dying man summons his brother-in-law; the brother-in-law visits the scene of murder, and there spiritually communicates with his sister, the widow, who is corporeally in that scene, and then sees further details of the scene after death, which he does not understand, and which are not explained to him.

Fantastic though this explanation seems, it is not easy to hit on a simpler one which will cover the facts as stated. Could we accept it, we should have a kind of transition between two groups of cases, which although apparently so different may form parts of a continuous series. I mean the cases where the dreamer visits a distant scene, and the cases where another spirit visits the dreamer.

Taking, then, Dr. Bruce's case to bridge the interval between these two groups, I go on to a case which properly belongs to the *second*, though it still has much in common with the *first*. I shall quote Mrs. Storie's narrative at full length in the text; because the case is, in my judgment, both evidentially very strong, and also, in the naïveté of its confusion, extremely suggestive of the way in which these psychical communications are made. Mrs. Storie, who is now dead, was, by the testimony of Edmund Gurney, Professor Sidgwick, and others, a witness eminently deserving of trust; and, besides a corroboration from her husband of the manifestation of a troubled dream, before the event was known, we have the actual notes written down by her, as she informed us, the day, or the day after, the news of the fatal accident arrived, solely for her own use, and unmistakably reflecting the incoherent impressiveness of the broken vision. These notes form the narrative given in *Phantasms of the Living* (vol. i. p. 370) which I reproduce here. The fact that the deceased brother was a *twin* of Mrs. Storie's adds interest to the case, since one clue (a vague one as yet) to the causes directing and determining telepathic communications lies in what seems their exceptional frequency between *twins;* — the closest of all relations.

HOBART TOWN, *July* 1874.

On the evening of the 18th July, I felt unusually nervous. This seemed to begin [with the occurrence of a small domestic annoyance] about half past eight o'clock. When I went to my room I even felt as if some one was there. I fancied, as I stepped into bed, that some one *in thought* tried to stop me. At 2 o'clock I woke from the following dream. It seemed like in dissolving views. In a twinkle of light I saw a railway, and the puff of the engine. I thought, "What's going on up there? Travelling? I wonder if any of us are travelling and I dreaming of it." *Some one* unseen by me answered, "No; something quite different — something wrong." "I don't like to look at these things," I said. Then I saw behind and above my head William's upper half reclining, eyes and mouth half shut; his chest moved forward convulsively, and he raised his right arm. Then he bent forward, saying, "I suppose I should move out of this." Then I saw him lying, eyes shut, on the ground, flat. The chimney of an engine at his head. I called in excitement, "That will strike him!" The *some one* answered "Yes — well, here's what it was"; and immediately I saw William sitting in the open air — faint moonlight — on a raised place sideways. He raised his right arm, shuddered, and said, "I can't go on, or back, *No.*" Then he seemed lying flat. I cried out, "Oh! Oh!" and others seemed to echo, "Oh! Oh!" He seemed then upon his elbow, saying, "Now it comes." Then as if struggling to rise, turned twice round quickly, saying, "Is it the train? *the train, the train,*" his right shoulder reverberating as if struck from behind. He fell back like fainting; his eyes rolled. A large dark object came between us like panelling of wood, and rather in the dark something rolled over, and like an arm was thrown up, and the whole thing went away with a *swish.* Close beside me on the ground there seemed a long dark object. I called out, "They've left something behind; it's like a man." It then raised its shoulders and head, and fell down again. The same *some one* answered, "*Yes, sadly.*" [? "*Yes,*" sadly.] After a moment I seemed called on to look up, and said, "Is that *thing* not away yet?" Answered, "*No.*" And in front, in light, there was a railway compartment in which sat Rev. Mr. Johnstone, of Echuca. I said, "What's he doing there?" Answered, "He's there." A railway porter went up to the window asking, "Have you seen any of ——." I caught no more, but I *thought* he referred to the *thing* left behind. Mr. Johnstone seemed to answer "*No*"; and the man went quickly away — I thought to look for it. After all this the *some one* said close to me, "Now I'm going." I started, and at once saw

{ a tall dark figure at my head }
{ William's back at my side. } He put his right hand (in grief) over his face, and the other almost touching my shoulder, he crossed in front, looking stern and solemn. There was a flash from the eyes, and I caught

a glimpse of a fine pale face like ushering him along, and indistinctly another. I felt frightened, and called out, "Is he angry?" "Oh, no." "Is he going away?" Answered, "*Yes*," by the same *some one*, and I woke with a loud sigh, which woke my husband, who said, "What is it?" I told him I had been dreaming "something unpleasant" — named a "railway," and dismissed it all from my mind as a dream. As I fell asleep again I fancied the *some one* said, "It's all gone," and another answered, "I'll come and remind her."

The news reached me one week afterwards. The accident had happened to my brother on the same night about half past 9 o'clock. Rev. Mr. Johnstone and his wife were actually in the train which struck him. He was walking along the line which is raised two feet on a level country. He seemed to have gone 16 miles — must have been tired and sat down to take off his boot, which was beside him, dozed off and was very likely roused by the sound of the train; 76 sheep-trucks had passed without touching him, but some wooden projection, likely the step, had touched the *right* side of his head, bruised his right shoulder, and killed him instantaneously. The night was very dark. I believe now that the *some one* was (from something in the *way* he spoke) William *himself*. The face with him was white as alabaster and something like this [a small sketch pasted on] in profile. There were many other thoughts or words seemed to pass, but they are too many to write down here.

The voice of the *some one* unseen seemed *always above* the figure of William which I saw. And when I was shown the compartment of the carriage with Mr. Johnstone, the *some one* seemed on a line between me and it — *above* me.

[In an account-book of Mrs. Storie's, on a page headed July 1874, we find the 18th day marked, and the words, "Dear Willie died," and "Dreamed, dreamed of it all," appended.

The first letter, from the Rev. J. C. Johnstone to the Rev. John Storie, announcing the news of the accident, is lost. The following are extracts from his second and third letters on the subject: —]

ECHUCA, 10*th August* 1874.

The place where Hunter was killed is on an open plain, and there was consequently plenty of room for him to escape the train had he been conscious; but I think Meldrum's theory is the correct one, that he had sat down to adjust some bandages on his leg and had thoughtlessly gone off to sleep. There is only one line of rails, and the ground is raised about 2 feet — the ground on which the rails rest. He had probably sat down on the edge, and lain down backwards so as to be within reach of some part of the train. It was not known at the time that an accident had occurred. Mrs. Johnstone and myself were in the train. Meldrum says he was not very much crushed. The top of the skull was struck off, and some ribs were broken under the armpit on one side. His body was found on the Sunday morning by a herd-boy from the adjoining station.

The exact time at which the train struck poor Hunter must have been about 9.55 P.M., and his death must have been instantaneous.

[The above corresponds with the account of the inquest in the *Riverine Herald* for July 22nd. The *Melbourne Argus* also describes the accident as having taken place on the night of Saturday, the 18th.

The following remarks are taken from notes made by Professor Sidgwick, during an interview with Mrs. Storie, in April 1884, and by Mrs. Sidgwick after another interview in September 1885: —]

Mrs. Storie cannot regard the experience exactly as a dream, though she woke up from it. She is sure that it did not grow more definite in recollection afterwards. She never had a series of scenes in a dream at any other time; and she has never had anything like a hallucination. They were introduced by a voice in a whisper, not recognised as her brother's. He had sat on the bank as he appeared in the dream. The engine she saw behind him had a chimney of peculiar shape, such as she had not at that time seen; and she remembers that Mr. Storie thought her foolish about insisting on the chimney — unlike (he said) any which existed; but he informed her when he came back from Victoria, where her brother was, that engines of this kind had just been introduced there. She had no reason to think that any conversation between the porter and the clergyman actually occurred. The persons who seemed to lead her brother away were not recognised by her, and she only saw the face of one of them.

Mr. Storie confirms his wife having said to him at the time of the dream, "What is that light?" Before writing the account first quoted, she had just mentioned the dream to her husband, but had not described it. She desired not to think of it, and also was unwilling to worry him about it because of his Sunday's work. This last point, it will be observed, is a confirmation of the fact that the dream took place on the Saturday night; and "it came out clearly" (Mrs. Sidgwick says) "that her recollection about the Saturday night was an independent recollection, and not read back after the accident was known." The strongly nervous state that preceded the dream was quite unique in Mrs. S.'s experience. But as it appeared that, according to her recollection, it commenced at least an hour before the accident took place, it must be regarded as of no importance evidentially. The feeling of a presence in the room was also quite unique.

"Here," says Gurney, "the difficulty of referring the true elements of the dream to the agent's mind [is very great]. For Mr. Hunter was asleep; and even if we can conceive that the image of the advancing engine may have had some place in his mind, the presence of Mr. Johnstone could not have been perceived by him. But it is possible, of course, to regard this last item of correspondence as accidental, even though the dream was telepathic. It will be observed that the dream followed the accident by about four hours; such *deferment* is, I think, a strong point in favour of telepathic, as opposed to independent, clairvoyance."

I propose as an alternative explanation, — for reasons which I endeavour to justify in later chapters, — that the deceased brother, aided by some other dimly discerned spirit, was endeavouring to present to Mrs. Storie a series of pictures representing his death — as realised *after* his death. I add this last clause, because one of the marked points in the dream was the presence in the train of Mr. Johnstone of Echuca — a fact which (as Gurney remarks) the dying man could not possibly know.

I have dwelt on these two cases of Dr. Bruce and Mrs. Storie, because the reader will, I think, come to feel, as our evidence unrolls itself, that he has here complex experiences which are confirmed at various points by simpler experiences, in such a way as to make these stories seem a confused but an intimate transcript of what other narratives show in hints and glimpses alone.

In Mrs. Storie's case the whole experience, as we have seen, presented itself as a *dream;* yet as a dream of quite unusual type, like a series of pictures presented to the sleeper who was still conscious that she was lying in bed. In other cases the "psychical invasion" of the spirit either of a living or of a deceased person seems to set up a variety of sleep-waking states — both in agent and percipient. In one bizarre narrative a man dreaming that he has returned home is *heard* in his home calling for hot water — and has himself a singular sense of "bilocation" between the railway carriage and his bedroom.[1] In another curious case is recorded a kind of *encounter* in dreamland, apparently more or less remembered by both persons.[2]

An invasion of this type coming upon a sleeping person is apt to induce some change in the sleeper's state, which, even if he regards it as a complete awakening, is generally shown not to be so in fact by the dreamlike character of his own recorded feelings and utterances. Gurney called these "Borderland Cases," and the whole collection in *Phantasms of the Living* will repay perusal. I introduce one such case in Appendix IV. E, as being at once very perplexing and, I think, very strongly attested. I knew Mr. and Mrs. T., who certainly were seriously anxious for complete

[1] *Phantasms of the Living*, vol. ii. p. 105 [428 A].
[2] *Phantasms of the Living*, vol. ii. p. 154 [428 D].

The cases of Mrs. Manning (*Journal* S.P.R., vol. xii. p. 100 [428 B]) and Mr. Newnham (*Phantasms of the Living*, vol. i. p. 225 [428 C]) are somewhat similar. See also *Proceedings* S.P.R., vol. xi. p. 444 [428 E] and *Journal* S.P.R., vol. viii. p. 128 [428 F].

accuracy, and who had (as the narrative shows) made a brief memorandum and consulted various persons on the incident at the time.

These cases of invasion by the spirits of living persons pass on into cases of invasion by the dying, the impression being generally that of the presence of the visitant in the percipient's surroundings.[1] Sometimes the phantasm is seen as nearly as can be ascertained at the time of death. But there is no perceptible break in the series at this point. Some appear shortly after death, but before the death is known to the percipient. [See Appendix IV. F]. Finally, there are cases when the appearance takes place some time after death, but presents features unknown to the percipient.[2]

We have now briefly reviewed certain phenomena of sleep from a standpoint somewhat differing from that which is commonly taken. We have not (as is usual) fixed our attention primarily on the *negative* characteristics of sleep, or the extent to which it lacks the capacities of waking hours. On the contrary, we have regarded sleep as an independent phase of personality, existing with as good a right as the waking phase, and dowered with imperfectly expressed faculties of its own. In investigating those faculties we have been in no wise deterred by the fact of the apparent uselessness of some of them for our waking ends. *Useless* is a pre-scientific, even an anti-scientific term, which has perhaps proved a greater stumbling-block to research in psychology than in any other science. In science the *use* of phenomena is to prove laws, and the more bizarre and trivial the phenomena, the greater the chance of their directing us to some law which has been overlooked till now. In reviewing the phenomena of sleep, then, we found in the first place that it possesses a specific recuperative energy which the commonly accepted data of physiology and psychology cannot explain. We saw that in sleep there may be an increased co-ordination or centralisation of muscular control, and also an increased vividness of entencephalic perception, indicating a more intimate appreciation of intra-peripheral changes than is manifest in waking life. In accordance with this view, we found that the dreaming self may undergo sensory and emotional experiences apparently more intense than those of vigilance, and may produce thereby lasting effects upon the waking body and mind. Similarly again, we saw that that specific impress on body and mind which we term memory may in sleeping or hypnotic states be both wider in range and fuller in content than the evocable memory of the waking day. Nay, not memory only, but power of inference, of

[1] *Phantasms of the Living*, vol. i. p. 365; *ibid.*, p. 453 [429 A and B].
[2] See, for example, *Journal* S.P.R., vol. viii. p. 123 [429 F].

argument, may be thus intensified, as is shown by the solution in sleep of problems which have baffled waking effort.

All these are fragmentary indications, — useless for practical purposes if you will, — of sleeping faculty exercised on the same order of things as waking faculty, and with comparable or even superior power. But we were bound to push our inquiry further still — we were bound to ask whether the self of sleep showed any faculty of a quite different order from that by which waking consciousness maintains the activity of man. We found that this was so indeed; that there was evidence that the sleeping spirit was susceptible of relations unfettered by spatial bonds; of telæsthetic perception of distant scenes; of telepathic communication with distant persons, or even with spirits of whom we can predicate neither distance nor nearness, since they are released from the prison of the flesh.

The inference which all this evidence suggests is entirely in accordance with the hypothesis on which my whole work is based.

I have assumed that man is an organism informed or possessed by a soul. This view obviously involves the hypothesis that we are living a life in two worlds at once; a planetary life in this material world, to which the organism is intended to react; and also a cosmic life in that spiritual or metetherial world, which is the native environment of the soul. From that unseen world the energy of the organism needs to be perpetually replenished. That replenishment we cannot understand: we may figure it to ourselves as a protoplasmic process; — as some relation between protoplasm, ether, and whatever is beyond ether, on which it is at present useless to speculate.

Admitting, for the sake of argument, these vast assumptions, it will be easy to draw the further inference that it may be needful that the soul's attention should be frequently withdrawn from the business of earthly life, so as to pursue with greater intensity what we may call its protoplasmic task, — the maintenance of the fundamental, pervading connection between the organism and the spiritual world. Nay, this profounder condition, as responding to more primitive, more fundamental needs, will itself be more primitive than the waking state. And this is so: sleep is the infant's dominant phase: the pre-natal state resembles sleep rather than waking; and so does the whole life-condition of our lowly ancestors. And as the sleeping state is the more *primitive*, so also is it the more *generalised*, and the more *plastic*. Out of this dreamy abeyance between two worlds, the needs of the material world are constantly developing some form of alert activity, some faculty which was *potential* only until search for food and the defence against enemies compelled a closer heed to "the life of relation," lest the relation should become only that of victim to devourer.

We shall thus have two phases of personality developing into separate purposes and in separate directions from a parent stem. The waking personality will develop external sense organs and will fit itself progressively for the life of relation to the external world. It will endeavour to attain an ever completer control over the resources of the personality, and it will culminate in what we term *genius* when it has unified the subliminal as far as possible with the supraliminal in its pursuit of deliberate waking ends.

The sleeping personality will develop in ways less easy to foresee. What, on any theory, will it aim at, beyond the familiar intensification of recuperative power? We can only guess, on my theory, that its development will show some increasing trace of the soul's less exclusive absorption in the activity of the organism. The soul has withdrawn from the specialised material surface of things (to use such poor metaphor as we can) into a realm where the nature of the connection between matter and spirit — whether through the intermediacy of the ether or otherwise — is more profoundly discerned. That same withdrawal from the surface which, while it diminishes power over complex muscular processes, increases power over profound organic processes, may at the same time increase the soul's power of operating in that spiritual world to which sleep has drawn it nearer.

On this view of sleep, be it observed, there will be nothing to surprise us in the possibility of increasing the proportion of the sleeping to the waking phase of life by hypnotic suggestion. All we can say is that, while the soul must insist on at least the minimum quantity of sleep needful to keep the body alive, we can see no superior limit to the quantity of sleep which it may choose to take, — the quantity of attention, that is, which it may choose to give to the special operations of sleep as compared with those of waking life.

At this point we must for the present pause. The suggested hypothesis will indeed cover the actual facts as to sleep adduced in this chapter. But it covers them by virtue of assumptions too vast to be accepted without further confirmation. It must necessarily be our duty in later chapters to trace the development of the sleeping personality in both the directions indicated above; — in the direction of organic recuperation through the hypnotic trance, and in the direction of the soul's independent operation through that form of trance which leads to possession and to ecstasy. We shall begin at once in the next chapter to trace out that great experimental modification of sleep, from which, under the names of mesmerism or of hypnotism, results of such conspicuous practical value have already been won.

CHAPTER V

HYPNOTISM

εἵλετο δὲ ῥάβδον, τῇ τ' ἀνδρῶν ὄμματα θέλγει,
ὧν ἐθέλει, τοὺς δ' αὖτε καὶ ὑπνώοντας ἐγείρει.

. — HOMER.

IN the last chapter we were led on to adopt a conception of sleep which, whether or not it prove ultimately in any form acceptable by science, is at any rate in deep congruity with the evidence brought forward in this work. Our human life, in this view, exists and energises, at the present moment, both in the material and in the spiritual world. Human personality, as it has developed from lowly ancestors, has become differentiated into two phases; one of them mainly adapted to material or planetary, the other to spiritual or cosmic operation. The subliminal self, mainly directing the sleeping phase, is able either to rejuvenate the organism by energy drawn in from the spiritual world; — or, on the other hand, temporarily and partially to relax its connection with that organism, in order to expatiate in the exercise of supernormal powers; — telepathy, telesthæsia, ecstasy.

Such were the suggestions of the evidence as to dream and vision; such, I may add, will be seen to be the suggestions of *spontaneous somnambulism*, which has not yet fallen under our discussion. Yet claims so large as these demand corroboration from observation and experiment along many different lines of approach. Some such corroboration we have, in anticipatory fashion, already acquired. Discussing in Chapter II. the various forms of disintegration of personality, we had frequent glimpses of beneficent subliminal powers. We saw the deepest stratum of the self intervening from time to time with a therapeutic object, or we caught it in the act of exercising, even if aimlessly or sporadically, some faculty beyond supraliminal reach. And we observed, moreover, that the agency by which these subliminal powers were invoked was generally the *hypnotic trance*. Of the nature of that trance I then said nothing; It was manifest only that here was some kind of induced or artificial somnambulism, which seemed to systematise that beneficial control of the organism which spontaneous sleep-waking states had exercised in a fitful way. It must plainly be our business to understand *ab initio* these hypnotic phenomena; to push as far as may be what seems like an experimental evolution of the sleeping phase of personality.

Let us suppose, then, that we are standing at our present point, but with no more knowledge of hypnotic phenomena than existed in the boyhood of Mesmer. We shall know well enough what, as experimental psychologists, we desire to do; but we shall have little notion of how to set about it. We desire to summon at our will, and to subdue to our use, these rarely emergent sleep-waking faculties. On their physical side, we desire to develop their inhibition of pain and their reinforcement of energy; on their intellectual side, their concentration of attention; on their emotional side, their sense of freedom, expansion, joy. Above all, we desire to get hold of those supernormal faculties — telepathy and telæsthesia — of which we have caught fitful glimpses in somnambulism and in dream.

Yet to such hopes as these the so-called "experience of ages" (generally a very short and scrappy induction!) will seem altogether to refuse any practical outcome. History, indeed, — with the wonted vagueness of history, — will offer us a long series of stories of the strange sanative suggestion or influence of man on man; — beginning, say, with David and Saul, or with David and Abishag, and ending with Valentine Greatrakes, — or with the Stuarts' last touch for the King's evil. But in knowledge of how actually to set about it, we should still be just on the level of the Seven Sages.[1]

And now let the reader note this lesson on the unexhausted possibilities of human organisms and human life. Let him take his stand at one of the modern centres of hypnotic practice, — in Professor Bernheim's hospital-ward, or Dr. van Renterghem's *clinique;* let him see the hundreds of patients thrown daily into hypnotic trance, in a few moments, and as a matter of course; and let him then remember that this process, which now seems as obvious and easy as giving a pill, was absolutely unknown not only to Galen and to Celsus, but to Hunter and to Harvey; and when at last discovered was commonly denounced as a fraudulent fiction, almost up to the present day. Nay, if one chances to have watched as a boy some cure effected in Dr. Elliotson's Mesmeric Hospital, before neglect

---

[1] Long ago Solon had said, apparently of mesmeric cure —

Τὸν δὲ κακῶς ποδνουσι κυνέμενος ἀγγελέας τε
ἀρέμενος χαρεῖν αἶρα τίθηρ' ὑγιῆ.

and calumny had closed that too early effort for human good; — if one has seen popular indifference and professional prejudice check the new healing art for a generation; — is not one likely to have imbibed a deep distrust of all *a priori* negations in the matter of human faculty; — of all *obiter dicta* of eminent men on subjects with which they do not happen to be acquainted? Would not one, after such an experience, rather choose (with Darwin) "the fool's experiment" than any immemorial ignorance which has stiffened into an unreasoning incredulity?

Mesmer's experiment was almost a "fool's experiment," and Mesmer himself was almost a charlatan. Yet Mesmer and his successors, — working from many different points of view, and following many divergent theories, — have opened an ever-widening way, and have brought us now to a position where we can fairly hope, by experiments made no longer at random, to reproduce and systematise most of those phenomena of spontaneous somnambulism which once seemed to lie so tantalisingly beyond our grasp.

That promise is great indeed; yet it is well to begin by considering precisely how far it extends. We must not suppose that we shall at once be subduing to our experiment a central, integrated, reasonable Self.

We must be content (at first at any rate) if we can affect the personality in the same limited way as hysteria and somnambulism have affected it; but yet can act deliberately and usefully where these have acted hurtfully and at random. It is enough to hope that we may inhibit pain, as it is inhibited for the hysteric; or concentrate attention, as it is concentrated for the somnambulist; or change the tastes and passions, as these are changed in alternating personalities; or (best of all) recover and fix something of that supernormal faculty of which we have caught fugitive glimpses in vision and dream. Our proof of the origination of any phenomenon in the deeper strata of our being must lie in the intrinsic nature of the faculty exhibited; — not in the wisdom of its actual direction. *That* must often depend on the order given from above the threshold; just as the magic mill of the fable continues magical, although, for lack of the proper formula to stop it, it be still grinding out superfluous salt at the bottom of the sea.

This brief introduction will, I hope, show that hypnotism is no disconnected or extraneous insertion into experimental psychology, but rather a summary name for a group of necessary, though empirical and isolated, attempts to bring under control that range of submerged faculty which has already from time to time risen into our observation. The inquiry has been mainly the work of a few distinguished men, who have each of them pushed some useful ideas as far as they could, but whose work has not been adequately supported by successors.

I should much doubt whether there have been a hundred men in all countries together, at the ordinary level of professional intelligence, who during the century since Mesmer have treated hypnotism as the serious study of their lives. Some few of the men who have so treated it have been men of great force and strong convictions; and it will be found that there has consequently been a series of sudden developments of groups of phenomena, differing much from each other, but corresponding with the special beliefs and desires of the person who headed each movement in turn. I will mention some of the chief examples, so as to show the sporadic nature of the efforts made, and the great variety of the phenomena elicited.

The first name that must be mentioned is, of course, that of Mesmer himself. He believed primarily in a sanative effluence, and his method seems to have been a combination of passes, suggestion, and a supposed "metallotherapy" or "magneto-therapy" — the celebrated *baquet* — which no doubt was merely a form of suggestion. His results, though very imperfectly described, seem to have been peculiar to himself. The *crise·*which many of his patients underwent sounds like a hysterical attack; but there can be no doubt that rapid improvement in symptoms often followed it, or he would not have made so great an impression on *savants* as well as on the fashionable world of Paris. To Mesmer, then, we owe the first conception of the therapeutic power of a sudden and profound nervous change. To Mesmer, still more markedly, we owe the doctrine of a nervous influence or effluence passing from man to man, — a doctrine which, though it must assume a less exclusive importance than he assigned to it, cannot, in my view, be altogether ignored or denied.

The leading figure among his immediate successors, the Marquis de Puységur, seems from his writings[1] to have been one of the ablest and most candid men who have practised mesmerism; and he was one of the very few who have conducted experiments, other than therapeutic, on a large scale. The somnambulic state may also be said to have been his discovery; and he obtained clairvoyance or telæsthesia in so many instances, and recorded them with so much of detail, that it is hard to attribute all to malobservation, or even to telepathy from persons present. Other observers, as Bertrand, a physician of great promise, followed in the same track, and this brief period was perhaps the most fertile in disinterested experiments

[1] *Recherches Physiologiques sur l'Homme* (Paris, 1811); *Mémoires pour servir à l'Histoire et à l'Establissement du Magnétisme Animal; Du Magnétisme Animal considéré dans ses Rapports avec diverses branches de la Physique Générale;* etc.

that our subject has yet known. Much was then done in Germany also; and there, too, there is scattered testimony to supernormal powers.[1]

Next came the era of Elliotson in England, and of Esdaile in his hospital at Calcutta. Their method lay in mesmeric passes, Elliotson's object being mostly the direct cure of maladies, Esdaile's a deep anæsthesia, under which he performed hundreds of serious operations. His success in this direction was absolutely unique; — was certainly (setting aside supernormal phenomena) the most extraordinary performance in mesmeric history. Had not his achievements been matters of official record, the apparent impossibility of repeating them would probably by this time have been held to have disproved them altogether.

The next great step which hypnotism made was actually regarded by Elliotson and his group as a hostile demonstration. When Braid discovered that hypnosis could be induced without passes, the mesmerists felt that their theory of a sanative effluence was dangerously attacked. And this was true; for that theory has in fact been thrown into the shade, — too completely so, in my opinion, — first by the method used in Braid's earlier work of the production of hypnotic phenomena by means of the upward and inward squint, and secondly, by the much wider and more important discovery of the efficacy of mere *suggestion*, set forth in his later writings. Braid's hypnotic experience differed much from that of hypnotists before and after him. His early method of the convergent squint produced results which no one else has been able to produce; and the state which it induced appeared in his view to arrest and dissipate even maladies of which neither hypnotist nor patient had thought as capable of cure. But he afterwards abandoned this method in favour of simple verbal suggestion, as he found that what was required was merely to influence the ideas of his patients. He showed further that all so-called phrenological phenomena and the supposed effects of magnets, metals, etc., could be produced equally well by suggestion.[2] He also laid stress on the subject's power both of resisting the commands of the operator and of inducing hypnotic effects in himself without the aid of an operator. To my mind the most important novelty brought out by Braid was the possibility of self-hypnotisation by concentration of will. This inlet into human faculty,

---

[1] See Nasse's *Zeitschrift für Hypnotismus, passim*.

[2] This later work of Braid's has been generally overlooked, and his theories were stated again as new discoveries by recent observers who ignored what he had already accomplished. See Dr. Bramwell's paper on " James Braid, his Work and Writings," in *Proceedings* S.P.R., vol. xii. pp. 127–166. This contains a complete list of Braid's writings, and references to his work by other writers. See also the references to Braid's work and theories in Dr. Bramwell's *Hypnotism*.

in some ways the most important of all, has been as yet but slackly followed. But it is along with Braid's group of ideas that I should place those of an able but much inferior investigator, Dr. Fahnestock, although it is not clear that the latter knew of Braid's work. His book, *Statuvolism, or Artificial Somnambulism* (Chicago, 1871), has received less attention than it merits; — partly perhaps from its barbarous title, partly from the crudities with which it is encumbered, and partly from the fact of its publication at what was at that date a town on the outskirts of civilisation. Fahnestock seems to have obtained by self-suggestion with healthy persons results in some ways surpassing anything since recorded.

There is no reason to doubt these results, except the fact that they have not yet been repeated with equal success; and my present purpose is to show how little importance can as yet be attached in the history of hypnotic experiment to the mere absence thus far of successful repetition.

The next great stage was again strikingly different. It was mainly French; the impulse was given largely by Professor Charles Richet, whose work has proved singularly free from narrowness or misconception; but the movement was developed in a special and a very unfortunate direction by Charcot and his school. It is a remarkable fact that although Charcot was perhaps the only man of eminence whose professional reputation has ever been raised by his dealings with hypnotism, most of his work thereon is now seen to have been mistaken and aberrant, — a mere following of a blind alley, from which his disciples are now gradually returning. Charcot's leading phenomena (as with several of his predecessors above mentioned) were of a type which has seldom since been obtained. The once celebrated "three stages" of the *grand hypnotisme* are hardly anywhere now to be seen. But in this case the reason is not that other hypnotists could not obtain the phenomena if they would; it is rather (as I have already indicated) that experience has convinced them that the sequences and symptoms on which Charcot laid stress were merely very elaborate products of the long-continued, and, so to say, endemic suggestions of the Salpêtrière.

We come next to the movement which is now on the whole dominant, and to which the greatest number of cures may at present be credited. The school of Nancy — which originated with Liébeault, and which is now gradually merging into a general consensus of hypnotic practice — threw aside more and more decisively the supposed "somatic signs" of Charcot, — the phenomena of neuro-muscular irritability and the like, which he regarded as the requisite proof of hypnosis; — until Bernheim boldly affirmed that hypnotic trance was no more than sleep, and that hypnotic suggestion was at once the sole cause of hypnotic responsiveness and yet was undifferentiated from mere ordinary advisory speech. This was unfortunately too good to be true. Not one sleep in a million is really hypnosis; not one suggestion in a million reaches or influences the subliminal self. If Bernheim's theories, in their extreme form, were true, there would by this time have been no sufferers left to heal.

What Bernheim has done is to cure a number of people without mesmeric passes, and without any special predisposing belief on either side, — beyond a trust in his own power. And this is a most valuable achievement, especially as showing how much may be *dispensed with* in hypnotic practice — to how simple elements it may be reduced.

"Hypnotic trance," says Bernheim, in effect, "is ordinary sleep; hypnotic suggestion is ordinary command. You tell the patient to go to sleep, and he goes to sleep; you tell him to get well, and he gets well immediately." Even thus (one thinks) has one heard the conjuror explaining "how it's done," — with little resulting hope of emulating his brilliant performance. An ordinary command does *not* enable an ordinary man to get rid of his rheumatism, or to detest the previously too acceptable taste of brandy. In suggestion, in short, there must needs be something more than a name; a profound nervous change must needs be started by some powerful nervous stimulus from without or from within. Before contenting ourselves with Bernheim's formula, we must consider yet again what change we want to effect, and whether hypnotists have actually used any form of stimulus which was likely to effect it.

According to Bernheim we are all naturally suggestible, and what we want to effect through suggestion is increased suggestibility. But let us get rid for the moment of that oracular word. What it seems to mean here is mainly a readier obedience of the organism to what we wish it to do. The sleep or trance with which hypnotism is popularly identified is not essential to our object, for the subliminal modifications are sometimes attained without any trace of somnolence. Let us consider, then, whether any known nervous stimuli, either massive or specialised, tend to induce — not mere sleep or catalepsy — but that kind of ready modifiability, — of *responsiveness* both in visible gesture and in invisible nutritive processes, — for the sake of which hypnosis is in serious practice induced.

Now of the external stimuli which influence the whole nervous system the most conspicuous are narcotic drugs. Opium, alcohol, chloroform, cannabis indica, etc., affect the nerves in so many strange ways that one might hope that they would be of use as hypnotic agents. And some observers have found that slight chloroformisation rendered subjects more suggestible. Janet has cited one case where suggestibility was developed during recovery from delirium tremens. Other hypnotisers (as Bramwell) have found chloroform fail to render patients hypnotisable; and alcohol is generally regarded as a positive hindrance to hypnotic susceptibility. More experiment with various narcotics is much needed; but thus far the scantiness of proof that narcotics help towards hypnosis goes rather against the view that hypnosis is a direct physiological sequence from any form of external stimulus.

The apparent resemblance, indeed, between narcosis and hypnosis diminishes on a closer analysis. A stage may occur both in narcotised and in hypnotised subjects where there is incoherent, dream-like mentation; but in the narcotised subject this is a step towards inhibition of the whole nervous energy — the highest centres being paralysed first; whereas in hypnosis the inhibition of supraliminal faculty seems often at least to be merely a necessary preliminary to the liberation of fresh faculty which presently manifests itself from a profounder region of the self.

Next take another group of massive effects produced on the nervous system by external stimuli; — those forms, namely, of trance and cataplexy which are due to sudden shock. With human beings this phenomenon varies from actual death from failure of heart-action, or paralysis, or *stupor attonitus* (a recognised form of insanity), any of which may result from a mere alarming sight or unwelcome announcement, down to the cataleptic immobility of a Salpêtrière patient, when she hears a sudden stroke on the gong.

Similar phenomena in certain animals, as frogs, beetles, etc., are well known. It is doubtful, however, whether any of these sudden disablements should be classed as true hypnoses. It has not, I think, been shown that in any case they have induced any real responsiveness to control, or power of obeying suggestion; unless it be (as in some Salpêtrière cases) a form of suggestion so obvious and habitual that the obedience thereto may be called part of the actual cataplexy itself. Thus the "wax-like flexibility" of the cataleptic, whose arms remain in the position where you place them, must not be regarded as a readier obedience to control, but rather as a state which involves not a more but a less alert and capable responsiveness of the organism to either external or internal stimuli.

So with regard to animals — crocodiles, frogs, and the like. I hold theoretically that animals are probably hypnotisable and suggestible; and the records of Rarey's horse-taming, etc., seem to point in that direction.[1]

---

[1] See also the *Zoist* (Vol. viii. pp. 156, 297–299) for cases of mesmerisation of animals. In his *Thérapeutique Suggestive*, 1891 (pp. 246–68), Dr. Liébeault gives an account of his experiments with infants [513 B and C].

But in the commoner experiments with frogs, where mere passivity is produced, the resemblance seems to extend only to the lethargic stage in human beings,[1] and what relation that lethargy bears to suggestibility is not, I think, really known; although I shall later on suggest some explanation on psychological grounds.

It seems plain, at any rate, that it must be from stimuli applied to men and not to animals, and from stimuli of a special and localised rather than of a massive kind, that we shall have to learn whatever can be learnt as to the genesis of the true hypnotic control.

Now there exists a way of inducing hypnosis in some hysterical persons which seems intermediate between massive and localised stimulations. It is indeed a local stimulation; but there seems no reason beyond some deep-seated caprice of the organism why the special tract which is thus sensitive should have become developed in that direction.

I speak of the induction of trance in certain subjects by pressure upon so-called *hypnogenous zones*. These zones form a curious development of hysterical *cliniques*. Their starting-point is the well-known phenomenon of patches of anæsthesia found upon hysterical subjects — the "witch-marks" of our ancestors.

So far as we at present know, the situation of these "marks" is altogether capricious. It does not apparently depend, that is to say, upon any central lesion, in the same way as do the "referred pains," familiar in deep-seated organic complaints, which manifest themselves by superficial patches of tenderness, explicable by the distribution of nerve-trunks. The anæsthetic patches are an example of what I have called the irrational self-suggestions of the hypnotic stratum; — determined by dream-like fancies rather than necessitated by purely physiological antecedents.

Quite in accordance with this view, we find that under favourable conditions — especially in a hospital of hysterics — these anomalous patches or zones develop and specialise themselves in various ways. Under Dr. Pitres at Bordeaux (for example), we have *zones hystérogènes, zones hypnogènes, zones hypnofrénatrices*, etc.; that is to say, he finds that pressure on certain spots in certain subjects will bring on or will check hysterical accesses, or accesses of what is ranked as hypnotic sleep. There is no doubt that this sleep does in certain subjects follow instantly upon the pressure of certain spots, — constant for each subject, but different for one subject and for another; — and this without any conscious co-operation, or even foreknowledge, on the patient's part. Stated thus nakedly, this seems

[1] See Dr. Bramwell's discussion of the subject. (*Proceedings* S.P.R., vol. xii. p. 213) [513 A].

the strongest possible instance of the induction of hypnosis by localised stimulus. The reader, however, will at once understand that in my view there is here no simple physiological sequence of cause and effect. I must regard the local pressure as a mere *signal* — an appeal to the pre-formed capacities of lawlessly acting centres in the hypnotic stratum. A scrap of the self has decided, in dreamlike fashion, that pressure on a certain point of the body's surface shall produce sleep; — just as it has decided that pressure on that same point or on some other point shall *not* produce pain. Self-suggestion, and no mere physiological nexus, is responsible for the sleep or the hysterical access which follows the touch. The anæsthetic patches are here a direct, but a capriciously chosen avenue to the subliminal being, and the same random self-suggestiveness which is responsible for frequent determinations that hysterical subjects shall *not* be hypnotised has in this case decided that they *shall* be hypnotised, if you go about it in exactly the right way.

Next in order among forms of localised stimulus used for inducing hypnosis may be placed *monotonous stimulation,* — to whatever part of the body it be applied. It was at one time the fashion to attribute almost all hypnotic phenomena to this cause, and Edmund Gurney and I endeavoured to point out the exaggeration.[1] Of this presently; but first let us consider the few cases where the monotonous stimulation has undoubtedly been of a kind to affect the organism strongly. The late Dr. Auguste Voisin, of Paris, was perhaps more markedly successful than any physician in producing hypnosis in extreme cases; — in maniacal persons especially, whose attention it seemed impossible to fix. He often accomplished this by holding their eyes open with the blepharostat, and compelling them to gaze, sometimes for hours together, at a brilliant electric light. Exhaustion produces tranquillity and an almost comatose sleep — in which the physician has often managed to give suggestions of great value. This seems practically the only class of cases where a directly physiological antecedent for the sleep can be proved; and even here the provable effect is rather the exhaustion of morbid excitability than any direct induction of suggestibility. This dazzling process is generally accompanied with vigorous verbal suggestion; and it is, of course, quite possible that the patients might have been thrown into hypnosis by that suggestion alone, had their minds been capable at first of sufficient attention to receive it.

Braid's upward and inward squint has an effect of the same deadening kind as the long gazing at a light, and helps in controlling wandering

[1] This view unfortunately dominates Professor M'Kendrick's article on "Hypnotism" in the *Encyclopædia Britannica.*

attention; but Braid himself in later years (as mentioned above) attributed his hypnotic successes wholly to *suggestion*.

From monotonous excitations which, whatever their part in inducing hypnosis, are, at any rate, such as can sensibly affect the organism, I come down to the trivial monotonies of watch-tickings, "passes," etc., which are still by a certain school regarded as capable of producing a profound change in the nervous condition of the person before whose face the hypnotiser's hands are slowly waved for ten or twenty minutes. I regard this as a much exaggerated view. The clock's ticking, for instance, if it is marked at all, is at least as likely to irritate as to soothe; and the constant experience of life shows that continued monotonous stimuli, say the throbbing of the screw at sea, soon escape notice and produce no hypnotic effect at all. It is true, indeed, that monotonous rocking sends some babies to sleep; but other babies are merely irritated by the process, and such soporific effect as rocking may possess is probably an effect on spinal centres or on the semicircular canals. It depends less on mere monotony than on massive movement of the whole organism.

I think, then, that there is no real ground for supposing that the trivial degree of monotonous stimulation produced by passes often repeated can induce in any ordinary physiological manner that "profound nervous change" which is recognised as the prerequisite condition of any hypnotic results. I think that passes are effectual generally as mere suggestions, and must *primâ facie* be regarded in that light, as they are, in fact, regarded by many experienced hypnotisers (as Milne Bramwell) who have employed them with good effect. Afterwards, when reason is given for believing in a telepathic influence or impact occasionally transmitted from the operator to the subject at a distance, we shall consider whether passes may represent some other form of the same influence, operating in close physical contiguity.

First, however, let us consider the point which we have now reached. We have successively dismissed various supposed modes of physiologically inducing hypnotic trance. We stand at present in the position of the Nancy school; — we have found nothing but *suggestion* which really induces the phenomena.

But on the other hand we cannot possibly regard the word suggestion as any real answer to the important question *how* the hypnotic responsiveness is induced, on *what* conditions it depends.[1]

[1] See Dr. Bramwell's discussion of the inadequacy of this explanation in his article "What is Hypnotism?" in *Proceedings* S.P.R., vol. xii. p. 224, also in his book on *Hypnotism* pp. 337–8.

It must be remembered that many of the results which follow upon suggestion are of a type which no amount of willingness to follow the suggestion could induce, since they lie quite outside the voluntary realm. However disposed a man may be to believe me, however anxious to please me, one does not see how that should enable him, for instance, to govern the morbidly-secreting cells in an eruption of erysipelas. He already fruitlessly wishes them to stop their inflammation; the mere fact of my expressing the same wish can hardly alter his cellular tissue.

Here, then, we come to an important conclusion which cannot well be denied, yet is seldom looked fully in the face. Suggestion from without must for the most part resolve itself into suggestion from within. Unless there be some telepathic or other supernormal influence at work between hypnotiser and patient (which I shall presently show ground for believing to be sometimes, though not often, the case), the hypnotiser can plainly do nothing by his word of command beyond starting a train of thought which the patient has in most cases started many times for himself with no result; the difference being that now at last the patient starts it again, and it *has* a result. But *why* it thus succeeds on this particular occasion, we simply do not know. We cannot predict when the result will occur; still less can we bring it about at pleasure.

Nay, we do not even know whether it might not be possible to dispense altogether with suggestion from outside in most of the cases now treated in this way, and merely to teach the patient to make the suggestions for himself. If there be no "mesmeric effluence" passing from hypnotiser to patient, the hypnotiser seems little more than a mere *objet de luxe;* — a personage provided simply to impress the imagination, who must needs become even absurdly useless so soon as it is understood that he has no other function or power.

Self-suggestion, whatever this may really mean, is thus in most cases, whether avowedly or not, at the bottom of the effect produced. It has already been used most successfully, and it will probably become much commoner than it now is; — or, I should rather say (since every one no doubt suggests to himself when he is in pain that he would like the pain to cease), I anticipate that self-suggestion, by being in some way better directed, will become more *effective*, and that the average of voluntary power over the organism will rise to a far higher level than it at present reaches. I believe that this is taking place even now; and that certain *schemes of self-suggestion*, so to call them, are coming into vogue, where patients in large masses are supplied with effective conceptions, which they thus impress repeatedly upon themselves without the need of a hypnotiser's attendance on each occasion. The "Miracles of Lourdes" and the cures effected by "Christian Science" fall, in my view, under this category. We have here suggestions given to a quantity of more or less suitable people *en masse*, much as a platform hypnotiser gives suggestions to a mixed audience, some of whom may then be affected without individual attention from himself. The suggestion of the curative power of the Lourdes water, for instance, is thus thrown out, partly in books, partly by oral addresses; and a certain percentage of persons succeed in so persuading themselves of that curative efficacy that when they bathe in the water they are actually cured.

These *schemes of self-suggestion*, as I have termed them, constitute one of the most interesting parts of my subject, but space forbids that I should enter into a discussion of them here. It is sufficient to point out that in order to make self-suggestion operative, no strong belief or enthusiasm, such as those schemes imply, is really necessary. No recorded cases of self-suggestion, I think, are more instructive than those published by Dr. Hugh Wingfield in *Proceedings* S.P.R., vol. v. p. 279. (The paper was printed anonymously.) Dr. Wingfield was a Demonstrator in Physiology in the University of Cambridge, and his subjects were mainly candidates for the Natural Sciences Tripos. In these cases there was no excitement of any kind, and no previous belief. The phenomena occurred incidentally during a series of experiments on other points, and were a surprise to every one concerned. The results achieved were partly automatic writing and partly phenomena of neuro-muscular excitability; — stiffening of the arms, and so forth. "It seems probable," says Dr. Wingfield, "that all phenomena capable of being produced by the suggestion of the hypnotiser can also be produced by self-suggestion in a self-suggestive subject."

Experiments like these — confirming with modern care the conclusions reached by Fahnestock and others at various points in hypnotic history — seem to me to open a new inlet into human faculty, as surprising in its way as those first wild experiments of Mesmer himself. Who would have supposed that a healthy undergraduate could "by an effort of mind" throw his whole body into a state of cataleptic rigidity, so that he could rest with his heels on one chair and his head on another? or that other healthy young men could "close their own eyes so that they were unable to open them," and the like? The trivial character of these laboratory experiments makes them physiologically the more remarkable. There is the very minimum of predisposing conditions, of excited expectation, or of external motive prompting to extraordinary effort. And the results are not subjective merely — relief of pain and so on — but are definite neuro-muscular changes, capable (as in the case of the head and heels on separate chairs) of unmistakable test.

Yet, important though these and similar experiments in self-suggestion may be, they do not solve our problem as to the ultimate origin and distribution of the faculty thus displayed. We know no better with self-suggestion than with suggestion from outside *why* it is that one man succeeds where others fail, or why a man who succeeds once fails in his next attempt. Within the ordinary range of physiolgical explanations nothing (I repeat) has as yet been discovered which can guide us to the true nature or exciting causes of this characteristic responsiveness of hypnosis. If we are to find any light, it must be in some direction which has as yet been little explored.

The hint which I have to offer here involves, I hope, something more than a mere change of appellation. I define suggestion as "successful appeal to the subliminal self"; — not necessarily to that self in its most central, most unitary aspect; but to some one at least of those strata of subliminal faculty which I have in an earlier chapter described. I do not indeed pretend that my explanation can enable us to reduce hypnotic success to a certainty. I cannot say why the process should be so irregular and capricious; but I can show that this puzzle is part and parcel of a wider mystery; — of the obscure relationships and interdependencies of the supraliminal and the subliminal self. In split personalities, in genius, in dreams, in sensory and motor automatisms, we find the same fitfulness, the same apparent caprice.

Leaving perforce this problem for the present unsolved, let us consider the various ways in which this conception of subliminal operation may throw light on the actual phenomena of hypnotism; — phenomena at present scattered in bewildering confusion.

The word *hypnotism* itself implies that some kind of *sleep* or trance is regarded as its leading characteristic. And although so-called hypnotic suggestions do often take effect in the waking state,[1] our usual test of the hypnotiser's success lies in the slumber — light or deep — into which his subject is thrown. It is, indeed, a slumber which admits at times of strange wakings and activities; but it is also manifestly profounder than the sleep which we habitually enjoy.

If sleep, then, be the phase of personality specially consecrated to subliminal operation, it follows that any successful appeal to the subliminal self will be likely to induce some form of sleep. And further, if that form

[1] See Dr. Bramwell's *Hypnotism*, p. 274.

of sleep be in fact not an inevitable result of physiological needs, but a response to a psychological appeal, it seems not unlikely that we should be able to communicate with it without interrupting it; — and should thus be able to guide or supplement subliminal operations, just as in genius the subliminal self guided or supplemented supraliminal operations.

Now I hold that in all the varied trances, lethargies, sleep-waking states, to which hypnotism introduces us, we see the subliminal self coming to the surface in ways already familiar, and displacing just so much of the supraliminal as may from time to time be needful for the performance of its own work. That work, I say, will be of a character which we know already; the difference is that what we have seen done spontaneously we now see done in response to our appeal.

Armed with this simplifying conception, — simplifying in spite of its frank admission of an underlying mystery, — we shall find no added difficulty in several points which have been the subjects of eager controversy. The *sequence* of hypnotic phenomena, the question of the *stages* of hypnotism, is one of these. I have already briefly described how Charcot propounded his three stages — lethargy, catalepsy, somnambulism — as though they formed the inevitable development of a physiological law; — and how completely this claim has now had to be withdrawn. Other schemes have been drawn out, by Liébeault, etc., but none of them seems to do more than reflect the experience of some one hypnotist's practice. The simplest arrangement is that of Edmund Gurney, who spoke only of an "alert stage" and a "deep stage" of hypnosis; and even here we cannot say that either stage invariably precedes the other. The alert stage, which often came first with Gurney's subjects, comes last in Charcot's scheme; and it is hardly safe to say more than that hypnotism is apt to show a series of changes from sleep-waking to lethargy and back again, and that the advanced stages show more of subliminal faculty than the earlier ones. There is much significance in an experiment of Dr. Jules Janet, who, by continued "passes," carried on Wittman, Charcot's leading subject, beyond her usual somnambulic state into a new lethargic state, and out again from thence into a new sleep-waking state markedly superior to the old.

Gurney held the view that the main distinction of kind between his "alert" and his "deep" stage of hypnosis was to be found in the domain of memory, while memory also afforded the means for distinguishing the hypnotic state as a whole from the normal one. As a general rule (though with numerous exceptions), the events of ordinary life are remembered in the trance, while the trance events are forgotten on waking, but tend to recur to the memory on rehypnotisation. But the most interesting part of his observations consisted in showing alternations of memory in the alert and deep stages of the trance itself; — the ideas impressed in the one sort of state being almost always forgotten in the other, and as invariably again remembered when the former state recurs. (*Proceedings* S.P.R. vol. ii., pp. 61 *et seq.* [523 A].) On experimenting further, he met with a stage in which there was a distinct third train of memory, independent of the others; — and this, of course, suggests a further doubt as to there being any fixed number of stages in the trance. The later experiments of Mrs. Sidgwick [523 B] on the same subject, in which eight or nine distinct trains of memory were found — each recurring when the corresponding stage of depth of the trance was reached — seem to show conclusively that the number may vary almost indefinitely. We have already seen that in cases of alternating personalities the number of personalities similarly varies, and the student who now follows or repeats Gurney's experiments, with the increased knowledge of split personalities which recent years have brought, cannot fail to be struck with the analogies between Gurney's artificial light and deep states, — with their separate chains of memory, — and those morbid alternating personalities, with their complex mnemonic cleavages and lacunæ, with which we dealt in Chapter II. The hypnotic stages are in fact secondary or alternating personalities of very shallow type, but for that very reason all the better adapted for teaching us from what kinds of subliminal disaggregation the more serious splits in personality take their rise.

And beneath and between these awakenings into limited, partial alertness lies that profound hypnotic trance which one can best describe as a scientific or purposive rearrangement of the elements of sleep; — a rearrangement in which what is helpful is intensified, what is merely hindering or isolating is removed or reduced. A man's ordinary sleep is at once unstable and irresponsive. You can wake him with a pinprick, but if you talk to him he will not hear or answer you, until you rouse him with the mere noise. That is sleep as the needs of our timorous ancestors determined that it should be.

Hypnotic sleep, on the contrary, is at once stable and responsive; strong in its resistance to such stimuli as it chooses to ignore; ready in its accessibility to such appeals as it chooses to answer.

Prick or pinch the hypnotised subject, and although some stratum of his personality may be aware, in some fashion, of your act, the sleep will generally remain unbroken. But if you speak to him, — or even speak before him, — then, however profound his apparent lethargy, there is something in him which will hear.[1]

All this is true even of earlier stages of trance. Deeper still lies the stage of highest interest; — that sleep-waking in which the subliminal self is at last set free, — is at last able not only to receive but to respond: when it begins to tell us the secrets of the sleeping phase of personality, beginning with directions as to the conduct of the trance or of the cure, and going on to who knows what insight into who knows what world afar?

Without, then, entering into more detail as to the varying forms which hypnosis at different stages may assume, I have here traced its central characteristic; — the development, namely, of the sleeping phase of personality in such fashion as to allow of some supraliminal guidance of the subliminal self.

We have here a definition of much wider purview than any which has been habitually applied to the process of hypnotisation or to the state of hypnosis. To test its validity, to explain its scope, we need a survey of hypnotic results much wider in range than any enumeration of the kind at present usual in text-books. Regarding hypnotic achievements mainly in their *mental* aspects, I must seek for some broad principle of classification which on the one hand may not be so exclusively moral as to be physiologically untranslatable, — like the distinction between vice and virtue; — or on the other hand so exclusively physiological as to be morally untranslatable, — like the distinction between cerebral anæmia and hyperæmia.

Perhaps the broadest contrast which is expressible in both moral and physiological terms is the contrast between check and stimulus, — between *inhibition* and *dynamogeny*. Not, indeed, that such terms as *check* and *stimulus* can be pressed in detail. The central power, — the ruling agency within the man which gives the command, — is no doubt the same in both cases. But the common contrast between negative and positive exhortations, — "this you shall *not* do," "this you *shall* do,"

---

[1] I am inclined to think that this is always the case. For a long time the lethargic state was supposed at the Salpêtrière to preclude all knowledge of what was going on; and I have heard Charcot speak before a deeply-entranced subject as if there were no danger of her gathering hints as to what he expected her to do. I believe that his patients did subliminally receive such hints, and work them out in their own hypnotic behaviour. On the other hand, I have heard the late Dr. Auguste Voisin, one of the most persistent and successful of hypnotisers, make suggestion after suggestion to a subject apparently almost comatose, — which suggestions, nevertheless, she obeyed as soon as she awoke.

— will help to give clearness to our review of the influences of hypnotism in its bearings on intelligence and character, — its psychological efficacy.

The most rudimentary form of restraint or inhibition lies in our effort to preserve the infant or young child from acquiring what we call "bad tricks." These morbid affections of motor centres, trifling in their inception, will sometimes grow until they are incurable by any régime or medicament; — nay, till an action so insignificant as sucking the thumb may work the ruin of a life.

In no direction, perhaps, do the results of suggestion appear more inexplicable than here. Nowhere have we a more conspicuous touching of a spring; — a more complete achievement, almost in a single moment, of the deliverance which years of painful effort have failed to effect.[1]

[1] According to Dr. Edgar Bérillon, who was the first systematically to apply the hypnotic method to the education of children (see his paper, "De la Suggestion envisagée au point de vue pédagogique" in the *Revue de l'Hypnotisme*, vol. i. (1887), p. 84), the percentage of those who can be hypnotised is more than 80, and he asserts that suggestibility varies directly as the intellectual development of the subject. He classes under four heads the affections which can be successfully treated by hypnotic suggestion. (See the *Revue de l'Hypnotisme*, July 1895.)

(1) Psychical derangements caused by acute diseases; in particular, insomnia, restlessness, nocturnal delirium, incontrollable vomiting, incontinence of urine and of fæces.

(2) Functional affections connected with nervous disease: chorea, tics, convulsions, anæsthesiæ, contractures and hysterical paresis, hysterical hiccough, blepharospasm.

(3) Psychical derangements, such as habit of biting nails, precocious impulsive tendencies, nocturnal terrors, speaking in sleep, kleptomania, nervousness, shyness.

(4) Chorea, hysteria, epilepsy, or mental derangements considered as resulting from the combination of several nervous diseases.

Scattered about in the *Revue de l'Hypnotisme* the reader will find numerous illustrative cases. Specially characteristic are those recorded in the number for July 1893, p. 11, and April 1895, p. 306.

For reports of hypnotic cure of onychophagy, see Bérillon, the articles already quoted; Bourdon, *Revue de l'Hypnotisme*, November 1895, p. 134; Bouflé, *Revue de l'Hypnotisme*, September 1898, p. 76.

For reports of hypnotic cure of even graver habits, see Van Renterghem and Van Eeden, *Psycho-Thérapie*, p. 250; Bernheim, *Revue de l'Hypnotisme*, December 1891, a case in which the habit had become quite automatic and irresistible, and where every other method of treatment had failed; also *De la Suggestion;* Schrenck-Notzing, *Die Suggestions-Therapie bei krankhaften Erscheinungen des Geschlechtssinnes;* Bérillon, *Revue de l'Hypnotisme*, July 1893, pp. 12, 14, 15; Bourdon, *Revue de l'Hypnotisme*, November 1895, pp. 136, 139, 140; Auguste Voisin, *Revue de l'Hypnotisme*, November 1887, p. 151.

For cures of *enuresis nocturna*, see Liébeault, *Revue de l'Hypnotisme*, September 1886, p. 71; Bérillon, *Revue de l'Hypnotisme*, June 1894, p. 359; Van Renterghem

These cases stand midway between ordinary therapeutics and moral suasion. No one can here doubt the importance of finding the shortest and swiftest path to cure. Nor is there any reason to think that cures thus obtained are less complete or permanent than if they had been achieved by gradual moral effort. These facts should be borne in mind throughout the whole series of the higher hypnotic effects, and should serve to dispel any anxiety as to the possible loss of moral training when cure is thus magically swift. Each of these effects consists, as we must suppose, in the modification of some group of nervous centres; and, so far as we can tell, that is just the same result which moral effort made above the conscious threshold more slowly and painfully attains. This difference, in fact, is like the difference between results achieved by diligence and results achieved by genius. Something valuable in the way of training, — some exercise in patience and resolve, — no doubt may be missed by the man who is "suggested" into sobriety; — in the same way as it was missed by the schoolboy Gauss, — writing down the answers to problems as soon as set, instead of spending on them a diligent hour. But moral progress is in its essence as limitless as mathematical; and the man who is thus carried over rudimentary struggles may still find plenty of moral effort in life to train his character and tax his resolution.

Among these morbid tricks *kleptomania* has an interest of its own, on account of the frequent doubt whether it is not put forward as a mere excuse for pilfering. It may thus happen that the cure is the best proof of the existence of the disease; and certain cures indicate that the impulse

and Van Eeden, *Psycho-thérapie.*; Paul Farez, *Revue de l'Hypnotisme*, August 1899, p. 53. This author recommends the method of suggestion in normal sleep.

Liébeault, in the *Revue de l'Hypnotisme* for January 1889, gives twenty-two cases in which hypnotic suggestion was used in the moral education of children from the age of fourteen months upwards, with the aim of curing, *e.g.* the habit of lying, excessive developments of emotions, such as fear and anger, and precocious or depraved appetites; and of improving the normal faculties of attention and memory. He reports ten cures, eight improvements, and four failures.

For other cases of moral education, see Bérillon, *De la suggestion et de ses applications à la pédagogie* (1887); *L'Hypnotisme et l'Orthopédie morale* (1898); *Revue de l'Hypnotisme*, December 1887, pp. 169–180, and December 1897, p. 162; Bernheim, *Revue de l'Hypnotisme*, November 1886, p. 129; Ladame, the same, June and July 1887; Voisin, the same, November 1888; De Jong, the same, September 1891; Bourdon, the same, August 1896; Van Renterghem and Van Eeden, *Psycho-thérapie*, p. 215. Nervous troubles in adults have often been cured by the same means. Thus, in the *Revue de l'Hypnotisme*, September 1899, p. 73, Dr. Vlavianos records a case of *tic convulsif* cured by hypnotic suggestion. Wetterstrand has used the same method with success (*loc. cit.*, p. 76). See also Janet, *Névroses et Idées Fixes*, vol. ii., part ii., chapter iii., " Les. Tics."

has veritably involved a morbid excitability of motor centres, acted on by special stimuli, — an *idée fixe* with an immediate outcome in act.[1]

Many words and acts of *violence* fall under the same category, in cases where the impulse to swear or to strike has acquired the unreasoning automatic promptness of a *tic*, and yet may be at once inhibited by suggestion. Many undesirable impulses in the realm of *sex* are also capable of being thus corrected or removed.

The stimulants and narcotics, to which our review next leads us, form a standing menace to human virtue. By some strange accident of our development, the impulse of our organisms towards certain drugs — alcohol, opium, and the like — is strong enough to overpower, in a large proportion of mankind, not only the late-acquired altruistic impulses, but even the primary impulses of self-regard and self-preservation. We are brought back, one may almost say, to the "chimiotaxy" of the lowest organisms, which arrange themselves inevitably in specific relation to oxygen, malic acid, or whatever the stimulus may be. We thus experience in ourselves a strange conflict between moral responsibility and molecular affinities; — the central will overborne by dumb unnumbered elements of our being. With this condition of things hypnotic suggestion deals often in a curious way. The suggestion is not generally felt as a strengthening of the central will. It resembles rather a molecular redisposition; it leaves the patient indifferent to the stimulus, or even disgusted with it. The man for whom alcohol has combined the extremes of delight and terror now lives as though in a world in which alcohol did not exist at all.[2]

Even for the slave of morphia the same sudden freedom is sometimes achieved. It has been said of victims to morphia-injection that a cure means death; — so often has suicide followed on the distress caused by giving up the drug. But in certain cases cured by suggestion it seems

---

[1] See Bérillon, *Revue de l'Hypnotisme*, September 1890, p. 75, and February 1896, p. 237; Regis, the same, May 1896; De Jong, the same, September 1891, p. 82; and Auguste Voisin, the same, November 1888, p. 130.

[2] See Otto Wetterstrand, *Der Hypnotismus und seine Anwendung in der praktischen Medicin;* Georg Ringier, *Erfolge des therapeutischen Hypnotismus in der Landpraxis;* Van Renterghem and Van Eeden, *Psycho-thérapie;* Auguste Forel, *Einige therapeutische Versuche mit dem Hypnotismus bei Geisteskranken;* Lloyd Tuckey, *Revue de l'Hypnotisme*, January 1897, p. 207; Ladame, *Revue de l'Hypnotisme*, November 1887, p. 131, and December 1887, p. 165; A. Voisin, *Revue de l'Hypnotisme*, vol. ii. (1888), p. 69, and vol. iii. (1889), p. 353; Vlavianos, *Revue de l'Hypnotisme*, June 1899, p. 361; Neilson, *Revue de l'Hypnotisme*, vol. vi. (1892), p. 17. Bérillon, *Le traitement psychologique de L'Alcoolisme*. Paris 1906. See also the works of Liébeault, Bernheim, and Milne Bramwell.

that no craving whatsoever has persisted after the sudden disuse of the drug. There is something here which is in one sense profounder than moral reform. There is something which suggests a spirit within us less injured than we might have feared by the body's degradation. The morphinomaniac *character* — the lowest type of subjection to a ruling vice — disappears from the personality in proportion as the drug is eliminated from the system. The shrinking outcast turns at once into the respectable man.[1]

But apart from troubles consequent on any intelligible instinct, any discoverable stimulus of pleasure, there are a multitude of impulses, fears, imaginations, one or more of which may take possession of persons not otherwise apparently unhealthy or hysterical, sometimes to an extent so distressing as to impel to suicide.

Some of these "phobies" have been often described of late years, — as, for instance, *agoraphobia*, which makes a man dread to cross an open space; and its converse *claustrophobia*, which makes him shrink from sitting in a room with closed doors; or the still more distressing *mysophobia*, which makes him constantly uneasy lest he should have become dirty or defiled.

All these disorders involve a kind of displacement or cramp of the attention; and for all of them, one may broadly say, hypnotic suggestion is the best and often the only cure. Suggestion seems to stimulate antagonistic centres; to open clogged channels; to produce, in short, however we imagine the process, a rapid disappearance of the insistent notion.

I have spoken of this effect as though it were mainly to be valued intellectually, as a readjustment of the dislocated attention. But I must note also that the moral results may be as important here as in the cases of inhibition of dipsomania and the like, already mentioned. These morbid fears which suggestion relieves may be ruinously degrading to a man's character. The ingredients of antipathy, of jealousy, which they sometimes contain, may make him dangerous to his fellows as well as loathsome to himself. One or two cases of the cure of morbid

---

[1] There are many instances of the cure of morphinomania. See especially the case recorded by Dr. Marot in the *Revue de l'Hypnotisme*, February 1893, on account of the psychological interest of the patient's own remarks.

Wetterstrand, out of fourteen cases, records eleven cures of morphinomania. In a paper in the *Revue de l'Hypnotisme*, November 1890, he discusses the benefit of prolonged hypnosis — causing the patient to sleep for a week or more at a time — which he tried in one case. See also Voisin, *Revue de l'Hypnotisme*, December 1886, p. 163.

jealousy are to my mind among the best records which hypnotism has to show.[1]

But this is not all. The treasure of memory is mixed with rubbish; the caution which experience has taught has often been taught too well; philosophic calm has often frozen into apathy. Plato would have the old men in his republic plied well with wine on festal days, that their tongues might be unloosed to communicate their wisdom without reserve. "Accumulated experience," it has been said with much truth in more modern language,[2] "hampers action, disturbs the logical reaction of the individual to his environment. The want of control which marks the decadence of mental power is [sometimes] itself undue control, a preponderance of the secondary over the primary influences."

Now the removal of shyness, or *mauvaise honte*, which hypnotic suggestion can effect, is in fact a *purgation of memory*, — inhibiting the recollection of previous failures, and setting free whatever group of aptitudes is for the moment required. Thus, for the boy called on to make an oration in a platform exhibition, hypnotisation sets free the *primary* instinct of garrulity without the restraining fear of ridicule. For the musical executant, on the other hand, a similar suggestion will set free the *secondary* instinct which the fingers have acquired, without the interference of the learner's puzzled, hesitating thoughts.

I may remark here (following Gurney and Bramwell) how misleading a term is *mono-ideism* for almost any hypnotic state. There is a *selection* of ideas to which the hypnotic subject will attend, and there is a *concentration* upon the idea thus selected; but those ideas themselves may be both complex and constantly shifting, and indeed this is just one of the ways in which the hypnotic trance differs from the somnambulic — in which it may happen that only a relatively small group of brain-centres are awake enough to act. The somnambulic servant-girl, for instance, may persist in laying the tea-table, whatever you say to her, and this may fairly be called mono-ideism; but the hypnotic subject (as Bramwell has justly insisted) can be made to obey simultaneously a greater number of separate commands than he could possibly attend to in waking life.

From these inhibitions of memory, — of attention as directed to the experiences of the past, — we pass on to attention as directed to the experiences of the present. And here we are reaching a central point; we are affecting the *macula lutea* (as it has been well called) of the mental

---

[1] See Dr. A. Dores, *Revue de l'Hypnotisme*, May 1899, p. 345; and Dr. Bourdon, the same, November 1893, p. 141 [557 A].

[2] Dr. Hill, *British Medical Journal*, July 4th, 1891.

field. Many of the most important of hypnotic results will be best described as modifications of *attention*.

Any modification of attention is of course likely to be at once a check and a stimulus; — a check to certain thoughts and emotions, a stimulus to others. And in many cases it will be the *dynamogenic* aspect of the change — the new vigour supplied in needed directions — which will be for us of greatest interest. Yet from the *inhibitive* side also we have already had important achievements to record. All these arrests and destructions of *idées fixes*, of which so much has been said, were powerful modifications of attention, although the limited field which they covered made it simpler to introduce them under a separate heading.

And even now it may not be without surprise that the reader finds described under the heading of *inhibition of attention* a phenomenon so considerable and so apparently independent as *hypnotic suppression of pain*. This induced *analgesia* has from the first been one of the main triumphs of mesmerism or hypnotism. All have heard that mesmerism will stop headaches; — that you can have a tooth out "under mesmerism" without feeling it. The rivalry between mesmerism and ether, as anæsthetic agents in capital operations, was a conspicuous fact in the medical history of early Victorian times. But the ordinary talk, at any rate of that day, seemed to assume that if mesmerism produced an effect at all it was an effect *resembling* that produced by narcotics — a modification of the intimate structure of the nerve or of the brain which rendered them for the time incapable of transmitting or of feeling painful sensations. The state of a man's nervous system, in fact, when he is poisoned by chloroform, or stunned by a blow, or almost frozen to death, or nearly drowned, etc., is such that a great part of it is no longer fit for its usual work, — is no longer capable of those prolongations of neurons, or whatever they be, which constitute its specific nervous activity. We thus get rid of pain by getting rid for the time of a great deal of other nervous action as well; and we have to take care lest by pushing the experiment too far we get rid of life into the bargain. But on the other hand, a man's nervous system, when hypnotic suggestion has rendered him incapable of pain, is quite as active and vigorous as ever, — quite as capable of transmitting and feeling pain, — although capable also of inhibiting it altogether. In a word, the hypnotic subject is *above* instead of *below* pain.

To understand this apparent paradox we must remind ourselves that pain probably originated as a warning of danger, — a warning which, while useful to active creatures with miscellaneous risks, has become only a mixed advantage to beings of more advanced intelligence and sensitivity. There are many occasions when, knowing it to be useless, we wish to shut off pain, to rise as definitely *above* it as our earliest ancestors were *below* it, or as the drunken or narcotised man is below it. This is just what hypnotic suggestion enables us to do.

Hypnotism attacks the real *origo mali;* — not, indeed, the pressure on the tooth-nerve, which can only be removed by extraction, but the representative power of the central sensorium which converts that pressure for us into pain. It *diverts attention* from the pain, as the excitement of battle might do; but diverts it without any competing excitement whatever. To this topic of *influence on attention* we shall have to recur again and again. For the present it may suffice if I refer the reader to a few cases — chosen from among some thousands where hypnotic practice has removed or obviated the distress or anguish till now unmistakably associated with various bodily incidents — from the extraction of a tooth to the great pain and peril of childbirth.[1]

This suppression of pain has naturally been treated from the therapeutic point of view, as an end in itself; and neither physician nor patient has been inclined to inquire exactly *what* has occurred; — what physiological or psychological condition has underlain this great subjective relief. Yet in the eye of experimental psychology the matter is far from a simple one. We are bound to ask *what* has been altered. Has there been a total *ablation*, or some mere *translation* of pain? What objective change

---

[1] In some articles in the *Revue Philosophique*, published in 1886 and 1887, Delbœuf describes some experiments which suggest that in many of the remarkable hypnotic cures recorded in the *Zoist* (as well as in modern cases) the removal of pain was probably an important element in the cure; see *e.g.* cures of inflammation (*Zoist*, vol. x. p. 347); of neuralgia and chronic rheumatism (vol. ix. pp. 76–79); of abdominal pains (vol. ix. p. 155); of tic douloureux (vol. viii. p. 186); of severe headaches (vol. x. p. 369); of eczema impetiginodes (vol. x. p. 96).

The general subject of hypnotic analgesia is strikingly illustrated by Esdaile's well-known work in the Indian hospitals; see his books, *Mesmerism in India* (London, 1846); *The Introduction of Mesmerism with Sanction of Government into the Public Hospitals of India* (2nd edit. London, 1856); *Natural and Mesmeric Clairvoyance* (London, 1852); and constant references to him in the *Zoist*.

For later cases see *British Medical Journal*, April 5th, 1890, p. 801; the same, February 28th, 1891, pp. 460–468.

See also Van Renterghem and Van Eeden's *Psycho-thérapie*, pp. 262–280.

See also the *Proceedings* S.P.R., vol. xii. p. 21, and the *Revue de l'Hypnotisme*, November 1891, p. 132; the same, 1895, p. 300; and for the discussion of a very interesting recent case of the cure of sycosis menti, see Bérillon, *Revue de l'Hypnotisme*, January 1896, p. 195; Delbœuf, *Revue de l'Hypnotisme*, February 1896, p. 225; Durand (de Gros), *Revue de l'Hypnotisme*, 1896, p. 37. It was also quoted in the *British Medical Journal* for November 16th, 1895.

on the bodily side has occurred in nerve or tissue? and, on the mental side, how far does the change in consciousness extend? How deep does it go? Does any subliminal knowledge of the pain persist?

The very imperfect answers which can at present be given to these questions may, at any rate, suggest directions for further inquiry.

(1) In the first place, it seems clear that when pain is inhibited in any but the most simple cases, a certain group of changes is produced whose *nexus* is psychological rather than physiological. That is to say, one suggestion seems to relieve at once all the symptoms which form one idea of pain or distress in the patient's mind; while another suggestion is often needed to remove some remaining symptom, which the patient regards as a different trouble altogether. The suggestion thus differs both from a specific remedy, which might relieve a specific symptom, and from a general narcotisation, which would relieve all symptoms equally. In making suggestions, moreover, the hypnotiser finds that he has to consider and meet the patient's own subjective feelings, describing the intended relief as the patient wishes it to be described, and not attempting technical language which the patient could not follow. In a word, it is plain that in this class, as in other classes of suggestion, we are addressing ourselves to a *mind*, an *intelligence*, which can of itself select and combine, and not merely to a tissue or a gland responsive in a merely automatic way.

(2) It will not then surprise us if, — pain being thus treated as a psychological entity, — there shall prove to be a certain psychological complexity in the response to analgesic suggestion.

By this I mean that there are occasional indications that some memory of the pain, say, of an operation has persisted in some stratum of the personality; — thus apparently indicating that there was somewhere an actual consciousness of the pain when the operation was performed.[1] We find accounts of the revival of pain in dreams after operations performed under chloroform.[2]

(3) Such experiences, if more frequent, might tempt us to suppose that the pain is not wholly abrogated, but merely translated to some stratum of consciousness whose experiences do not enter into our habitual chain of memories. Yet we possess (strangely enough) what seems direct evidence that the profoundest organic substratum of our being is by suggestion wholly freed from pain. It had long been observed that recoveries from operations performed in hypnotic trance were unusually benign; — there being less tendency to inflammation than when the patient had felt the

---

[1] See the *Revue de l'Hypnotisme*, August 1887.
[2] See the *Journal* S.P.R., vol. vi. p. 209 [535 A].

knife. The same observation — perhaps in a less marked degree — has since been made as to operations under chemical anæsthesia. The shock to the system, and the irritation to the special parts affected, are greatly diminished by chloroform. And more recently Professor Delbœuf, by an experiment of great delicacy on two symmetrical wounds, of which one was rendered painless by suggestion, has distinctly demonstrated that pain tends to induce and keep up inflammation.[1]

Thus it seems that pain is abrogated at once on the highest and on the lowest level of consciousness; yet possibly in some cases (though not usually[2]) persists obscurely in some stratum of our personality into which we gain only occasional and indirect glimpses. And if indeed this be so, it need in no way surprise us. We need to remember at every point that we have no reason whatever to suppose that we are cognisant of all the trains of consciousness, or chains of memory, which are weaving themselves within us. I shall never attain on earth — perhaps I never shall in any world attain — to any complete conspectus of the variously interwoven streams of vitality which are, in fact, obscurely present in my conception of myself.

It is to hypnotism in the first place that we may look for an increased power of analysis of these intercurrent streams, these irregularly superposed strata of our psychical being. In the meantime, this power of *inhibiting* almost any fraction of our habitual consciousness at pleasure gives for the first time to the ordinary man — if only he be a suggestible subject — a power of concentration, of *choice* in the exercise of faculty, such as up till now only the most powerful spirits — a Newton or an Archimedes — have been able to exert.

The man who sits down in his study to write or read, — in perfect safety and intent on his work, — continues nevertheless to be involuntarily and inevitably armed with all that alertness to external sights and sounds, and all that sensibility to pain, which protected his lowly ancestors at different stages of even pre-human development. It is much as though he were forced to carry about with him all the external defences which his forefathers have invented for their defence; — to sit at his writing-table clad in chain-mail and a respirator, and grasping an umbrella and a boomerang. Let him learn, if he can, inwardly as well as outwardly, to get rid of all that, to keep at his command only the half of his faculties which for his purpose is worth more than the whole. Dissociation and choice; — dissociation between elements which have always hitherto

---

[1] See the *Revue Philosophique*, 1886.
[2] See the *Proceedings* S.P.R., vol. xii. p. 193 [535 B].

ﾇextricably knit;—choice between faculties which till now we have
ﾇ all together or not at all;—such is the promise, such is the incipi-
ﾇmance of hypnotic plasticity in its aspect of *inhibitive suggestion*.
ﾇ now to the division of hypnotic achievement with which I next
ﾇo deal, namely, the *dynamogenic* results of hypnotic suggestion.
ﾇnese I shall arrange in an order resembling that which we try to follow
in education: — proceeding from external senses to internal sensory and
other central operations; and thence again to attention and will, and so
to character which is a kind of resultant of all these.

I will begin, then, with what seems the most external and measurable of
these different influences — the influence, namely, of suggestion upon man's
perceptive faculties;—its power to educate his external organs of sense.

This wide subject is almost untouched as yet; and there is no direction
in which one could be more confident of interesting results from further
experiment.

The exposition falls naturally into three parts, as suggestion effects
one or other of the three following objects:

    (1) Restoration of ordinary senses from some deficient condition.

    (2) Vivification of ordinary senses; — hyperæsthesiæ.

    (3) Development of new senses; — heteræsthesiæ.

(1) The first of these three headings seems at first sight to belong to
therapeutics rather than to psychology. It is, however, indispensable
as a preliminary to the other two heads; since by learning how and to what
extent suggestion can repair *defective* senses we have the best chance of
guessing at its *modus operandi* when it seems to excite the *healthy* senses
to a point beyond their normal powers.[1]

Two points may be mentioned here. Improvement of *vision* seems
sometimes to result from relaxation of an involuntary ciliary spasm, which
habitually over-corrects some defect of the lens. This is interesting,
from the analogy thus shown in quite healthy persons to the fixed ideas,
the subliminal errors and fancies characteristic of hysteria. The stratum
of self whose business it is to correct the mechanical defect of the eye has
in these instances done so amiss, and cannot set itself right. The corrected form of vision is as defective as the form of vision which it replaced.
But if the state of trance be induced, or if it occur spontaneously, it sometimes happens that the error is suddenly righted; the patient lays aside
spectacles; and since we must assume that the original defect of mechanism

---

[1] For cases bearing on this subject see Dr. Liébeault's *Thérapeutique Suggestive*,
pp. 64 *et seq.*; the *Revue de l'Hypnotisme*, January 1893; and *Proceedings* S.P.R.,
vol. xii. p. 177 [538 A and B].

remains, it seems that that defect is now perfectly instead of imperfectly met. This shows a subliminal adjusting power operating during trance more intelligently than the supraliminal intelligence had been able to operate during waking life.

Another point of interest lies in the effect of increased attention, as stimulated by suggestion, upon the power of hearing Dr. Liébeault[1] records two cases which are among the most significant that I know. If such susceptibility to self-suggestion could be reached by patients generally, there might be, with no miracle at all, a removal of perhaps half the annoyance which deafness inflicts on mankind.

I pass on to cases of the production by suggestion or self-suggestion of hyperæsthesia, — of a degree of sensory delicacy which overpasses the ordinary level, and the previous level of the subject himself.

The rudimentary state of our study of hypnotism is somewhat strangely illustrated by the fact that most of the experiments which show hyperæsthesia most delicately have been undertaken with a view of proving something else — namely, mesmeric *rapport*, or the mesmerisation of objects, or telepathy. In these cases the proof of *rapport*, telepathy, etc., generally just falls short, — because one cannot say that the action of the ordinary senses might not have reached the point necessary for the achievement, though there is often good reason to believe that the subject was supraliminally ignorant of the way in which he was, in fact, attaining the knowledge in question.

In these extreme cases, indeed, the explanation by hyperæsthesia is not always proved. There *may* have been telepathy, although one has not the right to assume telepathy, in view of certain slighter, but still remarkable, hyperæsthetic achievements, which are common subjects of demonstration. The ready recognition of *points de repère*, on the back of a card or the like, which are hardly perceptible to ordinary eyes, is one of the most usual of these performances.

In this connection the question arises as to the existence of physiological limits to the exercise of the ordinary senses. In the case of the eye a *minimum visibile* is generally assumed; and there is special interest in a case of clairvoyance versus cornea-reading, where, if the words were read (as appears most probable) from their reflection upon the cornea of the hypnotiser, the common view as to the *minimum visibile* is greatly stretched.[2]

---

[1] *Thérapeutique Suggestive*, pp. 64 *et seq.*

[2] See the *Revue Philosophique*, November 1886. The same case is discussed in *Mind* for January 1887 [539 A].

With regard to the other senses, whose mechanism is less capable of minute dissection, one meets problems of a rather different kind. What are the definitions of smell and touch? Touch is already split up into various factors — tactile, algesic, thermal; and thermal touch is itself a duplicate sense, depending apparently on one set of nerve-terminations adapted to perceive heat, and another set adapted to perceive cold. Taste is similarly split up; and we do not call anything taste which is not definitely referred to the mouth and adjacent regions. Smell is vaguer; and there are cognate sensations (like that of the presence of a cat) which are not referred by their subject to the nose. The study of hyperæsthesia does in this sense prepare the way for what I have termed heteræsthesia; in that it leaves us more cautious in definition as to what the senses are, it accustoms us to the notion that people become aware of things in many ways which they cannot definitely realise.

Let us now consider the evidence for heteræsthesia; — for the existence, that is to say, under hypnotic suggestion, of any form of sensibility decidedly different from those with which we are familiar. It would sound more accurate if one could say "demanding some end-organ different from those which we know that we possess." But we know too little of the range of perceptivity of these end-organs in the skin which we are gradually learning to distinguish — of the heat-feeling spots, cold-feeling spots, and the like — to be able to say for what purposes a new organ would be needed. For certain heteræsthetic sensations, indeed, as the perception of a magnetic field, one can hardly assume that any end-organ would be necessary. It is better, therefore, to speak only of modes of sensibility.

Looking at the matter from the evolutionary point of view, the question among sensations was one of the development of the fittest; that is to say that, as the organism became more complex and needed sensations more definite than sufficed for the protozoon, certain sensibilities got themselves defined and stereotyped upon the organism by the evolution of end-organs.[1] Others failed to get thus externalised; but may, for aught we know, persist nevertheless in the central organs; — say, for instance, in what for man are the optic or olfactory tracts of the brain. There will then be no apparent reason why these latent powers should not from time to time receive sufficient stimulus, either from within or from without, to make them perceptible to the waking intelligence, or perceptible at least in states (like trance) of narrow concentration.

[1] Nagel suggests that there may have been at a certain stage *mixed sense-organs*, by means of which two or three sensations were perceived simultaneously.

As the result of these considerations, I approach alleged heteræsthesiæ of various kinds with no presumption whatever against their real occurrence. Yet on the other hand, my belief in the extent of possible *hyperæsthesia* continually suggests to me that the apparently new perceptions may only consist of a mixture of familiar forms of perception, pushed to a new extreme, and centrally interpreted with a new acumen, while there is no doubt that many experiments supposed to furnish evidence of such new perceptions merely illustrate the effect of suggestion or self-suggestion.

Without, however, presuming to criticise past evidence wholesale, I yet hope that the experience now attained may lead to a much greater number of well-guarded experiments in the near future. In Appendix V.A, I very briefly present the actual state of this inquiry. In default of any logical principle, I shall there divide these alleged forms of sensibility according as they are excited by inorganic objects on the one hand, or by organisms (dead or living) on the other.

In the meantime I pass on to that group of the dynamogenic effects of suggestion which affect the more central vital operations — either the vaso-motor system, or the neuro-muscular system, or the central sensory tracts. The effects of suggestion on character — induced changes to which we can hardly guess the nervous concomitant — will remain to be dealt with later.

First, then, as to the effects of suggestion on the vaso-motor system. Simple effects of this type form the commonest of "platform experiments." The mesmerist holds ammonia under his subject's nose, and tells him it is rose-water. The subject smells it eagerly, and his eyes do not water. The suggestion, that is to say, that the stinging vapour is inert has inhibited the vaso-motor reflexes which would ordinarily follow, and which no ordinary effort of will could restrain. *Vice versâ*, when the subject smells rose-water, described as ammonia, he sneezes and his eyes water. These results, which his own will could not produce, follow on the mesmerist's word. No one who sees these simple tests applied can doubt the genuineness of the influence at work. We find then, as might be expected, that action on glands and secretions constitutes a large element in hypnotic therapeutics. The literature of suggestion is full of instances where a suppressed secretion has been restored at a previously arranged moment, almost with "astronomical punctuality." And yet in what memory is that command retained? by what signal is it announced? or by what agency obeyed?

In spite of this underlying obscurity, common to every branch of suggestion, these vaso-motor phenomena are by this time so familiar that no further description of them is necessary.

This delicate responsiveness of the vaso-motor system has given rise to some curious spontaneous phenomena, and has suggested some experiments, which are probably as yet in their infancy. The main point of interest is that at this point spontaneous self-suggestion, and subsequently suggestion from without, have made a kind of first attempt at the modification of the human organism in what may be called fancy directions, — at the production of a change which has no therapeutic aim, and so to say, no physiological unity; but which is guided by an intellectual caprice along lines with which the organism is not previously familiar. I speak of the phenomenon commonly known as "stigmatisation," from the fact that its earliest spontaneous manifestations were suggested by imaginations brooding on the stigmata of Christ's passion; — the marks of wounds in hands and feet and side. This phenomenon, which was long treated both by *savants* and by devotees as though it must be either fraudulent or miraculous, — *ou supercherie, ou miracle*, — is now found (like a good many other phenomena previously deemed subject to that dilemma) to enter readily within the widening circuit of natural law. Stigmatisation is, in fact, a form of vesication; and suggested vesication — with the quasi-burns and real blisters which obediently appear in any place and pattern that is ordered — is a high development of that same vaso-motor plasticity of which the ammonia-rose-water experiment was an early example.[1]

---

[1] For a circumstantial English account of the well-known case of Louise Lateau, see *Macmillan's Magazine*, vol. xxiii. pp. 488 *et seq.*

Three cases of the production of cruciform marks reported by Dr. Biggs, of Lima, appeared in the *Journal* S.P.R., vol. iii. p. 100.

Another remarkable American case of stigmatisation was reported in the *Courier-Journal*, Louisville, Ky., December 7th, 1891, on the authority of Dr. M. F. Coomes and several other physicians.

See also the case of Ilma S. recorded in Dr. R. von Krafft-Ebing's *Experimental Study in Hypnotism.*

Dr. P. Janet describes somewhat similar experiments in *L'Automatisme Psychologique* (see p. 166 *et seq.*).

Again, somewhat similar is a case recorded by Dr. J. Rybalkin in the *Revue de l'Hypnotisme*, June 1890 (p. 361), in which a post-hypnotic suggestion to the subject to burn his arm at a stove — really unlighted — produced blisters as of a burn.

Hæmorrhage and bleeding stigmata were several times produced in the famous subject, Louis Vivé, by verbal suggestion alone. (Drs. Bourru and Burot, *Comptes Rendus de la Société de Biologie*, July 12th, 1885; and Dr. Mabille, *Progrès Médical*, August 29th, 1885.)

The group of suggestive effects which we reach next in order is a wide and important one. The education of the *central sensory faculties*, — of our power of inwardly representing to ourselves sights and sounds, etc., — is not less important than the education of the external senses. The powers of construction and combination which our central organs possess differ more widely in degree in different healthy individuals than the degrees of external perception itself. And the stimulating influence of hypnotism on *imagination* is perhaps the most conspicuous phenomenon which the whole subject offers; yet it has been little dwelt upon, save from one quite superficial point of view.

Every one knows that a hypnotised subject is easily hallucinated; — that if he is told to see a non-existent dog, he sees a dog, — that if he is told *not* to see Mr. A., he sees everything in the room, Mr. A. excepted. Common and conspicuous, I say, as this experiment is, even the scientific observer has too often dealt with it with the shallowness of the platform lecturer. The lecturer represents this induced hallucinability simply as an odd illustration of his own power over the subject. "I tell him to forget his name, and he forgets his name; I tell him that he has a baby on his lap, and he sees and feels and dandles it." At the best, such a hallucination is quoted as an instance of "mono-ideism." But the real kernel of the phenomenon is not the inhibition but the dynamogeny; — not the abstraction of attention or imagination from other topics, but the increased power which imagination gains under suggestion; — the development of faculty, useless, if you will, in that special form of imagining the baby, but faculty mentally of a high order — faculty in one shape or another essential to the production of almost all the most admired forms of human achievement.

On this theme I shall have much to say; yet here again it will be convenient to defer fuller discussion until I review what I have termed "sensory automatism" in a more general way. We shall then see that this quickened imaginative faculty is not educed by hypnosis alone; that it is a part of the equipment of the subliminal self, and will be better treated

Professor Beaunis (*Recherches Expérimentales*, etc., Paris, 1886, p. 29) produced redness and cutaneous congestion in his subject, Mlle. A. E., by suggestion, and the experiment was repeated on the same subject by the present writer and Edmund Gurney in September 1885 (see *Proceedings* S.P.R., vol. iv. p. 167).

It appears that there is at present at the Salpêtrière a *stigmatisée*, the development of whose stigmata has been watched by Dr. Janet under copper shields with glass windows inserted in them (*Revue de l'Hypnotisme*, December 1900, p. 190).

Other cases are recorded in the *Revue de l'Hypnotisme*, June 1890, p. 353; the same February 1892, p. 251 [543 A to H].

at length in connection with other spontaneous manifestations. Enough
here to have pointed out the main fact; for when pointed out it can hardly
be disputed, although its significance for the true comprehension of hypnotic phenomena has been too often overlooked.

Yet here, and in direct connection with hypnotism, certain special
features of hallucinations need to be insisted upon, both as partly explaining certain more advanced hypnotic phenomena, and also as suggesting
lines of important experiment. The first point is this.

Post-hypnotic hallucinations can be *postponed* at will. That is to
say, a constant watchfulness is exercised by the subject, so that if, for
example, the hypnotiser tells him that he will (when awakened) poke
the fire when the hypnotiser has coughed three times, the awakened subject, although knowing nothing of the order in his waking state, will be
on the look-out for the coughs, amid all other disturbances, and will poke
the fire at the fore-ordained signal.[1] Moreover, when the post-hypnotic
suggestion is executed there will often be a slight momentary relapse into
the hypnotic state, and the subject will not afterwards be aware that he
has (for instance) poked the fire at all. This means that the suggested
act belongs properly to the hypnotic, not to the normal chain of memory;
so that its performance involves a brief reappearance of the subliminal
self which received the order.

Another characteristic of these suggested hallucinations tells in exactly
the same direction. It is possible to suggest no mere isolated picture,
— a black cat on the table, or the like, — but a whole complex series of
responses to circumstances not at the time predictable. This point is
well illustrated by what are called "negative hallucinations" or "systematised anæsthesiæ." Suppose, for instance, that I tell a hypnotised
subject that when he awakes there will be no one in the room with him
but myself. He awakes and remembers nothing of this order, but sees
me alone in the room. Other persons present endeavour to attract his
attention in various ways. Sometimes he will be quite unconscious of
their noises and movements; sometimes he will perceive them, but will
explain them away, as due to other causes, in the same irrational manner
as one might do in a dream. Or he may perceive them, be unable to
explain them, and feel considerable terror until the "negative hallucination" is dissolved by a fresh word of command. It is plain, in fact, throughout, that some element in him is at work all the time in obedience to the
suggestion given, — is keeping him by ever fresh modifications of his
illusion from discovering its unreality. Nothing could be more charac-

---

[1] See *Proceedings* S.P.R., vol. iv. pp. 268-323 [551 A].

teristic of what I have called a "middle-level centre" of the subliminal self — of some element in his nature which is potent and persistent without being completely intelligent; — a kind of dream-producer, ready at any moment to vary and defend the dream.

Another indication of the subliminal power at work to produce these hallucinations is their remarkable *range* — a range as wide, perhaps, as that over which therapeutic effects are obtainable by suggestion. The post-hypnotic hallucination may affect not sight and hearing alone (to which spontaneous hallucinations are in most cases confined), but all kinds of vaso-motor responses and organic sensations — cardiac, stomachic, and the like — which no artifice can affect in a waking person. The legendary flow of perspiration with which the flatterer sympathises with his patron's complaint of heat — *si dixeris " Æstuo," sudat* — is no exaggeration if applied to the hypnotic subject, who will often sweat and shiver at your bidding as you transplant him from the Equator to frosty Caucasus.

Well, then, given this strength and vigour of hallucination, one sees a possible extension of knowledge in more than one direction. To begin with, by suggestion to the subject that he is feeling or doing something which is beyond his normal range of faculties, we may perhaps enable him to perceive or to act as thus suggested.

What we need is to address to a sensitive subject a series of strong suggestions of the increase of his sensory range and power. We must needs begin by suggesting hallucinatory sensations: — the subject should be told that he perceives some stimulus which is, in fact, too feeble for ordinary perception. If you can make him *think* that he perceives it, he probably will after a time perceive it; the direction given to his attention heightening either peripheral or central sensory faculty. You may then be able to attack the question as to how far his specialised end-organs are really concerned in the perception; — and it may then be possible to deal in a more fruitful way with those alleged cases of *transposition of senses* which have so great a theoretical interest as being apparently intermediate between hyperæsthesia and telæsthesia or clairvoyance. If we once admit (as I, of course, admit) the reality of telæsthesia, it is just in some such way as this that we should expect to find it beginning.

I start from the thesis that the perceptive power within us precedes and is independent of the specialised sense-organs, which it has developed for earthly use.

νοῦς ὁρᾶ καὶ νοῦς ἀκούει· τἆλλα κωφὰ καὶ τυφλά.

I conceive further that under certain circumstances this primary telæsthetic faculty resumes direct operations, in spite of the fleshly barriers which are constructed so as to allow it to operate through certain channels alone. And I conceive that in thus resuming exercise of the wider faculty, the incarnate spirit will be influenced or hampered by the habits or self-suggestions of the more specialised faculty; so that there may be apparent *compromises* of different kinds between telæsthetic and hyperæsthetic perception, — as the specialised senses endeavour, as it were, to retain credit for the perception which is in reality widening beyond their scope.

In this attitude of mind, then, I approach the recorded cases of trans-position of special sense.[1]

Two main hypotheses have been put forward as a general explanation of such cases, neither of which seems to me quite satisfactory. (1) The common theory would be that these are merely cases of erroneous self-suggestion; — that the subject really sees with the eye, but thinks that he sees with the knee, or the stomach, or the finger-tips. This may prob-ably have been so in many, but not, I think, in all instances. (2) Dr. Prosper Despine and others suppose that, while the accustomed cerebral centres are still concerned in the act of sight, the finger-end (for example) acts for the nonce as the end-organ required to carry the visual sensation to the brain. I cannot here get over the mechanical difficulty of the absence of a lens. However hyperæsthetic the finger-end might be (say) to light and darkness, I can hardly imagine its acting as an organ of definite sight.

My own suggestion (which, for aught I know, may have been made before) is that the finger-end is no more a true organ of sight than the arbitrary "hypnogenous zone" is a true organ for inducing trance. I think it possible that there may be actual telæsthesia, — not necessarily involving any perception by the bodily organism; — and that the spirit which thus perceives in wholly supernormal fashion may be under the impression that it is perceiving through some bizarre corporeal channel — as the knee or the stomach. I think, therefore, that the perception may not be *optical* sight at all, but rather some generalised telæsthetic perception represented as visual, but *incoherently* so represented; so that it may be referred to the knee instead of the retina. And here again, as at several previous points in my argument, I must refer the reader to what will be said in my chapter on *Possession* by external spirits (Chapter IX.) to illustrate the operation even of the subject's own spirit acting without external aid.

[1] Professor Fontan's experiments described in the *Revue Philosophique*, August 1887, cannot lightly be set aside. An account of his experiments is given in *Proceedings* S.P.R vol. ii. p. 263–268. [549 D]. See also the works of Pététin, Durand, Foissac, and Despine, especially *Observations de Médecine Pratique*, pp. 45, 62, and *Etude Scientifique sur Somnambulisme*, p. 167.

And now I come to the third main type of the dynamogenic efficacy of suggestion: its influence, namely, on *attention*, on *will*, and on *character* — character, indeed, being largely a resultant of the direction and persistence of voluntary attention.

It will be remembered that for convenience' sake I have discussed the dynamogenic effect of suggestion first upon the external senses, then upon the internal sensibility, — the mind's eye, the mind's ear, and the imagination generally; — and now I am turning to similar effects exercised upon that central power which reasons upon the ideas and images which external and internal senses supply, which chooses between them, and which reacts according to its choice. These are "highest-level centres," which I began by saying that the hypnotist could rarely hope to reach; — since those spontaneous somnambulisms which the hypnotic trance imitates and develops do so seldom reach them. We have, however, already found a good deal of intelligence of a certain kind in hypnotic phenomena; what we do here is to pass from one stage to another and higher stage of consciousness of intelligent action.

To explain this statement, let us dwell for a moment upon the degree of intelligence which is sometimes displayed in those modifications of the organism which suggestion effects. Take, for instance, the formation of a cruciform blister, as recorded by Dr. Biggs, of Lima.[1] In this experiment the hypnotised subject was told that a red cross would appear on her chest every Friday during a period of four months. For the carrying out of this suggestion an unusual combination of capacities was needed; — the capacity of directing physiological changes in a new way, and also, and combined therewith, the capacity of recognising and imitating an abstract, arbitrary, non-physiological idea, such as that of *cruciformity*.

All this, in my view, is the expression of *subliminal* control over the organism — more potent and profound than *supraliminal*, and exercised neither blindly nor wisely, but with intelligent caprice.

Bearing this in mind as we go on to suggestions more directly affecting central faculty, in which *highest-level* centres begin to be involved, we need not be surprised to find an intermediate stage in which high faculties are used in obedience to suggestion, for purely capricious ends.

I speak of *calculations* subliminally performed in the carrying out of post-hypnotic suggestions.

These suggestions *à échéance* — commands, given in the trance, to do something under certain contingent circumstances, or after a certain time has elapsed — form a very convenient mode of testing the amount

[1] See *Journal* S.P.R., vol. iii. p. 100 [543 B].

of mentation which can be started and carried out without the intervention of the supraliminal consciousness. Experiments have been made
in this direction by three men especially who have in recent times done
some of the best work on the psychological side of hypnotism, namely,
Edmund Gurney, Delbœuf, and Milne Bramwell.

Dr. Milne Bramwell's experiments[1] (to mention these as a sample of
the rest) were post-hypnotic suggestions involving arithmetical calculations; the entranced subject, for instance, being told to make a cross when
20,180 minutes had elapsed from the moment of the order. Their primary
importance lay in showing that a subliminal or hypnotic memory persisted across the intervening gulf of time, — days and nights of ordinary
life, — and prompted obedience to the order when at last it fell due. But
incidentally, as I say, it became clear that the subject, whose arithmetical
capacity in common life was small, worked out these sums subliminally
a good deal better than she could work them out by her normal waking
intelligence.

Of course, all that was needed for such simple calculations was close
attention to easy rules; but this was just what the waking mind was unable
to give, at least without the help of pencil and paper. If we lay this long
and careful experiment side by side with the accounts already given of
the solution of problems in somnambulic states, it seems clear that there
is yet much to be done in the education of subliminal memory and acumen
as a help to supraliminal work.

Important in this connection is Dr. Dufay's account of help given to
an actress in the representation of her *rôles* by hypnotisation.[2] It seems
obvious that stage-fright is just the kind of nervous annoyance from which
hypnotisation should give relief. Somewhat similarly I believe some
persons can secure a cheap substitute for genius on stage or platform,
evoking by suggestion or self-suggestion a helpful subliminal uprush.
Here again, the hypnotisation is a kind of extension of "secondary automatism," — of the familiar lapse from ordinary consciousness of movements (walking, pianoforte-playing, etc.), which have been very frequently
performed. The possibilities thus opened up are very great: no less than
the combination by mankind of the stability of instinct with the plasticity
of reason. There seems no reason why man's range of automatism should
not thus be largely increased in two main ways: many things now unpleasant
to do might be done with indifference, and many things now difficult to
do might be done with ease.

[1] See *Proceedings* S.P.R., vol. xii. pp. 176–203 [551 C].
[2] *Revue Philosophique*, September 1888 [552 A].

And now let us pass on from these specialised influences of suggestion on certain kinds of attention to its influence on attention generally, as needed, for instance, in education. If we can arrest the shifting of the mental focus to undesired ideational centres in at all the same way as we can arrest the choreic or fidgetty shiftings of motor impulse to undesired motor centres, we shall have done perhaps as much for the world's ordinary work as if we had raised the average man's actual intelligence a step higher in the scale. We shall have checked waste, although we may not have improved quality. The well-known case of Dr. Forel's warders,[1] who were enabled by hypnotic suggestion to sleep soundly by the side of the patients they had to watch, and wake only when the patients required to be restrained, shows us how by this means the attention may be concentrated on selected impressions and waste of energy be avoided in a way that could hardly be compassed by any ordinary exercise of the will.

How far, indeed, we can go in actually *heightening* intelligence by suggestion we have yet to learn. We must not expect to add a cubit to intellectual any more than to physical stature. Limitations at birth must prevent our developing the common man into a Newton; but there seems no reason why we should not bring up his practical achievements much nearer than at present to the maximum of his innate capacity.[2]

In passing on from the influence of suggestion on *attention* to its influence on *will*, I am not meaning to draw any but the most every-day distinction between these two forms of inward concentration. The point, in fact, which I wish now to notice is rather a matter of common observation than a provable and measurable phenomenon. I speak of the energy and resolution with which a hypnotic suggestion is carried out; — the *ferocity*, even, with which the entranced subject pushes aside the opposition of much more powerful men. I do not, indeed, assert that he would thus risk very serious injury; for I believe (with Bramwell and others) that there does exist somewhere within him a knowledge that the whole proceeding is a mere experiment. But, nevertheless, he actually risks something; he behaves, in short, as a confident, resolute man would behave, and this however timid and unaggressive his habitual character may be. I believe that much advantage may yet be drawn from this confident temper. We can thus inhibit the acquired self-distrust and shyness of the supraliminal self, and get the subliminal self concentrated upon some

[1] *Revue de l'Hypnotisme*, vol. vi. p. 357 [553 A].

[2] For illustrative instances see *Brain*, Summer Number 1900, p. 207, *Revue de l'Hypnotisme*, January 1889, and Bérillon, *De la suggestion et de ses applications à la pédagogie* (1887) [553 B]. See also Bérillon, *La Psychologie du Courage et l'Éducation du Caractère*. Paris 1905.

task which may be as difficult as we please; — which may, if we can adjust it rightly, draw out to the uttermost the innate powers of man.

It has been supposed that the mere fact of being hypnotised tended to weaken the will; that the hypnotised person fell inevitably more and more under the control of the hypnotiser, and even that he could at last be induced to commit crimes by suggestion. In his article "What is Hypnotism?"[1] Dr. Milne Bramwell shows on how small a foundation of fact these fanciful theories have been erected. It may suffice to say here that nothing is easier, either for subject or for hypnotiser, than to *avert* undue influence. A trusted friend has only to suggest to the hypnotised subject that *no one else* will be able to affect him, and the thing is done. As to the crimes supposed to be committed by hypnotised persons under the influence of suggestion, the evidence for such crimes, in spite of great efforts made to collect it and set it forth, remains, I think, practically *nil*.

This fact, I must add, is quite in harmony with the views expressed in the present chapter. For it implies that the higher subliminal centres (so to term them) never really abdicate their rule; that they may indeed remain passive while the middle centres obey the experimenter's caprice, but are still ready to resume their control if such experiment should become really dangerous to the individual. And this runs parallel with common experience in the spontaneous somnambulisms. The sleeper may perform apparently rash exploits; but yet, unless he be suddenly awakened, serious accidents are very rare. Nevertheless, both in spontaneous and in induced somnambulism, accidents *may* occur; nor should any experiment be undertaken in a careless or jesting spirit.

But the rôle of the hypnotiser, as our command over hypnotic artifice increases, is likely to become continually smaller in proportion to the rôle played by the subject himself. Especially must this be so where the object is to strengthen the subject's own power of will. All that can be done from *without* in such a case is to imbue the man's spirit with the sense of its unexhausted prerogatives, — the strength which he may then employ, not only to avert pain or anxiety, but in any active direction which his original nature itself admits.

These last words may naturally lead us on to our next topic: the influence of suggestion on *character*, — on that function of combined attention and will, which is, of course, also ultimately a function of the possibilities latent in the individual germ.

First of all, then, and going back to the evidence already given as to

[1] *Proceedings* S.P.R., vol. xii. pp. 204–58 [555 B]. See also his book on *Hypnotism*, pp. 425–32.

the cure of the victims of morphia, we may say with truth that *there* we have seen as tremendous a moral *lift* — as sudden an elevation from utter baseness to at least normal living — as can be anywhere presented to us.

Here, then, the question arises as to the possible range of such sudden reformations. Did we succeed with the morphinomaniac only because his was a *functional*, and not an *organic*, degradation?

And may it not be a much harder task to create honesty, purity, unselfishness in a brain whose very conformation must keep the spirit that thinks through it nearly on the level of the brute? The question is of the highest psychological interest; the answer, though as yet rudimentary, is unexpectedly encouraging. The examples given in Appendix V. B show that if the subject is hypnotisable, and if hypnotic suggestion be applied with sufficient persistency and skill, no depth of previous baseness and foulness need prevent the man or woman whom we charge with "moral insanity," or stamp as a "criminal-born," from rising into a state where he or she can work steadily, and render services useful to the community.[1]

I purposely limit my assertion to these words. We must still work within the bounds of natural capacity. Just as we cannot improvise a genius, we cannot improvise a saint. But what experience seems to show is that we can *select* from the lowest and poorest range of feelings and faculties enough of sound feeling, enough of helpful faculty, to keep the man in a position of moral stability, and capable of falling in with the common labours of his kind.

And here we approach a point of much interest. Hypnotic suggestion or self-suggestion is not an agency which stands wholly alone. It melts into the suasion of ordinary life. Ministers of religion as well as physicians have always wielded with authority the suasive power. From the crude animistic dances and ceremonies of the savage up to the "missions" and "revivals" in English and American churches and chapels, we find sudden and exciting impressions on mind and sense called into play for the purpose of producing religious and moral change.[2] Among the lower races especially these exciting reunions often involve both hysterical and hypnotic phenomena. There are sometimes convulsive accesses and there is sometimes the milder phenomenon of a deep restorative sleep. The influence exerted upon the convert is intermediate between hypnotic

[1] See also the *Revue de l'Hypnotisme*, January 1889, September 1890, November 1886, November 1888, for cases reported by Liébeault, Bérillon, Bernheim, and Voisin.
[2] See Mr. Fryer's paper on "The Welsh Revival of 1904-5," in *Proceedings* S.P.R., vol. xix. p. 80.

artifice, dependent on trance-states for access to subliminal plasticity, and ordinary moral suasion, addressed primarily to ordinary waking reason.

Let us pause here to consider the point which we have already reached. We began by defining hypnotism as the empirical development of the sleeping phase of man's personality. In that sleeping phase the most conspicuous element—the most obvious function of the subliminal self—is the repair of wasted tissues, the physical, and therefore also largely the moral, refreshment and rejuvenation of the tired organism.

But we found reason to believe that the subliminal self has other functions to fulfil during sleep. Those other functions are concerned in some unknown way with the spiritual world; and the indication of their exercise is given by the sporadic occurrence, in the sleeping phase, of supernormal phenomena. Such phenomena, as we shall presently see, occur also at various points in hypnotic practice. To them we must now turn, if our account of the phenomena of induced somnambulism is to be complete.

Yet here, in order to give completeness to our intended review, we shall need a certain apparent extension of the scope of this chapter. We shall need to consider a group of cases which might have been introduced at various points in our scheme, but which are perhaps richest in their illustrations of the supernormal phenomena of hypnotism.

Spontaneous somnambulisms,—those crude uprushes of incoherent subliminal faculty which sometimes break through the surface of sleep,—seem to occupy a kind of midway position among the various phenomena through which our inquiry has thus far carried us.

The somnambulism often *starts* as an exaggerated dream; it *develops* into a kind of secondary personality. The thoughts and impulses which the upheaval raises into manifestations — the psychical output — resemble sometimes the inspirations of genius, sometimes the follies of hysteria. And, finally, the spontaneous sleep-waking state itself is manifestly akin to hypnosis, — is sometimes actually interchangeable with the induced somnambulisms of the hypnotic trance. The *chain of memory* which repeated spontaneous somnambulisms gradually form, — while lying quite outside the primary or waking memory, — will often be found to form a part of the *hypnotic* memory, which gradually accretes in similar fashion from repeated hypnosis.

For one form of sleep-waking capacity we are already prepared by what has been said in Chapter IV. of the solution of problems in sleep. This is one of the ways in which we can watch the gradual merging of a vivid dream into a definite somnambulic act. The solution of a problem (as we have seen) may present itself merely as a sentence or a diagram, constructed in dream and remembered on waking. Or the sleeper (as in various cases familiar in text-books) may rise from bed and *write out* the chain of reasoning, or the sermon, or whatever it may be. Or again, in rarer cases the somnambulic output may take the form of oratory, and edifying discourses may be delivered by a preacher whom no amount of shaking or pinching will silence or, generally, even interrupt. This, so to speak, is genius with a vengeance; this is a too persistent uprush of sub-liminal zeal, co-operating even out of season with the hortatory instincts of the waking self.

The group of sleep-waking cases which we may next discuss illustrates a natural evolution of the faculty of the sleeping phase of personality. The subliminal self, exercising in sleep a profounder *influence* over the organism than the supraliminal can exert, may also be presumed to possess a profounder *knowledge* of the organism — of its present, and therefore of its future — than the supraliminal self enjoys.

There are cases[1] in which the somnambulic personality is discerned throughout as a wiser self — advising a treatment, or at least foreseeing future developments of the disease with great particularity. Of course, in such a case prediction is often simply a form of suggestion; the symptom occurs simply because it has been ordained beforehand. In the case of cures of long-standing disease the sagacity which foresees probably co-operates with the control which directs the changes in the organism.

The next stage is a very important one. We come to the manifesta-tion in spontaneous sleep-waking states of manifestly supernormal powers, — sometimes of telepathy, but more commonly of clairvoyance or telæs-thesia. Unfortunately, these cases have been, as a rule, very insufficiently observed. Still, it appears that in spontaneous somnambulism there is frequently some indication of supernormal powers, though the observers — even if competent in other ways — have generally neglected to take account of the hyperæsthesia and heightening of memory and of general intelligence that often accompany the state.

Before leaving this subject of spontaneous sleep-waking states I ought briefly to mention a form of trance with which we shall have to deal more at length in a later chapter. I speak of trance ascribed to *spirit-possession*. As will be seen, I myself fully adopt this explanation in a small number

---

[1] See Puységur, *Recherches sur l'Homme dans le Somnambulisme* (Paris, 1811); Pététin, *Electricité Animale* (Paris, 1808); Despine, *Observations de Médecine Pra-tique* (1838), and *Journal* S.P.R., vol. ix. p. 333.

of the cases where it is put forward. Yet I do not think that spirit-agency is necessarily present in all the trances even of a true subject of possession. With all the leading sensitives — with D. D. Home, with Stainton Moses, with Mrs. Piper and with others — I think that the depth of the trance has varied greatly on different occasions, and that sometimes the subliminal self of the sensitive is vaguely simulating, probably in an unconscious dream-like way, an external intelligence. This hypothesis suggested itself to several observers in the case especially of D. D. Home, with whom the moments of strong characterisation of a departed personality, though far from rare, were yet scattered among tracts of dreamy improvisation which suggested only the utterance of Home's subliminal self. However we choose to interpret these trances, they should be mentioned in comparison with all the other sleep-waking states. They probably form the best transition between those shallow somnambulisms, on the one hand, which are little more than a vivid dream, and those profound trances, on the other hand, in which the native spirit quits, as nearly as may be, the sensitive's organism, and is for the time replaced, as nearly as may be, by an invading spirit from that unseen world.

This brief review of non-hypnotic somnambulisms has not been without its lessons. It has shown us that the supernormal powers which we have traced in each of the preceding chapters in turn do also show themselves, in much the same fashion, in spontaneous sleep-waking states of various types. We must now inquire how far they occur in sleep-waking states experimentally induced.

And here the very fact of *induction* suggests to us a question specially applicable to the hypnotic state itself. Is hypnosis ever supernormally induced? Can any one, that is to say, be thrown into hypnotic trance by a telepathic impact? or, to phrase it more generally, by any influence, inexplicable by existing science, which may pass from man to man?

In the first place one may say that of the anti-mesmeric schools of opinion, the "purely physiological" school has on the whole failed, the "purely suggestive" school has triumphantly succeeded. The school of Nancy, reinforced by hypnotists all over Europe, has abundantly proved that "pure suggestion" (whatever that be) is the determining cause of a very large proportion of hypnotic phenomena. That is beyond dispute; and the two other schools, the "pure physiologists" and the "mesmerists" alike, must now manage to prove as best they can that their favourite methods play any real part in the induction of any case of hypnosis. For to the pure suggestionist, monotonous stimulation and mesmeric passes are alike in themselves inert, are alike mere facilitations of suggestion, acting not directly on the patient's organism, but rather on his state of mental expectation.

I reply that there is absolutely no need to go as far as this. In admitting suggestion as a *vera causa* of hypnosis, we are recognising a cause which, if we really try to grasp it, resolves itself into *subliminal operation, brought about we know not how.* So far, therefore, from negativing and excluding any obscure and perhaps supernormal agency, the suggestion theory leaves the way for any such agency broadly open. Some unknown cause or other must determine whether each suggestion is to "take" or no; and that unknown cause must presumably act somehow upon the subliminal self. We should have something like a real explanation of suggestion, if we could show that a suggestion's success or failure was linked with some telepathic impact from the suggester's mind, or with some mesmeric effluence from his person.

I know well that in many cases we can establish no link of this kind. In Bernheim's rapid hospital practice there seems no opportunity to bring the hypnotist's will, or the hypnotiser's organism, into any effective *rapport* with the subject. Rather, the subject seems to do all that is wanted for himself almost instantaneously. He often falls into the suggested slumber almost before the word "*Dormez!*" has left the physician's mouth. But on the other hand, this is by no means the only type of hypnotic success. Just as in the mesmeric days, so also now there are continual instances where much more than the mere command has been needed for effective hypnotisation. Persistence, proximity, passes — all these prove needful still in the practice even of physicians who place no faith at all in the old mesmeric theory.

The fact is, that since the days of those old controversies between mesmerists proper and hypnotists proper, the conditions of the controversy have greatly changed. The supposed mesmeric effluence was then treated as an entirely isolated, yet an entirely physiological phenomenon. There was supposed to be a kind of radiation or infection passing from one nervous system to another. It was of this that Cuvier (for instance) was convinced; it was this theory which Elliotson defended in the *Zoist* with a wealth of illustration and argument to which little justice has even yet been done. Yet it was hard to prove *effluence* as opposed to *suggestion*, because where there was proximity enough for effluence to be effective there was also proximity enough for suggestion to be possible. Only in some few circumstances, — such as Esdaile's mesmerisation of a blind

man over a wall,[1] — was it possible to claim that the mesmeric trance had
been induced without any suspicion whatever on the subject's part that
the mesmerist was trying to entrance him.

Since those days, however, the evidence for *telepathy* — for psychical
influence from a distance — has grown to goodly proportions. A new
form of experiment has been found possible, from which the influence
of suggestion can be entirely excluded. It has now, as I shall presently
try to show, been actually proved that the hypnotic trance can be induced
from a distance so great, and with precautions so complete, that telepathy
or some similar supernormal influence is the only efficient cause which can
be conceived.

I subjoin one of a series of experiments in this "telepathic hypnotism."
(See Appendix V. C.) These experiments are not easy to manage, since
it is essential at once to prevent the subject from suspecting that the experiment is being tried, and also to provide for his safety in the event of its
success. In Dr. Gibert's experiment, for instance, it was a responsible
matter to bring this elderly woman in her dream-like state through the
streets of Havre. It was needful to provide her with an unnoticed escort;
and, in fact, several persons had to devote themselves for some hours to
a single experiment.

I have cited first this experiment at a distance, without attempting
to analyse the nature of the suggestion given or power employed by the
hypnotist. Of course it is plain that if one can thus influence unexpectant
persons from a distance there must be sometimes some kind of power
actually exercised by the hypnotiser; — something beyond the mere tact
and impressiveness of address, which is all that Bernheim and his followers
admit or claim. Evidence of this has been afforded by the occasional
production of organic and other effects in hypnotised subjects by the
unuttered will of the operator when near them. The ingenious experiments of Gurney[2] in the production of local rigidity and anæsthesia were
undertaken to test whether the agency employed were more in the nature
of an effort of will or, — as the early mesmerists claimed, — of an emission
of actual "mesmeric fluid" or physical effluence of some sort. Gurney
was inclined to think that his results could not be explained solely by
mental suggestion or telepathy, because the physical proximity of the
operator's hand seemed necessary to produce them, and he thought it
probable that they were due to a direct nervous influence, exercised through

---

[1] *Natural and Mesmeric Clairvoyance*, pp. 227–28; quoted in *Phantasms of the Living*, vol. i. p. 88.

[2] See *Proceedings* S.P.R., vol. v. (1888), pp. 14–17. [569 A.]

the hand of the operator, but not perceptible through the ordinary sensory channels. Mrs. Sidgwick's experiments [1] of the same kind, however, in which success was obtained when the operator was standing with folded arms several feet away from the subject, removed Gurney's main objection to the telepathic explanation. The fact that a thick sheet of glass over the subject's hands did not interfere with the results also afforded some presumption against the hypothesis of a physical influence; and Mrs. Sidgwick pointed out that the delicate discrimination involved in the specific limitations of the effects is much more easily attributable to mental suggestion, through the action of the operator's mind on that of the subject, than to any direct physical influence on the latter's nerves.

It is, however, in my view, by no means improbable that effluences, as yet unknown to science, but perceptible by sensitive persons as the telepathic impulse is perceptible, should radiate from living human organisms. I see no reason to assume that the varied and concordant statements made by patients in the *Zoist* and early mesmeric works merely reflect subjective fancies. I have myself performed and witnessed experiments on intelligent persons expressly designed to test whether or no the sensation following the hand was a mere fancy. It seems to me hardly likely that persons who have never experienced other purely subjective sensations, and who are expressly alive to the question here at issue, should nevertheless again and again feel the classical tingling, etc., along the track of the hypnotiser's passes without any real external cause. To assume that all which they feel is a mere result of suggestion, may be a premature attempt at simplifying modes of supernormal communication which, in fact, are probably not simpler but more complex than any idea which we have as yet formed of them.

And here at last we arrive at what is in reality the most interesting group of inquiries connected with the hypnotic trance.

We have just seen that the subliminal state of the hypnotised subject may be approached by ways subtler than mere verbal suggestion — by telepathic impacts and perhaps by some effluence of kindred supernormal type. We have now to trace the supernormal elements in the hypnotic *response*. Whether those elements are most readily excited by a directly subliminal appeal, or whether they depend mainly on the special powers innate in the hypnotised person, we can as yet but imperfectly guess. We can be pretty sure, at any rate, that they are not often evoked in answer to any rapid and, so to say, perfunctory hypnotic suggestion; they do not spring up in miscellaneous hospital practice; they need an education and

[1] See *Proceedings* S.P.R., vol. viii. pp. 536-596. [569 B.]

a development which is hardly bestowed on one hypnotised subject in a hundred. The first stage of this response lies in a subliminal relation established between the subject and his hypnotiser, and manifesting itself in what is called *rapport*, or in *community of sensation*. The earlier stages of *rapport* — conditions when the subject apparently hears or feels the hypnotiser only, and so forth — arise probably from mere self-suggestion or from the suggestions of the operator, causing the conscious attention of the subject to be exclusively directed to him. Indications of the possible development of a real link between the two persons may rather be found in the cases where there is provable community of sensation, — the hypnotised subject tasting or feeling what the hypnotiser (unknown to the subject) does actually at that moment taste or feel.

We have thus brought the hypnotised subject up to the point of knowing supernormally, at any rate, the superficial sensations of his hypnotiser. From that starting-point, — or, at any rate, from some supernormal perception of narrow range, — his cognition widens and deepens. He may seem to discern some picture of the past, and may retrace the history of some object which he holds in his hand, or he may seem to wander in spirit over the habitable globe, and to bring back knowledge of present facts discernible by no other means. Perhaps he seems to behold the future, predicting oftenest the organic history of some person near him; but sometimes discerning, as it were pictorially, scattered events to which we can guess at no attainable clue. For all this there is already more of positive evidence than is generally realised; nor (I must repeat) is there any *negative* evidence which might lead us to doubt that further care in developing hypnotic subjects may not at any moment be rewarded in the same way. We have here, in fact, a successful branch of investigation which has of late years been practically dropped from mere inattention to what has been done already, — mere diversion of effort to the easier and more practical triumphs of suggestive therapeutics.[1]

The next group of cases to which I pass relate chiefly to knowledge of present facts. I may first refer to some experiments in thought-transference with hypnotised persons[2] analogous to the experiments with persons in a normal condition recorded in my next chapter. Here the subject

---

[1] Beginning with cases partly retrocognitive, the reader is referred to *Proceedings* S.P.R., vol. vii. pp. 30–99; *Zoist*, vol. vii. pp. 95–101 [572 A and B].

[2] The longest and most important series of experiments in thought-transference with hypnotised subjects, carried out by members of the S.P.R., are those of Professor and Mrs. Sidgwick. *Proceedings* S.P.R., vol. vi. pp. 128–70; and vol. viii. pp. 536–96 [573 A].

seems simply to become aware telepathically of the thoughts of his hypnotiser, the hypnotic condition - perhaps facilitating the transfer of the impression. Next come the cases of what used to be called "travelling clairvoyance" in the hypnotic state. These are more like the partially retrocognitive cases in that they cannot be traced with certainty to the contemporary thoughts of any particular person. In travelling clairvoyance we seem to have a development of "invasive dreams," — of those visions of the night in which the sleeper seems to visit distant scenes and to bring back intelligence otherwise unattainable. These distant hypnotic visions seem to develop out of thought-transference; thus the subject may discern an imaginary picture as it is conceived in the hypnotiser's mind. Thence he may pass on and discern a true contemporaneous scene,[1] unknown to any one present, and in some few cases there is an element of apparent prevision in the impression.[2]

Our survey of that important, though inchoate, appeal to the subliminal self which passes under the name of hypnotism is now nearly as complete — in its brief sketchy form — as the present state of knowledge permits.

I have attempted to trace the inevitable *rise* of hypnotism — its necessary development out of the spontaneous phenomena which preceded and which might so naturally have suggested it. I have shown, nevertheless, its almost accidental initiation, and then its rapid development in ways which no single experimenter has ever been able to correlate or to foresee. I am bound to say something further as to its prospect in the future. A systematic appeal to the deeper powers in man — conceived with the generality with which I have here conceived it — cannot remain a mere appanage of medical practice. It must be fitted on in some way to the whole serious life of man; it must present itself to him as a development of faiths and instincts which lie already deep in his heart. In other words, there must needs be some *scheme of self-suggestion,* — some general theory which can give the individual a basis for his appeal, whether he regards that appeal as directed to an intelligence outside himself or to his own inherent faculties and informing soul. These helps to the power of generalisation — to the feeling of confidence — we must consider now.

The schemes of self-suggestion which have actually been found effective have covered, not unnaturally, a range as wide as all the superstition and

---

[1] *Proceedings* S.P.R., vol. vii. pp. 199-220; Dr. Fahnestock's *Statuvolism*, pp. 117-35, 221-32 [573 B, C and D].

[2] *Zoist*, vol. xii. pp. 149-52 [573 F].

all the religion of men. That is to say that each form of supernatural belief in turn has been utilised as a means of securing that urgently-needed temporal blessing — relief from physical pain. We see the same tendency running through fetichistic, polytheistic, monotheistic forms of belief. Beginning with fetichistic peoples, we observe that *charms* of various kinds, — inert objects, arbitrary gestures, meaningless words, — have probably been actually the most general means which our race has employed for the cure of disease. We know how long some forms of primitive belief persisted in medicine, — as, for example, the doctrine of *likenesses*, or the cure of a disease by some object supposed to resemble its leading symptom. What is, however, even more remarkable is the efficacy which charms still continue in some cases to possess, even when they are worn merely as an experiment in self-suggestion by a person who is perfectly well aware of their intrinsic futility. Experiments on this subject seem to show that the mere continual contact of some small unfamiliar object will often act as a reminder to the subliminal self, and keep, at any rate, some nervous disturbances in check. Until one reads these modern examples, one can hardly realise how veritably potent for good may have been the savage amulet, the savage incantation.

The transition from fetichistic to polytheistic conceptions of cure is, of course, a gradual one. It may be said to begin when curative properties are ascribed to objects not arbitrarily, nor on account of the *look* of the objects themselves, but on account of their having been blessed or handled by some divine or semi-divine personage, or having formed part of his body or surroundings during some incarnation. Thus Lourdes water, bottled and exported, is still held to possess curative virtue on account of the Virgin's original blessing bestowed upon the Lourdes spring. But generally the influence of the divine or divinised being is more directly exercised, as in oracles, dreams, invisible touches, or actual *theophanies*, or appearances of the gods to the adoring patient. It will be seen as we proceed how amply the tradition of Lourdes has incorporated these ancient aids to faith.

But at this point our modern experience suggests to us a remarkable interpolation in the antique chain of ideas. It is now alleged that departed persons need not exert influence through their dead bones alone, nor yet only by their supposed intermediacy with higher powers. There intervenes, in fact, the whole topic of *spirit-healing*, — which cannot, however, be treated fully here.

Next in the ascending scale from polytheism to monotheism we come to the "Miracles of Lourdes," to which I have just alluded, where the supposed healer is the Virgin Mary, reverenced as semi-divine. This form of belief, however, retains (as has been said) some affinity with fetichism, since the actual *water* from the Lourdes spring, supposed to have been blessed by the Virgin, is an important factor in the cures.[1]

Much further removed from primitive belief is the appeal made by Christian scientists to the aid of Jesus Christ; — either as directly answering prayer, or as enabling the worshippers to comprehend the infinite love on which the universe is based, and in face of which pain and sickness become a vain imagination or even a sheer nonentity. To the readers of this chapter, however, there will be nothing surprising in my own inclination to include all these efforts at health under the general category of schemes of self-suggestion.

In my view they are but crude attempts at a practical realisation of the essential truth that it is possible by a right disposition of our own minds to draw energy from an environing world of spiritual life.

It seems, at least, that no real explanation of hypnotic vitalisation can, in fact, be given except upon the general theory supported in this work — the theory that a world of spiritual life exists, an environment profounder than those environments of matter and ether which in a sense we know. Let us look at this hypothesis a little more closely. When we say that an organism exists in a certain environment, we mean that its energy, or some part thereof, forms an element in a certain system of cosmic forces, which represents some special modification of the ultimate energy. The life of the organism consists in its power of interchanging energy with its environment, — of appropriating by its own action some fragment of that pre-existent and limitless Power. We human beings exist in the first place in a world of matter, whence we draw the obvious sustenance of our bodily functions.

We exist also in a world of ether; — that is to say, we are constructed to respond to a system of laws, — ultimately continuous, no doubt, with the laws of matter, but affording a new, a generalised, a profounder conception of the Cosmos. So widely different, indeed, is this new aspect of things from the old, that it is common to speak of the ether as a newly-known environment. On this environment our organic existence depends as absolutely as on the material environment, although less obviously. In ways which we cannot fathom, the ether is at the foundation of our physical being. Perceiving heat, light, electricity, we do but recognise in certain conspicuous ways, — as in perceiving the "X rays" we recognise

[1] See "Mind-Cure, Faith-Cure, and the Miracles of Lourdes," by A. T. Myers, M.D., F.R.C.P., and F. W. H. Myers, *Proceedings* S.P.R., vol. ix. pp. 160-210.

in a way less conspicuous, — the pervading influence of etherial vibrations which in range and variety far transcend our capacity of response.

Within, beyond, the world of ether, — as a still profounder, still more generalised aspect of the Cosmos, — must lie, as I believe, the world of spiritual life. That the world of spiritual life does not depend upon the existence of the material world I hold as now proved by actual evidence. That it is in some way continuous with the world of ether I can well suppose. But for our minds there must needs be a "critical point" in any such imagined continuity; so that the world where life and thought are carried on apart from matter, must certainly rank again as a new, a *metetherial* environment. In giving it this name I expressly imply only that from our human point of view it lies after or beyond the ether, as metaphysic lies after or beyond physics. I say only that what does not originate in matter or in ether originates *there;* but I well believe that beyond the ether there must be not one stage only, but countless stages in the infinity of things.

On this hypothesis there will be an essential concordance between *all* views — spiritual or materialistic — which ascribe to any direction of attention or will any practical effect upon the human organism. "The prayer of faith shall save the sick," says St. James. "There is nothing in hypnotism but suggestion," says Bernheim. In my clumsier language these two statements (setting aside a possible telepathic element in St. James' words) will be expressible in identical terms. "There will be effective therapeutical or ethical self-suggestion whenever by any artifice subliminal attention to a bodily function or to a moral purpose is carried to some unknown pitch of intensity which draws energy from the metetherial world."

A great practical question remains, to which St. James' words supply a direct, though perhaps an inadequate answer, while Bernheim's words supply no answer at all.

What is this saving faith to be, and how is it to be attained? Can we find any sure way of touching the spring which moves us so potently, at once from without and from within? Can we propose any form of self-suggestion effective for all the human race? any controlling thought on which all alike can fix that long-sought mountain-moving faith?

Assuredly no man can extemporise such a faith as this. Whatever form it may ultimately take, it must begin as the purification, the intensification, of the purest, the intensest beliefs to which human minds have yet attained. It must invoke the whole strength of all philosophies, of all religions; — not indeed the special arguments or evidence adduced for each, which lie outside my present theme, but all the spiritual energy by which in truth they live. And so far as this purpose goes, of drawing strength from the unseen, if one faith is true, all faiths are true; in so far at least as human mind can grasp or human prayer appropriate the unknown metetherial energy, the inscrutable Grace of God.

CHAPTER VI

SENSORY AUTOMATISM

Βλέπομεν γὰρ ἄρτι δι' ἐσόπτρου ἐν αἰνίγματι.

EACH of the several lines of inquiry pursued in the foregoing chapters has brought indications of something transcending sensory experience in the reserves of human faculty; and we have come to a point where we need some further colligating generalisation — some conception under which these scattered phenomena may be gathered in their true kinship.

Some steps at least towards such a generalisation the evidence to be presented in these next chapters may allow us to take. Considering together, under the heading of sensory and motor *automatism*, the whole range of that subliminal action of which we have as yet discussed fragments only, we shall gradually come to see that its distinctive faculty of telepathy or telæsthesia is in fact an introduction into a realm where the limitations of organic life can no longer be assumed to persist. Considering, again, the evidence which shows that that portion of the personality which exercises these powers during our earthly existence does actually continue to exercise them after our bodily decay, *we shall recognise a relation — obscure but indisputable — between the subliminal and the surviving self.*

I begin, then, with my definition of *automatism*, as the widest term under which to include the range of subliminal emergences into ordinary life. The turbulent uprush and downdraught of hysteria; the helpful uprushes of genius, co-operating with supraliminal thought; the profound and recuperative changes which follow on hypnotic suggestion; these have been described under their separate headings. But the main mass of subliminal manifestations remains undescribed. I have dealt little with veridical hallucinations, not at all with automatic writing, nor with the utterances of spontaneous trance. The products of inner vision or inner audition externalised into quasi-percepts, — these form what I term *sensory automatisms*. The messages conveyed by movement of limbs or hand or tongue, initiated by an inner motor impulse beyond the conscious will — these are what I term *motor automatisms*. And I claim that when all these are surveyed together their essential analogy will be recognised beneath much diversity of form. They will be seen to be *messages* from the subliminal to the supraliminal self; endeavours — conscious or unconscious — of submerged tracts of our personality to present to ordinary waking thought fragments of a knowledge which no ordinary waking thought could attain.

I regard supraliminal life merely as a *privileged case* of personality; a special phase of our personality, which is easiest for us to study, because it is simplified for us by our ready consciousness of what is going on in it; yet which is by no means necessarily either central or prepotent, could we see our whole being in comprehensive view.

Now if we thus regard the whole supraliminal personality as a special case of something much more extensive, it follows that we must similarly regard all human faculty, and each sense severally, as mere special or privileged cases of some more general power.

All human terrene faculty will be in this view simply a selection from faculty existing in the metetherial world; such part of that antecedent, even if not individualised, faculty as may be expressible through each several human organism.

Each of our special senses, therefore, may be conceived as straining towards development of a wider kind than earthly experience has as yet allowed. And each special sense is both an internal and an external sense; involves a tract of the brain, of unknown capacity, as well as an end-organ, whose capacity is more nearly measurable. The relation of this internal, mental, mind's-eye vision to non-sensory psychological perception on the one hand, and to ocular vision on the other hand, is exactly one of the points on which some profounder observation will be seen to be necessary. One must at least speak of "mind's eye" perception in these sensory terms, if one is to discuss it at all.

But ordinary experience at any rate assumes that the end-organ alone can acquire fresh information, and that the central tract can but combine this new information already sent in to it. This must plainly be the case, for instance, with optical or acoustic knowledge; — with such knowledge as is borne on waves of ether or of air, and is caught by a terminal apparatus, evolved for the purpose. But observe that it is by no means necessary that all seeing and all hearing should be through eye or ear.

The vision of our dreams — to keep to vision alone for greater simplicity — is non-optical vision. It is usually generated in the central brain, not sent up thither from an excited retina. Optical laws can only by a stretch of terms be said to apply to it at all.

Let us attempt some rough conspectus, which may show something of the relation in which central and peripheral vision stand to each other.

We start from a region below the specialisation of visual faculty. The study of the successive dermal and nervous modifications which have led up to that faculty belongs to Biology, and all that our argument needs here is to point out that the very fact that this faculty has been developed in a germ, animated by metetherial life, indicates that some perceptivity from which sight could take its origin pre-existed in the originating, the unseen world. We know vaguely how vision differentiated itself peripherally, with the growing sensibility of the pigment-spot to light and shadow. But there must have been a cerebral differentiation also, and also a psychological differentiation, namely, a gradual shaping of a distinct feeling from obscure feelings, whose history we cannot recover.

Yet I believe that we have still persistent in our brain-structure some dim vestige of the transition from that early undifferentiated continuous sensitivity to our existing specialisation of sense. Probably in all of us, though in some men much more distinctly than in others, there exist certain *synæsthesiæ* or concomitances of sense-impression, which are at any rate not dependent on any recognisable link of association.[1] My present point is that such synæsthesiæ stand on the dividing line between percepts externally and internally originated. These irradiations of sensitivity,

[1] For a true synæsthetic or "sound-seer,"—to take the commonest form of these central repercussions of sensory shock,—there is a connection between sight and sound which is instinctive, complex, and yet for our intelligence altogether arbitrary.

But sound-seeing is only a conspicuous example of synæsthesiæ which exist in as yet unexplored variety. When we find that there are gradated, peremptory, inexplicable associations connecting sensations of light and colour with sensations of temperature, smell, taste, muscular resistance, etc., we are led to conclude that we are dealing, not with the casual associations of childish experience, but with some reflection or irradiation of specialised sensations which must depend upon the connate structure of the brain itself.

This view is consistent with the results of an *Enquête sur l'audition colorée* recently conducted by Professor Flournoy, from which it appears that of 213 persons presenting these associations only 48 could assign the date of their origin; and is supported by a case described in the *Revue de l'Hypnotisme*, December 1892, p. 185, where a man who had long exhibited a limited form of *audition colorée* developed *gustation colorée* in addition when in a low state of health.

See also the "Report of the International Congress of Experimental Psychology, Second Session, London, 1892," pp. 10-20 (Williams & Norgate, London, 1892), and the *American Journal of Psychology* for April 1900 (vol. xi. pp. 377-404).

sometimes apparently congenital, cannot, on the one hand, be called a purely mental phenomenon. Nor again can they be definitely classed under external vision; since they do sometimes follow upon a mental process of association. It seems safer to term them *entencephalic*, on the analogy of *entoptic*, since they seem to be due to something in brain-structure, much as entoptic percepts are due to something in the structure of the eye.

I will, then, start with the synæsthesiæ as the most generalised form of inward perception, and will pass on to other classes which approach more nearly to ordinary external vision.

From these entencephalic photisms we seem to proceed by an easy transition to the most inward form of unmistakable entoptic vision — which is therefore the most inward form of all external vision — the flash of light consequent on electrisation of the optic nerve. Next on our outward road we may place the phosphenes caused by pressure on the optic nerve or irritation of the retina. Next Purkinje's figures, or shadows cast by the blood-vessels of the middle layer upon the bacillary layer of the retina. Then *muscæ volitantes*, or shadows cast by motes in the vitreous humour upon the fibrous layer of the retina.

Midway, again, between entoptic and ordinary external vision we may place *after-images;* which, although themselves perceptible with shut eyes, presuppose a previous retinal stimulation from without; — forming, in fact, the entoptic sequelæ of ordinary external vision.

Next comes our ordinary vision of the external world — and this, again, is pushed to its highest degree of externality by the employment of artificial aids to sight. He who gazes through a telescope at the stars has mechanically improved his end-organs to the furthest point now possible to man.

And now, standing once more upon our watershed of entencephalic vision, let us trace the advancing capacities of internal vision. The forms of vision now to be considered are virtually independent of the eye; they can persist, that is to say, after the destruction of the eye, if only the eye has worked for a few years, so as to give visual education to the brain. We do not, in fact, fully know the limits of this independence, which can only be learnt by a fuller examination of intelligent blind persons than has yet been made. Nor can we say with certainty how far in a seeing person the eye is in its turn influenced by the brain. I shall avoid postulating any "retropulsive current" from brain to retina, just as I have avoided any expression more specific than "the brain" to indicate the primary seat of sight. The arrangement here presented, as already explained, is a

psychological one, and can be set forth without trespassing on contro-
verted physiological ground.

We may take *memory-images* as the simplest type of internal vision.
These images, as commonly understood, introduce us to no fresh knowledge; they preserve the knowledge gained by conscious gaze upon the
outer world. In their simplest spontaneous form they are the *cerebral*
sequelæ of external vision, just as after-images are its *entoptic* sequelæ.
These two classes of vision have been sometimes confounded, although
the distinction is a marked one. Into the cerebral storage of impressions one element habitually enters which is totally absent from the mere
retinal storage, namely, a psychical element — a rearrangement or
generalisation of the impressions retinally received.

Next we come to a common class of memory-images, in which the
subliminal rearrangement is particularly marked. I speak of *dreams* —
which lead us on in two directions from memory-images; in the direction
of *imagination-images*, and in the direction of *hallucinations*. Certain
individual dreams, indeed, of rare types point also in other directions
which later on we shall have to follow. But dreams *as a class* consist of
confused memory-images, reaching a kind of low hallucinatory intensity,
a glow, so to say, sufficient to be perceptible in darkness.

I will give the name of *imagination-images* to those conscious re-
combinations of our store of visual imagery which we compose either for
our mere enjoyment, as "waking dreams," or as artifices to help us to the
better understanding of facts of nature confusedly discerned. Such, for
instance, are imagined geometrical diagrams; and Watt, lying in bed in a
dark room and conceiving the steam-engine, illustrates the utmost limit
to which voluntary internal visualisation can go.

Here at any rate the commonly admitted category of stages of inward
vision will close. Thus far and no farther the brain's capacity for presenting visual images can be pushed on under the guidance of the conscious
will of man. It is now my business to show, on the contrary, that we
have here reached a mere intermediate point in the development of *internal*
vision. These imagination-images, valuable as they are, are merely attempts to control supraliminally a form of vision which — as spontaneous
memory-images have already shown us — is predominantly subliminal.
The memory-images welled up from a just-submerged stratum; we must
now consider what other images also well upward from the same hidden
source.

To begin with, it is by no means certain that some of Watt's images
of steam-engines did not well up from that source, — did not emerge ready-

made into the supraliminal mind while it rested in that merely *expectant* state which forms generally a great part of invention. We have seen in Chapter III. that there is reason to believe in such a conveyance in the much inferior mental processes of calculating boys, etc., and also in the mental processes of the painter. In short, without pretending to judge of the proportion of voluntary to involuntary imagery in each several creative mind, we must undoubtedly rank the spontaneously emergent visual images of genius as a further stage of internal vision.

And now we have reached, by a triple road, the verge of a most important development of inward vision — namely, that vast range of phenomena which we call *hallucination*. Each of our last three classes had led up to hallucination in a different way. *Dreams* actually *are* hallucinations; but they are usually hallucinations of low intensity; and are only rarely capable of maintaining themselves for a few seconds (as hypnopompic illusions) when the dreamer wakes to the stimuli of the material world. *Imagination-images* may be carried to a hallucinatory pitch by good visualisers.[1] And the *inspirations of genius* — Raphael's San Sisto is the classical instance — may present themselves in hallucinatory vividness to the astonished artist.

A hallucination, one may say boldly, is in fact a *hyperæsthesia;* and generally a *central* hyperæsthesia. That is to say, the hallucination is in some cases due indirectly to peripheral stimulation; but often also it is the result of a stimulus to "mind's-eye vision," which sweeps the idea onwards into visual form, regardless of ordinary checks.

Here, then, is a comprehensive and reasonable way of regarding these multifarious hallucinations or sensory automatisms. They are phenomena which must neither be feared nor ignored, but rather controlled and interpreted. Nor will that interpretation be an easy matter. The interpretation of the symbols by which the retina represents the external world has been, whether for the race or for the individual, no short or simple process. Yet ocular vision is in my view a simple, easy, privileged case of vision generally; and the symbols which represent our internal percepts of an immaterial world are likely to be far more complex than any impressions from the material world on the retina.

All inward visions are like symbols abridged from a picture-alphabet. In order to understand any one class of hallucinations we ought to have all classes before us. At the lower limit of the series, indeed, the analysis of the physician should precede that of the psychologist. We already know to some extent, and may hope soon to know more accurately, what

[1] See *Proceedings* S.P.R., vol. viii. p. 480 [610 A].

sensory disturbance corresponds to what nervous lesion.   Yet these violent disturbances of inward perception — the snakes of the drunkard, the scarlet fire of the epileptic, the jeering voices of the paranoiac — these are perhaps of too gross a kind to afford more than a kind of neurological introduction to the subtler points which arise when hallucination is unaccompanied by any observable defect or malady.

It is, indeed, obvious enough that the more idiognomonic the hallucination is, the more isolated from any other disturbance of normality, the greater will be its psychological interest. *An apparently spontaneous modification of central percepts* — what phenomenon could promise to take us deeper into the mystery of the mind?

Yet until quite recently — until, in short, Edmund Gurney took up the inquiry in 1882 — this wide, important subject was treated, even in serious text-books, in a superficial and perfunctory way. Few statistics were collected; hardly anything was really known; rather there was a facile assumption that all hallucinations or sensory automatisms *must* somehow be due to physical malady, even when there was no evidence whatever for such a connection. I must refer my readers to Gurney's résumé in his chapter on "Hallucinations" in *Phantasms of the Living*, if they would realise the gradual confused fashion in which men's minds had been prepared for the wider view soon to be opened, largely by Gurney's own statistical and analytical work. The wide collection of first-hand experiences of sensory automatisms of every kind which he initiated, and which the S.P.R. "Census of Hallucinations" continued after his death, has for the first time made it possible to treat these phenomena with some surety of hand.[1]

The results of these inquiries show that a great number of sensory automatisms occur among sane and healthy persons, and that for many of these we can at present offer no explanation whatever. For some of them, however, we can offer a kind of explanation, or at least an indication of a probable determining cause, whose mode of working remains wholly obscure.

Thus, in some few instances, although there is no disturbance of health, there seems to be a predisposition to the externalisation of figures or sounds. Since this in no way interferes with comfort, we must simply class it as

---

[1] The "Census of Hallucinations" was undertaken in 1889, by a Committee of the S.P.R., under the direction of Professor Sidgwick, and consisting of himself and Mrs. Sidgwick, Dr. A. T. Myers, Mr. F. Podmore, Miss A. Johnson, and the present writer. The full report of the committee was published in 1894. (*Proceedings* S.P.R., vol. x. pp. 25-422.) A summary of the report is given in the original edition. [612 A.]

an idiosyncratic central hyperæsthesia — much like the tendency to extremely vivid dreams, which by no means always implies a poor quality of sleep.

In a few instances, again, we can trace moral predisposing causes — expectation, grief, anxiety.

These causes, however, turn out to be much less often effective than might have been expected from the popular readiness to invoke them. In two ways especially the weakness of this predisposing cause is impressed upon us. In the first place, the bulk of our percipients experience their hallucinations at ordinary unexciting moments; traversing their more anxious crises without any such phenomenon. In the second place, those of our percipients whose hallucination is in fact more or less coincident with some distressing external event, seldom seem to have been predisposed to the hallucination by a knowledge of the event. For the event was generally unknown to them when the corresponding hallucination occurred.

This last remark, it will be seen, introduces us to the most interesting and important group of percipients and of percepts; the percipients whose gift constitutes a fresh faculty rather than a degeneration; the percepts which are *veridical* — which are (as we shall see cause to infer) in some way generated by some event outside the percipient's mind, so that their correspondence with that event conveys some new fact, in however obscure a form. It is this group, of course, which gives high importance to the whole inquiry; which makes the study of inward vision no mere curiosity, but rather the opening of an inlet into forms of knowledge to which we can assign no bound.

Now these telepathic hallucinations will introduce us to very varying forms of inward vision. It will be well to begin their study by recalling and somewhat expanding the thesis already advanced: that man's *ocular* vision is but a special or privileged case of visual power, of which power his *inner* vision affords a more extensive example.

Ocular vision is the perception of material objects, in accordance with optical laws, from a definite point in space. Our review of hallucinations has already removed two of these limitations. If I see a hallucinatory figure — and figures seen in *dreams* come under this category — I see something which is not a material object, and I see it in a manner not determined by optical laws. A dream-figure may indeed seem to *conform* to optical laws; but that will be the result of self-suggestion, or of organised memories, and will vary according to the dreamer's visualising power. While a portrait-painter may see a face in dream which he can paint from memory when he wakes, the ordinary man's dream-percept will be vague, shifting, and unrememberable.

Similarly, if I see a subjective hallucinatory figure "out in the room," its aspect is not *determined* by optical laws (it may even seem to stand *behind* the observer, or otherwise *outside* his visual field), but it will more or less *conform* — by my mere self-suggestion, if by nothing else — to optical laws; and, moreover, it will still seem to be seen from a fixed point in space, namely, from the stationary observer's eyes or brain.

All this seems fairly plain, so long as we are admittedly dealing with hallucinatory figures whose origin must be in the percipient's own mind. But so soon as we come to quasi-percepts which we believe to exist or to originate somewhere outside the percipient's mind, our difficulties come thick and fast.

If there be some external origin for our inward vision (which thereby becomes *veridical*) we must not any longer assume that all veridical inward vision starts or is exercised from the same point. If it gets hold of *facts* (veridical impressions or pictures, not mere subjective fancies), we cannot be sure *a priori* whether it somehow goes to find the facts, or the facts come to find it. Again, we cannot any longer take for granted that it will be cognisant only of phantasmal or immaterial percepts. If it can get at phantasmal percepts outside the organism, may it not get at *material* percepts also? May it not see distant houses, as well as the images of distant souls?

Hazardous as these speculations may seem, they nevertheless represent an attempt to get our notions of supersensory things as near down to our notions of sensory things as we fairly can. Whatever may be our ultimate conception of an ideal world, we must not for the present attempt to start from any standpoint too far removed from the temporal and spatial existence which alone we know.

As telepathy is a conception intermediate between the apparent isolation of minds here communicating only as a rule through material organs, and the ultimate conception of the unity of all mind, so the conception which I am about to propose, of a recognition of space without our concomitant subjection to laws of matter, is strictly intermediate between man's incarnate condition and the condition which we may imagine him ultimately to attain. We cannot possibly infer *a priori* that all recognition of space must needs disappear with the disappearance of the particular bodily sensations by means of which our conception of space has been developed. But we can imagine that a spirit should be essentially *independent* of space, and yet capable of recognising it.

Provisionally admitting this view, let us consider what range we are now led to assign to inner vision, when it is no longer merely subjective but veridical; bringing news to the percipient of actual fact outside his own organism.

We infer that it may represent to us (1) material objects; or (2) symbols of immaterial things; (3) in ways not necessarily accordant with optical laws; and (4) from a point of view not necessarily located within the organism, by means of what I have called a *psychical excursion*. I will take an illustration from a case which is recorded in detail in *Proceedings* S.P.R., vol. vii. p. 41 [666 C].

A Mrs. Wilmot has a vision of her husband in a cabin in a distant steamer. Besides her husband, she sees in the cabin a stranger (who was in fact present there), with certain material details. Now here I should say that Mrs. Wilmot's inner vision discerned material objects, from a point of view outside her own organism. But, on the other hand, although the perception came to her in visual terms, I do not suppose that it was really *optical*, that it came through the eye.

Mrs. Wilmot might believe, say, that her husband's head concealed from her some part of the berth in which he lay; but this would not mean a real optical concealment, but only a special direction of her attention, guided by preconceived notions of what would be optically visible from a given point.

As we proceed further we shall see, I think, in many ways how needful is this *excursive* theory to explain *many* telepathic and *all* telæsthetic experiences; *many*, I mean, of the cases where two minds are in communication, and *all* the cases where the percipient learns material facts (as words in a closed book, etc.) with which no other known mind is concerned.

Another most important corollary of this excursive theory must just be mentioned here. If there be spiritual excursion to a particular point of space, it is conceivable that this should involve not only the migrant spirit's perception *from* that point, but also perception of that point by persons materially present near it. That point may become a *phantasmogenetic centre*, as well as a centre of outlook. In plain words, if A has spiritually invaded B's room, and there sees B, B on his part may see A symbolically standing there; and C and D if present may see A as well.

This hint, here thrown out as an additional argument for the excursive theory, will fall to be developed later on. For the present we must confine our attention to our immediate subject: the range of man's inner vision, and the means which he must take to understand, to foster, and to control it.

The first and simplest step in the control of inner vision is the repression by hypnotic suggestion of degenerative hallucinations. It is a noteworthy fact that such of these as are at all curable are much more often curable by hypnotism than in any other way.

The next step is one to which, as the reader of my chapter on hypnotism already knows, I attribute an importance much greater than is generally accorded to it. I refer to the hypnotiser's power not only of controlling but of *inducing* hallucinations in his subject.

As I have already said, the evocation of hallucinations is commonly spoken of as a mere example of the subject's *obedience* to the hypnotiser. "I tell my subject to raise his arm, and he raises it; I tell him to see a tiger in the room, and he sees one accordingly." But manifestly these two incidents are not on the same level, and only appear to be so through a certain laxity of language. The usage of speech allows me to say, "I will make my subject lift his arm," although I am of course unable to affect the motor centres in his brain which start that motion. But it is so easy for a man to lift his arm that my speech takes that familiar power for granted, and notes only his readiness to lift it when I tell him — the hypnotic complaisance which prompts him to obey me if I suggest this trivial action. But when I say, "I will make him see a tiger," I take for granted a power on his part which is *not* familiar, which I have no longer a right to assume. For under ordinary circumstances my subject simply *cannot* see a tiger at will; nor can I affect the visual centres which might enable him to do so. All that I can ask him to do, therefore, is to choose this particular way of indicating that in his hypnotic condition he has become able to stimulate his central sensory tracts more powerfully than ever before.

And not only this. His hallucinations are in most cases elaborate products — complex images which must have needed intelligence to fashion them — although the process of their fashioning is hidden from our view. In this respect they resemble the inspirations of genius. For here we find again just what we found in those inspirations — the uprush of a complex intellectual product, performed beneath the threshold, and projected ready-made into ordinary consciousness. The uprushing stream of intelligence, indeed, in the man of genius flowed habitually in conformity with the superficial stream. Only rarely does the great conception intrude itself upon him with such vigour and such untimeliness as to bring confusion and incoherence into his ordinary life. But in the case of these induced hallucinations the incongruity between the two streams of intelligence is much more marked. When a subject, for instance, is trying to keep down some post-hypnotic hallucinatory suggestion, one can watch the smooth surface of the supraliminal river disturbed by that suggestion as though by jets of steam from below, which sometimes merely break in bubbles, but sometimes force themselves up bodily through the superficial film.

It is by considering hallucinations in this generalised manner and among these analogies, that we can best realise their absence of necessary connection with any bodily degeneration or disease. Often, of course, they accompany disease; but that is only to say that the central sensory tracts, like any other part of the organism, are capable of morbid as well as of healthful stimulus. Taken in itself, the mere fact of the quasi-externalisation of a centrally initiated image indicates strong central stimulation, and absolutely nothing more. There is no physiological law whatever which can tell us what degree of vividness our central pictures may assume consistently with health — short of the point where they get to be so indistinguishable from external preceptions that, as in madness, they interfere with the rational conduct of life. That point no well-attested case of veridical hallucinations, so far as my knowledge goes, has yet approached.

It was, of course, natural that in the study of these phantasms, as elsewhere, the therapeutic interest should have preceded the psychological, but in the newer practical study of *eugenics* — the study which aims at improving the human organism, instead of merely conserving it — experimental psychology is indispensable, and one branch of this is the experimental study of mental visions.

Let us consider whether, apart from such a rare and startling incident as an actual hallucination, there is any previous indication of a habit of receiving, or a power of summoning, pictures from a subliminal storehouse? Any self-suggestion, conscious or unconscious, which places before the supraliminal intelligence visual images apparently matured elsewhere?

Such indications have not been wanting. In the chapter on Genius, and in the chapter on Sleep, we have traced the existence of many classes of these pictures; all of them ready, as it would seem, to manifest themselves on slight inducement. *Dream-figures* will rise in any momentary blur of consciousness; *inspirations* will respond to the concentrated desire or the mere passing emotion of the man of genius; *after-images* will recur, under unknown conditions, long after the original stimulus has been withdrawn; *memory-images* will surge up into our minds with even unwished-for vividness; the brilliant exactness of *illusions hypnagogiques* will astonish us in the revealing transition from waking to sleep.

All is prepared, so to say, for some empirical short-cut to a fuller control of these subjacent pictures; just as before Mesmer and Puységur all was prepared for an empirical short-cut to trance, somnambulism, suggestibility.

All that we want is to hit on some simple empirical way of bringing out the correlation between all these types of sub acent vision, just as mesmerism was a simple empirical way of bringing out the correlation between various trances and sleep-waking states.

Crystal-vision, then, like hypnotic trance, might have been gradually evolved by a series of reasoned experiments, along an unexceptionable scientific road.

In reality, of course, this prehistoric practice must have been reached in some quite different way. It does not fall within the scope of this book to trace the various streams of divination which converge into Dr. Dee's magic, and "the attracting of spirits into the ball." But it is really to the Elizabethan Dr. Dee — one of the leading *savants* of his time — that the credit must be given of the first systematic attempt to describe, analyse, and utilise these externalised pictures.[1]

I will describe briefly the general type of the experiment, and we shall see how near we can get to a psychological explanation.

Let the observer gaze, steadily but not fatiguingly, into some speculum, or clear depth, so arranged as to return as little reflection as possible. A good example of what is meant will be a glass ball enveloped in a black shawl, or placed in the back part of a half-opened drawer; so arranged, in short, that the observer can gaze into it with as little distraction as may be from the reflection of his own face or of surrounding objects. After he has tried (say) three or four times, for ten minutes or so at a time — preferably in solitude, and in a state of mental passivity — he will perhaps begin to see the glass ball or crystal *clouding*, or to see some figure or picture apparently *in* the ball. Perhaps one man or woman in twenty will have some slight occasional experience of this kind; and perhaps one in twenty of these seers (the percentages must as yet be mainly guess-work) will be able by practice to develop this faculty of inward vision up to a point where it will sometimes convey to him information not attainable by ordinary means.

How comes it, in the first place, that he sees any figure in the crystal at all? Common hypnotic experiments supply two obvious answers, each of which no doubt explains some part of the phenomena.

[1] For prehistoric and historic crystal-gazing see Mr. Andrew Lang's *Making of Religion*, and Miss Goodrich-Freer's "Recent Experiments in Crystal-Vision," *Proceedings* S.P.R., vol. v. p. 486 [620 A].

In the first place, we know that the hypnotic trance is often induced by gazing at some small bright object. This may or may not be a mere effect of suggestion; but it certainly sometimes occurs, and the "scryer" consequently may be partially hypnotised, and in a state which facilitates hallucinations.

In the second place, a hypnotised subject — hypnotised but in a fully alert state — can often be caused by suggestion to see (say) a portrait upon a blank card; and will continue to see that portrait on that card, after the card has been shuffled with others; thus showing that he discerns with unusual acuteness such *points de repère*, or little guiding marks, as may exist on the surface of even an apparently blank card.

Correspondently with the *first* of these observations, we find that crystal-vision is sometimes accompanied by a state of partial hypnotisation, perhaps merging into trance. This has been the case with various French hysterical subjects; and not only with them but with that exceptionally sound and vigorous observer, Mr. J. G. Keulemans. His evidence (in *Proceedings* S.P.R., vol. viii. pp. 516–521) is just what one would have expected *a priori* on such a matter.

Correspondently with the *second* of the above observations, we find that *points de repère* do occasionally seem to determine crystal visions.

This, again, has been noticed among the French hysterical subjects; and not only with them, but with another among our best observers, Mrs. Verrall.

These things being so — both these causes being apparently operative along the whole series of "scryers," or crystal-gazers, from the most unstable to the most scientific — one might be tempted to assume that these two clues, if we could follow them far enough, would explain the whole group of phenomena. Persons who have not *seen* the phenomena, indeed, can hardly be persuaded to the contrary. But the real fact is, as even those who have seen much less of crystal-gazing than I have will very well know, that these explanations cannot be stretched to cover a quarter — perhaps not even a tenth — of the phenomena which actually occur.

Judging both from the testimony of scryers themselves, and from the observations of Dr. Hodgson and others (myself included), who have had many opportunities of watching them, it is very seldom that the gaze into the glass ball induces any hypnotic symptoms whatever. It does not induce such symptoms with successful scryers any more than with unsuccessful. Furthermore, there is no proof that the gift of crystal-vision goes along with hypnotic sensibility. The most that one can say is that the gift often goes along with *telepathic* sensibility; but although telepathic sensibility may sometimes be quickened by hypnotism, we have no proof that those two forms of sensitiveness habitually go together.

The ordinary attitude of the scryer, I repeat, is one of complete detachment; an interested and often puzzled scrutiny and analysis of the figures which display themselves in swift or slow succession in the crystal ball.

This last sentence applies to the theory of *points de repère* as well. As a general rule, the crystal vision, however meaningless and fantastic, is a thing which changes and develops somewhat as a dream does; following, it may be, some trivial chain of associations, but not maintaining, any more than a dream maintains, any continuous scheme of line or colour. At the most, the scraps of reflection in the crystal could only *start* such a series of pictures as this. And the start, the initiation of one of these series, is often accompanied by an odd phenomenon mentioned above — a *milky clouding* of the crystal, which obscures any fragments of reflected images, and from out of which the images of the vision gradually grow clear. I cannot explain this clouding. It occurs too often and too independently to be a mere effect of suggestion. It does not seem to depend on any optical condition — to be, for instance, a result of change of focus of the eye, or of prolonged gazing. It is a picture like other pictures; it may come when the eyes are quite fresh (nor ought they ever to be strained); and it may persist for some time, so that the scryer looks away and back again, and sees it still. It comes at the beginning of a first series of pictures, or as a kind of drop scene between one series of pictures and another. Its closest parallel, perhaps, is the mist or cloud out of which phantasmal figures, "out in the room," sometimes seem to form themselves.

Moreover, the connection, if one can so call it, between the crystal and the vision is a very variable one. Sometimes the figures seem clearly defined within the crystal and limited thereby; sometimes all perception of the crystal or other speculum disappears, and the scryer seems clairvoyantly introduced into some group of life-sized figures. Nay, further, when the habit of gazing is fully acquired, some scryers can dispense with any speculum whatever, and can see pictures in mere blackness; thus approximating to the seers of "faces in the dark," or of *illusions hypnagogiques*.

On the whole it seems safest to attempt at present no further explanation of crystal-gazing than to say that it is an empirical method of developing internal vision; of externalising pictures which are associated with changes in the sensorial tracts of the brain, due partly to internal stimuli, and partly to stimuli which may come from minds external to the scryer's own. The hallucinations thus induced appear to be absolutely harmless.

I at least know of no kind of injury resulting from them; and I have probably heard of most of the experiments made in England, with any scientific aim or care, during the somewhat limited revival of crystal-gazing which has proceeded for the last few years.

The crystal picture is what we must call (for want of knowledge of determining causes) a *random* glimpse into inner vision, a reflection caught at some odd angle from the universe as it shines through the perturbing medium of that special soul. Normal and supernormal knowledge and imaginings are blended in strangely mingled rays. Memory, dream, telepathy, telæsthesia, retrocognition, precognition, all are there. Nay, there are indications of spiritual communications and of a kind of ecstasy.[1]

We cannot pursue all these phenomena at once. In turning, as we must now turn, to the *spontaneous* cases of sensory automatism — of every type of which the *induced* visions of the crystal afford us a foretaste — we must needs single out first some fundamental phenomenon, illustrating some principle from which the rarer or more complex phenomena may be in part at least derived. Nor will there be difficulty in such a choice. Theory and actual experience point here in the same direction. If this inward vision, this inward audition, on whose importance I have been insisting, are to have any such importance — if they are to have any validity at all — if their contents are to represent anything more than dream or meditation — they must receive knowledge from other minds or from distant objects; — knowledge which is *not* received by the external organs of sense. Communication must exist from the subliminal to the subliminal as well as from the supraliminal to the supraliminal parts of the being of different individual men. Telepathy, in short, must be the prerequisite of all these supernormal phenomena.

Actual experience, as we shall presently see, confirms this view of the place of telepathy. For when we pass from the induced to the spontaneous phenomena we shall find that these illustrate before all else this transmission of thought and emotion directly from mind to mind.

Now as to telepathy, there is in the first place this to be said, that such a faculty must absolutely exist somewhere in the universe, if the universe contains any unembodied intelligences at all. If there be any life less rooted in flesh than ours — any life more spiritual (as men have supposed that a higher life would be), then either it must not be *social* life — there can be no exchange of thought in it at all — or else there must exist some

---

[1] It is right also to state, although I cannot here discuss the problems involved, that I believe these visions to be sometimes seen by more than one person, simultaneously or successively.

method of exchanging thought which does not depend upon either tongue or brain.

Thus much, one may say, has been evident since man first speculated on such subjects at all. But the advance of knowledge has added a new presumption — it can be no more than a presumption — to all such cosmic speculations. I mean the presumption of *continuity*. Learning how close a tie in reality unites man with inferior lives, — once treated as something wholly alien, impassably separated from the human race — we are led to conceive that a close tie may unite him also with superior lives, — that the series may be fundamentally unbroken, the essential qualities of life the same throughout. It used to be asked whether man was akin to the ape or to the angel. I reply that the very fact of his kinship with the ape is proof presumptive of his kinship with the angel.

It is natural enough that man's instinctive feeling should have anticipated any argument of this speculative type. Men have in most ages believed, and do still widely believe, in the reality of prayer; that is, in the possibility of telepathic communication between our human minds and minds above our own, which are supposed not only to understand our wish or aspiration, but to impress or influence us inwardly in return.

So widely spread has been this belief in prayer that it is somewhat strange that men should not have more commonly made what seems the natural deduction — namely, that if our spirits can communicate with higher spirits in a way transcending sense, they may also perhaps be able in like manner to communicate with each other. The idea, indeed, has been thrown out at intervals by leading thinkers — from Augustine to Bacon, from Bacon to Goethe, from Goethe to Tennyson.

Isolated experiments from time to time indicated its practical truth. Yet it is only within the last few years that the vague and floating notion has been developed into definite theory by systematic experiment.

To make such experiment possible has indeed been no easy matter. It has been needful to elicit and to isolate from the complex emotions and interactions of common life a certain psychical element of whose nature and working we have beforehand but a very obscure idea.

If indeed we possessed any certain method of detecting the action of telepathy, — of distinguishing it from chance coincidence or from unconscious suggestion, — we should probably find that its action was widely diffused and mingled with other more commonplace causes in many incidents of life. We should find telepathy, perhaps, at the base of many sympathies and antipathies, of many wide communities of feeling; operating, it may be, in cases as different as the quasi-recognition of some

friend in a stranger seen at a distance just before the friend himself
unexpectedly appears, and the *Phêmê* or Rumour which in Hindostan
or in ancient Greece is said to have often spread far an inexplicable
knowledge of victory or disaster.

But we are obliged, for the sake of clearness of evidence, to set aside,
when dealing with experimentation, all these mixed emotional cases, and
to start from telepathic communications intentionally planned to be so
trivial, so devoid of associations or emotions, that it shall be impossible
to refer them to any common memory or sympathy; to anything save a
direct transmission of idea, or impulse, or sensation, or image, from one
to another mind.

The reader who has studied the evidence originally set forth in Chapters II. and III. of *Phantasms of the Living* will, I trust, carry away a
pretty clear notion of what can at present actually be done in the way of
experimental transferences of small definite ideas or pictures from one or
more persons — the "agent" or "agents" — to one or more persons —
the "percipient" or "percipients."[1] In these experiments actual *contact*
has been forbidden, to avoid the risk of unconscious indications by pressure.
It is at present still doubtful how far close proximity really operates in aid
of telepathy, or how far its advantage is a mere effect of self-suggestion —
on the part either of agent or of percipient. Some few pairs of experi-
menters have obtained results of just the same type at distances of half
a mile or more.[2] Similarly, in the case of induction of hypnotic trance,
Dr. Gibert attained at the distance of nearly a mile results which are usually
supposed to require close and actual presence. [See Appendix V. C.]

We must clearly realise that in telepathic experiment we encounter
just the same difficulty which makes our results in hypnotic therapeutics

[1] See also *Proceedings* S.P.R., vol. i. pp. 263-283; vol. ii. pp. 1-5, 24-42, 189-200;
vol. iii. pp. 424-452, where a full record will be found of Mr. Malcolm Guthrie's experiments [630 B]. Also *Proceedings* S.P.R., vol. xi. pp. 2-17 [630 C], for Mr. Henry G.
Rawson's experiments. Others are recorded in the *Proceedings* S.P.R., vol. i. pp.
161-167 and 174-215. See also those of Herr Max Dessoir (*Proceedings* S.P.R., vol. iv.
p. 111, and vol. v. p. 355); Herr Anton Schmoll and M. Etienne Mabire (*ibid.* vol. iv. p.
324 and vol. v. p. 169); Mr. J. W. Smith (*ibid.* vol. ii. p. 207); Sir Oliver Lodge (*ibid.* vol.
vii. p. 374); Dr. A. Blair Thaw (*ibid.* vol. viii. p. 422); Dr. von Schrenck-Notzing (*ibid.*
vol. vii. p. 3); Professor Richet (*ibid.* vol. v. p. 18). See also *Phantasms of the Living*,
vol. i. pp. 32-34, and vol. ii. pp. 653-654. Also the experiments of Professor and
Mrs. Sidgwick (*Proceedings*, vol. vi. and vol. viii.) already referred to in Chapter V.

[2] See Mr. F. Podmore's *Apparitions and Thought-transference*, Chapter V. [630
D, etc.]; also *Proceedings* S.P.R., vol. xi. p. 455 [630 F]; and *Journal* S.P.R., vol. vii.
pp. 325-329 [630 E]; *ibid.* pp. 234-237, pp. 299-306 and pp. 311-319; and vol.
xii. p. 223 (March 1906).

so unpredictable and irregular.   We do not know how to get our suggestions to *take hold* of the subliminal self.   They are liable to fail for two
main reasons.   Either they somehow never *reach* the subliminal centres
which we wish to affect, or they find those centres preoccupied with some
self-suggestion hostile to our behest.   This source of uncertainty can only
be removed by a far greater number of experiments than have yet been
made — experiments repeated until we have oftener struck upon the happy
veins which make up for an immense amount of sterile exploration.   Meantime we must record, but can hardly interpret.   Yet there is one provisional interpretation of telepathic experiment which must be noticed thus
early in our discussion, because, if true, it may conceivably connect our
groping work with more advanced departments of science, while, if seen
to be inadequate, it may bid us turn our inquiry in some other direction.
I refer to the suggestion that telepathy is propagated by "brain-waves";
or, as Sir W. Crookes has more exactly expressed it, by ether-waves of
even smaller amplitude and greater frequency than those which carry the
X rays.   These waves are conceived as passing from one brain to another,
and arousing in the *second* brain an excitation or image similar to the
excitation or image from which they start in the *first*.   The hypothesis
is an attractive one; because it fits an agency which certainly exists, but
whose effect is unknown, to an effect which certainly exists, but whose
agency is unknown.

In this world of vibrations it may seem at first the simplest plan to
invoke a vibration the more.   It would be rash, indeed, to affirm that any
phenomenon perceptible by men may not be expressible, in part at least,
in terms of ethereal undulations.   But in the case of telepathy the analogy
which suggests this explanation, the obvious likeness between the picture
emitted (so to say) by the agent and the picture received by the percipient
— as when I fix my mind on the two of diamonds, and he sees a mental
picture of that card — goes but a very short way.   One has very soon
to begin assuming that the percipient's mind *modifies* the picture despatched
from the agent: until the likeness between the two pictures becomes a
quite symbolical affair.   We have seen that there is a continuous transition from experimental to spontaneous telepathy; from our transferred
pictures of cards to monitions of a friend's death at a distance.   These
monitions may indeed be pictures of the dying friend, but they are seldom
such pictures as the decedent's brain seems likely to project in the form in
which they reach the percipient.   Mr. L.— to take a well-known case
in our collection (*Phantasms of the Living*, vol. i. p. 210) — dies of heart
disease when in the act of lying down undressed, in bed.   At or about

the same moment Mr. N. J. S. sees Mr. L. standing beside him with a cheerful air, dressed for walking and with a cane in his hand. One does not see how a system of undulations could have transmuted the physical facts in this way.

A still greater difficulty for the vibration-theory is presented by *collective* telepathic hallucinations. It is hard to understand how A can emit a pattern of vibrations which, radiating equally in all directions, shall affect not only his distant friend B, but also the strangers C and D, who happen to be standing near B ; — and affect no other persons, so far as we know, in the world.

The above points have been fair matter of argument almost since our research began. But as our evidence has developed, our conception of telepathy has needed to be more and more generalised in other and new directions, — still less compatible with the vibration theory. Three such directions may be briefly specified here — namely, the relation of telepathy (*a*) to telæsthesia or clairvoyance, (*b*) to time, and (*c*) to disembodied spirits. (*a*) It is increasingly hard to refer all the scenes of which percipients become aware to the action of any given mind which is perceiving those distant scenes. This is especially noticeable in crystal-gazing experiments. (*b*) And these crystal visions also show what, from the strict telepathic point of view, we should call a great laxity of time relations. The scryer chooses his own time to look in the ball; — and though sometimes he sees events which are taking place at the moment, he may also see past events, — and even, as it seems, future events. I at least cannot deny *precognition*, nor can I draw a definite line amid these complex visions which may separate precognition from telepathy (see *Proceedings* S.P.R., vol. xi. pp. 408–593). (*c*) Precognition itself may be explained, if you will, as telepathy from disembodied spirits; — and this would at any rate bring it under a class of phenomena which I think all students of our subject must before long admit. Admitting here, for argument's sake, that we do receive communications from the dead which we should term telepathic if we received them from the living, it is of course open to us to conjecture that these messages also are conveyed on ether-waves. But since those waves do not at any rate emanate from material brains, we shall by this time have got so far from the original brain-wave hypothesis that few will care still to defend it.

I doubt, indeed, whether we can safely say of telepathy anything more definite than this: *Life has the power of manifesting itself to life.* The laws of life, as we have thus far known them, have been only laws of life when already associated with matter. Thus limited, we have learnt little

as to Life's true nature. We know not even whether Life be only a directive Force, or, on the other hand, an effective Energy. We know not in
what way it operates on matter. We can in no way define the connection
between our own consciousness and our organisms. Just here it is, I
should say, that telepathic observations ought to supply us with some
hint. From the mode in which some element of one individual life, —
apart from material impact, — gets hold of another organism, we may
in time learn something of the way in which our own life gets hold of our
own organism, — and maintains, intermits, or abandons its organic sway.[1]

The hypothesis which I suggested in *Phantasms of the Living* itself,
in my "Note on a possible mode of psychical interaction," seems to me
to have been rendered increasingly plausible by evidence of many kinds
since received; evidence of which the larger part falls outside the limits
of this present work. I still believe — and more confidently than in 1886
— that a "psychical invasion" does take place; that a "phantasmogenetic
centre" is actually established in the percipient's surroundings; that some
movement bearing some relation to space as we know it is actually accomplished; and some presence is transferred, and may or may not be discerned by the invaded person; some perception of the distant scene in
itself is acquired, and may or may not be remembered by the invader.

But the words which I am here beginning to use carry with them associations from which the scientific reader may well shrink. Fully realising
the offence which such expressions may give, I see no better line of excuse
than simply to recount the way in which the gradual accretion of evidence
has obliged me, for the mere sake of covering all the phenomena, to use
phrases and assumptions which go far beyond those which Edmund
Gurney and I employed in our first papers on this inquiry in 1883.

When in 1882 our small group began the collection of evidence bearing
upon "veridical hallucinations" — or apparitions which coincided with
other events in such a way as to suggest a causal connection — we found
scattered among the cases from the first certain types which were with
difficulty reducible under the conception of telepathy pure and simple —
even if such a conception could be distinctly formed. Sometimes the apparition was seen by more than one percipient at once — a result which
we could hardly have expected if all that had passed were the transference
of an impression from the agent's mind to another mind, which then bodied

[1] It is plain that on this view there is no theoretical reason for limiting telepathy to
human beings. For aught we can say, the impulse may pass between man and the
lower animals, or between the lower animals themselves. See *Journal* S.P.R., vol. xi.
pp. 278–290 and pp. 323–4; the same, vol. xii. pp. 21–3; the same, vol. iv. p. 289;
and *Proceedings* S.P.R., vol. xiv. p. 285.

forth that impression in externalised shape according to laws of its own structure. There were instances, too, where the percipient seemed to be the agent also — in so far that it was he who had an impression of having somehow visited and noted a distant scene, whose occupant was not necessarily conscious of any immediate relation with him. Or sometimes this "telepathic clairvoyance" developed into "reciprocity," and each of the two persons concerned was conscious of the other; — the *scene* of their encounter being the same in the vision of each, or at least the experience being in some way common to both. These and cognate difficulties were present to my mind from the first; and in the above-mentioned "Note on a suggested mode of psychical interaction," included in vol. ii. of *Phantasms of the Living*, I indicated briefly the extension of the telepathic theory to which they seemed to me to point.

Meantime cases of certain other definite types continued to come steadily to hand, although in lesser numbers than the cases of apparition at death. To mention two important types only — there were apparitions of the so-called *dead*, and there were cases of *precognition*. With regard to each of these classes, it seemed reasonable to defer belief until time should have shown whether the influx of first-hand cases was likely to be permanent; whether independent witnesses continued to testify to incidents which could be better explained on these hypotheses than on any other. Before Edmund Gurney's death in 1888 our cases of apparitions and other manifestations of the dead had reached a degree of weight and consistency which, as his last paper showed, was beginning to convince him of their veridical character; and since that date these have been much further increased; and especially have drawn from Mrs. Piper's and other trance-phenomena an unexpected enlargement and corroboration. The evidence for communication from the departed is now in my personal estimate quite as strong as that for telepathic communication between the living; and it is moreover evidence which inevitably alters and widens our conception of telepathy between living men.

The evidence for precognition, again, was from the first scantier, and has advanced at a slower rate. It has increased steadily enough to lead me to feel confident that it will have to be seriously reckoned with; but I cannot yet say — as I do say with reference to the evidence for messages from the departed — that almost every one who accepts our evidence for telepathy at all, must ultimately accept this evidence also. It must run on at any rate for some years longer before it shall have accreted a convincing weight.

But at whatever point one or another inquirer may happen at present to stand, I urge that this is the reasonable course for conviction to follow. First analyse the miscellaneous stream of evidence into definite types; then observe the frequency with which these types recur, and let your sense of their importance gradually grow, if the evidence grows also.

Now this mode of procedure evidently excludes all definite *a priori* views, and compels one's conceptions to be little more than the mere grouping to which the facts thus far known have to be subjected in order that they may be realised in their *ensemble*.

"What definite reason do I know why this should *not* be true?" — this is the question which needs to be pushed home again and again if one is to realise — and not in the ordinary paths of scientific speculation alone — how profound our ignorance of the Universe really is.

My own ignorance, at any rate, I recognise to be such that my notions of the probable or improbable in the Universe are not of weight enough to lead me to set aside any facts which seem to me well attested, and which are not shown by experts actually to conflict with any better-established facts or generalisations. Wide though the range of established science may be, it represents, as its most far-sighted prophets are the first to admit, a narrow glance only into the unknown and infinite realm of law.

The evidence, then, leading me thus unresisting along, has led me to this main difference from our early treatment of veridical phantasms. Instead of starting from a root-conception of a telepathic impulse merely passing from mind to mind, I now start from a root-conception of the dissociability of the self, of the possibility that different fractions of the personality can act so far independently of each other that the one is not conscious of the other's action.

Naturally the two conceptions coincide over much of the ground. Where experimental thought-transference is concerned — even where the commoner types of coincidental phantasms are concerned — the second formula seems a needless and unprovable variation on the first. But as soon as we get among the difficult types — reciprocal cases, clairvoyant cases, collective cases, above all, manifestations of the dead — we find that the conception of a telepathic impulse as a message despatched and then left alone, as it were, to effect its purpose needs more and more of straining, of manipulation, to fit it to the evidence. On the other hand, it is just in those difficult regions that the analogies of other splits of personality recur, and that phantasmal or automatic behaviour recalls to us the behaviour of segments of personality detached from primary personality, but operating through the organism which is common to both.

The innovation which we are here called upon to make is to suppose that segments of the personality can operate in apparent separation from the organism. Such a supposition, of course, could not have been started without proof of telepathy, and could with difficulty be sustained without proof of survival of death. But, given telepathy, we have *some* psychical agency connected with man operating apart from his organism. Given survival, we have an element of his personality — to say the least of it — operating when his organism is destroyed. There is therefore no very great additional burden in supposing that an element of his personality may operate apart from his organism, while that organism still exists.

Ce n'est que le premier pas qui coûte. If we have once got a man's *thought* operating apart from his body — if my fixation of attention on the two of diamonds does somehow so modify another man's brain a few yards off that he seems to see the two of diamonds floating before him — there is no obvious halting-place on *his* side till we come to "possession" by a departed spirit, and there is no obvious halting-place on *my* side till we come to "travelling clairvoyance," with a corresponding visibility of my own phantasm to other persons in the scenes which I spiritually visit. No obvious halting-place, I say; for the point which at first seems abruptly transitional has been already shown to be only the critical point of a continuous curve. I mean, of course, the point where consciousness is duplicated — where each segment of the personality begins to possess a separate and definite, but contemporaneous stream of memory and perception. That these can exist concurrently in the same organism our study of hypnotism has already shown, and our study of motor automatisms will still further prove to us.

Dissociation of personality, combined with activity in the metetherial environment; such, in the phraseology used in this book, will be the formula which will most easily cover those actually observed facts of veridical apparition on which we must now enter at considerable length. And after this preliminary explanation I shall ask leave to use for clearness in my argument such words as are simplest and shortest, however vague or disputable their connotation may be. I must needs, for instance, use the word "spirit," when I speak of that unknown fraction of a man's personality — not the supraliminal fraction — which we discern as operating before or after death in the metetherial environment. For this conception I can find no other term, but by the word *spirit* I wish to imply nothing more definite than this. Of the spirit's relation to space, or (which is a part of the same problem) to its own spatial manifestation in definite form, something has already been said, and there will be more to say hereafter. And similarly those terms, *invader* or *invaded*, from whose strangeness and barbarity our immediate discussion began, will depend for their meaning upon conceptions which the evidence itself must gradually supply.

That evidence, as it now lies before us, is perplexingly various both in content and quality. For some of the canons needed in its analysis I have already referred the reader to extracts from Edmund Gurney's writings. Certain points must still be mentioned here before the narrative begins.

It must be remembered, in the first place, that all these veridical or coincidental cases stand out together as a single group from a background of hallucinations which involve no coincidence, which have no claim to veridicality. If purely subjective hallucinations of the senses affected insane or disordered brains alone, — as was pretty generally the assumption, even in scientific circles, when our inquiry began, — our task would have been much easier than it is. But while there can be no question as to the sound and healthy condition of the great majority of our percipients, Edmund Gurney's "Census of Hallucinations" of 1884, confirmed and extended by the wider inquiry of 1889-1892, showed a frequency, previously unsuspected, of scattered hallucinations among sane and healthy persons, the experience being often unique in a lifetime, and in no apparent connection with any other circumstance whatever.[1]

Since casual hallucinations of the sane, then, are thus *frequent*, we can hardly venture to assume that they are all *veridical*. And the existence of all these perhaps merely subjective hallucinations greatly complicates our investigation of veridical hallucinations. It prevents the mere existence of the hallucinations, however strangely interposed in ordinary life, from having any evidential value, and throws us upon evidence afforded by external coincidence; — on the mere fact, to put such a coincidence in its simplest form, that I see a phantom of my friend Smith at the moment when Smith is unexpectedly dying at a distance. A coincidence of this general type, if it occurs, need not be difficult to substantiate, and we have in fact substantiated it with more or less completeness in several hundred cases.

The *primâ facie* conclusion will obviously be that there is a causal connection between the death and the apparition. To overcome this presumption it would be necessary either to impugn the accuracy of the informant's testimony, or to show that chance alone might have brought about the observed coincidences.

On both of these questions there have been full and repeated discussions elsewhere. I need not re-argue them at length here, but will refer

[1] See *Proceedings* S.P.R., vol. x. pp. 25-422.

the reader to the "Report on the Census of Hallucinations," *Proceedings* S.P.R., vol. x., where every source of error as yet discovered has been pretty fully considered.

To that volume also I must refer him for a thorough discussion of the arguments for and against chance-coincidence. The conclusion to which the Committee unanimously came is expressed in the closing words: "Between deaths and apparitions of the dying person a connection exists which is not due to chance alone."

We have a right, I think, to say that only by another census of hallucinations, equally careful, more extensive, and yielding absolutely different results, could this conclusion be overthrown.

In forming this conclusion, apparitions at death are of course selected, because, death being an unique event in man's earthly existence, the coincidences between death and apparitions afford a favourable case for statistical treatment. But the coincidences between apparitions and crises other than death, although not susceptible of the same arithmetical precision of estimate, are, as will be seen, quite equally convincing. To this great mass of spontaneous cases we must now turn.

The arrangement of these cases is not easy; nor are they capable of being presented in one logically consequent series.

But the conception of *psychical invasion or excursion* on which I have already dwelt has at any rate this advantage, that it is sufficiently fundamental to allow of our arrangement of all our recorded cases — perhaps of all possible cases of apparition — in accordance with its own lines.

Our scheme will include all observable telepathic action, from the faint currents which we may imagine to be continually passing between man and man, up to the point — reserved for the following chapter — where one of the parties to the telepathic intercourse has definitely quitted the flesh. The *first* term in our series must be conveniently vague: the *last* must lead us to the threshold of the spiritual world.

I must begin with cases where the action of the excursive fragment of the personality is of the weakest kind — the least capable of affecting other observers, or of being recalled into the agent's own waking memory.

Such cases, naturally enough, will be hard to bring up to evidential level. It must depend on mere chance whether these weak and aimless psychical excursions are observed at all; or are observed in such a way as to lead us to attribute them to anything more than the subjective fancy of the observers.

How can a casual vision — say, of a lady sitting in her drawing-room,

— of a man returning home at six o'clock — be distinguished from memory-images on the one hand and from what I may term "expectation-images" on the other? The picture of the lady may be a slightly modified and externalised reminiscence; the picture of the man walking up to the door may be a mere projection of what the observer was hoping to see.

I have assumed that these phantoms coincided with no marked event. The lady may have been thinking of going to her drawing-room; the man may have been in the act of walking home; — but these are trivial circumstances which might be repeated any day.

Yet, however trivial, almost any set of human circumstances are sufficiently complex to leave room for coincidence. If the sitter in the drawing-room is wearing a distinctive article of dress, never seen by the percipient until it is seen in the hallucination; — if the phantasmal homeward traveller is carrying a parcel of unusual shape, which the real man does afterwards unexpectedly bring home with him; — there may be reason to think that there is a causal connection between the apparent agent's condition at the moment, and the apparition.

In Appendix VI. A, I quote one of these "arrival-cases," so to term them, where the peculiarity of dress was such as to make the coincidence between vision and reality well worth attention. The case is interesting also as one of our earliest examples of a psychical incident carefully recorded at the time; so that after the lapse of nearly forty years it was possible to correct the percipient's surviving recollection by his contemporary written statement.

In these *arrival* cases, there is, I say, a certain likelihood that the man's mind may be fixed on his return home, so that his phantasm is seen in what might seem both to himself and to others the most probable place.[1] But there are other cases where a man's phantasm is seen in a place where there is no special reason for his appearing, although these places seem always to lie within the beat and circuit of his habitual thought.

In such cases there are still possible circumstances which may give reason to think that the apparition is causally connected with the apparent agent. The phantasm of a given person may be seen *repeatedly* by different percipients, or it may be seen *collectively* by several persons at a time; or it may combine both these evidential characteristics, and may be seen several times and by several persons together.

Now considering the rarity of phantasmal appearances, considering that not one person in (say) five thousand is ever phantasmally seen at all; the mere fact that a given person's phantasm is seen even *twice*, by different

[1] See also *Phantasms of the Living* vol. ii. p. 96 [§ 653], and for an auditory case, *ibid.* p. 100 [§ 655].

percipients (for we cannot count a second appearance to the *same* percipient as of equal value), is in itself a remarkable fact; while if this happens
three or four times (as in the case of Mrs. Hawkins)[1] we can hardly ascribe
such a sequence of rare occurrences to chance alone.

Again, impressive as is the *repetition* of the apparition in these cases,
it is yet less so to my mind than the *collective* character of some of the perceptions. In Mrs. Hawkins's first case there were two simultaneous
percipients, and in Canon Bourne's first case (given in Appendix VI. B)
there were three.

And we now come to other cases, where the percipience has been collective, although it has not been repeated. There is a case[2] where two
persons at one moment — a moment of no stress or excitement whatever
— see the phantasm of a third; that third person being perhaps occupied
with some supraliminal or subliminal thought of the scene in the midst
of which she is phantasmally discerned. Both the percipients supposed
at the moment that it was their actual sister whom they saw; and one can
hardly fancy that a mere act of tranquil recognition of the figure by one
percipient would communicate to the other percipient a telepathic shock
such as would make *her* see the same figure as well.

The question of the true import of collectivity of percipience renews
in another form that problem of *invasion* to which our evidence so often
brings us back. When two or three persons see what seems to be the
same phantom in the same place and at the same time, does that mean
that that special part of space is somehow modified? or does it mean that
a mental impression, conveyed by the distant agent — the phantom-
begetter — to one of the percipients is reflected telepathically from that
percipient's mind to the minds of the other — as it were secondary
— percipients? The reader already knows that I prefer the former
of these views. And I observe — as telling against that other view,
of psychical contagion — that in certain collective cases we discern no
probable link between any one of the percipient minds and the distant
agent.

In some of that group of collective cases which we are at this moment
considering, this absence of link is noticeable in a special way. There is
nothing to show that any thought or emotion was passing from agent to
percipients at the moment of the apparition. On the contrary, the

---

[1] *Phantasms of the Living*, vol. ii. p. 78 [§ 645]. See also *op. cit.*, p. 82 *et seq.*

[2] *Proceedings* S.P.R., vol. x. p. 306 [§ 646]. See also the case in *Phantasms of
the Living* (vol. ii. p. 217) [§ 647], where an apparition was seen *by its original* and
by others *at the same time*.

indication is that there is no necessary connection whatever between the agent's condition of mind at the moment and the fact that such and such persons observed his phantasm. The projection of the phantasm, if I may so term it, seems a matter wholly automatic on the agent's part, as automatic and meaningless as a dream.

Assuming, then, that this is so — that these *bilocations* or self-projections to a point apparently remote from one's body do occur without any appreciable stimulus from without, and in moments of apparent calm and indifference — in what way will this fact tend to modify previous conceptions?

It suggests that the continuous dream-life which we must suppose to run concurrently with our waking life is potent enough to effect from time to time enough of dissociation to enable some element of the personality to be perceived at a distance from the organism. How much of consciousness, if any, may be felt at the point where the excursive phantasm is seen, we cannot say. But the notion that a mere incoherent quasi-dream should thus become perceptible to others is fully in accordance with the theories suggested in this work. For I regard subliminal operation as *continuously* going on, and I hold that the degree of dissociation which can generate a perceptible phantasm is not necessarily a profound change, since that perceptibility depends so largely upon idiosyncrasies of agent and percipient as yet wholly unexplained.

That special idiosyncracy on the part of the agent which tends to make his phantasm easily visible has never yet, so far as I know, received a name, although for convenience' sake it certainly needs one. I propose to use the Greek word ψυχορραγῶ, which means strictly "to let the soul break loose," and from which I form the words *psychorrhagy* and *psychorrhagic*, on obvious analogies. When I say that the agents in these cases were born with the *psychorrhagic diathesis*, I express what I believe to be an important fact, physiological as well as psychological, in terms which seem pedantic, but which are the only ones which mean exactly what the facts oblige me to say. That which "breaks loose" on my hypothesis is not (as in the Greek use of the word) the whole principle of life in the organism; rather it is some psychical element probably of very varying character, and definable mainly by its power of producing a phantasm, perceptible by one or more persons, in some portion or other of space. I hold that this phantasmogenetic effect may be produced either on the mind, and consequently on the brain of another person — in which case he may discern the phantasm somewhere in his vicinity, according to his own mental habit or prepossession — or else directly on a portion of space, "out in the open," in which case several persons may simultaneously discern the phantasm in that actual spot.

Let us apply this view to one of our most bizarre and puzzling cases — that of Canon Bourne (see Appendix VI. B). Here I conceive that Canon Bourne, while riding in the hunting-field, was also subliminally dreaming of himself (imagining himself with some part of his submerged consciousness) as having had a fall, and as beckoning to his daughters — an incoherent dream indeed, but of a quite ordinary type. I go on to suppose that, Canon Bourne being born with the psychorrhagic diathesis, a certain psychical element so far detached itself from his organism as to affect a certain portion of space — near the daughters of whom he was thinking — to effect it, I say, not materially nor even optically, but yet in such a manner that to a certain kind of immaterial and non-optical sensitivity a phantasm of himself and his horse became discernible. His horse was of course as purely a part of the phantasmal picture as his hat. The non-optical distinctness with which the words printed inside his hat were seen indicates that it was some inner non-retinal vision which received the impression from the phantasmogenetic centre. The other phantasmal appearance of Canon Bourne chanced to affect only one percipient, but was of precisely the same character; and of course adds, so far as it goes, to the plausibility of the above explanation.

That explanation, indeed, suffers from the complexity and apparent absurdity inevitable in dealing with phenomena which greatly transcend known laws; but on the other hand it does in its way colligate Canon Bourne's case with a good many others of odd and varying types. Thus appearances such as Canon Bourne's are in my view exactly parallel to the *hauntings* ascribed to departed spirits. There also we find a psychorrhagic diathesis — a habit or capacity on the part of certain spirits of detaching some psychical element in such a manner as to form a phantasmal picture, which represents the spirit as going through some dream-like action in a given place.

The phantasmogenetic centre may thus, in my view, be equally well produced by an incarnate or by a discarnate spirit.

Again, my hypothesis of a real modification of a part of space, transforming it into a phantasmogenetic centre, applies to a phantasmal voice just as well as to a phantasmal figure. The voice is not heard acoustically any more than the figure is seen optically. Yet a phantasmal voice may in a true sense "come from" a given spot.

These psychorrhagic cases are, I think, important as showing us the earliest or feeblest stages of self-projection — where the dissociation belongs to the dream-stratum — implicating neither the supraliminal will nor the profounder subliminal strata.

And now let us pass on from these, which hardly concern anybody beyond the phantom-begetter himself — and do not even add anything to his own knowledge — to cases where there is some sort of communication from one mind to another, or some knowledge gained by the excursive spirit.

It is impossible to arrange these groups in one continuous logical series. But, roughly speaking, the degree in which the psychical collision is *recollected* on either side may in some degree indicate its *intensity*, and may serve as a guide to our provisional arrangement.

Following this scheme I shall begin with a group of cases which seem to promise but little information, — cases, namely, where A, the agent, in some way impresses or invades P, the percipient, — but nevertheless neither A nor P retains in supraliminal memory any knowledge of what has occurred.

Now to begin with we shall have no difficulty in admitting that cases of this type are likely often to occur. The psychical *rapprochement* of telepathy takes place, *ex hypothesi*, in a region which is subliminal for both agent and percipient, and from whence but few and scattered impressions rise for either of them above the conscious threshold. Telepathy will thus probably operate far more continuously than our scattered glimpses would in themselves suggest.

But how can we outside inquirers know anything of telepathic incidents which the principals themselves fail altogether to remember?

In ordinary life we may sometimes learn from bystanders incidents which we cannot learn from the principals themselves. Can there be bystanders who look on at a psychical invasion?

The question is of much theoretical import. On my view that there is a real transference of something from the agent, involving an alteration of some kind in a particular part of space, there might theoretically be some bystander who might discern that alteration in space more clearly than the person for whose benefit, so to say, the alteration was made. If, on the other hand, what has happened is merely a transference of some impulse "from mind to mind"; — then one can hardly understand how any mind except the mind aimed at could perceive the telepathic impression. Yet, in *collective* cases, persons in whom the agent feels no interest, nay, of whose presence along with the intended percipient he is not aware, do in fact receive the impression in just the same way as that intended percipient himself. This was explained by Gurney as probably due to a fresh telepathic transmission, — this time from the due or original percipient's mind to the minds of his neighbours of the moment.

Such a supposition, however, in itself a difficult one, becomes much more difficult when the telepathic impulse has never, so far as we know, penetrated into the due or intended percipient's mind at all. If in such a case a bystander perceives the invading figure, I must think that he perceives it merely as a bystander, — not as a person telepathically influenced by the intended percipient, who does not in fact perceive anything whatsoever. I quote in illustration a bizarre but well-attested case (see Appendix VI. C) which this explanation seems to fit better than any other.

In a somewhat similar case[1] there is strong attestation that a sailor, watching by a dying comrade, saw figures around his hammock, apparently representing the dying man's family, in mourning garb. The family, although they had no ordinary knowledge of the sailor's illness, had been alarmed by noises, etc., which rightly or wrongly they took as indications of some danger to him. I conceive, then, that the wife paid a psychical visit to her husband; and I take the mourning garb and the accompanying children's figures to be symbolical accompaniments, representing her thought, "My children will be orphans." I think this more likely than that the sailor's children also should have possessed this rare peculiarity of becoming perceptible at a distant point in space. And secondary figures, as we shall see later on, are not uncommon in such telepathic presentations. One may picture oneself as though holding a child by the hand, or even driving in a carriage and pair, as vividly as though carrying an umbrella or walking across a room; and one may be thus pictured to others.

And here I note a gradual transition to the next large class of cases on which I am about to enter. I am about to deal with *telæsthesia;* — with cases where an agent-percipient — for he is both in one — makes a clairvoyant excursion (of a more serious type than the mere psychorrhagies already described), and brings back some memory of the scene which he has psychically visited. Now, of course, it may happen that he fails to bring back any such memory, or that if he *does* bring it back, he tells no one about it. In such cases, just as in the telepathic cases of which I have just spoken, the excursive phantom may possibly be observed by a bystander, and the circumstances may be such as to involve some coincidence which negatives the supposition of the bystander's mere subjective fancy. Such, I think, is the case which I give in Appendix VI. D.

There is a similar case in *Phantasms of the Living*, vol. ii. p. 541, where

[1] See *Phantasms of the Living*, vol. ii. p. 144 [651 A] and *ibid.* p. 61 [§ 651].

a girl, who is corporeally present in a certain drawing-room, is seen phantasmally in a neighbouring grove, whither she herself presently goes and hangs herself.

Ponderings on projected suicide form perhaps the strongest instance of mental preoccupation with a particular spot. But of course, in our ignorance of the precise quality of thought or emotion needed to prompt a psychical excursion, we need not be surprised to find such an excursion observed on some occasions as trivial as the "arrival-case" of Col. Reed, with which I prefaced the mere psychorrhagic cases.

Again, there is a strange case,[1] which comes to us on good authority, where we must suppose one man's subliminal impulse to have created a picture of himself, his wife, a carriage and a horse, persistent enough to have been watched for some seconds at least by three observers in one place, and by a fourth and independent observer at another point in the moving picture's career. The only alternative, if the narrative be accepted as substantially true, will be the hypothesis before alluded to of the flashing of an impending scene, as in crystal-vision, from some source external to any of the human minds concerned. I need hardly at this point repeat that in my view the wife and the horse will be as purely a part of the man's conception of his own aspect or environment as the coat on his back.

And here, for purposes of comparison, I must refer to one of the most bizarre cases in our collection.[2] Four credible persons, to some extent independently, see a carriage and pair, with two men on the box and an inside occupant, under circumstances which make it impossible that the carriage was real. Now this vision cannot have been *precognitive;* nothing of the kind occurred for years after it, nor well *could* occur; and I am forced to regard it as the externalisation of some dream, whether of an incarnate or of a discarnate mind. The parallel between this case and the one mentioned above tends therefore to show that the first, in spite of the paraphernalia of wife, horse, and dog-cart, may have been the outcome of a single waking dream; — of the phantasmogenetic dissociation of elements of one sole personality.

In the cases which I have just been discussing there has been a psychical excursion, with its possibilities of clairvoyance; but the excursive element has not brought home any assignable knowledge to the supraliminal personality. I go on now to cases where such knowledge *has* thus been garnered. But here there is need of some further pause, to

---

[1] *Phantasms of the Living*, vol. ii. p. 97 [654 A].
[2] *Phantasms of the Living*, vol. ii. p. 194 [654 B].

consider a little in how many ways we can imagine that knowledge to be reached.

Firstly, the distant knowledge may, it would seem, be reached through hyperæsthesia, — an extended power of the ordinary senses. Secondly, it sometimes seems to come through crystal-gazing or its correlative shell-hearing, — artifices which seem to utilise the ordinary senses in a new way. And besides these two avenues to distant knowledge there is a *third*, the telepathic avenue, which, as we have already surmised, sometimes shades off into the purely telæsthetic; when no distant *mind*, but only the distant *scene*, seems to be attracting the excursive spirit. And in the *fourth* place we must remember that it is mainly in the form of *dream or vision* that the most striking instances of telæsthesia which I have as yet recorded have come. Can we in any way harmonise these various modes of perception? Can we discover any condition of the percipient which is common to all?

To a certain limited extent such co-ordination is possible. In each approach to telæsthesia in turn we find a tendency to something like a dream-excursion. Hyperæsthesia, in the first place, although it exists sometimes in persons wide awake, is characteristically an attribute of sleep-waking states.

We have seen in discussing hypnotic experiments that it is sometimes possible to extend the subject's perceptive faculty by gradual suggestion, so far as to transform a hyperæsthesia which can still be referred to the action of the sense-organs into a telæsthesia which cannot be so referred. It is observable that percipients in such cases sometimes describe their sensation as that of receiving an impression, or seeing a picture placed before them; sometimes as that of *travelling* and visiting the distant scene or person. Or the feeling may oscillate between these two sensations, just as the sense of *time-relation* in the picture shown may oscillate between past, present, and future.

To all these complex sensations the phenomena of crystal-gazing offer close analogies. I have already remarked on the curious fact that the simple artifice of gazing into a speculum should prove the avenue to phenomena of such various types. There may be very different origins even for pictures which in the crystal present very similar aspects; and certain sensations do also accompany these pictures; sensations not merely of *gazing* but sometimes (though rarely) of partial *trance;* and oftener of *bilocation;* — of psychical *presence* among the scenes which the crystal has indeed initiated, but no longer seems to limit or to contain.

The idea of psychical excursion thus suggested must, however, be

somehow reconciled with the frequently *symbolic* character of these visions.
The features of a crystal-vision seem often to be no mere transcription of
material facts, but an abbreviated selection from such facts, or even a bold
modification of such facts with a view of telling some story more quickly
and clearly. We are familiar with the same kind of succession of symbolical scenes in dream, or in waking reverie. And of course if an intelligence outside the crystal-gazer's mind is endeavouring to impress him,
this might well be the chosen way.

And moreover through all telæsthetic vision some element of similar
character is wont to run — some indication that *mind* has been at work
upon the picture — that the scene has not been presented, so to say, in
crude objectivity, but that there has been some *choice* as to the details
discerned; and some *symbolism* in the way in which they are presented.

Let us consider how these characteristics affect different theories of
the mechanism of clairvoyance. Let us suppose first that there is some
kind of transition from hyperæsthesia to telæsthesia, so that when peripheral sensation is no longer possible, central perception may be still
operating across obstacles otherwise insurmountable.

If this be the case, it seems likely that central perception will shape
itself on the types of perception to which the central tracts of the brain
are accustomed; and that the *connaissance supérieure*, the telæsthetic
knowledge, however it may really be acquired, will present itself mainly
as clairvoyance or clairaudience — as some form of sight or sound. Yet
these telæsthetic sights and sounds may be expected to show some trace
of their unusual origin. They may, for instance, be *imperfectly co-ordinated* with sights and sounds arriving through external channels; and,
since they must in some way be a translation of supernormal impressions
into sensory terms, they are likely to show something *symbolic* in character.

This tendency to subliminal symbolism, indeed, meets us at each point
of our inquiry. As an instance of it in its simplest form, I may mention
a case where a botanical student passing inattentively in front of the glass
door of a restaurant thought that he had seen *Verbascum Thapsus* printed
thereon. The real word was *Bouillon;* and that happens to be the trivial
name in French for the plant Verbascum Thapsus. The actual optical
perception had thus been subliminally transformed; the words Verbascum
Thapsus were the report to the inattentive supraliminal self by a subliminal self more interested in botany than in dinner.

Nay, we know that our own optical perception is in its own way highly symbolic. The scene which the baby sees instinctively, — which the impressionist painter manages to see by a sort of deliberate self-simplification, — is very different from the highly elaborate interpretation and selection of blotches of colour by which the ordinary adult figures to himself the visible world.

Now we adults stand towards this subliminal symbolism in much the same attitude as the baby stands towards our educated optical symbolism. Just as the baby fails to grasp the third dimension, so may we still be failing to grasp a fourth; — or whatever be the law of that higher cognisance which begins to report fragmentarily to man that which his ordinary senses cannot discern.

Assuredly then we must not take the fact that any knowledge comes to us symbolically as a proof that it comes to us from a mind outside our own. The symbolism may be the inevitable language in which one stratum of our personality makes its report to another. The symbolism, in short, may be either the easiest, or the only possible psychical record of actual objective fact; whether that fact be in the first instance discerned by our deeper selves, or be conveyed to us from other minds in this form; — elaborated for our mind's digestion, as animal food has been elaborated for our body's digestion, from a primitive crudity of things.

But again one must question, on general idealistic principles, whether there be in such cases any real distinction between symbolism and reality, — between subjective and objective as we commonly use those terms. The resisting matter which we see and touch has "solid" reality for minds so constituted as to have the same subjective feeling awakened by it. But to other minds, endowed with other forms of sensibility — minds possibly both higher and more numerous than our own — this solid matter may seem disputable and unreal, while thought and emotion, perceived in ways unknown to us, may be the only reality.

This material world constitutes, in fact, a "privileged case" — a simplified example — among all discernible worlds, so far as the perception of incarnate spirits is concerned. For discarnate spirits it is no longer a privileged case; to *them* it is apparently easier to discern thoughts and emotions by non-material signs.[1] But they need not therefore be wholly cut off from discerning material things, any more than incarnate spirits are wholly cut off from discerning immaterial things — thoughts and emotions symbolised in phantasmal form. "The ghost in man, the ghost that once was man," to use Tennyson's words, have each of them to over-

[1] See Chapter IX., *passim.*

come by empirical artifices certain difficulties which are of different type for each, but are not insurmountable by either.

These reflections, applicable at various points in our argument, have seemed specially needed when we had first to attack the meaning of the so-called "travelling clairvoyance," of which instances were given in the chapter on hypnotism. It was needful to consider how far there was a continuous transition between these excursions and directer transferences between mind and mind, — between telæsthesia and telepathy. It now seems to me that such a continuous transition may well exist, and that there is no absolute gulf between the supernormal perception of ideas as existing in other minds, and the supernormal perception of what we know as matter. All matter may, for aught we know, exist as an idea in some cosmic mind, with which mind each individual spirit may be in relation, as fully as with individual minds. The difference perhaps lies rather in the fact that there may be generally a *summons* from a cognate mind which starts the so-called agent's mind into action; his invasion may be in some way *invited;* while a spiritual excursion among inanimate objects only may often lack an impulse to start it. If this be so, it would explain the fact that such excursions have mainly succeeded under the influence of hypnotic suggestion.

We see in travelling clairvoyance,[1] just as we see in crystal-visions, a kind of fusion of all our forms of supernormal faculty. There is telepathy, telæsthesia, retrocognition, precognition; and in the cases reported by Cahagnet, which will be referred to in Chapter IX., there is apparently something more besides. We see, in short, that any empirical inlet into the metetherial world is apt to show us those powers, which we try to distinguish, coexisting in some synthesis by us incomprehensible. Here, therefore, just as with the crystal-visions, we have artificially to separate out the special class of phenomena with which we wish first to deal.

In these experiments, then, there seems to be an independent power of visiting almost any desired place, its position having been perhaps first explained by reference to some landmark already known. The clair-voyante (I use the female word, but in several cases a man or boy has shown this power) will frequently miss her way, and describe houses or scenes adjacent to those desired. Then if she — almost literally — gets on the scent, — if she finds some place which the man whom she is sent to

[1] See *Proceedings* S.P.R., vol. vii. pp. 30-99 [572 A and 573 B]; *op. cit.*, 199-220 [573 C]; *Zoist*, vol. vii. pp. 95-101, vol. ix. p. 234, vol. xii. pp. 249-52; and Dr. Fahnestock's *Statuvolism*, especially pp. 127-35 and 221-32.

seek has some time traversed, — she follows up his track with greater ease, apparently recognising past events in his life as well as present circumstances.

In these prolonged experimental cases there is thus time enough to allow of the clairvoyante's traversing certain places, such as empty rooms, factories, and the like, whither no assignable link from any living person could draw her. The evidence to prove telæsthesia, unmixed with telepathy, has thus generally come *incidentally* in the course of some experiment mainly telepathic in character.

These long clairvoyant wanderings are more nearly paralleled by *dreams* than by waking hallucinations.

In a case which I will here quote a physician is impressed, probably in dream, with a picture of a special place in a street, where something is happening, which, though in itself unemotional — merely that a man is standing and talking in the street — is of moment to the physician, who wants to get unobtrusively into the man's house.

From *Phantasms of the Living*, vol. i. p. 267. The case is there described as coming "from a Fellow of the College of Physicians, who fears professional injury if he were 'supposed to defend opinions at variance with general scientific belief,' and does not therefore allow his name to appear."

May 20th, 1884.

Twenty years ago [abroad] I had a patient, wife of a parson. She had a peculiar kind of delirium which did not belong to her disease, and perplexed me. The house in which she lived was closed at midnight, that is — the outer door had no bell. One night I saw her at nine. When I came home I said to my wife, "I don't understand that case; I wish I could get into the house late." We went to bed rather early. At about one o'clock I got up. She said, "What are you about? are you not well?" I said, "Perfectly so." "Then why get up?" "Because I can get into that house." "How, if it is shut up?" "I see the proprietor standing under the lamp-post this side of the bridge, with another man." "You have been dreaming." "No, I have been wide awake; but dreaming or waking, I mean to try." I started with the firm conviction that I should find the individual in question. Sure enough there he was under the lamp-post, talking to a friend. I asked him if he was going home. (I knew him very well.) He said he was, so I told him I was going to see a patient, and would accompany him. I was positively ashamed to explain matters; it seemed so absurd that I knew he would not believe me. On arriving at the house I said, "Now I am here, I will drop in and see my patient." On entering the room I found the maid giving her a tumbler of strong grog. The case was clear; it was as I suspected — delirium from drink. The next day I delicately spoke to the husband about

it. He denied it, and in the afternoon I received a note requesting me
not to repeat the visits. Three weeks ago I was recounting the story
and mentioned the name. A lady present said: "That is the name of the
clergyman in my parish, at B., and his wife is in a lunatic asylum from
drink!"

In conversation with Gurney, the narrator explained that the vision
— though giving an impression of externality and seen, as he believes,
with open eyes — was not definably located in space. He had never
encountered the proprietor in the spot where he saw him, and it was not
a likely thing that he should be standing talking in the streets at so late
an hour.

In this case we cannot consider either the drunken patient or the indifferent proprietor as in any sense the *agent*. Somehow or other the
physician's own persistent wish to get some such opportunity induced a
collaboration of his subliminal with his supraliminal self, akin to the
inspirations of genius. Genius, however, operates within ordinary sensory limits; while in this physician's case the subliminal self exercised its
farthest-reaching supernormal powers.

With this again may be compared a case in *Phantasms of the Living*
(vol. ii. p. 368), where a dreamer seems to himself to be present in the
Thames Tunnel during a fatal accident, which did in fact occur during
that night. Here again the drowned workman — who was quite unknown
to the distant dreamer — can hardly be called an *agent;* yet it may have
been the excitement surrounding his death which attracted the dreamer's
spirit to that scene, as a conflagration might attract a waking night-
wanderer.

There are, on the other hand, a good many cases where a scene
thus discerned in a flash is one of special interest to the percipient,
although no one in the scene may have actually wished to transfer it to
him.

A case again of a somewhat different type is the sudden waking vision
of Mr. Gottschalk,[1] who sees in a circle of light the chalked hands and
ruffled wrists of Mr. Courtenay Thorpe — a well-known actor — who
was opening a letter of Mr. Gottschalk's in that costume at the time.
Trivial in itself, this incident illustrates an interesting class of cases, where
a picture very much like a crystal-vision suddenly appears on a wall or
even in the air with no apparent background.

I know one or two persons who have had in their lives one single round
or oval hallucinatory picture of this kind, of which no interpretation was

---

[1] *Phantasms of the Living*, vol. ii. p. 31 [662 B].

apparent,—a curious indication of some subliminal predisposition towards this somewhat elaborate form of message.

Somewhat like Mr. Gottschalk's projection of his picture upon a background of dark air is the experience of Mrs. Taunton.[1] In this case the phantasm was perfectly external; yet it certainly did not hold to the real objects around the same relation as a figure of flesh and blood would have held; it was in a peculiar way transparent. Gurney regards this transparency as indicating *imperfect externalisation* of the hallucinatory image.

My own phrase, "imperfect *co-ordination* of inner with outward vision," comes to much the same thing, and seems specially applicable to Mrs. Taunton's words: "The appearance was not transparent or filmy, but perfectly solid-looking; *and yet I could somehow see the orchestra, not through, but behind it.*" There are a few cases where the percipient seems to see a hallucinatory figure *behind* him, out of the range of optical vision.[2] There is of course no reason why this should not be so, — even if a part of space external to the percipient's brain should be actually affected.

Mr. Searle's case also is very interesting.[3] Here Mrs. Searle faints when visiting a house a few miles from Mr. Searle's chambers in the Temple. At or about the same time, he sees as though in a looking-glass, upon a window opposite him, his wife's head and face, white and bloodless.

Gurney suggests that this was a transference from Mrs. Searle's mind simply of "the *idea* of fainting," which then worked itself out into perception in an appropriate fashion.

Was it thus? Or did Mr. Searle in the Temple see with inner vision his wife's head as she lay back faint and pallid in Gloucester Gardens? Our nearest analogy here is plainly crystal-vision; and crystal-visions, as we have observed, point both ways. Sometimes the picture in the crystal is conspicuously symbolical; sometimes it seems a transcript of an actual distant scene.

There are two further problems which occur as we deal with each class of cases in turn, — the problem of time-relations and the problem of spirit-agency. Can an incident be said to be seen clairvoyantly if it is seen some hours after it occurred? Ought we to say that a scene is clairvoyantly visited, or that it is spiritually shown, if it represents a still chamber of death,[4] where no emotion is any longer stirring; but to which the freed spirit might desire to attract the friend's attention and sympathy?

---

[1] *Phantasms of the Living*, vol. ii. p. 37 [662 D].
[2] See *Journal* S.P.R., vol. vii. p. 25 [665 A].
[3] *Phantasms of the Living*, vol. ii. p. 35 [662 C].
[4] See *Phantasms of the Living*, vol. i. p. 265 [§ 664].

Such problems cannot at present be solved; nor, as I have said, can any one class of these psychical interchanges be clearly demarcated from other classes. Recognising this, we must explain the central characteristics of each group in turn, and show at what points that group appears to merge into the next.

And now we come to that class of cases where B. invades A, and A perceives the invasion; but B retains no memory of it in supraliminal life. From one point of view, as will be seen, this is just the reverse of the class last discussed — where the invader remembered an invasion which the invaded person (when there was one) did not perceive.

We have already discussed some cases of this sort which seemed to be *psychorrhagic* — to have occurred without will or purpose on the part of the invader. What we must now do is to collect cases where there may probably have been some real projection of will or desire on the invader's part, leading to the projection of his phantasm in a manner recognisable by the distant friend whom he thus invades — yet without subsequent memory of his own. These cases will be intermediate between the *psychorrhagic* cases already described and the *experimental* cases on which we shall presently enter.

In the case of Canon Warburton — in Chapter IV. — the person undergoing the accident did recollect having had a vivid thought of his brother at the moment; — while his brother on the other hand was startled from a slight doze by the vision of the scene of danger as then taking place; — the steep stairs and the falling figure. This is an acute crisis, much resembling impending death by drowning, etc.; and the apparition may be construed either way — either as a scene clairvoyantly discerned by Canon Warburton, owing, as I say, to a spasmodic tightening of his psychical link with his brother, or as a sudden *invasion* on that brother's part, whose very rapidity perhaps helped to prevent his remembering it.

The case given in Appendix VI. E is interesting, both evidentially and from its intrinsic character. The narrative, printed in *Phantasms of the Living*, on the authority of one only of the witnesses concerned, led to the discovery of the *second* witness — whom we had no other means of finding — and has been amply corroborated by her independent account.

The case stands about midway between psychorrhagic cases and intentional self-projections, and is clearly of the nature of an *invasion*, since the phantasm was seen by a stranger as well as by the friend, and seemed to both to be moving about the room. The figure, that is to say, was adapted to the percipient's environment.

Cases of this general character, both visual and auditory, occupy a great part of *Phantasms of the Living*, and others have been frequently quoted in the S.P.R. *Journal* during recent years.[1]

Of still greater interest is the class which comes next in order in my ascending scale of apparent *intensity;* the cases, namely, where there is recollection on both sides, so that the experience is *reciprocal.*[2] These deserve study, for it is by noting under what circumstances these spontaneously reciprocal cases occur that we have the best chance of learning how to produce them experimentally. It will be seen that there have been various degrees of tension of thought on the agent's part.

And here comes in a small but important group — the group of what I may call death-compacts prematurely fulfilled. We shall see in the next chapter that the exchange of a solemn promise between two friends to appear to one another, if possible, after death is far from being a useless piece of sentiment. Such posthumous appearances, it is true, may be in most cases impossible, but nevertheless there is real ground to believe that the previous tension of the will in that direction makes it more likely that the longed-for meeting shall be accomplished. If so, this is a kind of *experiment*, and an experiment which all can make.

Now we have two or three cases where this compact has been made, and where an apparition has followed — but before and not after the agent's death — at the moment, that is to say, of some dangerous accident, when the sufferer was perhaps all but drowned, or was stunned, or otherwise insensible.[3]

Lastly, the lessons of these spontaneous apparitions have been confirmed and widened by actual experiment. It is plain that just as we are not confined to noting small spontaneous telepathic transferences when they occur, but can also endeavour to reproduce them by experiment, so also we can endeavour to reproduce experimentally these more advanced telepathic phenomena of the invasion of the presence of the percipient by the agent. It is to be hoped, indeed, that such experiment may become one of the most important features of our inquiry. The type of the experiment is somewhat as follows. The intending agent endeavours by an effort at self-concentration, made either in waking hours or just before sleep, to render himself perceptible to a given person at a distance, who, of course, must have no reason to expect a phantasmal visit at that hour.

[1] For examples of various types see *Journal* S.P.R., vol. vii. p. 25; vol. v. p. 68, and *op. cit.*, p. 147 [665 A, B and C].

[2] See *Phantasms of the Living*, vol. ii. p. 162; *op. cit.*, p. 164; *Proceedings* S.P.R., vol. vii. p. 41 [666 A, B and C].

[3] See *Phantasms of the Living*, vol. i. p. 527, for example [667 A].

Independent records must be made on each side, of all attempts made, and of all phantoms seen. The evidential point is, of course, the coincidence between the *attempt* and the *phantom*, whether or not the agent can afterwards remember his own success.[1]

Now the *experimental* element here is obviously very incomplete. It consists in little more than in a concentrated desire to produce an effect which one can never explain, and seldom fully remember. I have seen no evidence to show that any one can claim to be an adept in such matters — has learned a method of thus appearing at will.[2] We are acting in the dark. Yet nevertheless the mere fact that on some few occasions this strong desire has actually been followed by a result of this extremely interesting kind is one of the most encouraging phenomena in our whole research. The successes indeed have borne a higher proportion to the failures than I should have ventured to hope. But nowhere is there more need of persistent and careful experimentation; — nowhere, I may add, have emotions quite alien from Science — mere groundless fears of seeing anything unusual — interfered with more disastrous effect. Such fears, one hopes, will pass away, and the friend's visible image will be recognised as a welcome proof of the link that binds the two spirits together.

The case which I quote in Appendix VI. F illustrates both the essential harmlessness — nay, naturalness — of such an experiment, and the causeless fear which it may engender even in rational and serious minds.

In these experimental apparitions, which form, as it were, the *spolia opima* of the collector, we naturally wish to know all that we can about each detail in the experience. Two important points are the *amount of effort* made by the experimenter, and the degree of his *consciousness of success*. The amount of effort in Mr. S. H. B.'s case (for instance) seems to have been great; and this is encouraging, since what we want is to be assured that the tension of will has really some power. It seems to act in much the same way as a therapeutic suggestion from the conscious self; one can never make sure that any given self-suggestion will "take"; but, on the whole, the stronger the self-suggestions, the better the result. It is therefore quite in accordance with analogy that a suggestion from

[1] For cases see the second edition of *Phantasms of the Living*, vol. i. p. lxxxi; *Proceedings* S.P.R., vol. x. pp. 270, 273, and 418; *Forum*, March 1900; *Journal* S.P.R., vol. iv. p. 217; vol. vii. p. 99 [668 A to G]. See also *Phantasms of the Living*, vol. i. p. 104 and vol. ii. p. 675; and the *Journal* S.P.R., vol. iii. p. 307.

[2] Some such power as this is frequently claimed in oriental books as attainable by mystic practices. We have not thus far been fortunate enough to discover any performances corresponding to these promises.

without, given to a hypnotised person, should be the most promising way of inducing these self-projections. It should be strongly impressed on hypnotised subjects that they can and must temporarily "leave the body," as they call it, and manifest themselves to distant persons — the consent, of course, of both parties to the experiment having been previously secured.

Of this type were Dr. Backman's experiments with his subject "Alma,"[1] and although that series of efforts was prematurely broken off, it was full of promise. There were some slight indications that Alma's clairvoyant excursions were sometimes perceptible to persons in the scenes psychically invaded; and there was considerable and growing evidence to her own retention in subsequent memory of some details of those distant scenes.

By all analogy, indeed, that subsequent memory should be an eminently *educable* thing. The carrying over of recollections from one stratum of personality into another — as hypnotic experiment shows us — is largely a matter of patient suggestion. It would be very desirable to hypnotise the person who had succeeded in producing an experimental apparition, of Mr. S. H. B.'s type, and to see if he could then recall the psychical excursion. Hypnotic states should be far more carefully utilised in connection with all these forms of self-projection.

In these self-projections we have before us, I do not say the most useful, but the most extraordinary achievement of the human will. What can lie further outside any known capacity than the power to cause a semblance of oneself to appear at a distance? What can be a more *central* action — more manifestly the outcome of whatsoever is deepest and most unitary in man's whole being? Here, indeed, begins the justification of the conception expressed at the beginning of this chapter; — that we should now see the subliminal self no longer as a mere chain of eddies or backwaters, in some way secluded from the main stream of man's being, but rather as itself the central and potent current, the most truly identifiable with the man himself. Other achievements have their manifest limit; where is the limit here? The spirit has shown itself in part dissociated from the organism; to what point may its dissociation go? It has shown some independence, some intelligence, some permanence. To what degree of intelligence, independence, permanence, may it conceivably attain? Of all vital phenomena, I say, this is the most significant; this self-projection is the one definite act which it seems as though a man might perform equally well before and after bodily death.

[1] See *Proceedings* S.P.R., vol. vii. pp. 199–220 [573 C].

CHAPTER VII

PHANTASMS OF THE DEAD

οὐκέτι πρόσω
ἀβάταν ἅλα κιόνων ὑπὲρ Ἡρακλέος περᾶν εὐμαρές.
. . . θυμέ, τίνα πρὸς ἀλλοδαπὰν
ἄκραν ἐμὸν πλόον παραμείβεαι;
— PINDAR

THE course of our argument has gradually conducted us to a point of capital importance. A profound and central question, approached in irregular fashion from time to time in previous chapters, must now be directly faced. From the actions and perceptions of spirits still in the flesh, and concerned with one another, we must pass on to inquire into the actions of spirits no longer in the flesh, and into the forms of perception with which men still in the flesh respond to that unfamiliar and mysterious agency.

There need, I hope, be no real break here in my previous line of argument. The subliminal self, which we have already traced through various phases of growing sensitivity, growing independence of organic bonds, will now be studied as sensitive to yet remoter influences; — as maintaining an independent existence even when the organism is destroyed. Our subject will divide itself conveniently under three main heads. *First,* it will be well to discuss briefly the nature of the evidence to man's survival of death which may theoretically be obtainable, and its possible connections with evidence set forth in previous chapters. *Secondly,* — and this must form the bulk of the present chapter, — we need a classified exposition of the main evidence to survival thus far obtained; — so far, that is to say, as sensory automatism — audition or apparition — is concerned; for motor automatism — automatic writing and trance-utterance — must be left for later discussion. *Thirdly,* there will be need of some consideration of the meaning of this evidence as a whole, and of its implications alike for the scientific and for the ethical future of mankind. Much more, indeed, of discussion (as well as of evidence) than I can furnish will be needed before this great conception can be realised or argued from with

the scientific thoroughness due to its position among fundamental cosmical laws. Considering how familiar the notion — the vague shadowy
notion — of "immortality" has always been, it is strange indeed that so
little should have been done in these modern days to grasp or to criticise
it; — so little, one might almost say, since the *Phædo* of Plato.

Beginning, then, with the inquiry as to what kind of evidence ought
to be demanded for human survival, we are met first by the bluff statement which is still often uttered even by intelligent men, that *no* evidence
would convince them of such a fact; "neither would they be persuaded
though one rose from the dead."

Extravagant as such a profession sounds, it has a meaning which we
shall do well to note. These resolute antagonists mean that no new
evidence can carry conviction to them unless it be *continuous* with old
evidence; and that they cannot conceive that evidence to a world of spirit
can possibly be continuous with evidence based upon our experience of
a world of matter. I agree with this demand for continuity; and I agree
also that the claims usually advanced for a spiritual world have not only
made no attempt at continuity with known fact, but have even ostenta-
tiously thrown such continuity to the winds. The popular mind has
expressly desired something startling, something outside Law and above
Nature. It has loved, if not a *Credo quia absurdum*, at least a *Credo
quia non probatum*. But the inevitable retribution is a deep insecurity
in the conviction thus attained. Unsupported by the general fabric of
knowledge, the act of faith seems to shrink into the background as that
great fabric stands and grows.

I can hardly too often repeat that my object in these pages is of a quite
opposite character. Believing that all cognisable Mind is as continuous
as all cognisable Matter, my ideal would be to attempt for the realm of
mind what the spectroscope and the law of gravitation have effected for
the realm of matter, and to carry that known cosmic uniformity of substance and interaction upwards among the essences and operations of
an unknown spiritual world. And in order to explore these unreachable
altitudes I would not ask to stand with the theologian on the summit of
a "cloud-capt tower," but rather on plain earth at the measured base
of a trigonometrical survey.

If we would measure such a base, the jungle must be cleared to begin
with. Let us move for a while among first definitions; trying to make
clear to ourselves what kind of thing it is that we are endeavouring to trace
or discover. In popular parlance, we are looking out for *ghosts*. What
connotation, then, are we to give to the word "ghost" — a word which

has embodied so many unfounded theories and causeless fears? It would be more satisfactory, in the present state of our knowledge, simply to collect facts without offering speculative comment. But it seems safer to begin by briefly pointing out the manifest errors of the traditional view; since that tradition, if left unnoticed, would remain lodged in the background even of many minds which have never really accepted it.

Briefly, then, the popular view regards a "ghost" as *a deceased person permitted by Providence to hold communication with survivors*. And this short definition contains, I think, at least three unwarrantable assumptions.

In the first place, such words as *permission* and *Providence* are simply neither more nor less applicable to this phenomenon than to any other. We conceive that all phenomena alike take place in accordance with the laws of the universe, and consequently by permission of the Supreme Power in the universe. Undoubtedly the phenomena with which we are dealing are in this sense permitted to occur. But there is no *a priori* reason whatever for assuming that they are permitted in any especial sense of their own, or that they form exceptions to law, instead of being exemplifications of law. Nor is there any *a posteriori* reason for supposing any such inference to be deducible from a study of the phenomena themselves. If we attempt to find in these phenomena any poetical justice or manifest adaptation to human cravings, we shall be just as much disappointed as if we endeavoured to find a similar satisfaction in the ordinary course of terrene history.

In the second place, we have no warrant for the assumption that the phantom seen, even though it be somehow *caused* by a deceased person, *is* that deceased person, in any ordinary sense of the word. Instead of appealing to the crude analogy of the living friend who, when he has walked into the room, *is* in the room, we shall find for the ghost a much closer parallel in those hallucinatory figures or phantasms which living persons can sometimes project at a distance.

But experience shows that when — as with these *post-mortem* phantoms — the deceased person has gone well out of sight or reach there is a tendency, so to say, to *anthropomorphose* the apparition; to suppose that, as the deceased person is not provably anywhere else, he is probably here; and that the apparition is bound to behave accordingly. All such assumptions must be dismissed, and the phantom must be taken on its merits, as indicating merely a certain connection with the deceased, the precise nature of that connection being a part of the problem to be solved.

And in the third place, just as we must cease to say that the phantom *is* the deceased, so also must we cease to ascribe to the phantom the motives by which we imagine that the deceased might be swayed. We must therefore exclude from our definition of a ghost any words which assume its intention to communicate with the living. It may bear such a relation to the deceased that it can reflect or represent his presumed wish to communicate, or it may not. If, for instance, its relation to his *post-mortem* life be like the relation of my dreams to my earthly life, it may represent little that is truly his, save such vague memories and instincts as give a dim individuality to each man's trivial dreams.

Let us attempt, then, a truer definition. Instead of describing a "ghost" as a dead person permitted to communicate with the living, let us define it as *a manifestation of persistent personal energy*, or as an indication that some kind of force is being exercised after death which is in some way connected with a person previously known on earth. In this definition we have eliminated, as will be seen, a great mass of popular assumptions. Yet we must introduce a further proviso, lest our definition still seem to imply an assumption which we have no right to make. It is theoretically possible that this force or influence, which after a man's death creates a phantasmal impression of him, may indicate no continuing action on his part, but may be some residue of the force or energy which he generated while yet alive. There may be *veridical after-images* — such as Gurney hints at (*Proceedings* S.P.R., vol. v. p. 417) when in his comments on the recurring figure of an old woman — seen on the bed where she was murdered — he remarks that this figure suggests not so much "any continuing local interest on the part of the deceased person, as the survival of a mere image, impressed, we cannot guess how, on we cannot guess what, by that person's physical organism, and perceptible at times to those endowed with some cognate form of sensitiveness."

Strange as this notion may seem, it is strongly suggested by many of the cases of *haunting* which do not fall within the scope of the present chapter. We shall presently find that there is strong evidence for the recurrence of the same hallucinatory figures in the same localities, but weak evidence to indicate any purpose in most of these figures, or any connection with bygone individuals, or with such tragedies as are popularly supposed to start a ghost on its career. In some of these cases of frequent, meaningless recurrence of a figure in a given spot, we are driven to wonder whether it can be some deceased person's past frequentation of that spot, rather than any fresh action of his after death, which has generated what I have termed the veridical after-image — veridical in the sense that it communicates information, previously unknown to the percipient, as to a former inhabitant of the haunted locality.

Such are some of the questions which our evidence suggests. And I may point out that the very fact that such bizarre problems should present themselves at every turn does in a certain sense tend to show that these apparitions are not purely subjective things, — do not originate merely in the percipient's imagination. For they are not like what any man would have imagined. What man's mind does tend to fancy on such topics may be seen in the endless crop of fictitious ghost stories, which furnish, indeed, a curious proof of the persistence of preconceived notions. For they go on being framed according to canons of their own, and deal with a set of imaginary phenomena quite different from those which actually occur. The actual phenomena, I may add, could scarcely be made romantic. One true "ghost story" is apt to be very like another, and most of them to be fragmentary and apparently meaningless. Their meaning, that is to say, lies in their conformity, not to the mythopœic instinct of mankind, which fabricates and enjoys the fictitious tales, but to some unknown law, not based on human sentiment or convenience at all.

And thus, absurdly enough, we sometimes hear men ridicule the phenomena which actually do happen, simply because those phenomena do not suit their preconceived notions of what ghostly phenomena ought to be; — not perceiving that this very divergence, this very unexpectedness, is in itself no slight indication of an origin *outside* the minds which obviously were so far from anticipating anything of the kind.

And in fact the very qualities which are most apt to raise derision are such as the evidence set forth in the earlier chapters of this work might reasonably lead us to expect. For I hold that now for the first time can we form a conception of ghostly communications which shall in any way consist or cohere with more established conceptions; which can be presented as in any way a development of facts which are already experimentally known. Two preliminary conceptions were needed — conceptions in one sense ancient enough; but yet the first of which has only in this generation found its place in science, while the second is as yet awaiting its brevet of orthodoxy. The first conception is that with which hypnotism and various automatisms have familiarised us, — the conception of multiplex personality, of the potential coexistence of many states and many memories in the same individual. The second is the conception of telepathy; of the action of mind on mind apart from the ordinary organs of sense; and especially of its action by means of hallucinations; by the generation of veridical phantasms which form, as it were, messages from men still in the flesh. And I believe that these two conceptions are in this way connected, that the telepathic message generally starts from, and generally impinges upon, a subconscious or submerged stratum in both agent and percipient.[1] Wherever there is hallucination, whether delusive or veridical, I hold that a message of some sort is forcing its way upwards from one stratum of personality to another, — a message which may be merely dreamlike and incoherent, or which may symbolise a fact otherwise unreachable by the percipient personality. And the mechanism seems much the same whether the message's path be continued within one individual or pass between two; whether A's own submerged self be signalling to his emergent self, or B be telepathically stimulating the hidden fountains of perception in A. If anything like this be true, it seems plainly needful that all that we know of abnormal or supernormal communications between minds, or states of the same mind, still embodied in flesh, should be searched for analogies which may throw light on this strangest mode of intercourse between embodied and disembodied minds.

A communication (if such a thing exists) from a departed person to a person still on earth is, at any rate, a communication from a mind in one state of existence to a mind in a very different state of existence. And it is, moreover, a communication from one mind to another which passes through some channel other than the ordinary channels of sense, since on one side of the gulf no material sense-organs exist. It will apparently be an extreme instance of both these classes — of communications between state and state,[2] and of telepathic communications; and we ought, therefore, to approach it by considering the less advanced cases of both these types.

On what occasions do we commonly find a mind conversing with another mind not on the same plane with itself? — with a mind inhabiting in some sense a different world, and viewing the environment with a difference of outlook greater than the mere difference of character of the two personages will account for?

The first instance of this sort which will occur to us lies in spontaneous somnambulism, or colloquy between a person asleep and a person awake.

---

[1] See *Phantasms of the Living*, vol. i. p. 231.

[2] Some word is much needed to express communications between one state and another, *e.g.* between the somnambulic and the waking state, or, in hypnotism, the cataleptic and the somnambulic, etc. The word "methectic" (μεθεκτικὸς) seems to me the most suitable, especially since μέθεξις happens to be the word used by Plato (Parm. 132 D.) for participation between ideas and concrete objects. Or the word "inter-state" might be pressed into this new duty.

And observe here how slight an accident allows us to enter into converse with a state which at first sight seems a type of incommunicable isolation. "Awake, we share our world," runs the old saying, "but each dreamer inhabits a world of his own." Yet the dreamer, apparently so self-enclosed, may be gently led, or will spontaneously enter, into converse with waking men.

The somnambulist, or rather the somniloquist — for it is the talking rather than the walking which is the gist of the matter — is thus our first natural type of the *revenant*.

And observing the habits of somnambulists, we note that the degree in which they can communicate with other minds varies greatly in different cases. One sleep-waker will go about his customary avocations without recognising the presence of any other person whatever; another will recognise certain persons only, or will answer when addressed, but only on certain subjects, his mind coming into contact with other minds only on a very few points. Rarely or never will a somnambulist spontaneously notice what other persons are doing, and adapt his own actions thereto.

Next let us turn from natural to induced sleep-waking, from idiopathic somnambulism to the hypnotic trance. Here, too, throughout the different stages of the trance, we find a varying and partial (or elective) power of communication. Sometimes the entranced subject makes no sign whatever; sometimes he seems able to hear and answer one person, or certain persons, and not others; sometimes he will talk freely to all; but, however freely he may talk, he is not exactly his waking self, and as a rule he has no recollection, or a very imperfect recollection, in waking life of what he has said or done in his trance.

Judging, then, from such analogy as communications from one living state to another can suggest to us, we shall expect that the communication of a disembodied or discarnate person with an incarnate, if such exist, will be subject to narrow limitations, and very possibly will not form a part of the main current of the supposed discarnate consciousness.

These preliminary considerations are applicable to any kind of alleged communication from the departed — whether well or ill evidenced; whether conveyed in sensory or in motor form.

Let us next consider what types of communication from the dead our existing evidence of communications among the living suggests to us as analogically possible. It appears to me that there is an important parallelism running through each class of our experiments in automatism and each class of our spontaneous phenomena. Roughly speaking, we may say that our experiment and observation up to this point have comprised five different stages of phenomena, viz., (I.) hypnotic suggestion; (II.) telepathic experiments; (III.) spontaneous telepathy during life; (IV.) phantasms at death; (V.) phantasms after death. And we find, I think, that the same types of communication meet us at each stage; so that this recurrent similarity of types raises a presumption that the underlying mechanism of manifestation at each stage may be in some way similar.

Again using a mere rough form of division, we shall find three main forms of manifestation at each stage: (1) hallucinations of the senses; (2) emotional and motor impulses; (3) definite intellectual messages.

(I.) And first let us start from a class of experiments into which telepathy does not enter, but which exhibit in its simplest form the mechanism of the automatic transfer of messages from one stratum to another of the same personality. I speak, of course, of post-hypnotic suggestions. Here the agent is a living man, operating in an ordinary way, by direct speech. The unusual feature lies in the condition of the percipient, who is hypnotised at the time, and is thus undergoing a kind of dislocation of personality, or temporary upheaval of a habitually subjacent stratum of the self. This hypnotic personality, being for the time at the surface, receives the agent's verbal suggestion, of which the percipient's waking self is unaware. Then afterwards, when the waking self has resumed its usual upper position, the hypnotic self carries out at the stated time the given suggestion,—an act whose origin the upper stratum of consciousness does not know, but which is in effect a message communicated to the upper stratum from the now submerged or subconscious stratum on which the suggestion was originally impressed.

And this message may take any one of the three leading forms mentioned above;—say a hallucinatory image of the hypnotiser or of some other person; or an impulse to perform some action; or a definite word or sentence to be written automatically by the waking self, which thus learns what order has been laid upon the hypnotic self while the waking consciousness was in abeyance.

(II.) Now turn to our experiments in thought-transference. Here again the agent is a living man; but he is no longer operating by ordinary means, — by spoken words or visible gestures. He is operating on the percipient's subconscious self by means of a telepathic impulse, which he desires, indeed, to project from himself, and which the percipient may desire to receive, but of whose *modus operandi* the ordinary waking selves of agent and percipient alike are entirely unaware.

Here again we may divide the messages sent into the same three main classes. First come the hallucinatory figures — always or almost always of himself — which the agent causes the percipient to see. Secondly come impulses to act, telepathically impressed, as when the hypnotiser desires his subject to come to him at an hour not previously notified. And thirdly, we have a parallel to the post-hypnotic writing of definite words or figures in our own experiments on the direct telepathic transmission of words, figures, cards, etc., from the agent, using no normal means of communication, to the percipient, either in the hypnotised or in the waking state.

(III.) We come next to the spontaneous phantasms occurring during life. Here we find the same three broad classes of messages, with this difference, that the actual apparitions, which in our telepathic experimentation are thus far unfortunately rare, become now the most important class. I need not recall the instances given in Chapters IV. and VI., etc., where an agent undergoing some sudden crisis seems in some way to generate an apparition of himself seen by a distant percipient. Important also in this connection are those apparitions of the *double,* where some one agent is seen repeatedly in phantasmal form by different percipients at times when that agent is undergoing no special crisis.

Again, among our telepathic impressions generated (spontaneously, not experimentally) by living agents, we have cases, which I need not here recapitulate, of pervading sensations of distress; or impulses to return home, which are parallel to the hypnotised subject's impulse to approach his distant hypnotiser, at a moment when that hypnotiser is willing him to do so.

And thirdly, among these telepathic communications from the living to the living, we have definite sentences automatically written, communicating facts which the distant person knows, but is not consciously endeavouring to transmit.

(IV.) Passing on to phantasms which cluster about the moment of death, we find our three main classes of cases still meeting us. Our readers are familiar with the *visual* cases, where there is an actual apparition of the dying man, seen by one or more persons; and also with the *emotional and motor* cases, where the impression, although powerful, is not definitely sensory in character. And various cases also have been published where the message has consisted of definite words, not always externalised as an auditory hallucination, but sometimes automatically *uttered* or automatically *written* by the percipient himself, as in the case communicated by Dr. Liébeault (see Appendix VIII. C), where a girl writes the message announcing her friend's death at the time when that friend is, in fact, dying in a distant city.

(V.) And now I maintain that in these post-mortem cases also we find the same general classes persisting, and in somewhat the same proportion. Most conspicuous are the actual *apparitions*, with which, indeed, the following pages will mainly deal. It is very rare to find an apparition which seems to impart any verbal message; but a case of this kind has been given in Appendix IV. F. As a rule, however, the apparition is of the apparently automatic, purposeless character, already so fully described. We have also the *emotional and motor* class of post-mortem cases;[1] and these may, perhaps, be more numerous in proportion than our collection would indicate; for it is obvious that impressions which are so much less definite than a visual hallucination (although they may be even more impressive to the percipient himself) can rarely be used as evidence of communication with the departed.

But now I wish to point out that, besides these two classes of post-mortem manifestations, we have our *third* class also still persisting; we have definite verbal messages which at least purport, and sometimes, I think, with strong probability, to come from the departed.

I have, indeed, for the reader's convenience, postponed these motor cases to a subsequent chapter, so that the evidence here and now presented for survival will be very incomplete. Yet, at any rate, we are gradually getting before us a fairly definite task. We have in this chapter to record and analyse such sensory experiences of living men as seem referable to the action of some human individuality persisting after death. We have also obtained some preliminary notion as to the kind of phenomena for which we can hope, especially as to what their probable limitations must be, considering how great a gulf between psychical states any communication must overpass.

Let us now press the actual evidential question somewhat closer. Let us consider, for it is by no means evident at first sight, what conditions a visual or auditory phantasm is bound to fulfil before it can be regarded as indicating *primâ facie* the influence of a discarnate mind. The discussion may be best introduced by quoting the words in which Edmund Gurney opened it in 1888.[2] The main evidential lines as there laid down retain their validity, although the years which have since passed have greatly augmented the testimony, and in so doing have illustrated yet other tests of true post-mortem communication, — to which we shall presently come.

---

[1] See for example Mr. Cameron Grant's case. (*Proceedings* S.P.R., vol. viii. p. 202.)

[2] *Proceedings* S.P.R., vol. v. pp. 404-408.

"It is evident that in alleged cases of apparitions of the dead, the point which we have held to distinguish certain apparitions of *living* persons from purely subjective hallucinations is necessarily lacking. That point is *coincidence* between the apparition and some critical or exceptional condition of the person who seems to appear; but with regard to the dead, we have no independent knowledge of their condition, and therefore never have the opportunity of observing any such coincidences.

"There remain three, and I think only three, conditions which might establish a presumption that an apparition or other immediate manifestation of a dead person is something more than a mere subjective hallucination of the percipient's senses. Either (1) more persons than one might be independently affected by the phenomenon; or (2) the phantasm might convey information, afterwards discovered to be true, of something which the percipient had never known; or (3) the appearance might be that of a person whom the percipient himself had never seen, and of whose aspect he was ignorant, and yet his description of it might be sufficiently definite for identification. But though one or more of these conditions would have to be fully satisfied before we could be convinced that any particular apparition of the dead had some cause external to the percipient's own mind, there is one more general characteristic of the class which is sufficiently suggestive of such a cause to be worth considering. I mean the disproportionate number of cases which occur *shortly after* the death of the person represented. Such a time-relation, if frequently enough encountered, might enable us to argue for the objective origin of the phenomenon in a manner analogous to that which leads us to conclude that many phantasms of the living have an objective (a telepathic) origin. For, according to the doctrines of probabilities, a hallucination representing a known person would not *by chance* present a definite time-relation to a special cognate event — viz., the death of that person — in more than a certain percentage of the whole number of similar hallucinations that occur; and if that percentage is decidedly exceeded, there is reason to surmise that some other cause than chance — in other words, some objective origin for the phantasm — is present."

But on the other hand, a phantasm representing a person whose death is recent is specially likely to arouse interest and, in cases where the death is previously known to the percipient, his emotional state may be considered a sufficient cause of the hallucination.

"If, then," Gurney continues, "we are to draw any probable conclusion as to the objective nature of *post-mortem* appearances and communications (or of some of them) from the fact of their special frequency soon after death, we must confine ourselves to cases where the fact of death has been unknown to the percipient at the time of his experience. Now, in these days of letters and telegrams, people for the most part hear of the deaths of friends and relatives within a very few days, sometimes within a very few hours, after the death occurs; so that appearances of the sort required would, as a rule, have to follow very closely indeed on the death. Have we evidence of any considerable number of such cases?

"Readers of *Phantasms of the Living* will know that we have. In a number of cases which were treated in that book as examples of telepathic transference from a dying person, the person was actually dead at the time that the percipient's experience occurred; and the inclusion of such cases under the title of *Phantasms of the Living* naturally occasioned a certain amount of adverse criticism. Their inclusion, it will be remembered, required an assumption which cannot by any means be regarded as certain. We had to suppose that the telepathic transfer took place just before, or exactly at, the moment of death; but that the impression remained latent in the percipient's mind, and only after an interval emerged into his consciousness, whether as waking vision or as dream or in some other form. Now, as a provisional hypothesis, I think that this assumption was justified. For in the first place, the moment of death is, in time, the central point of a cluster of abnormal experiences occurring to percipients at a distance, of which some *precede*, while others follow, the death; it is natural, therefore, to surmise that the same explanation will cover the whole group, and that the motive force in each of its divisions lies in a state of the 'agent' prior to bodily death. In the second place, some of the facts of experimental thought-transference countenance the view that 'transferred impressions' may be latent for a time before the recipient becomes aware of them; and recent discoveries with respect to the whole subject of automatism and 'secondary intelligence' make it seem far less improbable than it would otherwise have seemed that telepathy may take effect first on the 'unconscious' part of the mind.[1] And in the third place, the period of supposed latency has in a good many instances been a period when the person affected was in activity, and when his mind and senses were being solicited by other things; and in such cases it is specially easy to suppose that the telepathic impression did not get the right conditions for rising into consciousness until a season of silence and *recueillement* arrived.[2] But though the theory of latency has thus a good deal to be said for it, my colleagues and I are most anxious not to be supposed to be putting forward as a dogma what must be regarded at present merely as a working hypothesis. Psychical research is of all subjects the one where it is most important to avoid this error, and to keep the mind open for new interpretations of the facts. And in the present instance there are certain definite objections which may fairly be made to the hypothesis that a telepathic impression derived from a dying person may emerge after hours of latency. The experimental cases to which I have referred as analogous are few and uncertain, and, moreover, in them the period of latency has been measured

---

[1] In some experimental cases, it will be remembered, the impression takes effect through the *motor*, not the *sensory*, system of the recipient, as by automatic writing, so that he is never directly aware of it at all.

[2] See, for instance, case 500, *Phantasms of the Living*, vol. ii. p. 462.

by seconds or minutes, not by hours. And though, as I have said, some
of the instances of apparent delay among the death-cases might be accounted for by the fact that the percipient's mind or senses needed to
be withdrawn from other occupations before the manifestation could
take place, there are other instances where this is not so, and where no
ground at all appears for connecting the delay with the percipient's
condition. On the whole, then, the alternative hypothesis — that the
condition of the phenomenon on the 'agent's' side (be it psychical or
be it physical) is one which only comes into existence at a distinct
interval after death, and that the percipient really is impressed at the
moment, and not before the moment, when he is conscious of the impression — is one which must be steadily kept in view.

"So far I have been speaking of cases where the interval between the
death and the manifestation was so short as to make the theory of latency
possible. The rule adopted in *Phantasms of the Living* was that this
interval must not exceed twelve hours. But we have records of a few
cases where this interval has been greatly exceeded, and yet where the fact
of the death was still unknown to the percipient at the time of his
experience. The theory of latency cannot reasonably be applied to cases
where weeks or months divide the vision (or whatever it may be) from
the moment of death, which is the latest at which an ordinary[1] telepathically transferred idea could have obtained access to the percipient. And
the existence of such cases — so far as it tends to establish the reality
of objectively-caused apparitions of the dead — diminishes the objection
to conceiving that the appearances, etc., which have very shortly *followed*
death have had a different causation from those which have coincided
with or very shortly *preceded* it. For we shall not be inventing a wholly
new class for the former cases, but only provisionally shifting them from
one class to another — to a much smaller and much less well-evidenced
class, it is true, but one nevertheless for which we have evidence enough
to justify us in expecting more."

This, as I conceive, is a sound method of proceeding from ground
made secure in *Phantasms of the Living* — and traversed in my own just
previous chapter — to cases closely analogous, save for that little difference
in *time-relations*, that occurrence in the hours which follow, instead of the
hours which precede, bodily dissolution, which counts for so much in
our insight into cosmic law.[2]

---

[1] I mean by "ordinary" the classes which are recognised and treated of in *Phantasms of the Living*. But if the departed survive, the possibility of thought-transference between them and those who remain is of course a perfectly tenable hypothesis.
"As our telepathic theory is a psychical one, and makes no physical assumptions,
it would be perfectly applicable (though the *name* perhaps would be inappropriate)
to the conditions of disembodied existence." — *Phantasms*, vol. i. p. 512.

[2] Certain statistics as to these time-relations are given by Edmund Gurney as
follows (*Proceedings* S.P.R., vol. v. p. 408): "The statistics drawn from the first-
hand records in *Phantasms of the Living* as to the time-relation of appearances, etc.,

The hypothesis of *latency* which thus meets us *in limine* in this inquiry will soon be found inadequate to cover the facts. Yet it will be well to dwell somewhat more fully upon its possible range.

If we examine the proportionate number of apparitions observed at various periods before and after death, we find that they increase very rapidly for the few hours which precede death, and decrease gradually during the hours and days which follow, until after about a year's time they become merely sporadic.

Yet one more point must be touched on, to avoid misconception of the phrase cited above, that "the moment of death is the centre of a cluster of abnormal experiences, of which some precede, while others follow, the death." Gurney, of course, did not mean to assume that the act of death itself was the cause of all these experiences. Those which occur before death may be caused or conditioned, not by the death itself, but by the abnormal state, as of coma, delirium, etc., which preceded the death. This we say because we have many instances where veridical phantasms have coincided with moments of *crisis* — carriage-accidents and the like — occurring to distant agents, but not followed by death. Accordingly we find that in almost all cases where a phantasm, apparently veridical, has *preceded* the agent's death, that death was the result of disease and not of accident. To this rule there are very few exceptions. There is a case given in *Phantasms of the Living* (vol. ii. p. 52), where the phantasm seems on the evidence to have preceded by about half an hour (longitude allowed for) a sudden death by drowning. In this case the percipient was in a Norfolk farmhouse, the drowning man — or agent — was in a storm off the island of Tristan d'Acunha; and we have suggested that an error of clocks or of observation may account for the discrepancy. In another case the death was in a sense a violent one, for it was a suicide; but the morbidly excited state of the girl a few hours before death — when

occurring in close proximity to deaths, are as follows: — In 134 cases the coincidence is represented as having been exact, or, when times are specifically stated, close to within an hour. In 104 cases it is not known whether the percipient's experience preceded or followed the death; such cases cannot be taken account of for our present purpose. There remain 78 cases where it appears that there was an interval of more than an hour; and of these 38 preceded and 40 followed the death. Of the 38 cases where the percipient's experience preceded the death (all of which, of course, took place during a time when the "agent" was seriously ill), 19 fell within twenty-four hours of the death. Of the 40 cases where the percipient's experience followed the death, all followed within an interval of twenty-four hours, and in only one (included by mistake) was the twelve hours' interval certainly exceeded, though there are one or two others where it is possible that it was slightly exceeded."

her phantasm was seen — was in itself a state of crisis. But there are also a few recorded cases (none of which were cited in *Phantasms of the Living*) where a phantasm or double of some person has been observed some days previous to that person's accidental death. The evidence obtained in the Census of Hallucinations, however, tended to show that cases of this sort are too few to suggest even *primâ facie* a causal connection between the death and the apparition (see *Proceedings* S.P.R. vol. x. p. 331).

I now proceed briefly to review some of the cases where the interval between death and phantasm has been measurable by minutes or hours.

It is not easy to get definite cases where the interval has been measurable by *minutes;* for if the percipient is at a distance from the agent we can seldom be sure that the clocks at both places have been correct, and correctly observed; while if he is *present* with the agent we can rarely be sure that the phantasm observed is more than a mere subjective hallucination. Thus we have several accounts of a rushing sound heard by the watcher of a dying man just after his apparent death, or of some kind of luminosity observed near his person; but this is just the moment when we may suppose some subjective hallucination likely to occur, and if one person's senses alone are affected we cannot allow much evidential weight to the occurrence.[1]

There are some circumstances, however, in which, in spite of the fact that the death is already known, a hallucination occurring shortly afterwards may have some slight evidential value. Thus we have a case where a lady who knew that her sister had died a few hours previously, but who was not herself in any morbidly excited condition, seemed to see some one enter her own dining-room, opening and shutting the door. The percipient (who had never had any other hallucination) was much astonished when she found no one in the dining-room; but it did not till some time afterwards occur to her that the incident could be in any way

---

[1] The *Proceedings* of the American Society for Psychical Research (vol. i. p. 405) contain a case where a physician and his wife, sleeping in separate but adjoining rooms, are both of them awakened by a bright light. The physician sees a figure standing in the light; his wife, who gets up to see what the light in her husband's room may be, does not reach that room till the figure has disappeared. The figure is not clearly identified, but has some resemblance to a patient of the physician's, who has died suddenly (from hemorrhage) about three hours before, calling for her doctor, who did not anticipate this sudden end. Even this resemblance did not strike the percipient until after he knew of the death, and the defect in *recognition* weakens the case evidentially.

connected with her recent loss. This reminds us of a case (ii. p. 694 [1]) where the Rev. R. M. Hill sees a tall figure rush into the room, which alarms and surprises him, then vanishes before he has time to recognise it. An uncle, a tall man, dies about that moment, and it is remarked that although Mr. Hill knew his uncle to be ill, the anxiety which he may have felt would hardly have given rise to an unrecognised and formidable apparition.

There are cases also where a percipient who has had an apparition of a friend shortly after that friend's known death has had *veridical* hallucinations at other times, and has never had any hallucination of purely subjective origin. Such a percipient may naturally suppose that his apparition of the departed friend possessed the same veridical character which was common to the rest, although it was not *per se* evidential, since the fact of the death was already known.

For the present, however, it will be better to return to the cases which are free from this important *primâ facie* drawback — cases where the percipient was, at any rate, unaware that the death, which the phantasm seemed to indicate, had in fact taken place.

In the first place, there are a few cases where a percipient is informed of a death by a veridical phantasm, and then some hours afterwards a similar phantasm differing perhaps in detail, recurs.

Such was the case of Archdeacon Farler (i. p. 414), who *twice* during one night saw the dripping figure of a friend who, as it turned out, had been drowned during the previous day. Even the first appearance was several hours after the death, but this we might explain by the latency of the impression till a season of quiet. The second appearance may have been a kind of recrudescence of the first; but if the theory of latency be discarded, so that the *first* appearance (if more than a mere chance coincidence) is held to depend upon some energy excited by the deceased person after death, it would afford some ground for regarding the *second* appearance as also veridical. The figure in this case was once more seen a fortnight later, and on this occasion, as Archdeacon Farler informs me, in ordinary garb, with no special trace of accident.

A similar repetition occurs in seven other cases recorded in *Phantasms of the Living.*[2]

---

[1] The references in this and the two following pages are to *Phantasms of the Living*.

[2] See the cases of Major Moncrieff (i. p. 415); of Mr. Keulemans (i. p. 444), where the second phantasm was held by the percipient to convey a fresh veridical picture; of Mr. Hernaman (i. p. 561), where, however, the agent was alive, though dying, at

Turning now to the cases where the phantasm is not repeated, but occurs some hours after death, let us take a few narratives where the interval of time is pretty certain, and consider how far the hypothesis of *latency* looks probable in each instance.

Where there is no actual hallucination, but only a feeling of unique *malaise* or distress following at a few hours' interval on a friend's death at a distance, as in Archdeacon Wilson's case (i. p. 280), it is very hard to picture to ourselves what has taken place. Some injurious shock communicated to the percipient's brain at the moment of the agent's death may conceivably have slowly worked itself into consciousness. The delay may have been due, so to say, to physiological rather than to psychical causes.

Next take a case like that of Mrs. Wheatcroft (i. p. 420), or of Mrs. Evens (ii. p. 690), or Sister Bertha (quoted below in Appendix VII. F), where a definite hallucination of sight or sound occurs some hours after the death, but in the middle of the night. It is in a case of this sort that we can most readily suppose that a "telepathic impact" received during the day has lain dormant until other excitations were hushed, and has externalised itself as a hallucination after the first sleep, just as when we wake from a first sleep some subject of interest or anxiety, which has been thrust out of our thoughts during the day, will often well upwards into consciousness with quite a new distinctness and force. But on the other hand, in the case (for instance) of Mrs. Teale (ii. p. 693), there is a deferment of some eight hours, and then the hallucination occurs while the percipient is sitting wide awake in the middle of her family. And in one of the most remarkable dream-cases in our collection (given in Chapter IV.), Mrs. Storie's experience does not resemble the mere emergence of a latent impression. It is long and complex, and suggests some sort of clairvoyance; but if it be "telepathic clairvoyance," that is, a picture transferred from the decedent's mind, then it almost requires us to suppose that a *post-mortem* picture was thus transferred, a view of the accident and its consequences *fuller* than any which could have flashed through

the time of the appearance; see also the cases of Mrs. Ellis (ii. p. 59); of Mrs. D. (ii. p. 467); of Mrs. Fairman (ii. p. 482), and of Mr. F. J. Jones (ii. p. 500), where the death was again due to drowning, and the act of dying cannot, therefore, have been very prolonged. We may note also Mrs. Reed's case (ii. p. 237), Captain Ayre's (ii. p. 256) and Mrs. Cox's (ii. p. 235). In the case of Miss Harriss (ii. p. 117) a hallucinatory *voice*, about the time of the death, but not suggesting the decedent, is followed by a dream the next night, which presents the dead person as in the act of dying. One or two other cases might be added to this list, and it is plain that the matter is one towards which observation should be specially directed.

the dying man's mind during his moment of sudden and violent death from "the striking off of the top of the skull" by a railway train.

If once we assume that the deceased person's mind could continue to act on living persons after his bodily death, then the confused horror of the series of pictures which were presented to Mrs. Storie's view — mixed, it should be said, with an element of *fresh departure* which there was nothing in the accident itself to suggest — would correspond well enough to what one can imagine a man's feelings a few hours after such a death to be. This is trespassing, no doubt, on hazardous ground; but if once we admit communication from the other side of death as a working hypothesis, we must allow ourselves to imagine something as to the attitude of the communicating mind, and the least violent supposition will be that that mind is still in part at least occupied with the same thoughts which last occupied it on earth. It is possible that there may be some interpretation of this kind for some of the cases where a funeral scene, or a dead body, is what the phantasm presents. There is a remarkable case (i. p. 265) [§ 664] where a lady sees the body of a well-known London physician — about ten hours after death — lying in a bare unfurnished room (a cottage hospital abroad). Here the description, as we have it, would certainly fit best with some kind of telepathic clairvoyance prolonged after death — some power on the deceased person's part to cause the percipient to share the picture which might at that moment be occupying his own mind.

It will be seen that these phenomena are not of so simple a type as to admit of our considering them from the point of view of *time-relations* alone. Whatever else, indeed, a "ghost" may be, it is probably one of the most complex phenomena in nature. It is a function of two unknown variables — the incarnate spirit's sensitivity and the discarnate spirit's capacity of self-manifestation. Our attempt, therefore, to study such intercourse may begin at either end of the communication — with the percipient or with the agent. We shall have to ask, How does the incarnate mind receive the message? and we shall have to ask also, How does the discarnate mind originate and convey it?

Now it is by pressing the *former* of these two questions that we have, I think, the best chance at present of gaining fresh light. So long as we are considering the incarnate mind we are, to some extent at least, on known ground; and we may hope to discern analogies in some other among that mind's operations to that possibly most perplexing of all its operations, which consists in taking cognisance of messages from unembodied minds, and from an unseen world. I think, therefore, that "the surest way, though most about," as Bacon would say, to the comprehension of this sudden and startling phenomenon lies in the study of other rare mental phenomena which can be observed more at leisure, just as "the surest way, though most about," to the comprehension of some blazing inaccessible star has lain in the patient study of the spectra of the incandescence of terrestrial substances which lie about our feet. I am in hopes that by the study of various forms of subliminal consciousness, subliminal faculty, subliminal perception, we may ultimately obtain a conception of our own total being and operation which may show us the incarnate mind's perception of the discarnate mind's message as no isolated anomaly, but an orderly exercise of natural and innate powers, frequently observed in action in somewhat similar ways.

It is, I say, from this human or terrene side that I should prefer, were it possible, to study in the first instance all our cases. Could we not only share but interpret the percipient's subjective feelings, could we compare those feelings with the feelings evoked by ordinary vision or telepathy among living men, we might get at a more intimate knowledge of what is happening than any observation from outside of the details of an apparition can supply. But this, of course, is not possible in any systematic way; occasional glimpses, inferences, comparisons, are all that we can attain to as yet. On the other hand, it is comparatively easy to arrange the whole group of our cases in some series depending on their observed external character and details. They can, indeed, be arranged in more than one series of this kind — the difficulty is in selecting the most instructive. That which I shall here select is in some points arbitrary, but it has the advantage of bringing out the wide range of variation in the clearness and content of these apparitional communications, here arranged mainly in a descending series, beginning with those cases where fullest knowledge or purpose is shown, and ending with those where the indication of intelligence becomes feeblest, dying away at last into vague sounds and sights without recognisable significance.

But I shall begin by referring to a small group of cases,[1] which I admit to be anomalous and non-evidential — for we cannot prove that they were more than subjective experiences — yet which certainly should not be lost, filling as they do, in all their grotesqueness, a niche in our series otherwise as yet vacant. If man's spirit is separated at death from his organism, there must needs be cases where that separation, although apparently, is not really complete. There must be subjective sensations corresponding to the objective external facts of apparent death and subsequent resuscitation. Nor need it surprise those who may

---

[1] See *Phantasms of the Living*, vol. ii. p. 305; *Proceedings* S.P.R., vol. viii. p. 180; *ibid.* p. 194.

have followed my general argument, if those subjective sensations should prove to be dreamlike and fantastic. Here, as so often in our inquiries, the very oddity and unexpectedness of the details — the absence of that solemnity which one would think the dying man's own mind would have infused into the occasion — may point to the existence of some reality beneath the grotesque symbolism of the transitional dream.

The transitional dream, I call it, for it seems to me not improbable — remote though such a view may be from current notions — that the passage from one state to another may sometimes be accompanied with some temporary lack of adjustment between experiences taking place in such different environments — between the systems of symbolism belonging to the one and to the other state. But the reason why I refer to the cases in this place is that here we have perhaps our nearest possible approach to the sensations of the spirit which is endeavouring to manifest itself; — an inside view of a would-be apparition. The narratives suggest, moreover, that spirits recently freed from the body may enjoy a fuller perception of earthly scenes than it is afterwards possible to retain, and that thus the predominance of apparitions of the *recently* dead may be to some extent explained.

We have, indeed, very few cases where actual apparitions give evidence of any *continuity* in the knowledge possessed by a spirit of friends on earth. Such evidence is, naturally enough, more often furnished by automatic script or utterance. But there is one case (which I give in Appendix VII. A) where a spirit is recorded as appearing repeatedly — in guardian-angel fashion — and especially as foreseeing and sympathising with the survivor's future marriage.

Among repeated apparitions this case at present stands almost alone; its parallels will be found when we come to deal with the persistent "controls," or alleged communicating spirits, which influence trance-utterance or automatic script. A case bearing some resemblance to it, however, is given in *Proceedings* S.P.R., vol. viii. p. 233, the main difference being that the repeated communications are there made in *dream*, and in *Proceedings* S.P.R., vol. v. p. 450, [714 A], is recorded another case, where the deceased person seems to make repeated efforts to impress on survivors a wish prompted by continued affection.

Less uncommon are the cases where an apparition, occurring singly and not repeated, indicates a continued knowledge of the affairs of earth. That knowledge, indeed, runs mainly, as we shall presently see, in two directions. There is often knowledge of some circumstance connected with the deceased person's own death, as the appearance of his body after dissolution, or the place of its temporary deposit or final burial. And there is often knowledge of the impending or actual death of some friend of the deceased person's. On the view here taken of the gradual passage from the one environment into the other, both these kinds of knowledge seem probable enough. I think it likely that some part of the consciousness after death may for some time be dreamily occupied with the physical scene. And similarly, when some surviving friend is gradually verging towards the same dissolution, the fact may be readily perceptible in the spiritual world. When the friend has actually died, the knowledge which his predecessor may have of his transition is knowledge appertaining to events of the next world as much as of this.

But apart from this information, acquired perhaps on the borderland between two states, apparitions do sometimes imply a perception of more definitely terrene events, such as the moral crises (as marriage, grave quarrels, or impending crimes) of friends left behind on earth. In *Proceedings* S.P.R., vol. vi. p. 25 [716 A], is a case of impressive warning, in which the phantom was seen by two persons, one of whom had already had a less evidential experience.

In another case of similar type,[1] the message, while felt by the percipient to be convincing and satisfactory, was held too private to be communicated in detail. It is plain that just in the cases where the message is most intimately veracious, the greatest difficulty is likely to be felt as to making it known to strangers.

I have already given a case (Appendix VII. A) where a departed spirit seems to show a sympathetic anticipation of a marriage some time before it is contemplated. In another case (*Journal* S.P.R., vol. v. p. 10), the percipient, Mrs. V., describes a vision of a mother's form suspended, as it were, in a church where her son is undergoing the rite of confirmation. That vision, indeed, might have been purely subjective, as Mrs. V. was familiar with the departed mother's aspect; though value is given to it by the fact that Mrs. V. has had other experiences which included evidential coincidences.

From these instances of knowledge shown by the departed of events which seem wholly terrene, I pass to knowledge of events which seem in some sense more nearly concerned with the spirit-world. We have, as already hinted, a considerable group of cases where a spirit seems to be aware of the *impending death* of a survivor.[2] In some few of those

---

[1] See *Proceedings* S.P.R., vol. viii. p. 236 [716 B].

[2] See for instance *Proceedings* S.P.R., vol. vi. p. 20; the same, vol. xi. p. 429 and *Phantasms of the Living*, vol. ii. p. 208 [717 A, B and C].

cases the foreknowledge is entirely inexplicable by any such foresight as we mortals can imagine, but in the case given in Appendix VII. B, though the family did not foresee the death, a physician might, for aught we know, have been able to anticipate it. However explained, the case is one of the best-attested, and in itself one of the most remarkable, that we possess.

I place next by themselves a small group of cases which have the interest of uniting the group just recounted, where the spirit anticipates the friend's departure, with the group next to be considered, where the spirit welcomes the friend already departed from earth. This class forms at the same time a natural extension of the clairvoyance of the dying exemplified in some "reciprocal" cases (e.g. in the case of Miss W., where a dying aunt has a vision of her little niece who sees an apparition of her at the same time; see *Phantasms of the Living*, vol. ii. p. 253). Just as the approaching severance of spirit from body there aided the spirit to project its observation among incarnate spirits at a distance upon this earth, so here does that same approaching severance enable the dying person to see spirits who are already in the next world. It is not very uncommon for dying persons to say, or to indicate when beyond speech, that they see spirit friends apparently near them. But, of course, such vision becomes evidential only when the dying person is unaware that the friend whose spirit he sees has actually departed, or is just about to depart, from earth. Such a conjuncture must plainly be rare; it is even rather surprising that these "Peak in Darien" cases, as Miss Cobbe has termed them in a small collection which she made some years ago, should be found at all. We can add to Miss Cobbe's cases two of fair attestation. (*Proceedings* S.P. R., vol. iii. p. 93, and vol. xiv. p. 288 [718 A and B]).

From this last group, then, there is scarcely a noticeable transition to the group where departed spirits manifest their knowledge that some friend who survived them has now passed on into their world. That such recognition and welcome does in fact take place, later evidence, drawn especially from trance-utterances, will give good ground to believe. Only rarely, however, will such welcome — taking place as it does in the spiritual world — be reflected by apparitions in *this*. When so reflected, it may take different forms, from an actual utterance of sympathy, as from a known departed friend, down to a mere silent presence, perhaps inexplicable except to those who happen to have known some long predeceased friend of the decedent's.

I quote in Appendix VII. C one of the most complete cases of this type, which was brought to us by the Census of Hallucinations.

There are other cases more or less analogous to this. In one[1] the apparition of a dying mother brings the news of her own death and that her baby is living. In another[2] a mother sees a vision of her son being drowned and also an apparition of her own dead mother, who tells her of the drowning. In this case, the question may be raised as to whether the second figure seen may not have been, so to say, *substitutive* — a symbol in which the percipient's own mind clothed a telepathic impression of the actual decedent's passage from earth. Such a view might perhaps be supported by some anomalous cases where news of the death is brought by the apparition of a person still living, who, nevertheless, is not by any normal means aware of the death. (See the case of Mrs. T., already given in Appendix IV. E.)

But such an explanation is not always possible. In the case of Mrs. Bacchus,[3] for instance, both the deceased person and the phantasmal figure were previously unknown to the percipient. This case — the last which Edmund Gurney published — comes from an excellent witness. The psychical incident which it seems to imply, while very remote from popular notions, would be quite in accordance with the rest of our present series. A lady dies; her husband in the spirit-world is moved by her arrival; and the direction thus given to his thought projects a picture of him, clothed as in the days when he lived with her, into visibility in the house where her body is lying. We have thus a dream-like recurrence to earthly memories, prompted by a revival of those memories which had taken place in the spiritual world. The case is midway between a case of *welcome* and a case of *haunting*.

I now come to a considerable group of cases where the departed spirit shows a definite knowledge of some fact connected with his own earth-life, his death, or subsequent events connected with that death. The knowledge of subsequent events, as of the spread of the news of his death, or as to the place of his burial, is, of course, a greater achievement (so to term it) than a mere recollection of facts known to him in life, and ought strictly, on the plan of this series, to be first illustrated. But it will be seen that all these stages of knowledge cohere together; and their connection can better be shown if I begin at the lower stage, — of mere earth-memory. Now here again, as so often already, we shall have to wait for automatic script and the like to illustrate the full extent of the deceased person's possible memory. Readers of the utterances, for instance, of

---

[1] *Proceedings* S.P.R., vol. x. p. 214 [719 A].
[2] *Phantasms of the Living*, vol. i. p. 449 [719 B].
[3] See *Proceedings* S.P.R., vol. v. pp. 422–26 [§ 720].

"George Pelham" (see Chapter IX.) will know how full and accurate may be these recollections from beyond the grave. Mere apparitions, such as those with which we are now dealing, can rarely give more than one brief message, probably felt by the deceased to be of urgent importance.

A well-attested case where the information communicated in a vision proved to be definite, accurate, and important to the survivors is given in Appendix VII. D. In the same Appendix another case in this group is also quoted. It illustrates the fact that the cases of deepest interest are often the hardest for the inquirer to get hold of.

In this connection I may refer again to Mrs. Storie's dream of the death of her brother in a railway accident, given in Chapter IV. While I think that Gurney was right — in the state of the evidence at the time *Phantasms of the Living* was written — in doing his best to bring this incident under the head of telepathic clairvoyance, I yet feel that the knowledge since gained makes it impossible for me to adhere to that view. I cannot regard the visionary scene as wholly reflected from the mind of the dying man. I cannot think, in the first place, that the vision of Mr. Johnstone — interpolated with seeming irrelevance among the details of the disaster — did only by accident coincide with the fact that that gentleman really *was* in the train, and with the further fact that it was *he* who communicated the fact of Mr. Hunter's death to Mr. and Mrs. Storie. I must suppose that the communicating intelligence was aware of Mr. Johnstone's presence, and at least guessed that upon him (as a clergyman) that task would naturally fall. Nor can I pass over as purely symbolic so important a part of the vision as the *second figure*, and the scrap of conversation, which seemed to be half heard. I therefore consider that the case falls among those where a friend recently departed appears in company of some other friend, dead some time before.

We have thus seen the spirit occupied shortly after death with various duties or engagements, small or great, which it has incurred during life on earth. Such ties seem to prompt or aid its action upon its old surroundings. And here an important reflection occurs. Can we *prepare* such a tie for the departing spirit? Can we create for it some welcome and helpful train of association which may facilitate the self-manifestation which many souls appear to desire? I believe that we can to some extent do this. At an early stage of our collection, Edmund Gurney was struck by the unexpectedly large proportion of cases where the percipient informed us that there had been a *compact* between himself and the deceased person that whichever passed away first should try to appear to the other. "Considering," he adds, "what an extremely small number of persons make such a compact, compared with those who do not, it is difficult to resist the conclusion that its existence has a certain efficacy."

Let us now review the compact-cases given in *Phantasms of the Living* and consider how far they seem to indicate *ante-mortem* or *post-mortem* communication. The twelve cases there recorded are such as fell, or may have fallen, within twelve hours of the death. In three of these cases, the agent whose phantasm appeared was certainly still alive. In most of the other cases the exact time relation is obscure; in a few of them there is strong probability that the agent was already dead. The inference will be that the existence of a promise or compact may act effectively both on the subliminal self before death and also probably on the spirit after death.

This conclusion is confirmed by several other cases, one of which is given in Appendix VII. E. This case suggests an important practical reflection. When a compact to appear, if possible, after death is made, it should be understood that the appearance need not be to the special partner in the compact, but to any one whom the agent can succeed in impressing. It is likely enough that many such attempts, which have failed on account of the surviving friend's lack of appropriate sensitivity, might have succeeded if the agent had tried to influence some one already known to be capable of receiving these impressions.[1] There is a case given in *Proceedings* S.P.R., vol. v. p. 440, in which a lady, having made a compact with her husband and also with a friend, her phantom is seen after her death by her husband and daughter and the latter's nurse, collectively; but not by the friend, who was living elsewhere.

Again, we cannot tell how long the spirit may continue the effort, or, so to say, renew the experiment. In a case recorded in *Proceedings* S.P.R., vol. x. p. 378, the compact is fulfilled after a space of five years. In another case,[2] there had been no formal compact; but there is an attempt to express gratitude on an anniversary of death; and this implies the same kind of mindful effort as the fulfilment of a definite promise.

I have now traced certain *post-mortem* manifestations which reveal a recollection of events known at death, and also a persistence of purpose in carrying out intentions formed before death. In this next group I shall trace the knowledge of the departed a little further, and shall discuss some cases where they appear cognisant of the aspect of their bodies after death, or of the scenes in which those bodies are temporarily deposited or finally laid. Such knowledge may appear trivial,—unworthy the atten-

---

[1] The cases recorded in *Phantasms of the Living*, vol. ii. p. 216, and *Proceedings* S.P.R., vol. x. p. 263 [727 A and B] may be regarded as deflected fulfilments.

[2] *Proceedings* S.P.R., vol. x. p. 383. See also *ibid*. p. 371 and vol. viii. p. 214 [728 A and B and § 726].

tion of spirits transported into a higher world.   But it is in accordance with the view of a gradual transference of interests and perceptions, — a period of intermediate confusion, such as may follow especially upon a death of a sudden or violent kind, or perhaps upon a death which interrupts very strong affections.

Thus we have already (Appendix VII. B) encountered one striking case of this type, — the *scratch on the cheek*, perceived by the departed daughter, as we may conjecture, by reason of the close sympathy which united her to the mother who was caring for her remains.

There are also two cases closely resembling each other, though from percipients in widely different parts of the world, where a clairvoyant vision seems to be presented of a tranquil death-chamber.   In that of Mr. Hector of Valencia, South Australia (see *Phantasms of the Living*, vol. i. p. 353), the percipient sees in a dream his father dying in the room he usually occupied, with a candle burning on a chair by his bed; and the father is found dead in the morning, with a candle by his bedside in the position seen in the dream.   There is not, however, in this case any sure indication that the dead or dying person was cognisant of his own body's aspect or surroundings.   There may have been a clairvoyant excursion on the percipient's part, evoked by some impulse from the agent which did not itself develop into distinctness.[1]

But in certain cases of violent death there seems to have been an intention on the deceased person's part to show the condition in which his body is left.   Such was Mrs. Storie's dream, or rather series of visions referred to earlier in this chapter.   Such are the cases given in *Phantasms of the Living*, vol. i. p. 365 [429 A], and *Proceedings* S.P.R., vol. iii. (1885) p. 95 [§ 730].   Here, too, may be placed two cases — those of Dr. Bruce (in Appendix IV. D) and Miss Hall (*Journal* S.P.R., vol. vii. p. 173 [731 A]) — where there are *successive* pictures of a death and the subsequent arrangement of the body.   The *milieux* of the percipients, the nature of the deaths, are here again totally disparate; yet we seem to see the same unknown laws producing effects closely similar.

In Dr. Bruce's case one might interpret the visions as coming to the percipient through the mind of his wife, who was present at the scene of the murder.   But this explanation would be impossible in Miss Hall's case.   Rather it seems as though some telepathic link, set up between the dying brother and the sister, had been maintained after death until all duties had been fulfilled to the departed.   The case reminds one of the old Homeric notions of the restless appeal of unburied comrades.

[1] For the other case see *Phantasms of the Living*, vol. i. p. 265.

In the case of Mrs. Green (*Proceedings* S.P.R., vol. v. p. 420 [429 D]), we come across an interesting problem.   Two women are drowned under very peculiar circumstances.   A friend has apparently a clairvoyant vision of the scene, yet not at the moment when it occurred, but many hours afterwards, and about the time when another person, deeply interested, heard of the death.   It is therefore possible to suppose that the apparently clairvoyant scene was in reality impressed telepathically on the percipient by another living mind.   I think, however, that both the nature of the vision and certain analogies, which will appear later in our argument, point to a different view, involving an agency both of the dead and of the living.   I conjecture that a current of influence may be started by a deceased person, which, however, only becomes strong enough to be perceptible to its object when reinforced by some vivid current of emotion arising in living minds.   I do not say that this is yet provable; yet the hint may be of value when the far-reaching interdependencies of telepathy between the two worlds come to be better understood.

Two singular cases in this group remain, where the departed spirit, long after death, seems preoccupied with the spot where his bones are laid. The first of these cases (*Journal* S.P.R., vol. vi. p.230 [733 A]) approaches farce; the second (in which the skeleton of a man who had probably been murdered about forty years before was discovered by means of a dream; see *Proceedings* S.P.R., vol. vi. p. 35), stands alone among our narratives in the tragedy which follows on the communication.   Mr. Podmore in an article in the same volume (p. 303) suggests other theories to account for this case without invoking the agency of the dead; but to me the least impossible explanation is still the notion that the murdered man's dreams harked back after all those years to his remote unconsecrated grave.   I may refer further to another case (in *Proceedings* S.P.R., vol. iv. p. 155, footnote) where feelings of horror and depression were constantly experienced in a room over which a baby's body was afterwards found.   This case makes, perhaps, for another explanation — depending not so much on any *continued* influence of the departed spirit as on some *persistent* influence inhering in the bones themselves — deposited under circumstances of terror or anguish, and possibly in some way still radiating a malignant memory.   Bizarre as this interpretation looks, we shall find some confirmation of such a possibility in our chapter on Possession.   Yet another case belonging to the same group (*Proceedings* S.P.R., vol. v. p. 418) supplies a variant on this view; suggesting, as Edward Gurney has remarked, the local imprintation of a tragic picture, by *whom* and upon *what* we cannot tell.

I think it well to suggest even these wild conjectures; so long as they are understood to be conjectures and nothing more. I hold it probable that those communications, of which telepathy from one spirit to another forms the most easily traceable variety, are in reality infinitely varied and complex, and show themselves from time to time in forms which must for long remain quite beyond our comprehension.

The next class of cases in this series well illustrates this unexpectedness. It has only been as the result of a gradual accumulation of concordant cases that I have come to believe there is some reality in the bizarre supposition that the departed spirit is sometimes specially aware of the time at which news of his death is about to reach some given friend.[1] Proof of such knowledge on his part is rendered harder by the alternative possibility that the friend may by clairvoyance become aware of a letter in his own proximity. As was shown in *Phantasms of the Living*, there is some evidence for such clairvoyance even in cases where the letter seen is quite unimportant.

Again, there are cases where the percipient states that a cloud of unreasonable depression fell upon him about the time of his friend's death at a distance, and continued until the actual news arrived; when, instead of becoming intensified, it lifted suddenly. In one or two such cases there was an actual presence or apparition, which seemed to hang about until the news arrived, and then disappeared. Or, on the other hand, there is sometimes a happy vision of the departed preluding the news, as though to prepare the percipient's mind for the shock (*Proceedings* S.P.R., vol. iii. p. 90 [735 A]). The suggested inference is that in such cases the spirit's attention is more or less continuously directed to the survivor until the news reaches him. This does not, of course, explain how the spirit learns as to the arrival of the news; yet it makes that piece of knowledge seem a less isolated thing.

Having thus referred to a number of cases where the apparition shows varying degrees of knowledge or memory, I pass on to the somewhat commoner type, where the apparition lacks the power or the impulse to communicate any message much more definite than that all-important one — of his own continued life and love. These cases, nevertheless, might be subdivided on many lines. Each apparition, even though it be momentary, is a phenomenon complex in more ways than our minds can follow. We must look for some broad line of demarcation, which may apply to a great many different incidents, while continuing to some extent

[1] For cases illustrating this, see *Proceedings* S.P.R., vol. v. p. 409 [§ 734]; also *Proceedings* S.P.R., vol. viii. p. 220; *ibid.* p. 218; *Phantasms of the Living*, vol. ii. p. 690; and *Proceedings* S.P.R., vol. x. p. 373 [§ 736 and 736 A, B and C].

the series which we have already been descending — from knowledge and purpose on the deceased person's part down to vagueness and apparent automatism.

Such a division — gradual, indeed, but for that very reason the more instructive — exists between *personal* and *local* apparitions; between manifestations plainly intended to impress the minds of certain definite survivors and manifestations in accustomed haunts, some of which, indeed, may be destined to impress survivors, but which degenerate and disintegrate into sights and sounds too meaningless to prove either purpose or intelligence.

Let us look, then, for these characteristics, not expecting, of course, that our series will be logically simple; for it must often happen that the personal and local impulses will be indistinguishable, as when the desired percipient is inhabiting the familiar home. But we may begin with some cases where the apparition has shown itself in some scene altogether strange to the deceased person.

We have had, of course, some cases of this type already. Such was the case of the apparition with the *red scratch* (Appendix VII. B); such too was the apparition in the Countess Kapnist's carriage (Appendix VII. E). Such cases, indeed, occur most frequently — and this fact is itself significant — among the higher and more developed forms of manifestation. Among the briefer, less-developed apparitions with which we have now to deal, invasions by the phantasm of quite unknown territory are relatively few. I will begin by referring to a curious case, where the impression given is that of a spiritual presence which seeks and finds the percipient, but is itself too confused for coherent communication (Mrs. Lightfoot's case, *Phantasms of the Living*, vol. i. p. 453 [429 B]). It will be seen that this narrative is thoroughly in accordance with previous indications of a state of posthumous *bewilderment* supervening before the spirit has adjusted its perceptions to the new environment.

In cases like Mrs. Lightfoot's, where the percipient's surroundings are unknown to the deceased person, and especially in cases where the intimation of a death reaches the percipient when *at sea*, there is plainly nothing except the percipient's own personality to guide the spirit in his search. We have several narratives of this type. In one of these — Archdeacon Farler's, already referred to (p. 227), the apparition appears *twice*, the second appearance at least being subsequent to the death. It is plain that if in such a case the *second* apparition conveys no fresh intelligence, we cannot prove that it is more than a subjective recrudescence of the *first*. Yet analogy is in favour of its veridical character, since we have cases where successive manifestations *do* bring fresh knowledge, and seem to show a continued effort to communicate.[1]

Then, again, there are *auditory* cases where the phantasmal speech has occurred in places not known to the deceased person. (*Proceedings S.P.R.*, vol. iii. p. 90, and vol. v. p. 455.)

One specially impressive characteristic of apparitions (as has been already remarked) is their occasional *collectivity* — the fact that more percipients than one sometimes see or hear the phantasmal figure or voice simultaneously. When one is considering the gradual decline in definiteness and apparent purpose from one group of apparitions to another, it is natural to ask whether this characteristic — in my view so important — is found to accompany especially the higher, more intelligent manifestations.

I cannot find that this is so. On the contrary, it is, I think, in cases of mere *haunting* that we oftenest find that the figure is seen by several persons at once, or else (a cognate phenomenon) by several persons successively. I know not how to explain this apparent tendency. Could we admit the underlying assumptions, it would suit the view that the "haunting" spirits are "earthbound," and thus somehow nearer to matter than spirits more exalted. Yet instances of collectivity are scattered through all classes of apparitions; and the irregular appearance of a characteristic which seems to us so fundamental affords another lesson how great may be the variety of inward mechanism in cases which to us might seem constructed on much the same type.

I pass on to a group of cases which are both personal and local; although the personal element in most of them — the desire to manifest to the friend — may seem more important than the local element — the impulse to revisit some accustomed haunt.

In the case which I shall now cite the deceased person's image is seen simultaneously by several members of his own household, in his own house. Note the analogy to a collective crystal vision.[2]

The account is taken from *Phantasms of the Living*, vol. ii. p. 213. It is given by Mr. Charles A. W. Lett, of the Military and Royal Naval Club, Albemarle Street, W.

---

[1] See for instance *Journal* S.P.R., vol. vii. p. 173.

[2] This analogy suggests itself still more forcibly in the remarkable case recorded in *Journal* S.P.R., vol. xii. p. 17. Here the visions, seen in a mirror, were perceived simultaneously, though not quite in the same way, by four witnesses, and lasted for an appreciable length of time.

On the 5th April 1873 my wife's father, Captain Towns, died at his residence, Cranbrook, Rose Bay, near Sidney, N. S. Wales. About six weeks after his death my wife had occasion, one evening about nine o'clock, to go to one of the bedrooms in the house. She was accompanied by a young lady, Miss Berthon, and as they entered the room — the gas was burning all the time — they were amazed to see, reflected as it were on the polished surface of the wardrobe, the image of Captain Towns. It was barely half figure, the head, shoulders, and part of the arms only showing — in fact, it was like an ordinary medallion portrait, but life-size. The face appeared wan and pale, as it did before his death, and he wore a kind of grey flannel jacket, in which he had been accustomed to sleep. Surprised and half alarmed at what they saw, their first idea was that a portrait had been hung in the room, and that what they saw was its reflection; but there was no picture of the kind.

Whilst they were looking and wondering, my wife's sister, Miss Towns, came into the room, and before either of the others had time to speak she exclaimed, "Good gracious! Do you see papa?" One of the house-maids happened to be passing downstairs at the moment, and she was called in, and asked if she saw anything, and her reply was, "Oh, miss! the master." Graham — Captain Towns' old body servant — was then sent for, and he also immediately exclaimed, "Oh, Lord save us! Mrs. Lett, it's the Captain!" The butler was called, and then Mrs. Crane, my wife's nurse, and they both said what they saw. Finally, Mrs. Towns was sent for, and, seeing the apparition, she advanced towards it with her arm extended as if to touch it, and as she passed her hand over the panel of the wardrobe the figure gradually faded away, and never again appeared, though the room was regularly occupied for a long time after.

These are the simple facts of the case, and they admit of no doubt; no kind of intimation was given to any of the witnesses; the same question was put to each one as they came into the room, and the reply was given without hesitation by each. It was by the merest accident that I did not see the apparition. I was in the house at the time, but did not hear when I was called.   C. A. W. LETT.

We, the undersigned, having read the above statement, certify that it is strictly accurate, as we both were witnesses of the apparition.

SARA LETT.
SIBBIE SMYTH (*nee* TOWNS).

Gurney writes: —

Mrs. Lett assures me that neither she nor her sister ever experienced a hallucination of the senses on any other occasion. She is positive that the recognition of the appearance on the part of each of the later witnesses was *independent*, and not due to any suggestion from the persons already in the room.

There is another collective case which is noticeable from the fact that the departed spirit appears to influence two persons at a distance from

each other in a concordant way, so that one of them becomes conscious
of the appearance to the other.[1] Compare with this the incident given
at the end of Appendix VII. G, when Miss Campbell has a vision of her
friend seeing an apparition at a time when this is actually occurring.[2]

The case given in Appendix VII. F — which comes from excellent
informants — is one of those which correspond most nearly to what one
would *desire* in a posthumous message. I may refer also to General Campbell's case (in *Proceedings* S.P.R., vol. v. p. 476) in which a long continued
series of unaccountable noises and an apparition twice seen by a child in
the house suggested to the narrator the agency of his dead wife. The
case, which depends for its evidential force on a great mass of detail, is
too long for me to quote; but it is worth study, as is any case where there
seems evidence of persistent effort to manifest, meeting with one knows
not what difficulty. It may be that in such a story there is nothing but
strange coincidence, or it may be that from records of partially successful
effort, renewed often and in ambiguous ways, we shall hereafter learn
something of the nature of that curtain of obstruction which now seems
so arbitrary in its sudden lifting, its sudden fall.

I will conclude this group by referring the reader to three cases closely
similar, all well attested, and all of them capable of explanation either on
local or personal grounds. In the first (*Phantasms of the Living*, vol. ii.
p. 619 [744 A]) an apparition is seen by two persons in a house in
Edinburgh, a few hours before the death of a lady who had lived there,
and whose body was to be brought back to it. In the second (*Proceedings* S.P.R., vol. vi. p. 57 [744 B]) the dead librarian haunts his library,
but in the library are members of his old staff. In the third (*Phantasms
of the Living*, vol. i. p. 212 [§ 744]), the dead wife loiters round her
husband's tomb, but near it passes a gardener who had been in her
employ.

In this last case the apparition was seen about seven and a half hours
after the death. This, as Gurney remarked, makes it still more difficult
to regard the case as a telepathic impression transmitted at the moment
of death, and remaining latent in the mind of the percipient. The incident suggests rather that Bard, the gardener, had come upon Mrs. de

[1] See the *Proceedings* of the American Society for Psychical Research, vol. i. p. 446
[741 A].

[2] In the case recorded in *Proceedings* S.P.R., vol. viii. p. 173 [§ 742], the decedent
would appear to be satisfying both a local and a personal attraction. See also the
cases given in *Proceedings* S.P.R., vol. iii. p. 93, and vol. v. p. 437 [742 A], which
are somewhat similar.

Fréville's spirit, so to say, unawares.   One cannot imagine that she specially wished him to see her, and to see her engaged in what seems so needless and undignified a retracing of currents of earthly thought. Rather this seems a rudimentary *haunting* — an incipient lapse into those aimless, perhaps unconscious, reappearances in familiar spots which may persist (as it would seem) for many years after death.

A somewhat similar case is that of Colonel Crealock (in *Proceedings* S.P.R., vol. v. p. 432) where a soldier who had been dead some hours was seen by his superior officer in camp at night rolling up and taking away his bed.

It is, indeed, mainly by dwelling on these intermediate cases, between a message-bringing apparition and a purposeless haunt, that we have most hope of understanding the typical haunt which, while it has been in a sense the most popular of all our phenomena, is yet to the careful inquirer one of the least satisfactory.   One main evidential difficulty generally lies in identifying the haunting figure, in finding anything to connect the history of the house with the vague and often various sights and sounds which perplex or terrify its flesh and blood inhabitants.   We must, at any rate, rid ourselves of the notion that some great crime or catastrophe is always to be sought as the groundwork of a haunt of this kind.   To that negative conclusion our cases concordantly point us.[1] The apparition is most often seen by a stranger, several months after the death, with no apparent reason for its appearance at that special time.   This last point is of interest in considering the question whether the hallucinatory picture could have been projected from any still incarnate mind.   In one case — the vision of the Bishop of St. Brieuc (given in *Proceedings* S.P.R., vol. v. p. 460), there *was* such a special reason — the Bishop's body, unknown to the percipient, was at that moment being buried at the distance of a few miles.   Mr. Podmore suggests (*op. cit.*, vol. vi. p. 301) that it was from the minds of the living mourners that the Bishop's phantasm was generated.   That hypothesis may have its portion of truth; the surrounding emotion may have been one of the factors which made the apparition possible.   But the assumption that it was the only admissible factor — that the departed Bishop's

[1] See, however, Sir Arthur Beecher's case (*Proceedings* S.P.R., vol. iii. p. 110) where there was at least a rumour of some crime.   In Mrs. M.'s case, too (*Proceedings* S.P.R., vol. viii. p. 178) and Mrs. Pennée's (*Proceedings* S.P.R., vol. vi. p. 60) there is some indication of past troubles in which the percipients, of course, were in no way concerned.   But in no other cases has there been anything, as far as we know, which could trouble the departed spirit with importunate memories of his earthly home.

own possible agency must be set aside altogether — lands us, I think, in difficulties greater than those which we should thus escape. The reader who tries to apply it to the apparitions quoted in my earlier groups will find himself in a labyrinth of complexity. Still more will this be the case in dealing with the far fuller and more explicit *motor* communications, by automatic writing or speech, which we shall have to discuss in the two next chapters. Unless the actual evidence be disallowed in a wholesale manner, we shall be forced, I think, to admit the continued action of the departed as a main element in these apparitions.

I do not say as the *only* element. I myself hold, as already implied, that the thought and emotion of living persons does largely intervene, as aiding or conditioning the independent action of the departed. I even believe that it is possible that, say, an intense fixation of my own mind on a departed spirit may aid that spirit to manifest at a special moment — and not even to me, but to a percipient more sensitive than myself. In the boundless ocean of mind innumerable currents and tides shift with the shifting emotion of each several soul.

But now we are confronted by another possible element in these vaguer classes of apparitions, harder to evaluate even than the possible action of incarnate minds. I mean the possible *results* of past mental action, which, for aught we know, may persist in some perceptible manner, without fresh reinforcement, just as the results of past bodily action persist. This question leads to the still wider question of *retrocognition*, and of the relation of psychical phenomena to *time* generally — a problem whose discussion cannot be attempted here.[1] Yet we must remember that such possibilities exist; they may explain certain phenomena into which little of fresh intelligence seems to enter, as, for instance, the alleged persistence, perhaps for years, of meaningless sounds in a particular room or house.

And since we are coming now to cases into which this element of meaningless sound will enter largely, it seems right to begin their discussion with a small group of cases where there is evidence for the definite agency of some dying or deceased person in connection with inarticulate sounds, or I should rather say of the *connection* of some deceased person with the sounds; since the best explanation may perhaps be that they are *sounds of welcome* — before or after actual death — corresponding to those *apparitions of welcome* of which we have already had specimens. One of our

---

[1] For a discussion of this problem, illustrated by a large number of cases, see my article on "Retrocognition and Precognition" in the *Proceedings* S.P.R., vol. xi. pp. 334–593.

cases (see *Phantasms of the Living*, vol. ii. p. 639 [§ 747]) is remarkable in that the auditory hallucination — a sound as of female voices gently singing — was heard by five persons, by four of them, as it seems, independently, and in two places, on different sides of the house. At the same time, one person — the Eton master whose mother had just died, and who was therefore presumably in a frame of mind more prone to hallucination than the physician, matron, friend, or servants who actually did hear the singing — himself heard nothing at all. In this case the physician felt no doubt that Mrs. L. was actually dead; and in fact it was during the laying out of the body that the sounds occurred.

I have already discussed (Chapter VI.) the nature of these phantasmal sounds; — nor is it contrary to our analogies that the person most deeply concerned in the death should in this case fail to hear them. But the point on which I would here lay stress is that phantasmal sounds — even non-articulate sounds — may be as clear a manifestation of personality as phantasmal figures. Among non-articulate noises music is, of course, the most pleasing; but sounds, for instance, which imitate the work of a carpenter's shop, may be equally human and intelligent. In some of the cases of this class we see apparent attempts of various kinds to simulate sounds such as men and women — or manufactured, as opposed to natural, objects — are accustomed to produce. To claim this humanity, to indicate this intelligence, seems the only motive of sounds of this kind.[1]

These sounds, in their rudimentary attempt at showing intelligence, are about on a level with the exploits of the "Poltergeist," where coals are thrown about, water spilt, and so forth. Poltergeist phenomena, however, seldom coincide with the ordinary phenomena of a haunt. We have one remarkable case (*Journal* S.P.R., vol. ix. p. 280-84 [868 B]) where Poltergeist phenomena coincide with a death, and a few cases where they are supposed to follow on a death; but, as a rule, where figures appear there are no movements; and where there are movements no apparition is seen. If alleged Poltergeist phenomena are always fraudulent, there would be nothing to be surprised at here. If, as I suspect, they are sometimes genuine, their dissociation from visual hallucinations may sometimes afford us a hint of value.

---

[1] See, however, Mrs. Sidgwick's remarks (*Proceedings* S.P.R., vol. iii. pp. 79–80), as to the rarity of any indication of intelligence in such sounds, and the possibility of reading more intelligence into them than they really possess. There is now, of course, more evidence as to these sounds than there was at the date of Mrs. Sidgwick's paper (1885).

But after Poltergeists have been set aside, — after a severe line has been drawn excluding all those cases (in themselves singular enough) where the main phenomena observed consist of non-articulate sounds, — there remains a great mass of evidence to haunting, — that is, broadly speaking, to the fact that there are many houses in which more than one person has independently seen phantasmal figures, which usually, though not always, bear at least some resemblance to each other.[1] The facts thus baldly stated are beyond dispute. Their true interpretation is a very difficult matter. Mrs. Sidgwick gives four hypotheses, which I must quote at length as the first serious attempt ever made (so far as I know) to collect and face the difficulties of this problem, so often, but so loosely, discussed through all historical times. (From *Proceedings* S.P.R., vol. iii. pp. 146–8.)

"I will, therefore, proceed briefly to state and discuss the only four theories that have occurred to me.

"The two which I will take first in order assume that the apparitions are due to the agency or presence of the spirits of deceased men.

"There is first the popular view, that the apparition is something belonging to the external world — that, like ordinary matter, it occupies and moves through space, and would be in the room whether the percipient were there to see it or not. This hypothesis involves us in many difficulties, of which one serious one — that of accounting for the clothes of the ghost — has often been urged, and never, I think, satisfactorily answered. Nevertheless, I am bound to admit that there is some little evidence tending to suggest this theory. For instance, in the account,[2] of which I have given an abstract, of the weeping lady who has appeared so frequently in a certain house, the following passage occurs: — 'They went after it (the figure) together into the drawing-room; it then came out, and went down the aforesaid passage (leading to the kitchen), but was the next minute seen by another Miss [M.] . . .come up the outside steps from the kitchen. On this particular day, Captain [M.'s] married daughter happened to be at an upstairs window . . . and independently

[1] Thus Mrs. Sidgwick, even as far back as 1885 (*Proceedings* S.P.R., vol. iii. p. 142), writes: "I can only say that having made every effort — as my paper will, I hope, have shown — to exercise a reasonable scepticism, I yet do not feel equal to the degree of unbelief in human testimony necessary to avoid accepting, at least provisionally, the conclusion that there are, in a certain sense, haunted houses, *i.e.*, that there are houses in which similar quasi-human apparitions have occurred at different times to different inhabitants, under circumstances which exclude the hypothesis of suggestion or expectation."

[2] This case is given in Appendix VII. G.

saw the figure continue her course across the lawn and into the orchard.'
A considerable amount of clear evidence to the appearance of ghosts to
independent observers in successive points in space would certainly afford
a strong argument for their having a definite relation to space; but in
estimating evidence of this kind it would be necessary to know how far
the observer's attention had been drawn to the point in question. If
it had been a real woman whom the Miss [M.'s] were observing, we should
have inferred, with perfect certainty, from our knowledge that she could
not be in two places at once, that she had been successively, in a certain
order, in the places where she was seen by the three observers. If they
had noted the moments at which they saw her, and comparing notes afterwards, found that according to these notes they had all seen her at the
same time, or in some other order to that inferred, we should still feel
absolute confidence in our inference, and should conclude that there must
be something wrong about the watches or the notes. From association
of ideas, it would be perfectly natural to make the same inference in the
case of a ghost which looks exactly like a woman. But in the case of
the ghost the inference would not be legitimate, because, unless the particular theory of ghosts which we are discussing be true, there is no reason,
so far as we know, why it should not appear in two or more places at once.
Hence, in the case of the ghost, a well-founded assurance that the appearances were successive would require a careful observation of the times,
which, so far as I know, has never been made. On the whole, therefore,
I must dismiss the popular theory as not having, in my opinion, even a
primâ facie ground for serious consideration.

"The theory that I will next examine seems to me decidedly more
plausible, from its analogy to the conclusion to which I am brought by
the examination of the evidence for phantasms of the living. This theory
is that the apparition has no real relation to the external world, but is a
hallucination caused in some way by some communication, without the
intervention of the senses, between the disembodied spirit and the percipient, its form depending on the mind either of the spirit or of the percipient, or of both. In the case of haunted houses, however, a difficulty
meets us that we do not encounter, or at least rarely encounter, in applying
a similar hypothesis to explain phantasms of the living, or phantasms
of the dead other than fixed local ghosts. In these cases we have generally to suppose a simple *rapport* between mind and mind, but in a haunted
house we have a *rapport* complicated by its apparent dependence on locality.
It seems necessary to make the improbable assumption, that the spirit
is interested in an entirely special way in a particular house (though

possibly this interest may be of a subconscious kind), and that his interest in it puts him into connection with another mind, occupied with it in the way that that of a living person actually there must consciously or unconsciously be, while he does not get into similar communication with the same, or with other persons elsewhere.

"If, notwithstanding these difficulties, it be true that haunting is due in any way to the agency of deceased persons, and conveys a definite idea of them to the percipients through the resemblance to them of the apparition, then, by patiently continuing our investigations, we may expect, sooner or later, to obtain a sufficient amount of evidence to connect clearly the commencement of hauntings with the death of particular persons, and to establish clearly the likeness of the apparition to those persons. The fact that almost everybody is now photographed ought to be of material assistance in obtaining evidence of this latter kind.

"My third theory dispenses with the agency of disembodied spirits, but involves us in other and perhaps equally great improbabilities. It is that the first appearance is a purely subjective hallucination, and that the subsequent similar appearances, both to the original percipient and to others, are the result of the first appearance; unconscious expectancy causing them in the case of the original percipient, and some sort of telepathic communication from the original percipient in the case of others. In fact, it assumes that a tendency to a particular hallucination is in a way infectious. If this theory be true, I should expect to find that the apparently independent appearances after the first depended on the percipient's having had some sort of intercourse with some one who had seen the ghost before, and that any decided discontinuity of occupancy would stop the haunting. I should also expect to find, as we do in one of the cases I have quoted, that sometimes the supposed ghost would follow the family from one abode to another, appearing to haunt them rather than any particular house.

"The fourth theory that I shall mention is one which I can hardly expect to appear plausible, and which, therefore, I only introduce because I think that it corresponds best to a certain part of the evidence; — and, as I have already said, considering the altogether tentative way in which we are inevitably dealing with this obscure subject, it is as well to express definitely every hypothesis which an impartial consideration of the facts suggests. It is that there is something in the actual building itself — some subtle physical influence — which produces in the brain that effect which, in its turn, becomes the cause of a hallucination. It is certainly difficult on this hypothesis alone to suppose that the hallucinations of different people would be similar, but we might account for this by a combination of this hypothesis and the last. The idea is suggested by the case, of which I have given an abstract, where the haunting continued through more than one occupancy, but changed its character; and if there be any truth in the theory, I should expect in time to obtain a good deal more evidence of this kind, combined with evidence that the same persons do not as a rule encounter ghosts elsewhere. I should also expect evidence to be forthcoming supporting the popular idea that repairs and alterations of the building sometimes cause the haunting to cease."[1]

These hypotheses — none of which, as Mrs. Sidgwick expressly states (*op. cit.*, p. 145), seemed to herself satisfactory — did nevertheless, I think, comprise all the deductions which could reasonably be made from the evidence as it at that time stood. A few modifications, which the experience of subsequent years has led me to introduce, can hardly be said to afford further *explanation*, although they state the difficulties in what now seems to me a more hopeful way.

In the first place then — as already explained in Chapter VI. — I in some sense fuse into one Mrs. Sidgwick's two first hypotheses by my own hypothesis of actual presence, actual spatial changes induced in the metetherial, but not in the material world. I hold that when the phantasm is discerned by more than one person at once (and on some other, but not all other occasions) it is actually effecting a change in that portion of space where it is perceived, although not, as a rule, in the matter which occupies that place. It is, therefore, not optically nor acoustically perceived; perhaps no rays of light are reflected nor waves of air set in motion; but an unknown form of supernormal perception, not necessarily acting through the sensory end-organs, comes into play. In the next place, I am inclined to lay stress on the parallel between these narratives of haunting and those phantasms of the living which I have already classed as *psychorrhagic*.

---

[1] In an earlier part of this paper, I mentioned cases of haunted houses where the apparitions are various, and might therefore all of them be merely subjective hallucinations, sometimes, perhaps, caused by expectancy. It is, of course, also possible to explain these cases by the hypothesis we are now discussing. Another class of cases is, perhaps, worth mentioning in this connection. We have in the collection two cases of what was believed by the narrators to be a quite peculiar feeling of discomfort, in houses where concealed and long since decomposed bodies were subsequently found. Such feelings are seldom clearly defined enough to have much evidential value, for others, at any rate, than the percipient; even though mentioned beforehand, and definitely connected with the place where the skeleton was. But if there be really any connection between the skeleton and the feeling, it may possibly be a subtle physical influence such as I am suggesting. — E. M. S.

In each case, as it seems to me, there is an involuntary detachment of some element of the spirit, probably with no knowledge thereof at the main centre of consciousness. Those "haunts by the living," as they may be called, where, for instance, a man is seen phantasmally standing before his own fireplace, seem to me to be repeated, perhaps more readily, after the spirit is freed from the flesh.

Again, I think that the curious question as to the influence of certain *houses* in generating apparitions may be included under the broader heading of Retrocognition. That is to say, we are not here dealing with a special condition of certain houses, but with a branch of the wide problem as to the relation of supernormal phenomena to *time*. Manifestations which occur in haunted houses depend, let us say, on something which has taken place a long time ago. In what way do they depend on that past event? Are they a sequel, or only a residue? Is there fresh operation going on, or only fresh perception of something already accomplished? Or can we in such a case draw any real distinction between a continued action and a continued perception of a past action? The closest parallel, as it seems to me, although not at first sight an obvious one, lies between these phenomena of haunting, these persistent sights and sounds, and certain phenomena of crystal-vision and of automatic script, which also seem to depend somehow upon long-past events, — to be their sequel or their residue. One specimen case I give in Appendix (VII. G), where the connection of the haunting apparition with a certain person long deceased may be maintained with more than usual plausibility. From that level the traceable connections get weaker and weaker, until we come to phantasmal scenes where there is no longer any even apparent claim to the contemporary agency of human spirits. Such a vision, for instance, as that of a line of spectral deer crossing a ford, may indeed, if seen in the same place by several independent observers, be held to be something more than a mere subjective fancy; but what in reality such a picture signifies is a question which brings us at once to theories of the permanence or simultaneity of all phenomena in a timeless Universal Soul.

Such conceptions, however difficult, are among the highest to which our mind can reach. Could we approach them more nearly, they might deeply influence our view, even of our own remote individual destiny. So, perhaps, shall it some day be; at present we may be well satisfied if we can push our knowledge of that destiny one step further than of old, even just behind that veil which has so long hung impenetrably before the eyes of men.

Here, then, is a natural place of pause in our inquiry.

The discussion of the ethical aspect of these questions I have postponed to my concluding chapter. But one point already stands out from the evidence—at once so important and so manifest that it seems well to call attention to it at once — as a solvent more potent than any Lucretius could apply to human superstition and human fears.

In this long string of narratives, complex and bizarre though their details may be, we yet observe that the character of the appearance varies in a definite manner with their distinctness and individuality. Haunting phantoms, incoherent and unintelligent, may seem restless and unhappy. But as they rise into definiteness, intelligence, individuality, the phantoms rise also into love and joy. I cannot recall one single case of a proved posthumous combination of intelligence with wickedness. Such evil as our evidence will show us — we have as yet hardly come across it in this book — is scarcely more than monkeyish mischief, childish folly. In dealing with automatic script, for instance, we shall have to wonder whence come the occasional vulgar jokes or silly mystifications. We shall discuss whether they are a kind of dream of the automatist's own, or whether they indicate the existence of unembodied intelligences on the level of the dog or the ape. But, on the other hand, all that world-old conception of Evil Spirits, of malevolent Powers, which has been the basis of so much of actual devil-worship and of so much more of vague supernatural fear; — all this insensibly melts from the mind as we study the evidence before us.

Hunc igitur terrorem animi tenebrasque necessest
Non radii solis, neque lucida tela diei
Discutiant sed, naturæ species ratioque.

Here surely is a fact of no little meaning. Our narratives have been collected from men and women of many types, holding all varieties of ordinary opinion. Yet the upshot of all these narratives is to emphasise a point which profoundly differentiates the scientific from the superstitious view of spiritual phenomena. The terror which shaped primitive theologies still tinges for the populace every hint of intercourse with disembodied souls. The transmutation of savage fear into scientific curiosity is of the essence of civilisation. Towards that transmutation each separate fragment of our evidence, with undesigned concordance, indisputably tends. In that faintly opening world of spirit I can find nothing worse than living men; I seem to discern not an intensification but a disintegration of selfishness, malevolence, pride. And is not this a natural result of any cosmic moral evolution? If the selfish man (as Marcus Antoninus has it) "is a kind of boil or imposthume upon the universe," must not his egoistic impulses suffer in that wider world a sure, even if a painful, decay; finding no support or sustenance among those permanent forces which maintain the stream of things?

I have thus indicated one point of primary importance on which the undesignedly coincident testimony of hundreds of first-hand narratives supports a conclusion, not yet popularly accepted, but in harmony with the evolutionary conceptions which rule our modern thought. Nor does this point stand alone. I can find, indeed, no guarantee of absolute and idle bliss; no triumph in any exclusive salvation. But the student of these narratives will, I think, discover throughout them uncontradicted indications of the persistence of Love, the growth of Joy, the willing submission to Law.

These indications, no doubt, may seem weak and scattered in comparison with the wholesale, thorough-going assertions of philosophical or religious creeds. Their advantage is that they occur incidentally in the course of our independent and cumulative demonstration of the profoundest cosmical thesis which we can at present conceive as susceptible of any kind of scientific proof. Cosmical questions, indeed, there may be which are in themselves of deeper import than our own survival of bodily death. The nature of the First Cause; the blind or the providential ordering of the sum of things; — these are problems vaster than any which affect only the destinies of men. But to whatever moral certainty we may attain on those mightiest questions, we can devise no way whatever of bringing them to scientific test. They deal with infinity; and our modes of investigation have grasp only on finite things.

But the question of man's survival of death stands in a position uniquely intermediate between matters capable and matters incapable of proof. It is in itself a definite problem, admitting of conceivable proof which, even if not technically rigorous, might amply satisfy the scientific mind. And at the same time the conception which it involves is in itself a kind of avenue and inlet into infinity. Could a proof of our survival be obtained, it would carry us deeper into the true nature of the universe than we should be carried by an even perfect knowledge of the material scheme of things. It would carry us deeper both by achievement and by promise. The discovery that there was a life in man independent of blood and brain would be a cardinal, a dominating fact in all science and in all philosophy. And the prospect thus opened to human knowledge, in this or in other worlds, would be limitless indeed.

CHAPTER VIII

MOTOR AUTOMATISM

Μηκέτι μόνον συμπνεῖν τῷ περιέχοντι ἀέρι, ἀλλ' ἤδη καὶ συμφρονεῖν
τῷ περιέχοντι πάντα νοερῷ.
— MARCUS AURELIUS.

At this point, one may broadly say, we reach the end of the phenomena
whose existence is vaguely familiar to popular talk. And here, too, I
might fairly claim, the evidence for my primary thesis, — namely, that
the analysis of man's personality reveals him as a spirit, surviving death,
— has attained an amplitude which would justify the reader in accepting
that view as the provisional hypothesis which comes nearest to a comprehensive co-ordination of the actual facts. What we have already recounted
seems, indeed, impossible to explain except by supposing that our inner
vision has widened or deepened its purview so far as to attain some
glimpses of a spiritual world in which the individualities of our
departed friends still actually subsist.

The reader, however, who has followed me thus far must be well aware
that a large class of phenomena, of high importance, is still awaiting discussion. *Motor* automatisms, — though less familiar to the general public
than the phantasms which I have classed as *sensory* automatisms, — are
in fact even commoner, and even more significant.

Motor automatisms, as I define them, are phenomena of very wide
range. We have encountered them already many times in this book. We
met them in the first place in a highly developed form in connection with
multiplex personality in Chapter II. Numerous instances were there
given of motor effects, initiated by secondary selves without the knowledge
of the primary selves, or sometimes in spite of their actual resistance. All
motor action of a secondary self is an automatism in this sense, in relation
to the primary self. And of course we might by analogy extend the use
of the word still further, and might call not only post-epileptic acts, but
also maniacal acts, automatic; since they are performed without the initiation of the presumedly sane primary personality. Those degenerative

phenomena, indeed, are not to be discussed in this chapter. Yet it will be well to pause here long enough to make it clear to the reader just what motor automatisms I am about to discuss as *evolutive* phenomena, and as therefore falling within the scope of this treatise; — and what kind of relation they bear to the dissolutive motor phenomena which occupy so much larger a place in popular knowledge.

In order to meet this last question, I must here give more distinct formulation to a thesis which has already suggested itself more than once in dealing with special groups of our phenomena.

It may be expected that supernormal vital phenomena will manifest themselves as far as possible through the same channels as abnormal or morbid vital phenomena, when the same centres or the same synergies are involved.

To illustrate the meaning of this theorem, I may refer to a remark long ago made by Edmund Gurney and myself in dealing with "Phantasms of the Living," or veridical hallucinations, generated (as we maintained), not by a morbid state of the percipient's brain, but by a telepathic impact from an agent at a distance. We observed that if a hallucination — a subjective image — is to be excited by this distant energy, it will probably be most readily excited in somewhat the same manner as the morbid hallucination which follows on a cerebral injury. We urged that this is *likely* to be the case — we showed ground for supposing that it *is* the case — both as regards the mode of evolution of the phantasm in the percipient's brain, and the mode in which it seems to present itself to his senses.

And here I should wish to give a much wider generality to this principle, and to argue that if there be within us a secondary self aiming at manifestation by physiological means, it seems probable that its readiest *path of externalisation* — its readiest outlet of visible action — may often lie along some track which has already been shown to be a line of low resistance by the disintegrating processes of disease. Or, varying the metaphor, we may anticipate that the partition of the primary and the secondary self will lie along some plane of cleavage which the *morbid* dissociations of our psychical synergies have already shown themselves disposed to follow. If epilepsy, madness, etc., tend to *split up* our faculties in certain ways, automatism is likely to split them up in ways somewhat resembling these.

But in what way then, it will be asked, do you distinguish the supernormal from the merely abnormal? Why assume that in these aberrant states there is anything besides hysteria, besides epilepsy, besides insanity?

The answer to this question has virtually been given in previous chapters of this book. The reader is already accustomed to the point of view which regards all psychical as well as all physiological activities as necessarily either developmental or degenerative, tending to evolution or to dissolution. And now, whilst altogether waiving any teleological speculation, I will ask him hypothetically to suppose that an evolutionary *nisus*, something which we may represent as an effort towards self-development, self-adaptation, self-renewal, is discernible especially on the psychical side of at any rate the higher forms of life. Our question, Supernormal or abnormal? — may then be phrased, Evolutive or dissolutive? And in studying each psychical phenomenon in turn we shall have to inquire whether it indicates a mere degeneration of powers already acquired, or, on the other hand, the "promise and potency," if not the actual possession, of powers as yet unrecognised or unknown.

Thus, for instance, Telepathy is surely a step in *evolution*.[1] To learn the thoughts of other minds without the mediation of the special senses, manifestly indicates the possibility of a vast extension of psychical powers. And any knowledge which we can amass as to the conditions under which telepathic action takes place will form a valuable starting-point for an inquiry as to the evolutive or dissolutive character of unfamiliar psychical states.[2]

For example, we may learn from our knowledge of telepathy that the superficial aspect of certain stages of psychical evolution, like the superficial aspect of certain stages of physiological evolution, may resemble mere

[1] To avoid misconception, I may point out that this view in no way negatives the possibility that telepathy (or its correlative telergy) may be in some of its aspects commoner, or more powerful, among savages than among ourselves. Evolutionary processes are not necessarily *continuous*. The acquirement by our lowly-organised ancestors of the sense of *smell* (for instance) was a step in evolution. But the sense of smell probably reached its highest energy in races earlier than man; and it has perceptibly declined even in the short space which separates civilised man from existing savages. Yet if, with some change in our environment, the sense of smell again became useful, and we reacquired it, this would be none the less an evolutionary process because the evolution had been interrupted.

[2] I do not wish to assert that *all* unfamiliar psychical states are necessarily evolutive or dissolutive in any assignable manner. I should prefer to suppose that there are states which may better be styled *allotropic;* — modifications of the arrangements of nervous elements on which our conscious identity depends, but with no more conspicuous *superiority* of the one state over the other than (for instance) charcoal possesses over graphite or graphite over charcoal. But there may also be states in which the (metaphorical) carbon becomes *diamond;* — with so much at least of *advance* on previous states as is involved in the substitution of the crystalline for the amorphous structure.

inhibition, or mere *perturbation*. But the inhibition may involve latent dynamogeny, and the perturbation may mask evolution. The hypnotised subject may pass through a lethargic stage before he wakes into a state in which he has gained *community of sensation* with the operator; somewhat as the silkworm (to use the oldest and the most suggestive of all illustrations) passes through the apparent torpor of the cocoon-stage before evolving into the moth. Again, the automatist's hand (as we shall presently see) is apt to pass through a stage of inco-ordinated movements, which might almost be taken for choreic, before it acquires the power of ready and intelligent writing. Similarly the development, for instance, of a tooth may be preceded by a stage of indefinite aching, which might be ascribed to the formation of an abscess, did not the new tooth ultimately show itself. And still more striking cases of a *perturbation which masks evolution* might be drawn from the history of the human organism as it develops into its own maturity, or prepares for the appearance of the fresh human organism which is to succeed it.

Analogy, therefore, both physiological and psychical, warns us not to conclude that any given psychosis is merely degenerative until we have examined its results closely enough to satisfy ourselves whether they tend to bring about any enlargement of human powers, to open any new inlet to the reception of objective truth. If such there prove to be, then, with whatever morbid activities the psychosis may have been intertwined, it contains indications of an evolutionary *nisus* as well.

These remarks, I hope, may have sufficiently cleared the ground to admit of our starting afresh on the consideration of such motor automatisms as are at any rate not morbid in their effect on the organism, and which I now have to show to be *evolutive* in character. I maintain that we have no valid ground for assuming that the movements which are *not* due to our conscious will must be less important, and less significant, than those that *are*. We observe, of course, that in the organic region the movements which are *not* due to conscious will are really the most important of all, though the voluntary movements by which a man seeks food and protects himself against enemies are also of great practical importance — he must first live and multiply if he is to learn and know. But we must guard against confusing importance for immediate practical life with importance for science — on which even practical life ultimately depends. As soon as the task of living and multiplying is no longer all-engrossing, we begin to change our relative estimate of values, and to find that it is not the broad and obvious phenomena, but the residual and elusive phenomena, which are oftenest likely to introduce us to new avenues of knowledge.　I wish to persuade my readers that this is quite as truly the case in psychology as in physics.

As a first step in our analysis, we may point out certain main characters which unite in a true class all the automatisms which we are here considering — greatly though these may differ among themselves in external form.

In the first place, then, our automatisms are *independent* phenomena; they are what the physician calls *idiognomonic*.　That is to say, they are not merely symptomatic of some other affection, or incidental to some profounder change.　The mere fact, for instance, that a man writes messages which he does not consciously originate will not, when taken alone, prove anything beyond this fact itself as to the writer's condition.　He may be perfectly sane, in normal health, and with nothing unusual observable about him.　This characteristic — provable by actual observation and experiment — distinguishes our automatisms from various seemingly kindred phenomena.　Thus we may have to include in our class the occasional automatic utterance of words or sentences.　But the continuous exhausting vociferation of acute mania does not fall within our province; for those shouts are merely *symptomatic;* nor, again, does the *cri hydrocéphalique* (or spontaneous meaningless noise which sometimes accompanies water on the brain); for that, too, is no independent phenomenon, but the direct consequence of a definite lesion.　Furthermore, we shall have to include in our class certain simple movements of the hands, coordinated into the act of writing.　But here, also, our definition will lead us to exclude *choreic* movements, which are merely symptomatic of nervous malnutrition; or which we may, if we choose, call *idiopathic*, as constituting an independent malady.　But our automatisms are not *idiopathic* but *idiognomonic;* they may indeed be associated with or facilitated by certain states of the organism, but they are neither a symptom of any other malady, nor are they a malady in themselves.

Agreeing, then, that our peculiar class consists of automatisms which are idiognomonic, — whose existence does not necessarily imply the existence of some profounder affection already known as producing them, — we have still to look for some more positive bond of connection between them, some quality common to all of them, and which makes them worth our prolonged investigation.

This we shall find in the fact that they are all of them *message-bearing* or *nunciative* automatisms.　I do not, of course, mean that they all of them bring messages from sources external to the automatist's own mind. In some cases they probably do this; but as a rule the so-called messages seem more probably to originate within the automatist's own persona. Why, then, it may be asked, do I call them *messages?* We do not usually speak of a man as sending a message to himself. The answer to this question involves, as we shall presently see, the profoundest conception of these automatisms to which we can as yet attain. They present themselves to us as messages communicated from one stratum to another stratum of the same personality. Originating in some deeper zone of a man's being, they float up into superficial consciousness, as deeds, visions, words, ready-made and full-blown, without any accompanying perception of the elaborative process which has made them what they are.

Can we then (we may next ask) in any way predict the possible *range* of these motor automatisms? Have we any limit assignable *a priori*, outside which it would be useless to look for any externalisation of an impulse emanating from sub-conscious strata of our being?

The answer to this must be that no such limit can be with any confidence suggested. We have not yet learnt with any distinctness even how far the wave from a *consciously*-perceived stimulus will spread, or what changes its motion will assume. Still less can we predict the limitations which the resistance of the organism will impose on the radiation of a stimulus originated within itself. We are learning to consider the human organism as a practically infinite complex of interacting vibrations; and each year adds many new facts to our knowledge of the various transformations which these vibrations may undergo, and of the unexpected artifices by which we may learn to cognise some stimulus which is not directly felt.

A few concrete instances will make my meaning plainer. And my first example shall be taken from those experiments in *muscle-reading* — less correctly termed mind-reading — with which the readers of the *Proceedings* of the S.P.R. are already familiar. Let us suppose that I am to hide a pin, and that some accomplished muscle-reader is to take my hand and find the pin by noting my muscular indications.[1] I first hide the pin in the hearth-rug; then I change my mind and hide it in the bookshelf. I fix my mind on the bookshelf, but resolve to make no guiding movement. The muscle-reader takes my hand, leads me first to the rug, then to the bookshelf, and finds the pin. Now, what has happened in this case? What movements have I made?

Firstly, I have made no *voluntary* movement; and secondly, I have made no *conscious involuntary* movement. But, thirdly, I have made an *unconscious involuntary* movement which directly depended on conscious

[1] See, for instance, *Proceedings* S.P.R., vol. i. p. 291.

ideation. I strongly thought of the bookshelf, and when the bookshelf was reached in our vague career about the room I made a movement — say rather a tremor occurred — in my hand, which, although beyond both my knowledge and my control, was enough to supply to the muscle-reader's delicate sensibility all the indication required. All this is now admitted, and, in a sense, understood; we formulate it by saying that my conscious ideation contained a motor element; and that this motor element, though inhibited from any conscious manifestation, did yet inevitably externalise itself in a peripheral tremor.

But, fourthly, something more than this has clearly taken place. Before the muscle-reader stopped at the bookshelf he stopped at the rug. I was no longer consciously thinking of the rug; but the idea of the pin in the rug must still have been reverberating, so to say, in my sub-conscious region; and this unconscious memory, this unnoted reverberation, revealed itself in a peripheral tremor nearly as distinct as that which (when the bookshelf was reached) corresponded to the strain of conscious thought.

This tremor, then, was in a certain sense a message-bearing automatism. It was the externalisation of an idea which, once conscious, had become unconscious, though in the slightest conceivable degree — namely, by a mere slight escape from the field of direct attention.

Having, then, considered an instance where the automatic message passes only between two closely-adjacent strata of consciousness, externalising an impulse derived from an idea which has only recently sunk out of consciousness and which could easily be summoned back again; — let us find our next illustration in a case where the line of demarcation between the strata of consciousness through which the automatic message pierces is distinct and impassable by any effort of will.

Let us take a case of *post-hypnotic suggestion;* — say, for instance, an experiment of Edmund Gurney's (see *Proceedings* S.P.R., vol. iv. p. 319). The subject had been trained to write with planchette, after he had been awakened, the statements which had been made to him when in the hypnotic trance. He wrote the desired words, or something like them, but while he wrote them his waking self was entirely unaware of what his hand was writing. Thus, having been told in the trance, "It has begun snowing again," he wrote, after waking, "It begun snowing," while he read aloud, with waking intelligence, from a book of stories, and was quite unconscious of what his hand (placed on a planchette behind a screen) was at the same time writing.

Here we have an automatic message of traceable origin; a message implanted in the hypnotic stratum of the subject's self, and cropping up

— like a fault — in the waking stratum, — externalised in automatic movements which the waking self could neither predict nor guide.

Yet once more. In the discussion which will follow we shall have various instances of the transformation (as I shall regard it) of psychical shock into definite muscular energy of apparently a quite alien kind. Such transformations of so-called psychical into physical force — of will into motion — do of course perpetually occur within us.

For example, I take a child to a circus; he sits by me holding my hand; there is a discharge of musketry and his grip tightens. Now in this case we should call the child's tightened grip automatic. But suppose that, instead of merely holding my hand, he is trying with all his might to squeeze the dynamometer, and that the sudden excitation enables him to squeeze it harder — are we then to describe that extra squeeze as automatic? or as voluntary?

However phrased, it is the fact (as amply established by M. Féré and others [1]) that excitations of almost any kind — whether sudden and startling or agreeable and prolonged — do tend to increase the subject's dynamometrical power. In the first place, and this is in itself an important fact, the average of squeezing-power is found to be greater among educated students than among robust labouring men, thus showing that it is not so much developed muscle as active brain which renders possible a sudden concentration of muscular force. But more than this; M. Féré finds that with himself and his friends the mere listening to an interesting lecture, or the mere stress of thought in solitude, or still more the act of writing or of speech, produces a decided increase of strength in the grip, especially of the right hand. The same effect of dynamogeny is produced with hypnotic subjects, by musical sounds, by coloured light, especially red light, and even by a hallucinatory suggestion of red light. "All our sensations," says M. Féré in conclusion, "are accompanied by a development of potential energy, which passes into a kinetic state, and externalises itself in motor manifestations which even so rough a method as dynamometry is able to observe and record."

I would beg the reader to keep these words in mind. We shall presently find that a method apparently even rougher than dynamographic tracings may be able to interpret, with far greater delicacy, the automatic tremors which are coursing to and fro within us. If once we can get a spy into the citadel of our own being, his rudest signalling will tell us more than our subtlest inferences from outside of what is being planned and done within.

[1] *Sensation et Mouvement*, par Ch. Féré. Paris: Alcan, 1887.

And now having to deal with what I define as messages conveyed by one stratum in man to another stratum, I must first consider in what general ways human messages can be conveyed. Writing and speech have become predominant in the intercourse of civilised men, and it is to writing and speech that we look with most interest among the communications of the subliminal self. But it does not follow that the subliminal self will always have such complex methods at its command. We have seen already that it often finds it hard to manage the delicate co-ordinations of muscular movement required for writing, — that the attempt at automatic script ends in a thump and a scrawl.

The subliminal self like the telegraphist begins its effort with full knowledge, indeed, of the alphabet, but with only weak and rude command over our muscular adjustments. It is therefore *a priori* likely that its easiest mode of communication will be through a repetition of simple movements, so arranged as to correspond to letters of the alphabet.

And here, I think, we have attained to a conception of the mysterious and much-derided phenomenon of "table-tilting" which enables us to correlate it with known phenomena, and to start at least from an intelligible basis, and on a definite line of inquiry.

A few words are needed to explain what are the verifiable phenomena, and the less verifiable hypotheses, connoted by such words as "table-turning," "spirit-rapping," and the like.

If one or more persons of a special type — at present definable only by the question-begging and barbarous term "mediumistic" — remain quietly for some time with hands in contact with some easily movable object, and desiring its movement, that object will sometimes begin to move. If, further, they desire it to indicate letters of the alphabet by its movements, — as by tilting once for *a*, twice for *b*, etc., it will often do so, and answers unexpected by any one present will be obtained.

Thus far, whatever our interpretation, we are in the region of easily reproducible facts, which many of my readers may confirm for themselves if they please.

But beyond the simple movements — or table-turning — and the intelligible responses — or table-tilting — both of which are at least *primâ facie* physically explicable by the sitters' unconscious pressure, without postulating any unknown physical force at all, — it is alleged by many persons that further physical phenomena occur; namely, that the table moves in a direction, or with a violence, which no unconscious pressure can explain; and also that percussive sounds or "raps" occur, which no unconscious action, or indeed no agency known to us, could produce.

These raps communicate messages like the tilts, and it is to them that the name of "spirit-rapping" is properly given. But spiritualists generally draw little distinction between these four phenomena — mere table-turning, responsive table-tilting, movements of inexplicable vehemence, and responsive raps — attributing all alike to the agency of departed spirits of men and women, or at any rate to disembodied intelligences of some kind or other.

I am not at present discussing the physical phenomena of Spiritualism, and I shall therefore leave on one side all the alleged movements and noises of this kind for which unconscious pressure will not account. I do not prejudge the question as to their real occurrence; but assuming that such disturbances of the physical order do occur, there is at least no *primâ facie* need to refer them to disembodied spirits. If a table moves when no one is touching it, this is not obviously more likely to have been effected by my deceased grandfather than by myself. We cannot tell how *I* could move it; but then we cannot tell how *he* could move it either. The question must be argued on its merits in each case; and our present argument is not therefore vitiated by our postponement of this further problem.

M. Richet [1] was, I believe, the first writer, outside the Spiritualistic group, who so much as showed any practical knowledge of this phenomenon, still less endeavoured to explain it. Faraday's well-known explanation of table-turning as the result of the summation of many unconscious movements — obviously true as it is for some of the simplest cases of table-movement — does not touch this far more difficult question of the origination of these intelligent messages, conveyed by distinct and repeated movements of some object admitting of ready displacement. The ordinary explanation — I am speaking, of course, of cases where fraud is not in question — is that the sitter unconsciously sets going and stops the movements so as to shape the word in accordance with his expectation. Now that he unconsciously sets going and stops the movements is part of my own present contention, but that the word is thereby shaped in accordance with his expectation is often far indeed from being the case. To those indeed who are familiar with automatic *written* messages, this question as to the unexpectedness of the *tilted* messages will present itself in a new light. If the written messages originate in a source beyond the automatist's supraliminal self, so too may the tilted messages; — even though we admit that the tilts are caused by his hand's pressure of the table just as directly as the script by his hand's manipulation of the pen.

[1] *La Suggestion Mentale* (see *Proceedings* S.P.R., vol. ii. pp. 239 sqq.).

One piece of evidence showing that *written* messages are not always the mere echo of expectation is a case[1] where *anagrams* were automatically written, which their writer was not at once able to decipher. Following this hint, I have occasionally succeeded in getting anagrams tilted out for myself by movements of a small table which I alone touched.

This is a kind of experiment which might with advantage be oftener repeated; for the extreme incoherence and silliness of the responses thus obtained does not prevent the process itself from being in a high degree instructive. Here, again (as in automatic writing), a man may hold colloquy with his own dream — may note in actual juxtaposition two separate strata of his own intelligence.

I shall not at present pursue the discussion of these tilted responses beyond this their very lowest and most rudimentary stage. They almost immediately suggest another problem, for which our discussion is hardly ripe, the participation, namely, of several minds in the production of the same automatic message. There is something of this difficulty even in the explanation of messages given when the hands of two persons are touching a planchette; but when the instrument of response is large, and the method of response simple, as with table-tilting, we find this question of the influence of more minds than one imperatively recurring.

Our immediate object, however, is rather to correlate the different attainable modes of automatic response in some intelligible scheme than to pursue any one of them through all its phases. We regarded the table-tilting process as in one sense the simplest, the least differentiated form of motor response. It is a kind of *gesture* merely, though a gesture implying knowledge of the alphabet. Let us see in what directions the movement of response becomes more specialised, — as gesture parts into pictorial art and articulate speech. We find, in fact, that a just similar divergence of impulses takes place in automatic response. On the one hand the motor impulse specialises itself into *drawing;* on the other hand it specialises itself into *speech*. Of automatic drawing I have already said something (Chapter III.). Automatic speech will receive detailed treatment in Chapter IX. At present I shall only briefly indicate the position of each form of movement among cognate automatisms.

Some of my readers may have seen these so-called "spirit-drawings," — designs, sometimes in colour, whose author asserts that he drew them without any plan, or even knowledge of what his hand was going to do. This assertion may be quite true, and the person making it may be

[1] See *Proceedings* S.P.R., vol. ii. pp. 226–31 [830 A].

perfectly sane.[1] The drawings so made will be found curiously accordant with what the view which I am explaining would lead us to expect. For they exhibit a fusion of arabesque with ideography; that is to say, they partly resemble the forms of ornamentation into which the artistic hand strays when, as it were, dreaming on the paper without definite plan; and partly they afford a parallel to the early attempts at symbolic self-expression of savages who have not yet learnt an alphabet. Like savage writing, they pass by insensible transitions from direct pictorial symbolism to an abbreviated ideography, mingled in its turn with writing of a fantastic or of an ordinary kind.

And here, before we enter on the study of automatic writing, I must refer to two great historic cases of automatism, which may serve as a kind of prologue to what is to follow. One case, that of Socrates, is a case of monitory *inhibition;* the other, that of Jeanne d'Arc, of monitory *impulse.*

The Founder of Science himself — the permanent type of sanity, shrewdness, physical robustness, and moral balance — was guided in all the affairs of life by a monitory Voice, — by "the Dæmon of Socrates." This is a case which can never lose its interest, a case which has been vouched for by the most practical, and discussed by the loftiest intellect of Greece, — both of them intimate friends of the illustrious subject; — a case, therefore, which one who endeavours to throw new light on hallucination and automatism is bound, even at this distance of time, to endeavour to explain.[2] And this is the more needful, since a treatise was actually written, a generation ago, as "a specimen of the application of the science of psychology to the science of history," arguing from the records of the δαιμόνιον in Xenophon and Plato that Socrates was in fact insane.[3]

I believe that it is now possible to give a truer explanation; to place these old records in juxtaposition with more instructive parallels; and to show that the messages which Socrates received were only advanced

[1] See Mr. Wilkinson's book *Spirit Drawings: a Personal Narrative.* But, of course, like other automatic impulses, this impulse to decorative or symbolical drawing is sometimes seen at its maximum in insane patients. Some drawings of an insane patient, reproduced in the *American Journal of Psychology*, June 1888, show a noticeable analogy (in my view a *predictable* analogy) with some of the "spirit-drawings" above discussed. See also the Martian landscapes of Hélène Smith, in Professor Flournoy's *Des Indes à la planète Mars.*

[2] An account of recorded instances of Socratic monitions and some discussion of them is given in the original edition (§ 813, 814).

[3] *Du Démon de Socrate*, etc., by L. F. Léut, Membre de l'Institut. Nouvelle édition, 1856.

examples of a process which, if supernormal, is not abnormal, and which characterises that form of intelligence which we describe as *genius*.

The story of Socrates I take as a signal example of *wise automatism;* of the possibility that the messages which are conveyed to the supraliminal mind from subliminal strata of the personality, — whether as sounds, as sights, or as movements, — may sometimes come from far beneath the realm of dream and confusion, — from some self whose monitions convey to us a wisdom profounder than we know.

Similarly in the case of Joan of Arc, I believe that only now, with the comprehension which we are gradually gaining of the possibility of an impulse from the mind's deeper strata which is so far from madness that it is wiser than our sanity itself, — only now, I repeat, can we understand aright that familiar story.

Joan's condemnation was based on her own admissions; and the Latin *procès-verbal* still exists, and was published from the MS. by M. Quicherat, 1841-9, for the French Historical Society.[1] Joan, like Socrates, was condemned mainly on the ground, or at least on the pretext of her monitory voices: and her Apology remarkably resembles his, in its resolute insistence on the truth of the very phenomena which were being used to destroy her. Her answers are clear and self-consistent, and seem to have been little, if at all, distorted by the recorder. Few pieces of history so remote as this can be so accurately known.

Fortunately for our purpose, her inquisitors asked her many questions as to her voices and visions; and her answers enable us to give a pretty full analysis of the phenomena which concern us.

I. The voices do not begin with the summons to fight for France. Joan heard them first at thirteen years of age, — as with Socrates also the voice began in childhood. The first command consisted of nothing more surprising than that "she was to be a good girl, and go often to church." After this the voice — as in the case of Socrates — intervened frequently, and on trivial occasions.

II. The voice was accompanied at first by a light, and sometimes afterwards by figures of saints, who appeared to speak, and whom Joan appears to have both seen and felt as clearly as though they had been living persons. But here there is some obscurity; and Michelet thinks that on one occasion the Maid was tricked by the courtiers for political ends. For she asserted (apparently without contradiction) that several persons, including the

[1] For other authorities see Mr. Andrew Lang's paper in *Proceedings* S.P.R., vol. xi. pp. 198-212.

Archbishop of Rheims, as well as herself, had seen an angel bringing to the King a material crown.[1]

III. The voices came mainly when she was awake, but also sometimes roused her from sleep; a phenomenon often observed in our cases of "veridical hallucination." "Ipsa dormiebat, et vox excitabat eam." (Quicherat, i., p. 62.)

IV. The voice was not always fully intelligible (especially if she was half awake); — in this respect again resembling some of our recorded cases, both visual and auditory, where, on the view taken in *Phantasms of the Living*, the externalisation has been incomplete. "Vox dixit aliqua, sed non omnia intellexit." (Quicherat, i., p. 62.)

V. The predictions of the voice, so far as stated, were mainly fulfilled; viz., that the siege of Orleans would be raised; that Charles VII. would be crowned at Rheims; that she herself would be wounded; but the prediction that there would be a great victory over the English within seven years was not fulfilled in any exact way, although the English continued to lose ground. In short, about so much was fulfilled as an ardent self-devoted mind might have anticipated; much indeed that might have seemed irrational to ordinary observers, but nothing which actually needed a definite prophetic power. Here, again, we are reminded of the general character of the monitions of Socrates. And yet in Joan's case, more probably than in the case of Socrates, there may have been one singular exception to this general rule. She knew by monition that there was a sword "retro altare" — somewhere behind the altar — in the Church of St. Catherine of Fierbois. "Scivit ipsum ibi esse per voces": — she sent for it, nothing doubting, and it was found and given to her. This was a unique incident in her career. Her judges asked whether she had not once found a cup, and a missing priest, by help of similar monitions, but this she denied; and it is remarkable that no serious attempt was made either to show that she had claimed this clairvoyant power habitually, or, on the other hand, to invalidate the one instance of it which she did in effect claim. It would be absurd to cite the alleged discovery of the sword as in itself affording a proof of clairvoyance, any more than Socrates' alleged intimation of the approaching herd of swine.[2] But when we are considering monitions given in more recent times it will be well to remember that it is in this direction that some supernormal extension of knowledge seems possibly traceable.

The cases of Socrates and of Joan of Arc, on which I have just dwelt,

[1] On this point, see Mr. Lang's paper referred to above.
[2] See Plutarch's *De genio Socratis*.

might with almost equal fitness have been introduced at certain other points of my discussion. At first sight, at any rate, they appear rather like sensory than like motor automatisms, — like hallucinations of hearing rather than like the motor impulses which we are now about to study. Each case, however, approaches motor automatism in a special way.

In the case of Socrates the "sign" seems to have been not so much a definite voice as a sense of *inhibition*. In the case of Joan of Arc the voices were definite enough, but they were accompanied — as such voices sometimes are, but sometimes are *not* — with an overmastering impulse to *act* in obedience to them. These are, I may say, palmary cases of inhibition and of impulse: and inhibition and impulse are at the very root of motor phenomena.

They show moreover the furthest extent of the claim that can be made for the agency of the subliminal self, apart from any external influence, — apart from telepathy from the living, or possession by the departed. Each of those other hypotheses will claim its own group of cases; but we must not invoke them until the resources of subliminal wisdom are manifestly overtaxed.

These two famous cases, then, have launched us on our subject in the stress of a twofold difficulty in logical arrangement. We cannot always answer these primary questions, Is the subliminal impulse sensory or motor? is it originated in the automatist's own mind, or in some mind external to him?

In the first place, we must reflect that, if the subliminal self really possesses that profound power over the organism with which I have credited it, we may expect that its "messages" will sometimes express themseves in the form of deep organic modifications — of changes in the vaso-motor, the circulatory, the respiratory systems. Such phenomena are likely to be less noted or remembered as *coincidental*, from their very indefiniteness, as compared, for instance, with a phantasmal appearance; but we have, nevertheless, records of various telepathic cases of deep cœnesthetic disturbance, of a profound *malaise* which must, one would think, have involved some unusual condition of the viscera.[1]

In cases, too, where the telepathic impression has ultimately assumed a definite sensory form, some organic or emotional phenomena have been noted, being perhaps the *first* effects of the telepathic impact, whether from the living or from the dead.[2]

[1] See *Phantasms of the Living*, vol. i., Chapter VII, *passim*.
[2] See *Proceedings* of the American S.P.R., vol. i. p. 397; *Proceedings* S.P.R., vol. ix. pp. 33 and 35 [817 A, B, and C].

And here I may mention an experience of Lady de Vesci's, who described to me in conversation a feeling of *malaise*, defining itself into the urgent need of definite action — namely, the despatch of a telegram to a friend who was in fact then dying at the other side of the world.[1] Such an impulse had one only parallel in her experience, which also was telepathic in a similar way.

Similar sensory disturbances are sometimes reported in connection with an important form of motor automatism, — that of "dowsing" or discovering water by means of the movement of a rod held in the hands of the automatist, — already treated of in Appendix V. A.

A small group of cases may naturally be mentioned here. From two different points of view they stand for the most part at the entrance of our subject. I speak of motor inhibitions, prompted at first by subliminal memory, or by subliminal hyperæsthesia, but merging into telæsthesia or telepathy. Inhibitions — sudden arrests or incapacities of action — (more or less of the Socratic type) — form a simple, almost rudimentary, type of motor automatisms. And an inhibition — a sudden check on action of this kind — will be a natural way in which a strong but obscure impression will work itself out. Such an impression, for instance, is that of *alarm*, suggested by some vague sound or odour which is only subliminally perceived. And thus in this series of motor automatisms, just as in our series of dreams, or in our series of sensory automatisms, we find ourselves beginning with cases where the subliminal self merely shows some slight extension of memory or of sensory perception, — and thence pass insensibly to cases where no "cryptomnesia" will explain the facts known in the past, and no hyperæsthesia will explain the facts discerned in the present.

We may most of us have observed that if we perform any small action to which there are objections, which we have once known but which have altogether passed from our minds, we are apt to perform it in a hesitating, inefficient way.

Similarly there are cases where some sudden muscular impulse or inhibition has probably depended on a subliminal perception or interpretation of a sound which had not reached the supraliminal attention. For instance, two friends walking together along a street in a storm just evade by sudden movements a falling mass of masonry. Each thinks that he has received some *monition* of the fall; each asserting that he heard no noise whatever to warn him. Here is an instance where subliminal

---

[1] The case is recorded in *Journal* S.P.R., vol. v. p. 136 [817 D].

perception may have been slightly quicker and more delicate than supraliminal, and may have warned them just in time.

In the case which I now quote (from *Proceedings* S.P.R., vol. xi. p. 416) there may have been some subliminal hyperæsthesia of hearing which dimly warned Mr. Wyman of the approach of the extra train.[1]

Mr. Wm. H. Wyman writes to the Editor of the *Arena* as follows: —

DUNKIRK, N. Y., *June 26th*, 1891.

Some years ago my brother was employed and had charge as conductor and engineer of a working train on the Lake Shore and Michigan Southern Railway, running between Buffalo and Erie, which passes through this city (Dunkirk, N. Y.). I often went with him to the Grave Bank, where he had his headquarters, and returned on his train with him. On one occasion I was with him, and after the train of cars was loaded, we went together to the telegraph office to see if there were any orders, and to find out if the trains were on time, as he had to keep out of the way of all regular trains. After looking over the train reports and finding them all on time, we started for Buffalo. As we approached near Westfield Station, running about 12 miles per hour, and when within about one mile of a long curve in the line, my brother all of a sudden shut off the steam, and quickly stepping over to the fireman's side of the engine, he looked out of the cab window, and then to the rear of his train to see if there was anything the matter with either. Not discovering anything wrong, he stopped and put on steam, but almost immediately again shut it off and gave the signal for breaks and stopped. After inspecting the engine and train and finding nothing wrong, he seemed very much excited, and for a short time he acted as if he did not know where he was or what to do. I asked what was the matter. He replied that he did not know, when, after looking at his watch and orders, he said that he felt that there was some trouble on the line of the road. I suggested that he had better run his train to the station and find out. He then ordered his flagman with his flag to go ahead around the curve, which was just ahead of us, and he would follow with the train. The flagman started and had just time to flag an extra express train, with the General Superintendent and others on board, coming full 40 [forty] miles per hour. The Superintendent inquired what he was doing there, and if he did not receive orders to keep out of the way of the extra. My brother told him that he had not received orders and did not know of any extra train coming; that we had both examined the train reports before leaving the station. The train then backed to the station, where it was found that no orders had been given. The train despatcher was at once discharged from the road, and from that time to this both my brother and myself are unable to account for his stopping the train as he did. I consider it quite a mystery, and cannot give or find any intelligent reason for it. Can you suggest any?

The above is true and correct in every particular.

[1] For a somewhat similar case, possibly due to hyperæsthesia of hearing, see *American Journal of Psychology*, vol. iii. p. 435 (September 1890).

In other cases again some subliminal sense of smell may be conjectured.[1]

Tactile sensibility, too, must be carefully allowed for. The sense of varying resistance in the air may reach in some seeing persons, as well as in the blind, a high degree of acuteness.[2]

But there are cases of sudden motor inhibition where no warning can well have been received from hyperæsthetic sensation, where we come, as it seems, to telæsthesia or to spirit guardianship.

(From *Proceedings* S.P.R., vol. xi. p. 459.)

Four years ago, I made arrangements with my nephew, John W. Parsons, to go to my office after supper to investigate a case. We walked along together, both fully determined to go up into the office, but just as I stepped upon the door sill of the drug store, in which my office was situated, some invisible influence stopped me instantly. I was much surprised, felt like I was almost dazed, the influence was so strong, almost like a blow, I felt like I could not make another step. I said to my nephew, "John, I do not feel like going into the office now; you go and read Flint and Aitken on the subject." He went, lighted the lamp, took off his hat, and just as he was reaching for a book the report of a large pistol was heard. The ball entered the window near where he was standing, passed near to and over his head, struck the wall and fell to the floor. Had I been standing where he was, I would have been killed, as I am much taller than he. The pistol was fired by a man who had an old grudge against me, and had secreted himself in a vacant house near by to assassinate me.

This impression was unlike any that I ever had before. All my former impressions were slow in their development, grew stronger and stronger, until the maximum was reached. I did not feel that I was in any danger, and could not understand what the strong impression meant. The fellow was drunk, had been drinking for two weeks. If my system had been in a different condition—I had just eaten supper—I think I would have received along with the impression some knowledge of the character of the danger, and would have prevented my nephew from going into the office.

I am fully satisfied that the invisible and unknown intelligence did the best that could have been done, under the circumstances, to save us from harm.

D. J. PARSONS, M.D., Sweet Springs, Mo.

(The above account was received in a letter from Dr. D. J. Parsons, dated *December 15th*, 1891.)

[1] See *Proceedings* S.P.R., vol. xi. pp. 419 and 421 [821 A].

[2] See *Proceedings* S.P.R., vol. xi, p. 422 and 423 [§§ 822 and 823]; also a case given in *Proceedings* S.P.R., vol. viii. p. 345, where a lady hurrying up to the door of a lift, is stopped by seeing a figure of a man standing in front of it, and then finds that the door is open, leaving the well exposed, so that she would probably have fallen down it, if she had not been checked by the apparition.

Statement of Dr. J. W. PARSONS.

About four years ago my uncle, Dr. D. J. Parsons, and I were going to supper, when a man halted us and expressed a desire for medical advice. My uncle requested him to call the next morning, and as we walked along he said the case was a bad one and that we would come back after supper and go to the office and examine the authorities on the subject. After supper we returned, walked along together on our way to the office, but just as we reached the door of the drug store he very unexpectedly, to me, stopped suddenly, which caused me to stop too; we stood there together a few seconds, and he remarked to me that he did not feel like going into the office then, or words to that effect, and told me to go and examine Flint and Aitken. I went, lit the lamp, and just as I was getting a book, a pistol was fired into the office, the ball passing close to my head, struck the east wall, then the north, and fell to the floor.

This 5th day of July, 1891.

JOHN W. PARSONS [Ladonia, Texas.]

In the next group of cases, we reach a class of massive motor impulses which are almost entirely free from any sensory admixture.

Take for instance the case of Mr. Garrison, who left a religious meeting in the evening, and walked eighteen miles under the strong impulse to see his mother, and found her dead. The account is given in the *Journal* S.P.R., vol. viii. p. 125 [§ 825].

In another case, that of Major Kobbé (given in *Phantasms of the Living*, vol. i. p. 288), the percipient was prompted to visit a distant cemetery, without any conscious reason, and there found his father, who had, in fact, for certain unexpected reasons, sent to his son, Major Kobbé, a request (accidentally *not received*) to meet him at that place and hour.

In a third case, Mr. Skirving (see *Phantasms of the Living*, vol. i. p. 285 [825 A]) was irresistibly compelled to leave his work and go home — *why*, he knew not — at the moment when his wife was in fact calling for him in the distress of a serious accident. See also a case given in *Phantasms of the Living*, vol. ii. p. 377, where a bricklayer has a sudden impulse to run home, and arrives just in time to save the life of his little boy, who had set himself on fire.

This special sensibility to the *motor* element in an impulse recalls to us the special susceptibilities to different forms of hallucination or suggestion shown by different hypnotic subjects. Some can be made to see, some to hear, some to act out the conception proposed to them. Dr. Bérillon [1] has even shown that certain subjects who seem at first quite refractory to hypnotisation are nevertheless at once obedient, even in the waking state, to

[1] *Revue de l'Hypnotisme*, March 1893, p. 268.

a motor suggestion. This was the case both with a very strong man, with weak men and women, and with at least one subject actually suffering from locomotor ataxy. Thus the loss of supraliminal motor control over certain muscular combinations may actually lead to *motor suggestibility* as regards those combinations; just as the loss of supraliminal sensation in some anæsthetic patch may lead to a special subliminal sensitiveness in the very directions where the superficial sensibility has sunk away. On the other hand, a specially well-developed motor control may predispose in a similar way; — as for instance, the subject who can sing already is more easily made to sing by suggestion. We must, then, await further observations before we can pretend to say beforehand with which automatist the messages will take a sensory, and with which a motor form.

Still less can we explain the special predisposition of each experimenter to one or more of the common kinds of motor automatism — as automatic speech, automatic writing, table movements, raps, and so forth. These forms of messages may themselves be variously combined; and the contents of a message of any one of these kinds may be purely dream-like and fantastic, or may be veridical in various ways.

Let us enumerate the modes of subliminal motor message as nearly as we can in order of their increasing specialisation.

1. We may place first the massive motor impulses (like Mr. Garrison's) which mark a kind of transition between cœnesthetic affections and motor impulses proper. There was here no impulse to special movement of any limb; but an impulse to reach a certain place by ordinary methods.

2. Next, perhaps, in order of specialisation come the simple subliminal muscular impulses which give rise to table-tilting and similar phenomena.

3. Musical execution, subliminally initiated, might theoretically be placed next; although definite evidence of this is hard to obtain, since the threshold of consciousness with musical performers is notoriously apt to be shifting and indefinite. ("When in doubt, play with your fingers, and not with your head.")

4. Next we may place automatic drawing and painting. This curious group of messages has but seldom a telepathic content, and, as was suggested in Chapter III., is more akin to *genius* and similar non-telepathic forms of subliminal faculty.[1]

5. Next comes automatic writing, on which much remains to be said in this chapter.

[1] When the automatic drawings have any telepathic or other supernormal content, they are usually associated with automatic writing. Compare the case of Mr. Cameron Grant (*Phantasms of the Living*, vol. ii. p. 690).

6. Automatic *speech*, which would not seem to be *per se* a more developed form of motor message than automatic script, is often accompanied by profound changes of memory or of personality which raise the question of "inspiration" or "possession"; — for the two words, however different their theological import, mean much the same thing from the standpoint of experimental psychology.

7. I must conclude my list with a class of motor phenomena which I shall here merely record in passing, without attempting any explanation. I allude to raps, and to those telekinetic movements of objects whose real existence is still matter of controversy.

Comparing this list of motor automatisms with the sensory automatisms enumerated in Chapter VI., we shall find a certain general tendency running through each alike. The sensory automatisms began with vague unspecialised sensations. They then passed through a phase of definition, of specialisation on the lines of the known senses. And finally they reached a stage beyond these habitual forms of specialisation: beyond them, as of wider reach, and including in an apparently unanalysable act of perception a completer truth than any of our specialised forms of perception could by itself convey. With motor messages, too, we begin with something of similar vagueness. They, too, develop from modifications of the percipient's general organic condition, or cœnesthesia; and the first dim telepathic impulse apparently hesitates between several channels of expression. They then pass through various definitely specialised forms; and finally, as we shall see when automatic script is considered, they, too, merge into an unanalysable act of cognition in which the motor element of the message has disappeared. But these motor messages point also in another even more perplexing direction. They lead, as I have said above, towards the old idea of *possession;* — using the word simply as an expression for some form of temporary manifestation of some veritably distinct and alien personality through the physical organism of some man or woman, as is well exemplified in many cases of automatic writing. In Europe and America the phenomenon of automatic writing first came into notice as an element in so-called "modern spiritualism" about the middle of the nineteenth century; but the writings of W. Stainton Moses — about 1870–80 — were perhaps the first continuous series of such messages which could be regarded as worthy of serious attention. Mr. Moses — a man whose statements could not be lightly set aside — claimed for them that they were the direct utterances of departed persons, some of them lately dead, some dead long ago. However they were really to be explained, they strongly impressed Edmund Gurney and myself and added to our desire to work at the subject in as many ways as we could.

It was plain that these writings could not be judged aright without a wide analysis of similar scripts, — without an experimental inquiry into what the human mind, in states of somnambulism or the like, could furnish of written messages, apart from the main stream of consciousness. By his experiments on writing obtained in different stages of hypnotic trance, Gurney acted as the pioneer of a long series of researches which, independently set on foot by Professor Pierre Janet in France, have become of high psychological, and even medical, importance. What is here of prime interest is the indubitable fact that fresh personalities can be artificially and temporarily created, which will write down matter quite alien from the first personality's character, and even matter which the first personality never knew. That matter may consist merely of reminiscences of previous periods when the second personality has been in control. But, nevertheless, if these writings are shown to the primary personality, he will absolutely repudiate their authorship — alleging not only that he has no recollection of writing them, but also that they contain allusions to facts which he never knew. Some of these messages, indeed, although their source is so perfectly well defined — although we know the very moment when the secondary personality which wrote them was called into existence — do certainly look more alien from the automatist in his normal state than many of the messages which claim to come from spirits of lofty type. It is noticeable, moreover, that these manufactured personalities sometimes cling obstinately to their fictitious names, and refuse to admit that they are in reality only aspects or portions of the automatist himself. This must be remembered when the persistent *claim* to some spiritual identity — say Napoleon — is urged as an argument for attributing a series of messages to that special person.

What has now been said may suffice as regards the varieties of mechanism — the different forms of motor automatism — which the messages employ. I shall pass on to consider the *contents* of the messages, and shall endeavour to classify them according to their apparent sources.

A. In the first place, the message may come from the percipient's own mind; its contents being supplied from the resources of his ordinary memory, or of his more extensive subliminal memory; while the *dramatisation* of the message — its assumption of some other mind as its source — will resemble the dramatisations of dream or of hypnotic trance.

Of course the absence of facts unknown to the writer is not in itself a proof that the message does not come from some other mind. We cannot be sure that other minds, if they can communicate, will always be at the pains to fill their messages with evidential facts. But, equally of course, a message devoid of such facts must not, on the strength of its mere assertions, be claimed as the product of any but the writer's own mind.

B. Next above the motor messages whose content the automatist's own mental resources might supply, we may place the messages whose content seems to be derived telepathically from the mind of some other person still living on earth; that person being either conscious or unconscious of transmitting the suggestion.

C. Next comes the possibility that the message may emanate from some unembodied intelligence of unknown type — other, at any rate, than the intelligence of the alleged agent. Under this heading come the views which ascribe the messages on the one hand to "elementaries," or even devils, and on the other hand to "guides" or "guardians" of superhuman goodness and wisdom.

D. Finally we have the possibility that the message may be derived, in a more or less direct manner, from the mind of the agent — the departed friend — from whom the communication does actually claim to come.

My main effort has naturally been thus far directed to the proof that there are messages which do *not* fall into the lowest class, *A* — in which class most psychologists would still place them all. And I myself — while reserving a certain small portion of the messages for my other classes — do not only admit but assert that the great majority of such communications represent the subliminal workings of the automatist's mind alone. It does not, however, follow that such messages have for us no interest or novelty. On the contrary, they form an instructive, an indispensable transition from psychological introspection of the old-fashioned kind to the bolder methods on whose validity I am anxious to insist. The mind's subliminal action, as thus revealed, differs from the supraliminal in ways which no one anticipated, and which no one can explain. There seem to be subliminal tendencies setting steadily in certain obscure directions, and bearing as little relation to the individual characteristics of the person to the deeps of whose being we have somehow penetrated as profound ocean-currents bear to waves and winds on the surface of the sea.[1]

---

[1] See James's *Psychology*, vol. i. p. 394: "One curious thing about trance utterances is their generic similarity in different individuals. . . . It seems exactly as if one author composed more than half of the trance messages, no matter by whom they are uttered. Whether all sub-conscious selves are peculiarly susceptible to a certain stratum of the *Zeitgeist*, and get their inspiration from it, I know not." See

Another point also, of fundamental importance, connected with the powers of the subliminal self, will be better deferred until a later chapter. I have said that a message containing only facts normally known to the automatist must not, on the strength of its mere assertions, be regarded as proceeding from any mind but his own. This seems evident; but the converse proposition is not equally indisputable. We must not take for granted that a message which *does* contain facts not normally known to the automatist must therefore come from some mind other than his own. If the subliminal self can acquire supernormal knowledge at all, it may obtain such knowledge by means other than telepathic impressions from other minds. It may assimilate its supernormal nutriment also by a directer process — it may devour it not only cooked but raw. Parallel with the possibilities of reception of such knowledge from the influence of other embodied or disembodied minds lies the possibility of its own clairvoyant perception, or active absorption of some kind, of facts lying indefinitely beyond its supraliminal purview.

Now, as I have said, the great majority of the nunciative or message-bearing motor automatisms originate in the automatist's own mind, and do not involve the exercise of telepathy or telæsthesia, or any other super-normal faculty; but they illustrate in various ways the coexistence of the subliminal with the supraliminal self, its wider memory, and its independent intelligence.

I need not here multiply instances of the simpler and commoner forms of this type, and I will merely quote in illustration one short case recounted by Mr. H. Arthur Smith (author of *The Principles of Equity*, and a member of the Council of the Society for Psychical Research) who has had the patience to analyse many communications through "Planchette."

(From *Proceedings* S.P.R., vol. ii. p. 233.)[1] Mr. Smith and his nephew

the account of automatic and impressional script, by Mr. Sidney Dean, which Professor James goes on to quote, and which is closely parallel to (for instance) Miss A.'s case, to be referred to below, although the one series of messages comes from the hand of a late member of Congress, "all his life a robust and active journalist, author, and man of affairs," and the other from a young lady with so different a history and *entourage*.

[1] Some other cases of Mr. Smith's will be found in this volume. See also *Proceedings* S.P.R., vol. iii. p. 25 [§ 831] for a case of Prof. Sidgwick's, and *Proceedings* S.P.R., vol. ii. pp. 226–231 for the complex "Clelia" case. Other cases of imaginary personalities are to be found in the accounts of possession which have come down to us from the "Ages of Faith." See for example the auto-biography of Sœur Jeanne des Anges (*Bibliothèque Diabolique* [collection Bourneville] Paris, 1886).

placed their hands on the Planchette, and a purely fantastic name was given as that of the communicating agency.

Q. "Where did you live?" A. "Wem." This name was quite unknown to any of us. I am sure it was to myself, and as sure of the word of the others as of that of any one I know.

Q. "Is it decided who is to be Archbishop of Canterbury?" A. "Yes."

Q. "Who?" A. "Durham." As none of us remembered his name, we asked.

"What is his name?" A. "Lightfoot." Of course, how far the main statement is correct, I don't know. The curiosity at the time rested in the fact that the name was given which none of us could recall, but was found to be right.

Now, this is just one of the cases which a less wary observer might have brought forward as evidence of spirit agency. An identity, it would be said, manifested itself, and gave an address which none present had ever heard. But I venture to say that there cannot be any real proof that an educated person has never heard of Wem. A permanent recorded fact, like the name of a town which is to be found (for instance) in Bradshaw's Guide, may at any moment have been presented to Mr. Smith's eye, and have found a lodgment in his subliminal memory.

Similarly in the answers "Durham" and "Lightfoot" we are reminded of cases where in a dream we ask a question with vivid curiosity, and are astonished at the reply; which nevertheless proceeds from *ourselves* as undoubtedly as does the inquiry. The prediction in this case was wrong.

What we have been shown is an independent activity of the subliminal self holding colloquies with the supraliminal, and nothing more. Yet we shall find, if we go on accumulating instances of the same general type, that traces of telæsthesia and telepathy begin insensibly to show themselves; not at first with a distinctness or a persistence sufficient for actual proof, but just in the same gradual way in which indications of supernormal faculty stole in amid the disintegration of split personalities; or in which indications of some clairvoyant outlook stole in amid the incoherence of dream. Many of these faint indications, valueless, as I have said, for purely evidential purposes, are nevertheless of much theoretical interest, as showing how near is the subliminal self to that region of supernormal knowledge which for the supraliminal is so definitely closed.[1]

Mr. Schiller's case (see *Proceedings* S.P.R., vol. iv. pp. 216–224) [832 A] is a good example of these obscure transitions between normal and supernormal, and introduces us to several phenomena which we

---

[1] For the description of a curious case combining various motor automatisms in a very unusual way, see *Proceedings* S.P.R., vol. ix. p. 182 [§ 833].

shall afterwards find recurring again and again in independent quarters. Dramatisation of fictitious personalities, for instance, which forms so marked a feature in Professor Flournoy's celebrated case (to be discussed later), begins in this series of experiments, conducted throughout with a purely scientific aim, and with no sort of belief in the imaginary "Irktomar" and the rest. It seems as though this "objectivation of types" were part of a romance which some inscrutable but childish humorist was bent on making up. The "cryptomnesia" shown in this case through the reproduction of scraps of old French with which the automatist had no conscious acquaintance, reached a point at which (as again in Professor Flournoy's case) one is almost driven to suspect that it was aided by some slight clairvoyance on the part of the subliminal self.

Indeed as the cases become increasingly complex, one wonders to what extent this strange manufacture of inward romances can be carried. There is, I may say, a great deal more of it in the world than is commonly suspected. I have myself received so many cases of these dramatised utterances — as though a number of different spirits were writing in turn through some automatist's hand — that I have come to recognise the operation of some law of dreams, so to call it, as yet but obscurely understood. The alleged personalities are for the most part not only unidentified, but purposely unidentifiable; they give themselves romantic or ludicrous names, and they are produced and disappear as lightly as puppets on a mimic stage. The main curiosity of such cases lies in their very persistence and complexity; it would be a waste of space to quote any of the longer ones in such a way as to do them justice. And, fortunately, there is no need for me to give any of my own cases; since a specially good case has been specially well observed and reported in a book with which many of my readers are probably already acquainted, — Professor Flournoy's *Des Indes à la planète Mars: Etude sur un cas de Somnambulisme avec Glossolalie* (Paris and Geneva, 1900). I shall here make some comments on that striking record, which all students of these subjects ought to study in detail.

It happens, no doubt, to any group which pursues for many years a somewhat unfamiliar line of inquiry, that those of their points which are first assailed get gradually admitted, so that as they become interested in new points they may scarcely observe what change has taken place in the reception of the old. The reader of early volumes of the *Proceedings* S.P.R. will often observe this kind of progress of opinion. And now Professor Flournoy's book indicates in a remarkable way how things have

moved in the psychology of the last twenty years.   The book — a model
of fairness throughout — is indeed, for the most part, critically *destructive*
in its treatment of the quasi-supernormal phenomena with which it deals.
But what a mass of conceptions a competent psychologist now takes for
granted in this realm, which the official science of twenty years ago would
scarcely stomach our hinting at!

One important point may be noticed at once as decisively corroborating
a contention of my own made long ago, and at a time when it probably
seemed fantastic to many readers.   Arguing for the potential *continuity* of
subliminal mentation (as against those who urged that there were only
occasional flashes of submerged thought, like scattered dreams), I said
that it would soon be found needful to press this notion of a continuous
subliminal self to the utmost, if we were not prepared to admit a continuous
spiritual guidance or possession.   Now, in fact, with Professor Flournoy's
subject the whole discussion turns on this very point.   There is unques-
tionably a continuous and complex series of thoughts and feelings going
on beneath the threshold of consciousness of Mlle. "Hélène Smith."   Is
this submerged mentation due in any degree or in any manner to the operation of spirits other than Mlle. Smith's own?   That is the broad question;
but it is complicated here by a subsidiary question: whether, namely, any
previous incarnations of Mlle. Smith's — other phases of her own spiritual
history, now involving complex relationship with the past — have any
part in the crowd of personalities which seem struggling to express themselves through her quite healthy organism.

Mlle. Smith, I should at once say, is not,[1] and never has been, a paid
medium.   At the date of M. Flournoy's book, she occupied a leading post
on the staff of a large *maison de commerce* at Geneva, and gave séances to
her friends simply because she enjoyed the exercise of her mediumistic
faculties, and was herself interested in their explanation.

Her organism, I repeat, is regarded, both by herself and by others, as
a quite healthy one.   Mlle. Smith, says Professor Flournoy, declares distinctly that she is perfectly sound in body and mind — in no way lacking
in equilibrium — and indignantly repudiates the idea that there is any
hurtful anomaly or the slightest danger in mediumship as she practises it.

"It is far from being demonstrated," he continues, "that mediumship is a pathological phenomenon.   It is abnormal, no doubt, in the
sense of being *rare, exceptional;* but rarity is not morbidity.   The few
years during which these phenomena have been seriously and scientifically

---

[1] For Mlle. Smith's later history, see Professor Flournoy's *Nouvelles Observations sur un cas de Somnambulisme*, Geneva, 1902.

studied have not been enough to allow us to pronounce on their true nature. It is interesting to note that in the countries where these studies have been pushed the furthest, in England and America, the dominant view among the *savants* who have gone deepest into the matter is not at all unfavourable to mediumship; and that, far from regarding it as a special case of hysteria, they see in it a faculty superior, advantageous, healthy, of which hysteria is a form of degenerescence, a pathological parody, a morbid caricature."

The phenomena which this sensitive presents (Hélène Smith is Professor Flournoy's pseudonym for her) cover a range which looks at first very wide, although a clearer analysis shows that these varieties are more apparent than real, and that self-suggestion will perhaps account for all of them.

There is, to begin with, every kind of automatic irruption of subliminal into supraliminal life. As Professor Flournoy says (p. 45): "Phenomena of hypermnesia, divinations, mysterious findings of lost objects, happy inspirations, exact presentiments, just intuitions, teleological (purposive or helpful) automatisms, in short, of every kind; she possesses in a high degree this small change of genius — which constitutes a more than sufficient compensation for the inconvenience resulting from those distractions and moments of absence of mind which accompany her visions; and which, moreover, generally pass unobserved."

At séances — where the deeper change has no inconveniences — Hélène undergoes a sort of self-hypnotisation which produces various lethargic and somnambulistic states. And when she is alone and safe from interruption she has spontaneous visions, during which there may be some approach to ecstasy. At the séances she experiences positive hallucinations, and also negative hallucinations, or systematised anæsthesiæ, so that, for instance, she will cease to see some person present, especially one who is to be the recipient of messages in the course of the séance. "It seems as though a dream-like incoherence presided over this preliminary work of disaggregation, in which the normal perceptions are arbitrarily split up or absorbed by the subconscious personality — eager for materials with which to compose the hallucinations which it is preparing." Then, when the séance begins, the main actor is Hélène's guide *Léopold* (a pseudonym for Cagliostro) who speaks and writes through her, and is, in fact, either her leading spirit-control or (much more probably) her most developed form of secondary personality.

"Leopold," says Professor Flournoy (p. 134), "certainly manifests a very honourable and amiable side of Mlle. Smith's character, and in taking him as her 'guide' she has followed inspirations which are doubtless among the highest in her nature."

The high moral quality of these automatic communications, on which Professor Flournoy thus insists, is a phenomenon worth consideration.

I do not mean that it is specially strange in the case of Mlle. Smith. But the almost universally high moral tone of genuinely automatic utterances has not, I think, been sufficiently noticed or adequately explained.

In evidential messages — where there is real reason to believe that an identified spirit is communicating — there is a marked and independent consensus on such matters as these spirits profess themselves able to discuss.

And again in non-evidential messages — in communications which probably proceed from the automatist's subliminal self — I hold that there is a remarkable and undesigned concordance in high moral tone, and also in avoidance of certain prevalent tenets, which many of the automatists do supraliminally hold as true. But I also insist that these subliminal messages, even when not incoherent, are generally dream-like, and often involve tenets which (though never in my experience base or immoral) are unsupported by evidence, and are probably to be referred to mere self-suggestion.

Prominent among such tenets is one which forms a large part of Mlle. Smith's communications; namely, the doctrine of *reincarnation*, or of successive lives spent by each soul upon this planet.

The simple fact that such was probably the opinion both of Plato and of Virgil shows that there is nothing here which is alien to the best reason or to the highest instincts of men. Nor, indeed, is it easy to realise any theory of the *direct creation* of spirits at such different stages of advancement as those which enter upon the earth in the guise of mortal man. There *must*, one feels, be some kind of continuity — some form of spiritual Past. Yet for reincarnation there is at present no valid evidence; and it must be my duty to show how its assertion in any given instance — Mlle. Smith's included — constitutes in itself a strong argument in favour of self-suggestion rather than extraneous inspiration as the source of the messages in which it appears.

Whenever civilised men have received what they have regarded as a revelation (which has generally been somewhat fragmentary in its first delivery) they have naturally endeavoured to complete and systematise it as well as they could. In so doing they have mostly aimed at three objects: (1) to *understand* as much as possible of the secrets of the universe; (2) to *justify* as far as possible Heaven's dealings with men; and (3) to

appropriate as far as possible the favour or benefit which the revelation
may show as possibly accruing to believers. For all these purposes the
doctrine of reincarnation has proved useful in many countries and times.
But in no case could it seem more appropriate than in this last revelation
(so to term it) through automatic messages and the like. And as a matter
of history, a certain vigorous preacher of the new faith, known under the
name of Allan Kardec, took up reincarnationist tenets, enforced them (as
there is reason to believe) by strong suggestion upon the minds of various
automatic writers, and set them forth in dogmatic works which have had
much influence, especially among Latin nations, from their clarity, symmetry, and intrinsic reasonableness. Yet the data thus collected were
absolutely insufficient, and the *Livre des Esprits* must simply rank as the
premature formulation of a new religion — the premature systematisation
of a nascent science.

I follow Professor Flournoy in believing that the teaching of that work
must have directly or indirectly influenced the mind of Mlle. Smith, and
is therefore responsible for her claim to these incarnations previous to that
which she now undergoes or enjoys.

On the general scheme here followed, each incarnation, if the last has
been used aright, ought to represent some advance in the scale of being.
If one earth-life has been misused, the next earth-life ought to afford opportunity for expiation — or for further practice in the special virtue which
has been imperfectly acquired. Thus Mlle. Smith's present life in a humble
position may be thought to atone for her overmuch pride in her last incarnation — as Marie Antoinette.

But the mention of Marie Antoinette suggests the risk which this
theory fosters — of assuming that one is the issue of a distinguished line
of spiritual progenitors; insomuch that, with whatever temporary sets-
back, one is sure in the end to find oneself in a leading position.

Pythagoras, indeed, was content with the secondary hero Euphorbus
as his bygone self. But in our days Dr. Anna Kingsford and Mr. Edward
Maitland must needs have been the Virgin Mary and St. John the Divine.
And Victor Hugo, who was naturally well to the front in these self-multi-
plications, took possession of most of the leading personages of antiquity
whom he could manage to string together in chronological sequence. It
is obvious that any number of re-born souls can play at this game; but
where no one adduces any evidence it seems hardly worth while to go on.
Even Pythagoras does not appear to have adduced any evidence beyond
his *ipse dixit* for his assertion that the alleged shield of Euphorbus had in
reality been borne by that mythical hero. Meantime the question as to

reincarnation has actually been put to a very few spirits who have given some real evidence of their identity. So far as I know, no one of these has claimed to know anything personally of such an incident; although all have united in saying that their knowledge was too limited to allow them to generalise on the matter.

Hélène's controls and previous incarnations — to return to our subject — do perhaps suffer from the general fault of aiming too high. She has to her credit a control from the planet Mars; one pre-incarnation as an Indian Princess; and a second (as I have said) as Marie Antoinette.

In each case there are certain impressive features in the impersonation; but in each case also careful analysis negatives the idea that we can be dealing with a personality really revived from a former epoch, or from a distant planet; — and leaves us inclined to explain everything by "cryptomnesia" (as Professor Flournoy calls submerged memory), and that subliminal inventiveness of which we already know so much.

The *Martian* control was naturally the most striking at first sight. Its reality was supported by a Martian language, written in a Martian alphabet, spoken with fluency, and sufficiently interpreted into French to show that such part of it, at any rate, as could be committed to writing was actually a grammatical and coherent form of speech.

And here I reach an appropriate point at which to remark that this book of Professor Flournoy's is not the first account which has been published of Mlle. Hélène. Professor Lemaître, of Geneva, printed two papers about her in the *Annales des Sciences Psychiques*: first, a long article in the number for March–April, 1897 — then a reply to M. Lefébure in the number for May–June, 1897. In these papers he distinctly claims supernormal powers for Mlle. Hélène, implying a belief in her genuine possession by spirits, and even in her previous incarnations, and in the extra-terrene or ostensibly Martian language. I read these papers at the time, but put them aside as inconclusive, mainly because that very language, on which M. Lemaître seemed most to rely, appeared to me so obviously factitious as to throw doubt on all the evidence presented by an observer who could believe that denizens of another planet talked to each other in a language corresponding in every particular with simple French idioms, and including such words as *quisa* for *quel*, *quisé* for *quelle*, *vétèche* for *voir*, *vèche* for *vu;* — the fantastic locutions of the nursery. M. Lemaître remarks, as a proof of the consistency and reality of the extra-terrene tongue, "L'un des premiers mots que nous ayons eus, *métiche*, signifiant *monsieur*, se retrouve plus tard avec le sens de *homme*." That is to say, having transmogrified *monsieur* into *métiche*, Hélène further transmutes *les messieurs* into *cie mětichě;* — in naïve imitation of ordinary French usage. And this tongue is supposed to have sprung up independently of all the influences which have shaped terrene grammar in general or the French idiom in particular! And even after Professor Flournoy's analysis of this absurdity I see newspapers speaking of this Martian language as an impressive phenomenon! They seem willing to believe that the evolution of another planet, if it has culminated in conscious life at all, can have culminated in a conscious life into which we could all of us enter affably, with a suitable Ollendorff's phrase-book under our arms; — "*eni cie mětichě ont qudě,*" — "ici les hommes (messieurs) sont bons," — "here the men are good"; — and the rest of it.

To the student of automatisms, of course, all this irresistibly suggests the automatist's own subliminal handiwork. It is a case of "glossolaly," or "speaking with tongues"; and we have no modern case—no case later than the half-mythical Miracles of the Cevennes—where such utterance has proved to be other than gibberish. I have had various automatic hieroglyphics shown to me, with the suggestion that they may be cursive Japanese, or perhaps an old dialect of Northern China; but I confess that I have grown tired of showing these fragments to the irresponsive expert, who suggests that they may also be vague reminiscences of the scrolls in an Oriental tea-tray.

It seems indeed to be a most difficult thing to get telepathically into any brain even fragments of a language which it has not learnt. A few simple Italian, and even Hawaiian, words occur in Mrs. Piper's utterances, coming apparently from departed spirits (*Proceedings* S.P.R., vol. xiii. pp. 337 and 384 [960 A and § 961]), but these, with some Kaffir and Chinese words given through Miss Browne (*Proceedings* S.P.R., vol. ix. pp. 124–127 [871 A]), form, I think, almost the only instances which I know. And, speaking generally, whatever is elaborate, finished, pretentious, is likely to be of subliminal facture; while only things scrappy, perplexed, and tentative, have floated to us veritably from afar.

I need not here go into the details of the Hindow preincarnation or of the more modern and accessible characterisation of Marie Antoinette, but will pass on to certain minor, but interesting phenomena, which Professor Flournoy calls *teleological automatisms*. These are small acts of helpfulness — *beneficent synergies*, as we might term them, in contrast with the *injurious synergies*, or combined groups of *hurtful* actions, with which hysteria has made us familiar.[1]

[1] We have already printed several incidents of this type in our *Proceedings* and *Journal*. (See, for instance, *Proceedings* S.P.R., vol. viii. p. 344 [818 A].)

"One day," says Professor Flournoy (p. 35), "Miss Smith, when desiring to lift down a large and heavy object which lay on a high shelf, was prevented from doing so because her raised arm remained for some seconds as though petrified in the air and incapable of movement. She took this as a warning, and gave up the attempt. At a subsequent séance Leopold stated that it was he who had thus fixed Hélène's arm to prevent her from grasping this object, which was much too heavy for her and would have caused her some accident.

"Another time, a shopman, who had been looking in vain for a certain pattern, asked Hélène if by chance she knew what had become of it. Hélène answered mechanically and without reflection — 'Yes, it has been sent to Mr. J.' (a client of the house). At the same time she saw before her the number 18 in large black figures a few feet from the ground, and added instinctively, 'It was sent eighteen days ago.' [This was in the highest degree improbable, but was found to be absolutely correct.] Leopold had no recollection of this, and does not seem to have been the author of this cryptomnesic automatism."

A similar phenomenon has also been noted (p. 87) when warning is conveyed by an actual phantasmal figure. Mlle. Smith has seen an *apparition* of Leopold, barring a particular road, under circumstances which make it probable that Mlle. Smith would on that day have had cause to regret taking that route.

This case of Professor Flournoy's, then — this classical case, as it may already be fairly termed — may serve here as our culminant example of the free scope and dominant activity of the unassisted subliminal self. The telepathic element in this case, if it exists, is relatively small; what we are watching in Mlle. Hélène Smith resembles, as I have said, a kind of exaggeration of the submerged constructive faculty, — a hypertrophy of genius — without the innate originality of mind which made even the dreams of R. L. Stevenson a source of pleasure to thousands of readers.

In reference to the main purpose of this work, such cases as these, however curious, can be only introductory to automatisms of deeper moment. In our attempt to trace an evolutive series of phenomena indicating ever higher human faculty, the smallest telepathic incident, — the most trivial proof, if proof it be, of communication received without sensory intermediation from either an incarnate or a discarnate mind outweighs in importance the most complex ramifications and burgeonings of the automatist's own submerged intelligence.

I pass on, then, to evidence which points, through motor automatisms, to supernormal faculty; and I shall begin by referring the reader to certain experiments (due to Professor Richet) in the simplest of all forms of motor automatism, viz., table-tilting, with results which only telepathy can explain. (See Appendix VIII. A.)

Trivial though they seem, such experiments may with a little care be made absolutely conclusive. Had Professor Richet's friends, for example, been willing to prolong this series, we might have had a standing demonstration of telepathy, reproducible at will.[1]

And now I pass on to some experiments with Planchette, in which an element of telepathy was shown. The following account from Mrs. Alfred Moberly, Tynwald, Hythe, Kent, is corroborated, with some additional examples, by two other ladies present at the time. (From *Proceedings* S.P.R., vol. ii. p. 235.)

May 9th, 1884.

The operators were placed out of sight of the rest of the company, who selected — in silence — a photograph, one of an albumful, and fixed their attention on it. We — the operators — were requested to keep our minds a blank as far as possible and follow the first involuntary motion of the Planchette. In three out of five cases it wrote the name or initial or some word descriptive of the selected portrait. We also obtained the signatures to letters selected in the same manner. We both knew perfectly well that *we* were writing — not the spirits, as the rest of the company persist to this day in believing — but had only the slightest idea what the words might prove to be.

We have tried it since, and generally with some curious result. A crucial test was offered by two gentlemen in the form of a question to which we couldn't possibly guess the answer. "Where's Toosey?" The answer came, "In Vauxhall Road." "Toosey," they explained, was a pet terrier who had disappeared; suspicion attaching to a plumber living in the road mentioned, who had been working at the house and whose departure coincided with Toosey's.

Of course, in the case of the inquiry after the lost dog, we may suppose that the answer given came from the questioner's own mind. Mrs. Moberly and her friends seem to have been quite aware of this; and were little likely to fall into the not uncommon error of asking Planchette, for instance, what horse will win the Derby, and staking, perhaps, some pecuniary consideration on the extremely illusory reply.[2]

And now we come to the palmary case of the late Rev. P. H. Newnham, Vicar of Maker, Devonport, who was personally known to Edmund Gurney and myself, and was a man in all ways worthy of high respect.

---

[1] A somewhat similar but less complex set of experiments by Mr. G. M. Smith is given in the *Journal* S.P.R., vol. v. pp. 318–320 [843 B].

[2] For further cases see *Proceedings* S.P.R., vol. iii. pp. 2 and 5 [§§ 845 and 847].

The long series of communications between Mr. Newnham and his wife, which date back to 1871, and whose contemporaneous written record is preserved in the archives of the S.P.R., must, I think, always retain their primacy as early and trustworthy examples of a telepathic transference where the percipient's automatic script answers questions penned by the agent in such a position that the percipient could not in any normal manner discern what those questions were. No part of our evidence seems to me more worthy of study than this.[1]

It must be distinctly understood that Mrs. Newnham did not see or hear the questions which Mr. Newnham wrote down.[2] The fact, therefore, that her answers bore any relation to the questions shows that the sense of the questions was telepathically conveyed to her. This is the leading and important fact. The *substance* of the replies written is also interesting, and Mr. Newnham has some good comments thereon. But even had the replies contained no facts which Mrs. Newnham could not have known, this would not detract from the main value of the evidence, which consists in the fact that *Mrs. Newnham's hand wrote replies clearly and repeatedly answering questions which she neither heard nor saw.*

In this case we have the advantage of seeing before us the entire series of questions and answers, and thus of satisfying ourselves that the misses (which in that case are very few) are marked as well as the hits, and consequently that the coincidences between question and

---

[1] See *Proceedings* S.P.R., vol. iii. pp. 8–23 [849 A]. For a series of experiments on a smaller scale but analogous to these see *Proceedings* S.P.R., vol. ix. (1893), pp. 61–64.

[2] Mr. Newnham procured for me two autograph letters from eye-witnesses of some of the experiments, who do not, however, wish their names to be published. One writer says: "You wrote the question on a slip of paper and put it under one of the ornaments of the chimney-piece — no one seeing what you had written. Mrs. Newnham sat apart at a small table. I recollect you kept a book of the questions asked and answers given, as you thought some new power might be discovered, and you read me from it some of the results. I remember particularly questions and answers relating to the selection of a curate for B. My wife and her sister saw experiments conducted in this manner. Mrs. Newnham and you were sitting at different tables." Another eye-witness writes: "I and my sister were staying at ——, and were present at many of the Planchette experiments of Mr. and Mrs. Newnham. Mr. and Mrs. Newnham sat at different tables some distance apart, and in such a position that it was quite impossible Mrs. Newnham could see what question was written down. The subject of the questions was never mentioned even in a whisper. Mr. Newnham wrote them down in pencil and sometimes passed them to me and my sister to see, but not often. Mrs. Newnham immediately answered the questions. Though not always correct, they (the answers) always referred to the questions. Mr. Newnham copied out the pencil questions and answers verbatim each day into a diary."

answer are at any rate not the result of chance. In several other cases which I have known, where the good faith of the informants has been equally above question, the possibility of an explanation by chance alone has been a more important element in the problem. All our evidence has tended to show that the telepathic power itself is a variable thing; that it shows itself in flashes, for the most part spontaneously, and seldom persists through a series of deliberate experiments. And if an automatist possessing power of this uncertain kind has exercised it at irregular moments and with no scientific aim; — and has kept, moreover, no steady record of success and failure; — then it becomes difficult to say that even some brilliant coincidences afford cogent proof of telepathic action.[1]

I pass on to a small group of cases which form a curious transition from these communications *inter vivos* to communications which I shall class as coming from the dead. These are cases where the message professes to come from a deceased person, but shows internal evidence of having come, telepathically, from the mind of some one present, or, indeed, from some living person at a distance. (See the case given in Appendix VIII. B.)

But this, although a real risk, is by no means the only risk of deception which such messages involve. The communication may conceivably come from some unembodied spirit indeed, but not from the spirit who is claimed as its author.

The reader who wishes to acquaint himself with this new range of problems cannot do better than study the record of the varied experiences of automatic writing which have been intermingled with Miss A.'s crystal-visions, etc.[2]

There is no case that I have watched longer than Miss A.'s; — none where I have more absolute assurance of the scrupulous probity of the principal sensitive herself and of the group who share the experiments; — but none also which leaves me more often baffled as to the unseen source of the information given. There is a knowledge both of the past and of the future, which seems capriciously limited, and is mingled with mistakes, yet on the other hand is of a nature which it is difficult to refer to any individual human mind, incarnate or discarnate. We meet here some of the first indications of a possibility that discarnate spirits com-

---

[1] For further cases see *Proceedings* S.P.R., vol. ix, p. 44 [851 A]; *ibid.* p. 48 [852]; *ibid.* p. 64 [853]; *ibid.* p. 65 [854]. Also *Proceedings* S.P.R., vol. ii. p. 236; vol. vi. pp. 112–115 [855 and 856]; vol. xi. pp. 477–481 [852 B]; vol. ix. pp. 67–70 [857 A and 858 A].

[2] See *Proceedings* S.P.R., vol. ix. (1893) pp. 73–92 [859 A and 625 C].

municating with us have occasional access to certain sources of knowledge which even to themselves are inscrutably remote and obscure.

The written diagnoses and prognoses given by the so-called "Semirus," often without Miss A.'s even seeing the patient or hearing the nature of his malady, have become more and more remarkable. Miss A. and her friends do not wish these private matters to be printed, and I cannot therefore insist upon the phenomena here. Yet in view of the amount of telæsthesia which Miss A.'s various automatisms reveal, it should first be noted that human organisms seem especially pervious to such *vue à distance.* "Semirus," "Gelalius," etc., are obvious pseudonyms; and neither Semirus' prescriptions nor Gelalius' cosmogony contain enough of indication to enable us to grasp their origin.[1]

From the communications of these remote personages I go on to certain messages avowedly coming from persons more recently departed, and into which something more of definite personality seems to enter. One element of this kind is *handwriting;* there are many cases where resemblance of handwriting is one of the evidential points alleged. Now proof of identity from resemblance of handwriting may conceivably be very strong. But in estimating it we must bear two points in mind. The first is that (like the resemblances of so-called "spirit-photographs" to deceased friends) it is often very loosely asserted. One needs, if not an expert's opinion, at least a careful personal scrutiny of the three scripts — the automatist's voluntary and his automatic script, and the deceased person's script — before one can feel sure that the resemblance is in more than some general scrawliness. This refers to the cases where the automatist has provably never seen the deceased person's handwriting. Where he *has* seen that handwriting, we have to remember (in the second place) that a hypnotised subject can frequently imitate any known handwriting far more closely than in his waking state; and that consequently we are bound to credit the subliminal self with a mimetic faculty which may come out in these messages without any supraliminal guidance whatever on the automatist's part. In *Proceedings* S.P.R., vol. v. pp. 549–65 [864 A], is an account of a series of experiments by Professor Rossi-Pagnoni at Pesaro, into which the question of handwriting enters. The account illustrates automatic utterance as well as other forms of motor automatism, and possibly also telekinetic phenomena. The critical dis-

[1] For another series of messages which afford an interesting field for the discussion of the rival hypotheses of "cryptomnesia" and spirit-control, see *Journal* S.P.R., vol. iv. p. 319; *op. cit.* p. 174; and *Proceedings* S.P.R., vol. ix. p. 92 [§§ 860, 861 and 862 A].

cussion of the evidence by Mr. H. Babington Smith, to whom we are indebted for the account, shows with what complex considerations we have to deal in the questions now before us.

I now cite a few cases where the point of central interest is the announcement of a death unknown to the sitters.[1]

In Appendix VIII. C is given a case which we received from Dr. Lié-beault, of Nancy, and which was first published in *Phantasms of the Living* (vol. i. p. 293), where it was regarded as an example of a spontaneous telepathic impulse proceeding directly from a dying person. I now regard it as more probably due to the action of the spirit after bodily death.

I shall next give a *résumé* of a case of curious complexity received from M. Aksakof; — an automatic message written by a Mdlle. Stramm, informing her of the death of a M. Duvanel. The principal incidents may here be disentangled as follows: —

Duvanel dies by his own hand on January 15th, 1887, in a Swiss village, where he lives alone, having no relations except a brother living at a distance, whom Mdlle. Stramm had never seen (as the principal witness, M. Kaigorodoff, informs us in a letter of May 1890).

Mdlle. Stramm's father does not hear of Duvanel's death till two days later, and sends her the news in a letter dated January 18th, 1887.

Five hours after Duvanel's death an automatic message announcing it is written at the house of M. Kaigorodoff, at Wilna in Russia, by Mdlle. Stramm, who had certainly at that time received no news of the event.

From what mind are we to suppose that this information came?

(1) We may first attempt to account for Mdlle. Stramm's message on the theory of *latency*. We may suppose that the telepathic message came from the dying man, but did not rise into consciousness until an opportunity was afforded by Mdlle. Stramm's sitting down to write automatically.

But to this interpretation there is an objection of a very curious kind. The message written by Mdlle. Stramm was not precisely accurate. Instead of ascribing Duvanel's death to suicide, it ascribed it to a stoppage of blood, "un engorgement de sang."

And when M. Stramm, three days after the death, wrote to his daughter in Russia to tell her of it, he also used the same expression, "un engorgement de sang," thus disguising the actual truth in order to spare the feelings of his daughter, who had formerly refused to marry Duvanel, and who (as her father feared) might receive a painful shock if she learnt the tragic nature of his end. There was, therefore, a singular coincidence between the automatic and the normally-written message as to the death; — a coincidence which looks as though the same mind had been

[1] For further examples see the cases given in *Proceedings* S.P.R., vol. vi. pp. 355–57; vol. viii. pp. 242–48; *Journal* S.P.R., vol. iii. pp. 216–19; vol. ix. pp. 65–8; vol. ix. pp. 280–84 [868 A and B, 869 A and B, § 873].

at work in each instance. But that mind cannot have been M. Stramm's ordinary mind, as he was not supraliminally aware of Duvanel's death at the time when the first message was written. It may, however, be supposed that his subliminal self had received the information of the death telepathically, had transmitted it in a deliberately modified form to his daughter, while it remained latent in himself, and had afterwards influenced his supraliminal self to modify the information in the same way when writing to her.

(2) But we must also consider the explanation of the coincidence given by the intelligence which controlled the automatic writing. That intelligence asserted itself to be a brother of Mdlle. Stramm's, who died some years before. And this "Louis" further asserted that he had himself influenced M. Stramm to make use of the same euphemistic phrase, with the object of avoiding a shock to Mdlle. Stramm; for which purpose it was needful that the two messages should agree in ascribing the death to the same form of sudden illness.

Now if this be true, and the message did indeed come from the deceased "Louis," we have an indication of continued existence, and continued knowledge of earthly affairs, on the part of a person long dead.

But if we consider that the case, as presented to us, contains no proof of "Louis'" identity, so that "Louis" may be merely one of those arbitrary names which the automatist's subliminal intelligence seems so prone to assume; then we must suppose that Duvanel was actually operative on two occasions after death, first inspiring in Mdlle. Stramm the automatic message, and then modifying in M. Stramm the message which the father might otherwise have sent.

I next quote a case in Appendix VIII. D which illustrates the continued terrene knowledge on the part of the dead of which other instances were given in the last chapter.

And lastly, I give in Appendix VIII. E a case which in one respect stands alone. It narrates the success of a direct experiment, — a test-message planned before death, and communicated after death, by a man who held that the hope of an assurance of continued existence was worth at least a resolute effort, whatever its result might be. His tests, indeed, were two, and both were successful. One was the revealing of the place where, before death, he hid a piece of brick marked and broken for special recognition, and the other was the communication of the contents of a short letter which he wrote and sealed before death. We may say that the information was certainly not possessed supraliminally by any living person. There are two other cases (*Proceedings* S.P.R., vol. vi. pp. 353-355, and *op. cit.* vol. viii. pp. 238–242 [876 A and B]) where information given through automatists may hypothetically be explicable by telepathy from the living, although, indeed, in my own view, it probably emanated from the deceased as alleged. In one of these cases the place where a missing will had been hidden was revealed to the automatist, but it is not clear whether the will was actually discovered or not before the auto-. matic writing was obtained (although the automatist was unaware of its discovery), and in any case, apparently, its whereabouts was known to some living person who had hidden it, and may not have been known to the deceased before death.

In the other case the whereabouts of a missing note of hand was revealed to the automatists, and even if this could be regarded as absolutely unknown supraliminally to any living person, it is not by any means certain that the fact was known before death to the deceased person from whom the message purported to come.

These cases, therefore, are not such strong evidence for personal identity as the one to which I have referred above, and which I have given, as recording what purports to be the successful accomplishment of an experiment which every one may make; — which every one *ought* to make; — for, small as may be the chances of success, a few score of distinct successes would establish a presumption of man's survival which the common sense of mankind would refuse to explain away.

Here, then, let us pause and consider to what point the evidence contained in this chapter has gradually led us. We shall perceive that the motor phenomena have confirmed, and have also greatly extended, the results to which the cognate sensory phenomena had already pointed. We have already noted, in each of the two states of sleep and of waking, the variously expanding capacities of the subliminal self. We have watched a hyperæsthetic intensification of ordinary faculty, — leading up to telæsthesia, and to telepathy, from the living and from the departed. Along with these powers, which, on the hypothesis of the soul's independent existence, are at least within our range of analogical conception, we have noted also a precognitive capacity of a type which no fact as yet known to science will help us to explain.

Proceeding to the study of motor automatisms, we have found a *third* group of cases which independently confirm in each of these lines in turn the results of our analysis of sensory automatisms both in sleep and in waking. Evidence thus convergent will already need no ordinary boldness of negative assumption if it is to be set aside. But motor automatisms have taught us much more than this. At once more energetic and more persistent than the sensory, they oblige us to face certain problems which the lightness and fugitiveness of sensory impressions allowed us in some measure to evade. Thus when we discussed the mechanism (so to call it) of visual and auditory phantasms, two competing conceptions presented themselves for our choice, — the conception of *telepathic impact*, and the conception of *psychical invasion*. Either (we said) there was an influence exerted by the agent on the percipient's mind, which so stimulated the sensory tracts of his brain that he externalised that impression as a quasi-percept, or else the agent in some way modified an actual portion of space where (say) an apparition was discerned, perhaps by several percipients at once.

Phrased in this manner, the telepathic impact seemed the less startling, the less extreme hypothesis of the two, — mainly, perhaps, because the picture which it called up was left so vague and obscure. But now instead of a fleeting hallucination we have to deal with a strong and lasting impulse — such, for instance, as the girl's impulse to *write*, in Dr. Liébeault's case (Appendix VIII. C): — an impulse which seems to come from the depths of the being, and which (like a post-hypnotic suggestion) may override even strong disinclination, and keep the automatist uncomfortable until it has worked itself out. We may still call this a *telepathic impact*, if we will, but we shall find it hard to distinguish that term from a *psychical invasion*. This strong, yet apparently alien, motor innervation corresponds in fact as closely as possible to our idea of an *invasion* — an invasion no longer of the room only in which the percipient is sitting, but of his own body and his own powers. It is an invasion which, if sufficiently prolonged, would become a *possession;* and it both unites and intensifies those two earlier conjectures;—of telepathic impact on the percipient's mind, and of "phantasmogenetic presence" in the percipient's surroundings. What seemed at first a mere impact is tending to become a persistent control; what seemed an incursion merely into the percipient's environment has become an incursion into his organism itself.

As has been usual in this inquiry, this slight forward step from vagueness to comparative clearness of conception introduces us at once to a whole series of novel problems. Yet, as we have also learnt to expect, some of our earlier phenomena may have to be called in with advantage to illustrate phenomena more advanced.

In cases of split personality, to begin with, we have seen just the same phenomena occurring where certainly no personality was concerned save the percipient's own. We have seen a section of the subliminal self partially or temporarily dominating the organism; perhaps controlling permanently one arm alone; [1] or perhaps controlling intermittently

---

[1] See the "Report of Dr. Ira Barrows on the case of Miss Anna Winsor." An account of Professor James' inquiry into the case will be found in *Proceedings* of the American S.P.R., vol. i. p. 552 [237 A].

the whole nervous system; — and all this with varying degrees of displacement of the primary personality.

Similarly with post-hypnotic suggestion. We have seen the subliminal self ordered to write (say) "It has left off raining" — and thereupon writing the words without the conscious will of the automatist — and again with varying degrees of displacement of the waking self. The step hence to such a case as Mrs. Newnham's is thus not a very long one. Mrs. Newnham's subliminal self, exercising supernormal faculty, and by some effort of its own, acquires certain facts from Mr. Newnham's mind, and uses her hand to write them down automatically. The great problem here introduced is how the subliminal self acquires the facts, rather than how it succeeds in writing them down when it has once acquired them.

But as we go further we can no longer limit the problem in this way, — to the activities of the automatist's subliminal self. We cannot always assume that some portion of the automatist's personality gets at the supernormal knowledge by some effort of its own. Our evidence, as we know, has pointed decisively to telepathic impacts or influences from without. What, then, is the mechanism here? Are we still to suppose that the automatist's subliminal self executes the movements — obeying somehow the bidding of the impulse from without? or does the external agent, who sends the telepathic message, himself execute the movements also, directly using the automatist's arm? And if telekinetic movements accompany the message (a subject thus far deferred, but of prime importance), are we to suppose that these also are effected by the percipient's subliminal self, under the guidance of some external spirit, incarnate or discarnate? or are they effected directly by that external spirit?

We cannot really say which of these two is the easier hypothesis.

From one point of view it may seem simpler to keep as long as we can to that acknowledged *vera causa*, the automatist's subliminal self; and to collect such observations as may indicate any power on its part of producing physical effects outside the organism. Such scattered observations occur at every stage, and even Mrs. Newnham (I may briefly observe in passing) thought that her pencil, when writing down the messages telepathically derived from her husband, was moved by something other than the ordinary muscular action of the fingers which held it. On the other hand, there seems something very forced in attributing to an external spirit's agency impulses and impressions which seem intimately the automatist's own, and at the same time refusing to ascribe to that external agency phenomena which take place outside the automatist's organism, and which present themselves to him as objective facts, as much outside his own being as the fall of the apple to the ground.

Reflecting on such points — and once admitting this kind of interaction between the automatist's own spirit and an external spirit, incarnate or discarnate — we find the possible combinations presenting themselves in perplexing variety; — a variety both of agencies on the part of the invading spirit, and of effects on the part of the invaded spirit and organism.

What is that which invades? and what is that which is displaced or superseded by this invasion? In what ways may two spirits co-operate in the possession and control of the same organism?

These last words — control and possession — remind us of the great mass of vague tradition and belief to the effect that spirits of the departed may exercise such possession or control over the living. To those ancient and vague beliefs it will be our task in the next chapter to give a form as exact and stable as we can. And observe with how entirely novel a preparation of mind we now enter on that task. The examination of "possession" is no longer to us, as to the ordinary civilised inquirer, a merely antiquarian or anthropological research into forms of superstition lying wholly apart from any valid or systematic thought. On the contrary, it is an inquiry directly growing out of previous evidence; directly needed for the full comprehension of known facts as well as for the discovery of facts unknown. We need, (so to say), to analyse the spectrum of helium, as detected in the sun, in order to check and correct our spectrum of helium as detected in the Bath waters. We are obliged to seek for certain definite phenomena in the spiritual world in order to explain certain definite phenomena of the world of matter.

CHAPTER IX

TRANCE, POSSESSION, AND ECSTASY

Vicit iter durum pietas.
— VIRGIL.

Possession, to define it for the moment in the narrowest way, is a more developed form of Motor Automatism. The difference broadly is, that in Possession the automatist's own personality does for the time altogether disappear, while there is a more or less complete *substitution* of personality; writing or speech being given by a spirit through the entranced organism. The change which has come over this branch of evidence since the present work was first projected, in 1888, is most significant. There existed indeed, at that date, a good deal of evidence which pointed in this direction,[1] but for various reasons most of that evidence was still possibly explicable in other ways. Even the phenomena of Mr. W. S. Moses left it possible to argue that the main "controls" under which he wrote or spoke when entranced were self-suggestions of his own mind, or phases of his own deeper personality. I had not then had the opportunity, which the kindness of his executors after his death afforded to me, of studying the whole series of his original note-books, and forming at first-hand my present conviction that spiritual agency was an actual and important element in that long sequence of communications. On the whole, I did not then anticipate that the theory of possession could be presented as more than a plausible speculation, or as a supplement to other lines of proof of man's survival of death.

The position of things, as the reader of the S.P.R. *Proceedings* knows, has since that time undergone a complete change. The trance-phenomena of Mrs. Piper — so long and so carefully watched by Dr. Hodgson and others — formed, I think, by far the most remarkable mass of psychical evidence till then adduced in any quarter. And more recently other series of trance-phenomena with other "mediums" — though

---

[1] The cases of Swedenborg, Cahagnet's subject, D. D. Home, and Stainton Moses will be discussed in the course of this chapter.

still incomplete — have added materially to the evidence obtained through Mrs. Piper. The result broadly is that these phenomena of possession are now the most amply attested, as well as intrinsically the most advanced, in our whole repertory.

Nor, again, is the mere increment of direct evidence, important though that is, the sole factor in the changed situation. Not only has direct evidence grown, but indirect evidence, so to say, has moved to meet it. The notion of personality — of the control of organism by spirit — has gradually been so modified that Possession, which passed till the other day as a mere survival of savage thought, is now seen to be the consummation, the furthest development of many lines of experiment, observation, reflection, which the preceding chapters have opened to our view.

Let us then at once consider what the notion of possession does actually claim. It will be better to face that claim in its full extent at once, as it will be seen that the evidence, while rising through various stages, does in the end insist on all that the ancient term implies. The leading modern cases, of which Stainton Moses and Mrs. Piper may be taken as types, are closely analogous, presenting many undesigned coincidences, some of which come out only on close examination.

The claim, then, is that the automatist, in the first place, falls into a trance, during which his spirit partially "quits his body:" enters at any rate into a state in which the spiritual world is more or less open to its perception; and in which also — and this is the novelty — it so far ceases to occupy the organism as to leave room for an invading spirit to use it in somewhat the same fashion as its owner is accustomed to use it.

The brain being thus left temporarily and partially uncontrolled, a disembodied spirit sometimes, but not always, succeeds in occupying it; and occupies it with varying degrees of control. In some cases (Mrs. Piper) two or more spirits may simultaneously control different portions of the same organism.

The controlling spirit proves his identity mainly by reproducing, in speech or writing, facts which belong to *his* memory and not to the automatist's memory. He may also give evidence of supernormal perception of other kinds.

His manifestations may differ very considerably from the automatist's normal personality. Yet in one sense it is a process of selection rather than of addition; the spirit selects what parts of the brain-machinery he will use, but he cannot get out of that machinery more than it is constructed to perform. The spirit can indeed produce facts and names unknown to the automatist; but they must be, as a rule, such facts and names as the automatist could easily have repeated, had they been known to him: — not, for instance, mathematical formulæ or Chinese sentences, if the automatist is ignorant of mathematics or of Chinese.

After a time the control gives way, and the automatist's spirit returns. The automatist, awaking, may or may not remember his experiences in the spiritual world during the trance. In some cases (Swedenborg) there is this memory of the spiritual world, but no possession of the organism by an external spirit. In others (Cahagnet's subject) there is utterance during the trance as to what is being discerned by the automatist, yet no memory thereof on waking. In others (Mrs. Piper) there is neither utterance as a rule, or at least no prolonged utterance, by the automatist's own spirit, nor subsequent memory; but there is writing or utterance during the trance by controlling spirits.

Now this seems a strange doctrine to have reached after so much disputation. For it simply brings us back to the creeds of the Stone Age. We have come round again to the primitive practices of the shaman and the medicine-man; — to a doctrine of spiritual intercourse which was once œcumenical, but has now taken refuge in African swamps and Siberian tundras and the snow-clad wastes of the Red Indian and the Esquimaux. If, as is sometimes advised, we judge of the worth of ideas by tracing their *origins*, no conception could start from a lower level of humanity. It might be put out of court at once as unworthy of civilised men.

Fortunately, however, our previous discussions have supplied us with a somewhat more searching criterion. Instead of asking in what age a doctrine originated — with the implied assumption that the more recent it is, the better — we can now ask how far it is in accord or in discord with a great mass of actual recent evidence which comes into contact, in one way or another, with nearly every belief as to an unseen world which has been held at least by western men. Submitted to this test, the theory of possession gives a remarkable result. It cannot be said to be inconsistent with any of our proved facts. We know absolutely nothing which negatives its possibility.

Nay, more than this. The theory of possession actually supplies us with a powerful method of co-ordinating and explaining many earlier groups of phenomena, if only we will consent to explain them in a way which at first sight seemed extreme in its assumptions — seemed unduly prodigal of the marvellous. Yet as to that difficulty we have learnt by this time that no explanation of psychical phenomena is really simple, and that our best clue is to get hold of some group which seems to admit of one interpretation only, and then to use that group as a *point de repère* from which to attack more complex problems.

Now I think that the Moses-Piper group of trance-phenomena cannot be intelligently explained on any theory except that of possession. And I therefore think it important to consider in what way earlier phenomena have led up to possession, and in what way the facts of possession, in their turn, affect our view of these earlier phenomena.

If we analyse our observations of possession, we find two main factors — the central operation, which is the control by a spirit of the sensitive's organism; and the indispensable prerequisite, which is the partial and temporary desertion of that organism by the percipient's own spirit.

Let us consider first how far this withdrawal of the living man's spirit from his organism has been rendered conceivable by evidence already obtained.

First of all, the splits, and substitutions of phases of personality with which our second chapter made us familiar have great significance for *possession* also.

We have there seen some secondary personality, beginning with slight and isolated sensory and motor manifestations, yet going on gradually to complete predominance, — complete control of all supraliminal manifestation.

The mere collection and description of such phenomena has up till now savoured of a certain boldness. The idea of tracing the possible mechanism involved in these transitions has scarcely arisen.

Yet it is manifest that there must be a complex set of laws concerned with such alternating use of brain-centres; — developments, one may suppose, of those unknown physical laws underlying ordinary memory, of which no one has formed as yet even a first rough conception.

An ordinary case of ecmnesia may present problems as insoluble in their way as those offered by spirit-possession itself. There may be in ecmnesia periods of life absolutely and permanently extruded from memory; and there may be also periods which are only temporarily thus extruded. Thus on Wednesday and Thursday I may be unaware of what I learnt and did on Monday and Tuesday; and then on Friday I may recover Monday's and Tuesday's knowledge, as well as retaining Wednesday's and Thursday's, so that my brain-cells have taken on, so to say, two separate lines of education since Sunday — that which began on Monday, and that which began on Wednesday. These intercurrent educations may have been naturally discordant, and may be fused in all kinds of ways in the ultimate synthesis.

These processes are completely obscure; and all that can be said is that their mechanism probably belongs to the same unknown series of operations which ultimately lead to that completest break in the history of the brain-cells which consists in their intercalary occupation by an external spirit.

Passing on to *genius*, which I discussed in my third chapter, it is noticeable that there also there is a certain degree of temporary substitution of one control for another over important brain-centres. We must here regard the subliminal self as an entity partially distinct from the supraliminal, and its occupation of these brain-centres habitually devoted to supraliminal work is a kind of possession, which illustrates, in yet another way the rapid metastasis of psychical product (so to term it) of which these highest centres are capable. The highest genius would thus be the completest *self-possession*, — the occupation and dominance of the whole organism by those profoundest elements of the self which act from the fullest knowledge, and in the wisest way.

The next main subject which fell under our description was *sleep*. And this state—the normal state which most resembles trance—has long ago suggested the question which first hints at the possibility of ecstasy, namely, What becomes of the soul during sleep? I think that our evidence has shown that sometimes during apparent ordinary sleep the spirit may travel away from the body, and may bring back a memory, more or less confused, of what it has seen in this clairvoyant excursion. This may indeed happen for brief flashes during waking moments also. But ordinary sleep seems to help the process; and deeper states of sleep—spontaneous or induced—seem still further to facilitate it. In the coma preceding death, or during that "suspended animation" which is sometimes taken for death, this travelling faculty has seemed to reach its highest point.

I have spoken of deeper states of sleep, "spontaneous or induced," and here the reader will naturally recall much that has been said of ordinary somnambulism, much that has been said of hypnotic trance. Hypnotic trance has created for us, with perfect facility, situations externally indistinguishable from what I shall presently claim as true possession. A quasi-personality, arbitrarily created, may occupy the organism, responding to speech or sign in some characteristic fashion, although without producing any fresh verifiable facts as evidence to the alleged identity. Nay, sometimes, as in a few of the Pesaro experiments (see *Proceedings* S.P.R., vol. v. pp. 563–565), there may be indications that something of a new personality is there. And on the other hand, the sensitive's own spirit often claims to have been absent elsewhere, — much in the fashion in which it sometimes imagines itself to have been absent during ordinary sleep, but with greater persistence and lucidity.

Our inquiry into the nature of what is thus alleged to be seen in sleep and cognate states has proved instructive. Sometimes known earthly scenes appear to be revisited — with only such alteration as may have taken place since the sleeper last visited them in waking hours. But sometimes also there is an admixture of an apparently *symbolical* element. The earthly scene includes some element of human action, which is presented in a selected or abbreviated fashion, as though some mind had been concerned to bring out a special significance from the complex story. Sometimes this element becomes quite dominant; phantasmal figures are seen; or there may be a prolonged symbolical representation of an entry into the spiritual world.

Cases like these do of course apparently support that primitive doctrine of the spirit's actual wandering in space. On the other hand, this notion has become unwelcome to modern thought, which is less unwilling to believe in some telepathic intercourse between mind and mind in which space is not involved. For my own part, I have already explained that I think that the evidence to an at least apparent movement of some kind in space must outweigh any mere speculative presumption against it. And I hold that these new experiences of possession fall on this controversy with decisive force. It is so strongly claimed, in every instance of possession, that the sensitive's own spirit must in some sense *vacate* the organism, in order to allow another spirit to enter, — and the evidence for the reality of possession is at the same time so strong, — that I think that we must argue back from this spatial change as a relatively certain fact, and must place a corresponding interpretation on earlier phenomena. Such an interpretation, if once admitted, does certainly meet the phenomena in the way most accordant with the subjective impressions of the various percipients.

As we have already repeatedly found, it is the bold evolutionary hypothesis which best fixes and colligates the scattered facts. We encounter in these studies phenomena of degeneration and phenomena of evolution. The degenerative phenomena are explicable singly and in detail as declensions in divergent directions from an existing level. The evolutive phenomena point, on the other hand, to new generalisations; — to powers previously unrecognised towards which our evidence *converges* along constantly multiplying lines.

This matter of psychical excursion from the organism ultimately involves the extremest claim to novel faculty which has ever been advanced for men. For it involves, as we shall see, the claim to *ecstasy:* — to a wandering vision which is not confined to this earth or this material world alone, but introduces the seer into the spiritual world and among communities higher than any which this planet knows. The discussion of this transportation, however, will be better deferred until after the evidence for possession has been laid before the reader at some length.

Continuing, then, for the present our analysis of the idea of possession, we come now to its specific feature, — the occupation by a spiritual agency of the entranced and partially vacated organism. Here it is that our previous studies will do most to clear our conceptions. Instead of at once leaping to the question of what spirits in their essence are, — of what they can do and cannot do, — of the antecedent possibility of their re-entry into matter, and the like, — we must begin by simply carrying the idea of telepathy to its furthest point. We must imagine telepathy becoming as central and as intense as possible; — and we shall find that of two diverging types of telepathic intercourse which will thus present themselves, the one will gradually correspond to possession, and the other to ecstasy.

But here let us pause, and consider what is the truest conception which we are by this time able to form of telepathy. The *word* has been a convenient one; the *central notion* — of communication beyond this range of sense — can at any rate thus be expressed in simple terms. But nevertheless there has been nothing to assure us that our real comprehension of telepathic processes has got much deeper than that verbal definition. Our conception of telepathy, indeed, to say nothing of telæsthesia, has needed to be broadened with each fresh stage of our evidence. That evidence at first revealed to us certain transmissions of thoughts and images which suggested the passage of actual etherial vibrations from brain to brain. Nor indeed can any one say at any point of our evidence that etherial vibrations are demonstrably *not* concerned in the phenomena. We cannot tell how far from the material world (to use a crude phrase) some etherial agency may possibly extend. But telepathic phenomena are in fact soon seen to overpass any development which imaginative analogy can give to the conception of etherial radiation from one material point to another.

For from the mere transmission of isolated ideas or pictures there is, as my readers know, a continuous progression to impressions and apparitions far more persistent and complex. We encounter an influence which suggests no mere impact of etherial waves, but an intelligent and responsive *presence*, resembling nothing so much as the ordinary human intercourse of persons in bodily nearness. Such visions or auditions, inward or externalised, are indeed sometimes felt to involve an even closer contact of spirits than the common intercourse of earth allows. One could hardly assign etherial undulations as their cause without assigning that same mechanism to all our emotions felt towards each other, or even to our control over our own organisms.

Nay, more. There is — as I have striven to show — a further progression from these telepathic intercommunications between living men to intercommunications between living men and discarnate spirits. And this new thesis, — in every way of vital importance, — while practically solving one problem on which I have already dwelt, opens also a possibility of the determination of another problem, nowise accessible until now. In the first place, we may now rest assured that telepathic communication is not necessarily propagated by vibrations proceeding from an ordinary material *brain*. For the discarnate spirit at any rate has no such brain from which to start them.

So much, in the first place, for the *agent's* end of the communication.

And in the second place, we now discern a possibility of getting at the *percipient's* end; of determining whether the telepathic impact is received by the *brain* or by the *spirit* of the living man, or by both inseparably, or sometimes by one and sometimes by the other.

On this problem, I say, the phenomena of automatic script, of trance-utterance, of spirit-possession, throw more of light than we could have ventured to hope.

Stated broadly, our trance-phenomena show us to begin with that several currents of communication can pass at once from discarnate spirits to a living man; — and can pass in very varying ways. For clearness' sake I will put aside for the present all cases where the telepathic impact takes an externalised or sensory form, and will speak only of intellectual impressions and motor automatisms.

Now these may pass through all grades of apparent *centrality*. If a man, awake and in other respects fully self-controlled, feels his hand impelled to scrawl words on a piece of paper, without consciousness of motor effort *of his own*, the impulse does not seem to him a *central* one, although some part of his brain is presumably involved. On the other hand, a much less conspicuous invasion of his personality may feel much more central; — as, for instance, a premonition of evil, — an inward heaviness which he can scarcely define. And so the motor automatism goes on until it reaches the point of *possession;* — that is to say, until the man's own consciousness is absolutely in abeyance, and every part of his body is utilised by the invading spirit or spirits. What happens in such conditions to the man's ruling principle — to his own spirit — we must consider presently. But so far as his organism is concerned, the invasion seems complete: and it indicates a power which is indeed telepathic in a true sense; — yet not quite in the sense which we originally attached to the word. We first thought of telepathy as of a communication between two minds, whereas what we have here looks more like a communication between a mind and a body, — an external mind, in place of the mind which is accustomed to rule that particular body.

There is in such a case no apparent communication between the discarnate mind and the *mind* of the automatist. Rather there is a kind of contact between the discarnate mind and the *brain* of the automatist, in so far that the discarnate mind, pursuing its own ends, is helped up to a certain point by the accumulated capacities of the automatist's brain; — and similarly is hindered by its incapacities.

Yet here the most characteristic element of telepathy, I repeat, seems to have dropped out altogether. There is no perceptible communion between the mind of the entranced person and any other mind whatever. He is *possessed*, but is kept in unconsciousness, and never regains memory of what his lips have uttered during his trance.

But let us see whether we have thus grasped all the trance-phenomena; — whether something else may not be going on, which is more truly, more centrally telepathic.

To go back to the earliest stage of telepathic experience, we can see well enough that the experimental process might quite possibly involve two different factors. The percipient's mind must somehow receive the telepathic impression; — and to this reception we can assign no definite physical correlative; — and also the percipient's motor or sensory centres must receive an excitation; — which excitation may be communicated, for aught we know, either by his own mind in the ordinary way, or by the agent's mind in some direct way, — which I may call *telergic*, thus giving a more precise sense to a word which I long ago suggested as a kind of correlative to *telepathic*. That is to say, there may even in these apparently simple cases be first a transmission from agent to percipient in the spiritual world, and then an action on the percipient's physical brain, of the same type as spirit-possession. This action on the physical brain may be due either to the percipient's own spirit, or subliminal self, or else directly to the agent's spirit. For I must repeat that the phenomena of possession seem to indicate that the extraneous spirit acts on a man's organism in very much the same way as the man's own spirit habitually acts on it. One must thus practically regard the body as an instrument upon which a spirit plays; — an ancient metaphor which now seems actually our nearest approximation to truth.

Proceeding to the case of telepathic or veridical apparitions, we see the same hints of a double nature in the process; — traces of two elements mingling in various degrees. At the spiritual end there may be what we have called "clairvoyant visions," — pictures manifestly symbolical, and not located by the observer in ordinary three-dimensional space. These seem analogous to the views of the spiritual world which the sensitive enjoys during entrancement. Then comes that larger class of veridical apparitions where the figure seems to be externalised from the percipient's mind, some stimulus having actually been applied, — whether by agent's or percipient's spirit, — to the appropriate brain-centre. These cases of "sensory automatism" resemble those experimental transferences of pictures of cards, etc. And beyond these again, on the physical or rather the ultra-physical side, come those *collective* apparitions which in my view involve some unknown kind of modification of a certain portion of space not occupied by any organism, — as opposed to a modification of centres in one special brain. Here comes in, as I hold, the gradual transition from subjective to objective, as the portion of space in question is modified in a manner to affect a larger and larger number of percipient minds.

Now when we proceed from these apparitions of the living to apparitions of the departed, we find very much the same types persisting still. We find symbolical *visions* of departed persons, and of scenes among which they seem to dwell. We find externalised *apparitions* or phantasms of departed persons, — indicating that some point in the percipient's brain has been stimulated by his own or by some other spirit. And finally, as has already been said, we find that in certain cases of possession these two kinds of influence are simultaneously carried to an extreme. The percipient automatist of earlier stages becomes no longer a percipient but an automatist pure and simple, — so far as his body is concerned, — for his whole brain — not one point alone — seems now to be stimulated and controlled by an extraneous spirit, and he is not himself aware of what his body writes or utters. And meantime his spirit, partially set free from the body, may be purely percipient; — may be enjoying that other spiritual form of communication more completely than in any type of vision which our description had hitherto reached.

This point attained, another analogy, already mentioned, will be at once recalled. There is another class of phenomena, besides telepathy, of which this definition of possession at once reminds us. We have dealt much with *secondary personalities*, — with severances and alternations affecting a man's own spirit, in varying relation with his organism. Félida X.'s developed secondary personality, for instance (Appendix II. C), might be defined as another fragment — or another synthesis — of Félida's spirit acting upon her organism in much the same way as the original fragment — or the primary synthesis — of her spirit was wont to act upon it.

Plainly, this analogy is close enough to be likely to lead to practical confusion. On what grounds can we base our distinctions? What justifies us in saying that Félida X.'s organism was controlled only by another modification of her own personality, but that Mrs. Piper's is controlled by George Pelham (see page 330 *et seq.*)? May there not be any amount of self-suggestion, colouring with the fictitious hue of all kinds of identities what is in reality no more than an allotropic form of the entranced person himself? Is even the possession by the new personality of some fragments of fresh knowledge any proof of spirit-control? May not that knowledge be gained clairvoyantly or telepathically, with no intervention of any spirit other than of living men?

Yes, indeed, we must reply, there *is* here a danger of confusion, there *is* a lack of any well-defined dividing line. While we must decide on general rules, we must also keep our minds open to possible exceptions.

On the negative side, indeed, general rules will carry us a good way. We must *not* allow ourselves to ascribe to spirit-control cases where no new knowledge is shown in the trance state. And this rule has at once an important consequence, — a consequence which profoundly modifies the antique idea of possession. I know of no evidence, — reaching in any way our habitual standard, — either for angelic, for diabolical, or for hostile possession.

And here comes the question: What attitude are we to assume to savage cases of possession? Are we to accept as genuine the possession of the Esquimaux, the Chinaman, — nay, of the Hebrew of old days?

Chinese possession is a good example, as described in Dr. Nevius' book (on *Demon Possession and Allied Themes*, an account of which by Professor Newbold is given in *Proceedings* S.P.R., vol. xiii. p. 602 [912 A]). I agree with Professor Newbold in holding that no proof has been shown that there is more in the Chinese cases than that hysterical duplication of personality with which we are so familiar in France and elsewhere.

A devil is not a creature whose existence is independently known to science; and from the accounts the behaviour of the invading devils seems due to mere self-suggestion. With uncivilised races, even more than among our own friends, we are bound to insist on the rule that there must be some supernormal knowledge shown before we may assume an external influence. It may of course be replied that the character shown by the "devils" was fiendish and actually *hostile* to the possessed person. Can we suppose that the tormentor was actually a fraction of the tormented?

I reply that such a supposition, so far from being absurd, is supported by well-known phenomena both in insanity and in mere hysteria.

Especially in the Middle Ages, — amid powerful self-suggestions of evil and terror, — did these quasi-possessions reach an intensity and violence which the calm and sceptical atmosphere of the modern hospital checks and discredits. The devils with terrifying names which possessed Sœur Angélique of Loudun [1] would at the Salpêtrière under Charcot in our days have figured merely as stages of "clounisme" and "attitudes passionelles."

And even now these splits of personality seem occasionally to destroy all sympathy between the normal individual and a divergent fraction. No great sympathy was felt by Léonie II. for Léonie I. [2] And Dr. Morton Prince's case [3] shows us the deepest and ablest of the personalities of his "Miss Beauchamp" positively spiteful in its relation to her main identity.

Bizarre though a house thus divided against itself may seem, the moral dissidence is merely an exaggeration of the moral discontinuity observable in the typical case of Mrs. Newnham. [4] *There* the secondary intelligence was merely tricky, not malevolent. But its trickiness was wholly alien from Mrs. Newnham's character, — was something, indeed, which she would have energetically repudiated.

It seems, therefore, — and the analogy of dreams points in this direction also, — that our moral nature is as easily split up as our intellectual nature, and that we cannot be any more certain that the minor current of personality which is diverted into some new channel will retain *moral* than that it will retain *intellectual* coherence.

[1] *Bibliothèque Diabolique* (Collection Bourneville). Paris: Aux Bureaux du Progrès Medical, 1886 [832 B].

[2] See Professor Janet's paper in the *Revue Philosophique*, March, 1888. The case is also constantly referred to in his *L'Automatisme Psychologique*.

[3] See page 49.

[4] See page 288.

To return once more to the Chinese devil-possessions. Dr. Nevius asserts, though without adducing definite proof, that the possessing devils sometimes showed supernormal knowledge. This is a better argument for their separate existence than their fiendish temper is; but it is not in itself enough. The knowledge does not seem to have been specially appropriate to the supposed informing spirit. It seems as though it may have depended upon heightened memory, with possibly some slight telepathic or telæsthetic perception. Heightened memory is thoroughly characteristic of some hysterical phases; and even the possible traces of telepathy (although far the most important feature of the phenomena, if they really occurred) are, as we have seen, not unknown in trance states (like Léonie's) where there is no indication of an invading spirit.

Temporary control of the organism by a widely divergent fragment of the personality, self-suggested in some dream-like manner into hostility to the main mass of the personality, and perhaps better able than that normal personality to reach and manipulate certain stored impressions, — or even certain supernormal influences, — such will be the formula to which we shall reduce the invading Chinese devil, as described by Dr. Nevius, — and *probably* the great majority of supposed devil-possessions of similar type.

The great majority, no doubt, but perhaps not *all*. It would indeed be matter for surprise if such trance-phenomena as those of Mrs. Piper and other modern cases had appeared in the world without previous parallel. Much more probable is it that similar phenomena have occurred sporadically from the earliest times, — although men have not had enough of training to analyse them.

And, in fact, among the endless descriptions of trance-phenomena with which travellers furnish us, there are many which include points so concordant with our recent observations that we cannot but attach some weight to coincidences so wholly undesigned.[1] But although this may be admitted, I still maintain that the only invaders of the organism

---

[1] One important point of similarity is the concurrence in some savage ceremonies of utterance through an invading spirit and travelling clairvoyance exercised meantime by the man whose organism is thus invaded. The uncouth spirit shouts and bellows, presumably with the lungs of the medicine-man, hidden from view in profound slumber. Then the medicine-man awakes, — and tells the listening tribe the news which his sleep-wanderings, among gods or men, have won.

If this indeed be thus, it fits in strangely with the experience of our modern seers, — with the spiritual interchange which takes place when a discarnate intelligence occupies the organism and meantime the incarnate intelligence, temporarily freed, awakes to wider percipience, — in this or in another world.

who have as yet made good their title have been human, and have been friendly; and with this clearance should, I think, vanish the somewhat grim associations which have gathered around the word *possession*.

Assuming, then, as I think we at present may assume, that we have to deal only with spirits who have been men like ourselves, and who are still animated by much the same motives as those which influence us, we may briefly consider, on similar analogical grounds, what range of spirits are likely to be able to affect us, and what difficulties they are likely to find in doing so. Of course, actual experience alone can decide this; but nevertheless our expectations may be usefully modified if we reflect beforehand how far such changes of personality as we already know can suggest to us the limits of these profounder substitutions.

What, to begin with, do we find to be the case as to addition of faculty in alternating states? How far do such changes bring with them unfamiliar powers?

Reference to the recorded cases will show us that existing faculty may be greatly quickened and exalted. There may be an increase both in actual perception and in power of remembering or reproducing what has once been perceived. There may be increased control over muscular action, — as shown, for instance, in improved billiard-playing, — in the secondary state. But there is little evidence of the acquisition — telepathy apart — of any actual mass of fresh knowledge, — such as a new language, or a stage of mathematical knowledge unreached before. We shall not therefore be justified by analogy in expecting that an external spirit controlling an organism will be able easily to modify it in such a way as to produce speech in a language previously unknown. The brain is used as something between a typewriter and a calculating machine. German words, for instance, are not mere combinations of letters, but specific formulæ; they can only seldom and with great difficulty be got out of a machine which has not been previously fashioned for their production.

Consider, again, the analogies as to *memory*. In the case of alternations of personality, memory fails and changes in what seems a quite capricious way. The gaps which then occur recall (as I have said) the *eomnesiæ* or blank unrecollected spaces which follow upon accidents to the head, or upon crises of fever, when all memories that belong to a particular person or to a particular period of life are clean wiped out, other memories remaining intact. Compare, again, the memory of waking life which we retain in *dream*. This too is absolutely capricious; — I may forget my own name in a dream, and yet remember perfectly the kind of chairs in my dining-room. Or I may remember the chairs, but locate them in some one else's house. No one can predict the kind of confusion which may occur.

We have also the parallel of *somnambulic utterance*. In talking with a somnambulist, be the somnambulism natural or induced, we find it hard to get into continuous colloquy on our own subjects. To begin with, he probably will not speak continuously for long together. He drops back into a state in which he cannot express himself at all. And when he does talk, he is apt to talk only on his own subjects; — to follow out his own train of ideas, — interrupted rather than influenced by what *we* say to *him*. The difference of *state* between waking and sleep is in many ways hard to bridge over.

We have thus three parallelisms which may guide and limit our expectations. From the parallelism of possession with split personalities we may infer that a possessing spirit is not likely to be able to inspire into the recipient brain ideas or words of very unfamiliar type. From the parallelism of possession with dream we may infer that the memory of the possessing spirit may be subject to strange omissions and confusions. From the parallelism with somnambulism we may infer that colloquy between a human observer and the possessing spirit is not likely to be full or free, but rather to be hampered by difference of state, and abbreviated by the difficulty of maintaining psychical contact for long together.

These remarks will, I hope, prepare the reader to consider the problems of possession with the same open-mindedness which has been needed for the study of previous problems attacked in the present work.

But before we can proceed to the actual evidence there is another aspect of possession which must be explained. A group of phenomena are involved which have in various ways done much to confuse and even to retard our main inquiry, but which, when properly placed and understood, are seen to form an inevitable part of any scheme which strives to discover the influence of unseen agencies in the world we know.

In our discussion of all telepathic and other supernormal influence I have thus far regarded it mainly from the psychological and not from the physical side. I have spoken as though the field of supernormal action has been always the metetherial world. Yet true as this dictum may be in its deepest sense, it cannot represent the *whole* truth "for beings such as we are, in a world like the present." For us every psychological fact has (so far as we know) a physical side; and metetherial events, to be perceptible to us, must somehow affect the world of matter.

In sensory and motor automatisms, then, we see effects, supernormally initiated, upon the world of matter.

Imprimis, of course, and in ordinary life our own spirits (their existence once granted) affect our own bodies and are our standing examples of spirit affecting matter. Next, if a man receives a telepathic impact from another incarnate spirit which causes him to see a phantasmal figure, that man's brain has, we may suppose, been directly affected by his own spirit rather than by the spirit of the distant friend. But it may not always be true even in the case of sensory automatisms that the distant spirit has made a suggestion merely to the percipient's spirit which the percipient's own spirit carries out; and in motor automatisms, as they develop into *possession*, there are indications, as I have already pointed out, that the influence of the agent's spirit is *telergic* rather than telepathic, and that we have extraneous spirits influencing the human brain or organism. That is to say, they are producing movements in matter; — even though that matter be organised matter and those movements molecular.

So soon as this fact is grasped, — and it has not always been grasped by those who have striven to establish a fundamental difference between spiritual influence on our spirits and spiritual influence on the material world, — we shall naturally be prompted to inquire whether inorganic matter as well as organic ever shows the agency of extraneous spirits upon it. The reply which first suggests itself is, of course, in the negative. We are constantly dealing with inorganic matter, and no hypothesis of spiritual influence exerted on such matter is needed to explain our experiments. But this is a rough general statement, hardly likely to cover phenomena so rare and fugitive as many of those with which in this inquiry we deal. Let us begin, so to say, at the other end; not with the broad experience of life, but with the delicate and exceptional cases of *possession* of which we have lately been speaking.

Suppose that a discarnate spirit, in temporary possession of a living organism, is impelling it to motor automatisms. Can we say *a priori* what the limits of such automatic movements of that organism are likely to be, in the same way as we can say what the limits of any of its voluntary movements are likely to be? May not this extraneous spirit get more motor power out of the organism than the waking man himself can get out of it? It would not surprise us, for example, if the movements in trance showed increased *concentration;* if a dynamometer (for instance) was more forcibly squeezed by the spirit acting through the man than by the man himself. Is there any other way in which one would imagine that a spirit possessing me could use my vital force more skilfully than I could use it myself?

I do not know how my will moves my arm; but I know by experience that my will generally moves only my arm and what my arm can touch; — whatever objects are actually in contact with the "protoplasmic skeleton" which represents the life of my organism. Yet I can sometimes move objects not in actual contact, as by melting them with the heat or (in the dry air of Colorado) kindling them with the electricity, which my fingers emit. I see no very definite limit to this power. I do not know all the forms of energy which my fingers might, under suitable training, emit.

And now suppose that a possessing spirit can use my organism more skilfully than I can. May he not manage to emit from that organism some energy which can visibly move ponderable objects not actually in contact with my flesh? That would be a phenomenon of possession not very unlike its other phenomena; — and it would be *telekinesis*.

By that word (due to M. Aksakoff) it is convenient to describe what have been called "the physical phenomena of spiritualism," as to whose existence as a reality, and not as a system of fraudulent pretences, fierce controversy has raged for half a century, and is still raging.

The interest excited in the ordinary public by these phenomena has, as is well known, fostered much fraud, to expose and guard against which has been one of the main tasks of the S.P.R.[1]

Indeed, the persistent simulation of telekinesis has, naturally enough, inspired persistent doubt as to its genuine occurrence even in cases where simulation has been carefully guarded against, or is antecedently improbable. And thus while believing absolutely in the occurrence of telekinetic phenomena, I yet hold that it would be premature to press them upon my readers' belief, or to introduce them as an integral part of my general expository scheme. From one point of view, their detailed establishment, as against the theory of fraud, demands an expert knowledge of conjuring and other arts which I cannot claim to possess. From another point of view, their right comprehension must depend upon a knowledge of the relations between matter and ether such as is now only dimly adumbrated by the most recent discoveries; — for instance, discoveries as to previously unsuspected forms of radiation.

In a long Appendix, viz., "Scheme of Vital Faculty"[2] — originally

---

[1] See *Modern Spiritualism; a History and a Criticism*, by Frank Podmore (Methuen and Co., London, 1902).

[2] In this edition the Synopsis alone is given. See Appendix IX. A.

written with reference to the manifestations through Mr. Stainton Moses — I have tried to prepare the way for future inquiries; to indicate in what directions a better equipped exploration may hereafter reap rich reward. Even that tentative sketch, perhaps, may have been too ambitious for my powers in the present state not only of my own, but of human knowledge; and in this chapter I shall allude to telekinetic phenomena only where unavoidable, — owing to their inmixture into phenomena more directly psychological, — and in the tone of the historian rather than of the scientific critic.

* * * * * * * * * * * *[1]

The way has now been so far cleared for our cases of Possession that at least the principal phenomena claimed have been (I hope) made intelligible, and shown to be concordant with other phenomena already described and attested. It will be best, however, to consider first some of the more rudimentary cases before going on to our own special instances of possession, — those of Mr. Stainton Moses or Mrs. Piper.

We have already seen that there is no great gulf between the sudden incursions, the rapid messages of the dead, with which we are already familiar, and incursions so intimate, messages so prolonged, as to lay claim to a name more descriptive than that of motor automatisms.

And similarly no line of absolute separation can be drawn between the brief psychical *excursions* previously described, and those more prolonged excursions of the spirit which I would group under the name of ecstasy.

In the earlier part of this book I have naturally dwelt rather on the evidence for supernormal acquisition of knowledge than on the methods of such acquisition, and my present discussion must needs be restricted to a certain extent in the same way. We must, however, attempt some provisional scheme of classification, though recognising that the difficulties of interpretation which I pointed out in Chapter IV., when endeavouring to distinguish between telepathy and telæsthesia, meet us again in dealing with possession and ecstasy. We may not, that is, be able to say, as regards a particular manifestation, whether it is an instance of incipient possession, or incipient ecstasy, or even whether the organism is being "controlled" directly by some extraneous spirit or by its own

---

[1] The asterisks indicate the end of the part of this chapter which was consecutively composed by the author. The rest of the chapter consists chiefly of fragments written by him at different times.

incarnate spirit. It is from the extreme cases that we form our categories. But now that we have reached some conception of what is involved in ecstasy and possession, we can interpret some earlier cases in this new light. Such experiences, for instance, as those of Mr. Mamtchitch (Appendix VII. A) and Miss Conley (Appendix VII. D), suggest a close kinship to the more developed cases of Mr. Moses and Mrs. Piper.

In other cases it may be clear that no control of any discarnate spirit is involved, but there seems to be something like incipient possession by the subliminal self or incarnate spirit. From this point of view the first case given in Appendix IX. B is of undoubted psychological interest. If it is not a case of thought-transference from Miss C. to Mrs. Luther (possibly between their subliminal selves during sleep), we must assume that a very remarkable recrudescence of latent memory occurred to the latter independently, at the same time that a similar though less remarkable revival of memory occurred to the former. But I introduce the case here simply as suggestive of the momentary domination of the subliminal over the supraliminal self.

In Professor Thoulet's case [1] we find a fuller control by the subliminal self, with a manifestation of knowledge suggesting some spiritual excursion; in Mr. Goodall's case there seems to be a telepathic conversation between his subliminal self controlling his utterance and some perhaps discarnate spirit; and finally, in Mr. Wilkie's case, there is the definite superposition, as it were, of a discarnate spirit's message upon the automatist in such a way that we are led to wonder whether it was the *mind* or the *brain* of the automatist that received the message. The first step apparently is the abeyance of the supraliminal self and the dominance of the subliminal self, which may lead in rare cases to a form of trance (or of what we have hitherto called secondary personality) where the whole body of the automatist is controlled by his own subliminal self, or incarnate spirit, but where there is no indication of any relation with discarnate spirits. The next form of trance is where the incarnate spirit, whether or not maintaining control of the whole body, makes excursions into or holds telepathic intercourse with the spiritual world. And, lastly, there is the trance of possession by another, a discarnate spirit. We cannot, of course, always distinguish between these three main types of trance — which, as we shall see later, themselves admit of different degrees and varieties.

The most striking case known to me of the first form of trance —

[1] This as well as the next two cases mentioned are given in Appendix IX. B.

possession by the subliminal self — is that of the Rev. C. B. Sanders,[1] whose trance-personality has always called itself by the name of "X + Y = Z." The life of the normal Mr. Sanders has apparently been passed in the environment of a special form of Presbyterian doctrine, and there seems to have been a fear on the part of Mr. Sanders himself lest the trance manifestations of which he was the subject should conflict with the theological position which he held as a minister; and indeed for several years of his early suffering "he was inclined to regard his peculiar case of affliction as the result of Satanic agency." On the part of some of his friends also there seems to be a special desire to show that "X + Y = Z" was not heterodox. Under these circumstances it is perhaps not surprising that we find so much reticence in "X + Y = Z" concerning his own relations to the normal Mr. Sanders, whom he calls "his casket." What little explanation is offered seems to be in singular harmony with one of the main tenets advanced in this book, since the claim made by "X + Y = Z" is obviously that he represents the incarnate spirit of Mr. Sanders exercising the higher faculties which naturally pertain to it, but which can be manifested to the full only when it is freed from its fleshly barriers. This frequently occurs, he says, in dying persons, who describe scenes in the spiritual world, and in his own experience when "his casket" is similarly affected, and the bodily obstructions to spiritual vision are removed.

In this case, then, the subliminal self seems to take complete control of the organism, exercising its own powers of telepathy and telæsthesia, but showing no evidence of direct communication with discarnate spirits. We must now pass on to the most notable recent case where such communication has been claimed, — that of Swedenborg, — to whose exceptional trance-history and attempt to give some scientific system to his experiences of ecstasy I referred in Chapter I.

The *evidential* matter which Swedenborg has left behind him is singularly scanty in comparison with his pretensions to a communion of many years with so many spirits of the departed. But I think that the half-dozen "evidential cases" scattered through his memoirs are stamped with the impress of truth, — and I think, also, that without some true experience of the spiritual world Swedenborg could not have entered into that atmosphere of truth in which even his worst errors are held in solution. Swedenborg's writings on the world of spirits fall in the

[1] See *X + Y = Z; or, The Sleeping Preacher of North Alabama. Containing an account of most wonderful mysterious mental phenomena, fully authenticated by living witnesses.* By the Rev. G. W. Mitchell. (New York: W. C. Smith, 67 John Street, 1876) [934 A].

main into two classes, — albeit classes not easily divided. There are *experiential* writings and there are *dogmatic* writings. The first of these classes contains accounts of what he saw and felt in that world, and of such inferences with regard to its laws as his actual experience suggested. Now, speaking broadly, all this mass of matter, covering some hundreds of propositions, is in substantial accord with what has been given through the most trustworthy sensitives since Swedenborg's time. It is indeed usual to suppose that they have all been influenced by Swedenborg; and although I feel sure that this was not so in any direct manner in the case of the sensitives best known to myself, it is probable that Swedenborg's alleged experiences have affected modern thought more deeply than most modern thinkers know.

On the other hand, the *second* or purely *dogmatic* class of Swedenborg's writings, — the records of instruction alleged to have been given to him by spirits on the inner meaning of the Scriptures, etc., — these have more and more appeared to be mere arbitrary fancies; — mere projections and repercussions of his own preconceived ideas.

On the whole, then, — with some stretching, yet no contravention, of conclusions independently reached, — I may say that Swedenborg's story, — one of the strangest lives yet lived by mortal men, — is corroborative rather than destructive of the slowly rising fabric of knowledge of which he was the uniquely gifted, but uniquely dangerous, precursor.

It seemed desirable here to refer thus briefly to the doctrinal teachings of Swedenborg, but I shall deal later with the general question how much or how little of the statements of "sensitives" about the spiritual world — whether based on their own visions or on the allegations of their "controlling spirits" — are worthy of credence. In the case of Swedenborg there was at least some evidence, of the kind to which we can here appeal, of his actual communication with discarnate spirits;[1] but in most other cases of alleged ecstasy there is little or nothing to show that the supposed revelations are not purely subjective. (See, *e.g.*, the revelations of Alphonse Cahagnet's sensitives, described in his *Arcanes de la vie future dévoilées*.)[2] At most, these visions must be regarded as a kind of symbolical representation of the unseen world.[3]

---

[1] For Kant's evidence in regard to the supernormal powers of Swedenborg, see "Dreams of a Spirit Seer," by Immanuel Kant, translated by E. F. Goerwitz; edited by Frank Sewall (London: Swan Sonnenschein & Co.; New York: The Macmillan Co., 1900) [936 A].

[2] See also an account of the "Seeress of Prevorst," translated from the German by Mrs. Crowe, and published in London in 1845 [936 B].

[3] See *Proceedings* S.P.R., vol. xi. p. 560 [936 C].

Among Cahagnet's subjects, however, there was one young woman, Adèle Maginot, who not only saw heavenly visions of the usual post-Swedenborgian kind, but also obtained evidential communications — not unlike those of Mrs. Piper — purporting to come from discarnate spirits. Fortunately these were recorded with unusual care and thoroughness by Cahagnet, and the case thus becomes one of considerable importance for our inquiries. A general account of Cahagnet's work has recently been given in the *Proceedings* S.P.R. (vol. xiv. p. 50) by Mr. Podmore, who, though finding it "almost impossible to doubt that Adèle's success was due to some kind of supernormal faculty," thinks it might be accounted for by telepathy from living persons. It appears that in all her trances Adèle — like Mr. Sanders — was controlled by her own subliminal self — that is to say, her supraliminal self became dormant, under "magnetism" by Cahagnet, while her subliminal self in trance-utterance manifested a knowledge which was, as I incline to think from its analogies with more developed cases, obtained from the spiritual world. That this knowledge should be mixed with much that was erroneous or unverifiable is not surprising.

It is also interesting to note the occurrence in this case of circumstances which in their general character have become so habitual in trances of "mediumistic" type that they are not only found in genuine subjects, but are continually being simulated by the fraudulent. I refer to the so-called "taking on of the death conditions" of a communicating spirit, who, as Adèle stated, died of suffocation. "Adèle chokes as this man choked, and coughed as he did. . . . I was obliged to release her by passes; she suffered terribly."

I need scarcely say that this suggests incipient possession. There were occasional analogous instances in the early trances of Mrs. Piper, when Phinuit was the controlling influence (see *Proceedings* S.P.R., vol. viii. p. 98, Professor Barrett Wendell's account; and vol. xiii. p. 384). Other points of similarity between the accounts of the entranced Adèle and the utterances of Phinuit will be apparent to the student of the records.

The next case to be considered, and so far one of the most important, is that of D. D. Home.

The study of such records as are available of Home's psychical phenomena leaves me with the conviction that, — apart altogether from the telekinetic phenomena with which they were associated, — his trance-utterances belong to the same natural order as those, for instance, of Mr. Moses and Mrs. Piper. There are, however, important differences between these cases, — differences which should be of special instruction to us in endeavouring to comprehend the possession that completely excludes the subliminal self, and to appreciate the difficulty of obtaining this complete possession.

Thus in Home's case the subliminal self seems, throughout the longest series of séances of which we have a record, to have been the spirit chiefly controlling him during the trance and acting as intermediary for other spirits, who occasionally, however, took complete possession.

In Mrs. Piper's case, as we shall see, the subliminal self is very little in direct evidence; its manifestations form a fleeting interlude between her waking state and her possession by a discarnate spirit. In Mr. Moses' case, the subliminal self was rarely in direct evidence at all when he was entranced; but we infer from these other cases that it was probably dominant at some stage of his trance, even if at other times it was excluded or became completely dormant.

And if, in Home's case, as there seems reason to suppose, the subliminal self may have participated with discarnate spirits in the production of telekinetic phenomena, as well as in the communication of tests of personal identity, it is not improbable that the subliminal self of Mr. Moses may also have been actively concerned in both these classes of phenomena.

But, although I attribute much value to what evidence exists in the case of Home, it cannot but be deplored that the inestimable chance for experiment and record which this case afforded was almost entirely thrown away by the scientific world. Unfortunately the record is especially inadequate in reference to Home's trances and the evidence for the personal identity of the communicating spirits. His name is known to the world chiefly in connection with the telekinetic phenomena which are said to have occurred in his presence, and the best accounts of which we owe to Sir William Crookes. It is not my intention, as I have already explained, to deal with these, but it must be understood that they form an integral part of the manifestations in this case, as in the case of Stainton Moses. For detailed accounts of them the reader should consult the history of Home's life and experiences.[1]

[1] The chief sources of information as to D. D. Home's life and experiences are the following works: —

Incidents in my Life, by D. D. Home (1st edition, London, 1863; 2nd edition, 1864; second series, 1872).

D. D. Home: His Life and Mission, by Madame Dunglas Home (London, 1888).

The Gift of D. D. Home, by Madame Dunglas Home (London, 1890).

Report on Spiritualism of the Committee of the London Dialectical Society (London,

To the history of William Stainton Moses I now turn. Here the evidence for the telekinetic phenomena is comparatively slight, since they occurred almost exclusively in the presence of a small group of intimate personal friends, and were never scrutinised and examined by outside witnesses as were Home's manifestations. On the other hand, we have detailed records of Mr. Moses' whole series of experiences, while in the case of Home, as I have said, the record is very imperfect. As to the telekinetic phenomena, Mr. Moses himself regarded them as a mere means to an end, in accordance with the view urged on him by his "controls," — that they were intended as proofs of the power and authority of these latter, while the real message lay in the religious teaching imparted to him.

It was on May 9th, 1874, that Edmund Gurney and I met Stainton Moses for the first time, through the kindness of Mrs. Cowper-Temple (afterwards Lady Mount-Temple), who knew that we had become interested in "psychical" problems, and wished to introduce us to a man of honour who had recently experienced phenomena, due wholly to some gift of his own, which had profoundly changed his conception of life.

Here was a man of University education, of manifest sanity and probity, who vouched to us for a series of phenomena, — occurring to himself, and with no doubtful or venal aid, — which seemed at least to prove, in confusedly intermingled form, three main theses unknown to Science. These were (1) the existence in the human spirit of hidden powers of insight and of communication; (2) the personal survival and near presence of the departed; and (3) interference, due to unknown agencies, with the ponderable world. He spoke frankly and fully; he showed his note-books; he referred us to his friends; he inspired a belief which was at once sufficient, and which is still sufficient, to prompt to action.

1871). This contains the evidence of the Master of Lindsay, — now Earl of Crawford and Balcarres, — and others.

Experiences in Spiritualism with Mr. D. D. Home, by Viscount Adare (now Lord Dunraven; privately printed).

Researches in the Phenomena of Spiritualism, by William Crookes, F.R.S. Reprinted from the *Quarterly Journal of Science* (London, 1874).

Notes of Séances with D. D. Home, by William Crookes, F.R.S. (*Proceedings* S.P.R., vol. vi. p. 98.)

See also a review by Professor Barrett and the present writer of Madame Home's first book, *D. D. Home: His Life and Mission*, in the *Journal* S.P.R., vol. iv. pp. 101–136; a briefer review of her second book, *The Gift of D. D. Home*, in the *Journal* S.P.R., vol. iv. p. 249; and a note on "The Character of D. D. Home" in the *Journal* S.P.R., vol. vi. p. 176; also an article by Mr. Hamilton Aidé, "Was I hypnotised?" in the *Nineteenth Century* for April 1890.

The experiences which Stainton Moses had undergone had changed his views, but not his character. He was already set in the mould of the hard-working, conscientious, dogmatic clergyman, with a strong desire to do good, and a strong belief in preaching as the best way to do it. For himself the essential part of what I have called his "message" lay in the actual words automatically uttered or written, — not in the accompanying phenomena which really gave their uniqueness and importance to the automatic processes. In a book called *Spirit Teachings* he collected what he regarded as the real fruits of those years of mysterious listening in the vestibule of a world unknown.

My original impressions as regards Mr. Moses were strengthened by the opportunity which I had of examining his unpublished MSS. after his death on September 5th, 1892. These consist of thirty-one note-books — twenty-four of automatic script, four of records of physical phenomena, and three of retrospect and summary. In addition to these, the material available for a knowledge of Mr. Moses' experiences con-sists of his own printed works, and the written and printed statements of witnesses to his phenomena.

Of this available material a detailed account will be found in *Proceedings* S.P.R., vol. ix. pp. 245-352, and vol. xi. pp. 24-113, together with a brief record of Mr. Moses' life.

With the even tenor of this straightforward and reputable life was inwoven a chain of mysteries which, as I think, in what way soever they be explained, make it one of the most extraordinary which our century has seen. For its true history lies in that series of physical mani-festations which began in 1872 and lasted for some eight years, and that series of automatic writings and trance-utterances which began in 1873, received a record for some ten years, and did not, as is believed, cease altogether until the earthly end was near.

These two series were intimately connected; the physical phenomena being avowedly designed to give authority to the speeches and writings which professed to emanate from the same source. There is no ground for separating the two groups, except the obvious one that the automatic phenomena are less difficult of credence than the physical; but, for rea-sons already stated, it has seemed to me desirable to exclude the latter from detailed treatment in this work. They included the apparent pro-duction of such phenomena as intelligent raps, movements of objects untouched, levitation, disappearance and reappearance of objects, pas-sage of matter through matter, direct writing, sounds supernormally made on instruments, direct sounds, scents, lights, objects materialised,

hands materialised (touched or seen). Mr. Moses was sometimes, but
not always, entranced while these physical phenomena were occurring.
Sometimes he was entranced and the trance-utterance purported to be
that of a discarnate spirit. At other times, especially when alone, he
wrote automatically, retaining his own ordinary consciousness meanwhile, and carrying on lengthy discussions with the "spirit influence"
controlling his hand and answering his questions, etc. As a general rule
the same alleged spirits both manifested themselves by raps, etc., at Mr.
Moses' sittings with his friends, and also wrote through his hand when
he was alone. In this, as in other respects, Mr. Moses' two series of writings — when alone and in company — were concordant, and, so to say,
complementary; — explanations being given by the writing of what had
happened at the séances. When "direct writing" was given at the
séances the handwriting of each alleged spirit was the same as that
which the same spirit was in the habit of employing in the automatic
script. The claim to individuality was thus in all cases decisively made.

Now the personages thus claiming to appear may be divided roughly
into three classes: —

A. — First and most important are a group of persons recently deceased, and sometimes manifesting themselves at the séances before
their decease was known through any ordinary channel to any of the
persons present. These spirits in many instances give tests of identity,
mentioning facts connected with their earth-lives which are afterwards
found to be correct.

B. — Next comes a group of personages belonging to generations
more remote, and generally of some distinction in their day. Grocyn,
the friend of Erasmus, may be taken as a type of these. Many of these
also contribute facts as a proof of identity, which facts are sometimes
more correct than the conscious or admitted knowledge of any of the
sitters could supply. In such cases, however, the difficulty of proving
identity is increased by the fact that most of the correct statements are
readily accessible in print, and may conceivably have either been read
and forgotten by Mr. Moses, or have become known to him by some
kind of clairvoyance.

C. — A third group consists of spirits who give such names as Rector,
Doctor, Theophilus, and, above all, Imperator. These from time to
time reveal the names which they assert to have been theirs in earth-life.
These concealed names are for the most part both more illustrious, and
more remote, than the names in Class B, — and were withheld by Mr.
Moses himself, who justly felt that the assumption of great names is

likely to diminish rather than to increase the weight of the communication.

I now pass on to consider briefly the nature of the evidence that the alleged spirits were what they purported to be, as described, in the first place, in Mr. Moses' books of automatic writing. The contents of these books consist partly of messages tending to prove the identity of communicating spirits; partly of discussions or explanations of the physical phenomena; and partly of religious and moral disquisitions.

These automatic messages were almost wholly written by Mr. Moses' own hand, while he was in a normal waking state. The exceptions are of two kinds. (1) There is one long passage, alleged by Mr. Moses to have been written by himself while in a state of trance. (2) There are, here and there, a few words alleged to be in "direct writing"; — written, that is to say, by invisible hands, but in Mr. Moses' presence; as several times described in the notes of séances where other persons were present.

Putting these exceptional instances aside, we find that the writings generally take the form of a dialogue, Mr. Moses proposing a question in his ordinary thick, black handwriting. An answer is then generally, though not always, given; written also by Mr. Moses, and with the same pen, but in some one of various scripts which differ more or less widely from his own. Mr. Moses' own description of the process, as given in the preface to *Spirit Teachings*, may be studied with advantage.

A prolonged study of the MS. books has revealed nothing inconsistent with this description. I have myself, of course, searched them carefully for any sign of confusion or alteration, but without finding any; and I have shown parts of them to various friends, who have seen no points of suspicion. It seems plain, moreover, that the various entries were made at or about the dates to which they are ascribed. They contain constant references to the séances which went on concurrently, and whose dates are independently known; and in the later books, records of some of these séances are interspersed in their due places amongst other matter. The MSS. contain also a number of allusions to other contemporaneous facts, many of which are independently known to myself.

I think, moreover, that no one who had studied these entries throughout would doubt the originally private and intimate character of many of them. The tone of the spirits towards Mr. Moses himself is habitually courteous and respectful. But occasionally they have some criticism which pierces to the quick, and which goes far to explain to me Mr. Moses' unwillingness to have the books fully inspected during his lifetime. He did, no doubt, contemplate their being at least read by friends after his death; and there are indications that there may have been a still more private book, now doubtless destroyed, to which messages of an intimate character were sometimes consigned.

Indeed, the questions at issue, as to these messages, refer not so much to their *genuineness* as to their *authenticity*, in the proper sense of those words. That they were written down in good faith by Mr. Moses as proceeding from the personages whose names are signed to them, there can be little doubt. But as to whether they did really proceed from those personages or no there may in many cases be very great doubt; — a doubt which I, at least, shall be quite unable to remove. By the very conditions of the communication they cannot show commanding intellect, or teach entirely new truths, since their manifestations are *ex hypothesi* limited by the capacity — not by the previous *knowledge*, but by the previous *capacity* — of the medium. And if they give facts not consciously known to the medium — facts however elaborate — it may, of course, be suggested that these facts have been *subliminally acquired* by the medium through some unconscious passage of the eye over a printed page, or else that they are *clairvoyantly learnt*, without the agency of any but the medium's own mind, though acting in a supernormal fashion.

The case of Hélène Smith has shown us how far-reaching may be the faculties of hyperæsthesia and hypermnesia in the subliminal self; but in view of the then general ignorance of the scientific world on this subject, it is not surprising that both Mr. Moses and his friends absolutely rejected this explanation of his phenomena, and that the evidence appeared to them more conclusive than it possibly can to us. Whether or not the alleged spirits were concerned, — as may sometimes, of course, have been the case, — we can hardly avoid thinking that the subliminal self of the medium played at least a considerable part in the communications.

In two cases the announcement of a death was made to Mr. Moses, when the news was apparently not known to him by any normal means. One of these is the case of President Garfield (*Proceedings* S.P.R., vol. xi. p. 100). The other (see my article in *Proceedings* S.P.R., vol. xi. pp. 96 *et seq.*) is in some ways the most remarkable of all, from the series of chances which have been needful in order to establish its veracity. Specially noticeable in this case is the resemblance of the handwriting of the script to that of the alleged control, a lady whose writing was almost certainly unknown to Mr. Moses. Both to the lady's son and to myself the resemblance appeared incontestable, and our opinion was confirmed by Dr. Hodgson, who was an expert in such matters.

And now we must briefly go through the points which make such messages as were received by Mr. Moses *prima facie* evidential, which indicate, that is to say, that they actually do come in some way from their alleged source. A brief recapitulation of the main stages of evidential quality in messages given by automatic writing or by trance-utterances is all that will be needed here.

(1) Evidentially lowest comes the class of messages which is by far the most common; messages, namely, in which, although some special identity may be claimed, all the facts given have been consciously known to the automatist. Here we may well suppose that his own personality alone is concerned, and that the messages have a *subliminal*, but not an *external* source.

(2) Next above these come messages containing facts likely to be known to the alleged spirit, and not consciously known to the automatist; but which facts may nevertheless have some time been noted by the automatist, even unwittingly, and may have thus obtained lodgment in his subliminal memory.

(3) Next come facts which can be proved, — with such varying degrees of certainty as such negative proof allows, — never to have been in any way known to the automatist; but which nevertheless are easily to be found in books; so that they may have been learnt clairvoyantly by the automatist himself, or learnt and communicated to him by some mind other than that of the alleged spirit.

(4) Next come facts which can be proved, with similar varying degrees of certainty according to the circumstances, never to have been known to the automatist, or recorded in print; but which were known to the alleged spirit and can be verified by the memories of living persons.

(5) Above this again would come that class of *experimental* messages, or posthumous letters, of which we have as yet very few good examples, where the departed person has before death arranged some special test — some fact or sentence known only to himself, which he is to transmit after death, if possible, as a token of his return.

(6) Thus much for the various kinds of verbal messages, which can be kept and analysed at leisure. We must now turn to evidence of a different and not precisely comparable kind. In point of fact it is not these inferences from written matter which have commonly been most efficacious in compelling the survivor's belief in the reality of the friend's return. Whether logically or no, it is not so much the written message that he trusts, but some phantom of face and voice that he knew so well.

It is this familiar convincing presence, — ἵκτο δὲ θέσκελον ἀυτῷ, — on which the percipient has always insisted, since Achilles strove in vain to embrace Patroclus' shade.

How far such a phantasm is in fact a proof of any real action on the part of the spirit thus recognised is a problem which has been dealt with already in Chapter VII. The upshot of our evidence to my mind is that although the apparition of a departed person cannot *per se* rank as evidence of his presence, yet this is not a shape which purely hallucinatory phantasms seem often to assume; and if there be any corroborative evidence, as, for instance, writing which claims to come from the same person, the chance that he is really operative is considerable. In Mr. Moses' case almost all the figures which he saw brought with them some corroboration by writing, trance-utterance, gesture-messages (as where a figure makes signs of assent or dissent), or raps.

(7) And this brings us to a class largely represented in Mr. Moses' series, where writings professing to come from a certain spirit are supported by physical phenomena of which that spirit claims also to be the author. Whether such a line of proof can ever be made logically complete or no, one can imagine many cases where it would be practically convincing to almost all minds. Materialisations of hands, or direct writing in the script of the departed, have much of actual cogency; and these methods, with others like them, are employed by Mr. Moses' "controls" in their efforts to establish their own identities. Physical phenomena in themselves, however, carry no proof of an intelligence outside that of the sensitive himself, and, as I have said, may in many cases be a mere extension of his own ordinary muscular powers, and not due to any external agency at all.

If we confine ourselves to the verbal messages, we find that the cases most fully represented in the records of Mr. Moses are limited to the first three classes mentioned above, and those which come under the fourth class — verifiable facts of which there is no printed record and which it is practically certain that the medium could never have known — are comparatively few. This may partly be accounted for by the small number of sitters with Mr. Moses and the fact that they were his personal friends. The records of Mrs. Piper, on the other hand, to which we now turn, are especially rich in incidents that fall under the fourth heading, and the evidential value of the verbal messages in this case is, therefore, much greater than in the case of Mr. Moses. Whereas for Mr. Moses the identity of many of his communicators rested largely upon their being guaranteed by Imperator and his group of helpers, — in the case of Mrs. Piper the spirits of some recently-departed friends who have given much evidence of their identity appear to maintain the independent reality and guiding control over Mrs. Piper of these same intelligences — Imperator, Rector, Doctor, and others — that Mr. Moses claimed as ruling in his own experience.

The case of Mrs. Piper differs in two important respects from that of W. Stainton Moses or D. D. Home. In the first place no telekinetic phenomena have occurred in connection with her trance-manifestations; and in the second place her supraliminal self shows no traces of any supernormal faculty whatsoever. She presents an instance of automatism of the extreme type where the "possession" is not merely local or partial, but affects, so to say, the whole psychical area, — where the supraliminal self is for a time completely displaced, and the whole personality appears to suffer intermittent change. In other words, she passes into a trance, during which her organs of speech or writing are "controlled" by other personalities than the normal waking one. Occasionally, either just before or just after the trance, the subliminal self appears to take some control of the organism for a brief interval; but with this exception the personalities that speak or write during her trance claim to be discarnate spirits.

Mrs. Piper's trances may be divided into three stages: (1) Where the dominant controlling personality was known as "Dr. Phinuit" and used the vocal organs almost exclusively, communicating by *trance-utterance*, 1884-91.

(2) Where the communications were made chiefly by automatic writing in the trance under the supervision more particularly of the control known as "George Pelham," or "G. P.," although "Dr. Phinuit" usually communicated also by speech during this period, 1892-96.

(3) Where supervision is alleged to be exercised by Imperator, Doctor, Rector, and others already mentioned in connection with the experiences of Mr. Moses, and where the communications have been mainly by writing, but occasionally also by speech. This last stage, which began early in 1897, still continues, and the final outcome remains to be seen.

I proceed now to indicate in further detail the nature of the evidence and the character of the manifestations themselves, and begin by quoting from Dr. Hodgson (*Proceedings* S.P.R., vol. xiii. pp. 367-68) a brief statement of some of the historical facts of the case.

Mrs. Piper has been giving sittings for a period extending over thirteen [now, 1901, seventeen] years. Very early in her trance history she came under the attention of Professor James, who sent many persons to her as strangers, in most cases making the appointments himself, and in no case giving their names. She came to some extent under my own supervision in 1887, and I also sent many persons to her, in many cases accompanying them and recording the statements made at their sittings, and taking all the care that I could to prevent Mrs. Piper's obtaining any knowledge beforehand of who the sitters were to be. In 1889-90 Mrs. Piper gave a series of sittings in England under the supervision of Dr. Walter Leaf and Mr. Myers and Professor Lodge, where also the most careful precautions possible were taken to ensure that the sitters went as strangers to Mrs. Piper. Further sittings were supervised by myself in 1890-91 after Mrs. Piper's return to America. Many persons who had sittings in the course of these earlier investigations were convinced that they were actually receiving communications from their "deceased" friends through Mrs. Piper's trance, but although the special investigators were satisfied, from their study of the trance-phenomena themselves and a careful analysis of the detailed records of the sittings, that some supernormal power was involved, there was no definite agreement as to their precise significance. And to myself it seemed that any hypothesis that was offered presented formidable difficulties in the way of its acceptance. In the course of these earlier investigations the communications were given almost entirely through the speech-utterance of the trance-personality known as Phinuit, and even the best of them were apt to include much matter that was irrelevant and unlike the alleged communicators, while there were many indications that Phinuit himself was far from being the kind of person in whom we should be disposed to place implicit credence.

During the years 1892-96 inclusive, I exercised a yet closer supervision of Mrs. Piper's trances than I had done in previous years, continuing to take all the precautions that I could as regards the introduction of persons as strangers. This period was marked by a notable evolution in the quality of the trance results, beginning early in 1892. The character of the manifestations changed with the development of automatic writing in the trance, and with what was alleged to be the continual rendering of active assistance by the communicator whom I have called G. P. [George Pelham]. As a result of this it appeared that communicators were able to express their thoughts directly through the writing by Mrs. Piper's hand, instead of conveying them more dimly and partially through Phinuit as intermediary; and the advice and guidance which they, apparently, received from G. P. enabled them to avoid much of the confusion and irrelevancy so characteristic of the earlier manifestations.

I do not propose here to discuss the hypothesis of fraud in this case, since it has been fully discussed by Dr. Hodgson, Professor William James, Professor Newbold of Pennsylvania University, Dr. Walter Leaf, and Sir Oliver Lodge.[1] I merely quote, as a summary of the argument, a

[1] See *Proceedings* S.P.R., vol. vi. pp. 436–659; vol. viii. pp. 1–167; vol. xiii. pp. 284–582; vol. xiv. pp. 6–78; vol. xv. pp. 16–52; vol. xvi. pp. 1–649.

few words of Professor James, from *The Psychological Review*, July, 1898, pp. 421-22: —

Dr. Hodgson considers that the hypothesis of fraud cannot be seriously maintained. I agree with him absolutely. The medium has been under observation, much of the time under close observation, as to most of the conditions of her life, by a large number of persons, eager, many of them, to pounce upon any suspicious circumstance for [nearly] fifteen years. During that time, not only has there not been one single suspicious circumstance remarked, but not one suggestion has ever been made from any quarter which might tend positively to explain how the medium, living the apparent life she leads, could possibly collect information about so many sitters by natural means. The scientist who is confident of "fraud" here, must remember that in science as much as in common life a hypothesis must receive some positive specification and determination before it can be profitably discussed, and a fraud which is no assigned kind of fraud, but simply "fraud" at large, fraud *in abstracto*, can hardly be regarded as a specially scientific explanation of concrete facts.

Unfortunately we have no contemporary records of what occurred during Mrs. Piper's earliest trances; nor practically any information as to the first manifestations of the Phinuit personality. It seems clear at least that the *name* Phinuit was the result of suggestion at these earliest trances (see *Proceedings* S.P.R., vol. viii. pp. 46-58), and many may think it most probable that the Phinuit "control" was nothing more than a secondary personality of Mrs. Piper. But, according to the statements (for which there is of course no evidence) made by "Imperator," Phinuit was an "earth-bound" or inferior spirit, who had become confused and bewildered in his first attempts at communication, and had, as we say, "lost his consciousness of personal identity." That such an occurrence is not uncommon in this life is plain from the cases to which I have drawn attention in Chapter II. of this book, and we cannot prove it to be impossible that profound memory disturbances should be produced in an inexperienced discarnate spirit when first attempting to communicate with us through a material organism. Be that as it may, the Phinuit personality has not manifested either directly or indirectly since January 1897, when "Imperator" claimed the supervision of Mrs. Piper's trances.

There were various cases of alleged direct "control" by spirits other than Phinuit during the first stage of Mrs. Piper's trance history. But such cases were not usual, and on the whole, although there seemed to be abundant proof of some supernormal faculty which demanded at least the hypothesis of thought-transference from living persons both near and distant, and suggested occasionally some power of telæsthesia or perhaps even of premonition, yet the main question with which we are now concerned, — whether Mrs. Piper's organism was controlled, directly or indirectly, by discarnate spirits who could give satisfactory evidence of their identity, — remained undecided.

More important, as regards this question of personal identity, is the series of sittings which formed the second stage of Mrs. Piper's trance history, in the years 1892-96, (of which a detailed account is given in *Proceedings* S.P.R., vol. xiii. pp. 284-582, and vol. xiv. pp. 6-49), where the chief communicator or intermediary was G. P. This G. P., whose name (although, of course, well known to many persons) has been altered for publication into "George Pelham," was a young man of great ability, mainly occupied in literary pursuits. Although born an American citizen, he was a member of a noble English family. I never met him, but I have the good fortune to include a number of his friends among my own, and with several of these I have been privileged to hold intimate conversation on the nature of the communications which they received. I have thus heard of many significant utterances of G. P.'s, which are held too private for print; and I have myself been present at sittings where G. P. manifested. For the full discussion of the evidence tending to prove the identity of G. P., I refer my readers to the original report in the *Proceedings* S.P.R. I quote here a general summary, given by Dr. Hodgson several years later, of the whole series of his manifestations. (From *Proceedings* S.P.R., vol. xiii. pp. 328-330.)

On the first appearance of the communicating G. P. to Mr. Hart in March 1892, he gave not only his own name and that of the sitter, but also the names of several of their most intimate common friends, and referred specifically to the most important private matters connected with them. At the same sitting reference was made to other incidents unknown to the sitters, such as the account of Mrs. Pelham's taking the studs from the body of G. P. and giving them to Mr. Pelham to be sent to Mr. Hart, and the reproduction of a notable remembrance of a conversation which G. P. living had with Katharine, the daughter of his most intimate friends, the Howards. These were primary examples of two kinds of knowledge concerning matters unknown to the sitters, of which various other instances were afterwards given; knowledge of events connected with G. P. which had occurred since his death, and knowledge of special memories pertaining to the G. P. personality before death. A week later, at the sitting of Mr. Vance, he made an appropriate inquiry after the sitter's son, and in reply to inquiries rightly specified that the sitter's son had been at college with him, and further correctly gave a correct description of the sitter's summer home as the place of a special visit. This, again, was paralleled by many later instances where appropriate inquiries were made and remembrances recalled concerning

other personal friends of G. P. Nearly two weeks later came his most
intimate friends, the Howards, and to these, using the voice directly,
he showed such a fulness of private remembrance and specific knowledge
and characteristic intellectual and emotional quality pertaining to G. P.
that, though they had previously taken no interest in any branch of psychical research, they were unable to resist the conviction that they were
actually conversing with their old friend G. P. And this conviction
was strengthened by their later experiences. Not least important, at
that time, was his anxiety about the disposal of a certain book and about
certain specified letters which concern matters too private for publication.
He was particularly desirous of convincing his father, who lived in Washington, that it was indeed G. P. who was communicating, and he soon
afterwards stated that his father had taken his photograph to be copied,
as was the case, though Mr. Pelham had not informed even his wife of
this fact. Later on he reproduced a series of incidents, unknown to
the sitters, in which Mrs. Howard had been engaged in her own home.
Later still, at a sitting with his father and mother in New York, a further
intimate knowledge was shown of private family circumstances, and
at the following sitting, at which his father and mother were not present,
he gave the details of certain private actions which they had done in the
interim. At their sitting, and at various sittings of the Howards, appropriate comments were made concerning different articles presented which
had belonged to G. P. living, or had been familiar to him; he inquired
after other personal articles which were not presented at the sittings,
and showed intimate and detailed recollections of incidents in connection
with them. In points connected with the recognition of articles with
their related associations of a personal sort, the G. P. communicating,
so far as I know, has never failed. Nor has he failed in the recognition
of personal friends. I may say generally that out of a large number of
sitters who went as strangers to Mrs. Piper, the communicating G. P.
has picked out the friends of G. P. living, precisely as the G. P. living
might have been expected to do [thirty cases of recognition out of at least
one hundred and fifty persons who have had sittings with Mrs. Piper
since the first appearance of G. P., and no case of false recognition], and
has exhibited memories in connection with these and other friends which
are such as would naturally be associated as part of the G. P. personality,
which certainly do not suggest in themselves that they originate otherwise, and which are accompanied by the emotional relations which were
connected with such friends in the mind of G. P. living. At one of his
early communications G. P. expressly undertook the task of rendering
all the assistance in his power towards establishing the continued existence of himself and other communicators, in pursuance of a promise
of which he himself reminded me, made some two years or more before
his death, that if he died before me and found himself "still existing,"
he would devote himself to prove the fact; and in the persistence of his
endeavour to overcome the difficulties in communicating as far as possible, in his constant readiness to act as amanuensis at the sittings, in the
effect which he has produced by his counsels, — to myself as investigator,

and to numerous other sitters and communicators, — he has, in so far as I can form a judgment in a problem so complex and still presenting so much obscurity, displayed all the keenness and pertinacity which were eminently characteristic of G. P. living.

Finally the manifestations of this G. P. communicating have not been of a fitful and spasmodic nature, they have exhibited the marks of a continuous living and persistent personality, manifesting itself through a course of years, and showing the same characteristics of an independent intelligence whether friends of G. P. were present at the sittings or not. I learned of various cases where in my absence active assistance was rendered by G. P. to sitters who had never previously heard of him, and from time to time he would make brief pertinent reference to matters with which G. P. living was acquainted, though I was not, and sometimes in ways which indicated that he could to some extent see what was happening in our world to persons in whose welfare G. P. living would have been specially interested.

The sitter called Mr. Hart, to whom G. P. first manifested, died at Naples three years afterwards, and communicated, with the help of G. P., on the second day after his death. An account of his communications is given in *Proceedings* S.P.R., vol. xiii. pp. 353-57.

There are numerous instances in the reports in the *Proceedings* (see vol. vi. pp. 647-50; vol. viii. pp. 15-26; vol. xiii., *passim;* and vol. xvi. pp. 131-3), of the giving of information unknown to the sitters and afterwards verified. A striking illustration of this occurred in the case of the lady called "Elisa Mannors," whose near relatives and friends concerned in the communications were known to myself. On the morning after the death of her uncle, called F. in the report, she described an incident in connection with the appearance of herself to her uncle on his deathbed. I quote Dr. Hodgson's account of this (*Proceedings* S.P.R., vol. xiii. p. 378, footnote).

The notice of his [F.'s] death was in a Boston morning paper, and I happened to see it on my way to the sitting. The first writing of the sitting came from Madame Elisa, without my expecting it. She wrote clearly and strongly, explaining that F. was there with her, but unable to speak directly, that she wished to give me an account of how she had helped F. to reach her. She said that she had been present at his deathbed, and had spoken to him, and she repeated what she had said, an unusual form of expression, and indicated that he had heard and recognised her. This was confirmed in detail in the only way possible at that time, by a very intimate friend of Madame Elisa and myself, and also of the nearest surviving relative of F. I showed my friend the account of the sitting, and to this friend, a day or two later, the relative, who was present at the death-bed, stated spontaneously that F. when dying said that he saw Madame Elisa who was speaking to him, and he repeated what she was saying. The expression so repeated, which the relative quoted to my friend, was that which I had received from Madame Elisa through Mrs. Piper's trance, when the death-bed incident was of course entirely unknown to me.

Rare are the "Peak in Darien" cases (see page 233), but cases like this are rarer still.

With regard to the last of the three periods of Mrs. Piper's trance-history, the only detailed published accounts are contained in Professor Hyslop's report of his sittings in *Proceedings* S.P.R., vol. xvi.[1] But neither his records nor the manuscript records which I have seen contain any proof of the personal identity of the alleged spirits called "Imperator," "Doctor," "Rector," etc., or any proof of the identity of these intelligences with those claimed by Mr. Moses. (See *Proceedings* S.P.R., vol. xiii. pp. 408-9.) Whether any such proof will be forthcoming in the future remains to be seen, — or indeed, whether proof or disproof for us at present is even possible.

We must now try to form some more definite idea — based not on preconceived theories but on our actual observation of trances — of the processes of possession.

Let us try to realise what kind of feat it is which we are expecting the disembodied spirit to achieve. Such language, I know, again suggests the medicine-man's wigwam rather than the study of the white philosopher. Yet can we feel sure that the process in our own minds which has (as we think) refined and spiritualised man's early conceptions of an unseen world has been based upon any observed facts?

In dealing with matters which lie outside human experience, our only clue is some attempt at *continuity* with what we already know. We cannot, for instance, form independently a reliable conception of life in an unseen world. That conception has never yet been fairly faced from the standpoint of our modern ideas of continuity, conservation, evolution. The main notions that have been framed of such survival have been framed first by savages and then by *a priori* philosophers.

The savage made his own picture first. And he at any rate dimly felt after a principle of continuity; although he applied it in the crudest fashion. Yet the happy hunting-ground and the faithful dog were conceptions not more arbitrary and unscientific than that eternal and unimaginable worship *in vacuo* which more accredited teachers have proclaimed. And, passing on to modern philosophic conceptions, one may say that where

[1] For a discussion of Professor Hyslop's report see *Proceedings* S.P.R., vol. xvii. pp. 331-388.

the savage assumed *too little* difference between the material and the spiritual world the philosopher has assumed *too much*. He has regarded the gulf as too unbridgeable; he has taken for granted too clean a sweep of earthly modes of thought. Trying to shake off time, space, and definite form, he has attempted to transport himself too magically to what may be in reality an immensely distant goal.

What, then, is to be our conception of identity prolonged beyond the tomb? In earth-life the actual body, in itself but a subordinate element in our thought of our friend, did yet by its physical continuity override as a symbol of identity all lapses of memory, all changes of the character within. Yet it was memory and character, — the stored impressions upon which he reacted, and his specific mode of reaction, — which made our veritable friend. How much of memory, how much of character, must he preserve for our recognition?

Do we ask that either he or we should remember always, or should remember all? Do we ask that his memory should be expanded into omniscience and his character elevated into divinity? And, whatever heights he may attain, do we demand that he should reveal to us? Are the limitations of our material world no barrier to him?

It is safest to fall back for the present upon the few points which these communications do seem to indicate. The spirit, then, is holding converse with a living man, located in a certain place at a certain moment, and animated by certain thoughts and emotions. The spirit (to which I must give a neuter pronoun for greater clearness) in some cases can find and follow the man as it pleases. It is therefore in some way cognizant of space, although not conditioned by space. Its mastery of space may perhaps bear somewhat the same relation to our eyesight as our eyesight bears to the gropings of the blind. Similarly, the spirit appears to be partly cognizant of our *time*, although not wholly conditioned thereby. It is apt to see as *present* both certain things which appear to us as past and certain things which appear to us as future.

Once more, the spirit is at least partly conscious of the thought and emotions of its earthly friend, so far as directed towards itself; and this not only when the friend is in the presence of the sensitive, but also (as G. P. has repeatedly shown) when the friend is at home and living his ordinary life.

Lastly, it seems as though the spirit had some occasional glimpses of material fact upon the earth (as the contents of drawers and the like), not manifestly proceeding through any living mind. I do not, however, recall any clear evidence of a spirit's perception of material facts which provably have never been known to any incarnate mind whatever.

Accepting this, then, for argument's sake, as the normal condition of a spirit in reference to human things, what process must it attempt if it wishes to communicate with living men? That it *will* wish to communicate seems probable enough, if it retains not only memory of the loves of earth, but actual fresh consciousness of loving emotion directed towards it after death.

Seeking then for some open avenue, it discerns something which corresponds (in G. P.'s phrase) to a *light* — a glimmer of translucency in the confused darkness of our material world. This "light" indicates a *sensitive* — a human organism so constituted that a spirit can temporarily *inform* or *control* it, not necessarily interrupting the stream of the sensitive's ordinary consciousness; perhaps using a hand only, or perhaps, as in Mrs. Piper's case, using voice as well as hand, and occupying all the sensitive's channels of self-manifestation. The difficulties which must be inherent in such an act of control are thus described by Dr. Hodgson: —

"If, indeed, each one of us is a 'spirit' that survives the death of the fleshly organism, there are certain suppositions that I think we may not unreasonably make concerning the ability of the discarnate 'spirit' to communicate with those yet incarnate. Even under the best of conditions for communication — which I am supposing for the nonce to be possible — it may well be that the aptitude for communicating clearly may be as rare as the gifts that make a great artist, or a great mathematician, or a great philosopher. Again, it may well be that, owing to the change connected with death itself, the 'spirit' may at first be much confused, and such confusion may last for a long time; and even after the 'spirit' has become accustomed to its new environment, it is not an unreasonable supposition that if it came into some such relation to another living human organism as it once maintained with its own former organism, it would find itself confused by that relation. The state might be like that of awaking from a prolonged period of unconsciousness into strange surroundings. If my own ordinary body could be preserved in its present state, and I could absent myself from it for days or months or years, and continue my existence under another set of conditions altogether, and if I could then return to my own body, it might well be that I should be very confused and incoherent at first in my manifestations by means of it. How much more would this be the case were I to return to *another* human body. I might be troubled with various forms of aphasia and agraphia, might be particularly liable to failures of inhibition, might find the conditions oppressive and exhausting, and my state of mind would probably be of an automatic and dreamlike character. Now, the communicators through Mrs. Piper's trance exhibit precisely the kind of confusion and incoherence which it seems to me we have some reason *a priori* to expect if they are actually what they claim to be."

At the outset of this chapter I compared the phenomena of possession with those of alternating personalities, of dreams, and of somnambulism. Now it seems probable that the thesis of multiplex personality — namely, that no known current of man's consciousness exhausts his whole consciousness, and no known self-manifestation expresses man's whole potential being — may hold good both for embodied and for unembodied men, and this would lead us to expect that the manifestations of the departed, — through the sensory automatisms dealt with in Chapter VII., and the motor automatisms considered in Chapter VIII., up to the completer form of possession illustrated in the present chapter, — would resemble those fugitive and unstable communications between widely different strata of personality of which embodied minds offer us examples. G. P. himself appears to be well aware of the dreamlike character of the communications, which, indeed, his own style often exemplifies. Thus he wrote on February 15th, 1894: —

"Remember we share and always shall have our friends in the dream-life, *i.e.* your life so to speak, which will attract us for ever and ever, and so long as we have any friends *sleeping* in the material world; you to us are more like as we understand sleep, you look shut up as one in prison, and in order for us to get into communication with you, we have to enter into your sphere, as one like yourself, asleep. This is just why we make mistakes, as you call them, or get confused and muddled."

Yet even this very difficulty and fragmentariness of communication ought in the end to be for us full of an instruction of its own. We are here actually witnessing the central mystery of human life, unrolling itself under novel conditions, and open to closer observation than ever before. We are seeing a mind use a brain. The human brain is in its last analysis an arrangement of matter expressly adapted to being acted upon by a spirit; but so long as the accustomed spirit acts upon it the working is generally too smooth to allow us a glimpse of the mechanism. *Now*, however, we can watch an unaccustomed spirit, new to the instrument, installing itself and feeling its way. The lessons thus learnt are likely to be more penetrating than any which mere morbid interruptions of the accustomed spirit's work can teach us. In aphasia, for instance,

we can watch with instruction special difficulties of utterance, supervening on special injuries to the brain. But in *possession* we perceive
the controlling spirit actually engaged in overcoming somewhat similar
difficulties — writing or uttering the wrong word, and then getting hold
of the right one — and sometimes even finding power to explain to us
something of the minute verbal mechanism (so to term it) through whose
blocking or dislocation the mistake has arisen.

And we may hope, indeed, that as our investigations proceed, and as
we on this side of the fateful gulf, and the discarnate spirits on the other,
learn more of the conditions necessary for perfect control of the brain
and nervous system of intermediaries, — the communications will grow
fuller and more coherent, and reach a higher level of unitary consciousness.

Among the cases of trance discussed in this chapter, we have found
intimately interwoven with the phenomena of possession many instances
of its correlative, — ecstasy. Mrs. Piper's fragmentary utterances and
visions during her passage from trance to waking life, — utterances and
visions that fade away and leave no remembrance in her waking self;
Stainton Moses' occasional visions, his journeys in the "spirit world" which
he recorded on returning to his ordinary consciousness; Home's entrancement and converse with the various controls whose messages he gave;
— all these suggest actual excursions of the incarnate spirit from its organism. The theoretical importance of these spiritual excursions is,
of course, very great. It is, indeed, so great that most men will hesitate
to accept a thesis which carries us straight into the inmost sanctuary
of mysticism; which preaches "a precursory entrance into the most holy
place, as by divine transportation."

Yet I think that this belief, although extreme, is not, at the point to
which our evidence has carried us, in any real way improbable. To
put the matter briefly, if a spirit from outside can enter the organism,
the spirit from inside can go out, can change its centre of perception and
action, in a way less complete and irrevocable than the change of death.
Ecstasy would thus be simply the complementary or correlative aspect
of spirit-control. Such a change need not be a *spatial* change, any more
than there need be any *spatial* change for the spirit which invades the
deserted organism. Nay, further: if the incarnate spirit can in this manner change its centre of perception in response (so to say) to a discarnate
spirit's invasion of the organism, there is no obvious reason why it should
not do so on other occasions as well. We are already familiar with "travelling clairvoyance," a spirit's change of centre of perception among
the scenes of the material world. May there not be an extension of

travelling clairvoyance to the spiritual world? a spontaneous transfer of the centre of perception into that region from whence discarnate spirits seem now to be able, on their side, to communicate with growing freedom?

The conception of *ecstasy* — at once in its most literal and in its most lofty sense—has thus developed itself, almost insensibly, from several concurrent lines of actual modern evidence. It must still, of course, be long before we can at all adequately separate, — I can hardly say the objective from the subjective element in the experience, for we have got beyond the region where the meaning of those words is clear,—but the element in the experience which is recognised and responded to by spirits other than the ecstatic's, from the element which belongs to his own spirit alone.

In the meantime, however, the fact that this kind of communion of ecstasy has been, in preliminary fashion, rendered probable is of the highest importance for our whole inquiry. We thus come directly into relation with the highest form which the various religions known to men have assumed in the past.

It is hardly a paradox to say that the evidence for ecstasy is stronger than the evidence for any other religious belief. Of all the subjective experiences of religion, ecstasy is that which has been most urgently, perhaps to the psychologist most convincingly, asserted; and it is not confined to any one religion. From a psychological point of view, one main indication of the importance of a subjective phenomenon found in religious experience will be the fact that it is common to all religions. I doubt whether there is any phenomenon, except ecstasy, of which this can be said. From the medicine-man of the lowest savages up to St. John, St. Peter, St. Paul, with Buddha, Mahomet and Swedenborg on the way, we find records which, though morally and intellectually much differing, are in psychological essence the same.

At all stages alike we find that the spirit is conceived as quitting the body; or, if not quitting it, at least as greatly expanding its range of perception in some state resembling trance. Observe, moreover, that on this view all genuine recorded forms of ecstasy are akin, and all of them represent a real fact.

To our embodied souls the matter round us seems real and self-existent; to souls emancipated it is but the sign of the degree which we have reached, and thus the highest task of science must be to link and co-ordinate the symbols appropriate to our terrene state with the symbols appropriate to the state immediately above us. Nay, one might push this truth to paradox, and maintain that of all earth's inspired spirits it has been the least divinised, the least lovable, who has opened the surest path for men.

Religions have risen and die again; philosophy, poetry, heroism, answer only indirectly the prime need of men. Plotinus, "the eagle soaring above the tomb of Plato," is lost to sight in the heavens   Conquering and to conquer, the Maid rides on through other worlds than ours.   Virgil himself, "light among the vanished ages, star that gildest yet this earthly shore," sustains our spirit, as I have said, but indirectly, by filling still our fountain of purest intellectual joy.   But the prosaic Swede, — his stiff mind prickly with dogma, — the opaque cell-walls of his intelligence flooded cloudily by the irradiant day, — this man as by the very limitations of his faculty, by the practical humility of a spirit trained to acquire but not to generate truth ,— has awkwardly laid the corner-stone, grotesquely sketched the elevation of a temple which our remotest posterity will be upbuilding and adorning still.   For he dimly felt that man's true passage and intuition from state to state depends not upon individual ecstasy, but upon comprehensive law; while yet all law is in fact but symbol; adaptation of truth timeless and infinite to intelligences of lower or higher range.

Beyond us still is mystery; but it is mystery lit and mellowed with an infinite hope.   We ride in darkness at the haven's mouth; but sometimes through rifted clouds we see the desires and needs of many generations floating and melting upwards into a distant glow, "up through the light of the seas by the moon's long-silvering ray."

The high possibilities that lie before us should be grasped once for all, in order that the dignity of the quest may help to carry the inquirer through many disappointments, deceptions, delays.   But he must remember that this inquiry must be extended over many generations; nor must he allow himself to be persuaded that there are byways to mastery. I will not say that there cannot possibly be any such thing as occult wisdom, or dominion over the secrets of nature ascetically or magically acquired.   But I will say that every claim of this kind which my colleagues or I have been able to examine has proved deserving of complete mistrust; and that we have no confidence here any more than elsewhere in any methods except the open, candid, straightforward methods which the spirit of modern science demands.

All omens point towards the steady continuance of just such labour as has already taught us all we know.   Perhaps, indeed, in this complex of interpenetrating spirits our own effort is no individual, no transitory thing.   That which lies at the root of each of us lies at the root of the Cosmos too.   Our struggle is the struggle of the Universe itself; and the very Godhead finds fulfilment through our upward-striving souls.

CHAPTER X

EPILOGUE

Ἐδόκει τίς μοι γυνὴ προσελθοῦσα καλὴ καὶ εὐειδής, λευκὰ ἱμάτια ἔχουσα, καλέσαι με καὶ εἰπεῖν, Ὦ Σώκρατες, Ἤματί κεν τριτάτῳ Φθίην ἐρίβωλον ἴκοιο.— Πλάτωνος Κρίτων.

THE task which I proposed to myself at the beginning of this work is now, after a fashion, accomplished. Following the successive steps of my programme, I have presented, — not indeed all the evidence which I possess, and which I would willingly present, — but enough at least to illustrate a continuous exposition, and as much as can be compressed into two volumes, with any hope that these volumes will be read at all. [1] I have indicated also the principal inferences which that evidence immediately suggests. Such wider generalisations as I may now add must needs be dangerously speculative; they must run the risk of alienating still further from this research many of the scientific minds which I am most anxious to influence.

This risk, nevertheless, I feel bound to face. For two reasons, — or, I should perhaps say, for one main reason seen under two aspects, — I cannot leave this obscure and unfamiliar mass of observation and experiment without some words of wider generalisation, some epilogue which may place these new discoveries in clearer relation to the existing schemes of civilised thought and belief.

In the first place, I feel that some such attempt at synthesis is needful for the practical purpose of enlisting help in our long inquiry. As has been hinted more than once, the real drag upon its progress has been not opposition but indifference. Or if indifference be too strong a word, at any rate the interest evoked has not been such as to inspire to steady independent work anything like the number of coadjutors who would have responded to a new departure in one of the sciences which all men have learnt to respect. The inquiry falls between the two stools of religion and science; it cannot claim support either from the "religious world" or from the Royal Society. Yet even apart from the instinct

[1] The original unabridged edition was published in two volumes.

of pure scientific curiosity (which surely has seldom seen such a field opening before it), the mighty issues depending on these phenomena ought, I think, to constitute in themselves a strong, an exceptional appeal. I desire in this book to emphasise that appeal; — not only to produce conviction, but also to attract co-operation. And actual converse with many persons has led me to believe that in order to attract such help, even from scientific men, some general view of the moral upshot of all the phenomena is needed; — speculative and uncertain though such a general view must be.

Again, — and here the practical reason already given expands into a wider scope, — it would be unfair to the evidence itself were I to close this work without touching more directly than hitherto on some of the deepest faiths of men. The influence of the evidence set forth in this book should not be limited to the conclusions, however weighty, which that evidence may be thought to establish. Rather these discoveries should prompt, as nothing else could have prompted, towards the ultimate achievement of that programme of scientific dominance which the *Instauratio Magna* proclaimed for mankind. Bacon foresaw the gradual victory of observation and experiment — the triumph of actual analysed fact — in every department of human study; — in every department save one. The realm of "Divine things" he left to Authority and Faith. I here urge that that great exemption need be no longer made. I claim that there now exists an incipient method of getting at this Divine knowledge also, with the same certainty, the same calm assurance, with which we make our steady progress in the knowledge of terrene things. The authority of creeds and Churches will thus be replaced by the authority of observation and experiment. The impulse of faith will resolve itself into a reasoned and resolute imagination, bent upon raising even higher than now the highest ideals of man.

Most readers of the preceding pages will have been prepared for the point of view thus frankly avowed. Yet to few readers can that point of view at first present itself otherwise than as alien and repellent. Philosophy and orthodoxy will alike resent it as presumptuous; nor will science readily accept the unauthorised transfer to herself of regions of which she has long been wont either to deny the existence, or at any rate to disclaim the rule. Nevertheless, I think that it will appear on reflection that some such change of standpoint as this was urgently needed, — nay, was ultimately inevitable.

I need not here describe at length the deep disquiet of our time. Never, perhaps, did man's spiritual satisfaction bear a smaller proportion to his needs. The old-world sustenance, however earnestly administered, is too unsubstantial for the modern cravings. And thus through our civilised societies two conflicting currents run. On the one hand health, intelligence, morality, — all such boons as the steady progress of planetary evolution can win for man, — are being achieved in increasing measure. On the other hand this very sanity, this very prosperity, do but bring out in stronger relief the underlying *Welt-Schmerz*, the decline of any real belief in the dignity, the meaning, the endlessness of life.

There are many, of course, who readily accept this limitation of view; who are willing to let earthly activities and pleasures gradually dissipate and obscure the larger hope. But others cannot thus be easily satisfied. They rather resemble children who are growing too old for their games; — whose amusement sinks into an indifference and discontent for which the fitting remedy is an initiation into the serious work of men.

A similar crisis has passed over Europe once before. There came a time when the joyful naïveté, the unquestioning impulse of the early world had passed away; when the worship of Greeks no more was beauty, nor the religion of Romans Rome. Alexandrian decadence, Byzantine despair, found utterance in many an epigram which might have been written to-day. Then came a great uprush or incursion from the spiritual world, and with new races and new ideals Europe regained its youth.

The unique effect of that great Christian impulse begins, perhaps, to wear away. But more grace may yet be attainable from the region whence that grace came. Our age's restlessness, as I believe, is the restlessness not of senility but of adolescence; it resembles the approach of puberty rather than the approach of death.

What the age needs is not an abandonment of effort, but an increase; the time is ripe for a study of unseen things as strenuous and sincere as that which Science has made familiar for the problems of earth. For now the scientific instinct, — so newly developed in mankind, — seems likely to spread until it becomes as dominant as was in time past the religious; and if there be even the narrowest chink through which man can look forth from his planetary cage, our descendants will not leave that chink neglected or unwidened. The scheme of knowledge which can commend itself to such seekers must be a scheme which, while it *transcends* our present knowledge, steadily *continues* it; — a scheme not catastrophic, but evolutionary; not promulgated and closed in a moment, but gradually unfolding itself to progressive inquiry.

Must there not also be a continuous change, an unending advance in the human ideal itself? so that Faith must shift her standpoint from the brief Past to the endless Future, not so much caring to supply the lacunæ of tradition as to intensify the conviction that there is still a higher life to work for, a holiness which may be some day reached by grace and effort as yet unknown.

It may be that for some generations to come the truest faith will lie in the patient attempt to unravel from confused phenomena some trace of the supernal world; — to find thus at last "the substance of things hoped for, the evidence of things not seen." I confess, indeed, that I have often felt as though this present age were even unduly favoured; — as though no future revelation and calm could equal the joy of this great struggle from doubt into certainty; — from the materialism or agnosticism which accompany the first advance of Science into the deeper scientific conviction that there is a deathless soul in man. I can imagine no other crisis of such deep delight. But after all this is but like the starving child's inability to imagine anything sweeter than his first bite at the crust. Give him but *that*, and he can hardly care for the moment whether he is fated to be Prime Minister or ploughboy.

Equally transitory, equally dependent on our special place in the story of man's upward effort, is another shade of feeling which many men have known. They have felt that uncertainty gave scope to faith and courage in a way which scientific assurance could never do. There has been a stern delight in the choice of virtue, — even though virtue might bring no reward. This joy, like the joy of Columbus sailing westward from Hierro, can hardly recur in precisely the same form. But neither (to descend to a humbler comparison) can we grown men again give ourselves up to learning in the same spirit of pure faith, without prefigurement of result, as when we learnt the alphabet at our mother's knees. Have we therefore relaxed since then our intellectual effort? Have we felt that there was no longer need to struggle against idleness when once we knew that knowledge brought a sure reward?

Endless are the varieties of lofty joy. In the age of Thales, Greece knew the delight of the first dim notion of cosmic unity and law. In the age of Christ, Europe felt the first high authentic message from a world beyond our own. In our own age we reach the perception that such messages may become continuous and progressive; — that between seen and unseen there is a channel and fairway which future generations may learn to widen and to clarify. Our own age may seem the best to us; so will their mightier ages seem to them.

> "'Talia saecla' suis dixerunt 'currite' fusis
> Concordes stabili Fatorum numine Parcae."

Spiritual evolution: — that, then, is our destiny, in this and other worlds; — an evolution gradual with many gradations, and rising to no assignable close. And the passion for Life is no selfish weakness, it is a factor in the universal energy. It should keep its strength unbroken even when our weariness longs to fold the hands in endless slumber; it should outlast and annihilate the "pangs that conquer trust." If to the Greeks it seemed a λιποταξία — a desertion of one's post in battle — to quit by suicide the life of earth, how much more craven were the desire to desert the Cosmos, — the despair, not of this planet only, but of the Sum of Things!

Nay, in the infinite Universe man may now feel, for the first time, at home. The worst fear is over; the true security is won. The worst fear was the fear of spiritual extinction or spiritual solitude; the true security is in the telepathic law.

Let me draw out my meaning at somewhat greater length.

As we have dwelt successively on various aspects of telepathy, we have gradually felt the conception enlarge and deepen under our study. It began as a quasi-mechanical transference of ideas and images from one to another brain. Presently we found it assuming a more varied and potent form, as though it were the veritable ingruence or invasion of a distant mind. Again, its action was traced across a gulf greater than any space of earth or ocean, and it bridged the interval between spirits incarnate and discarnate, between the visible and the invisible world. There seemed no limit to the distance of its operation, or to the intimacy of its appeal.

ἐν θήρσιν ἐν βροτοῖσιν ἐν θεοῖς ἄνω.

This Love, then, which (as Sophocles has it) rules "beasts and men and gods" with equal sway, is no matter of carnal impulse or of emotional caprice. Rather it is now possible to define Love (as we have already defined Genius) in terms which convey for us some new meaning in connection with phenomena described in this work. Genius, as has been already said, is a kind of exalted but undeveloped clairvoyance. The subliminal uprush which inspires the poet or the musician presents to him a deep, but vague perception of that world unseen, through which the seer or the sensitive projects a narrower but an exacter gaze. Somewhat similarly, Love is a kind of exalted but unspecialised telepathy; — the simplest and most universal expression of that mutual gravitation or kinship of spirits which is the foundation of the telepathic law.

This is the answer to the ancient fear; the fear lest man's fellowships

be the outward and his solitude the inward thing; the fear lest all close
linking with our fellows be the mere product of the struggle for existence,
— of the tribal need of strength and cohesion; — the fear that if love and
virtue thus arose, love and virtue may thus likewise perish. It is an
answer to the dread that separate centres of conscious life must be
always strangers, and often foes; their leagues and fellowships interested
and illusory; their love the truce of a moment amid infinite inevitable
war.

Such fears, I say, vanish when we learn that it is the soul in man which
links him with other souls; the body which dissevers even while it seems
to unite; so that "no man liveth to himself nor dieth to himself," but
in a sense which goes deeper than metaphor, "We are every one members
one of another." Like atoms, like suns, like galaxies, our spirits are
systems of forces which vibrate continually to each other's attractive
power.

All this as yet is dimly adumbrated; it is a first hint of a scheme of
thought which it may well take centuries to develop. But can we suppose
that, when once this conception of the bond between all souls has taken
root, men will turn back from it to the old exclusiveness, the old controversy? Will they not see that this world-widening knowledge is both old
and new, that *die Geisterwelt ist nicht verschlossen?* that always have
such revelations been given, but develop now into a mightier meaning,
—with the growth of wisdom in those who send them, and in us who
receive?

Surely we have here a conception, at once wider and exacter than ever
before, of that "religious education of the world" on which theologians
have been fain to dwell. We need assume no "supernatural interference" no "plan of redemption." We need suppose only that the same
process which we observe to-day has been operating for ages between
this world and the next.

Let us suppose that whilst incarnate men have risen from savagery
into intelligence, discarnate men have made on their part a like advance.
Let us suppose that they have become more eager and more able to use,
for communication with earth, the standing laws of relation between
the spiritual and the material Universe.

At first, on such a hypothesis, certain automatic phenomena will occur,
but will not be purposely modified by spirit power. Already and always
there must have been points of contact where unseen things impinged
upon the seen. Always there would be "clairvoyant wanderings," where
the spirit of *shaman* or of medicine-man discerned things distant upon

earth by the spirit's excursive power. Always there would be apparitions at death, — conscious or unconscious effects of the shock which separated soul from body; and always "hauntings," — where the spirit, already discarnate, revisited, as in a dream perceptible by others, the scenes which once he knew.

From this groundwork of phenomena developed (to take civilised Europe alone) the oracular religion first, the Christian later. The golden gifts of Crœsus to Delphi attested the clairvoyance of the Pythia as strongly, perhaps, as can be expected of any tradition which comes to us from the morning of history.

And furthermore, do we not better understand at once the uniqueness and the reality of the Christian revelation itself, when we regard it as a culmination rather than an exception, — as destined not to destroy the cosmic law, but to fulfil it? Then first in human history came from the unseen a message such as the whole heart desired; — a message adequate in its response to fundamental emotional needs not in that age only, but in all ages that should follow. *Intellectually* adequate for all coming ages that revelation could not be; — given the laws of mind, incarnate alike and discarnate, — the evolution, on either side of the gulf of death, of knowledge and power.

No one at the date of that revelation suspected that uniformity, that continuity of the Universe which long experience has now made for us almost axiomatic. No one foresaw the day when the demand for miracle would be merged in the demand for higher law.

This newer scientific temper is not confined, as I believe, to the denizens of this earth alone. The spiritual world meets it, as I think our evidence has shown, with eager and strenuous response. But that response is made, and must be made, along the lines of our normal evolution. It must rest upon the education, the disentanglement, of that within us mortals which exists in the Invisible, a partaker of the undying world. And on our side and on theirs alike, the process must be steady and continuous. We have no longer to deal with some isolated series of events in the past, — interpretable this way or that, but in no way renewable, — but rather with a world-wide and actual condition of things, recognisable every year in greater clearness, and changing in directions which we can better and better foresee. This new aspect of things needs something of new generalisation, of new forecast, — it points to a provisional synthesis of religious belief which may fitly conclude the present work.

PROVISIONAL SKETCH OF A RELIGIOUS SYNTHESIS

ὄλβιος ὅστις ἰδὼν ἐκεῖνα κοῖλαν
εἶσιν ὑπὸ χθόνα· οἶδεν μὲν βίου κεῖνος τελευτάν,
οἶδεν δὲ διόσδοτον ἀρχάν.
                                        — PINDAR.

I see ground for hoping that we are within sight of a religious synthesis, which, although as yet provisional and rudimentary, may in the end meet more adequately than any previous synthesis the reasonable needs of men. Such a synthesis cannot, I think, be reached by a mere predominance of any one existing creed, nor by any eclectic or syncretic process. Its prerequisite is the actual acquisition of new knowledge whether by discovery or by revelation — knowledge discerned from without the veil or from within — yet so realised that the main forms of religious thought, by harmonious expansion and development, shall find place severally as elements in a more comprehensive whole. And enough of such knowledge has, I think, been now attained to make it desirable to submit to my readers the religious results which seem likely to follow.

With such a purpose, our conception of religion should be both profound and comprehensive. I will use here the definition already adopted of religion as the sane and normal response of the human spirit to all that we know of cosmic law; that is, to the known phenomena of the universe, regarded as an intelligible whole. For on the one hand I cannot confine the term to any single definite view or tradition of things unseen. On the other hand, I am not content to define religion as "morality tinged with emotion," lest morality *per se* should seem to hang in air, so that we should be merely gilding the tortoise which supports the earth. Yet my definition needs some further guarding if it is to correspond with our habitual use of language. Most men's subjective response to their environment falls below the level of true religious thought. It is scattered into cravings, or embittered by resentment, or distorted by superstitious fear. But of such men I do not speak; rather of men in whom the great pageant has inspired at least some vague out-reaching toward the Source of All; men for whom knowledge has ripened into meditation, and has prompted high desire. I would have Science first sublimed into Philosophy, and then kindled by Religion into a burning flame. For, from my point of view, man cannot be too religious. I desire that the environing, the interpenetrating universe, — its energy, its life, its love, — should illume in us, in our low degree, that which we ascribe to the World-Soul, saying, "God is Love," "God is Light." The World-Soul's infinite energy of omniscent benevolence should become in us an enthusiasm of adoring co-operation, — an eager obedience to whatsoever with our best pains we can discern as the justly ruling principle — τὸ ἡγεμονικόν — without us and within.

Yet if we form so high an ideal of religion, — raising it so far above any blind obedience or self-seeking fear that its submission is wholly willing, and its demand is for spiritual response alone, — we are bound to ask ourselves whether it is right and reasonable to be religious, to regard with this full devotion a universe apparently imperfect and irresponsive, and a Ruling Principle which so many men have doubted or ignored.

The pessimist holds the view that sentient existence has been a deplorable blunder in the scheme of things. The egotist at least *acts* upon the view that the universe has no moral coherence, and that "each for himself" is the only indisputable law. I am sanguine enough to think that the answer to the pessimist and the egotist has by our new knowledge been made complete. There remains, indeed, a difficulty of subtler type, but instinctive in generous souls. "The world," such an one may say, "is a mixed place, and I am plainly bound to do my best to improve it. But am I bound to feel — can any bribe of personal happiness justify me in feeling — *religious enthusiasm* for a universe in which even one being may have been summoned into a sentiency destined to inescapable pain?"

The answer to this ethical scruple must be a matter largely of faith. If indeed we knew that this earthly life was all, or (far worse) that it was followed for any one soul by endless pain, we could not without some moral jugglery ascribe perfection of both power and goodness to a personal or impersonal First Cause of such a doom. But if we believe that endless life exists for all, with infinite possibilities of human redress and of divine justification, then it seems right to assume that the universe is either already (in some inscrutable fashion) wholly good, or is at least in course of becoming so; since it may be becoming so in part through the very ardour of our own faith and hope.

I do but mention these initial difficulties; I shall not dwell on them here. I speak to men who have determined, whether at the bidding of instinct or of reason, that it is well to be religious; well to approach in self-devoted reverence an infinite Power and Love. Our desire is simply to find the least unworthy way of thinking of matters which inevitably transcend and baffle our finite thought.

And here, for the broad purpose of our present survey, we may divide the best religious emotion of the world in triple fashion; tracing three main streams of thought, — streams which on the whole run parallel, and which all rise, as I believe, from some source in the reality of things.

First, then, I place that obscure consensus of independent thinkers in many ages and countries which, to avoid any disputable title, I will here call simply the Religion of the Ancient Sage. Under that title (though Lao Tzŭ is hardly more than a name) it has been set forth to us in brief summary by the great sage and poet of our own time; and such words as Natural Religion, Pantheism, Platonism, Mysticism, do but express or intensify varying aspects of its main underlying conception. That conception is the coexistence and interpenetration of a real or spiritual with this material or phenomenal world; a belief driven home to many minds by experiences both more weighty and more concordant than the percipients themselves have always known. More weighty, I say, for they have implied the veritable nascency and operation of a "last and largest sense"; a faculty for apprehending, not God, indeed (for what finite faculty can apprehend the Infinite?), but at least some dim and scattered tokens and prefigurements of a true world of Life and Love. More *concordant* also; and this for a reason which till recently would have seemed a paradox. For the mutual corroboration of these signs and messages lies not only in their fundamental agreement up to a certain point, but in their inevitable divergence beyond it; — as they pass from things felt into things imagined; from actual experience into dogmatic creed.

The Religion of the Ancient Sage is of unknown antiquity. Of unknown antiquity also are various Oriental types of religion, culminating in historical times in the Religion of Buddha. For Buddhism all interpenetrating universes make the steps upon man's upward way; until deliverance from illusion leaves the spirit merged ineffably in the impersonal All. But the teaching of Buddha has lost touch with reality; it rests on no basis of observed or of reproducible fact.

On a basis of observed facts, on the other hand, Christianity, the youngest of the great types of religion, does assuredly rest. Assuredly those facts, so far as tradition has made them known to us, do tend to prove the superhuman character of its Founder, and His triumph over death; and thus the existence and influence of a spiritual world, where men's true citizenship lies. These ideas, by common consent, lay at the origin of the Faith. Since those first days, however, Christianity has been elaborated into codes of ethic and ritual adapted to Western civilisation; — has gained (some think) as a rule of life what it has lost as a simplicity of spirit.

From the unfettered standpoint of the Ancient Sage the deep concordance of these and other schemes of religious thought may well outweigh their formal oppositions. And yet I repeat that it is not from any mere welding of these schemes together, nor from any choice of the best points in existing syntheses, that the new synthesis for which I hope must be born. It must be born from new-dawning knowledge; and in that new knowledge I believe that each great form of religious thought will find its indispensable — I may almost say its predicted — development. Our race from its very infancy has stumbled along a guarded way; and now the first lessons of its early childhood reveal the root in reality of much that it has instinctively believed.

What I think I know, therefore, I am bound to tell; I must give the religious upshot of observation and experiment in such brief announcement as an audience like this [1] has a right to hear, even before our discoveries can be laid in full before the courts of science for definite approval.

The *religious upshot*, I repeat: — for I cannot here reproduce the mass of evidence which has been published in full elsewhere. Its general character is by this time widely known. Observation, experiment, inference, have led many inquirers, of whom I am one, to a belief in direct or telepathic intercommunication, not only between the minds of men still on earth, but between minds or spirits still on earth and spirits departed. Such a *discovery* opens the door also to *revelation*. By discovery and by revelation — by observation from without the veil, and by utterance from within — certain theses have been provisionally established with regard to such departed souls as we have been able to encounter. First and chiefly, I at least see ground to believe that their state is one of endless evolution in wisdom and in love. Their loves of earth persist; and most of all those highest loves which seek their outlet in adoration and worship. We do not find, indeed, that support is given by souls in bliss to any special scheme of terrene theology. Thereon they know less than we mortal men have often fancied that we knew. Yet from their step of vantage-ground in the Universe, at least, they see that it is good. I do not mean that they know either of an end or of an explanation of evil. Yet evil to them seems less a terrible than a slavish thing. It is embodied in no mighty Potentate; rather it forms an isolating mad-

---

[1] The Synthetic Society, before which these pages were first read as a paper in March 1899.

ness from which higher spirits strive to free the distorted soul. There needs no chastisement of fire; self-knowledge is man's punishment and his reward; self-knowledge, and the nearness or the aloofness of companion souls. For in that world love is actually self-preservation; the Communion of Saints not only adorns but constitutes the Life Everlasting. Nay, from the law of telepathy it follows that that communion is valid for us here and now. Even now the love of souls departed makes answer to our invocations. Even now our loving memory — love is itself a prayer — supports and strengthens those delivered spirits upon their upward way. No wonder; since we are to them but as fellow-travellers shrouded in a mist; "neither death, nor life, nor height, nor depth, nor any other creature," can bar us from the hearth-fire of the universe, or hide for more than a moment the inconceivable oneness of souls.

And is not this a fresh instalment, or a precursory adumbration, of that Truth into which the Paraclete should lead? Has any world-scheme yet been suggested so profoundly corroborative of the very core of the Christian revelation? Jesus Christ "brought life and immortality to light." By His appearance after bodily death He proved the deathlessness of the spirit. By His character and His teaching He testified to the Fatherhood of God. So far, then, as His unique message admitted of evidential support, it is here supported. So far as He promised things unprovable, that promise is here renewed.

I venture now on a bold saying; for I predict that, in consequence of the new evidence, all reasonable men, a century hence, will believe the Resurrection of Christ, whereas, in default of the new evidence, no reasonable men, a century hence, would have believed it. The ground of this forecast is plain enough. Our ever-growing recognition of the continuity, the uniformity of cosmic law has gradually made of the alleged *uniqueness* of any incident its almost inevitable refutation. Ever more clearly must our age of science realise that any relation between a material and a spiritual world cannot be an ethical or emotional relation alone; that it must needs be a great structural fact of the Universe, involving laws at least as persistent, as identical from age to age, as our known laws of Energy or of Motion. And especially as to that central claim, of the soul's life manifested after the body's death, it is plain that this can less and less be supported by remote tradition alone; that it must more and more be tested by modern experience and inquiry. Suppose, for instance, that we collect many such histories, recorded on first-hand evidence in our critical age; and suppose that all these narratives break down on analysis; that they can all be traced to hallucination, misdescription, and other persistent sources of error; — can we then expect reasonable men to believe that this marvellous phenomenon, always vanishing into nothingness when closely scrutinised in a modern English scene, must yet compel adoring credence when alleged to have occurred in an Oriental country, and in a remote and superstitious age? Had the results (in short) of "psychical research" been purely negative, would not Christian evidence — I do not say Christian *emotion*, but Christian *evidence* — have received an overwhelming blow?

As a matter of fact, — or, if you prefer the phrase, in my own personal opinion, — our research has led us to results of a quite different type. They have not been negative only, but largely positive. We have shown that amid much deception and self-deception, fraud and illusion, veritable manifestations do reach us from beyond the grave. The central claim of Christianity is thus confirmed, as never before. If our own friends, men like ourselves, can sometimes return to tell us of love and hope, a mightier Spirit may well have used the eternal laws with a more commanding power. There is nothing to hinder the reverent faith that, though we be all "the Children of the Most Highest," He came nearer than we, by some space by us immeasurable, to That which is infinitely far. There is nothing to hinder the devout conviction that He of His own act "took upon Him the form of a servant," and was made flesh for our salvation, foreseeing the earthly travail and the eternal crown. "Surely before this descent into generation," says Plotinus,[1] "we existed in the intelligible world; being other men than now we are, and some of us Gods; clear souls, and minds unmixed with all existence; parts of the Intelligible, nor severed thence; nor are we severed even now."

It is not thus to less of reverence that man is summoned, but to more. Let him keep hold of early sanctities; but let him remember also that once again "a great sheet has been let down out of heaven"; and lo! neither Buddha nor Plato is found common or unclean.

Nay, as to our own soul's future, when that first shock of death is past, it is in Buddhism that we find the more inspiring, the truer view. That Western conception of an instant and unchangeable bliss or woe — a bliss or woe determined largely by a man's beliefs, in this earthly ignorance, on matters which "the angels desire to look into" — is the bequest of a pre-Copernican era of speculative thought. In its Mahomedan travesty, we see the same scheme with outlines coarsened into grotesqueness; — we see it degrade the cosmic march and profluence into a manner of children's play.

[1] *Enn.* vi. 4, 14.

Meantime the immemorial musings of unnumbered men have dreamt of a consummation so far removed that he who gazed has scarcely known whether it were Nothingness or Deity. With profoundest fantasy, the East has pondered on the vastness of the world that now is, of the worlds that are to be. What rest or pasture for the mind in the seven days of Creation, the four rivers of Paradise, the stars "made also"? The farther East has reached blindly forth towards astronomical epochs, sidereal spaces, galactic congregations of inconceivable Being. Pressed by the incumbency of ancestral gods (as the Chinese legend tells us), it has "created by one sweep of the imagination a thousand Universes, to be the Buddha's realm."

The sacred tale of Buddha, developed from its earlier simplicity by the shaping stress of many generations, opens to us the whole range and majesty of human fate. "The destined Buddha has desired to be a Buddha through an almost unimaginable series of worlds." No soul need ever be without that hope. "The spirit-worlds are even now announcing the advent of future Buddhas, in epochs too remote for the computation of men." No obstacles without us can arrest our way. "The rocks that were thrown at Buddha were changed into flowers." Not our own worst misdoings need beget despair. "Buddha, too, had often been to hell for his sins." The vast complexity of the Sum of Things need not appal us. "Beneath the bottomless whirlpool of existences, behind the illusion of Form and Name," we, too, like Buddha, may discover and reveal "the perfection of the Eternal Law." Us, too, like Buddha, the cosmic welcome may await; as when "Earth itself and the laws of all worlds" trembled with joy "as Buddha attained the Supreme Intelligence, and entered into the Endless Calm."

I believe that some of those who once were near to us are already mounting swiftly upon this heavenly way. And when from that cloud encompassing of unforgetful souls some voice is heard, — as long ago, — there needs no heroism, no sanctity, to inspire the apostle's ἐπιθυμία εἰς τὸ ἀναλῦσαι, the desire to lift our anchor, and to sail out beyond the bar. What fitter summons for man than the wish to live in the memory of the highest soul that he has known, now risen higher; — to lift into an immortal security the yearning passion of his love? "As the soul hasteneth," says Plotinus,[1] "to the things that are above, she will ever forget the more; unless all her life on earth leave a memory of things done well. For even here may man do well, if he stand clear of the cares of earth. And he must stand clear of their memories too; so that one may rightly speak

[1] Enn. iv. 3, 27.

of a noble soul as forgetting those things that are behind. And the shade of Hêraklês, indeed, may talk of his own valour to the shades, but the true Hêraklês in the true world will deem all that of little worth; being transported into a more sacred place, and strenuously engaging, even above his strength, in those battles in which the wise engage." Can we men now on earth claim more of sustainment than lies in the incipient communion with those enfranchised souls? What day of hope, of exaltation, has dawned like this, since the message of Pentecost?

Yet a durable religious synthesis should do more than satisfy man's immediate aspiration. It should be in itself progressive and evolutionary; it should bear a promise of ever deeper holiness, to answer to the long ages of heightening wisdom during which our race may be destined to inhabit the earth. This condition has never yet been met. No scheme, indeed, could meet it which was not based upon recurrent and developing facts. To such facts we now appeal. We look, not backward to fading tradition, but onward to dawning experience. We hope that the intercourse, now at last consciously begun — although as through the mouth of babes and sucklings, and in confused and stammering speech — between discarnate and incarnate souls, may through long effort clarify into a directer communion, so that they shall teach us all they will.

Science, then, need be no longer fettered by the limitations of this planetary standpoint; nor ethics by the narrow experience of a single life. Evolution will no longer appear as a truncated process, an ever-arrested movement upon an unknown goal. Rather we may gain a glimpse of an ultimate incandescence where science and religion fuse in one; a cosmic evolution of Energy into Life, and of Life into Love, which is Joy. Love, which is Joy at once and Wisdom; — we can do no more than ring the changes on terms like these, whether we imagine the transfiguration and apotheosis of conquering souls, or the lower, but still sacred, destiny which may be some day possible for souls still tarrying here. We picture the perfected soul as the Buddha, the Saviour, the *aurai simplicis ignem*, dwelling on one or other aspect of that trinal conception of Wisdom, Love, and Joy. For souls not yet perfected but still held on earth I have foretold a growth in *holiness*. By this I mean no unreal opposition or forced divorcement of sacred and secular, of flesh and spirit. Rather I define holiness as the joy too high as yet for our enjoyment; the wisdom just beyond our learning; the rapture of love which we still strive to attain. Inevitably, as our link with other spirits strengthens, as the life of the organism pours more fully through the individual cell, we shall feel love more ardent, wider wisdom, higher joy; perceiving that this organic unity

of Soul, which forms the inward aspect of the telepathic law, is in itself
the Order of the Cosmos, the Summation of Things. And such devotion may find its flower in no vain self-martyrdom, no cloistered resigna-
tion, but rather in such pervading ecstasy as already the elect have known;
the Vision which dissolves for a moment the corporeal prison-house;
"the flight of the One to the One."

"So let the soul that is not upworthy of that vision contemplate the
Great Soul; freed from deceit and every witchery, and collected into calm.
Calmed be the body for her in that hour, and the tumult of the flesh;
ay, all that is about her, calm; calm be the earth, the sea, the air, and
let Heaven itself be still. Then let her feel how into that silent heaven
the Great Soul floweth in. . . . And so may man's soul be sure of Vision,
when suddenly she is filled with light; for this light is from Him and is
He; and then surely shall one know His presence when, like a god of
old time, He entered into the house of one that calleth Him, and maketh
it full of light." "And how," concludes Plotinus, "may this thing be
for us? Let all else go." [1]

These heights, I confess, are above the stature of my spirit. Yet
for each of us is a fit ingress into the Unseen; and for some lesser man
the memory of one vanished soul may be beatific as of old for Plotinus
the flooding immensity of Heaven. And albeit no historical religion
can persist as a logical halting-place upon the endless mounting way
— that way which leads unbroken from the first germ of love in the heart
to an inconceivable union with the Divine — yet many a creed in turn
may well be close inwrought and inwoven with our eternal hope. What
wonder, if in the soul's long battle, some Captain of our Salvation shall
sometimes seem to tower unrivalled and alone? — οἷος γὰρ ἐρύετο Ἴλιον Ἕκτωρ.
And yet in no single act or passion can that salvation stand; far hence,
beyond Orion and Andromeda, the cosmic process works and shall work
for ever through unbegotten souls. And even as it was not in truth the
great ghost of Hector only, but the whole nascent race of Rome, which
bore from the Trojan altar the hallowing fire, so is it not one Saviour
only, but the whole nascent race of man — nay, all the immeasurable
progeny and population of the heavens — which issues continually from
behind the veil of Being, and forth from the Sanctuary of the Universe
carries the ever-burning flame: *Aeternumque adytis effert penetralibus ignem.*

[1] *Enn.* v. 2-3. The World-Soul is *supra grammaticam;* and Plotinus sometimes
uses a personal, sometimes an impersonal, locution to express what is infinitely beyond
the conception of personality, as it is infinitely beyond any human conception whatsoever.

APPENDICES

TO

CHAPTER II

II. A. It is well known that a great variety of slight causes — hunger, fatigue, slight poisoning by impure air, a small degree of fever, etc. — are sometimes enough to produce a transient perturbation of personality of the most violent kind.   I give as an instance the following account of a feverish experience, sent to me by the late Robert Louis Stevenson, from Samoa, in 1892 (and published in *Proceedings* S.P.R., vol. ix. p. 9).   In Stevenson's paper on his own dreams, alluded to in Chapter III, we have one of the most striking examples known to me of that helpful and productive subliminal uprush which I have characterised as the mechanism of genius. It is therefore, interesting to observe how, under morbid conditions, this temperament of genius — this ready permeability of the psychical diaphragm — transforms what might in others be a mere vague and massive discomfort into a vivid though incoherent message from the subliminal storm and fire.   The result is a kind of supraliminal duality, the perception at the same time of two personalities — the one rational and moral, the other belonging to the stratum of dreams and nightmare.

Vailima Plantation, Upoho, Samoan Islands,
July 14th, 1892.

Dear Mr. Myers, — I am tempted to communicate to you some experiences of mine which seem to me (ignorant as I am) of a high psychological interest.

I had infamous bad health when I was a child and suffered much from night fears; but from the age of about thirteen until I was past thirty I did not know what it was to have a high fever or to wander in my mind. So that these experiences, when they were renewed, came upon me with entire freshness; and either I am a peculiar subject, or I was thus enabled to observe them with unusual closeness.

Experience A.   During an illness at Nice I lay awake a whole night in extreme pain.   From the beginning of the evening *one part of my mind* became possessed of a notion so grotesque and shapeless that it may best be described as a form of words.   I thought the pain was, or was con-

356

nected with, a wisp or coil of some sort; I knew not of what it consisted nor yet where it was, and cared not; only I thought, if the two ends were brought together, the pain would cease. Now all the time, with *another part of my mind*, which I venture to think was *myself*, I was fully alive to the absurdity of this idea, knew it to be a mark of impaired sanity, and was engaged with *my other self* in a perpetual conflict. *Myself* had nothing more at heart than to keep from my wife, who was nursing me, any hint of this ridiculous hallucination; the *other* was bound that she should be told of it and ordered to effect the cure. I believe it must have been well on in the morning before the fever (or *the other fellow*) triumphed, and I called my wife to my bedside, seized her savagely by the wrist, and looking on her with a face of fury, cried: "Why do you not put the two ends together and put me out of pain?"

Experience B. The other day in Sydney I was seized on a Saturday with a high fever. Early in the afternoon I began to repeat mechanically the sound usually written "mhn," caught myself in the act, instantly stopped it, and explained to my mother, who was in the room, my reasons for so doing. "That is the beginning of the mind to wander," I said, "and has to be resisted at the outset." I fell asleep and woke, and for the rest of the night repeated to myself mentally a nonsense word which I could not recall next morning. I had been reading the day before the life of Swift, and all night long one part of my mind (*the other fellow*) kept informing me that I was not repeating the word myself, but was only reading in a book that Swift had so repeated it in his last sickness. The temptation to communicate this nonsense was again strongly felt by *myself*, but was on this occasion triumphantly resisted, and my watcher heard from me all night nothing of Dean Swift or the word, nothing but what was rational and to the point. So much for the two consciousnesses when I can disentangle them; but there is a part of my thoughts that I have more difficulty in attributing. One part of my mind continually bid me remark the transrational felicity of the word, examined all the syllables, showed me that not one was in itself significant, and yet the whole expressed to a nicety the voluminous distress of one in a high fever and his annoyance at and recoil from the attentions of his nurses. It was probably the same part (and for a guess *the other fellow*) who bid me compare it with the nonsense words of Lewis Carroll as the invention of a lunatic with those of a sane man. But surely it was *myself* (and myself in a perfectly clear-headed state) that kept me trying all night to get the word by heart, on the ground that it would afterwards be useful in literature if I wanted to deal with mad folk. It must have been myself, I say, because *the other fellow* believed (or pretended to believe) he was reading the passage in a book where it could always be found again when wanted.

Experience C. The next night *the other fellow* had an explanation ready for my sufferings, of which I can only say that it had something to do with the navy, that it was sheer undiluted nonsense, had neither end nor beginning, and was insusceptible of being expressed in words. *Myself* knew this; yet I gave way, and my watcher was favoured with

some references to the navy.   Nor only that; *the other fellow* was annoyed
— or *I* was annoyed — on two inconsistent accounts: first, because he
had failed to make his meaning comprehensible; and second, because
the nurse displayed no interest.   *The other fellow* would have liked to
explain further; but *myself* was much hurt at having been got into this
false position, and would be led no further.

In cases A and C the illusion was amorphous.   I knew it to be so,
and yet succumbed to the temptation of trying to communicate it.   In
case B the idea was coherent, and I managed to hold my peace.   Both
consciousnesses, in other words, were less affected in case B, and both
more affected in cases A and C.   It is perhaps not always so: the illusion
might be coherent, even practical, and the rational authority of the mind
quite in abeyance.   Would not that be lunacy?

In case A I had an absolute knowledge that I was out of my mind,
and that there was no meaning in my words; these were the very facts
that I was anxious to conceal; and yet when I succumbed to the temptation of speaking my face was convulsed with anger, and I wrung my
watcher's wrist with cruelty.   Here is action, unnatural and uncharac-
teristic action, flowing from an idea in which I had no belief, and which
I had been concealing for hours as a plain mark of aberration.   Is it
not so with lunatics?

I have called the one person *myself*, and the other *the other fellow*.
It was myself who spoke and acted; the other fellow seemed to have no
control of the body or the tongue; he could only act through myself, on
whom he brought to bear a heavy strain, resisted in one case, triumphant
in the two others.   Yet I am tempted to think that I know the other
fellow; I am tempted to think he is the dreamer described in my Chapter
on Dreams to which you refer.   Here at least is a dream belonging to
the same period, but this time a pure dream, an illusion, I mean, that
disappeared with the return of the sense of sight, not one that persevered
during waking moments, and while I was able to speak and take my
medicine.   It occurred the day after case B and before case C.

Case D.   In the afternoon there sprang up a storm of wind with mon-
strous clouds of dust; my room looked on a steep hill of trees whose boughs
were all blowing in the same direction; the world seemed to pass by my
windows like a mill-race.   By this turmoil and movement I was confused,
but not distressed, and surprised not to be distressed; for even in good
health a high wind has often a painful influence on my nerves.   In the
midst of this I dozed off asleep.   I had just been reading Scott's "Life
of Dryden," and been struck with the fact that Dryden had translated
some of the Latin hymns, and had wondered that I had never remarked
them in his works.   As soon as I was asleep I dreamed a reason why
the sound of the wind and the sight of the flying dust had not distressed
me.   There was no wind, it seemed, no dust; it was only Dryden singing
his translated hymns in *one direction*, and all those who had blamed and
attacked him after the Revolution singing them in *another*.   This point
of the two directions is very singular and insane.   In part it meant that
Dryden was continuously flying past yet never passing my window in

the direction of the wind and dust, and all his detractors similarly flying past yet not passing towards the other side.   But it applied, besides this, both to the words and to the music in a manner wholly insusceptible of expression.

That was a dream; and yet how exactly it reproduces the method of *my other fellow* while I was awake.   Here is an explanation for a state of mind or body sought, and found, in a tissue of rabid, complicated, and inexpressible folly. — Yours very sincerely.

ROBERT LOUIS STEVENSON.

II. B.   A good example of the application of true scientific method to problems which doctors of the old school did not think worth their science is Dr. Janet's treatment of a singular problem which the mistakes of brutal ignorance turned in old times into a veritable scourge of our race. I speak of *demoniacal possession*, in which affliction Dr. Janet has shown himself a better than ecclesiastical exorcist.

I give here a typical case of pseudo-possession from *Névroses et Idées fixes* (vol. i. pp. 377–389): Achille, as Professor Janet calls him, was a timid and rather morbid young man, but he was married to a good wife, and nothing went specially wrong with him until his return from a business journey in 1890.   He then became sombre and taciturn — sometimes even seemed unable to speak — then took to his bed and lay murmuring incomprehensible words, and at last said farewell to his wife and children, and stretched himself out motionless for a couple of days, while his family waited for his last breath.

"Suddenly one morning, after two days of apparent death, Achille sat up in bed with his eyes wide open, and burst into a terrible laugh.   It was a convulsive laugh which shook all his limbs; an exaggerated laugh which twisted his mouth; a lugubrious, satanic laugh which went on for more than two hours.

"From this moment everything was changed.   Achille leapt from his bed and refused all attentions.   To every question he answered, 'There's nothing to be done! let's have some champagne; it's the end of the world!' Then he uttered piercing cries, 'They are burning me — they are cutting me to pieces!'"

After an agitated sleep, Achille woke up with the conviction that he was possessed with a devil.   And in fact his mouth now uttered blasphemies, his limbs were contorted, and he repeatedly made unsuccessful efforts at suicide.   Ultimately he was taken to the Salpêtrière, and placed under Professor Janet, who recognised at once the classic signs of possession.   The poor man kept protesting against the odious outrages on religion, which he attributed to a devil inside him, moving his tongue against his will. "Achille could say, like a celebrated victim of possession, Père Surin, 'It is as though I had two souls; one of which has been dispossessed of its body and the use of its organs, and is frantic at the sight of the other soul which has crept in.'"

It was by no means easy to get either at Achille or at his possessing devil. Attempts to hypnotise him failed, and any remonstrance was met with insult. But the wily psychologist was accustomed to such difficulties, and had resort to a plan too insidious for a common devil to suspect. He gently moved the hand of Achille in such a way as to suggest the act of writing, and having thus succeeded in starting automatic script, he got the devil thus to answer questions quietly put while the raving was going on as usual. "I will not believe in your power," said Professor Janet to the malignant intruder, "unless you give me a proof." "What proof?" "Raise the poor man's left arm without his knowing it." This was done — to the astonishment of poor Achille — and a series of suggestions followed, all of which the demon triumphantly and unsuspectingly carried out, to show his power. Then came the suggestion to which Professor Janet had been leading up. It was like getting the djinn into the bottle. "You cannot put Achille soundly to sleep in that arm-chair!" "Yes, I can!" No sooner said than done, and no sooner done than Achille was delivered from his tormentor — from his own tormenting self.

For there in that hypnotic sleep he was gently led on to tell all his story; and such stories, when told to a skilled and kindly auditor, are apt to come to an end in the very act of being told.

Achille had been living in a day-dream; it was a day-dream which had swollen to these nightmare proportions, and had, as it were, ousted his rational being; and in the deeper self-knowledge which the somnambulic state brings with it the dream and the interpretation thereof became present to his bewildered mind.

The fact was that on that fateful journey when Achille's troubles began he had committed an act of unfaithfulness to his wife. A gloomy anxiety to conceal this action prompted him to an increasing taciturnity, and morbid fancies as to his health grew on him until at last his day-dream led him to imagine himself as actually dead. "His two days' lethargy was but an episode, a chapter in the long dream."

What then was the natural next stage of the dream's development? "He dreamt that, now that he was dead indeed, the devil rose from the abyss and came to take him. The poor man, as in his somnambulic state he retraced the series of his dreams, remembered the precise instant when this lamentable event took place. It was about 11 A.M.: a dog barked in the court at the moment, incommoded, no doubt, by the smell of brimstone; flames filled the room; numbers of little fiends scourged the unhappy man, or drove nails into his eyes, and through the wounds in his body Satan entered in to take possession of head and heart."

From this point the pseudo-possession may be said to have begun. The fixed idea developed itself into sensory and motor automatisms — visions of devils, uncontrollable utterances, automatic script — ascribed by the automatist to the possessing devil within.

And now came the moment when the veracity, the utility, of this new type of psychological analysis was to be submitted to yet another test. From the point of view of the ordinary physician Achille's condition was almost hopeless. Physical treatment had failed, and death from exhaustion and misery seemed near at hand. Nor could any appeal have been effective which did not go to the hidden root of the evil, which did not lighten the load of morbid remorse from which the whole series of troubles had developed. Fortunately for Achille, he was in the hands of an unsurpassed minister to minds thus diseased. Professor Janet adopted his usual tactics — what he terms the *dissociation* and the gradual *substitution* of ideas. The incidents of the miserable memory were modified, were explained away, were slowly dissolved from the brooding brain, and the hallucinatory image of the offended wife was presented to the sufferer at what novelists call the psychological moment, with pardon in her eyes. "Such stuff as dreams are made of!" — but even by such means was Achille restored to physical and moral health; he leads now the life of normal man; he no longer "walketh in a vain shadow, and disquieteth himself in vain."

II. C.   I give here the case of Dr. Azam's often quoted patient, Félida X.[1] In this case the somnambulic life finally became the normal life; as the "second state," which appeared at first only in short, dreamlike accesses, gradually replaced the "first state," which finally recurred but for a few hours at long intervals.   But the point on which I wish to dwell is this: that Félida's second state was altogether *superior* to the first — physically superior, since the nervous pains which had troubled her from childhood dissappeared: and mentally superior, inasmuch as her morose, self-centred disposition was exchanged for a cheerful activity which enabled her to attend to her children and her shop much more effectively than when she was in the "état bête," as she called what was once the only

---

[1] For the fullest account of Félida, see *Hypnotisme, Double Conscience*, etc., par le Dr. Azam. Paris, 1887.

personality that she knew. In this case, then, which at the time Dr. Azam wrote — 1887 — was of nearly thirty years' standing, the spontaneous readjustment of nervous activities — the second state, no memory of which remained in the first state — resulted in an improvement profounder than could have been anticipated from any moral or medical treatment that we know. The case shows us how often the word "normal" means nothing more than "what happens to exist." For Félida's *normal* state was in fact her *morbid* state: and the new condition, which seemed at first a mere hysterical abnormality, brought her at last to a life of bodily and mental sanity which made her fully the equal of average women of her class.

A very complete account of the case, reproducing in full almost the whole of Dr. Azam's report, is given in Dr. A. Binet's *Altérations de la Personnalité* (pp. 6-20), and I briefly summarise this here: —

Félida was born at Bordeaux, in 1843, of healthy parents. Towards the age of thirteen years she began to exhibit symptoms of hysteria. When about fourteen and a half she used suddenly to feel a pain in her forehead, and then to fall into a profound sleep for some ten minutes, after which she woke spontaneously in her secondary condition. This lasted an hour or two; then the sleep came on again, and she awoke in her normal state. The change at first occurred every five or six days. As the hysterical symptoms increased, Dr. Azam was· called in to attend her in 1858.

His report of that time states that in the primary state she appears very intelligent and fairly well educated; of a melancholy disposition, talking little, very industrious; constantly thinking of her maladies and suffering acute pains in various parts of the body, especially the head — the *clou hystérique* being very marked; all her actions, ideas, and words perfectly rational. Almost every day what she calls her *crise* comes on spontaneously — often while she is sitting at her needlework — preceded by a brief interval of the profound sleep, from which no external stimulus can rouse her. On waking into the secondary state, she appears like an entirely different person, smiling and gay; she continues her work cheerfully or walks about briskly, no longer feeling all the pains she has just before been complaining of. She looks after her ordinary domestic duties, goes out, walks about the town, and pays calls; behaves in every way like an ordinary healthy girl.

In this condition she remembers perfectly all that has happened on previous occasions when she was in the same state, and also all the events of her normal life; whereas during her normal life she forgets absolutely the occurrences of the secondary state. She declares constantly that whatever state she is in at the moment is the normal one — her *raison* — while the other one is always her *crise*.

The change of character in the secondary state is strongly marked;

she becomes gay and vivacious — almost noisy; instead of being indifferent to everything, her sensibilities — both imaginative and emotional — become excessive. All her faculties appear more developed and more complete. The condition, in fact, is much superior to her ordinary one, as shown by the disappearance of her physical pains, and especially by the state of her memory.

She married early, and her *crises* became more frequent, though there were occasionally long intervals when they never came at all. But the secondary state, which in 1858 and 1859 only occupied about a tenth part of her life, gradually encroached more and more on the primary state, till the latter began to appear only at intervals and for a brief space of time.

In 1875 Dr. Azam, having for long lost sight of her, found her a mother of a family, keeping a shop. Now and then, but more and more rarely, occurred what she called her *crises* — really relapses into her *primary* condition. These were excessively inconvenient, since she forgot in them all the events of what was now her ordinary life, all the arrangements of her business, etc.; for instance, in going to a funeral, she had a *crise*, and consequently found it impossible to remember who the deceased person was. She had a great dread of these occurrences, though, by long practice, she had become very skilful at concealing them from every one but her husband; and the transition periods in passing from one state to another, during which she was completely unconscious, were now so short as to escape general notice. A peculiar feeling of pressure in the head warned her that the *crise* was coming, and she would then, for fear of making mistakes in her business, hastily write down whatever facts she most needed to keep in mind.

While the primary state lasted, she relapsed into the extreme melancholy and depression that characterised her early life, these being, in fact, now aggravated by her troublesome amnesia. She also lost her affection for her husband and children, and suffered from many hysterical pains and other symptoms which were much less acute in the secondary state. By 1887, however, the primary state only occurred every month or two, lasting only for a few hours at a time.

APPENDICES

TO

CHAPTER IV

IV. A. From *Proceedings* S.P.R., vol. viii. p. 389; related by Mr. Herbert J. Lewis, 19 Park Place, Cardiff.

In September 1880, I lost the landing order of a large steamer containing a cargo of iron ore, which had arrived in the port of Cardiff. She had to commence discharging at six o'clock the next morning. I received the landing order at four o'clock in the afternoon, and when I arrived at the office at six I found that I had lost it. During all the evening I was doing my utmost to find the officials of the Custom House to get a permit, as the loss was of the greatest importance, preventing the ship from discharging. I came home in a great degree of trouble about the matter, as I feared that I should lose my situation in consequence.

That night I dreamed that I saw the lost landing order lying in a crack in the wall under a desk in the Long Room of the Custom House.

At five the next morning I went down to the Custom House and got the keeper to get up and open it. I went to the spot of which I had dreamed, and found the paper in the very place. The ship was not ready to discharge at her proper time, and I went on board at seven and delivered the landing order, saving her from all delay.   HERBERT J. LEWIS.

I can certify to the truth of the above statement.

THOMAS LEWIS
(Herbert Lewis's father),
July 14th, 1884.   H. WALLIS.

[Mr. E. J. Newell, of the George and Abbotsford Hotel, Melrose, adds the following corroborative note: —]

August 14th, 1884.

I made some inquiries about Mr. Herbert Lewis's dream before I left Cardiff. He had been searching throughout the room in which the order was found. His theory as to how the order got in the place in which it was found, is that it was probably put there by some one (perhaps with malicious intent), as he does not see how it could have fallen so.

The fact that Mr. H. Lewis is exceedingly short-sighted adds to the probability of the thing which you suggest, that the dream was simply an unconscious act of memory in sleep.   On the other hand he does not believe it was there when he searched.   E. J. NEWELL.

Can there have been a momentary unnoticed spasm of the ciliary muscle, with the result of extending the range of vision?   It may suffice here to quote — that my suggestion may not seem too fantastic — a few lines from a personal observation of a somnambule by Dr. Dufay.[1]

"It is eight o'clock: several workwomen are busy around a table, on which a lamp is placed.   Mdlle. R. L. directs and shares in the work, chatting cheerfully meantime.   Suddenly a noise is heard; it is her head which has fallen sharply on the edge of the table.   This is the beginning of the access.   She picks herself up in a few seconds, pulls off her spectacles with disgust, and continues the work which she had begun; — having no further need of the concave glasses which a pronounced myopia renders needful to her in ordinary life; — and even placing herself so that her work is less exposed to the light of the lamp."   Similarly, and yet differently, Miss Goodrich-Freer has had an experience where the title of a book quite unknown to her, which she had vainly endeavoured to read where it lay at some distance from her, presented itself in the crystal.   In such a case we can hardly suppose any such spasmodic alteration in ocular conditions as may perhaps occur in trance.

IV. B.   This case was recorded by Professor W. Romaine Newbold of the University of Pennsylvania, in a paper entitled " Subconscious Reasoning," in the *Proceedings* S.P.R., vol. xii. pp. 11–20.

I give the following extracts: —

For [these] cases I am indebted to another friend and colleague, Dr. Herman V. Hilprecht, Professor of Assyrian in the University of Pennsylvania.   Both occurred in his own experience, and I write the account of the first from notes made by me upon his narrative.

During the winter, 1882—1883, he was working with Professor Friedrich Delitzsch, and was preparing to publish, as his dissertation, a text, transliteration, and translation of a stone of Nebuchadnezzar I. with notes. He accepted at that time the explanation given by Professor Delitzsch of the name Nebuchadnezzar — "*Nabû-kudûrru-usur*," "Nebo protect my mason's pad, or mortar board," *i.e.*, "my work as a builder."   One night, after working late, he went to bed about two o'clock in the morning. After a somewhat restless sleep, he awoke with his mind full of the thought that the name should be translated "Nebo protect my boundary."   He had a dim consciousness of having been working at his table in a dream, but could never recall the details of the process by which he arrived at this conclusion.   Reflecting upon it when awake, however, he at once saw that *kudûrru*, "boundary," could be derived from the verb *kadâru*,

[1] *Revue Scientifique*, 3ᵉ série, xxxii. p. 167.

to enclose. Shortly afterwards he published this translation in his dissertation, and it has since been universally adopted.

I quote this experience, in itself of a familiar type, on account of its interest when viewed in connection with the more curious dream next to be related. I was told of the latter shortly after it happened, and here translate an account written in German by Professor Hilprecht, August 8th, 1893, before the more complete confirmation was received.

"One Saturday evening, about the middle of March, 1893, I had been wearying myself, as I had done so often in the weeks preceding, in the vain attempt to decipher two small fragments of agate which were supposed to belong to the finger-rings of some Babylonian. The labour was much increased by the fact that the fragments presented remnants only of characters and lines, that dozens of similar small fragments had been found in the ruins of the temple of Bel at Nippur with which nothing could be done, that in this case furthermore I had never had the originals before me, but only a hasty sketch made by one of the members of the expedition sent by the University of Pennsylvania to Babylonia. I could not say more than that the fragments, taking into consideration the place in which they were found and the peculiar characteristics of the cuneiform characters preserved upon them, sprang from the Cassite period of Babylonian history (circa 1700–1140 B.C.); moreover, as the first character of the third line of the first fragment seemed to be KU, I ascribed this fragment, with an interrogation point, to King Kurigalzu, while I placed the other fragment, as unclassifiable, with other Cassite fragments upon a page of my book where I published the unclassifiable fragments. The proofs already lay before me, but I was far from satisfied. The whole problem passed yet again through my mind that March evening before I placed my mark of approval under the last correction in the book. Even then I had come to no conclusion. About midnight, weary and exhausted, I went to bed and was soon in deep sleep. Then I dreamed the following remarkable dream. A tall, thin priest of the old pre-Christian Nippur, about forty years of age and clad in a simple abba, led me to the treasure chamber of the temple, on its south-east side. He went with me into a small, low-ceiled room without windows, in which there was a large wooden chest, while scraps of agate and lapis-lazuli lay scattered on the floor. Here he addressed me as follows: 'The two fragments which you have published separately upon pages 22 and 26, belong together, are not finger-rings, and their history is as follows. King Kurigalzu (circa 1300 B.C.) once sent to the temple of Bel, among other articles of agate and lapis lazuli, an inscribed votive cylinder of agate. Then we priests suddenly received the command to make for the statue of the god Ninib a pair of earrings of agate. We were in great dismay, since there was no agate as raw material at hand. In order to execute the command there was nothing for us to do but cut the votive cylinder into three parts, thus making three rings, each of which contained a portion of the original inscription. The first two rings served as earrings for the statue of the god; the two fragments which have given you so much trouble are portions of them. If you will put the two together you will have confirmation of my words. But the third ring you have not yet found in the course of your excavations, and you never will find it.' With this, the priest disappeared. I awoke at once and immediately told my wife the dream that I might not forget it. Next morning — Sunday — I examined the fragments once more in the light of these disclosures, and to my astonishment found all the details of the dream precisely verified in so far as the means of verification were in my hands. The original inscription on the votive cylinder read: 'To the god Ninib, son of Bel, his lord, has Kurigalzu, pontifex of Bel, presented this.'

"The problem was thus at last solved. I stated in the preface that I had unfortunately discovered too late that the two fragments belonged together, made the corresponding changes in the Table of Contents, pp. 50 and 52, and, it being not possible to transpose the fragments, as the plates were already made, I put in each plate a brief reference to the other. (Cf. Hilprecht, 'The Babylonian Expedition of the University of Pennsylvania,' Series A, Cuneiform Texts, Vol. I., Part 1, 'Old Babylonian Inscriptions, chiefly from Nippur.')   "H. V. HILPRECHT."

Upon the priest's statement that the fragments were those of a votive cylinder, Professor Hilprecht makes the following comment: —

"There are not many of these votive cylinders. I had seen, all told, up to that evening, not more than two. They very much resemble the so-called seal cylinders, but usually have no pictorial representations upon them, and the inscription is not reversed, not being intended for use in sealing, but is written as it is read."

The following transliteration of the inscription, in the Sumerian language, will serve to give those of us who are unlearned in cuneiform languages an idea of the material which suggested the dream. The straight vertical lines represent the cuts by which the stone-cutter divided the original cylinder into three sections. The bracketed words are entirely lost, and have been supplied by analogy from the many similar inscriptions.

Line 1.	Dingir N	inib du	(mu)	To the god Ninib, child
" 2.	dingir	En-	(lil)	of the god Bel
" 3.	luga	l - a - ni	(ir)	his lord
" 4.	Ku-r	(i- galzu)		Kurigalzu
" 5.	pa-	(tesi dingir Enlil)		pontifex of the god Bel
" 6.	(in- na-	ba)		has presented it.

I translate also the following statement which Mrs. Hilprecht kindly made at my request.

"I was awakened from sleep by a sigh, immediately thereafter heard a spring from the bed, and at the same moment saw Professor Hilprecht hurrying into his study. Thence came the cry, 'It is so, it is so.' Grasping the situation, I followed him and satisfied myself in the midnight hour as to the outcome of his most interesting dream.[1]

                                    "J. C. HILPRECHT."

[1] An apparent discrepancy between Professor Hilprecht's account and that of Mrs. Hilprecht calls for explanation. Professor Hilprecht states that he verified his

At the time Professor Hilprecht told me of this curious dream, which was a few weeks after its occurrence, there remained a serious difficulty which he was not able to explain. According to the memoranda in our possession, the fragments were of different colours, and therefore could have scarcely belonged to the same object. The original fragments were in Constantinople, and it was with no little interest that I awaited Professor Hilprecht's return from the trip which he made thither in the summer of 1893. I translate again his own account of what he then ascertained.

"November 10th, 1895.

"In August 1893, I was sent by the Committee on the Babylonian Expedition to Constantinople, to catalogue and study the objects got from Nippur and preserved there in the Imperial Museum. It was to me a matter of the greatest interest to see for myself the objects which, according to my dream, belonged together, in order to satisfy myself that they had both originally been parts of the same votive cylinder. Halil Bey, the director of the museum, to whom I told my dream, and of whom I asked permission to see the objects, was so interested in the matter, that he at once opened all the cases of the Babylonian section, and requested me to search. Father Scheil, an Assyriologist from Paris, who had examined and arranged the articles excavated by us before me, had not recognised the fact that these fragments belonged together, and consequently I found one fragment in one case, and the other in a case far away from it. As soon as I found the fragments and put them together, the truth of the dream was demonstrated *ad oculos* — they had, in fact, once belonged to one and the same votive cylinder. As it had been originally of finely veined agate, the stone-cutter's saw had accidentally divided the object in such a way that the whitish vein of the stone appeared only upon the one fragment and the larger grey surface upon the other. Thus I was able to explain Dr. Peters's discordant description of the two fragments."

Professor Hilprecht is unable to say what language the old priest used in addressing him. He is quite certain that it was not Assyrian, and thinks it was either English or German.

There are two especial points of interest in this case, the character of the information conveyed, and the dramatic form in which it was put. The apparently novel points of information given were: —

1. That the fragments belonged together.
2. That they were fragments of a votive cylinder.
3. That the cylinder was presented by King Kurigalzu.
4. That it was dedicated to Ninib.
5. That it had been made into a pair of earrings.

dream on Sunday morning at the University; Mrs. Hilprecht that he verified it immediately upon awaking, in his library. Both statements are correct. He had a working copy in his library which he examined at once, but hurried to the University next morning to verify it by comparison with the authorised copy made from the originals. — W. R. N.

6. That the "treasure chamber" was located upon the south-east side of the temple.

A careful analysis reveals the fact that not one of these items was beyond the reach of the processes of associative reasoning which Professor Hilprecht daily employs. Among the possible associative consequents of the writing upon the one fragment, some of the associative consequents of the writing on the other were sub-consciously involved; the attraction of these identical elements brings the separate pieces into mental juxtaposition, precisely as the pieces of a "dissected map" find one another in thought. In waking life the dissimilarity of colour inhibited any tendency on the part of the associative processes to bring them together, but in sleep this difference of colour seems to have been forgotten — there being no mention made of it — and the assimilation took place. The second point is more curious, but is not inexplicable. For as soon as the fragments were brought into juxtaposition mentally, enough of the inscription became legible to suggest the original character of the object. This is true also of the third and fourth points. The source of the fifth is not so clear. Upon examining the originals, Professor Hilprecht felt convinced from the size of the hole still to be seen through the fragments that they could not have been used as finger-rings, and that they had been used as earrings, but the written description which he had before him at the time of his dream did not bring these points to view. Still, such earrings are by no means uncommon objects. Such a supposition might well have occurred to Professor Hilprecht in his waking state and, in view of the lack of positive confirmation, it would be rash to ascribe it to any supernormal power. The last point is most interesting. When he told me this story, Professor Hilprecht remembered that he had heard from Dr. John P. Peters, before he had the dream, of the discovery of a room in which were remnants of a wooden box, while the floor was strewn with fragments of agate and lapis-lazuli. The walls, of course, and ceiling have long since perished. The location, however, of the room he did not know, and suggested I should write to Dr. Peters and find out whether it was correctly given in his dream, and whether Dr. Peters had told him of it. Dr. Peters replied that the location given was correct, but, he adds, he told Professor Hilprecht all these facts as long ago as 1891, and thinks he provided him with a drawing of the room's relation to the temple. Of this Professor Hilprecht has no recollection. He thinks it probable that Dr. Peters told him orally of the location of the room, but feels sure that if any such plan was given him it would now be found among his papers. This is a point of no importance, however. We certainly cannot regard the location as ascertained by supernormal means.

IV. C. From *Proceedings* S.P.R., vol. xi. p. 505.

From Mr. Alfred Cooper, of 9 Henrietta Street, Cavendish Square, W.

[This account was orally confirmed by him to Mr. E. Gurney, June

6th, 1888. It is written by Mr. Cooper, but attested also by the Duchess of Hamilton.]

A fortnight before the death of the late Earl of L——, in 1882, I called upon the Duke of Hamilton, in Hill Street, to see him professionally. After I had finished seeing him we went into the drawing-room, where the Duchess was, and the Duke said to me, "Oh, Cooper; how is the Earl?"

The Duchess said, "What Earl?" and on my answering, "Lord L——," she replied, "That is very odd. I have had a most extraordinary vision. I went to bed, but after being in bed a short time, I was not exactly asleep, but thought I saw a scene as if from a play before me. The actors in it were Lord L——, in a chair, as if in a fit, with a man standing over him with a red beard. He was by the side of a bath, over which bath a red lamp was distinctly shown."

I then said, "I am attending Lord L—— at present; there is very little the matter with him; he is not going to die; he will be all right very soon."

Well, he got better for a week and was nearly well, but at the end of six or seven days after this I was called to see him suddenly. He had inflammation of both lungs.

I called in Sir William Jenner, but in six days he was a dead man. There were two male nurses attending on him; one had been taken ill. But when I saw the other the dream of the Duchess was exactly represented. He was standing near a bath over the Earl and, strange to say, his beard was red. There was the bath with the red lamp over it. It is rather rare to find a bath with a red lamp over it, and this brought the story to my mind.

The vision seen by the Duchess was told two weeks before the death of Lord L——. It is a most remarkable thing.

This account, written in 1888, has been revised by the [late] Duke of Manchester, father of the Duchess of Hamilton, who heard the vision from his daughter on the morning after she had seen it.

(Signed)　Mary Hamilton.
Alfred Cooper.

Her Grace had been reading and had just blown out the candle.
Her Grace has had many dreams which have come true years after.

Alfred Cooper.

[The Duchess only knew Lord L—— by sight, and had not heard that he was ill. She knew she was not asleep, for she opened her eyes to get rid of the vision and, shutting them, saw the same thing again.]

An independent and concordant account has been given to me (F. W. H. M.) orally by a gentleman to whom the Duchess related the dream on the morning after its occurrence.

IV. D. From *Phantasms of the Living*, vol. i. p. 383. The following account, which first appeared in a letter in the *Religio-Philosophical*

Journal, is from Dr. Bruce, of Micanopy, Fla., U.S.A. The case might be called "collective," but for the fact that one of the dreams, though vivid and alarming, was probably not so distinctive as was afterwards imagined, and, moreover, was possibly dreamt on the night *preceding* that on which the tragic event took place.

February 17th, 1884.

On Thursday, the 27th of December last, I returned from Gainesville (twelve miles from here) to my orange grove, near Micanopy. I have only a small plank house of three rooms at my grove, where I spend most of my time when the grove is being cultivated. There was no one in the house but myself at the time, and being somewhat fatigued with my ride, I retired to my bed very early, probably 6 o'clock; and, as I am frequently in the habit of doing, I lit my lamp on a stand by the bed for the purpose of reading. After reading a short time, I began to feel a little drowsy, put out the light, and soon fell asleep. Quite early in the night I was awakened. I could not have been asleep very long, I am sure. I felt as if I had been aroused intentionally, and at first thought some one was breaking into the house. I looked from where I lay into the other two rooms (the doors of both being open), and at once recognised where I was, and that there was no ground for the burglar theory; there being nothing in the house to make it worth a burglar's time to come after.

I then turned on my side to go to sleep again, and immediately felt a consciousness of a presence in the room, and, singular to state, it was not the consciousness of a live person, but of a spiritual presence. This may provoke a smile, but I can only tell you the facts as they occurred to me. I do not know how to better describe my sensations than by simply stating that I felt a consciousness of a spiritual presence. This may have been a part of the dream, for I felt as if I were dozing off again to sleep; but it was unlike any dream I ever had. I felt also at the same time a strong feeling of superstitious dread, as if something strange and fearful were about to happen. I was soon asleep again, or unconscious, at any rate, to my surroundings. Then I saw two men engaged in a slight scuffle: one fell fatally wounded — the other immediately disappeared. I did not see the gash in the wounded man's throat, but knew that his throat was cut. I did not recognise him, either, as my brother-in-law. I saw him lying with his hands under him, his head turned slightly to the left, his feet close together. I could, from the position in which I stood, see but a small portion of his face; his coat, collar, hair, or something partly obscured it. I looked at him the second time a little closer to see if I could make out who it was. I was aware it was some one I knew, but still could not recognise him. I turned, and then saw my wife sitting not far from him. She told me she could not leave until he was attended to. (I had got a letter a few days previously from my wife, telling me she would leave in a day or two, and was expecting every day a letter or telegram telling me when to meet her at the depôt.) My attention was struck by the surroundings of the dead man. He appeared to be lying on an elevated platform of some kind, surrounded by chairs, benches, and desks, reminding me somewhat of a schoolroom. Outside of the room in which he was lying was a crowd of people, mostly females, some of whom I thought I knew. Here my dream terminated. I awoke again about midnight; got up and went to the door to see if there were any prospect of rain; returned to my bed again, and lay there until nearly daylight before falling asleep again. I thought of my dream, and was strongly impressed by it. All strange, superstitious feelings had passed off.

It was not until a week or ten days after this that I got a letter from my wife, giving me an account of her brother's death. Her letter, which was written the day after his death, was mis-sent. The account she gave me of his death tallies most remarkably with my dream. Her brother was with a wedding party at the depôt at Markham station, Fauquier Co., Va. He went into a store near by to see a young man who kept a bar-room near the depôt, and with whom he had some words. He turned and left the man, and walked out of the store. The bar-room keeper followed him out, and without further words deliberately cut his throat. It was a most brutal and unprovoked murder. My brother-in-law had on his overcoat, with the collar turned up. The knife went through the collar and clear to the bone. He was carried into the store and laid on the counter, near a desk and show case. He swooned from loss of blood soon after being cut. The cutting occurred early Thursday night, December 27th. He did not die, however, until almost daylight, Saturday morning.

I have not had a complete account of my sister-in-law's dream. She was visiting a young lady, a cousin, in Kentucky. They slept together Friday night, I think, the night of her brother's death. She dreamed of seeing a man with his throat cut, and awoke very much alarmed. She awoke her cousin, and they got up and lighted the lamp and sat up until daylight. That day she received a telegram announcing her brother's death.

I cannot give you any certain explanation of these dreams. I do not believe that they are due to ordinary causes, but to causes of which science does not at present take cognisance. WALTER BRUCE.

In reply to inquiries, Dr. Bruce says: —

July 9th, 1884.

I have never had another dream similar to the one related in the letter. I have at times had dreams that were vivid, or from some cause impressed themselves upon my mind for a time, such as any one would be likely to have. I cannot call to mind, though, any of special importance, or with any bearing upon the dream in question.

I did not mention the dream to any one before receiving the letter confirming it. I live in rather a retired place in the country, and if I saw any one during that time to whom I would care to relate the dream, it did not occur to me to do so.

You ask me how my wife knew of the circumstances of her brother's death. She was visiting her relatives in Va. at the time, and was present when her brother died.

The following account is from Dr. Bruce's sister-in-law, Mrs. Stubbing: —

March 28th, 1885.

Whilst in Kentucky on a visit in the year 1883, I had a dream, in which I saw two persons — one with his throat cut. I could not tell who it was, though I knew it was somebody that I knew, and as soon as I heard of my brother's death, I said at once that I knew it was he that I had seen murdered in my dream; and though I did not hear how my brother died, I told my cousin, whom I was staying with, that I knew he had been murdered. This dream took place on Thursday or Friday night, I do not remember which. I saw the exact spot where he was murdered, and just as it happened. ANNIE S. STUBBING.

The Thursday and Friday night mentioned in this account are December 26th and 27th [27th and 28th], 1883. It was upon the Thursday night my dream occurred. WALTER BRUCE.

In reply to questions, Mrs. Stubbing says: —

Yes, I saw one man cut the other. The wound was told to me to be just like what I had seen in my dream. I received a telegram announcing the death of my brother on Saturday morning. No, I never had any such dream as that before.

IV. E. I quote the following case from *Phantasms of the Living*, vol. i. p. 425. The account was written by Mrs. T—— in 1883.

On November 18th, 1863, I was living near Adelaide, and not long recovered from a severe illness at the birth of an infant, who was then five months old. My husband had also suffered from neuralgia, and had gone to stay with friends at the seaside for the benefit of bathing. One night during his absence the child woke me about midnight; having hushed him off to sleep, I said, "Now, sir, I hope you will let me rest!" I lay down, and instantly became conscious of two figures standing at the door of my room. One, M. N. (these are not the real initials), whom I recognised at once, was that of a former lover, whose misconduct and neglect had compelled me to renounce him. Of this I am sure, that if ever I saw him in my life, it was then. I was not in the least frightened; but said to myself, as it were, "You never used to wear that kind of waistcoat." The door close to which he stood was in a deep recess close to the fireplace, for there was no grate; we burnt logs only. In that recess stood a man in a tweed suit. I saw the whole figure distinctly, but not the face, and for this reason: on the edge of the mantelshelf always stood a morocco leather medicine chest, which concealed the face from me. (On this being stated to our friends, the Singletons, they asked to go into the room and judge for themselves. They expressed themselves satisfied that would be the case to any one on the bed where I was.) I had an impression that this other was a cousin of M. N.'s, who had been the means of leading him astray while in the North of England. I never saw him in my life; he died in India.

M. N. was in deep mourning; he had a look of unutterable sorrow upon his face, and was deadly pale. He never opened his lips, but I read his heart as if it were an open book, and it said, "My father is dead, and I have come into his property." I answered, "How much you have grown like your father!" Then in a moment, *without appearing to walk*, he stood at the foot of the child's cot, and I saw *distinctly* the blueness of his eyes as he gazed on my boy, and then raised them to Heaven as if in prayer.

All vanished. I looked round and remarked a trivial circumstance, viz., that the brass handles of my chest of drawers had been rubbed very bright. Not till then was I conscious of having seen a spirit, but a feeling of awe (not fear) came over me, and I prayed to be kept from harm, although there was no reason to dread it. I slept tranquilly, and in the morning I went across to the parsonage and told the clergyman's wife what I had seen. She, of course, thought it was merely a dream. But no — if it were a dream should I not have seen him *as I had known him*, a young man of twenty-two, without beard or whiskers? But there was all the difference that sixteen years would make in a man's aspect.

On Saturday my husband returned, and my brother having ridden out to see us on Sunday afternoon, I told them both my vision as we sat together on the verandah. They treated it so lightly that I determined to write it down in my diary and see if the news were verified. And from that diary I am now quoting. Also I mentioned it to at least twelve or fourteen other people, and bid them await the result.

And surely enough, at the end of several weeks, my sister-in-law wrote that M. N.'s father died at C—— Common on November 18th, 1863, which exactly tallied with the date of the vision. He left £45,000 to be divided between his son and daughter, but the son has never been found.

Many people in Adelaide heard the story before the confirmation came, and I wrote and told M. N.'s mother. She was much distressed about it, fearing he was unhappy. She is now dead. My husband was profoundly struck when he saw my diary corresponding *exactly* to the news in the letter I had that moment received in his presence.

Gurney adds the following note: —

Mr. T. has confirmed to us the accuracy of this narrative, and Mrs. T. has shown to one of us a memorandum of the appearance of two figures, under date November 18th, in her diary of the year 1863, and a newspaper obituary confirms this as the date of the death. We learn from a gentleman who is a near relative of M. N.'s, that M. N., though long lost sight of, was afterwards heard of, and outlived his father.

I should not now take it for granted (as we did at the time when *Phantasms of the Living* was compiled) that the agent here "can apparently only have been the dying man." I think it possible, in the light of our now somewhat fuller knowledge, that M. N.'s spirit was aware of his father's death, — even though possibly M. N.'s supraliminal self may not have heard of it; — so that the invading presence in this case may have been the discarded lover himself, — dreaming on his own account at a distance from Mrs. T. The second figure I regard as having been an object in M. N.'s dream; — symbolical of his own alienation from Mrs. T. All this sounds fanciful; but I may remark here (as often elsewhere), that I think that we gain little by attempting to enforce our own ideas of simplicity upon narratives of this bizarre type.

IV. F.   From *Proceedings* S.P.R., vol. vi. p. 341.

Communicated by Fräulein Schneller, sister-in-law of the percipient, and known to F. W. H. M., January 1890.

DOBER UND PAUSE, SCHLESIEN, *December 12th*, 1889.

About a year ago there died in a neighbouring village a brewer called Wünscher, with whom I stood in friendly relations. His death ensued after a short illness, and as I seldom had an opportunity of visiting him, I knew nothing of his illness nor of his death. On the day of his death I went to bed at nine o'clock, tired with the labours which my calling as a farmer demands of me. Here I must observe that my diet is of a frugal kind; beer and wine are rare things in my house, and water, as usual, had been my drink that night. Being of a very healthy constitution, I fell asleep as soon as I lay down. In my dream I heard the deceased call out with a loud voice, "Boy, make haste and give me my boots." This awoke me, and I noticed that, for the sake of our child, my wife had left the light burning. I pondered with pleasure over my dream, thinking in my mind how Wünscher, who was a good-natured, humorous man, would laugh when I told him of this dream. Still thinking on it, I hear Wünscher's voice scolding outside, just under my window. I sit up in my bed at once and listen, but cannot understand his words. What can the brewer want? I thought, and I know for certain that I was much vexed with him, that he should make a disturbance in the night, as I felt convinced that his affairs might surely have waited till the morrow. Suddenly he comes into the room from behind the linen press, steps with long strides past the bed of my wife and the child's bed; wildly gesticulating with his arms all the time, as his habit was, he called out, "What do you say to this, Herr Oberamtmann? This afternoon at five o'clock I have died." Startled by this information, I exclaim, "Oh, that is not true!" He replied: "Truly, as I tell you; and, what do you think? They want to bury me already on Tuesday afternoon at two o'clock," accentuating his assertions all the while by his gesticulations. During this long speech of my visitor I examined myself as to whether I was really awake and not dreaming.

I asked myself: Is this a hallucination? Is my mind in full possession of its faculties? Yes, there is the light, there the jug, this is the mirror, and this the brewer; and I came to the conclusion: I am awake. Then the thought occurred to me, What will my wife think if she awakes and sees the brewer in our bedroom? In this fear of her waking up I turn round to my wife, and to my great relief I see from her face, which is turned towards me, that she is still asleep; but she looks very pale. I say to the brewer, "Herr Wünscher, we will speak softly, so that my wife may not wake up, it would be very disagreeable to her to find you here." To which Wünscher answered in a lower and calmer tone: "Don't be afraid, I will do no harm to your wife." Things do happen indeed for which we find no explanation — I thought to myself, and said to Wünscher: "If this be true, that you have died, I am sincerely sorry for it; I will look after your children." Wünscher stepped towards me, stretched out his arms and moved his lips as though he would embrace me; therefore I said in a threatening tone, and looking steadfastly at him with a frowning brow: "Don't come so near, it is disagreeable to me," and lifted my right arm to ward him off, but before my arm reached him the apparition had vanished. My first look was to my wife to see if she were still asleep. She was. I got up and looked at my watch, it was seven minutes past twelve. My wife woke up and asked me: "To whom did you speak so loud just now?" "Have you understood anything?" I said. "No," she answered, and went to sleep again.

I impart this experience to the Society for Psychical Research, in the belief that it may serve as a new proof for the real existence of telepathy. I must further remark that the brewer *had* died that afternoon at five o'clock, and was buried on the following Tuesday at two. — With great respect,   KARL DIGNOWITY
(Landed Proprietor).

The usual time for burial in Germany, adds Fräulein Schneller, is three days after death. This time may be prolonged, however, on application. There are no special *hours* fixed.

In conversation Fräulein S. described her brother-in-law as a man of strong practical sense and of extremely active habits.

We have received the "Sterbeurkunde" from the "Standesbeamte" Siegismund, Kreis Sagan, certifying that Karl Wünscher died Saturday, September 15th, 1888, at 4.30 P.M., and was buried Tuesday, September 18th, 1888, at 2 P.M.

Herr Dignowity writes again, January 18th, 1890: —

Frau Wünscher told me that the time of the burial was settled in the death-room immediately after Wünscher's death, because relations at a distance had to be summoned by telegram. Wünscher had suffered from inflammation of the lungs, which ended in spasm of the heart. During his illness his thoughts had been much occupied with me, and he often wondered what I should say if I knew how ill he was.

Finally, Frau Dignowity (born Schneller) writes from Pause, January 18th, 1890: —

I confirm that my husband told me on the morning of September 16th, 1888, that the brewer Wünscher had given him intimation of his death.

APPENDICES

TO

CHAPTER V

V. A.[1] The principal inorganic objects alleged to have elicited novel sensations are running water, metals, crystals and magnets; — including under this last heading the magnetism of the earth, as claimed to be felt differently by sleepers according as they lie in the north-south or in the east-west positions.

(1) The faculty of finding *running water* has the interest of being the first subliminal faculty which has been so habitually utilised for public ends as to form for its possessors a recognised and lucrative occupation.

An exhaustive and impartial survey of the existing evidence for the faculty of "dowsing" is given in Professor W. F. Barrett's two articles "On the so-called Divining Rod" in the *Proceedings* S.P.R., vol. xiii. pp. 2-282, and vol. xv. pp. 130-383.

From this it seems clear that this power of discovery is genuine, and is not dependent on the dowser's conscious knowledge or observation. It forms a subliminal uprush; but whether it is akin to *genius*, as being a subconscious manipulation of facts accessible through normal sensory channels, or to *heteræsthesia* (as resting on a specific sensibility to the proximity of running water), is a question which will be variously decided in each special case. The dowser, I should add, is not hypnotised before he finds the water. But (as Professor Barrett has shown) he is often thrown, presumably by self-suggestion, into a state much resembling light hypnotic trance. The perceptivity (we may say) of central organs, in an unfamiliar direction, is stimulated by concentrated attention, involving a certain disturbance or abeyance of perceptivity in other directions.

(2) I next take the case of metallæsthesia, — that alleged reaction to special metals which has often been asserted both in hypnotic and in hysterical cases. As a definite instance I will take the statement made by

[1] This appendix has been greatly abridged.

certain physicians attending Louis Vivé,[1] that while they supported him during a hysterical attack a gold ring on the finger of one of them touched him for some time and left a red mark, as of a burn, of whose origin the patient knew nothing. It is further alleged — and this is a quite separate point, although often confused with the first — that gold is distinguished by some subjects under conditions where no degree of sensitiveness to weight or temperature could have shown them that gold was near.

Now, as to the first point, e.g. the Louis Vivé incident, I can readily believe that the touch of gold, unknown to the subject's supraliminal consciousness, may produce a redness, subsequent pain, etc. All that is needed for this is a capricious self-suggestion, like any other hysterical idea. This self-suggestion might remain completely unknown to the waking self, which might be puzzled as to the cause of the redness and pain. The second claim, however, involves much more than this. If gold is recognised through a covering, for instance, or heated to the same point as other metals, so that no sensation of weight or temperature can help observation, this might possibly be by virtue of some sensibility more resembling the attraction of low organisms to specific substances whose chemical action on them we cannot determine, or to particular rays in the spectrum. I am not convinced that this has yet been proved; but I should not regard it as a priori impossible.

Medicamentous substances have also been claimed by many different hypnotists as exerting from a little distance, or when in sealed tubes, specific influences on patients. The phenomenon is of the same nature as the alleged specific influences of metals, — all being very possibly explicable as the mere freak of self-suggestion.

(3) Considering in the next place the alleged sensibility of certain persons to crystals and magnets, — known to be absolutely inert in relation to ordinary men, — we should note the alleged connection between the perception of magnets and that of running water.

Some experiments intended to test the reality of the "magnetic sense," and especially of the so-called "magnetic light" — luminous appearances described by Baron Reichenbach as being seen by his sensitives in the neighbourhood of magnets — were carried out by a Committee of the S.P.R., in 1883. After careful and repeated trials with forty-five "subjects" of both sexes and of ages between sixteen and sixty, only three of these professed to see luminous appearances.

The value of these experiments as evidence of a magnetic sense of

[1] See *Annales Médico-Psychologiques*, 1882, p. 75, and Dr. Berjon, *La grande Hystérie chez l'Homme*, Paris, 1886.

course depends primarily on whether the subjects had any means, direct or indirect, of knowing when the current was made or broken. The precautions taken to avoid this and the other conditions of the experiments are described in detail in the report of them in the *Proceedings* S.P.R., vol. i. pp. 230–37. See also a further note by the Chairman of the Committee, Professor W. F. Barrett, vol. ii. pp. 56–60.

(4) And next as to the heteræsthesiæ alleged to be evoked by dead organic substances, or by living organisms. We may begin by observing that some of our senses, at any rate, form the subjective expression of certain chemical reactions. But many kinds of chemical reactions go on in us besides those which, for example, form the basis of our sense of taste. And some persons are much more affected than others by certain special reactions, which from a purely chemical point of view may or may not be precisely the same for all. Some persons have a specific sensibility to certain foods, or to certain drugs; — the presence of which their stomach detects, and to which it responds with extraordinary delicacy. Now, if it were an important object to discover the presence of a certain drug, such a sensibility would be regarded as a precious gift, and the discovery might be quite as valuable when made by the stomach as it would have been if made by the nose. These are nascent heteræsthesiæ, which, however, are not fostered either by natural selection or by human care.

Of similar type are the specific sensibilities to the presence of certain plants or animals, — familiar in certain cases of "rose-asthma," "horse-asthma," and discomfort felt if a cat is in the room. These feelings have many causes. At one end there is ordinary mechanical irritation by solid particles. At the other end of the scale there is, of course, mere self-suggestion. But between the two there seems to be a kind of sensibility which is not purely self-suggestive, and not exactly olfactory, but resembles rather the instincts by which insects or other animals discern each other's neighbourhood.

(5) It is perhaps through some such power of discrimination that effects are produced on sensitive subjects by "mesmerised objects," — assuming, of course, that sufficient care has been taken to avoid their discovering by ordinary means that the objects have been specially manipulated in any way. See some experiments recorded in the *Proceedings* S.P.R., vol. i. pp. 260–262, and a description of Esdaile's experiments with mesmerised water in vol. iii. p. 409; also cases in the *Zoist*, *e.g.* vol. v. p. 129, and vol. v. p. 99.

(6) And now I pass on to medical clairvoyance, or the power of

diagnosing the present or past state of a living organism either from actual contact or even in the absence of the invalid, and from contact with some object which he has himself touched.

The early mesmerists, *e.g.* Puységur, Pététin, Despine, and Teste, all had the utmost faith in the faculty of their subjects to see their own disease and prescribe the right remedy. The same attitude of mind can be traced all through the *Zoist*. Fahnestock was perhaps the first to point out the ambiguity of this alleged introvision. "It is well known to me," he says, "that when a resolution is taken, a belief cherished, or a determination formed by persons while in the somnambulic state, that, when they awake, although they may know nothing about it or relative to it, they always do what has been so resolved or determined upon at the time appointed or specified" (*Statuvolism*, p. 203), and he quotes experiments to prove his point. With the knowledge we now possess of the extraordinary power of self-suggestion in producing all kinds of bodily symptoms, it is obvious that these cases cannot be adduced as evidence of anything more. A typical instance of one of these early observations is to be found in the *Zoist*, vol. x. p. 347. See also Puységur, *Recherches sur l'Homme dans le Somnambulisme* (Paris, 1811), pp. 140 *et seq.* and 214 *et seq.*; Pététin, *Electricité Animale* (Paris, 1808); Despine, *Observations de Médecine Pratique* (1838) — "Estelle nous a indiqué tous les soirs, dans sa crise, ce qu'il y avait à faire pour le lendemain, tant pour le régime alimentaire que pour les moyens médicamentaires" (p. 38).

V. B. Some of the most striking cases of moral reforms produced by hypnotic suggestion are those recorded by Dr. Auguste Voisin. For instance: —

In the summer of 1884, there was at the Salpêtrière a young woman of a deplorable type.[1] Jeanne Sch—— was a criminal lunatic, filthy in habits, violent in demeanour, and with a lifelong history of impurity and theft. M. Voisin, who was one of the physicians on the staff, undertook to hypnotise her on May 31st, at a time when she could only be kept quiet by the strait jacket and *bonnet d'irrigation*, or perpetual cold douche to the head. She would not — indeed, she could not — look steadily at the operator, but raved and spat at him. M. Voisin kept his face close to hers, and followed her eyes wherever she moved them. In about ten minutes a stertorous sleep ensued, and in five minutes more she passed into a sleep-waking state, and began to talk incoherently. The process was repeated on many days, and gradually she became sane when in the trance, though she still raved when awake. Gradually, too, she became able to obey in waking hours commands impressed on her in

[1] *Annales Médico-Psychologiques*, 1884, vol. ii. p. 289 *seqq.*

the trance — first trivial orders (to sweep the room and so forth), then orders involving a marked change of behaviour. Nay more; in the hypnotic state she voluntarily expressed repentance for her past life, made a confession which involved more evil than the police were cognisant of (though it agreed with facts otherwise known), and finally of her own impulse made good resolves for the future. Two years later, M. Voisin wrote to me (July 31st, 1886) that she was then a nurse in a Paris hospital, and that her conduct was irreproachable. It appeared, then, that this poor woman, whose history since the age of thirteen had been one of reckless folly and vice, had become capable of the steady, self-controlled work of a nurse at a hospital, the reformed character having first manifested itself in the hypnotic state, partly in obedience to suggestion, and partly as the natural result of the tranquillisation of morbid passions.

M. Dufour, the medical head of another asylum,[1] has adopted hypnotic suggestion as a regular element in his treatment. "Dès à présent," he says, "notre opinion est faite: sans crainte de nous tromper, nous affirmons que l'hypnotisme peut rendre service dans le traitement des maladies mentales." As was to be expected, he finds that only a small proportion of lunatics are hypnotisable; but the effect produced on these, whether by entrancement or suggestion, is uniformly good. His best subject is a depraved young man, who after many convictions for crimes (including attempted murder) has become a violent lunatic. "T.," says Dr. Dufour, "a été un assez mauvais sujet. Nous n'avons plus à parler au présent, tellement ses sentiments moraux ont été améliorés par l'hypnotisme." This change and amelioration of character (over and above the simple recovery of sanity) has been a marked feature in some of Dr. Voisin's cases as well.

See also a case given by Dr. Voisin in the *Revue de l'Hypnotisme*, vol. iii., 1889, p. 130.

V. C. The subject of these experiments in telepathic hypnotisation was Professor Pierre Janet's well-known subject, Madame B. The experiments were carried out with her at Havre, by Professer Janet and Dr. Gibert, a leading physician there, and described in the *Bulletins de la Société de Psychologie Physiologique*, Tome I., p. 24, and in the *Revue Philosophique*, August 1886.

I give the following extract from my own notes of experiments, April 20th to 24th, 1886, taken at the time in conjunction with Dr. A. T. Myers, and forming the bulk of a paper presented to the Société de Psychologie Physiologique on May 24th (also published in *Proceedings* S.P.R., vol. iv. pp. 131-37.

[1] Dr. E. Dufour, médecin en chef de l'asile Saint-Robert (Isère). See *Annales Médico-Psychologiques*, September 1886, p. 238, and *Contribution à l'étude de l'hypnotisme*, par le Dr. Dufour, Grenoble, 1887.

In the evening (22nd) we all dined at M. Gibert's, and in the evening M. Gibert made another attempt to put her to sleep at a distance from his house in the Rue Séry — she being at the Pavillon, Rue de la Ferme — and to bring her to his house by an effort of will. At 8.55 he retired to his study, and MM. Ochorowicz, Marillier, Janet, and A. T. Myers went to the Pavillon, and waited outside in the street, out of sight of the house. At 9.22 Dr. Myers observed Madame B. coming half-way out of the garden-gate, and again retreating. Those who saw her more closely observed that she was plainly in the somnambulic state, and was wandering about and muttering. At 9.25 she came out (with eyes persistently closed, so far as could be seen), walked quickly past MM. Janet and Marillier, without noticing them, and made for M. Gibert's house, though not by the usual or shortest route. (It appeared afterwards that the *bonne* had seen her go into the *salon* at 8.45, and issue thence asleep at 9.15; had not looked in between those times.[1]) She avoided lamp-posts, vehicles, etc., but crossed and recrossed the street repeatedly. No one went in front of her or spoke to her. After eight or ten minutes she grew much more uncertain in gait, and paused as though she would fall. Dr. Myers noted the moment in the Rue Faure; it was 9.35. At about 9.40 she grew bolder, and at 9.45 reached the street in front of M. Gibert's house. There she met him, but did not notice him, and walked into his house, where she rushed hurriedly from room to room on the ground-floor. M. Gibert had to take her hand before she recognised him. She then grew calm.

M. Gibert said that from 8.55 to 9.20 he thought intently about her, from 9.20 to 9.35 he thought more feebly; at 9.35 he gave the experiment up, and began to play billiards; but in a few minutes began to will her again. It appeared that his visit to the billiard-room had coincided with her hesitation and stumbling in the street. But this coincidence may of course have been accidental. . . .

Out of a series of twenty-five similar experiments nineteen were successful. The experiments were made at different times in the day and at varying intervals, in order to avoid the effects of expectancy in the subject.

[1] It was not unusual for her to sit in the *salon* in the evening, after the day's occupations were over.

APPENDICES

TO

CHAPTER VI

VI. A. This case is taken from *Phantasms of the Living*, vol. ii. p. 94, having been contributed by Colonel Bigge, of 2 Morpeth Terrace, S.W., who took the account out of a sealed envelope, in Gurney's presence, for the first time since it was written on the day of the occurrence.

An account of a circumstance which occurred to me when quartered at Templemore, Co. Tipperary, on 20th February 1847.

This afternoon, about 3 o'clock P.M., I was walking from my quarters towards the mess-room to put some letters into the letter-box, when I distinctly saw Lieut.-Colonel Reed, 70th Regiment, walking from the corner of the range of buildings occupied by the officers towards the mess-room door; and I saw him go into the passage. He was dressed in a brown shooting-jacket, with grey summer regulation tweed trousers, and had a fishing-rod and a landing-net in his hand. Although at the time I saw him he was about 15 or 20 yards from me, and although anxious to speak to him at the moment, I did not do so, but followed him into the passage and turned into the ante-room on the left-hand side, where I expected to find him. On opening the door, to my great surprise, he was not there; the only person in the room was Quartermaster Nolan, 70th Regiment, and I immediately asked him if he had seen the colonel, and he replied he had not; upon which I said, "I suppose he has gone upstairs," and I immediately left the room. Thinking he might have gone upstairs to one of the officers' rooms, I listened at the bottom of the stairs and then went up to the first landing-place; but not hearing anything I went downstairs again and tried to open the bedroom door, which is opposite to the ante-room, thinking he might have gone there; but I found the door locked, as it usually is in the middle of the day. I was very much surprised at not finding the colonel, and I walked into the barrack-yard and joined Lieutenant Caulfield, 66th Regiment, who was walking there; and I told the story to him, and particularly described the dress in which I had seen the colonel. We walked up and down the barrack-yard talking about it for about ten minutes, when, to my great surprise, never having kept my eye from the door leading to the mess-room (there is only one outlet from it), I saw the colonel walk into the barracks through the gate — which is in the opposite direction — accompanied by Ensign Willington, 70th

Regiment, in precisely the same dress in which I had seen him, and with a fishing-rod and a landing-net in his hand. Lieutenant Caulfield and I immediately walked to them, and we were joined by Lieut.-Colonel Goldie, 66th Regiment, and Captain Hartford, and I asked Colonel Reed if he had not gone into the mess-room about ten minutes before. He replied that he certainly had not, for that he had been out fishing for more than two hours at some ponds about a mile from the barracks, and that he had not been near the mess-room at all since the morning.

At the time I saw Colonel Reed going into the mess-room I was not aware that he had gone out fishing — a very unusual thing to do at this time of the year; neither had I seen him before in the dress I have described during that day. I had seen him in uniform in the morning at parade, but not afterwards at all until 3 o'clock — having been engaged in my room writing letters, and upon other business. My eyesight being very good, and the colonel's figure and general appearance somewhat remarkable, it is morally impossible that I could have mistaken any other person in the world for him. That I *did* see him I shall continue to believe until the last day of my existence.　　　　WILLIAM MATTHEW BIGGE,
Major, 70th Regiment.

[On July 17th, 1885, after Colonel Bigge had described the occurrence but before the account was taken from the envelope and read, he dictated the following remarks to Gurney: —]

When Colonel R. got off the car about a couple of hours afterwards, Colonel Goldie and other officers said to me, "Why, that's the very dress you described." They had not known where he was or how he was engaged. The month, February, was a most unlikely one to be fishing in. Colonel Reed was much alarmed when told what I had seen.

The quartermaster, sitting at the window, would have been bound to see a real figure; he denied having seen anything.

I have never had the slightest hallucination of the senses on any other occasion.

[It will be seen that these recent remarks exhibit two slips of memory. It is quite unimportant whether Colonel Reed was seen walking in at the gate or getting off a car. But in making the interval between the vision and the return two hours instead of ten minutes, the later account unduly diminishes the force of the case. If there is any justification at all for the provisional hypothesis that the sense of impending arrival is a condition favourable for the emission of a telepathic influence, it is of importance that, at the time when the phantasmal form was seen, Colonel Reed was not busy with his fishing, but was rapidly approaching his destination; for thus the incident, at any rate, gets the benefit of analogy with other cases.]

VI. B.　From the *Journal* S.P.R., vol. vi. p. 129. The case is recorded by the Misses H. M. and L. Bourne.

Additional evidence of the hallucinatory character of the figure seen is afforded by the details having been more clearly discernible than those of a real figure at the same distance would have been, and also by the second appearance, where the percipient had the impression of being transported to a different scene.

Miss L. Bourne writes: —

On February 5th, 1887, my father, sister, and I went out hunting. About the middle of the day my sister and I decided to return home with the coachman, while my father went on. Somebody came and spoke to us, and delayed us for a few moments. As we were turning to go home, we distinctly saw my father, waving his hat to us and signing us to follow him. He was on the side of a small hill, and there was a dip between him and us. My sister, the coachman, and myself all recognised my father, and also the horse. The horse looked so dirty and shaken that the coachman remarked he thought there had been a nasty accident. As my father waved his hat I clearly saw the Lincoln and Bennett mark inside, though from the distance we were apart it ought to have been utterly impossible for me to have seen it. At the time I mentioned seeing the mark in the hat, though the strangeness of seeing it did not strike me till afterwards.

Fearing an accident, we hurried down the hill. From the nature of the ground we had to lose sight of my father, but it took us very few seconds to reach the place where we had seen him. When we got there, there was no sign of him anywhere, nor could we see anyone in sight at all. We rode about for some time looking for him, but could not see or hear anything of him. We all reached home within a quarter of an hour of each other. My father then told us he had never been in the field, nor near the field, in which we thought we saw him, the whole of that day. He had never waved to us, and had met with no accident.

My father was riding the only white horse that was out that day.

LOUISA BOURNE.
H. M. Bourne.

The second signature was added later, with the words: "This was written by my sister and me together."

Miss H. M. Bourne enclosed the above in the following letter to Mrs. Dent, to whom we are indebted for the case: —

WESTON SUBEDGE, BROADWAY, WORCESTERSHIRE,
May 21st, 1891.

MY DEAR MRS. DENT, — Louisa has asked me send you the enclosed account of the impression she, the coachman, and I had of seeing papa on Paddy in the hunting-field. It was on the 5th February 1887 it happened, and in March the same year, when I was out walking alone, I thought I saw papa and Paddy stop at a little plantation of his close to, and look at the wall, which had fallen in [in] one part. He then appeared to ride a few yards towards me, but afterwards turned round and went

back past the plantation and out of sight. When I went in I asked him
if he had not seen me, and why he turned back, when it transpired he
had not been past that plantation all day, but had ridden home another
way. He said it must have been some one else on a white horse, and
asked where I was when I saw him, and then, not before, it dawned on
me that it was utterly impossible to see either plantation or wall from
where I was. Since then I have often been along the same road, and
stood, and looked, and wondered how it was I so distinctly saw the broken
wall and papa on the white horse; a turn in the road makes my having
really done so quite impossible. I am sorry I cannot give you the exact
date of this: I know it was in March 1887, but cannot remember the day,
except that it was *not* on the 5th. The other "experience" is, I always
think, far more interesting, as having been seen by three, and also from
the fact that Paddy was the only white or grey horse in the hunting-field
that day; so that unbelievers could not say it was some one else on a white
horse that we had mistaken. . . . 　　　　NINA M. BOURNE.

Mrs. Sidgwick writes: —

February 25th, 1892.

I saw Miss H. Bourne and her father this afternoon. Miss Bourne
told me the stories of her seeing her father, first with her sister, and later
by herself, and signed the account which she and her sister had, she says,
made out together about it. The groom who saw the figure at the same
time has since been dismissed, and cannot be asked for his evidence.
Canon Bourne remembers hearing of the matter the day it happened.
The groom rode up to the ladies as they were looking, and said: "The
Canon is beckoning, Miss, and I think you had better go to him; his horse
looks as if he had had a fall" (that is, muddy). The figure was beckoning to them with their father's usual (and peculiar) gesture. He is a
heavy man, and his white horse, adapted to carry weight, was quite unlike
any other horse in the neighbourhood. Every one agrees as to the impossibility of mistaking the horse. The horses of the neighbourhood
were well known to the neighbourhood in general and to the Miss Bournes
in particular, as they were at that time constantly out with the hounds.
The incident seems quite unaccountable.

VI. C. From *Phantasms of the Living*, vol. i. p. 214. We received
the first account of this case — the percipient's evidence — through the
kindness of Mrs. Martin, of Ham Court, Upton-on-Severn, Worcester.

ANTONY, TORPOINT, *December 14th*, 1882.

Helen Alexander (maid to Lady Waldegrave) was lying here very ill
with typhoid fever, and was attended by me. I was standing at the table
by her bedside, pouring out her medicine, at about 4 o'clock in the morning
of the 4th October 1880. I heard the call-bell ring (this had been heard
twice before during the night in that same week), and was attracted by
the door of the room opening, and by seeing a person entering the room
whom I instantly felt to be the mother of the sick woman. She had a

brass candlestick in her hand, a red shawl over her shoulders, and a flannel petticoat on which had a hole in the front. I looked at her as much as to say, "I am glad you have come," but the woman looked at me sternly, as much as to say, "Why wasn't I sent for before?" I gave the medicine to Helen Alexander, and then turned round to speak to the vision, but no one was there. She had gone. She was a short, dark person, and very stout. At about 6 o'clock that morning Helen Alexander died. Two days after her parents and a sister came to Antony, and arrived between 1 and 2 o'clock in the morning; I and another maid let them in, and it gave me a great turn when I saw the living likeness of the vision I had seen two nights before. I told the sister about the vision, and she said that the description of the dress exactly answered to her mother's, and that they had brass candlesticks at home exactly like the one described. There was not the slightest resemblance between the mother and daughter.

FRANCES REDDELL.

This at first sight might be taken for a mere delusion of an excitable or over-tired servant, modified and exaggerated by the subsequent sight of the real mother. If such a case is to have evidential force, we must ascertain beyond doubt that the description of the experience was given in detail before any knowledge of the reality can have affected the percipient's memory or imagination. This necessary corroboration has been kindly supplied by Mrs. Pole-Carew, of Antony, Torpoint, Devonport.

December 31st, 1883.

In October, 1880, Lord and Lady Waldegrave came with their Scotch maid, Helen Alexander, to stay with us. [The account then describes how Helen was discovered to have caught typhoid fever.] She did not seem to be very ill in spite of it, and as there seemed no fear of danger, and Lord and Lady Waldegrave had to go a long journey the following day (Thursday), they decided to leave her, as they were advised to do, under their friend's care.

The illness ran its usual course, and she seemed to be going on perfectly well till the Sunday week following, when the doctor told me that the fever had left her, but the state of weakness which had supervened was such as to make him extremely anxious. I immediately engaged a regular nurse, greatly against the wish of Reddell, my maid, who had been her chief nurse all through the illness, and who was quite devoted to her. However, as the nurse could not conveniently come till the following day, I allowed Reddell to sit up with Helen again that night, to give her the medicine and food, which were to be taken constantly.

At about 4.30 that night, or rather Monday morning, Reddell looked at her watch, poured out the medicine, and was bending over the bed to give it to Helen, when the call-bell in the passage rang. She said to herself, "There's that tiresome bell with the wire caught again." (It seems it did occasionally ring of itself in this manner.) At that moment, however, she heard the door open and, looking round, saw a very stout old woman walk in.　She was dressed in a night-gown and red flannel petticoat, and carried an old-fashioned brass candlestick in her hand.　The petticoat had a hole rubbed in it.　She walked into the room, and appeared to be going towards the dressing-table to put her candle down.　She was a perfect stranger to Reddell, who, however, merely thought, "This is her mother come to see after her," and she felt quite glad it was so, accepting the idea without reasoning upon it, as one would in a dream.　She thought the mother looked annoyed, possibly at not having been sent for before. She then gave Helen the medicine, and turning round, found that the apparition had disappeared, and that the door was shut.　A great change, meanwhile, had taken place in Helen, and Reddell fetched me, who sent off for the doctor, and meanwhile applied hot poultices, etc., but Helen died a little before the doctor came.　She was quite conscious up to about half an hour before she died, when she seemed to be going to sleep.

During the early days of her illness, Helen had written to a sister, mentioning her being unwell, but making nothing of it, and as she never mentioned any one but this sister, it was supposed by the household, to whom she was a perfect stranger, that she had no other relation alive. Reddell was always offering to write for her, but she always declined, saying there was no need, she would write herself in a day or two.　No one at home, therefore, knew anything of her being so ill, and it is, therefore, remarkable, that her mother, a far from nervous person, should have said that evening going up to bed, "I am sure Helen is very ill."

Reddell told me and my daughter of the apparition, about an hour after Helen's death, prefacing with, "I am not superstitious, or nervous, and I wasn't the least frightened, but her mother came last night," and she then told the story, giving a careful description of the figure she had seen.　The relations were asked to come to the funeral, and the father, mother, and sister came, and in the mother Reddell recognised the apparition, as I did also, for Reddell's description had been most accurate, even to the expression, which she had ascribed to annoyance, but which was due to deafness.　It was judged best not to speak about it to the mother, but Reddell told the sister, who said the description of the figure corresponded exactly with the probable appearance of her mother if roused in the night; that they had exactly such a candlestick at home, and that there was a hole in her mother's petticoat produced by the way she always wore it.　It seems curious that neither Helen nor her mother appeared to be aware of the visit.　Neither of them, at any rate, ever spoke of having seen the other, nor even of having dreamt of having done so.

F. A. POLE-CAREW.

[Frances Reddell states that she has never had any hallucination, or any odd experience of any kind, except on this one occasion.　The Hon. Mrs. Lyttelton, formerly of Selwyn College, Cambridge, who knows her, tells us that "she appears to be a most matter-of-fact person, and was apparently most impressed by the fact that she saw a hole in the mother's flannel petticoat, made by the busk of her stays, reproduced in the apparition."]

Now what I imagine to have happened here is this. The mother, anxious about her daughter, paid her a psychical visit during the sleep of both. In so doing she actually modified a certain portion of space, not materially nor optically, but in such a manner that persons perceptive in a certain fashion would discern in that part of space an image approximately corresponding to the conception of her own aspect latent in the invading mother's mind. A person thus susceptible happened to be in the room, and thus, as a bystander, witnessed a psychical invasion whose memory the invader apparently did not retain, while the invaded person — the due percipient — may or may not have perceived it in a dream, but died and left no sign of having done so.

VI. D. From the "Report on the Census of Hallucinations," *Proceedings* S.P.R., vol. x. p. 332. The account is given by Mrs. McAlpine.

GARSCADDEN, BEARDSDEN, GLASGOW, *April 20th*, 1892.

I remember in the June of 1889, I drove to Castleblaney, a little town in the county Monaghan, to meet my sister, who was coming by train from Longford. I expected her at three o'clock, but as she did not come with that train, I got the horse put up, and went for a walk in the demesne. The day was very warm and bright, and I wandered on under the shade of the trees to the side of a lake, which is in the demesne. Being at length tired, I sat down to rest upon a rock, at the edge of the water. My attention was quite taken up with the extreme beauty of the scene before me. There was not a sound or movement, except the soft ripple of the water on the sand at my feet. Presently I felt a cold chill creep through me, and a curious stiffness of my limbs, as if I *could* not move, though wishing to do so. I felt frightened, yet chained to the spot, and as if impelled to stare at the water straight in front of me. Gradually a black cloud seemed to rise, and in the midst of it I saw a tall man, in a suit of tweed, jump into the water and sink.

In a moment the darkness was gone, and I again became sensible of the heat and sunshine, but I was awed and felt "eerie" — it was then about four o'clock or so — I cannot remember either the exact time or date. On my sister's arrival I told her of the occurrence; she was surprised, but inclined to laugh at it. When we got home I told my brother; he treated the subject much in the same manner. However, about a week afterwards, Mr. Espie, a bank clerk (unknown to me), committed suicide by drowning in that very spot. He left a letter for his wife, indicating that he had for some time contemplated his death. My sister's memory of the event is the only evidence I can give. I did not see the account of the inquest at the time, and did not mention my strange experience to any one, saving my sister and brother.

F. C. McALPINE.

Mrs. McAlpine's sister writes: —

ROXBORO', *February 15th*, 1892.

I remember perfectly you meeting me in Castleblaney, on my way home from Longford, and telling me of the strange thing which happened in the demesne.   You know you were always hearing or seeing something and I paid little attention; but I remember it distinctly — your troubled expression more than the story.   You said a tall gentleman, dressed in tweed, walked past you, and went into a little inlet or creek.   I think, but am not sure, that you said he had a beard.   You were troubled about it, or looked so; and I talked of other things.   You told me while we were driving home.   I think, but I am not sure, that it was about the 25th or 27th of June 1889 that I left Longford.   I am sure of that being the day, but cannot remember the date.   *It was in June*, and on the 3rd of July, 1889, a Mr. Espie, a bank clerk, drowned himself in the lake in the demesne in 'Blaney.   I have no doubt that the day I came home you saw Mr. Espie's "fetch."

The following account is taken from a local paper, the *Northern Standard*, Saturday, July 6th, 1889: — ·

Sad Case of Suicide. — The town of Castleblaney was put into a fearful state of excitement when it became known on Wednesday last that Mr. Espy had committed siucide by drowning himself in the lake in the demesne.   Latterly, he was noticed to be rather dull and low in spirits, but no serious notice was taken of his conduct, nor had any one the most remote idea that he contemplated suicide.   On Wednesday morning he seemed in his usual health, and, as was customary with him, walked down to get his newspaper on the arrival of the 9.45 train from Dublin.   He met Mr. Fox (in whose office he has been for years) at the station, and having procured his paper walked up to the office, wrote a note in which he stated what he was going to do, and indicating where his body would be found. This seemed to concern him a good deal, for he seemed very anxious that his body should be recovered without any delay.   He had fishing-tackle in his pocket, and having tied one end of a pike-line to a tree, and the other end round one of his legs, he threw himself into about three feet deep of water, where he was found shortly afterwards quite dead, and before the note that he had left in the office had been opened.

It would be possible, no doubt, to explain this appearance as simply precognitive — as a picture from the future impressed in some unknown way upon the percipient's inner vision.   There are certain cases which strongly suggest this extreme hypothesis.   But it seems here simpler to assume that the unhappy man was already imagining his plunge into the lake when Mrs. McAlpine visited the shore, and that his intense thought effected a self-projection, conscious or unconscious, of some element of his being.

VI. E. From *Phantasms of the Living*, vol. ii. p. 239. Mrs. Elgee, of 18 Woburn Road, Bedford, gave the following account: —

March 1st, 1885.

In the month of November 1864, being detained in Cairo, on my way out to India, the following curious circumstance occurred to me: —

Owing to an unusual influx of travellers, I, with the young lady under my charge (whom we will call D.) and some other passengers of the outward-bound mail to India, had to take up our abode in a somewhat unfrequented hotel. The room shared by Miss D. and myself was large, lofty, and gloomy; the furniture of the scantiest, consisting of two small beds, placed nearly in the middle of the room and not touching the walls at all, two or three rush-bottomed chairs, a very small washing stand, and a large old-fashioned sofa of the settee sort, which was placed against one half of the large folding doors which gave entrance to the room. This settee was far too heavy to be removed, unless by two or three people. The other half of the door was used for entrance, and faced the two beds. Feeling rather desolate and strange, and Miss D. being a nervous person, I locked the door, and, taking out the key, put it under my pillow; but on Miss D. remarking that there might be a duplicate which could open the door from outside, I put a chair against the door, with my travelling bag on it, so arranged that, on any pressure outside, one or both must fall on the bare floor, and make noise enough to rouse me. We then proceeded to retire to bed, the one I had chosen being near the only window in the room, which opened with two glazed doors, almost to the floor. These doors, on account of the heat, I left open, first assuring myself that no communication from the outside could be obtained. The window led on to a small balcony, which was isolated, and was three stories above the ground.

I suddenly woke from a sound sleep with the impression that somebody had called me, and, sitting up in bed, to my unbounded astonishment, by the clear light of early dawn coming in through the large window before mentioned, I beheld the figure of an old and very valued friend whom I knew to be in England. He appeared as if most eager to speak to me, and I addressed him with, "Good gracious! how did you come here?" So clear was the figure, that I noted every detail of his dress, even to three onyx shirt-studs which he always wore. He seemed to come a step nearer to me, when he suddenly pointed across the room, and on my looking round, I saw Miss D. sitting up in her bed, gazing at the figure with every expression of terror. On looking back, my friend seemed to shake his head, and retreated step by step, slowly, till he seemed to sink through that portion of the door where the settee stood. I never knew what happened to me after this; but my next remembrance is of bright sunshine pouring through the window. Gradually the remembrance of what had happened came back to me, and the question arose in my mind, had I been dreaming, or had I seen a visitant from another world? — the bodily presence of my friend being utterly impossible. Remembering that Miss D. had seemed aware of the figure as well as myself, I determined to allow the test of my dream or vision to be whatever she said to me upon the subject, I intending to say nothing to her unless she spoke to me. As she seemed still asleep, I got out of bed, examined the door carefully, and found the chair and my bag untouched, and the key under my pillow; the settee had not been touched nor had that portion of the door against which it was placed any appearance of being opened for years.

Presently, on Miss D. waking up, she looked about the room, and, noticing the chair and bag, made some remark as to their not having been much use. I said, "What do you mean?" and then she said, "Why, that man who was in the room this morning must have got in somehow." She then proceeded to describe to me exactly what I myself had seen. Without giving any satisfactory answer as to what I had seen, I made her rather angry by affecting to treat the matter as a fancy on her part, and showed her the key still under my pillow, and the chair and bag untouched. I then asked her, if she was so sure that she had seen somebody in the room, did not she know who it was? "No," said she, "I have never seen him before, nor any one like him." I said, "Have you ever seen a photograph of him?" She said, "No." This lady never was told what I saw, and yet described exactly to a third person what we both had seen.

Of course, I was under the impression my friend was dead. Such, however, was not the case; and I met him some four years later, when, without telling him anything of my experience in Cairo, I asked him, in a joking way, could he remember what he was doing on a certain night in November 1864. "Well," he said, "you require me to have a good memory;" but after a little reflection he replied, "Why, that was the time I was so harassed with trying to decide for or against the appointment which was offered me, and I so much wished you could have been with me to talk the matter over. I sat over the fire quite late, trying to think what you would have advised me to do." A little cross-questioning and comparing of dates brought out the curious fact that, allowing for the difference of time between England and Cairo, his meditations over the fire and my experience were simultaneous. Having told him the circumstances above narrated, I asked him had he been aware of any peculiar or unusual sensation. He said none, only that he had wanted to see me very much.   E. H. ELGEE.

In answer to inquiries, Mrs. Elgee says:—

I fear it is quite impossible to get any information from Miss D. She married soon after we reached India, and I never met her since, nor do I know where she is, if alive. I quite understand the value of her corroboration; and at the time she told the whole circumstance to a fellow-traveller, who repeated it to me, and her story and mine agreed in every particular, save that to her the visitant was a complete stranger; and her tale was quite unbiassed by mine, as I always treated hers as a fancy, and *never* acknowledged I had been aware of anything unusual having taken place in our room at Cairo. I never have seen, or fancied I saw, any one before or since.

My visitant, also, is dead, or he would, I know, have added his testimony, small as it was, to mine.   He was a very calm, quiet, clever, scientific man, not given to vain fancies on any subject, and certainly was not aware of any desire of appearing to me.

The publication of *Phantasms of the Living* led fortunately to our obtaining the testimony of the second percipient, now Mrs. Ramsay, of Clevelands, Bassett, Southampton, whose account follows: —

July 1891.

I have been asked by a leading member of the Psychical Society to write down what I can remember of a strange experience that occurred no less than twenty-seven years ago.   I now do so as simply as I can, and to the best of my recollection.

In October 1864, I was travelling to India, going to rejoin my parents, from whom I had been separated twelve years, a kind friend — a Mrs. E. — having undertaken to chaperon me as far as Calcutta.   She was going out to join her husband, Major E., of the 23rd Royal Welsh Fusiliers. We started by a P. & O steamer — the *Ceylon* — from Southampton, and travelled by the overland route, *via* Alexandria and Cairo, to Suez.

We landed at Alexandria, and went by rail across the desert to Cairo. There all passengers had to sleep the night before proceeding on to Suez. Shepherd's Hotel was the best hotel then, and there was consequently a great rush to try and get rooms in it; but Mrs. E. and I, finding we could get no corner, decided, with two or three other passengers, to get accommodation in the Hôtel de l'Europe.   We felt somewhat nervous at the swarthy visages of the Arabs all round us, and for this reason selected our quarters on the very highest storey, thinking we should be more out of reach of robbers and thieves than if we were on the ground floor.   This is an important point to remember, as no one could have effected an entrance into our room from outside.   It was a bright moonlight night when we went to bed, and I can recollect as if it were yesterday this fact, that the shadow of a "pepul" tree was reflected on the wall opposite our beds — the leaves of the tree were trembling and shaking, as the leaves of a "pepul" always do, making the shadows dance about the wall.

Before we finally retired to rest we made the grandest arrangements for personal security!   The window looking out on to the street below was much too high up to be at all unsafe.   So we left that open (I think) but we closed our door very firmly indeed!   It was a large folding door, and opened *inwards*.   We locked it carefully, leaving the key in the lock; pushed an arm-chair against the middle of the door; and, to crown all, we balanced a hand-bag on one of the arms, with a bunch of keys in the lock thereof! so that if any intruder should venture to open that door, we should *know* of it at any rate! !   (But no one did venture, and we found everything in the morning exactly as we had left it.)   I remember that Mrs. E. was very careful about tucking her mosquito curtains all round, but I disliked the feeling of suffocation they gave, and put mine up; not realising, of course, in my inexperience, what the consequences would be for myself; for these small plagues of Egypt (!) soon descended upon me, nearly eating me up, and absolutely prevented sleep. This is another important fact to remember, for had I slept I might have dreamed, but, as it happened, I was wide awake. I was looking at the shadows of the tree shaking on the wall when gradually they seemed to merge into a form, which form took the shape of a man, not of an Arab, but of an English gentleman. Then this form glided into the room, advancing towards my chaperon, stretching out his hands as if in blessing, turned round, looked at me, sadly and sorrowfully (so I thought), and then vanished again into'the shadows as it came. I do not remember feeling terrified, only awed — the face was so kind and human, only the moonlight made it look very white. I did not wake Mrs. E., as she appeared to me to be asleep. I felt sure I had seen a vision, and something that had to do with her.

The next morning, while we were dressing, she remarked how odd I looked, and quite apart from the mosquito bites, I know I did. We had a good laugh over my comical appearance, for I had not scrupled to scratch the bites, until my forehead and face resembled a plum bun! I believe I then told her it was not strange that I should look odd, for I "had seen a ghost." She started violently, and asked me to tell her what I saw. I described it as best I could, and she said *she had seen* "*it*" *too*, and that she knew it to be the form and face of a valued friend. She was much disturbed about it — as, indeed, so was I, for I had never indulged in "hallucinations" and was not given to seeing visions.

We proceeded next day to join our ship at Suez, and when on board, it was a great relief to us to be able to tell it to a kind fellow-passenger. He was an absolute sceptic in all matters relating to the invisible world, but he was obliged to admit that it was the most extraordinary thing he had ever heard. . . . I should like to add that I have never, before or since, had any kind of vision.

Our experience at Cairo had this sequel, that Mrs. E.'s spirit-friend happened to be, at that very time, in great perplexity of mind — most anxious about some very important event in his life. He was sitting in his room one night in the month of October 1864, and a most intense yearning came over him for her advice and assistance — so great was it, that he felt as if an invisible power had drawn him into some spirit-state, in which he could and did see her.[1]

For a somewhat similar case, that of the apparition of General Frémont (too lengthy to quote here), I may refer the reader to the *Journal* S.P.R., vol. v. p. 54. The crisis there is the removal of long and wearing anxiety; the self-projection into the home-scene which now at last the General felt assured of being able to reach alive.

[1] I noted on this narrative at the time I received it: "This account is entirely concordant with the account written by Mrs. Ramsay before reading Mrs. Elgee's account in 1888, and abstracted by me for an article in *Murray's Magazine*. There was this discrepancy between Mrs. Elgee and Mrs. Ramsay, — that Mrs. Ramsay thought that the figure wore a beard, whereas Mrs. Elgee saw him as she knew him — with whiskers only. He certainly had no beard at the time."

VI. F.   From *Phantasms of the Living*, vol. i. pp. 104-109.   The following case was especially remarkable in that there were two percipients. The narrative was copied by Gurney from a MS. book of Mr. S. H. B.'s, to which he transferred it from an almanac diary, since lost.

On a certain Sunday evening in November 1881, having been reading of the great power which the human will is capable of exercising, I determined with the whole force of my being, that I would be present in spirit in the front bed-room on the second floor of a house situated at 22 Hogarth Road, Kensington, in which room slept two ladies of my acquaintance, viz., Miss L. S. V. and Miss E. C. V., aged respectively 25 and 11 years. I was living at this time at 23 Kildare Gardens, a distance of about three miles from Hogarth Road, and I had not mentioned in any way my intention of trying this experiment to either of the above ladies, for the simple reason that it was only on retiring to rest upon this Sunday night that I made up my mind to do so.   The time at which I determined I would be there was 1 o'clock in the morning, and I also had a strong intention of making my presence perceptible.

On the following Thursday I went to see the ladies in question, and in the course of conversation (without any allusion to the subject on my part) the elder one told me, that on the previous Sunday night she had been much terrified by perceiving me standing by her bedside, and that she screamed when the apparition advanced towards her, and awoke her little sister, who saw me also.

I asked her if she was awake at the time, and she replied most decidedly in the affirmative, and upon my inquiring the time of the occurrence, she replied, about 1 o'clock in the morning.

This lady, at my request, wrote down a statement of the event and signed it.

This was the first occasion upon which I tried an experiment of this kind, and its complete success startled me very much.

Besides exercising my power of volition very strongly, I put forth an effort which I cannot find words to describe.   I was conscious of a mysterious influence of some sort permeating in my body, and had a distinct impression that I was exercising some force with which I had been hitherto unacquainted, but which I can now at certain times set in motion at will.

S. H. B.

Of the original entry in the almanac diary, Mr. B. says: "I recollect having made it within a week or so of the occurrence of the experiment, and whilst it was perfectly fresh in my memory."

Miss Verity's account is as follows: —

January 18th, 1883.

On a certain Sunday evening, about twelve months since, at our house in Hogarth Road, Kensington, I distinctly saw Mr. B. in my room, about 1 o'clock.   I was perfectly awake and was much terrified.   I awoke my sister by screaming, and she saw the apparition herself.   Three days after, when I saw Mr. B., I told him what had happened, but it was some time before I could recover from the shock I had received; and the remembrance is too vivid to be ever erased from my memory.   L. S. VERITY.

In answer to inquiries, Miss Verity adds: "I had never had any hallucination of the senses of any sort whatever."

Miss E. C. Verity says: —

I remember the occurrence of the event described by my sister in the annexed paragraph, and her description is quite correct.   I saw the apparition which she saw, at the same time and under the same circumstances.
                                                  E. C. VERITY.

Miss A. S. Verity says: —

I remember quite clearly the evening my eldest sister awoke me by calling to me from an adjoining room; and upon my going to her bedside, where she slept with my youngest sister, they both told me they had seen S. H. B. standing in the room.   The time was about 1 o'clock.   S. H. B. was in evening dress, they told me.   A. S. VERITY.

Mr. B. does not remember how he was dressed on the night of the occurrence.

Miss E. C. Verity was asleep when her sister caught sight of the figure, and was awoke by her sister's exclaiming, "There is S."   The name had therefore met her ear before she herself saw the figure; and the hallucination on her part might thus be attributed to suggestion.   But it is against this view that she has never had any other hallucination, and cannot therefore be considered as predisposed to such experiences.   The sisters are both equally certain that the figure was in evening dress, and that it stood in one particular spot in the room.   The gas was burning low, and the phantasmal figure was seen with far more clearness than a real figure would have been.

"The witnesses" (says Gurney) "have been very carefully cross-examined by the present writer.   There is not the slightest doubt that their mention of the occurrence to S. H. B. was spontaneous.   They had not at first intended to mention it; but when they saw him, their sense of its oddness overcame their resolution.   Miss Verity is a perfectly sober-minded and sensible witness, with no love of marvels, and with a considerable dread and dislike of this particular form of marvel."

[I omit here for want of space the next case, in which Mr. S. H. B. attempted to appear in Miss Verity's house at two different hours on the same evening, and was seen there, at both the times fixed, by a married sister who was visiting in the house.]

Gurney requested Mr. B. to send him a note on the night that he intended to make his next experiment of the kind, and received the following note by the first post on Monday, March 24th, 1884.

March 22nd, 1884.

DEAR MR. GURNEY, — I am going to try the experiment to-night of making my presence perceptible at 44 Norland Square, at 12 P.M. I will let you know the result in a few days. — Yours very sincerely, S. H. B.

The next letter was received in the course of the following week: —

April 3rd, 1884.

DEAR MR. GURNEY, — I have a strange statement to show you, respecting my experiment, which was tried at your suggestion, and under the test conditions which you imposed.

Having quite forgotten which night it was on which I attempted the projection, I cannot say whether the result is a brilliant success, or only a slight one, until I see the letter which I posted you on the evening of the experiment.

Having sent you that letter, I did not deem it necessary to make a note in my diary, and consequently have let the exact date slip my memory.

If the dates correspond, the success is complete in every detail, and I have an account signed and witnessed to show you.

I saw the lady (who was the subject) for the first time last night, since the experiment, and she made a voluntary statement to me, which I wrote down at her dictation, and to which she has attached her signature. The date and time of the apparition are specified in this statement, and it will be for you to decide whether they are identical with those given in my letter to you. I have completely forgotten, but yet I fancy that they are the same. S. H. B.

This is the statement: —

44 NORLAND SQUARE, W.

On Saturday night, March 22nd, 1884, at about midnight, I had a distinct impression that Mr. S. H. B. was present in my room, and I distinctly saw him whilst I was quite widely awake. He came towards me, and stroked my hair. I *voluntarily* gave him this information, when he called to see me on Wednesday, April 2nd, telling him the time and the circumstances of the apparition, without any suggestion on his part. The appearance in my room was most vivid, and quite unmistakable.

L. S. VERITY.

Miss A. S. Verity corroborates as follows: —

I remember my sister telling me that she had seen S. H. B., and that he had touched her hair, *before* he came to see us on April 2nd.

A. S. V.

Mr. B.'s own account is as follows: —

On Saturday, March 22nd, I determined to make my presence perceptible to Miss V., at 44 Norland Square, Notting Hill, at 12 midnight, and as I had previously arranged with Mr. Gurney that I should post him a letter on the evening on which I tried my next experiment (stating the time and other particulars), I sent a note to acquaint him with the above facts.

About ten days afterwards I called upon Miss V., and she voluntarily told me, that on March 22nd, at 12 o'clock midnight, she had seen me so vividly in her room (whilst widely awake) that her nerves had been much shaken, and she had been obliged to send for a doctor in the morning.

S. H. B.

Unfortunately Mr. B.'s intention to produce the impression of touching the percipient's hair is not included in his written account. On August 21st, 1885, he wrote to Gurney, "I remember that I had this intention"; and Gurney remembered that, very soon after the occurrence, he mentioned this as one of the points which made the success "complete in every detail"; and that he recommended him in any future trial to endeavour instead to produce the impression of some spoken phrase.

On this case, Gurney observes: —

It will be observed that in all these instances the conditions were the same — the agent concentrating his thoughts on the object in view before going to sleep. Mr. B. has never succeeded in producing a similar effect when he has been awake. And this restriction as to time has made it difficult to devise a plan by which the phenomenon could be tested by independent observers, one of whom might arrange to be in the company of the agent at a given time, and the other in that of the percipient. Nor is it easy to press for repetitions of the experiment, which is not an agreeable one to the percipient, and is followed by a considerable amount of nervous prostration. Moreover, if trials were frequently made with the same percipient, the value of success would diminish; for any latent expectation on the percipient's part might be argued to be itself productive of the delusion, and the coincidence with the agent's resolve might be explained as accidental. We have, of course, requested Mr. B. to try to produce the effect on ourselves; but though he has more than once made the attempt, it has not succeeded.

APPENDICES

TO

CHAPTER VII

VII. A. The account of this case, given by Mr. E. Mamtchitch, is taken from the "Report on the Census of Hallucinations" in the *Proceedings* S.P.R., vol. x. pp. 387–91.

ST. PETERSBURG, *April 29th*, 1891.

Comme il s'agira des apparitions de Palladia, je dois dire auparavant quelques mots sur sa personne. Elle était la fille d'un riche propriétaire russe, mort un mois avant sa naissance. Sa mère, dans son désespoir, voua son enfant futur au couvent. De là son nom, usité parmi les religieuses. Deux ans après, sa mère mourut, et l'orpheline, jusqu'à l'âge de 14 ans, fut élevée dans un couvent de Moscou par sa tante, qui en était la supérieure.

En 1870, étant encore étudiant à l'université de Moscou, je fis la connaissance du frère de Palladia, étudiant comme moi, et il fut souvent question entre nous de rendre à la société la nonne malgré soi; mais ce plan ne fut réalisé qu'en 1872. J'étais venu en été à Moscou, pour voir l'exposition, et j'y rencontrai par hasard le frère de Palladia. J'appris qu'il était en train de l'envoyer en Crimée pour cause de santé, et je le secondai de mon mieux. C'est alors que je vis Palladia pour la première fois; elle avait 14 ans; quoique haute de taille, elle était fort chétive et déjà poitrinaire. A la prière de son frère, j'accompagnai Palladia et sa sœur, Mme. P. S., en Crimée, où elles restèrent pour passer l'hiver et moi, deux semaines après, je revins à Kieff.

En été 1873 je rencontrai par hasard Palladia et sa sœur à Odessa, où elles étaient venues pour consulter les médecins, quoique Palladia avait l'air de se porter assez bien. Le 27 Août, pendant que je faisais la lecture aux deux dames, Palladia mourut subitement d'un anévrisme, à l'âge de 15 ans.

Deux ans après la mort de Palladia, en 1875, me trouvant à Kieff, il m'arriva, par une soirée du mois de Décembre, d'assister pour la première fois à une séance spiritique; j'entendis des coups dans la table; cela ne m'étonna nullement, car j'étais sûr que c'était une plaisanterie. De retour chez moi, je voulus voir si les mêmes coups se produiraient chez moi; je me mis dans la même pose, les mains sur la table. Bientôt des coups se firent entendre. Imitant le procédé dont j'avais été le temoin, je commençai à réciter l'alphabet; le nom de Palladia me fut indiqué. Je fus étonné, presque effrayé; ne pouvant me tranquilliser, je me mis de nouveau à la table, et je demandai à Palladia, qu'avait-elle à me dire? La réponse fut: "*Replacer l'ange, il tombe.*" Je ne compris pas de suite de quoi il s'agissait. Le fait est qu'elle est enterrée à Kieff, et j'avais entendu dire qu'on voulait mettre un monument sur sa tombe, mais je n'y avais jamais été, et je ne savais pas de quel genre était le monument. Après cette réponse, je ne me couchai plus, et dès que le jour parut je me rendis au cimetière. Non sans peine, avec l'aide du gardien, je découvris enfin la tombe enfouie sous la neige. Je m'arrêtai stupéfié: la statue en marbre de l'ange avec une croix était tout à fait de côté.

Depuis ce moment, il me fut prouvé à l'évidence qu'il y a un autre monde avec lequel, je ne sais comment, nous pouvons entrer en rapport, et dont les habitants peuvent nous donner de telles preuves de leur existence qu'elles désarment le scepticisme le plus tenace.

En Octobre, 1876, je me trouvais à Kieff, et j'étais en train de m'installer dans un nouveau logement (rue Prorésnaya) avec mon camarade de service au Ministère de la Justice, M. Potolof. On venait de m'apporter un pianino. Il fut placé dans la salle, et je me mis à jouer; il était à peu près 8 h. du soir; la salle où je jouais était éclairée par une lampe pendue au mur. A côté se trouvait mon cabinet de travail, éclairé aussi par une lampe. Je me rappelle très bien que j'étais de fort bonne humeur. Mon camarade, M. Potolof, était occupé à sa table, à l'autre bout du logis. Toutes les portes étaient ouvertes, et de sa place il pouvait voir très bien le cabinet et la salle où je jouais.[1] Jetant un regard vers la porte de mon cabinet de travail, je vis tout à coup Palladia. Elle se tenait au milieu de la porte, un peu de côté, avec le visage tourné vers moi. Elle me regardait tranquillement. Elle avait la même robe foncée qu'elle portait lorsqu'elle mourut en ma présence. Sa main droite pendait librement. Je voyais distinctement ses épaules et sa taille, mais ne me rappelle pas du bas de son habit, et avais-je vu les pieds? — peut-être, parce que tout le temps je lui regardais dans les yeux. En la voyant, j'avais tout à fait oublié que je voyais devant moi non une personne vivante, mais morte, tellement je la voyais distinctement; elle était éclairée de deux côtés; et d'autant plus j'ai la vue très bonne. Ma première sensation fut un frisson dans le dos. Je fus comme pétrifié et ma respiration fut suspendue; mais ce n'était pas un effet causé par le frayeur ou l'excitation, — c'était quelque chose d'autre. Je puis comparer cela à la sensation que j'éprouve quand je regarde en bas d'une grande hauteur; je sens alors une terrible anxiété et en même temps je ne puis me retenir de regarder, quelque chose m'attire invinciblement. Combien de temps Palladia resta devant moi, je ne saurais le dire, mais je me rappelle qu'elle fit un mouvement à droite et disparut derrière la porte du

---

[1] A plan enclosed shows a suite of four rooms, M. Potolof's study, the ante-room, the drawing-room, and M. Mamtchitch's study, all opening into one another, the three doors between them being in one straight line.

cabinet du travail.   Je me précipitai vers elle, mais dans la porte je m'arrêtai, car alors seulement je me rappelai qu'elle était déjà morte, et je craignai d'entrer, étant sûr de la revoir.   Dans ce moment mon camarade vint à moi et me demanda qu'est-ce que j'avais ?   Je lui dis ce qui venait de se passer; alors nous entrâmes au cabinet ou nous ne trouvâmes personne.   Mon camarade, ayant entendu la brusque interruption de mon jeu, avait levé la tête et, tant que je me rappelle, disait avoir vu aussi quelqu'un passer devant la porte de mon cabinet; mais, voyant mon excitation, il me dit, pour me tranquilliser, que probablement c'était Nikita, mon domestique, qui était venu arranger la lampe.   Nous allâmes immédiatement dans sa chambre, il n'y était pas; il était en bas, dans la cuisine, ou il préparait le samovar.   Voilà comment je vis Palladia pour la première fois, trois ans après sa mort.

Après la première apparition de Palladia, en Octobre, 1876, et jusqu'à présent, je la vois souvent.   Il arrive que je la vois trois fois par semaine, ou deux fois le même jour, ou bien un mois se passe sans la voir.   En résumé, voilà les traits principaux de ces apparitions.

(1) Palladia apparait toujours d'une façon inattendue, me prenant comme par surprise, juste au moment quand j'y pense le moins.

(2) Quand je veux la voir moi-même, j'ai beau y penser ou le vouloir — elle n'apparait pas.

(3) A de rares exceptions, son apparition n'a aucun rapport avec le courant de ma vie, comme présage ou avertissement de quelqu'événement insolite.

(4) Jamais je ne la vois en songe.

(5) Je la vois également quand je suis seul, ou en grande compagnie.

(6) Elle m'apparait toujours avec la même expression sereine des yeux; quelque fois avec un faible sourire.   Elle ne m'a jamais parlé, à l'exception de deux fois, que je vais raconter plus loin.

(7) Je la vois toujours dans la robe foncée qu'elle portait lorsqu'elle mourut sous mes yeux.   Je vois distinctement son visage, sa tête, les épaules et les bras, mais je ne vois pas ses pieds, ou plutôt je n'ai pas le temps de les examiner.

(8) Chaque fois, en voyant Palladia inopinément, je perds la parole, je sens du froid dans le dos, je pâlis, je m'écrie faiblement, et ma respiration s'arrête (c'est ce que me disent ceux qui par hasard m'ont observé pendant ce moment).

(9) L'apparition de Palladia se prolonge une, deux, trois minutes, puis graduellement elle s'efface et se dissout dans l'espace.

A présent je vais décrire trois cas d'apparitions de Palladia dont je me souviens bien.

(1) En 1879, à la fin de Novembre, à Kieff, j'étais assis à mon bureau à écrire un acte d'accusation; il était 8¼ du soir, la montre était devant moi sur la table.   Je me hâtais de finir mon travail, car à 9 h. je devais me rendre à une soirée.   Tout à coup, en face de moi, assise sur un fauteuil, je vis Palladia; elle avait le coude du bras droit sur la table et la tête appuyée sur la main.   M'étant remis de mon saisissement, je regardai la montre et je suivis le mouvement de l'aiguille à seconde, puis je relevai

les yeux sur Palladia; je vis qu'elle n'avait pas changé de pose et son coude se dessinait clairement sur la table. Ses yeux me regardaient avec joie et sérénité; alors pour la première fois je me décidai de lui parler: "Que sentez-vous à présent?" lui demandai-je. Son visage resta impassible, ses lèvres, tant que je me rappelle, restèrent immobiles, mais j'entendis distinctement sa voix prononcer le mot "Quiétude." "Je comprends," lui répondis-je, et effectivement, en ce moment, je comprenais toute la signification qu'elle avait mise dans ce mot. Encore une fois, pour être sûr que je ne rêvai pas, je regardai de nouveau la montre et je suivis les mouvements de l'aiguille à seconde; je voyais clairement comme elle se mouvait. Ayant rapporté mon regard sur Palladia, je remarquai qu'elle commençait déjà à s'effacer et disparaître. Si je m'étais avisé de noter immédiatement la signification du mot "Quiétude," ma mémoire aurait retenu tout ce qu'il y avait de nouveau et d'étrange. Mais à peine avais-je quitté la table pour monter en haut, chez mon camarade Apouktine, avec lequel nous devions aller ensemble, que je ne pus lui dire autre chose que ce que je viens d'écrire.

(2) En 1885, je demeurais chez mes parents, à une campagne du gouvernement de Poltava. Une dame de notre connaissance était venue passer chez nous quelques jours avec ses deux demoiselles. Quelque temps après leur arrivée, m'étant réveillé à l'aube du jour, je vis Palladia (je dormais dans une aile séparée ou j'étais tout seul). Elle se tenait devant moi, à cinq pas à peu près, et me regardait avec un sourire joyeux. S'étant approchée de moi, elle me dit deux mots: "J'ai été, j'ai vu," et tout en souriant disparut. Que voulaient dire ces mots, je ne pus le comprendre. Dans ma chambre dormait avec moi mon setter. Dès que j'aperçus Palladia, le chien hérissa le poil et avec glapissement sauta sur mon lit; se pressant vers moi, il regardait dans la direction où je voyais Palladia. Le chien n'aboyait pas, tandis que, ordinairement, il ne laissait personne entrer dans la chambre sans aboyer et grogner. Et toutes les fois, quand mon chien voyait Palladia, il se pressait auprès de moi, comme cherchant un refuge. Quand Palladia disparut et je vins dans la maison, je ne dis rien à personne de cette incident. Le soir de même jour, la fille aînée de la dame qui se trouvait chez nous me raconta qu'une chose étrange lui était arrivée ce matin: "M'étant réveillée de grand matin," me dit-elle, "j'ai senti comme si quelqu'un se tenait au chevet de mon lit, et j'entendis distinctement une voix me disant: 'Ne me crains pas, je suis bonne et aimante.' Je tournai la tête, mais je ne vis rien; ma mère et ma sœur dormaient tranquillement; cela m'a fort étonnée, car jamais rien de pareil ne m'est arrivé." Sur quoi je répondis que bien des choses inexplicables nous arrivent; mais je ne lui dit rien de ce que j'avais vu le matin. Seulement un an plus tard, quand j'étais déjà son fiancé, je lui fis part de l'apparition et des paroles de Palladia le même jour. N'était-ce pas elle qui était venue la voir aussi? Je dois ajouter que j'avais vu alors cette demoiselle pour la première fois et que je ne pensais pas du tout que j'allais l'épouser.

(3) En Octobre, 1890, je me trouvais avec ma femme et mon fils, âgé de deux ans, chez mes anciens amis, les Strijewsky, à leur campagne

du gouvernement de Woronèje. Un jour, vers les 7 h. du soir, rentrant de la chasse, je passai dans l'aile que nous habitons pour changer de toilette; j'étais assis dans une chambre éclairée par une grande lampe. La porte s'ouvrit et mon fils Olég accourut; il se tenait auprès de mon fauteuil, quand Palladia apparut tout à coup devant moi. Jetant sur lui un coup d'œil, je remarquai qu'il ne détachait pas les yeux de Palladia; se tournant vers moi et montrant Palladia du doigt, il prononça: "La tante." Je le pris sur les genoux et jetái un regard sur Palladia, mais elle n'était plus. Le visage d'Olég était tout à fait tranquil et joyeux; il commençait seulement à parler, ce qui explique la dénomination qu'il donna à Palladia.   EUGÈNE MAMTCHITCH.

Mrs. Mamtchitch writes: —

5 *Mai*, 1891.

Je me rappelle très bien que le 10 Juillet 1885, lorsque nous étions en visite chez les parents de M. E. Mamtchitch, je m'étais réveillée à l'aube du jour, car il avait été convenu entre moi et ma sœur que nous irions faire une promenade matinale. M'étant soulevée sur le lit, je vis que maman et ma sœur dormaient, et en ce moment je sentis comme si quelqu'un se tenait à mon chevet. M'étant tournée à demi — car je craignais de bien regarder — je ne vis personne; m'étant recouchée, j'entendis immédiatement, derrière et au dessus de ma tête, une voix de femme me disant doucement, mais distinctement: "Ne me crains pas, je suis bonne et aimante," et encore toute une phrase que j'oubliai à l'instant même. Immédiatement après je m'habillai et j'allai me promener. C'est étrange que ces paroles ne m'effrayèrent pas du tout. De retour, je n'en dis rien ni à ma mère, ni à ma sœur, car elles n'aimaient pas de telles choses et n'y croyaient pas; mais le soir du même jour, comme la conversation tourna sur le spiritisme, je racontai à M. M. ce qui venait de m'arriver le matin; il ne me répondit rien de particulier.

Je n'ai jamais eu aucune hallucination, ni avant, ni après cet incident, à l'exception d'un cas tout récent, quand je me suis vue moi-même, de quoi je parlerai une autre fois.   SOPHIE MAMTCHITCH.

Mr. Potolof writes to Mr. Aksakoff, through whom the case was sent: —

RUE SCHPALERNAYA, 26. S. PÉTERSBOURG, *le* 10 *Mai*, 1891.

MONSIEUR, — En réponse à votre lettre du 8 Mai et les questions que vous me posez relativement à l'incident avec M. E. Mamtchitch, lorsque dans les années 1876-77 nous habitions ensemble Kieff, rue Proresnaya, maison Barsky, je puis vous communiquer ce qui suit. Effectivement, je fus alors témoin comme M. M., pendant qu'il jouait un soir du piano quelque air mélancolique, s'interrompait brusquement (comme si après avoir fortement attaqué le clavier, ses mains s'étaient subitement affaissées), et lorsque je vins lui demander ce qui lui était arrivé, il me répondit qu'il venait de voir apparaître le fantôme de Palladia, se tenant derrière la draperie de la porte de la chambre contigue à celle où se trouvait le piano.   Je dois ajouter que notre appartement commun formait une enfilade de trois chambres, sans compter celle de l'entrée, qui occupait le milieu; je travaillais dans ma chambre, qui était à droite de celle de l'entrée, et je pouvais voir toute l'enfilade bien éclairée.   Ce qui me regarde personnellement, je ne vis en ce moment aucune figure humaine passer par les chambres de M. M., mais je ne nie pas que pour le tranquilliser j'essayai d'expliquer cet incident par l'entrée de notre domestique Nikita; il se peut aussi que, ne l'ayant pas trouvé dans nos appartements, nous allâmes le chercher en bas, dans la cuisine.   Voilà tout ce que je puis vous dire relativement à cet incident.   W. POTOLOF.

Note by Mr. Aksakoff: —

S. PÉTERSBOURG, *Le* 16|28 *Mai*, 1891.

Traduit des manuscrits russes de M. et Madame Mamtchitch, et de M. Potolof.   La première partie du manuscrit de M. Mamtchitch, jusqu'à la première apparition de Palladia, est abrégé.

J'avais rencontré M. Mamtchitch plusieurs fois, mais je n'avais aucune idée de ces apparitions constantes de Palladia.   M. Mamtchitch a vu aussi d'autres figures que celle de Palladia, mais je n'ai pas eu le temps d'en faire un mémorandum circonstantiel.   A. AKSAKOFF.

VII. B.   The account, which I quote from *Proceedings* S.P.R., vol. vi. p. 17, was sent in 1887 to the American Society for Psychical Research by Mr. F. G., of Boston.   Professor Royce and Dr. Hodgson vouch for the high character and good position of the informants; and it will be seen that, besides the percipient himself, his father and brother are first-hand witnesses as regards the most important point, — the effect produced by a certain symbolic item in the phantom's aspect.   Mr. G. writes: —

January 11*th*, 1888.

SIR, — Replying to the recently published request of your Society for actual occurrences of psychical phenomena, I respectfully submit the following remarkable occurrence to the consideration of your distinguished Society, with the assurance that the event made a more powerful impression on my mind than the combined incidents of my whole life. I have never mentioned it outside of my family and a few intimate friends, knowing well that few would believe it, or else ascribe it to some disordered state of my mind at the time; but I well know I never was in better health or possessed a clearer head and mind than at the time it occurred.

In 1867 my only sister, a young lady of eighteen years, died suddenly of cholera in St. Louis, Mo.   My attachment for her was very strong, and the blow a severe one to me.   A year or so after her death the writer became a commercial traveller, and it was in 1876, while on one of my Western trips, that the event occurred.

I had "drummed" the city of St. Joseph, Mo., and had gone to my room at the Pacific House to send in my orders, which were unusually large ones, so that I was in a very happy frame of mind indeed.   My thoughts, of course, were about these orders, knowing how pleased my house would be at my success. I had not been thinking of my late sister, or in any manner reflecting on the past. The hour was high noon, and the sun was shining cheerfully into my room. While busily smoking a cigar and writing out my orders, I suddenly became conscious that some one was sitting on my left, with one arm resting on the table. Quick as a flash I turned and distinctly saw the form of my dead sister, and for a brief second or so looked her squarely in the face; and so sure was I that it was she, that I sprang forward in delight, calling her by name, and, as I did so, the apparition instantly vanished. Naturally I was startled and dumbfounded, almost doubting my senses; but the cigar in my mouth, and pen in hand, with the ink still moist on my letter, I satisfied myself I had not been dreaming and was wide awake. I was near enough to touch her, had it been a physical possibility, and noted her features, expression, and details of dress, etc. She appeared as if alive. Her eyes looked kindly and perfectly natural into mine. Her skin was so life-like that I could see the glow or moisture on its surface, and, on the whole, there was no change in her appearance, otherwise than when alive.

Now comes the most remarkable *confirmation* of my statement, which cannot be doubted by those who know what I state actually occurred. This visitation, or whatever you may call it, so impressed me that I took the next train home, and in the presence of my parents and others I related what had occurred. My father, a man of rare good sense and very practical, was inclined to ridicule me, as he saw how earnestly I believed what I stated; but he, too, was amazed when later on I told them of a bright red line or *scratch* on the right-hand side of my sister's face, which I distinctly had seen. When I mentioned this my mother rose trembling to her feet and nearly fainted away, and as soon as she sufficiently recovered her self-possession, with tears streaming down her face, she exclaimed that I had indeed seen my sister, as no living mortal but herself was aware of that scratch, which she had accidentally made while doing some little act of kindness after my sister's death. She said she well remembered how pained she was to think she should have, unintentionally, marred the features of her dead daughter, and that, unknown to all, how she had carefully obliterated all traces of the slight scratch with the aid of powder, etc., and that she had never mentioned it to a human being from that day to this. In proof, neither my father nor any of our family had detected it, and positively were unaware of the incident, yet *I saw the scratch as bright as if just made.* So strangely impressed was my mother, that even after she had retired to rest she got up and dressed, came to me and told me *she knew* at least that I had seen my sister. A few weeks later my mother died, happy in her belief she would rejoin her favourite daughter in a better world.

In a further letter Mr. F. G. adds: —

There was nothing of a spiritual or ghostly nature in either the form or dress of my sister, she appearing perfectly natural, and dressed in clothing that she usually wore in life, and which was familiar to me. From her position at the table, I could only see her *from the waist up*, and her appearance and everything she wore is indelibly photographed in my mind. I even had time to notice the collar and little breastpin she wore, as well as the comb in her hair, after the style then worn by young ladies. The dress had no particular association for me or my mother, no more so than others she was in the habit of wearing; but *to-day, while I have forgotten all her other dresses, pins, and combs*, I could go to her trunk (which we have just as she left it) and pick out the very dress and ornaments she wore when she appeared to me, so well do I remember it.

You are correct in understanding that I returned home earlier than I had intended, as it had such an effect on me that I could hardly think of any other matter; in fact, I abandoned a trip that I had barely commenced, and, ordinarily, would have remained on the road a month longer.

Mr. F. G. again writes to Dr. Hodgson, January 23rd, 1888: —

As per your request, I enclose a letter from my father which is indorsed by my brother, confirming the statement I made to them of the apparition I had seen. I will add that my father is one of the oldest and most respected citizens of St. Louis, Mo., a retired merchant, whose winter residence is at ——, Ills., a few miles out by rail. He is now seventy years of age, but a remarkably well-preserved gentleman in body and mind, and a very learned man as well. As I informed you, he is slow to believe things that reason cannot explain. My brother, who indorses the statement, has resided in Boston for twelve years, doing business on —— Street, as per letter-head above, and the last man in the world to take stock in statements without good proof. The others who were present (including my mother) are now dead, or were then so young as to now have but a dim remembrance of the matter.

You will note that my father refers to the "scratch," and it was this that puzzled all, even himself, and which we have never been able to account for, further than that in some mysterious way I had actually seen my sister *nine years after death*, and had particularly noticed and described to my parents and family this bright red scratch, and which, beyond all doubt in our minds, was unknown to a soul save my mother, who had accidentally caused it.

When I made my statement, all, of course, listened and were interested; but the matter would probably have passed with comments that it was a freak of memory had not I asked about the scratch, and the instant I mentioned it my mother was aroused as if she had received an electric shock, as she had kept it secret from all, and *she alone* was able to explain it. My mother was a sincere Christian lady, who was for twenty-five years superintendent of a large infant class in her church, the Southern Methodist, and a directress in many charitable institutions, and was highly educated. No lady at the time stood higher in the city of St. Louis, and she was, besides, a woman of rare good sense.

I mention these points to give you an insight into the character and standing of those whose testimony, in such a case, is necessary.

(Signed)   F. G.

From Mr. H. G.: —

——, ILLS., *January 20th*, 1888.

DEAR F., — Yours of 16th inst. is received. In reply to your questions relating to your having seen our Annie, while at St. Joseph, Mo., I will state that I well remember the statement you made to family on your return home. I remember your stating how she looked in ordinary home dress, and particularly about the scratch (or red spot) on her face, which you could not account for, but which was fully explained by your mother. The spot was made while adjusting something about her head while in the casket, and covered with powder. All who heard you relate the phenomenal sight thought it was true. You well know how sceptical I am about things which reason cannot explain.

(Signed)   H. G. (father).

I was present at the time and indorse the above.

(Signed)   K. G. (brother).

The apparent *redness* of the scratch on the face of the apparition goes naturally enough with the look of life in the face. The phantom did not appear as a corpse, but as a blooming girl, and the scratch showed as it would have shown if made during life.

Dr. Hodgson visited Mr. F. G. later, and sent us the following notes of his interview: —

ST. LOUIS, Mo., *April 16th*, 1890.

In conversation with Mr. F. G., now forty-three years of age, he says that there was a very special sympathy between his mother, sister, and himself.

When he saw the apparition he was seated at a small table, about two feet in diameter, and had his left elbow on the table. The scratch which he saw was on the right side of his sister's nose, about three fourths of an inch long, and was a somewhat ragged mark. His home at the time of the incident was in St. Louis. His mother died within two weeks after the incident. His sister's face was hardly a foot away from his own. The sun was shining upon it through the open window. The figure disappeared like an instantaneous evaporation.

Mr. G. has had another experience, but of a somewhat different character. Last fall the impression persisted for some time of a lady friend of his, and he could not rid himself for some time of thoughts of her. He found afterwards that she died at the time of the curious persistence of his impression.

Mr. G. appears to be a first-class witness.   R. HODGSON.

I have ranked this case *primâ facie* as a perception by the spirit of her mother's approaching death. That coincidence is too marked to be explained away: the son is brought home in time to see his mother once more by perhaps the only means which would have succeeded; and the mother herself is sustained by the knowledge that her daughter loves and awaits her.   Mr. Podmore[1] has suggested, on the other hand, that the daughter's figure was a mere projection from the mother's mind: a conception which has scarcely any analogy to support it; for the one ancient case of Wesermann's projection of a female figure to a distance (*Journal* S.P.R., vol. iv. p. 217) remains, I think, the sole instance where an agent has generated a hallucinatory figure or group of figures which did not, at any rate, *include* his own.   I mean that he may spontaneously project a picture of himself as he is or dreams himself to be situated, perhaps with other figures round him, but not, so far as our evidence goes, the single figure of some one other than himself.   Whilst not assuming that this rule can have no exceptions, I see no reason for supposing that it has been transgressed in the present case.   Nay, I think that the very fact that the figure was not that of the corpse with the dull mark on which the mother's regretful thoughts might dwell, but was that of the girl in health and happiness, with the symbolic *red* mark worn simply as a test of identity, goes far to show that it was not the *mother's* mind from whence that image came.   As to the spirit's own knowledge of the fate of the body after death, there are other cases which show, I think, that this specific form of *post-mortem* perception is not unusual.

VII. C.   From *Proceedings* S.P.R., vol. x. pp. 380–82.
From Miss L. Dodson: —

September 14th, 1891.

On June 5th, 1887, a Sunday evening,[2] between eleven and twelve at night, being awake, my name was called three times.   I answered twice, thinking it was my uncle, "Come in, Uncle George, I am awake," but the third time I recognised the voice as that of my mother, who had been dead sixteen years.   I said, "Mamma!"   She then came round a screen near my bedside with two children in her arms, and placed them in my arms and put the bedclothes over them and said, "Lucy, promise me to take care of them, for their mother is just dead."   I said, "Yes, mamma."   She repeated, "*Promise* me to take care of them."   I replied, "Yes, I promise you"; and I added, "Oh, mamma, stay and speak to me, I am so wretched."   She replied, "Not yet, my child," then she seemed to go round the screen again, and I remained, feeling the children to be still in my arms, and fell asleep.   When I awoke there was nothing.   Tuesday morning, June 7th, I received the news of my sister-in-law's death.   She had given birth to a child three weeks before, which I did not know till after her death.

[1] See "Phantasms of the Dead from another point of view," *Proceedings* S.P.R., vol. vi. p. 291.
[2] We have ascertained that this date was a Sunday.

I was in bed, but not asleep, and the room was lighted by a gaslight in the street outside. I was out of health, and in anxiety about family troubles. My age was forty-two. I was quite alone. I mentioned the circumstance to my uncle the next morning. He thought I was sickening for brain fever. [I have had other experiences, but] only to the extent of having felt a hand laid on my head, and sometimes on my hands, at times of great trouble.   LUCY DODSON.

Mr. C. H. Cope, who sent the case, wrote in answer to our questions: —

BRUSSELS, *October 17th*, 1891.

I have received replies from Miss Dodson to your inquiries.

(1) "Yes [I was] perfectly awake [at the time]."

(2) "Was she in anxiety about her sister-in-law?" "None whatever; I did not know a second baby had been born; in fact, had not the remotest idea of my sister-in-law's illness."

(3) "Did she think at the time that the words about the children's mother having just died referred to her sister-in-law? Had she two children?" "No, I was at a total loss to imagine whose children they were."

(4) "I was living in Albany Street, Regent's Park, at the time. My sister-in-law, as I heard afterwards, was confined at St. André (near Bruges), and removed to Bruges three days prior to her death. (*N.B.* — She had two children including the new-born baby.)"

(5) "My late uncle only saw business connections, and having no relations or personal friends in London, save myself, would not have been likely to mention the occurrence to any one."

Mr. Cope also sent us a copy of the printed announcement of the death, which Miss Dodson had received. It was dated, "Bruges, June 7th, 1887," and gave the date of death as June 5th. He quotes from Miss Dodson's letter to him, enclosing it, as follows: "[My friend], Mrs. Grange, tells me she saw [my sister-in-law] a couple of hours prior to her death, which took place about nine o'clock on the evening of June 5th, and it was between eleven and twelve o'clock the same night my mother brought me the two little children."

Professor Sidgwick writes: —

November 23rd, 1892.

I have just had an interesting conversation with Miss Dodson and her friend, Mrs. Grange.

Miss Dodson told me that she was not thinking of her brother or his wife at this time, as her mind was absorbed by certain other matters. But the brother was an object of special concern to her, as her mother on her deathbed, in 1871, had specially charged her—and she had promised — to take care of the other children, especially this brother, who was then five years old. He had married in April, 1885, and she had not seen him since, though she had heard of the birth of his first child, a little girl, in January, 1886; and she had never seen his wife nor heard of the birth of the second child.

She is as sure as she can be that she was awake at the time of the experience. She knew the time by a clock in the room and also a clock outside. She heard this latter strike twelve afterwards, and the apparition must have occurred after eleven, because lights were out in front of the public-house. The children seemed to be with her a long time; indeed, they seemed to be still with her when the clock struck twelve. The room was usually light enough to see things in — *e.g.* to get a glass of water, etc. — owing to the lamp in the street, but the distinctness with which the vision was seen is not explicable by the real light. The children were of ages corresponding to those of her sister-in-law's children, *i.e.* they seemed to be a little girl and a baby newly born; the sex was not distinguished. She was not at all alarmed.

She heard from Mrs. Grange by letter, and afterwards orally from her brother, that her sister-in-law died between eight and nine the same night.

She never had any experience of the kind, or any hallucination at all before: but *since* she has occasionally felt a hand on her head in trouble.

Mrs. Grange told me that she was with the sister-in-law about an hour and a half before her death. She left her about seven o'clock, without any particular alarm about her; though she was suffering from inflammation after childbirth, and Mrs. Grange did not quite like her look; still her state was not considered alarming by those who were attending on her. Then about 8.30 news came to Mrs. Grange in her own house that something had happened at the sister-in-law's. As it was only in the next street, Mrs. Grange put on her bonnet and went round to the house, and found she was dead. She then wrote and told Miss Dodson.

VII. D. . From *Proceedings* S.P.R., vol. viii. pp. 200–205.[1]

The first report of the case appeared in *The Herald* (Dubuque, Iowa), February 11th, 1891, as follows: —

It will be remembered that on February 2nd, Michael Conley, a farmer living near Ionia, Chickasaw County, was found dead in an outhouse at the Jefferson house. He was carried to Coroner Hoffmann's morgue, where, after the inquest, his body was prepared for shipment to his late home. The old clothes which he wore were covered with filth from the place where he was found, and they were thrown outside the morgue on the ground.

His son came from Ionia, and took the corpse home. When he reached there, and one of the daughters was told that her father was dead, she fell into a swoon, in which she remained for several hours. When at last she was brought from the swoon, she said, "Where are father's old clothes? He has just appeared to me dressed in a white shirt, black clothes, and

---

[1] Some of the correspondence about the case given in the *Proceedings* is omitted here for want of space.

felt [mis-reported for *satin*] slippers, and told me that after leaving home he sewed a large roll of bills inside his grey shirt with a piece of my red dress, and the money is still there." In a short time she fell into another swoon, and when out of it demanded that somebody go to Dubuque and get the clothes. She was deathly sick, and is so yet.

The entire family considered it only a hallucination, but the physician advised them to get the clothes, as it might set her mind at rest. The son telephoned Coroner Hoffmann, asking if the clothes were still in his possession. He looked and found them in the backyard, although he had supposed they were thrown in the vault, as he had intended. He answered that he still had them, and on being told that the son would come to get them, they were wrapped in a bundle.

The young man arrived last Monday afternoon, and told Coroner Hoffmann what his sister had said. Mr. Hoffmann admitted that the lady had described the identical burial garb in which her father was clad, even to the slippers, although she never saw him after death, and none of the family had seen more than his face through the coffin lid. Curiosity being fully aroused, they took the grey shirt from the bundle, and within the bosom found a large roll of bills sewed with a piece of red cloth. The young man said his sister had a red dress exactly like it. The stitches were large and irregular, and looked to be those of a man. The son wrapped up the garments and took them home with him yesterday morning, filled with wonder at the supernatural revelation made to his sister, who is at present lingering between life and death.

Dr. Hodgson communicated with the proprietors of *The Herald*, and both they and their reporter who had written the account stated that it was strictly accurate. The coroner, Mr. Hoffmann, wrote to Dr. Hodgson on March 18th, 1891, as follows: —

In regard to the statements in the Dubuque *Herald*, about February 19th, about the Conley matter is more than true by my investigation. I laughed and did not believe in the matter when I first heard of it, until I satisfied myself by investigating and seeing what I did.

M. M. HOFFMANN, *County Coroner*.

Further evidence was obtained through Mr. Amos Crum, pastor of a church at Dubuque. The following statement was made by Mr. Brown, whom Mr. Crum described as "an intelligent and reliable farmer, residing about one mile from the Conleys."

IONIA, *July 20th*, 1891.

Elizabeth Conley, the subject of so much comment in the various papers, was born in Chickasaw township, Chickasaw County, Iowa, in March, 1863. Her mother died the same year. Is of Irish parentage; brought up, and is, a Roman Catholic; has been keeping house for her father for ten years.

On the 1st day of February, 1891, her father went to Dubuque, Iowa, for medical treatment, and died on the 3rd of the same month very suddenly. His son was notified by telegraph the same day, and he and I started the next morning after the remains, which we found in charge of Coroner Hoffmann.

He had 9 dollars 75 cents, which he had taken from his pocket-book. I think it was about two days after our return she had the dream or vision. She claimed her father had appeared to her, and told her there was a sum of money in an inside pocket of his undershirt. Her brother started for Dubuque a few days afterwards, and found the clothes as we had left them, and in the pocket referred to found 30 dollars in currency. These are the facts of the matter as near as I can give them.

GEORGE BROWN.

Mr. Crum wrote later: —

DUBUQUE, IOWA, *August 15th*, 1891.

DEAR MR. HODGSON, — I send you in another cover a detailed account of interview with the Conleys. I could not get the doctor.

I have had a long talk with Mr. Hoffmann about the Conley incident, and think you have all the facts — and they are *facts*.

The girl Lizzie Conley swooned. She saw her dead father; she heard from him of the money left in his old shirt; she returned to bodily consciousness; she described her father's burial dress, robe, shirt, and slippers exactly, though she had never seen them. She described the pocket in the shirt that had been left for days in the shed at the undertaker's. It was a ragged-edged piece of red cloth clumsily sewn, and in this pocket was found a roll of bills — 35 dollars in amount — as taken out by Mr. Hoffmann in presence of Pat Conley, son of the deceased, and brother of the Lizzie Conley whose remarkable dream or vision is the subject of inquiry.   AMOS CRUM, *Past. Univ. Ch.*

. . . I herewith transcribe my questions addressed to Miss Elizabeth Conley, and her replies to the same concerning her alleged dream or vision. . . .

On July 17th, about noon, I called at the Conley home near Ionia, Chickasaw County, Iowa, and inquired for Elizabeth Conley. She was present, and engaged in her domestic labours. When I stated the object of my call, she seemed quite reluctant for a moment to engage in conversation. Then she directed a lad who was present to leave the room. She said she would converse with me upon the matter pertaining to her father.

Q. What is your age? A. Twenty-eight.

Q. What is the state of your health? A. Not good since my father's death.

Q. What was the state of your health previous to his death? A. It was good. I was a healthy girl.

Q. Did you have dreams, visions, or swoons previous to your father's death? A. Why, I had *dreams*. Everybody has dreams.

Q. Have you ever made discoveries or received other information during your dreams or visions previous to your father's death? A. No.

Q. Had there been anything unusual in your dreams or visions previous to your father's death? A. No, not that I know of.

Q. Was your father in the habit of carrying considerable sums of money about his person? A. Not that I knew of.

Q. Did you know *before his death* of the pocket in the breast of the shirt worn by him to Dubuque? A. No.

Q. Did you wash or prepare that shirt for him to wear on his trip to Dubuque? A. No. It was a heavy woollen undershirt, and the pocket was stitched inside of the breast of it.

Q. Will you recite the circumstances connected with the recovery of money from clothing worn by your father at the time of his death? A. (after some hesitation) When they told me that father was dead I felt very sick and bad; I did not know anything. Then father came to me. He had on a white shirt and black clothes and slippers. When I came to, I told Pat [her brother] I had seen father. I asked him (Pat) if he had brought back father's old clothes. He said, "No," and asked me why I wanted them. I told him father said to me he had sewed a roll of bills inside of his grey shirt, in a pocket made of a piece of my old red dress. I went to sleep, and father came to me again. When I awoke I told Pat he must go and get the clothes.

Q. While in these swoons did you hear the ordinary conversations or noises in the house about you? A. No.

Q. Did you see your father's body after it was placed in its coffin? A. No; I did not see him after he left the house to go to Dubuque.

Q. Have you an education? A. No.

Q. Can you read and write? A. Oh yes, I can read and write; but I've not been to school much.

Q. Are you willing to write out what you have told me of this strange affair? A. Why, I've told you all I know about it.

She was averse to writing or to signing a written statement. During the conversation she was quite emotional, and manifested much effort to suppress her feelings. She is a little more than medium size, of Irish parentage, of Catholic faith, and shows by her conversation that her education is limited.

Her brother, Pat Conley, corroborates all that she has recited. He is a sincere and substantial man, and has no theory upon which to account for the strange facts that have come to his knowledge. In his presence Coroner Hoffmann, in Dubuque, found the shirt with its pocket of red cloth stitched on the inside with long, straggling, and awkward stitches, just as a dim-sighted old man or an awkward boy might sew it there. The pocket was about 7 [seven] inches deep, and in the pocket of that dirty old shirt that had lain in Hoffmann's back room was a roll of bills amounting to 35 dollars. When the shirt was found with the pocket, as described by his sister after her swoon, and the money as told her by the old man *after his death*, Pat Conley seemed dazed and overcome by the mystery. Hoffmann says the girl, after her swoon, described exactly the burial suit, shirt, coat or robe, and satin slippers in which the body was prepared for burial. She even described minutely the slippers, which were of a new pattern that had not been in the market here, and which the girl could never have seen a sample of; and she had not seen, and never saw, the body of her father after it was placed in the coffin, and if she had seen it she could not have seen his feet "in the nice black satin slippers" which she described. . . .   AMOS CRUM, *Pastor Univ. Church.*

If we may accept the details of this narrative, which seems to have been carefully and promptly investigated, we find that the phantasm communicates two sets of facts: one of them known only to strangers (the dress in which he was buried), and one of them known only to himself (the existence of the inside pocket and the money therein). In discussing from what mind these images originate it is, of course, important to note whether any living minds, known or unknown to the percipient, were aware of the facts thus conveyed.

There are few cases where the communication between the percipient and the deceased seems to have been more direct than here. The hard, prosaic reality of the details of the message need not, of course, surprise us. On the contrary, the father's sudden death in the midst of earthly business would at once retain his attention on money matters and facilitate his impressing them on the daughter's mind. One wishes that more could be learned of the daughter's condition when receiving the message. It seems to have resembled trance rather than dream.[1]

One other case in this group I must quote at length. It illustrates the fact that the cases of deepest interest are often the hardest for the inquirer to get hold of.

From the *Proceedings* S.P.R., vol. x. pp. 385-86.

The account of the percipient, Baron B. von Driesen, was written in November, 1890, and has been translated from the Russian by Mr. M. Petrovo-Solovovo, who sent us the case.

[Baron von Driesen begins by saying that he has never believed and does not believe in the supernatural, and that he is more inclined to attribute the apparition he saw to his "excited fancy" than to anything else. After these preliminary remarks he proceeds as follows: —]

I must tell you that my father-in-law, M. N. J. Ponomareff, died in the country. This did not happen at once, but after a long and painful illness, whose sharp phases had obliged my wife and myself to join him long before his death. I had not been on good terms with M. Ponomareff. Different circumstances, which are out of place in this narrative, had

---

[1] A dream in which a message of somewhat the same kind is given is recorded in the *Journal* S.P.R., vol. vii. p. 188. See also the old case of Dr. Binns, given in his *Anatomy of Sleep*, p. 462.

estranged us from each other, and these relations did not change until his death. He died very quietly, after having given his blessing to all his family, including myself. A liturgy for the rest of his soul was to be celebrated on the ninth day. I remember very well how I went to bed between one and two o'clock on the eve of that day, and how I read the Gospel before falling asleep. My wife was sleeping in the same room. It was perfectly quiet. I had just put out the candle when footsteps were heard in the adjacent room — a sound of slippers shuffling, I might say — which ceased before the door of our bedroom. I called out, "Who is there?" No answer. I struck one match, then another, and when after the stifling smell of the sulphur the fire had lighted up the room, I saw M. Ponomareff standing before the closed door. Yes, it was he, in his blue dressing-gown, lined with squirrel furs and only half-buttoned, so that I could see his white waistcoat and his black trousers. It was he undoubtedly. I was not frightened. They say that, as a rule, one is *not* frightened when seeing a ghost, as ghosts possess the quality of paralysing fear.

"What do you want?" I asked my father-in-law. M. Ponomareff made two steps forward, stopped before my bed, and said, "Basil Feodorovitch, I have acted wrongly towards you. Forgive me! Without this I do not feel at rest there." He was pointing to the ceiling with his left hand, whilst holding out his right to me. I seized this hand, which was long and cold, shook it, and answered, "Nicholas Ivanovitch, God is my witness that I have never had anything against you."

[The ghost of] my father-in-law bowed [or bent down], moved away, and went through the opposite door into the billard-room, where he disappeared. I looked after him for a moment, crossed myself, put out the candle, and fell asleep with the sense of joy which a man who has done his duty must feel. The morning came. My wife's brothers, as well as our neighbours and the peasants, assembled, and the liturgy was celebrated by our confessor, the Rev. Father Basil. But when all was over, the same Father Basil led me aside, and said to me mysteriously, "Basil Feodorovitch, I have got something to say to you in private." My wife having come near us at this moment, the clergyman repeated his wish. I answered, "Father Basil, I have no secrets from my wife; please tell us what you wished to tell me alone."

Then Father Basil, who is living till now in the Koi parish of the district of Kashin [Gov. of Tver], said to me in a rather solemn voice, "This night at three o'clock Nicholas Ivanovitch [Ponomareff] appeared to me and begged of me to reconcile him to you."

(Signed)   BARON BASIL DRIESEN.

Mr. Solovovo adds: —

The Baroness von Driesen is now dead, so that her evidence cannot be obtained. . . .

I also saw Baron Basil von Driesen himself, and spoke with him about M. Ponomareff's ghost. He stated to me that if he were going to die to-morrow, he should still be ready to swear to the fact of his having seen the apparition, or something to this effect. I asked him to obtain for me the clergyman's account, to whom I had already written before seeing Baron von Driesen (though not knowing him), but without receiving an answer — which is but natural, after all. Baron von Driesen kindly promised to procure for me the account in question, as it was then his intention to visit different estates in Central Russia, including the one that had belonged to M. Ponomareff.

Baron Nicholas von Driesen — Baron Basil's son — called on me a few days ago. He stated, with regard to the case in question, that it was necessary to see the clergyman in order to induce him to write an account of what had happened to him.

Baron N. von Driesen afterwards sent a note to Mr. Solovovo, stating that his grandfather (M. Ponomareff) died on November 21st, 1860; and the testimony of the priest was obtained later. Mr. Solovovo, who had already ascertained independently that the Rev. Basil Bajenoff had been a priest at Koi in the year 1861, and was there still, writes: —

The following is the translation of the Rev. Basil Bajenoff's statement: —

"Koi, *July 23rd [August 4th],* 1891.

"To the account I heard from Baron B. F. Driesen in the presence of his wife's brothers, MM. N. N., A. N., and I. N. Ponomareff, as to how M. Nicholas I. Ponomareff appeared to him in the night of November 29–30th, 1860, having died nine days before, and begged of the Baron to be reconciled to him, I may add that to me also did he appear *at the same time* and with the same request, which fact, before hearing the Baron's narrative, I communicated to all those present at the liturgy for the rest of the soul of the late M. N. I. Ponomareff.

"(Signed)   Basil Bajenoff,
"Priest of Trinity Church, at Koi, District of Kashin,
Government of Tver."

VII. E.   The following is quoted from the "Report on the Census of Hallucinations" in *Proceedings* S.P.R., vol. x. p. 284.

From Countess Eugénie Kapnist: —

June 24th, 1891.

A Talta, en Février, 1889, nous fîmes la connaissance de M. P. et de sa femme, passant la soirée chez des amis communs qui avaient tenu à nous réunir. A cette époque, M. P. souffrait déjà d'une phthisie assez avancée; il venait de perdre, à Pétersbourg, son frère, atteint de la même maladie. On pria ma sœur de faire un peu de musique, et elle choisit au hasard le Prélude de Mendelssohn. A mon étonnement je vis M. P. que nous ne connaissions que de ce soir, aller, très émotionné, prendre place auprès du piano, et suivre avec une espèce d'anxiété le jeu de ma sœur. Lorsqu'elle eut fini, il dit que pour quelques instants elle venait de faire ressusciter son frère, exécutant absolument de la même manière ce morceau, qu'il jouait fréquemment. Depuis, en voyant ma sœur,

il aimait particulièrement à causer avec elle.   Je puis certifier ainsi qu'elle
une conversation que nous eûmes à une soirée, au mois de Mars.   Nous
parlions de la mort, chose fréquente à Talta, toujours peuplée de malades:
— "Savez-vous," disait-il à ma sœur, "il me semble toujours que mon
esprit est très proche du vôtre; j'ai la certitude de vous avoir déjà connue;
nous avons dans la réalité une preuve que ce n'est pas en ce monde — ce
sera que je vous aurais vue durant quelqu'autre vie précédente" (il était
un peu spirite).   "Ainsi donc, si je meurs avant vous, ce qui est bien
probable, vu ma maladie, je reviendrai vers vous, si cela m'est possible,
et je vous apparaîtrai de façon à ne pas vous effrayer désagréablement."
Ma sœur lui répondit, prenant la chose très au sérieux, qu'elle lui rendrait
la pareille si elle mourait la première, et j'étais témoin de cette promesse
mutuelle.

Néanmoins nous fîmes à peine connaissance de maison; nous nous
rencontrions parfois chez des amis communs, et nous le voyions souvent
se promener sur le quai dans un paletot couleur noisette qui excitait
notre hilarité et qui nous resta dans la mémoire je ne sais plus pour-
quoi.   Au mois de Mai, nous partions de Talta, et depuis nous eûmes
tant d'impressions diverses, nous vîmes tant de monde, que jusqu'à
l'hiver suivant nous oubliâmes complétement M. P. et sa femme, qui
représentaient pour nous des connaissances comme on en a par cen-
taines dans la vie.

Nous étions à Pétersbourg.   Le 11 Mars, c'était un lundi de Carême
en 1890, nous allâmes au théâtre voir une représentation de la troupe
des Meiningner.   Je crois qu'on donnait *Le Marchand de Venise*.   Mlle.
B. était avec nous, venue de Tsarskoé à cette occasion.   La pièce ter-
minée, nous n'eûmes que le temps de rentrer à la maison changer de toilette,
après quoi nous accompagnâmes Mlle. B. à la gare.   Elle partait avec
le dernier train, qui quitte pour Tsarskoé Sélo à 1 heure de la nuit.   Nous
l'installâmes en wagon, et ne l'y laissâmes qu'après la seconde cloche
de départ.

Notre domestique allait bien en avant de nous, afin de retrouver notre
voiture, de manière que, gagnant le perron, nous la trouvâmes avancée
qui nous attendait.   Ma sœur s'assit la première; moi je la fis attendre,
descendant plus doucement les marches de l'escalier; le domestique tenait
la portière du landau ouverte.   Je montai à demi, sur le marchepied,
et soudain je m'arrêtai dans cette pose, tellement surprise que je ne compris plus ce qui m'arrivait.   Il faisait sombre dans la voiture, et pourtant en face de ma sœur, la regardant, je vis dans un petit jour gris qu'on
eût dit factice, s'éclaircissant vers le point qui attachait le plus mes yeux,
une figure à la silhouette émoussée, diaphane, plutôt qu'indécise.   Cette
vision dura un instant, pendant lequel, pourtant, mes yeux prirent connaissance des moindres détails de ce visage, qui me sembla connu: des
traits assez pointus, une raie un peu de côté, un nez prononcé, un menton
très maigre à barbe rare et d'un blond foncé.   Ce qui me frappe, lorsque
j'y pense à présent, c'est d'avoir vu les différentes couleurs, malgré que
la lueur grisâtre, qui éclairait à peine l'inconnu, eût été insuffisante pour
les distinguer dans un cas normal.   Il était sans chapeau, et en même

temps dans un paletot comme on en porte au sud — de couleur plutôt claire — noisette.   Toute sa personne avait un cachet de grande fatigue et de maigreur.

Le domestique, très étonné de ne pas me voir monter, arrêtée ainsi sur le marchepied, crut que j'avais marché dans ma robe et m'aida à m'asseoir, pendant que je demandais à ma sœur, en prenant place à côté d'elle, si c'était bien notre voiture? A tel point j'avais perdu la tête, ayant senti un vrai engourdissement de cerveau en voyant cet étranger installé en face d'elle, je ne m'étais pas rendu compte que, dans le cas d'une présence réelle d'un semblable vis-à-vis, ni ma sœur, ni le valet de pied ne resteraient si calmement à l'envisager.   Lorsque je fus assise, je ne vis plus rien, et je demandais à ma sœur: — "N'as-tu rien vu en face de toi?" "Rien du tout, et quelle idée as-tu eue de demander, en entrant dans la voiture, si c'était bien la nôtre?" répondit-elle en riant. Alors, je lui racontais tout ce qui précéde, décrivant minutieusement ma vision. "Quelle figure connue," disait-elle, "et à paletot noisette, cette raie de côté, où donc l'avons nous vue?   Pourtant nul ne ressemble ici à ta description"; et nous nous creusions la tête sans rien trouver. Rentrées à la maison, nous racontâmes ce fait à notre mère; ma description la fit aussi souvenir vaguement d'un visage analogue.   Le lendemain soir (12 Mars) un jeune homme de notre connaissance, M. M. S., vint nous voir.   Je lui répétais aussi l'incident qui nous était arrivé.   Nous en parlâmes beaucoup, mais inutilement; je ne pouvais toujours pas appliquer le nom voulu à la personnalité de ma vision, tout en me souvenant fort bien avoir vu un visage tout pareil parmi mes nombreuses connaissances; mais où et à quelle époque? Je ne me souvenais de rien, avec ma mauvaise mémoire qui me fait souvent défaut, à ce sujet. Quelques jours plus tard, nous étions chez la grandmère de M. M. S.: — "Savez-vous," nous dit-elle, "quelle triste nouvelle je viens de recevoir de Talta?   M. P. vient de mourir, mais on ne me donne pas de détails." Ma sœur et moi, nous nous regardâmes.   A ce nom, la figure pointue et le paletot noisette retrouvèrent leur possesseur.   Ma sœur reconnut en même temps que moi, grace à ma description précise.   Lorsque M. M. S. entra, je le priai de chercher dans les vieux journaux la date exacte de cette mort.   Le décès était marqué au 14 du mois de Mars, donc, deux jours *après* la vision que j'avais eue.   J'écrivis à Talta pour avoir des renseignements.   On me répondit qu'il gardait le lit depuis le 24 Novembre et qu'il avait été depuis dans un état de faiblesse extrême, mais le sommeil ne l'avait point quitté; il dormait si longtemps et si profondément, même durant les dernières nuits de son existence, que cela faisait espérer une amélioration.   Nous nous étonnions de ce que j'aie vu M. P., malgré sa promesse de se montrer à ma sœur.   Mais je dois ajouter ici qu'avant le fait décrit ci-dessus, j'avais été voyante un certain nombre de fois, mais cette vision est bien celle que j'ai distinguée le plus nettement, avec des détails minutieux, et avec les teintes diverses du visage humain, et même du vêtement.

COMTESSE EUGÉNIE KAPNIST.
COMTESSE INA KAPNIST.

The second signature is that of the sister who was present at the time. Mr. Michael Petrovo-Solovovo, who sent us the case, writes: —

I have much pleasure in certifying that the fact of Countess Kapnist's vision was mentioned, among others, to myself before the news of Mr. P.'s death came to Petersburg. I well remember seeing an announcement of his demise in the papers.

VII. F. From *Phantasms of the Living*, vol. i. p. 522, footnote. The account was written down, a few months after the occurrence, from the dictation of the percipient — Sister Bertha, Superior of the House of Mercy at Bovey Tracy, Newton Abbot — who read it through on December 29th, 1885, pronounced it correct, and signed it.

On the night of the 10th of November, 1861 (I do not know the exact hour), I was up in my bed watching, because there was a person not quite well in the next room. I heard a voice, which I recognised at once as familiar to me, and at first thought of my sister. It said, in the brightest and most cheerful tone, "I am here with you." I answered, looking and seeing nothing, "Who are you?" The voice said, "You mustn't know yet." I heard nothing more, and saw nothing, and am certain that the door was not opened or shut. I was not in the least frightened, and felt convinced that it was Lucy's [Miss Lucy Gambier Parry's] voice. I have never doubted it from that moment. I had not heard of her being worse; the last account had been good, and I was expecting to hear that she was at Torquay. In the course of the next day (the 11th), mother told me that she had died on the morning of the 10th, rather more than twelve hours before I heard her voice.

The narrator informs us that she has never in her life experienced any other hallucination of the senses. Mrs. Gambier Parry, of Highnam Court, Gloucester, step-mother and cousin of the "Lucy" of the narrative, writes: —

Sister Bertha (her name is Bertha Foertsch) had been living for many years as German governess to Lucy Anna Gambier Parry, and was her dearest friend. She came to us at once on hearing of Lucy's death, and told me of the mysterious occurrence of the night before.

VII. G. The following case is in some respects one of the most remarkable and best authenticated instances of "haunting" on record, although, as will be seen, the evidence for the identity of the apparition is inconclusive. The case was fully described in a paper entitled "Record of a Haunted House," by Miss R. C. Morton, in *Proceedings* S.P.R., vol. viii. pp. 311–332. Besides the account of the principal percipient, Miss R. C. Morton, the paper contains independent first-hand statements from six other witnesses, — a friend, Miss Campbell, a sister and brother of Miss

Morton's who lived in the house, a married sister who visited there, and two former servants; also plans of the whole house. For the full details I must refer the reader to the original paper; I have space here only for abbreviated extracts from Miss Morton's account.

An account of the case first came into my hands in December, 1884, and this with Miss Morton's letters to her friend, Miss Campbell, are the earliest written records. On May 1st, 1886, I called upon Captain Morton at the "haunted house," and afterwards visited him at intervals, and took notes of what he told me. I also saw Miss Morton and Miss E. Morton, and the two former servants whose accounts are given in Miss Morton's paper. The phenomena as seen or heard by all the witnesses were very uniform in character, even in the numerous instances where there had been no previous communication between the percipients. Miss Morton is a lady of scientific training, and was at the time her account was written (in April, 1892) preparing to be a physician. The name "Morton" is substituted for the real family name. With that exception the names and initials are the true ones.

After describing the house and garden, Miss Morton proceeds: —

It was built about the year 1860; the first occupant was Mr. S., an Anglo-Indian, who lived in it for about sixteen years. During this time, in the month of August, year uncertain, he lost his wife, to whom he was passionately attached, and to drown his grief took to drinking. About two years later, Mr. S. married again. His second wife, a Miss I. H., was in hopes of curing him of his intemperate habits, but instead she also took to drinking, and their married life was embittered by constant quarrels, frequently resulting in violent scenes. The chief subjects of dispute were the management of the children (two girls, and either one or two boys, all quite young) of the first Mrs. S., and the possession of her jewellery, to preserve which for her children, Mr. S. had some of the boards in the small front sitting-room taken up by a local carpenter and the jewels inserted in the receptacle so formed. Finally, a few months before Mr. S.'s death, on July 14th, 1876, his wife separated from him and went to live in Clifton. She was not present at the time of his death, nor, as far as is known, was she ever at the house afterwards. She died on September 23rd, 1878.

After Mr. S.'s death the house was bought by Mr. L., an elderly gentleman, who died rather suddenly within six months of going into it. The house then remained empty for some years — probably four.

During this time there is no direct evidence of haunting, but when inquiry was made later on much hearsay evidence was brought forward. In April 1882, the house was let by the representatives of the late Mr. L. to Captain Morton, and it is during his tenancy (not yet terminated) that the appearances recorded have taken place.

The family consists of Captain M. himself; his wife, who is a great invalid; neither of whom saw anything; a married daughter, Mrs. K., then about twenty-six, who was only a visitor from time to time, sometimes with, but more often without, her husband; four unmarried daughters, myself, then aged nineteen, who was the chief percipient and now give the chief account of the apparition; E. Morton, then aged eighteen; L. and M. Morton, then fifteen and thirteen; two sons, one of sixteen, who was absent during the greater part of the time when the apparition was seen; the other, then six years old.

My father took the house in March 1882, none of us having then heard of anything unusual about the house. We moved in towards the end of April, and it was not until the following June that I first saw the apparition.

I had gone up to my room, but was not yet in bed, when I heard some one at the door, and went to it, thinking it might be my mother. On opening the door, I saw no one; but on going a few steps along the passage, I saw the figure of a tall lady, dressed in black, standing at the head of the stairs. After a few moments she descended the stairs, and I followed for a short distance, feeling curious what it could be. I had only a small piece of candle, and it suddenly burnt itself out; and being unable to see more, I went back to my room.

The figure was that of a tall lady, dressed in black of a soft woollen material, judging from the slight sound in moving. The face was hidden in a handkerchief held in the right hand. This is all I noticed then; but on further occasions, when I was able to observe her more closely, I saw the upper part of the left side of the forehead, and a little of the hair above. Her left hand was nearly hidden by her sleeve and a fold of her dress. As she held it down a portion of a widow's cuff was visible on both wrists, so that the whole impression was that of a lady in widow's weeds. There was no cap on the head but a general effect of blackness suggests a bonnet, with a long veil or a hood.

During the next two years — from 1882 to 1884 — I saw the figure about half-a-dozen times; at first at long intervals, and afterwards at shorter, but I only mentioned these appearances to one friend, who did not speak of them to any one. During this period, as far as we know, there were only three appearances to any one else.

1. In the summer of 1882 to my sister, Mrs. K., when the figure was thought to be that of a Sister of Mercy who had called at the house, and no further curiosity was aroused. She was coming down the stairs rather late for dinner at 6.30, it being then quite light, when she saw the figure cross the hall in front of her, and pass into the drawing-room. She then asked the rest of us, already seated at dinner, "Who was that Sister of Mercy whom I have just seen going into the drawing-room?" She was told there was no such person, and a servant was sent to look; but the drawing-room was empty, and she was sure no one had come in. Mrs. K. persisted that she had seen a tall figure in black, with some white about it; but nothing further was thought of the matter.

2. In the autumn of 1883 it was seen by the housemaid about 10 P.M.,

she declaring that some one had got into the house, her description agreeing fairly with what I had seen; but as on searching no one was found,
her story received no credit.

3. On or about December 18th, 1883, it was seen in the drawing-
room by my brother and another little boy.　They were playing outside
on the terrace when they saw the figure in the drawing-room close to
the window, and ran in to see who it could be that was crying so bitterly.
They found no one in the drawing-room, and the parlour-maid told them
that no one had come into the house.

After the first time, I followed the figure several times downstairs
into the drawing-room, where she remained a variable time, generally
standing to the right hand side of the bow window.　From the drawing-
room she went along the passage towards the garden door, where she
always disappeared.

The first time I spoke to her was on January 29th, 1884.　"I opened
the drawing-room door softly and went in, standing just by it.　She came
in past me and walked to the sofa and stood still there, so I went up to her
and asked her if I could help her.　She moved, and I thought she was
going to speak, but she only gave a slight gasp and moved towards the
door.　Just by the door I spoke to her again, but she seemed as if she
were quite unable to speak.　She walked into the hall, then by the side
door she seemed to disappear as before."　(Quoted from a letter written
on January 31st.)　In May and June, 1884, I tried some experiments,
fastening strings with marine glue across the stairs at different heights
from the ground — of which I give a more detailed account later on.

I also attempted to touch her, but she always eluded me.　It was
not that there was nothing there to touch, but that she always seemed
to be *beyond* me, and if followed into a corner, simply disappeared.

During these two years the only *noises* I heard were those of slight
pushes against my bedroom door, accompanied by footsteps; and if I
looked out on hearing these sounds, I invariably saw the figure.　"Her
footstep is very light, you can hardly hear it, except on the linoleum, and
then only like a person walking softly with thin boots on."　(Letter on
January 31st, 1884.)　The appearances during the next two months
— July and August, 1884 — became much more frequent; indeed they
were then at their maximum, from which time they seem gradually to
have decreased, until now they seem to have ceased.

Of these two months I have a short record in a set of journal letters
written at the time to a friend.　On July 21st I find the following account.
"I went into the drawing-room, where my father and sisters were sitting
about nine in the evening, and sat down on a couch close to the bow window.　A few minutes after, as I sat reading, I saw the figure come in at
the open door, cross the room and take up a position close behind the
couch where I was.　I was astonished that no one else in the room saw
her, as she was so very distinct to me.　My youngest brother, who had
before seen her, was not in the room.　She stood behind the couch for
about half-an-hour, and then as usual walked to the door.　I went after
her, on the excuse of getting a book, and saw her pass along the hall,

until she came to the garden door, where she disappeared. I spoke to her as she passed the foot of the stairs, but she did not answer, although as before she stopped and seemed as though *about* to speak." On July 31st, some time after I had gone up to bed, my second sister E., who had remained downstairs talking in another sister's room, came to me saying that some one had passed her on the stairs. I tried then to persuade her that it was one of the servants, but next morning found it could not have been so, as none of them had been out of their rooms at that hour, and E.'s more detailed description tallied with what I had already seen.

On the night of August 1st, I again saw the figure. I heard the footsteps outside on the landing about 2 A.M. I got up at once, and went outside. She was then at the end of the landing at the top of the stairs, with her side view towards me. She stood there some minutes, then went downstairs, stopping again when she reached the hall below. I opened the drawing-room door and she went in, walked across the room to the couch in the bow window, stayed there a little, then came out of the room, went along the passage, and disappeared by the garden door. I spoke to her again, but she did not answer.

On the night of August 2nd the footsteps were heard by my three sisters and by the cook, all of whom slept on the top landing — also by my married sister, Mrs. K., who was sleeping on the floor below. They all said the next morning that they had heard them very plainly pass and repass their doors. The cook was a middle-aged and very sensible person; on my asking her the following morning if any of the servants had been out of their rooms the night before, after coming up to bed, she told me that she had heard these footsteps before, and that she had seen the figure on the stairs one night when going down to the kitchen to fetch hot water after the servants had come up to bed. She described it as a lady in widow's dress, tall and slight, with her face hidden in a handkerchief held in her right hand. Unfortunately we have since lost sight of this servant; she left us about a year afterwards on her mother's death, and we cannot now trace her. She also saw the figure outside the kitchen windows on the terrace-walk, she herself being in the kitchen; it was then about eleven in the morning, but having no note of the occurrence, I cannot now remember whether this appearance was subsequent to the one above mentioned.

These footsteps are very characteristic, and are not at all like those of any of the people in the house; they are soft and rather slow, though decided and even. My sisters would not go out on the landing after hearing them pass, nor would the servants, but each time when I have gone out after hearing them, I have seen the figure there.

On August 5th I told my father about her and what we had seen and heard. He was much astonished, not having seen or heard anything himself at that time — neither then had my mother, but she is slightly deaf, and is an invalid. He made inquiries of the landlord (who then lived close by) as to whether he knew of anything unusual about the house, as he had himself lived in it for a short time, but he replied that he had only been there for three months, and had never seen anything unusual. . . .

On the evening of August 11th we were sitting in the drawing-room with the gas lit but the shutters not shut, the light outside getting dusk, my brothers and a friend having just given up tennis, finding it too dark; my eldest sister, Mrs. K., and myself both saw the figure on the balcony outside, looking in at the window. She stood there some minutes, then walked to the end and back again, after which she seemed to disappear. She soon after came into the drawing-room, when I saw her, but my sister did not. The same evening my sister E. saw her on the stairs as she came out of a room on the upper landing.

The following evening, August 12th, while coming up the garden, I walked towards the orchard, when I saw the figure cross the orchard, go along the carriage drive in front of the house, and in at the open side door, across the hall and into the drawing-room, I following. She crossed the drawing-room and took up her usual position behind the couch in the bow window. My father came in soon after, and I told him she was there. He could not see the figure, but went up to where I showed him she was. She then went swiftly round behind him, across the room, out of the door, and along the hall, disappearing as usual near the garden door, we both following her. We looked out into the garden, having first to unlock the garden door, which my father had locked as he came through, but saw nothing of her.

On August 12th, about 8 P.M., and still quite light, my sister E. was singing in the back drawing-room. I heard her stop abruptly, come out into the hall, and call me. She said she had seen the figure in the drawing-room close behind her as she sat at the piano. I went back into the room with her and saw the figure in the bow window in her usual place. I spoke to her several times, but had no answer. She stood there for about ten minutes or a quarter of an hour; then went across the room to the door, and along the passage, disappearing in the same place by the garden door.

My sister M. then came in from the garden, saying she had seen her coming up the kitchen steps outside. We all three then went out into the garden, when Mrs. K. called out from a window on the first storey that she had just seen her pass across the lawn in front and along the carriage drive towards the orchard. This evening, then, altogether four people saw her. My father was then away, and my youngest brother was out.

On the morning of August 14th the parlour-maid saw her in the dining-room, about 8.30 A.M., having gone into the room to open the shutters. The room is very sunny, and even with all the shutters closed it is quite light, the shutters not fitting well, and letting sunlight through the cracks. She had opened one shutter, when, on turning round, she saw the figure cross the room. We were all on the look-out for her that evening, but saw nothing; in fact, whenever we had made arrangements to watch, and were especially expecting her, we never saw anything. This servant, who afterwards married, was interviewed by Mr Myers at her own house. . . .

On August 19th we all went to the seaside, and were away a month, leaving three servants in the house.

When we came back they said that they had heard footsteps and noises frequently, but as the stair-carpets were up part of the time and the house was empty, many of these noises were doubtless due to natural causes, though by them attributed to the figure.

The cook also spoke of seeing the figure in the garden, standing by a stone vase on the lawn behind the house.

During the rest of that year and the following, 1885, the apparition was frequently seen through each year, especially during July, August, and September. In these months the three deaths took place, viz.: — Mr. S., on July 14th, 1876; the first Mrs. S. in August, and the second Mrs. S. on September 23rd.

The apparitions were of exactly the same type, seen in the same places and by the same people, at varying intervals.

The footsteps continued, and were heard by several visitors and new servants who had taken the places of those who had left, as well as by myself, four sisters and brother; in all by about twenty people, many of them not having previously heard of the apparitions or sounds.

Other sounds were also heard in addition which seemed gradually to increase in intensity. They consisted of walking up and down on the second-floor landing, of bumps against the doors of the bedrooms, and of the handles of the doors turning. . . .

During this year, at Mr. Myers's suggestion, I kept a photographic camera constantly ready to try to photograph the figure, but on the few occasions I was able to do so, I got no result; at night, usually only by candle-light, a long exposure would be necessary for so dark a figure, and this I could not obtain. I also tried to communicate with the figure, constantly speaking to it and asking it to make signs, if not able to speak, but with no result. I also tried especially to *touch* her, but did not succeed. On cornering her, as I did once or twice, she disappeared.

Some time in the summer of this year (1886), Mrs. Twining, our regular charwoman, saw the figure, while waiting in the hall at the door leading to the kitchen stairs, for her payment. Until it suddenly vanished from her sight, as no real figure could have done, she thought it was a lady visitor who had mistaken her way. Mr. Myers interviewed her on December 29th, 1889, and has her separate account.

On one night in July 1886 (my father and I being away from home), my mother and her maid heard a loud noise in an unoccupied room over their heads. They went up, but seeing nothing and the noise ceasing, they went back to my mother's room on the first storey. They then heard loud noises from the morning-room on the ground floor. They then went half-way downstairs, when they saw a bright light in the hall beneath. Being alarmed, they went up to my sister E., who then came down, and they all three examined the doors, windows, etc., and found them all fastened as usual. My mother and her maid then went to bed. My sister E. went up to her room on the second storey, but as she passed the room where my two sisters L. and M. were sleeping, they opened their door to say that they had heard noises, and also seen what they described as the *flame* of a candle, without candle or hand visible, cross the room diagonally from corner to door. Two of the maids opened the doors of their two bedrooms, and said that they had also heard noises; they all five stood at their doors with their lighted candles for some little time. They all heard steps walking up and down the landing between them; as they passed they felt a sensation which they described as "a cold wind," though their candles were not blown about. They *saw* nothing. The steps then descended the stairs, re-ascended, again descended, and did not return.

In the course of the following autumn we heard traditions of earlier haunting, though, unfortunately, in no case were we able to get a first-hand account. . . .

We also now heard from a carpenter who had done jobs in the house in Mrs. S.'s time, that Mrs. S. had wished to possess herself of the first Mrs. S.'s jewels. Her husband had called him in to make a receptacle under the boards in the morning-room on the ground-floor, in which receptacle he placed the jewels, and then had it nailed down and the carpet replaced. The carpenter showed us the place. My father made him take up the boards; the receptacle was there, but empty. . . .

During the next two years, 1887 to 1889, the figure was very seldom seen, though footsteps were heard; the louder noises had gradually ceased. From 1889 to the present, 1892, so far as I know, the figure has not been seen at all; the lighter footsteps lasted a little longer, but even they have now ceased. The figure became much less substantial on its later appearances. Up to about 1886 it was so solid and life-like that it was often mistaken for a real person. It gradually became less distinct. At all times it intercepted the light; we have not been able to ascertain if it cast a shadow.

Proofs of Immateriality.

1. I have several times fastened fine strings across the stairs at various heights before going to bed, but after all others have gone up to their rooms. These were fastened in the following way: I made small pellets of marine glue, into which I inserted the ends of the cord, then stuck one pellet lightly against the wall and the other to the banister, the string being thus stretched across the stairs. They were knocked down by a very slight touch, and yet would not be felt by any one passing up or down the stairs, and by candle-light could not be seen from below. They were put at various heights from the ground from six inches to the height of the banisters, about three feet. I have twice at least seen the figure pass through the cords, leaving them intact.

2. The sudden and complete disappearance of the figure, while still in full view.

3. The impossibility of touching the figure. I have repeatedly followed it into a corner, when it disappeared, and have tried to suddenly pounce upon it, but have never succeeded in touching it or getting my hand up to it, the figure eluding my touch.

4. It has appeared in a room with the doors shut.

On the other hand, the figure was not called up by a desire to see it, for on every occasion when we had made special arrangements to watch for it, we never saw it. On several occasions we have sat up at night hoping to see it, but in vain, — my father, with my brother-in-law, myself with a friend three or four times, an aunt and myself twice, and my sisters with friends more than once; but on none of these occasions was anything seen. Nor have the appearances been seen after we have been talking or thinking much of the figure.

The figure has been connected with the second Mrs. S.; the grounds for which are: —

1. The complete history of the house is known, and if we are to connect the figure with any of the previous occupants, she is the only person who in any way resembled the figure.

2. The widow's garb excludes the first Mrs. S.

3. Although none of us had ever seen the second Mrs. S., several people who *had* known her identified her from our description. On being shown a photo-album containing a number of portraits, I picked out one of her sister as being most like that of the figure, and was afterwards told that the sisters were much alike.

4. Her step-daughter and others told us that she especially used the front drawing-room in which she continually appeared, and that her habitual seat was on a couch placed in similar position to ours.

5. The figure is undoubtedly connected with the house, none of the percipients having seen it anywhere else, nor had any other hallucination.

In writing the above account, my memory of the occurrences has been largely assisted by reference to a set of journal letters written [to Miss Campbell] at the time, and by notes of interviews held by Mr. Myers with my father and various members of our family.

R. C. MORTON.

Of the accounts given by the other witnesses, I quote only part of Miss Campbell's statement, as follows: —

77 CHESTERTON ROAD, NORTH KENSINGTON, W.,
March 31st, 1892.

. . . On the night on which Miss Morton first spoke to the figure, as stated in her account, I myself saw her telepathically. I was in my room (I was then residing in the North of England, quite one hundred miles away from Miss Morton's home), preparing for bed, between twelve and half-past, when I seemed suddenly to be standing close by the door of the housemaid's cupboard, so facing the short flight of stairs leading to the top landing. Coming down these stairs, I saw the figure, exactly as described, and about two steps behind Miss Morton herself, with a dressing-gown thrown loosely round her, and carrying a candle in her hand. A loud noise in the room overhead recalled me to my surroundings, and although I tried for some time I could not resume the impression. The black dress, dark head-gear, widow's cuffs and handkerchief were plainly visible, though the details of them were not given me by Miss Morton till afterwards, when I asked her whether she had not seen the apparition on that night. (Signed) CATHERINE M. CAMPBELL.

To this account Miss Morton adds: —

Miss Campbell was the friend to whom I first spoke of the apparition. She suggested to me that when next I saw her I should speak; but of course she had no idea when this would be. She wrote an account to me the next day of what she had seen, and asked me if I had not seen the figure that night; but naturally did not know that I *had* done so, until she received my reply. Miss Campbell asks me to say that this is the only vision she has had, veridical or otherwise.

APPENDICES

TO

CHAPTER VIII

VIII. A. Some early experiments in thought-transference through table-tilting were published by Professor Richet in the *Revue Philosophique* for December 1884. A critical discussion of these by Gurney appeared in the *Proceedings* S.P.R., vol. ii. pp. 239–64, and a briefer report in *Phantasms of the Living*, vol. i. pp. 72–81. I quote from the latter a description of the method used: —

The place of a planchette was taken by a table, and M. Richet prefaces his account by a succinct statement of the orthodox view as to "table-turning." Rejecting altogether the three theories which attribute the phenomena to wholesale fraud, to spirits, and to an unknown force, he regards the gyrations and oscillations of séance-tables as due wholly to the unconscious muscular contractions of the sitters. It thus occurred to him to employ a table as an indicator of the movements that might be produced by "mental suggestion." The plan of the experiments was as follows. Three persons (C, D, and E) took their seats in a semi-circle, at a little table on which their hands rested. One of these three was always a "medium" — a term used by M. Richet to denote a person liable to exhibit intelligent movements in which consciousness and will apparently take no part. Attached to the table was a simple electrical apparatus, the effect of which was to ring a bell whenever the current was broken by the tilting of the table. Behind the backs of the sitters at the table was another table, on which was a large alphabet, completely screened from the view of C, D, and E, even had they turned round and endeavoured to see it. In front of this alphabet sat A, whose duty was to follow the letters slowly and steadily with a pen, returning at once to the beginning as soon as he arrived at the end. At A's side sat B, with a note-book; his duty was to write down the letter at which A's pen happened to be pointing whenever the bell rang. This happened whenever one of the sitters at the table made the simple movement necessary to tilt it. Under these conditions, A and B are apparently mere automata. C, D, and E are little more, being unconscious of tilting the table, which appears to them to tilt itself; but even if they tilted it consciously, and with a conscious desire to dictate words, they have no means of ascertaining at what letter A's pen is pointing at any particular moment; and they might tilt for ever without producing more than an endless series of incoherent letters. Things being arranged thus, a sixth operator, F, stationed himself apart both from the tilting table and from the alphabet, and concentrated his thought on some word of his own choosing, which he had not communicated to the others. The three sitters at the first table engaged in conversation, sang, or told stories; but at intervals the table tilted, the bell rang, and B wrote down the letter which A's pen was opposite to at that moment. Now, to the astonishment of all concerned, these letters, when arranged in a series, turned out to produce a more or less close approximation to the word of which F was thinking.

VIII. B. The correspondent, Mr. G. E. Long, was known to Dr. Hodgson.

From *Proceedings* S.P.R., vol. ix. p. 65.

JERSEY CITY, N. J., *October 22nd*, 1888.

. . . I think I wrote you once that about two years ago I had received what was said to be a most convincing test of spirit-return, convincing to all except myself. A young lady, a Spiritualist and medium, though not a professional, nor one that ever received one cent in pay, by means of a lettered board and toy chair, she holding one leg of the chair and I another, while a third leg of the chair served as a pointer, gave the following by means of the chair: —

First the chair spelt out my name and showed a disposition to get in my lap; then it spelled out "CARY," and when I asked for the name of the "spirit" it spelt out "George (my name), you ought to know me as I am Jim." But I didn't, and said so. Then, without my looking at the board, it spelt out "Long Island, Jim Rowe," and "Don't you remember I used to carry you when you were a little fellow," or words to that effect. I had to acknowledge the truth of it and also to say that as he was an ignorant man he possibly intended "Cary" for carry. I must own I was puzzled for the moment. To make sure of his power I asked that he count the pickets in the fence outside of the house and I would go out and confirm his statement. Somehow he couldn't agree to this, and even the medium objected. As a last resort I asked how long he had been in the spirit land and the answer came, between thirteen and fourteen years.

Now to the sequel. First it occurred to me a day or two after, that while all the incidents given were correct, the name should have been given as ROE instead of ROWE. Second, I was upon Long Island this summer, and the matter coming to my mind I inquired how long Jim Roe had been dead, and was informed he died last winter; so when I received this test so convincing to the believers *the man was not dead.*

Yours truly,   GEO. E. LONG.

On October 26th, 1888, Mr. Long adds: —

I do not think that the medium was fraudulent. Her family consists of Mr. S. and three daughters, she being the youngest. I have found all to be hypnotic subjects, with the exception of the eldest daughter.

They are all believers in Spiritualism, the youngest having been the medium. They do not sit now, as it is claimed that the sittings, while rich in spiritualistic satisfaction, were productive of a state of poor health in the medium.

As I myself have obtained information supposed to have been impossible for me to have reached, I cannot say for certainty that she had not obtained information about Jim, but I don't believe she had. As the name Rowe was being spelled I sat with my eyes turned from the board and had in mind the name Scudder, and mentally followed the taps of the chair to S C U D—when the medium said, "The name Rowe is given," etc. This would seem to leave out any involuntary muscular action. Why Rowe should have been given instead of Roe is still another phase. I wonder whether, if any question of the Roe family had arisen, I would have had in mind the name of Rowe? If so, then she produced that which I had long while before been conscious of, but was at the time unconscious of, and had it coupled with an error in spelling that I might have been guilty of had I myself been called upon at that moment to spell it. Had she been fraudulent the probability is she would have spelt it correctly.

It seems to me that the basis of Spiritualism rests mainly upon this phenomenon which men and women in a supernormal condition produce, without understanding it, and credit it to spiritual agencies.

[A general corroboration of Mr. Long's memory of the incident is added from a lady present at the time, who does not now recall the details.]

VIII. C.   The following case, received from Dr. Liébeault, is quoted from *Phantasms of the Living*, vol. i. p. 293: —

NANCY, *September 4th,* 1885.

I hasten to write to you as to that case of thought-transference of which I spoke to you when you were present at my hypnotic séances at Nancy. The incident occurred in a French family from New Orleans, who had come to stay for some time at Nancy for business reasons. I had become acquainted with this family from the fact that M. G., its head, had brought to me his niece, Mlle. B., to be treated by hypnotism. She suffered from slight anæmia and from a nervous cough, contracted at Coblentz, in a High School where she was a teacher. I easily induced somnambulism, and she was cured in two sittings. The production of this hypnotic state suggested to the G. family (Mrs. G. was a spirit medium) and to Mlle. B. herself that she might easily become a medium. She set herself to the evocation of spirits (in which she firmly believed) by the aid of her pen, and at the end of two months she had become a remarkable writing medium. I have myself seen her rapidly writing page after page of what she called "messages," — all in well-chosen language and with no erasures, — while at the same time she maintained conversation with the people near her. An odd thing was that she had no knowledge whatever of what she was writing. "It must be a spirit," she would say, "which guides my hand; it is certainly not I."

One day, — it was, I think, February 7th, 1868, about 8 A.M., when just about to seat herself at table for breakfast, she felt a kind of need, an impulse which prompted her to write; — it was what she called a *trance*, — and she rushed off at once to her large note-book, where she wrote in pencil, with feverish haste, certain undecipherable words. She wrote the same words again and again on the pages which followed, and at last, as her agitation diminished, it was possible to read that a person called Marguérite was thus announcing her death. The family at once assumed that a young lady of that name, a friend of Mlle. B.'s and her companion and colleague in the Coblentz High School, must have just expired. They all came immediately to me, Mlle. B. among them, and we decided to verify the announcement of death that very day. Mlle. B. wrote to a young English lady who was also a teacher in that same school. She gave some other reason for writing; — taking care not to reveal the true motive of the letter. By return of post we received an answer in English, of which they copied for me the essential part. I found this answer in a portfolio hardly a fortnight ago, and have mislaid it again. It expressed the surprise of the English lady at the receipt of Mlle. B.'s unexpected and apparently motiveless letter. But at the same time the English correspondent made haste to announce to Mlle. B. that their common friend, Marguérite, had died on February 7th, at about 8 A.M. Moreover, the letter contained a little square piece of printed paper; — the announcement of death sent round to friends.

I need not say that I examined the envelope, and that the letter appeared to me to have veritably come from Coblentz. Yet I have since felt a certain regret. In the interests of science I ought to have asked the G. family to allow me to go with them to the telegraph office to inquire whether they had received a telegram early on February 7th. Science should feel no shame; truth does not dread exposure. My proof of the fact is ultimately a moral one: the honour of the G. family, — which has always appeared to me to be absolutely above suspicion.

A. A. Liébeault.

Upon these last sentences Gurney remarks that, apart from the improbability that the whole family would join in a conspiracy to deceive their friend, the nature of the answer received from Coblentz shows that the writer of it cannot have been aware that any telegraphic announcement had been sent. And it is in itself unlikely that the authorities of the school would have felt it necessary instantly to communicate the news to Mdlle. B.

VIII. D.   From *Proceedings* S.P.R., vol. vi. pp. 349–53. The narrative is a translation from an article in *Psychische Studien*, December 1889, pp. 572–77, by the Editor, the Hon. Alexander Aksakoff.

The case belongs not to the category of *facts which are known only to the deceased*, but to the category of those which *could only be imparted by the deceased*, for it relates to a political secret concerning a living person, which was revealed by an intimate friend of that living person for the purpose of saving him. I shall set forth this case in all possible detail, because I consider it a most convincing one in support of the Spiritualistic hypothesis. I will even express myself still more strongly. I consider that it affords as absolute a proof of identity as it is possible for evidence of this kind to present.

My readers are already acquainted with my sister-in-law, Mrs. A. von Wiesler, from the part she took in the family séances held with me in the years 1880–1883, after the decease of my wife. She has an only daughter, Sophie, who at the time of those séances was completing her studies. She had taken no part, either at our séances or at any others, and she had not read anything about Spiritualism. Her mother also had not joined in any séances except our own. One evening in October 1884, during the visit of a distant relative, the conversation turned upon Spiritualism, and in order to please him a trial with the table was arranged. This séance, however, gave no satisfactory result. It only showed that the two ladies were able to get something. On Tuesday evening, January 1st, 1885, Mrs. von Wiesler being alone with her daughter, in order to divert her mind from some matters which made her anxious, proposed to hold a little séance. An alphabet was written out on a sheet of paper, a saucer with a black line as pointer served as a planchette, and, behold, the name Andreas was indicated. This was quite natural, for Andreas was the name of Sophie's father, the deceased husband of Mrs. von Wiesler. The communication presented nothing remarkable, but it was nevertheless resolved to continue the séances once a week, on every Tuesday. For three weeks the character of the communications remained unchanged. The name Andreas was continually repeated.

But on the fourth Tuesday — January 22nd — in place of the customary name, Andreas, the name "Schura" was spelt out, to the great astonishment of both sitters. Then, by quick and precise movements of the pointer, these words were added: —

"It is given to thee to save Nikolaus."

"What does this mean?" asked the astonished ladies.

"He is compromised as Michael was, and will like him go to ruin. A band of good-for-nothing fellows are leading him astray."

"What can be done to counteract it?"

"Thou must go to the Technological Institute before three o'clock, let Nikolaus be called out, and make an appointment with him at his house."

This being all addressed to the young lady, Sophie, she replied that it would be difficult for her to carry out these directions on account of the slight acquaintanceship which existed between her and Nikolaus's family.

"Absurd ideas of propriety!" was "Schura's" indignant reply.

"But in what way shall I be able to influence him?" asked Sophie

"Thou wilt speak to him in my name."

"Then your convictions no longer remain the same?"

"Revolting error!" was the reply.

I must now explain the meaning of this mysterious communication.

"Schura" is the Russian pet name for Alexandrine. Nikolaus and Michael were her cousins. Michael, quite a young man, had unfortunately allowed himself to become entangled by the revolutionary ideas of our Anarchists or Socialists. He was arrested, tried, and condemned to imprisonment at a distance from St. Petersburg, where he lost his life in an attempt to escape. "Schura" loved him dearly, and fully sympathised with his political convictions, making no secret of it. After his death, which occurred in September 1884, she was discouraged in her revolutionary aspirations, and ended her life by poison, at the age of seventeen, on the 15th of January 1885, just one week before the séance above described. Nikolaus, Michael's brother, was then a student at the Technological Institute.

Mrs. von Wiesler and her daughter were aware of these circumstances, for they had long been acquainted with "Schura's" parents, and with those of her cousins, who belong to the best society of St. Petersburg. It will be obvious that I cannot publish the names of these families. I have also changed those of the young people. The acquaintanceship was, however, far from being intimate. They saw each other occasionally, but nothing more. Later I will give further details. We will now continue our narrative.

Naturally, neither Mrs. von Wiesler nor her daughter knew anything as to the views or secret conduct of Nikolaus. The communication was just as unexpected as it was important. It involved a great responsibility. Sophie's position was a very difficult one. The literal carrying out of "Schura's" demands was, for a young lady, simply impossible, merely from considerations of social propriety. What right could she have, on the ground of simple acquaintanceship, to interfere in family affairs of so delicate a character? Besides, it might not be true; or, quite simply and most probably, Nikolaus might deny it. What position would she then find herself in? Mrs. von Wiesler knew only too well, from the séances she had taken part in with me, how little dependence can be placed on Spiritualistic communications. She counselled her daughter, in the first place, to convince herself of "Schura's" identity. This advice was followed without any hesitation as one way out of the difficulty.

On the following Tuesday "Schura" manifested at once, and Sophie asked for a proof of her identity, to which "Schura" forthwith replied: —

"Invite Nikolaus, arrange a séance, and I will come."

It will be seen from this reply that "Schura," who during her life had learnt to despise the conventionalities of society, as is the custom among the Socialists, remained true to her character, and again demanded what was an impossibility. Nikolaus had never been in Mrs. von Wiesler's house. Sophie then asked for another proof of her identity, without Nikolaus being brought in at all, and requested that it might be a convincing one.

"I will appear to thee," was the reply.

"How?"

"Thou wilt see."

A few days later Sophie was returning home from a soirée; it was nearly 4 A.M. She was just retiring, and was at the door between her bedroom and the dining-room, there being no lights in the latter, when she saw on the wall of the dining-room, in sight of the door at which she stood, a luminous round spot, with, as it were, shoulders. This lasted for two or three seconds, and disappeared, ascending towards the ceiling. Sophie immediately assured herself that it was not the reflection of any light coming from the street.

At the séance on the following Tuesday, an explanation of this appearance being asked for, "Schura" replied: —

"It was the outline of a head with shoulders. I cannot appear more distinctly. I am still weak."

Many other details, which I have passed over, tended to convince Sophie of the reality of "Schura's" identity, yet she could not bring herself to carry out that which "Schura" desired her to do. She therefore proposed as a suitable compromise that she should acquaint Nikolaus's parents with what had occurred.

This proposal aroused "Schura's" strongest displeasure, expressed by violent movements of the saucer, and by the sentence: —

"That will lead to nothing"; —after which disparaging epithets followed, impossible to repeat here, especially applicable to persons of weak and irresolute character, with whom the energetic and decisive "Schura" had no patience — epithets which are not found in dictionaries, but which were expressions used by "Schura" in her lifetime, and characteristic of her. This was confirmed in the sequel.

Nevertheless Sophie continued to hesitate, and at each successive séance "Schura" insisted more and more imperatively that Sophie must act at once. This is very important to notice, as we shall see later. This want of resolution on the part of Sophie was ascribed by "Schura" to the influence of Mrs. von Wiesler. From the beginning "Schura" had seemed to bear a grudge against Mrs. von Wiesler. From the first séance she addressed Sophie only. She never permitted Mrs. von Wiesler to ask a question. Whenever she attempted to do so, she met with a — "Be silent — be silent!" Whereas in addressing Sophie she overwhelmed her with the tenderest expressions.

How great was the astonishment and consternation of the ladies, when at the séance on the 26th of February the first words were: —

"It is too late. Thou wilt repent it bitterly. The pangs of remorse will follow thee. Expect his arrest!"

These were "Schura's" last words. From this time she was silent. A séance was attempted on the following Tuesday, but there was no result. The séances of Mrs. von Wiesler and her daughter were from that time entirely given up.

While these séances were being held, Mrs. von Wiesler naturally kept me informed of what transpired, and consulted with me as to what was to be done in view of the extraordinary character of "Schura's" requests. Some time after they had ceased, Mrs. von Wiesler, to satisfy her own conscience and to comfort her daughter, resolved to communicate the whole episode to the parents of Nikolaus. They paid no attention to it. Nothing was elicited that any fault could be found with. The family were quite satisfied in regard to Nikolaus's conduct. But it is important to bear in mind the fact that these Spiritualistic communications were made known to the parents before the final issue. When during the remainder of the year everything went on happily, Sophie became fully convinced that all the communications were only lies, and formed a resolution that she would never again occupy herself with Spiritualistic séances.

Another year passed without any special event. But on the 9th of March, 1887, the secret police suddenly searched Nikolaus's rooms. He was arrested in his own house, and within twenty-four hours was exiled from St. Petersburg. It came out later that his crime was taking part in anarchical assemblies — assemblies which were held in the months of January and February 1885, exactly corresponding with the time when "Schura" was insisting that steps should *then* be taken to dissuade Nikolaus from taking part in such meetings. Only now were the communications of "Schura" estimated at their true value. The notes which Mrs. von Wiesler had made were read again and again by the families both of "Schura" and of Nikolaus. "Schura's" identity in all those manifestations was recognised as incontestably demonstrated, in the first place, by the main fact in relation to Nikolaus, by other intimate particulars, and also by the totality of the features which characterised her personality. This mournful occurrence fell like a fresh thunderclap on Nikolaus's family, and they had only to thank God that the errors of the young man were not followed by more fatal results.

In order to estimate this incident aright, it is of great importance to establish the relations which existed between the two young ladies. I have requested Madame and Mdlle. von Wiesler to give me on this, as on the previous points, a written memorandum in full detail; and from that memorandum I extract what follows [somewhat abridged here]: —

In December 1880 Madame von Wiesler and her daughter paid a Christmas visit to "Schura's" grandfather, Senator N., where Sophie saw "Schura" for the first time. Sophie was then about thirteen years old, and "Schura" even younger. Sophie was astonished to see "Schura's" writing-table covered with books [and had a talk with her about favourite authors]. The two girls often saw each other at a distance in the recreation-room of their school during the winter, but "Schura" was soon transferred to another school. [They met once at a country-house without exchanging a word, and saw each other once across a theatre. Sophie, in fact, had had one childish talk with "Schura"; Madame von Wiesler had never had any real talk with her.] Hence it is clear that the relations of these ladies with "Schura" were of the most distant kind, and that they could not know anything of her political secrets.

VIII. E.   From *Proceedings* S.P.R., vol. viii. pp. 248–51.[1]

[1] An account of this case appeared in an article by Herman Snow in the *Religio-Philosophical Journal* for January 31st, 1891, and Mr. Snow also sent us an earlier

The following letters were received from the principal witness, Mrs. Finney: —

ROCKLAND, MASS., *April 19th*, 1891.

MR. HODGSON, — DEAR SIR, — Some weeks ago I received from you a few lines asking me to give you an account of the communication received from Cousin Benja in spirit-life, some twenty-five years ago.

For weeks and months before my brother left the form we conversed freely on the subject of spirit communion and such matters, and one morning he requested me to bring him a small piece of brick, also pen and ink; he then made two marks on one side, and one on the other with the ink, then breaking the brick in two, gave me one piece, telling me at the time to take care of it, and some day he would hide the other piece away where no one but himself would know, and after leaving the form, if possible, would return in some way and tell me where it was. I could then compare them together, and it would be a test that he could return and communicate, and *my mind* could not have any influence over it, as I did not know where he put it.

After he left the form our anxiety was *very great* to hear and learn all we could of communicating with spirits, and for months we got nothing satisfactory.

We then commenced sitting at the table at home (mother and my-self), which we did for some little time; at last it commenced tipping, and by calling the alphabet spelled out where we could find the piece of brick that he put away, — that was the way we got the test. To us that was truth that spirits can and do communicate with us, and nothing but the influence and power of Benja could tell us that test. — Truly yours,

MRS. WM. A. FINNEY.

ROCKLAND, *May 3rd*, 1891.

MR. R. HODGSON, — DEAR SIR, — Yours of April 21st received, and I will add a few more lines as to statement of brother Benja's communication.

By calling the alphabet we spelled out: —

"You will find that piece of brick in the cabinet under the tomahawk. — BENJA."

I went to that room and took the key, unlocked the cabinet, which had not been touched by any one after he locked it and put away the key. There I found that piece of brick just as it had spelled out, and it corresponded with the piece I had retained, fitting on exactly where he broke it off the piece I had. It was wrapped in a bit of paper and tucked into a shell, and placed in the bottom of the cabinet *exactly under* the tomahawk, as was spelled out by the alphabet.

article on the subject which he had written in 1881, and of which his second account was a mere repetition. The facts were related to him by the Unitarian minister of the place where Mrs. Finney lived; and this third-hand account recorded by Mr. Snow fifteen years after the event closely coincides with Mrs. Finney's first-hand one, recorded twenty-five years after the event.

This is truth, and no power but Benja's could tell that.

Mother is not living; I am the only one of the family that is living. — Yours respectfully,   MRS. WM. A. FINNEY.

ROCKLAND, *May 11th,* 1891.

MR. R. HODGSON, — DEAR SIR, — Yours of 6th received. I will continue to say, in answer to your questions, that the piece of brick was entirely concealed in the shell, so that it could not be seen from outside of cabinet. It was wrapped in a piece of paper stuck together with muci-lage and tucked into the end of the shell, then a piece of paper gummed over that, so that nothing was visible from the shell. The shell was on the lower shelf of the cabinet, and only the top of the shell was visible outside the cabinet.

One more little incident I will mention, for to me it is as valuable as the other. He wrote me a letter (about the time he gave me the piece of brick) and sealed it, saying at the time it was not to be answered, but the contents of the letter to be told. I got that in the same way I did the other, by calling the alphabet and the table tipping. It was these words: —

"Julia! do right and be happy. — BENJA."

That was correct. Just the contents of my letter. I have no par-ticular objection as to giving my name, for I have stated nothing but the truth.

At my home in Kingston I have that little shell with the piece of brick, and if you would like them I will send them to you. Will place the brick into the shell as it was when I found it. Of course, the paper that was around it then is worn out years ago. The cabinet is disposed of.

                                    JULIA A. FINNEY.

Mrs. Finney further writes: —

ROCKLAND, *June 26th,* 1891.

I send you by express a box containing the letter and shell with the piece of brick. I have placed one piece in the shell just as it was when I found it, so you can see how nicely it was concealed in the shell. The papers that were around it then are worn out. You can retain them if you like, as I do not care for them now.

To me it is a positive truth that he did communicate to us, and our minds could have nothing to do with it.   J. A. FINNEY.

ROCKLAND, *July 19th,* 1891.

. . . The shell was placed on the same shelf with the tomahawk, and no other shells on that shelf. It was placed with the open side down, and the tomahawk stood directly over it. I cannot say why he did not tell us to look inside of the shell. We started to look as soon as he told ns. It was in the cabinet under the tomahawk. We did not wait for any more to be said.

I am not intimately acquainted with many public people. As to my integrity, will refer you to Rev. C. Y. de Normandie, of Kingston.

                                    J. A. FINNEY.

Dr. Hodgson writes: —

The shell is a large Triton, about ten inches long. The piece of brick was wrapped in folds of soft paper and tucked deeply into the recess. Another piece of paper was then gummed around the sides of the shell in the interior, so as absolutely to prevent the piece of brick from falling out. When I received the shell from Mrs. Finney and looked into the interior and shook the shell violently, there was nothing to indicate that the shell contained anything but the piece of gummed paper.

The piece of brick in the shell weighs one and a half ounces, and the piece of brick retained by Mrs. Finney weighs about two and a quarter ounces. The shell with the piece of brick and paper wrapping weighs about eleven and a half ounces.

Mrs. Finney also forwarded me the letter written by her brother. The shell and the pieces of brick and the letter are now all in my possession.

R. HODGSON.

We have a letter (in original) from the Rev. C. Y. de Normandie, of Kingston, Canada, to Mrs. Finney. "I expressed then," he says, speaking of a former note to Dr. Hodgson, which accidentally went astray, "that to the best knowledge I had of you and to my firm belief your word could be implicitly relied on. I felt confident that you would state a matter as you understood it, as you regarded it, without reference to the consequences; and that you would not be any more likely to be misled and deceived about a matter of that kind than others similarly situated."

APPENDICES

TO

CHAPTER IX

SCHEME OF VITAL FACULTY.

IX. A. The following scheme[1] is not put forth as expressing deliberate convictions, supported by adequate evidence. Its speculative character has, in fact, excluded it from my text, yet I hope that it may not be without its use. For many men the difficulty of belief is not so much in defect of trustworthy evidence as in the unintelligibility, the *incoherence* of the phenomena described, which prevents them from being retained in the mind or assimilated with previous knowledge.

I have felt myself the full force of this objection, and I believe that some effort to meet it has become absolutely needful. Undoubtedly a record of facts without theories is the first essential. But the facts individually are like "stones that fall down from Jupiter," — isolated marvels, each of which seems incredible until we have made shift to colligate them all.

Let us begin, then, by taking the most generalised view possible of all these phenomena. They appear, at any rate, to depend upon the presence of living human beings; and they are therefore in some sense phenomena of *life*. If, then, they are phenomena of life, they must be in some way derived from, or must bear some analogy to, the vital phenomena, the faculties and functions with which we are familiar in the experience of every day. Yet to say this brings us little nearer to our aim. Spirits may have ruled Mr. Moses' mind and body just as truly as our own conscious will rules our mind and body.[2] But the results which they produced were so different from any results which we can produce that it is hard to know where to begin the comparison. Is there not some middle term, some intermediate series, with which both these extreme series may have points of resemblance?

[1] In this edition the synopsis of the scheme alone is given.
[2] This appendix was written originally with a special view to the phenomena alleged to occur in the case of Mr. W. Stainton Moses.

It is here that we ought to feel the advantage of previous discussions on man's own supernormal faculties, — on the powers of the Self below the threshold of ordinary consciousness. We have traced these powers in detail; we have noted the extension of the normal spectrum of consciousness beyond both red and violet ends, in response to subliminal control. Perhaps the profounder conception of the Self thus gained may help us to bridge over that gulf between the performances of the ordinary man and those of the so-called medium which heretofore has involved so difficult a leap. We may find that the spirit's power over the organism which it controls or "possesses," — while possibly going much further than any subliminal power in the organism itself, as known to us, — may yet advance along similar lines, and receive explanation from hypnotic or telepathic phenomena. I will endeavour, then, to set side by side, in tabular form, the main heads of vital process or faculty as exercised (1) under normal or supraliminal control; (2) under subliminal and telepathic control; (3) under what is claimed as disembodied or spiritual control.

In arranging this scheme my first object is to bring all such phenomena as we actually have before us into intelligible connection; introducing by the way a few of the explanations given to Mr. Moses by his guides. Those explanations, however, are for the most part slight and vague, and our experimental knowledge of the phenomena is, of course, merely nascent and fragmentary. My scheme, therefore, cannot aim at complete logical arrangement. It must involve both repetitions and lacunæ; nor can it be such as the physiologist would care to sanction. But it will, at least, be a first attempt at a connected schedule or rational index of phenomena apparently so disparate that the very possibility of their interdependence is even now constantly denied.

SYNOPSIS OF VITAL FACULTY

I.

FIRST SERIES: — PHENOMENA SUPRALIMINALLY CONTROLLED, OR OCCURRING IN ORDINARY LIFE.

1. Supraliminal or empirical consciousness; aware only of the material world through sensory impressions.
2. Physical nutrition, including respiration.
    (a) Physiological and pathological processes and products.
3. Physical expenditure; action on material and etherial environment.
    (a) Mechanical work done at the expense of food assimilated.

(b) Production of heat, odour, sound, chemical changes, as the result of protoplasmic metabolism.

(c) Production of etherial disturbances; as emission of light and generation of electrical energy.

4. Action on the incarnation of life on the planet.

(a) Reproduction, as physiological division.

5. Mental nutrition; sensory receptivity.

(a) Ordinary sense-perception.

(b) Memory.

6. Mental expenditure; response to stimuli.

(a) Intra-cerebral response; ideation.

(b) Emotion; will; voluntary innervation.

7. Modifications of supraliminal personality.

(a) Birth; as physiological individuation.

(b) Sleep; with dreams, as oscillations of the conscious threshold.

(c) Metamorphoses; as of insects and amphibians; and polymorphism, as of hydrozoa; multiplex personality.

(d) Death; as physiological dissolution.

II.

SECOND SERIES: — PHENOMENA SUBLIMINALLY CONTROLLED.

1. Subliminal consciousness; obscurely aware of the transcendental world, through telepathic and telæsthetic impressions.

2. Physical nutrition modified by subliminal control.

(a) Suggestion, self-suggestion, psycho-therapeutics.

(b) Stigmatisation.

3. Physical expenditure modified by subliminal control.

(a) Mechanical work modified by psychical integration or disintegration; hysteria.

(b) Production of heat, and other specific effects upon matter, subliminally modified.

(c) Emission of light, and generation of electrical energy modified.

4. Action on the incarnation of life on the planet.

(a) Prenatal suggestion through intermediate organism of parent.

5. Mental nutrition (sensory and supersensory receptivity) subliminally controlled.

(a) Hyperæsthesia; anæsthesia; analgesia.

(b) Hypermnesia, manifested in dreams or automatisms.

(c) Telepathy; veridical hallucinations; sensory automatism.

(*d*) Telæsthesia or clairvoyance; perception of distant scenes; retrocognition; precognition.

6. Mental expenditure; response to stimuli modified by subliminal control.

    (*a*) Subliminal ideation; the inspirations of genius.

    (*b*) Motor automatism; concurrent consciousness; hyperboulia.

    (*c*) Extradition of will-power beyond the organism; telergy; self-projection.

7. Modifications of subliminal personality.

    (*a*) Birth; as spiritual individuation.

    (*b*) Sleep and trance; self-suggested or telepathically suggested; with clairvoyant visions.

    (*c*) Ecstasy.

    (*d*) Death; as irrevocable self-projection of the spirit.

III.

THIRD SERIES: — PHENOMENA CLAIMED AS SPIRITUALLY CONTROLLED.

1. Subliminal consciousness, discerning and influenced by disembodied spirits in a spiritual world, who co-operate in producing objective phenomena.

2. Physical nutrition modified by spirit-control.

    (*a*) Spirit-suggestion; psycho-therapeutics.

    (*b*) Stigmatisation.

    (*c*) Novel and purposive metastasis of secretion.

3. Physical expenditure modified by spirit-control.

    (*a*) Mechanical efficiency increased and fulcrum displaced.

    (*b*) Control over individual material molecules; resulting in abrogation of ordinary thermal laws, and in aggregation and disaggregation of matter.

    (*c*) Control over etherial manifestations; with possible effects in the domains of light, electricity, gravitation, and cohesion.

4. Action on the incarnation of life on the planet.

    (*a*) Pre-conceptual suggestion or self-suggestion.

    (*b*) Ectoplasy or Materialisation; temporary extradition or concentration of vital energy.

5. Mental nutrition modified by spirit-control.

    (*a*) Ordinary sensory perception spiritually controlled.

    (*b*) Memory controlled; retrocognition spiritually given.

    (*c*) Sensory automatism spiritually controlled; phantasms of the dead, etc.

(*d*) Telæsthesia developed into perception of spiritual environment; precognition.

6. Response to stimuli spiritually controlled.

    (*a*) Ideation inspired by spirits.

    (*b*) Motor automatism spiritually controlled; possession.

    (*c*) Extension of will-power into the spiritual world; prayer.

7. Modifications of personality from spiritual standpoint.

    (*a*) Birth; as descent into generation.

    (*b*) Sleep and trance induced, and visions inspired, by spirits.

    (*c*) Precursory emergence into completer personality; ecstasy with perception of spiritual world.

    (*d*) Death; as birth into completer personality.

    (*e*) Vital faculty fully exercised in spiritual world.

IX. B. (1) The following case is quoted from the *Journal* S.P.R., vol. v. p. 253. Professor Luther writes: —

HARTFORD, CONN., *March 2nd*, 1892.

. . . Miss C. is often in my study and consults my books freely, so that her dream was not remarkable. The dream of Mrs. L. (my wife) was also ordinary in character. The coincidence in time of the dreams may have been merely a coincidence. But that after these occurrences Mrs. L. should suddenly, without the least premeditation and without hesitation, take the right book and open it at the right page with the certainty of a somnambulist, seems to me strange. . . .

These events took place yesterday, last night, and this morning.

F. S. LUTHER

(Prof. Math., Trinity College).

Mrs. L. and Miss C. live at the same hotel and meet daily. Miss C. is engaged in writing an essay upon Emerson, and expresses to Mrs. L. her wish to obtain some particulars as to Emerson's private life. Mrs. L. regrets that she has no book treating of the subject. During the night following this conversation Mrs. L. dreams of handing Miss C. a book containing an article such as is desired, and Miss C. dreams of telling Mrs. L. that she had procured just the information which she had been looking for. Each lady relates to the other her dream when they meet at breakfast the next morning. Mrs. L. returns to her room, and, while certainly not consciously thinking of Emerson, suddenly finds in her mind the thought, "There is the book which Miss C. needs." She goes directly to a bookcase, takes down vol. xvii. of the *Century Magazine*, and opens *immediately* at the article, "The Homes and Haunts of Emerson." Mrs. L. had undoubtedly read this article in 1879, but she had never studied Emerson or his works, nor had she made any special effort to assist Miss C. in her search, though feeling a friend's interest in the proposed essay.

After receiving the book and hearing how it was selected, Miss C. relates her dream more fully, it appearing that she had seemed to be standing in front of Mrs. L.'s shelves with a large, illustrated book in her hands, and that in the book was something about Emerson.

Still later it is found that Miss C. had actually noticed the article in question while actually in the position reproduced in her dream. This, however, had happened about a month previous to the events just narrated, and before she had thought of looking up authorities as to Emerson, so that she had entirely forgotten the occurrence and the article. Neither did she, at that time, call Mrs. L.'s attention to the article, or mention Emerson.

According to the best information attainable, Miss C. was not thinking of her essay at the time when Mrs. L. felt the sudden impulse to take down a certain book. And perhaps it should be added that the volume is one of a complete set of the *Century* variously disposed upon Mrs. L.'s shelves.

[This account is signed by Professor Luther, Mrs. L., and Miss C.]

Of special interest are a few cases where the actual mechanism of some brief communication from the spiritual world seems to suggest and lead up to the mechanism which we shall afterwards describe either as ecstasy or as possession.

(2) I give here a case which suggests such knowledge as may be learnt in ecstasy; — as though a message had been communicated to a sleeper during some brief excursion into the spiritual world, — which message was remembered for a few moments, in symbolic form, and then rapidly forgotten, as the sleeper returned fully into the normal waking state. What is to be noted is that the personality of sleep, to which I attribute the spiritual excursion, seems at first to have been "controlling" the awakened organism. In other words, Professor Thoulet was partially entranced or *possessed* by his own spirit or subliminal self.

I quote from *Proceedings* S.P.R., vol. xi. pp. 503-5, a translation of the original account of the case in the *Annales des Sciences Psychiques* (September–October, 1891).

Professor Thoulet writes to Professor Richet as follows: —

April 17th, 1891.

. . . During the summer of 1867, I was officially the assistant, but in reality the friend, in spite of difference in age, of M. F., a former officer in the navy, who had gone into business. We were trying to set on foot again the exploitation of an old sulphur mine at Rivanazzaro, near Voghera, in Piedmont, which had been long abandoned on account of a falling in.

We occupied the same rooms, and our relations were those of father and son, or of elder and younger brother. . . .

I knew that Madame F., who lived at Toulon, and with whom I was slightly acquainted, would soon be confined. I cannot say I was indifferent about this fact, for it concerned M. F.; but it certainly caused me no profound emotion; it was a second child, all was going well, and M. F. was not anxious. I myself was well and calm. It is true that a few days before, in Burgundy, my mother had fallen out of a carriage; but the fall had no bad consequences, and the letter which informed me of it also told me there was no harm done.

M. F. and I slept in adjoining rooms, and as it was hot we left the door between them open. One morning I sprang suddenly out of bed, crossed my room, entered that of M. F., and awakened him by crying out, "You have just got a little girl; the telegram says . . ." Upon this I began to read the telegram. M. F. sat up and listened; but all at once I understood that I had been asleep, and that consequently my telegram was only a dream, not to be believed; and then, at the same time, this telegram, which was somehow in my hand and of which I had read about three lines aloud, word for word, seemed to withdraw from my eyes as if some one were carrying it off open; the words disappeared, though their image still remained; those which I had *pronounced* remained in my memory, while the rest of the telegram was only a *form*.

I stammered something; M. F. got up and led me into the dining-room, and made me write down the words I had pronounced; when I came to the lines which, though they had disappeared from my memory, still remained pictured in my eye, I replaced them by dots, making a sort of drawing of them. Remark that the telegram was not written in common terms; there were about six lines of it, and I had read more than two of them. Then, becoming aware of our rather incorrect costume, M. F. and I began to laugh, and went back to our beds.

Two or three days after I left for Torée; I tried in vain to remember the rest of the telegram; I went on to Turin, and eight or ten days after my dream I received the following telegram from M. F., "Come directly, you were right."

I returned to Rivanazzaro and M. F. showed me a telegram which he had received the evening before; I recognised it as the one I had seen in my dream; the beginning was exactly what I had written, and the end, which was exactly like my drawing, enabled me to read *again* the words which I saw *again*. Please remark that the confinement had taken place the evening before, and therefore the fact was not that I, being in Italy, had seen a telegram which already existed in France — this I might with some difficulty have understood — but that I had seen it ten days before it existed or could have existed; since the event it announced had not yet taken place. I have turned this phenomenon over in my memory and reasoned about it many times, trying to explain it, to connect it with something, with a previous conversation, with some mental tension, with an analogy, a wish, — and all in vain. M. F. is dead, and the paper I wrote has disappeared. If I were called before a court of justice about it, I could not furnish the shadow of a material proof, and again the two personalities which exist in me, the animal and the *savant*, have disputed on this subject so often that sometimes I doubt it myself. However, the animal, obstinate as an animal usually is, repeats incessantly that I have seen, and I have read, and it is useless for me to tell myself that if any one else told me such a story I should not believe it. I am obliged to admit that it happened.

J. THOULET,
Professor at the Faculté des Sciences at Nancy.

Professor Richet adds: —

M. Thoulet has lately confirmed all the details contained in his letter. He has no longer any written trace of this old story, but the recollection of it is perfectly clear. He assured me that he had *seen* and *read* the telegram like a real object. . . .

(3) And now I quote a case where a kind of conversation is indicated between the sleeper and some communicating spirit; — recalling the scraps of conversation sometimes overheard (as it were) between Mrs. Piper and some "control" when she is in the act of awaking from trance. These moments "between two worlds" are often, as will be seen, of high significance. In the case here cited we seem to see Mr. Goodall at first misapprehending a message, and himself automatically uttering the misapprehension, and then receiving the needed correction from his invisible interlocutor.

From *Proceedings* S.P.R., vol. v. pp. 453-5. The following narrative was communicated by Mr. Edward A. Goodall, of the Royal Society of Painters in Water Colours, London: —

May 1888.

At Midsummer, 1869, I left London for Naples. The heat being excessive, people were leaving for Ischia, and I thought it best to go there myself.

Crossing by steamer, I slept one night at Casamicciola, on the coast, and walked next morning into the town of Ischia.

Liking the hotel there better than my quarters of the previous night, I fetched my small amount of luggage by help of a man, who returned with me on foot beside an animal which I rode — one of the fine, surefooted, big donkeys of the country. Arrived at the hotel, and while sitting perfectly still in my saddle talking to the landlady, the donkey went down upon his knees as if he had been shot or struck by lightning, throwing me over his head upon the lava pavement. In endeavouring to save myself my right hand was badly injured. It soon became much swollen and very painful. A Neapolitan doctor on the spot said no bones were broken, but perfect rest would be needful, with my arm in a sling. Sketching, of course, was impossible, and with neither books, newspapers, nor letters I felt my inactivity keenly.

It must have been on my third or fourth night, and about the middle of it, when I awoke, as it seemed at the sound of my own voice, saying,

"I know I have lost my dearest little May." Another voice, which I in no way recognised, answered, "*No*, not May, but your *youngest boy.*"

The distinctness and solemnity of the voice made such a distressing impression upon me that I slept no more. I got up at daybreak, and went out, noticing for the first time telegraph-poles and wires.

Without delay I communicated with the postmaster at Naples, and by next boat received two letters from home. I opened them according to dates outside. The first told me that my youngest boy was taken suddenly ill; the second, that he was dead.

Neither on his account nor on that of any of my family had I any cause for uneasiness. All were quite well on my taking leave of them so lately. My impression ever since has been that the time of the death coincided as nearly as we could judge with the time of my accident.[1]

In writing to Mrs. Goodall, I called the incident of the voice a dream, as less likely perhaps to disturb her than the details which I gave on reaching home, and which I have now repeated.

My letters happen to have been preserved.

I have never had any hallucination of any kind, nor am I in the habit of talking in my sleep. I do remember once waking with some words of mere nonsense upon my lips, but the experience of the voice speaking to me was absolutely unique. 　　　EDWARD A. GOODALL.

Extracts from letters to Mrs. E. A. Goodall from Ischia: —

Wednesday, August 11th, 1869.

The postman brought me two letters containing sad news indeed. Poor little Percy. I dreamt some nights since the poor little fellow was taken from us. . . .

August 14th.

I did not tell you, dear, the particulars of my dream about poor little Percy.

I had been for several days very fidgety and wretched at getting no letters from home, and had gone to bed in worse spirits than usual, and in my dream I fancied I said: "I have lost my dearest little May." A strange voice seemed to say: "No, *not* May but your youngest boy," not mentioning his name. . . .

Mr. Goodall gave me verbally a concordant account of the affair, and several members of his family, who were present at our interview, recollected the strong impression made on him and them at the time.

(4) The next case is precisely a miniature case of possession.

From the *Journal* S.P.R., vol. viii. pp. 278-280.

"The following account" (writes Dr. Hodgson) "was sent to me by Mr. John E. Wilkie at the suggestion of one of our American members

---

[1] Mr. Goodall thinks that the mule's sudden fall, otherwise unexplainable, may have been due to terror at some apparition of the dying child.

who is well known to me, and who speaks in the highest terms of Mr. Wilkie as a witness:" —

Washington, D. C., *April 11th*, 1898.

In October 1895, while living in London, England, I was attacked by bronchitis in rather a severe form, and on the advice of my physician, Dr. Oscar C. De Wolf, went to his residence in 6 Grenville Place, Cromwell Road, where I could be under his immediate care. For two days I was confined to my bed, and about five o'clock in the afternoon of the third day, feeling somewhat better, I partially dressed myself, slipped on a heavy bath robe, and went down to the sitting-room on the main floor, where my friend, the doctor, usually spent a part of the afternoon in reading. A steamer chair was placed before the fire by one of the servants, and I was made comfortable with pillows. The doctor was present, and sat immediately behind me reading. I dropped off into a light doze, and slept for perhaps thirty minutes. Suddenly I became conscious of the fact that I was about to awaken; I was in a condition where I was neither awake nor asleep. I realised fully that I had been asleep, and I was equally conscious of the fact that I was not wide awake. While in this peculiar mental condition I suddenly said to myself: "Wait a minute. Here is a message for the doctor." At the moment I fancied that I had upon my lap a pad of paper, and I thought I wrote upon this pad with a pencil the following words: —

"Dear Doctor, — Do you remember Katy McGuire, who used to live with you in Chester? She died in 1872. She hopes you are having a good time in London."

Instantly thereafter I found myself wide awake, felt no surprise at not finding the pad of paper on my kneee, bcause I then realised that that was but the hallucination of a dream, but impressed with that feature of my thought which related to the message, I partly turned my head, and, speaking over my shoulder to the doctor, said: "Doctor, I have a message for you."

The doctor looked up from the *British Medical Journal* which he was reading, and said: "What's that?"

"I have a message for you," I repeated. "It is this: 'Dear Doctor: Do you remember Katy McGuire, who used to live with you in Chester? She died in 1872. She hopes you are having a good time in London.'"

The doctor looked at me with amazement written all over his face, and said: "Why, —— what the devil do you mean?"

"I don't know anything about it except that just before I woke up I was impelled to receive this message which I have just delivered to you."

"Did you ever hear of Katy McGuire?" asked the doctor.

"Never in my life."

"Well," said the doctor, "that's one of the most remarkable things I ever heard of. My father for a great many years lived at Chester, Mass. There was a neighbouring family named McGuire, and Katy McGuire, a daughter of this neighbour, frequently came over to our house, as the younger people in a country village will visit their neighbours, and used to assist my mother in the lighter duties about the house. I was absent from Chester from about 1869 to about 1873. I had known Katy, however, as a daughter of our neighbour and knew that she used to visit the house. She died some time during the absence I speak of, but as to the exact date of her death I am not informed."

That closed the incident, and although the doctor told me that he would write to his old home to ascertain the exact date of Katy's death, I have never heard from him further in the matter. I questioned him at the time as to whether he had recently thought of Katy McGuire, and he told me that her name had not occurred to him for twenty years, and that he might never have recalled it had it not been for the rather curious incident which had occurred. In my own mind I could only explain the occurrence as a rather unusual coincidence. I was personally aware of the fact that the doctor's old home had been Chester, Mass., and had frequently talked with him of his earlier experiences in life when he began practice in that city, but never at any time during these conversations had the name of this neighbour's daughter been mentioned, nor had the name of the neighbour been mentioned, our conversation relating entirely to the immediate members of the family, particularly the doctor's father, who was a noted practitioner in that district.

JOHN E. WILKIE.

Dr. De Wolf, in reply to Dr. Hodgson's first inquiry, wrote: —

6 GRENVILLE PLACE, CROMWELL ROAD, S.W., *April 29th*, 1898.

DEAR SIR, — In reply to your letter of the 27th inst., I regret that I cannot recall with any definite recollection the incident to which Mr. Wilkie refers.

I *do* remember that he told me one morning he had had a remarkable dream — or conference with some one who knew me when a young lad. — Very truly yours,   OSCAR C. DE WOLF.

Dr. Hodgson then sent Mr. Wilkie's account to Dr. De Wolf, with further inquiries, to which Dr. De Wolf replied as follows: —

6 GRENVILLE PLACE, CROMWELL ROAD, S.W., *May 4th*, 1898.

DEAR SIR, — Mr. Wilkie's statement is correct except as to unimportant detail. My father practised his profession of medicine, in Chester, Mass., for sixty years — dying in 1890. I was born in Chester and lived there until 1857, when I was in Paris studying medicine for four years. In 1861 I returned to America and immediately entered the army as surgeon and served until the close of the war in 1865. In 1866 I located in Northampton, Mass., where I practised my profession until 1873, when I removed to Chicago.

Chester is a hill town in Western Mass., and Northampton is seventeen miles distant. While in Northampton I was often at my father's house — probably every week — and during some of the years from 1866 to 1873 I knew Katy McGuire as a servant assisting my mother.

She was an obliging and pleasant girl and always glad to see me. She had no family in Chester (as Mr. Wilkie says) and I do not know where she came from. Neither do I know where or when she died — but I know she is dead. There is nothing left of my family in Chester. The old homestead still remains with me, and I visit it every year.

The strange feature (to me) of this incident is the fact that I had not thought of this girl for many years, and Mr. Wilkie was never within 500 miles of Chester.

We had been warm friends since soon after my location in Chicago, where he was connected with a department of the Chicago *Tribune*. I came to London in 1892 and Mr. Wilkie followed the next year as the manager of Low's *American Exchange*, 3 Northumberland Avenue. His family did not join him until 1895, which explains his being in my house when ill.

Mr. Wilkie is a very straightforward man and not given to illusions of any kind. He is now the chief of the Secret Service Department of the U.S. Government, Washington, D. C.

Neither of us were believers in spiritual manifestations of this character, and this event so impressed us that we did not like to talk about it, and it has been very seldom referred to when we met. — Very truly yours,

OSCAR C. DE WOLF.

INDEX

Lightning Source UK Ltd.
Milton Keynes UK
29 June 2010

156226UK00001B/103/P